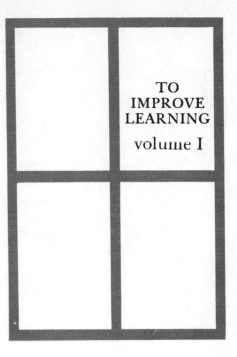

TO
IMPROVE
LEARNING
volume I

TO IMPROVE LEARNING

An Evaluation Of Instructional Technology

volume I

PART ONE
A Report by the Commission on
Instructional Technology

PART TWO
Instructional Technology:
Selected Working Papers on *The State of the Art*

EDITED BY
SIDNEY G. TICKTON

with the Staff of
the Academy for Educational Development, Inc.

R. R. BOWKER COMPANY, NEW YORK & LONDON 1970

Contents

PART ONE
A Report by the Commission on Instructional Technology

PART TWO
Instructional Technology: Selected Working Papers on *The State of the Art*

Selected Papers:

PART ONE

A Report
by the Commission
on Instructional Technology

Introduction

The report by the Commission on Instructional Technology, reproduced herein, grew out of Title III of the Public Broadcasting Act, but it goes far beyond the scope of that act. It reviews the use in the educational process not only of television, both closed circuit and regular broadcasting, but of all methods of communication.

The Committee on Education and Labor for many years has expressed a great interest in instructional technology, and has initiated programs in this area. Title III of the National Defense Education Act in its final form reflected congressional initiative. This was the first program of Federal financial assistance to help elementary and secondary schools take advantage of advanced communications technology. Over the years Congress has expanded the subject matters for which such equipment may be purchased and used.

In that same act we created a separate program of research into the uses of new media, as well as the dissemination of the results of that research. Subsequently the research activity has been absorbed into the regular cooperative research program.

In recent years this committee has authorized a parallel program for institutions of higher education, and, in Title II of the Elementary and Secondary Education Act, provided for grants to help purchase instructional materials, including those suitable for use in new media.

Publication of the present report does not imply endorsement of its recommendations in whole or in part. It does reflect the interest of the committee in all ideas for the improvement of educational quality and its delivery systems.

CARL D. PERKINS,
Chairman, Committee on Education and Labor

MEMBERS OF THE COMMISSION
ON INSTRUCTIONAL TECHNOLOGY

Commission On Instructional Technology

DEAR MR. FINCH:

We have the honor to present herewith the report prepared by the Commission on Instructional Technology.

This report is the result of the study requested in April 1968 by your predecessor, in response to Title III of the Public Broadcasting Act. However, in his first meeting with us, the Commissioner of Education broadened the scope of the study beyond the precise wording of Title III of the Act (a title for which a specific appropriation was not made) by saying:

"The scope of your work should be wide ranging. Every aspect of instructional technology and every problem which may arise in its development should be included in your study."

In the light of this mandate, the Commission has concerned itself with the whole gamut of instructional technology—old, new, and future; mechanical and electronic; automated and cybernated; from innovations in print technology to computers; from classrooms to multimedia centers.

In addition to investigating the status and potential of each medium, the Commission has studied instructional technology as a whole—as a system greater than the sum of the various media. Throughout the study, our focus has been on the potential use of technology to improve learning from preschool to graduate school to adult education.

This study has been directed by Sidney G. Tickton, executive vice president of the Academy for Educational Development; staff work was provided by other Academy officers and researchers, plus special consultants. Throughout, the Commission and its staff have had the advice and assistance of scholars, educators, specialists in educational technology, and business leaders. We thank them for their cooperation; many of the papers submitted by them will be published soon.

Respectfully yours,
COMMISSION ON INSTRUCTIONAL TECHNOLOGY

DAVID E. BELL	HAROLD B. GORES
ROALD F. CAMPBELL	A. LEON HIGGINBOTHAM
C. RAY CARPENTER	KERMIT C. MORRISSEY
NELL P. EURICH	KENNETH E. OBERHOLTZER

STERLING M. McMURRIN (Chairman)

The Honorable Robert H. Finch
Secretary of Health, Education, and Welfare
Washington, D. C.

What Is
Instructional
Technology?

"Instructional technology can be defined in two ways. In its more familiar sense, it means the media born of the communications revolution which can be used for instructional purposes alongside the teacher, textbook, and blackboard. In general, the Commission's report follows this usage. In order to reflect present-day reality, the Commission has had to look at the pieces that make up instructional technology: television, films, overhead projectors, computers, and the other items of 'hardware' and 'software' (to use the convenient jargon that distinguishes machines from programs). In nearly every case, these media have entered education independently, and still operate more in isolation than in combination.

The second and less familiar definition of instructional technology goes beyond any particular medium or device. In this sense, instructional technology is more than the sum of its parts. It is a systematic way of designing, carrying out, and evaluating the total process of learning and teaching in terms of specific objectives, based on research in human learning and communication, and employing a combination of human and nonhuman resources to bring about more effective instruction. The widespread acceptance and application of this broad definition belongs to the future." (From Chapter II, p. 27.)

> NOTE: The quotations included in the report were selected to illustrate the range of judgments and opinions about instructional technology, and do not necessarily represent the views of the Commission. The quotations are reprinted by permission of the authors, and are subject to the usual copyright restrictions; all rights are reserved on behalf of the authors. The examples that are not otherwise attributed, were compiled by the staff from various sources including their own observations.

> The repetition, sometimes verbatim, of ideas and statements in the report is intentional in order to make each section of the report complete in itself.

> Appendices A through E deal with specific aspects of instructional technology and are intended for the reader interested in further details on such matters as cost or the application of technology to special educational problems.

Summary

The Commission on Instructional Technology was established in the belief that technology, properly supported and wisely employed, could help meet some of the nation's most pressing educational needs. The Commission's task was to determine, in a study lasting more than a year, whether this belief in technology's value for education is justified; and, if it is justified, to recommend to the President and the Congress specific actions to provide for the most effective possible application of technology to American education.

The Commission took as the starting point of its study not technology, but learning. The heart of education is the student learning, and the value of any technology used in education must therefore be measured by its capacity to improve learning.

But today, we observed, learning in our schools and colleges is increasingly impeded by such troubles as the growing gap between education's income and needs, and the shortage of good teachers in the right places. Formal education is not responsive enough: the organization of schools and colleges takes too little account of even what is now known about the process of human learning, particularly of the range of individual differences among students. This condition makes schools particularly unresponsive to the needs of disadvantaged and minority-group children. Moreover, formal education is in an important sense outmoded—students learn outside schools in ways which differ radically from the ways they learn inside school. Educational institutions make scant use of the potent means of communication that modern society finds indispensable and that occupy so much of young people's out-of-school time.

Today technology touches only a small fraction of instruction. Colleges, universities, and schools have been using television, films, computers, or programmed texts in instruction, but to a limited extent. The results are mixed, with some institutions making a creative and sustained use of the new media while others, after an initial burst of enthusiasm, quickly lose interest.

Examining the impact of technology on American education in 1969 is like examining the impact of the automobile on American life when the Model T Ford first came on the market. The further ahead one looks, the more benefits technology seems to hold out for education. The Commission weighed future promise against present achievements, and examined the discrepancies between the science-fiction myths of instructional technology and the down-to-earth facts.

Obviously, the problems that confront education have no one solution. But learning might be significantly improved if the so-called second industrial revolution—the revolution of information processing and communication—could be harnessed to the tasks of instruction.

On the basis of present experience and informed projections, the Commission believes that technology could bring about far more productive use of the teacher's and the student's time. Of particular importance is its capacity to provide instruction that is truly tailored to each individual student; the traditional resources of teacher and textbook are not sufficiently flexible by themselves. Moreover, technology could help educators base instruction more systematically on what is known about learning and communication, not only guiding the basic research, but also providing the strategies for applying research findings.

There are other reasons for harnessing technology fully to the work of schools and colleges. New forms of communication give man new capacities. Instructional technology could extend the scope and power of instruction. It could help to bridge the gap between the outside world and the school, thus making learning more immediate and more relevant. Perhaps technology's greatest boon could be to make education more democratic. Access to the best teaching and the richest opportunities for learning is inevitably inequitable because of the constraints of economics, geography, or other factors having nothing to do with a student's ability to learn. Through television, film, and other forms of telecommunications, however, the remote rural college and the hard-pressed ghetto school could share the intellectual and esthetic advantages of the best institutions and the richest community resources.

In the conviction that technology can make education more productive, individual, and powerful, make learning more immediate, give instruction a more scientific base, and make access to education more equal, the Commission concludes that the nation should increase its investment in instructional technology, thereby upgrading the quality of education, and, ultimately, the quality of individuals' lives and of society generally.

Our study has shown that one-shot injections of a single technological medium are ineffective. At best they offer only optional "enrichment." Technology, we believe, can carry out its full potential for education only insofar as educators embrace instructional technology as a system and integrate a range of human and nonhuman resources into the total educational process.

To achieve such improvements, the knowledge of how people learn must be deepened, and the capacity to put that knowledge to effective use must be augmented. In the process the organization and governance of the entire educational enterprise may well have to be changed. So may the preparation and deployment of professionals and other highly trained specialists. To make instruction productive and responsive to individual students, the barriers that stand between the formal institutions of education and the larger community may have to be breached.

The changes required will probably be as thoroughgoing as those which industry underwent when it shifted from hand labor to mechanization. But a society hurtling into the age of the computer and the satellite can no longer be held back by an educational system which is limping along at the blackboard-and-textbook stage of communication.

The six recommendations proposed in Chapter V of this report comprise the initial steps which the Commission on Instructional Technology considers essential, beginning with a new agency to provide leadership and focus for concerted action. Recommendation #1 would establish the National Institutes of Education (N.I.E.) within the Department of Health, Education, and Welfare, with broad authorization to support and fund greatly strengthened programs in educational research, development, and application. The N.I.E. would consist of several constituent institutes, and through them make grants to universities and other independent research institutions, as well as conduct research itself. It would also sponsor several strong autonomous centers for research, development, and application, and a few comprehensive demonstration projects.

A National Institute of Instructional Technology (N.I.I.T.) should be established within the National Institutes of Education to work closely with existing agencies concerned with instructional technology and to establish such other regional centers and programs as it deems necessary (Recommendation #2). It would concentrate on research, development, and application of technology. One of its chief functions would be to encourage the production of a wide variety of good instructional materials.

The proposed National Institute of Instructional Technology should also take the lead in searching out, organizing, and preparing for distribution high-quality material, in all media, needed to improve education (Recommendation #3). To this end, the N.I.I.T. should consider establishing a center or "library" of educational resources. The center would take on additional responsibilities, such as helping school and college libraries transform themselves into comprehensive learning centers.

Projects to demonstrate the value of technology for instruction (Recommendation #4) would be initiated by the National Institute for Instructional Technology. These projects would concentrate funds and other resources on a few carefully selected communities or school districts, with the emphasis on pockets of poverty or minority-group deprivation. The school system of the District of Columbia might be invited to mount the first of such model demonstrations.

Improving the capacity of educators to make good use of technology would be a major function of the proposed National Institute of Instructional Technology. Recommendation #5 proposes the support of programs, based on stepped-up research and development, to train and retrain teachers, administrators, and a variety of specialists.

Recommendation #6 proposes a mechanism whereby the National Institute of Instructional Technology could bring education and industry together in a close working relationship to advance the effectiveness of instruction through technology.

The Commission has concluded that only the federal government can undertake the major responsibility for the expenditures for basic and applied research, development, and application required in the years immediately ahead. Furthermore, we believe that the minimum initial financing required to carry out the recommendations of this report is approximately $565 million. Of this about $150 million would be required to launch the National Institutes of Education and the National Institute of Instructional Technology. The remaining $415 million would be required for the first full year of operation, including approximately $250 million for the research, development, and application activities of the institutes, $25 million for the center or "library" of educational resources, $100 million for demonstration projects, and $40 million for the training of personnel. The aggregate amount suggested would equal no more than 1 percent of the projected total expenditures for American education in fiscal 1972.

In October 1968, before his election, President Nixon proposed the creation of a National Institute for the Educational Future. Mr. Nixon said: "This institute will take us into the space age in education. We are on the threshold of great changes, many brought about by the possibilities inherent in new technology."

The Commission believes that its proposals will help achieve this vision.

I.
Focus
on Learning

Dissatisfaction with American education is everywhere evident. Opinions as to what should be done often contradict each other. But there is a clear demand for action that will enhance the learning of the individual student, the effectiveness of schools and colleges, and ultimately the quality of the nation's life.

Since the late fifties, the federal government has granted billions of dollars to finance curriculum reforms, innovations of all kinds in thousands of schools, and a large program designed specifically to improve the instruction of the disadvantaged. Yet the outcome of much of this endeavor and expenditure has been, to put it mildly, disappointing. All too often innovations have been alterations in form rather than substance, soon to be dropped in favor of a later model.

More recently, radical critics (and many students) have begun to question the axioms of American education, suggesting revision of the compulsory education laws, competitive alternatives to the public schools, and abolition of traditional instructional procedures. Maverick educators have set up freedom schools, street academics in the big-city ghettos, schools without buildings or classrooms or conventionally organized programs.

But for all the fanfare, effort, money, and good will, the generality of schools and colleges is much the same as it was a generation ago. Many people, educators included, have come to the conclusion that fundamental and far-reaching changes must be made.

> The establishment in lower and secondary education is probably the most encrusted in the entire world. They still are teaching children as we were taught thirty years ago. A child today who comes into kindergarten has had from 3,000 to 4,000 hours sitting in front of that television tube, absorbing unstructured data that takes him way past Dick and Jane. And the system just doesn't respond to that.

> Robert H. Finch
> Secretary of Health,
> Education, and Welfare

The crisis in education has been a long time building. The iceberg image is unavoidable: most of the troubles have been with us for years—but nine-tenths submerged beneath a sea of public complacency and preoccupation with other matters. Today, however, no one can ignore the problems which are pressing in from every side.

To some extent the schools and colleges are victims of conditions beyond their control: rapid population growth and mobility, country-to-city migration, unpredictable economic and social changes wrought by technology, disproportionate military claims on the gross national product. Added to these are the pervasive malaise and uncharacteristic self-doubts manifest today in America especially among the young, a condition resulting from many factors—a long, unpopular war, poverty amid affluence, the bitter harvest of protracted racial injustice, and the menace of crime and violence. If education is sometimes made the scapegoat for the ills of society, the reason lies partly in the faith that most Americans from Jefferson's day to the present have had in the importance and power of education.

> Certainly it is not possible to spend any prolonged period visiting public-school classrooms without being appalled by the mutilation visible everywhere—mutilation of spontaneity, of joy in learning, of pleasure of creation, of sense of self. The public schools—those "killers of the dream," to appropriate a phrase of Lillian Smith's—are the kind of institution one cannot really dislike until one gets to know it well.

> Because they take the schools so much for granted, adults fail to appreciate what grim, joyless places most American schools are, how oppressive and petty are the rules by which they are governed, how intellectually sterile and aesthetically barren the atmosphere, what an appalling lack of civility obtains on the part of teachers and principals. The fact is that schools are not organized to facilitate *learning* (and certainly not joy in learning); they are organized and managed so as to facilitate order.

> Charles E. Silberman; Director
> The Carnegie Study for
> the Education of Educators

Against this troubled background the Commission on Instructional Technology was appointed and assigned its task—to examine the instructional uses of such media as television, computers, tapes, radio, and their relation to each other. Implicit in this charge may have been the hope that here, in the technology that had made America one of the most affluent and powerful nations in history, could be found the magic to transform American education. But the rationale for the Commission's study was more modest and realistic: *the belief that technology, properly supported and wisely employed, could help meet some of the nation's most pressing educational needs.*

The Commission's aims were:

a. To determine whether in fact this belief in technology's value for education is justified;

b. If it is justified, to recommend to the President and the Congress specific actions that may be taken to provide for the most effective possible application of technology to instruction.

Means and Ends

The Commission's mandate concerned the *means* of instruction—especially such newer means as television or computers. But in education as elsewhere means are inextricably involved with ends.

How can powerful means of instruction play their proper role in achieving desired ends, both the broad purposes of education and the proximate goals of classroom instruction, without becoming the dominant factor in the mixture? Technology has a way of shaping the ends it ostensibly serves. To date, man has not been entirely successful in harnessing the machine to humane ends. Instead, technological society has at times subjugated human values to mechanical efficiency. It has adjusted men to machines rather than machines to men, permitted communications media like television to stabilize at a low level, allowed industry and the automobile to foul and choke and scar the environment.

Are educators so conscientious and clever that there is no need to fear similar misuses of technology in education? It would hardly seem so. The dangers of dehumanization are as real for education as they are for other social institutions if schools and colleges fall prey to a technological order in which means determine ends.

As the current scene attests, there is also the constant need to make the *reality* of schools and colleges come closer to education's goals. Much of the pervasive student dissatisfaction today appears to stem from such discrepancies as those between the rhetoric of college catalogs and what actually takes place day after day in the classroom. Indeed, some critics hold that American education is already dehumanized without technology.

In determining the proper direction for America's educational institutions, the answers must be sought across the total spectrum of human interest, experience, and value. There is no single goal of education. Its purposes are many, to match the pluralistic structure of America itself.

Education should be concerned first with the well-being of the individual student and his capacity for a productive and happy life as a person and as a worker. But education must also be concerned with the well-being of the nation: its economic and social integrity, its political wisdom, its security and survival and growth. It must be concerned with the intellectual, artistic, and spiritual values by which men live and by which their judgments are made and their purposes defined. Education must help to answer the all-important question of how to achieve and preserve a genuinely free society in which men are authentic persons who are masters rather than slaves of the forces which help shape their world.

It is important to come to grips with these large matters in order to set the perspective and direction for schools and colleges. But instructional programs must also be shaped to fit more immediate ends, goals which lie within the reach of the student and teacher. The worth of instructional equipment, materials, and techniques must be judged in terms of their effectiveness in achieving these goals, as they relate to the basic types of personal experience—feelings and actions, as well as thought.

Quite properly, the prime concerns of schools and colleges are thought, reason, and knowledge. But American education runs the risk of neglecting the noncognitive facets of life. Western culture has a long tradition of preoccupation with knowledge, reason, and abstraction, a habit of mind that has produced a verbal-conceptual type of education that relies heavily on language and language skills. The ability to use words and mathematical symbols and to engage in logical discourse with complex ideas is for us the chief mark of educational achievement. The inner life of feeling and appreciation, and the moral, esthetic, and spiritual values associated with that life, deserve far more attention than they commonly receive, especially in formal education.

> *he is trying to think*
> *to teach them to think*
> *he tries it by a pond*
> *to tell them why he likes it*
> *to help them like it*
>
> *he teaches them*
> *he makes love to them*
> *he dies with them a little*
>
> *they ask no questions*
>
> *after a while they all go away*
>
> *"teechur,"*
> *by Dick Higgins*

In conducting our study we have tried to keep this imbalance in mind, looking for the potential values of instructional technology that go beyond the mere transmission of information.

Learning

Since the heart of education is the student learning, the value of any technology must be measured by its ability to facilitate learning. Learning therefore has been the Commission's touchstone throughout. All our studies, inquiries, research, and deliberations have begun and ended here: with the student as learner—whether he learns by himself, with fellow students, through a teacher, or through some other agent. This emphasis is consonant with the most promising advances in education. "Less teaching and more learning" has been a goal of enlightened educators since Comenius pleaded for it in the 17th century.

We have been making assumptions for centuries about how learning takes place, how it is motivated, and how the teacher should teach. I think we have reason to believe that most of those assumptions were wrong and that most significant learning has taken place *despite* teachers rather than because of them.

One only has to reflect on the magnificent way the infant learns how to understand and speak his native tongue without formal instruction or systematic teaching systems. Later on, when he is learning to read, under systematic tutelage with specially designed materials and large amounts of time devoted to it, he has much greater difficulty, and less success.

J. Richard Suchman
Educational Consultant

The Commission's focus on learning disclosed three significant conditions:

IMPEDED EDUCATION	Learning in American schools and colleges is impeded by such troubles as the increasing gap between education's income and needs, and shortages of good teachers in the right places.
UNRESPONSIVE EDUCATION	The organization of schools and colleges takes little account of even what is now known about the process of human learning, including the range of individual differences among learners and styles of learning. This condition makes schools particularly unresponsive to the needs of disadvantaged and minority-group students.
OUTMODED EDUCATION	The ways that students learn outside school differ radically from the ways they learn inside school. Formal education makes only limited use of the many means of communication which society at large finds indispensable.

Impeded Education

The factors which are impeding education will not yield to conventional remedies. To be sure, it would be a giant step forward if the nation could double or triple its educational budget, find the requisite manpower and leadership, and improve poor and mediocre institutions. Better-trained teachers and administrators, more modern facilities, better teaching materials in adequate supply—there is no denying that sharply stepped-up outlays of time, money, talent, and effort could go far to improve education and alleviate some of its grosser inequities and more obvious failures. But "more of the same"—or even "more of the same, but better"—will not get at the root of education's troubles.

> Education is beyond repair. What is needed is radical reform. This reform is to include the nature of the schooling process, the systems which control educational policy, and the institutions which prepare persons to be teachers.
>
> *Teachers for the Real World*
> B. Othanel Smith, et al, for
> the American Association of
> Colleges for Teacher Education

If under present methods education is impeded, if present arrangements of time, space, teacher and student role are incapable of resolving the major problems facing American education, the answers must lie in fundamental change.

Unresponsive Education

Researchers in human learning agree that individuals differ markedly in the ways they learn, in the speed at which they learn, in their motivation to learn, and in what they desire to learn. But educational institutions cater only fractionally to these individual differences. Even in the best schools, where students' achievements in the three R's and the standard subjects are well above grade, and resounding percentages graduate from high school to enter college, many thoughtful educators and outside observers believe that institutions have lost touch with the individual student.

Most schools and colleges are still locked into conventional patterns of grade structure, time span, and subject-matter division that fail to exploit each student's individual capacities, interests, and personality. Conventional practice is geared to some abstract "average" or "norm" that penalizes both the unusually gifted and the seemingly backward student as well as the spectrum that lies between.

> Schools are graded as an administrative convenience. Such an organizational pattern merely permits us to obtain prettier and neater statistical tables. The question from the state superintendent is, "How many children in the second grade?" Answer: "400." So what? There is at least a four-year achievement span among these children, and any "second grade" teacher can attest to this. There is no such thing as a "second grade." Such nomenclature merely provides information for census studies or reports to the country. It has nothing to do with the education of children.
>
> Robert M. Finley, Superintendent
> Glen Cove Public Schools,
> New York

How then can conditions of learning be designed that effectively respond to the individual differences among learners? Although research has pointed up these differences, it has not yet provided adequate guidelines for the design of individualized instruction. One thing, however, seems clear: the traditional mix of teacher, textbook, and blackboard is not sufficiently flexible by itself to make learning an individualized process. Differentiated types of instruction—with less rigid student groupings and a more flexible range of resources—are essential.

Individualized instruction does not mean the end of group instruction. It means shaping instruction to the needs and styles of the learners and the requirements of the subject matter. Instruction geared to the individual calls for many different arrangements, from independent study to large-group instruction.

Outmoded Education

Today's students are deluged by electronic media and many types of audiovisual communications: television and movies occupy more of their waking hours than any other single activity including school. The transistor radio pounds at their ears with the rock rhythms and lyrics to which they respond as they seldom do to conventional music and poetry. The telephone, the mass-circulation magazine, the paperback book, the phonograph and tape recorder—all are integral and intimate elements of their lives. They shape the ways in which young people think, determine whom they admire and whom they scorn, what and how they feel about love, war, life, death—and about education.

Children learn, from television and from the ads, just what is happening in the world, about the pill and IUD and organ transplantation and tissue propagation. They are learning about the possibility of test-tube babies while the schools are still cautiously producing a few carefully sterile remarks about reproduction.

The prewar generation grew up trained to "concentrate," to work in quiet libraries where people were punished for talking, to finish their lessons before they played records or turned on the radio.

The postwar generation has learned to read and study and think with several media going at once, TV showing a game with the sound turned off, the radio turned on to a radio commentator on the same game, a long-playing record providing background music, as ninth graders glued to the telephone compare notes on the problems they are doing.

Margaret Mead
Curator of Ethnology Emeritus
American Museum of
Natural History

As a result of this communications barrage, today's child has a world view entirely different from his parents'. To some observers, this change in sensibility makes formal education virtually obsolete as currently practiced. They argue that to compete for students' interest, educators must reconsider both what they teach and how they teach it. For example, the child who has absorbed the rudiments of space rocketry from live television broadcasts of the astronauts may not only resist covering the same topic in class; he may also find that other subjects seem pallid when presented by a harried, inexpert teacher unassisted by technology. Are we asking too much to insist that learning in school should be at least as interesting and relevant as the learning that goes on incessantly outside of school?

The young of many countries continue daily to manifest revulsion against the traditional effort to contain the educational processes in the bureaucratic and homogenized spaces of existing schools and colleges and curricula.

Young and old alike now live in unique service environments of information. It is a many-layered environment.

The inner layers are the familiar electric networks of telegraph and telephone and radio and TV. The outer layers are jet and satellite.

To go on building 19th century spaces for the storing and dissemination of classified information is perfectly natural. It is also fatal.

> Marshall McLuhan
> Director of the Center
> for Culture and Technology
> University of Toronto

Society employs a wide range of communications. America would almost stop functioning without telephones, computers, and jets. Communications technology has given man new powers that enable him not only to accomplish existing tasks more efficiently but also to undertake new tasks that were previously impossible. Space flights could not have taken place without the instantaneous computer calculations that control orbiting and reentry.

Learning and Instructional Technology

The multiple problems that confront American education have no single solution. But learning could be significantly improved if the technology and techniques of the so-called second industrial revolution—the revolution of information processing and communication—could be harnessed to the tasks of the schools and colleges.

> Can technology help the mediocre teacher or the one who really doesn't like young people? I suppose our major hope for computers and other technology is to compensate for the imperfections of those who can be trained to teach but who cannot be taught to be good teachers.

> John Caffrey, Director
> Commission on Administrative Affairs
> American Council on Education

Colleges, universities, and schools have been making a limited application of technology—television, films, computers, teaching machines—to instruction. How has this instructional technology fared? Has it shown the capabilities to tackle the complex problems of learning which can now be identified? Do the accomplishments of the various types of instructional technology justify the belief that "technology, properly supported and wisely employed, could help meet some of the nation's most pressing educational needs"?

II.
Instructional
Technology Today

Examining the impact of modern technology on instruction in 1969 is like examining the impact of the automobile on American life in 1908 when the Model T first came on the market, or the impact of technology on farming a decade after the appearance of Mc-Cormick's reaper. Western man may now be entering the post-industrial age, but his children attend schools and colleges that are just catching up with the industrial age, and have scarcely been brushed by the communications revolution. Indeed, the very term "instructional technology" is unfamiliar not only to the public at large but to many teachers and administrators as well.

> Instructional technology is today largely supplementary to the two primary media of instruction: the textbook and the teacher. Eliminate either of these and the educational system would be transformed. Eliminate all of the technology, and education would go on with hardly a missed lesson.
>
> Norman D. Kurland, Director
> Center on Innovation in Education
> New York State Education Department

Instructional technology can be defined in two ways. In its more familiar sense, it means the media born of the communications revolution which can be used for instructional purposes alongside the teacher, textbook, and blackboard. In general, the Commission's report follows this usage. In order to reflect present-day reality, the Commission has had to look at the pieces that make up instructional technology: television, films, overhead projectors, computers, and the other items of "hardware" and "software" (to use the convenient jargon that distinguishes machines from programs). In nearly every case, these media have entered education independently, and still operate more in isolation than in combination.

The second and less familiar definition of instructional technology goes beyond any particular medium or device. In this sense, instructional technology is more than the sum of its parts. It is a systematic way of designing, carrying out, and evaluating the total process of learning and teaching in terms of specific objectives, based on research in human learning and communication, and employing a combination of human and nonhuman resources to bring about more effective instruction. The widespread acceptance and application of this broad definition belongs to the future. Though only a limited number of institutions have attempted to design instruction using such a systematic, comprehensive approach, there is reason to believe that this approach holds the key to the contribution technology can make to the advancement of education. It became clear, in fact, as we pursued our study, that a major obstacle to instructional technology's fulfillment has been its application by bits and pieces.

Instructional technology, by either definition, includes a wide array of instruments, devices, and techniques, each with its particular problems, potential, and advocates. Note, however, that neither definition equates technology with "machines"—an easy mistake to make. To put prime emphasis on *equipment*—e.g., films, coaxial cable, teaching machines—can lead up a blind alley. Many observers believe, for instance, that fascination with the gadgetry of instructional television to the exclusion of the idea behind it has often led to stereotyped and impoverished uses of that medium.

> Has all of this made any real difference in what teachers do in classrooms, in how instruction is managed, and in how children learn in classrooms today? One could be gentle and say that the answer, like the schools, is pluralistic. But anyone who knows teachers and teaching and who visits schools will report a negative answer. In sum, it has made very little difference. What God hath wrought—from telegram to transistor—man has made little use of in the teaching-learning process that persists today in the classroom.

> Robert C. Snider
> Assistant Director, Division
> of Educational Technology
> National Education Association

Instructional Technology: Myth and Reality

In addition to encountering different views on the meaning of "instructional technology," the Commission also encountered many different judgments on instructional technology's present and potential role in American education. The education profession and the general public have been bombarded for some time with rosy predictions of how technology could quickly transform our schools and colleges. Such visions have been characterized as "the myths of instructional technology" by Anthony G. Oettinger, a linguist and mathematician associated with the Harvard Program on Technology and Society. He describes himself "not as a Luddite fearful of the Machine nor as a shrinking humanist living in the past, but as a scientist and engineer convinced that educational technology holds great promise."

Of his recent book *Run, Computer, Run* Mr. Oettinger has written: "My aim in analyzing the myths, the institutional failures, the brazen exploitations, the oppressive self-delusions that make a mockery of technological change in education is not to deny the promise, but to rescue it from unmerited disillusionment. I say there are no easy victories, no quick answers, no panaceas. If we are to realize the promise, we must not allow our human and material resources to be diverted into showy changes in form that will continue to block change in substance. Fundamental ignorance remains to be overcome in many realms that bear on the successful application of modern technology to education and we must therefore be prepared to encourage long-term investment in the exploration of diverse paths."

With changes coming so fast, definitive judgments and projections are almost impossible. While there is a convincing case for instructional technology as a cohesive, promising new approach to the whole problem of improving learning, examples are limited and largely unevaluated.

Technological devices already introduced into schools in recent years have had only peripheral impact, partly because educational technology is as yet much more primitive than is generally appreciated, so that fragile, unreliable, and expensive devices often gather dust in a classroom corner after an initial wave of enthusiasm has subsided.

Knowledge about how to apply the technology is even more primitive, in a number of respects. Even when machines work and classroom attitudes are attuned to their use, attempts to graft the new techniques to old curriculums have proved spectacularly unsuccessful and largely unrelieved as yet by imaginative technical and curriculum innovation tailored to the new demands and possibilities of education.

> Emmanuel G. Mesthene, Director
> Harvard University Program on
> Technology and Society

In American schools and colleges today the major source of instruction other than the teacher in person is the book, plus such immemorial accessories as charts and blackboards. Consider this simple calculation. There are fifty million pupils attending class an average of five hours a day, five days a week. In the aggregate, for the nation as a whole, the total comes to about 1,250,000,000 pupil class hours a week. All the films, filmstrips, records, programmed texts, television, and computer programs do not fill more than 5 percent of these class hours. Some experts put the figure at 1 percent or less. For higher education the estimated use of instructional technology is of the same order.

Most theorists who have contributed to the best thinking and writing in this field, describe motion pictures in education as noncinematic, pedantic, ineffective—produced by amateurs or unimaginative professionals for unimaginative educators who simply use dull films as substitutes for dull lectures.

> Robert W. Wagner, Chairman
> Department of Photography and Cinema
> Ohio State University

To generalize and oversimplify: *the present status of instructional technology in American education is low in both quantity and quality.* Rather than taking hold and gaining followers through successful demonstrations, many ambitious projects have faltered and failed. Rather than boldly exploring fresh strategies to stimulate learning, most projects have merely translated existing curricula and teaching techniques into the newer media. Rather than filling a functional role in a comprehensive approach to the design of instruction, most innovators have chosen or been forced to confine themselves to their own special medium or technique. Rather than moving into the center of the planning process in education, most technologically oriented educators are on its periphery.

The chief problems of using satellites for education are now ground problems, not space problems. The hardware has outrun the software. The tools are so fascinating that we have tended to watch them develop and marvel at them and to neglect the more mundane and messier questions of how to use them.

> Wilbur Schramm, Director
> Institute for Communication Research
> Stanford University

On the quantitative side, statistics are sketchy and often inconsistent. Furthermore, without uniform criteria, it is often difficult if not impossible to make useful comparisons or to arrive at sound conclusions on changing patterns of use. There is a glaring lack of data reliably indicating the actual *use* of the various technological media, as against their mere availability in an institution. There is no doubt about the rise in the number of tape recorders, record players, projectors, and filmstrips *available* for use. But the Commission learned again and again, from school superintendents and media experts, about the widespread failure of instructors to use equipment and materials (including expensive installations such as language laboratories bought with newly authorized federal funds). "Gathering dust" was the recurring phrase for what has happened to a great deal of technological equipment.

The evidence on the *quality* of most available programs is equally dispiriting. For example, the National Instructional Television Center, established a few years ago to winnow out and distribute good instructional television programs, found only a very small fraction of the programs scanned worthy of national distribution. Comparable judgments apply to most instructional media, from films to programmed instruction.

> As long as television represents for the schools only a public-address system with pictures, there is nothing but casual mediocrity to be expected.
>
> John W. Meaney
> Professor of Communication Arts
> University of Notre Dame

But there are recent reassuring examples, too, of good programming and wise applications of instructional technology. Some of these examples are coming out of the Research and Development Centers and the Regional Educational Laboratories funded by the federal government. The best foreshadow what technology's full contribution might be to education: they integrate a range of media old and new, exploiting the special qualities of each; they are based on sustained research and development, with plenty of feedback from field testing to enable needed change and improvements to be made. Moreover, they are designed so that the results can be carefully evaluated.

The fact is, then, that instructional technology is a mixed bag. It can be anything from an audiovisual graveyard in the basement of some school, to a successful computer-assisted course in Russian, to the extensive instructional television network in South Carolina.

> Twenty-two Stanford University students in an introductory Russian course during 1967-68 spent about 50 minutes a day, five days a week, at a computer console. A total of 135 lessons were specially prepared and presented to the students in a combined audio and teletype format. The students responded on a Model-33 teletype with a special keyboard containing the Cyrillic alphabet. During the period prior to the final examination, the computer assessed each student's performance and told him the areas in which he should concentrate his efforts. The student could redo any lesson or portion of a lesson at the computer console.

Costs of Instructional Technology

Any consideration of instructional technology in American education would be incomplete without a look at costs. Occasionally, technology saves money for schools or colleges—for instance, when closed-circuit television makes up for unavailable art or music teachers (as in Washington County, Maryland) or reproduces the lecturer in multiple classrooms (as in a number of public universities which use television to handle overflow freshman and sophomore classes). Many believe that wide-scale use of certain kinds of technology, with corresponding reduction of initial investment costs and well-planned operating procedures, could effect economies in education. But a true *technology of instruction* that integrates human and nonhuman resources into a comprehensive system to improve learning is unlikely to save money. Quality comes high.

> More dollars are spent in one week for programming three major television networks than in a year for all educational television.
>
> Newton N. Minow,
> former Chairman, Federal
> Communications Commission

To date, costs of large-scale demonstration projects making extensive use of technology have been substantial. The Midwest Program on Airborne Television Instruction cost $18 million (1961-1965). The Children's Television Workshop, which will start broadcasting in the fall of 1969, has estimated the cost of its initial series of 130 one-hour television programs at $8 million, including developmental costs. The Education Development Center spent approximately $6.5 million to develop a single high-school physics course. It also spent about $3.1 million to develop its widely acclaimed series of films on fluid mechanics, and about $8.1 million for its elementary-school science course.

The TV advertising budget for a fifty-second commercial selling a headache tablet is larger than the annual budget for public television.

Gabriel D. Ofiesh, Director
Center for Educational Technology
Catholic University of America

There are several factors which contribute to the high cost of instructional technology, on top of the large initial investment in complex equipment such as computers, television, and talking typewriters; specifically, the cost of:

1. Developing and testing high-quality programs.

2. Providing time for teachers to gain an understanding of technology, to learn the technical skills necessary, and to plan programs.

3. Employing media specialists and teacher aides.

4. Maintaining equipment.

Experiments which have not taken these factors into account have generally failed. Equipment too often wears out or succumbs to casual vandalism; no one is available to repair it quickly and few are willing to depend on it thereafter. Attempts to cut corners by not properly training teachers or by not hiring enough specialists can produce poor results or none at all. One teacher told the Commission that his school, a new institution fully equipped to integrate the most advanced technology into the curriculum, had to abandon the system after a year and a half because teachers were never trained in its use and technicians were lacking.

Today, the estimated costs of a computer-based instructional system, for example, vary enormously. While the cost of hardware can be approximated, estimates of the cost of effective, high-quality programs are meaningless until much more research and development work has been done. Professor Phil C. Lange of Teachers College, Columbia University, told the Commission: "Most of the figures that I see on computers just don't add up; the only way the figures do make sense is when there is an assumption of a statewide or regional monopoly using a standard curriculum for a fixed population."

There is an even more basic problem. The techniques of cost accounting used by educational institutions do not provide the necessary data. In general, schools and colleges conduct their business by methods that yield few valid measures to guide education's managers in choosing among a range of instructional options. John E. Dietrich and F. Craig Johnson of Michigan State University told the Commission:

> At present, cost data on educational technology are almost nonexistent. The lack of these data severely impedes the academic decision-making process. Regardless of costing procedures used, ways must be found to place costs of educational technology in perspective. Present inadequate cost data are frequently so subjective that they are nothing more than pious hopes. The time is here to come to grips, with the reality of cost analysis in the academic decision-making process.

The effort to establish effective procedures for determining instructional costs must be mounted. Its purpose has little relation to that once vaunted "cult of efficiency" that sought to bring business methods to bear on inefficient schools. The purpose of sensible economic practice in education has less to do with efficiency than with *effectiveness*. It is a question of education's turning out the highest-quality product possible—i.e., genuinely educated students—for the funds, talent, and time expended in their education.

Diagnosis

High cost and inadequate costing techniques are clearly a major cause of instructional technology's lack of impact on American schools and colleges. There are other causes important to identify. Some are quite tangible, such as insufficient time, talent, and resources to produce effective and imaginative programs; the inaccessibility of whatever good materials exist; lack of specialists in instructional technology; inadequate preparation and in-service training of teachers and administrators; the tendency of some commercial firms to sell educators hardware designed for noninstructional purposes. Other causes are less tangible but more fundamental—such as the lack of sustained, well-funded research and development in the teaching-learning process. Too little is known about how human beings learn, still less about how to apply what *is* known to the instructional process.

> There is considerable "religiosity" associated with instructional technology—those that are in the field seem to believe that the potential is just lying there waiting to be tapped. This reveals an underlying assumption: that the system is adaptable to instructional technology, and that operations in this area will be welcome. Such an assumption has not been wholeheartedly validated.
>
> > Richard E. Spencer
> > Professor of Educational Psychology
> > University of Illinois

Obstacles to a more extensive use of instructional technology also include negative teacher attitudes, lack of administrative commitment, the pervasive conservatism of the education establishment. The application of technology to something as "human" as schooling smacks of sacrilege to many Americans, especially teachers. Their opposition, or at least ambivalence, may well have been aggravated by overemphasis on mass instruction, machines, and gadgetry, and by the expression "teaching machine" (now pretty well supplanted by "programmed instruction").

Resistance to instructional technology among students and teachers appears to be in direct ratio to the grade level. This is borne out by observation as well as by such studies as have been made. Elementary-school children and teachers accept television or films far more readily than college students and teachers. ("I am a student. Do not fold, spindle, or mutilate," read the protesting campus signs.) Primarily, fears center around prospects of depersonalization, standardization, conformity, and the gradual elimination of whatever diversity now exists. High-school and college staffs are also constrained by rigid schedules, departmentalization, and to some measure by distrust of "outside" materials. Other negative attitudes toward instructional technology in both students and teachers stem not so much from visions of a dehumanized future as from actual unsatisfactory experiences with technology.

> In the Midwest a determined group of faculty members attempted to sabotage a newly installed computer system for recording grades by punching random holes in the cards used to report grades to the IBM machine. At yet another university an embattled registrar fought a proposal to introduce a streamlined computer registration system, arguing that his office could do the job more efficiently with traditional hand methods. Whether these reactions are justified or not, they serve as a reminder that institutions of higher education have begun to convert important

segments of their administrative procedure to electronic computers and that the effects of this conversion are being felt in all quarters of the academic community.

> Francis E. Rourke and Glenn E.
> Brooks, *The Managerial Revolution in Higher Education*

A 1969 poll, conducted for *Life* by Louis Harris and Associates, Inc., showed a large majority of high school students and their teachers eager for innovations. Both groups, for instance, wanted more field work outside the school and more opportunities to work directly in the community. But, according to the poll: "One innovation got an overwhelming thumbs-down from the students: teaching by films and closed-circuit television. The reason, they said, was that it cast them in a passive role and froze out class discussion." Contrasting with this sampling are some earlier studies on student attitudes toward instructional television (at Pennsylvania State University, for instance, and other colleges) that show students taking a favorable or at least neutral attitude toward television teaching. Generally the research shows that college students prefer small discussion classes to television, but prefer television to very large lecture classes.

There is a tendency among those working in the field of educational technology to assume that this is the only way to improve instruction and schools. I prefer an overall system that allows for alternate proven approaches, even if some of them are traditional. Look at some first-rate schools—Bronx High School of Science (New York City) and New Trier High School (Winnetka, Illinois) might serve as examples—and I suspect you will find that the human element, the human teacher, is still dominant.

> Mortimer Smith,
> Executive Director
> Council for Basic Education

The Commission faced the basic question of whether instructional technology's poor showing to date is evidence that it does *not* have potential value for improving education. Is education justified in resisting the advances of technology? The spectacular success of technology in multiplying productivity in other sectors of American society does not mean that it can or should do the same for education. The growing number of social critics who see technology's detrimental effects on American society (air and water pollution, scarred countryside, war machinery) fear that technology could have a comparable effect on education.

Indeed, if instructional technology merely provided more potent means of conducting education as usual, it would bring no great benefits. It should be encouraged only if it promises, on the basis of experience to date and on informed projections about the future, enhancement of students' learning and growth. The Commission therefore undertook to review that experience and examine those projections.

We have become victims of our own technological genius. But I am confident that the same energy and skill which gave rise to these problems can also be marshalled for the purpose of conquering them.

> President Richard M. Nixon

III.
Instructional Technology Tomorrow

The further one looks ahead, the more benefits technology seems to hold for education. At the core of the crystal ball is instruction that is truly tailored to the individual student. Patrick Suppes, director of the Institute for Mathematical Studies in the Social Sciences, Stanford University, foresees the time when "millions of school children will have access to what Philip of Macedon's son, Alexander, enjoyed as a royal prerogative: the personal services of a tutor as well-informed and responsive as Aristotle."

Tomorrow's student might "get" his education not within the confines of school or campus, but wherever he happened or wanted to be. Videotaped lessons could be played on a home television set. The computer opens up vast possibilities. It is predicted, for instance, that computer terminals, including teletypewriters with cathode-ray visual displays, might be located almost anywhere. A "suitcase" terminal could be connected by telephone line with a central computer. The student might engage the computer in a program of remedial instruction, drill, self-testing exercises, or a Socratic dialogue.

A broad technological innovation likely to affect instructional technology in the next decade is holography. This photographic technique, which may employ lasers, records wave fronts of light from an object. These are then used to reconstruct an image of the object in true three-dimensional form. This will make possible three-dimensional photographs, printed illustrations, projected slides, motion pictures, televised pictures, images at computer terminals, and microscopic slides.

It is likely that in the next ten years breakthroughs in the use of lasers, improvements in data transmission, storage, and retrieval, will play a part in a more widespread and more sophisticated use of communications satellites for direct broadcasts to schools and homes. This, along with improvements in computers, tape players, and film projectors, will greatly increase the potential for individualized instruction in audio and video forms, programmed and non-programmed.

Hugh F. Beckwith, President
Beckwith and Associates

Television and satellite systems could turn the student into an eyewitness of all manner of instructive events. Whether it were a national election, a student rebellion, a moon shot, an African lion hunt, or a Guru convention, the student would be able to observe what was happening as it happened.

The "schools" of tomorrow might also use technology to cultivate not only the student's cognitive powers, but his esthetic and moral development as well. George B. Leonard, in *Education and Ecstasy,* foresees academic courses that would enhance, through seemingly extraneous material, the central nervous system's capacity to make connections which are not necessarily conceptual, factual, or symbolic. He predicts the use of the computer as an artistic tool in its own right, and forecasts its use to incorporate brain-wave information in the creation of a total learning atmosphere of color and sound.

> The day when we can alter the intellectual capacity of children, and maybe of adults, through the use of drugs may come pretty soon—in all probability within ten years—since we are likely to develop chemical or pharmacological means for enhancing learning before we fully understand the biochemical processes of the brain. Eventually there may be a whole arsenal of drugs, each affecting a different part of the learning process, e.g., acquisition of information, short-term memory, long-term memory.

> Seminar on the Chemistry of
>   Learning and Memory, sponsored by
> the Institute for Development of
> Educational Activities, Inc., and the
> U.S. Office of Education

Another area ripe for change, say the forecasters, is information and library science. Tomorrow's information-seeker could query a system which could search a collective fund of global information, and deliver the answer within seconds. If a text were desired, it would be printed out. Educational managers would have access to up-to-the-minute information on student characteristics, behavior, and performance, as well as to the latest findings in learning research and to actual materials available for instruction.

> By proper planning and coordinated activity we can work toward a time when information is unrestrictedly and equally distributed to everyone, regardless of his location, status, or wealth. It may come to be considered one of the rights of man to have immediate access (by remote man-machine interfaces or the terminals of a network), wherever he is, to complete, correct, and undistorted information on any topic of his interest.

> James G. Miller
> Vice President, EDUCOM
> (Interuniversity Communications Council)

Such is the visionary, long-range prospect for achieving vast improvements in education through a full exploitation of technology. But the closer one focuses the telescope, the more clearly do the genuine obstacles, constraints, and flaws show up. Much of the confusion and fruitless controversy in this whole field, in fact, arises from the tendency to confuse the short-term outlook with the long-term outlook, and to use one inappropriately against the other. Thus, the long-range potential of computers in education encourages the advocacy of using equipment available but possibly unsuitable now. On the other hand, the failure of prototypes and poorly designed experiments encourages arguments that a particular medium—or even technology in general—has a limited potential for improving education in the future.

Even in the short run, however, instructional technology could strengthen our ability to deal with critical problems. For example, it could introduce an inspiriting change of pace and mode for the minority-group student in cases where the teacher, coming from a different cultural and economic background, fails to sympathize with him and his problems. It could help to accommodate students whose learning styles make them unresponsive to a solid diet of books and lectures. It could stimulate students who are accustomed to the kaleidoscopic diversity and excitement of out-of-school learning via television, radio, and recordings, and who are bored by conventional instruction.

Moreover, as a labor-intensive system, education is growing more expensive all the time without becoming more effective. With the vast repertoire of communications media available, it is high time instruction became more productive. If, as seems clear, some of the functions performed by human beings can be performed as well or better through other agencies, teachers could assume more versatile, differentiated, *human* roles in the schools.

A human being should not be wasted in doing what forty sheets of paper or two phonographs can do. Just because personal teaching is precious and can do what books and apparatus can not, it should be saved for its peculiar work.

Edward L. Thorndike (1912)

Various innovations have been introduced as ways to break out of the rigid system which marches students, lock-step fashion, through a series of identical classrooms in which teachers do most of the talking and students have little opportunity to respond. Among these innovations are team teaching and teacher aides, nongraded elementary and secondary schools, independent study, curricula focused on helping students discover things for themselves rather than on trying to tell them everything, and schools designed for maximum flexibility so that students can work alone, or in small groups, or take part in large-group instruction via diverse media.

The aim of all these innovations—organizational, curricular, and technological—is to adapt instruction more precisely to the needs of each individual student. Many people who have an aversion to organizing instruction scientifically and to bringing new technology into the schools and colleges fail to realize that the present system is in many respects mechanical and rigid. The vast differences in the ways students learn are disregarded when they are taught the same thing, in the same way, at the same time. There is no escaping the evidence that many students themselves feel little enthusiasm and even outright hostility for the present way schools and colleges are organized and instruction is handled. Many of them resent technology, but what they object to is usually technology patched on as an expedient for handling a large number of students. Or it is programming which merely reproduces conventional classroom teaching.

What instruction requires is an arrangement of resources whereby the student responds and learns, reaching new plateaus from which to climb to higher levels of understanding. Implicit in such an arrangement, if it is to be effective, is the adaptability of the process to the individual student's differences—in pace, temperament, background, and style of learning.

Technological media can perform many of the functions involved in this process:

- They can store information until it is needed or wanted;

- They can distribute it over distances to reach the student where he happens to be instead of bringing him to the teacher;

- They can present the information to the student through various senses and in many modes;

- They can give the student the opportunity to react to the material and respond in many ways.

In short, the student's opportunities for learning can be increased and enhanced by using a wide range of instructional technology. All the available resources for instruction, including the teacher, can work together to create conditions for maximum effective learning.

Much of the energy and intelligence which teachers currently expend in the classroom can be profitably shifted to working with students in tutorial and small group discussions, and to preparing potent materials which can then be stored, transmitted, and presented by nonhuman means.

A machine is not a sadist and does not suffer from rebuffs or redundancy. Nor does a student feel demeaned by having to take instruction from a person of another class or race or sex. For a boy who feels that, like Huckleberry Finn, he must light out for the Territory to prove his manhood, or for a black student who feels that a white teacher is subjecting him to counterfeit nurturance and thus making him even weaker and more deprived, or for a lower-class white student who feels a similar uneasiness at being helped, the machine can be a marvelously neutral substitute.

Few teachers are sadists; they are, however, human and naturally react to the adverse reactions of students and to the constraints of conventional school organization. The machine can spare both student and teacher.

> David Riesman
> Henry Ford II Professor
>   of Social Sciences
> Harvard University

Many people see instructional technology primarily as a way of recording, storing, transmitting, distributing, and displaying material. But equally important is its capacity for response and feedback and for reinforcement of learning. Some of the most fruitful uses of technology for instruction aim at carrying out these functions, in ways which may be beyond the capability of the teacher. Programmed learning, for example, provides immediate, constant, and infinitely patient feedback. Another quite different example is the use of videotapes in teacher education ("micro-teaching"), which gives teachers a new way to see themselves, to analyze small units of their own teaching, and to improve their methods as a result.

The Benefits of Instructional Technology

On the basis of present and past applications of instructional technology, and of informed projections by educators, scholars, and specialists, the Commission has summarized the potential benefits of instructional technology as follows:

1) TECHNOLOGY CAN MAKE EDUCATION MORE PRODUCTIVE

With the demand for education outstripping education's income, more effective and efficient learning is vital. Instructional technology has shown its ability to speed up the rate of learning. It can help the teacher make better use of his time. It can reduce the teacher's heavy burden of administrative tasks and take over some of the teacher's routine job of information transmission. Thus, the teacher would be able to spend more time on *teaching*—inspiring students to learn and encouraging them to apply newly acquired information in useful and interesting ways.

At the U. S. Navy's Memphis Air Training Center, where 25 courses use programmed instruction, training managers reduced training time by 28 percent after introducing programmed instruction and saved 235 man years in 1968 alone. At Fort Rucker, Alabama, the United States Army Aviation School redesigned the entire Helicopter Instrument Flight Course by converting academic instruction to programmed format and adapting the technique of programmed, self-paced instruction to flight and synthetic flight training. This redesign resulted in a significant reduction in course length.

> Lt. Col. Howard B. Hitchens
> Professor of Instructional
>   Communications
> U.S. Air Force Academy

2) TECHNOLOGY CAN MAKE EDUCATION MORE INDIVIDUAL

Group-paced and group-prescribed instruction seems to be a virtual necessity when resources are restricted to teacher and textbook. But technology properly applied opens up many different ways of learning. Individual differences can be taken seriously. The traditional rigid control and standardization of what students learn, how they learn, when and at what pace, is no longer necessary. One teacher per thirty students no longer has to be the dominant pattern for the public schools. The live lecture as the most common medium of instruction in higher education can now be questioned. Different combinations of teachers, students, materials, space, time, and dollars can respond more to actual learning needs and less to administrative convenience.

Freedom and self-direction have always been accepted as goals of American education. The use of technology in education can increase the alternatives and permit the student to find his own direction more easily. The pluralism of educational objectives in a democratic society can only be reached by using a plurality of means.

> A freshman botany course at Purdue University has been totally restructured with the aim of defining clearly all objectives. Students, teaching assistants, and academic and research colleagues have been consulted extensively, and all identifiable "busy work" has been eliminated. Most of the factual information is acquired through independent study in a specially designed learning center containing thirty booths. Each is equipped with a tape player, an 8mm movie projector, a microscope, live plants, test tubes, diagrams, and other materials pertinent to the week's study.

> Learning activities may include listening to short lectures, performing experiments, reading from texts and journals, studying demonstrations, viewing short films, discussions with the instructor and/or other students, microscope study, dissection of specimens, and any other study activity deemed helpful by the senior instructor or the student. Since the independent study is unscheduled, experiments do not have to be designed to fit into a three-hour time interval, and some experiments can take the form of miniature research projects.

> S. N. Postlethwait
> Professor of Biological Sciences
> Purdue University

3) TECHNOLOGY CAN GIVE INSTRUCTION A MORE SCIENTIFIC BASE

Instructional technology could provide the framework necessary for designing conditions of learning that are more closely based on what is known about how human beings learn. Research reveals, for example, the importance of reinforcement and reward in furthering learning: instructional technology can help make reinforcement and reward an integral part of learning. Instructional technology has the potential not only to guide research into asking the right questions, but also to apply research results to schools and colleges.

> Oakleaf Elementary School, located in a blue-collar suburb of Pittsburgh, has been operating an individually prescribed instruction program (IPI) since 1963. Research and development for the IPI curriculum originated in the federally funded R&D Center located at the University of Pittsburgh. The purpose of IPI is to enable each student to go through the curriculum at his own speed, working independently much of the time. Courses thus programmed are math, science, reading, and writing.

> At Oakleaf, the system is learner-centered and the role of the teacher has been sharply redefined. Little of the teacher's time is spent in lecturing to a group. Much of the information transmission takes place independently of the live teacher —through the media of booklets and worksheets and, in science, audiotape cartridges and three-dimensional manipulative equipment. The teacher's main tasks

are evaluating individual pupils' progress, preparing daily learning prescriptions for each child, and tutoring children on a one-to-one or small group basis.

4) TECHNOLOGY CAN MAKE INSTRUCTION MORE POWERFUL

New forms of communication give man added capability. Instructional technology can *extend* the possibilities of education. The live teacher cannot "say everything." A physical-education film using slow motion photography, a recording of diseased heart beats, or a videotape of a presidential press conference enables the teacher to communicate more to the learner.

The study of the 20th century need no longer be so dependent on written documents when technology enables the student to *see* New York City in the 1920s, or the battle of the Somme, or a Hitler speech in the Berlin Sports Palace. By stressing instruction through teacher and textbook alone, formal education has become overly verbal. Many students—particularly poor or minority-group children—are thus handicapped in their academic progress, finding themselves ill at ease with the kind of language, oral or written, which they encounter at school.

Teachers at our high school are committed to the concept that their students want to learn. So we took a careful look at their learning styles and turned to, among other things, the Tube. Our students watch as much as five hours a day, and they like it. It occupies their minds. And because that is precisely what *we* sought to do, many of the staff turned to TV. Closed-circuit television turned out to be an educational gold mine, for it allows us to address ourselves to our students' cry for relevance, to their surging interest in their identity as black Americans. It gives us a vehicle which capitalizes on how our kids like to learn and how they learn most readily.

Marcus Foster, former principal
Simon Gratz High School
North Philadelphia

5) TECHNOLOGY CAN MAKE LEARNING MORE IMMEDIATE

Instructional technology can help to bridge the gap between the world outside and the world inside the school. Television and xerography can bring immediacy to the learner. They can make possible a dynamic curriculum. If instructional technology is creatively applied, the student's route to knowledge and understanding can be more direct.

Knowledge and reality, filtered through the words of textbook and teacher, all too often reach the student as predigested conclusions, neatly packaged, and thoroughly divorced from what Alfred North Whitehead called the "radically untidy, ill-adjusted character" of reality.

"First-hand knowledge," Whitehead wrote, "is the ultimate basis of intellectual life. To a large extent book-learning conveys second-hand information, and as such can never rise to the importance of immediate practice. Our goal is to see the immediate events of our lives as instances of our general ideas."

It would, of course, be idle to interpret Whitehead's words as a wholesale attack on books and a prescient endorsement of television. Nonetheless the words quoted above are typical of educational philosophers' constant plea for immediacy and diversity, qualities which the newer media of instruction can bring to formal instruction.

In the spring of 1968, 17 ETV stations on the East Coast, 495 teachers, and 13,650 students participated in a live, interconnected educational simulation involving telephone feedback from classrooms during the broadcasts. "Cabinets in Crisis," developed by the Educational Division of WGBH-TV in Boston, was a simulation of the Yugoslav aid crisis of 1950. Political decision-makers in the United States, the Soviet Union, and Yugoslavia were played on television by students in Philadelphia, Rochester, and Boston. "Political advisors" in the classrooms communicated advice and votes to the TV studio teams by telephone and letter. The staff of WGBH reported to the Commission that participation and interest ran high:

"A group of students from Boston became so involved they came to the studio when it was all over and announced they could construct a much better TV simulation. We encouraged them to work on it during the summer and they have come up with an original simulation which is in fact an improvement on our first experiment."

6) *TECHNOLOGY CAN MAKE ACCESS TO EDUCATION MORE EQUAL.*

Equal access to rich learning environments is not possible without some recourse to technology. Through television or film nearly every school in America can have the luxury of seeing Sir Laurence Olivier play Othello. When the telecommunications network envisaged by the Interuniversity Communications Council (EDUCOM) is operational, the students and faculty of a small rural college can have direct access to the greatest libraries of the country. At the present time, via the National Library of Medicine's Medical Literature Analysis and Retrieval System (MEDLARS), doctors in Denver can obtain as much bibliographic information on recent medical literature as can doctors working in the hospital across the street from the computer center in Bethesda, Maryland.

Harvard has a beautiful Russian History Center and Pennsylvania has a beautiful South Asia Center. If I were in Pennsylvania and I wanted to know something about Russian history, obviously the best professor is at Harvard. But I can't see him.

There is no reason why the federal government couldn't allow the educational TV stations to get telephone wires at a lower rate than the networks pay, so that I could listen to that lecture whenever they give it at Harvard—listen to it in Pennsylvania and have everybody on the Coast listen to it. Right now it costs too much money.

Richard Clarke, freshman
University of Pennsylvania
CIT student seminar

Technology does not have to move people; it transmits the impact of people. The limits to improving instruction through technology are political, parochial, financial—they are not inherent in technology itself.

The Commission is convinced that technology properly employed could make education more productive, individual, and powerful, learning more immediate, instruction more scientifically based, and access to education more equal. *We have concluded, therefore, that this nation should make a far greater investment in instructional technology. We believe that such an investment will contribute to extending the scope and upgrading the quality of education, and that the results will benefit individuals and society.*

I believe that instructional technology offers unique and priceless opportunities to bring to every student in every classroom the kinds of knowledge, the kinds of experiences, the kinds of insights that can truly widen the dialogue and help find the common ground for solutions to our most pressing problems.

Wilbur J. Cohen, former
Secretary of Health,
Education, and Welfare

What form should this investment take? How should instructional technology be employed? What magnitude of investment should be made?

IV.
To Improve
Learning

To improve learning through the application of instructional technology requires a course of action that will:

- Deal with root problems, such as the advancement of the knowledge of how human beings learn and the application of these findings to instruction in schools and colleges.

- Support sustained research, development, and application projects.

- Apply technology to the most critical problems in education.

- Encourage alternative approaches to the solution of any given educational problem.

- Concentrate resources on action programs of high visibility.

- Create conditions which encourage scholars and specialists from various fields to work together.

The Commission proposes a course of action to meet these requirements. Top priority should go to the expansion and improvement of educational research and development and to the application of research findings to important practical problems in education. Finally, the results must be packaged for effective use by the schools and colleges.

It would seem that much of what we have so laboriously learned about educational theory and practice has been—to say the least—underadvertised, poorly packaged, and thinly distributed.

Thus, our first goal must be to get the good, new ideas and practices into use—and get them there quickly.

James E. Allen, Jr.
Assistant Secretary for Education
and Commissioner of Education
Department of Health, Education,
and Welfare

The Commission was strengthened in its conviction of the importance of research, development, and application by the findings of earlier and concurrent inquiries into this field. Similar conclusions were reached, for example, in the recent study, *Innovation in Education,* by the Committee for Economic Development (CED), and in the 1966 Congressional report on automation and technology in education; in the findings of the Harvard Program on Technology and Society; by outsiders at odds with the establishment as well as spokesmen for such groups as the American Educational Research Association; by a committee of the National Academy of Education; and in recommendations proposed to this Commission by scholars, the professions, industry, instructional technologists, and practicing educators.

The nation spends proportionately 20 times as much on health research—and about 60 times as much on defense research—as it does on education research.

U.S. Office of Education

Advances in educational research, development, and application have been made in recent years, as the Committee for Economic Development report noted: "Much has been learned about relating subject matter to instructional goals, refining the techniques of explanation, cultivating the capacity for discovery, and defining other aspects of the learning process." But the Committee for Economic Development added that much more needs to be known "if the schools are to continue to move ahead." It emphasized the importance of *development* as industry understands the process, of better ways to measure and evaluate the quality of instruction, and of concerted efforts to package, disseminate, and apply significant findings and likely hypotheses. Research findings must be brought to the schools under conditions and in forms that make them useful. There is no point in disseminating ideas which are not packaged for practical use.

We need a means of analyzing the needs of education on a systematic and national basis; and then of influencing the allocation of R&D resources according to these needs, whether the resources are in education itself, in nonprofit research organizations, or in industry. Further, whatever mechanism is developed for this purpose, it needs to be structured in such a way that the independence of local or state educational units is not jeopardized.

Robert W. Locke and
David Engler
McGraw-Hill Book Company

Harold Howe II, when he was U.S. Commissioner of Education, described education's research and development needs to a group of businessmen interested in the education market. Before the "revolution" in education, however desirable, could get very far, Mr. Howe said, much more would have to be known about the educational process: man has barely scratched the surface of man's ability to learn. While warning his audience that no miracles were around the corner, he stressed the double role that technology could play in dealing with the unanswered questions—both as an instrument of instruction and as a research instrument.

An agenda for educational research:

How can we reach the children of the slums, who have remained relatively untouched by traditional education?

How can we find out, for any group of youngsters, whether we are teaching them the right or wrong things?

Can those who learn well learn even more?

How can we decide, in view of the explosion of knowledge, what part of the whole field we ought to attempt to teach?

How do we reach those presently unmotivated to learn?

How do we evaluate and alter school organization?

How do we come to a real understanding of what intelligence is? And can intelligence be learned?

At what age should formal education begin? And do parents have a real job to do in this connection?

How do we improve the education of two million teachers without seriously interrupting their teaching careers?

How can we get the most out of the individual student's ability to teach himself?

> Harold Howe II, former
> U.S. Commissioner of Education

Comprehensive Approach

Research, development, and application (R. D. & A.) should, the Commission believes, form the core of a comprehensive approach to the improvement of learning. This comprehensive approach should include more and better training of teachers, administrators, and instructional technologists; the production of better materials; improved methods of access to instructional materials in all media; and more fruitful relationships between education and industry (see the six recommendations in Chapter V of this report).

> The major issues in the use of technology in education, as I see them, reside not so much in the development of technologies as in the re-education of teachers and educators in the value of technology as an aid to instruction. When educators look at technology as a resource for developing new alternatives and individualizing instruction, rather than as a dangerous, mechanistic intruder, then the existing wealth of technological developments will have its desired effect upon the world of education.

> Dwight W. Allen, Dean
> School of Education
> University of Massachusetts

The problems confronting American schools and colleges demand a cohesive, concerted attack. It is not the parts of the educational system that must be improved; it is the system in its totality. The key remedy is not computer-assisted instruction or team teaching or nongraded classes or educational parks or instructional television: it is innovations like these wisely integrated with each other and with teachers and the more traditional resources of education that may make the difference.

> Systematic application of communications technology to education provides the basis for developing new and economical means for coping with important educational problems. Technology—radio or television, for example—can communicate material that is carefully organized, documented, and planned. When technology can share with the teacher the responsibility for making the lesson effective, opportunities open up for designing and carrying out new instructional strategies.

> William G. Harley, President
> National Association of
> Educational Broadcasters

There are dangers, to be sure, in focusing prematurely and unremittingly on the "big picture." A comprehensive systems analysis is hardly required to know what has to be done to improve a ghetto classroom where the windowpanes fall in on the students and where there are no textbooks for the first six weeks of school. In these ghetto classrooms pictured so vividly in the news, in novels, movies, and official reports, as well as in the suburban class-rooms dissected by social critics such as John Holt and Edgar Friedenberg, in the colleges under increasing attack as sterile and irrelevant, in poorly equipped schools in the rural South, in predominantly Negro colleges, and in many other places—there is much obvious, everyday work needed to make American education decent and equitable.

At the beginning of this report, instructional technology was defined as "a systematic way of designing, carrying out, and evaluating the total process of learning and teaching in terms of specific objectives, based on findings from research in human learning and com-munication, and employing a combination of human and nonhuman resources to bring about more effective instruction." A significant improvement of learning depends on our ability to organize our efforts in accordance with this definition.

John W. Gardner, chairman of the Urban Coalition, said recently: "We have already developed and tested many of the ingredients of what will be a new era in education. But the pieces of the educational revolution are lying around unassembled. Perhaps in ten or twenty years we will be able to look back and find that these pieces have taken shape into one cohesive whole."

Much of the Commission's study has dealt, by necessity, with the pieces of this unassem-bled revolution. But the revolution must eventually be assembled if education is to generate its full benefits for American youth. The nation cannot wait. A massive effort, year after year for decades ahead, is needed. This conviction underlies the recommendations that fol-low.

V.
Recommendations

Recommendation #1

We Recommend:

A new institution—the National Institutes of Education (N.I.E.)—should be established by Congress within the Department of Health, Education, and Welfare, reporting directly to the Assistant Secretary for Education.

The National Institutes of Education should be broadly authorized to develop, support, and fund greatly strengthened programs in educational research, development, and application (R. D. & A.).

The National Institutes of Education should comprise several constituent institutes, through which grants would be made to universities and other independent research institutions. The institutes would also conduct research themselves. The N.I.E. should sponsor, among other things, several strong autonomous regional R. D. & A. centers, plus a small number of comprehensive demonstration projects.

The proposed National Institutes of Education—well-funded, broadly based, and building on present strengths and successful programs (public and private)—would give concentrated leadership and direction to a national effort to improve learning and teaching at every level of education. The organization should start with a few component institutes focused on critical areas. This report proposes the creation of a National Institute of Instructional Technology (see Recommendation #2), including a center or "library" of educational resources (see Recommendation #3). In addition, the National Institutes of Education might create other institutes, as for instance one concentrating on learning research, one on teaching and curriculum development, and another on educational organization, finance, and management. A prime function of the N.I.E. as the parent body would be to ensure close cooperation and feedback among the institutes. Their provinces would obviously overlap and it is important to avoid perpetuating conventional and unproductive divisions.

Instructional technology simultaneously draws from and contributes to an underlying science of learning. The technology of instruction is shaped by, as it will shape, the purposes and the substance of education. Unless technological means are harnessed to humane ends, with full regard for individual diversity and needs, no real benefit will accrue to society—indeed, the reverse is more likely.

Furthermore, instructional technology is integrally involved with the process of learning and the genuine individualization of learning. Any sharp distinction, then, between research and development in instructional technology, on the one hand, and research and development in the basics of education, on the other, appears to us to be arbitrary. In fact, this very division has contributed to the disappointing impact thus far of instructional technology—so frequently heralded, so seldom realized down the years since 1913 when Edison proclaimed the motion picture as the prospective agent of complete school reform.

The National Institutes of Education and its component institutes would undertake a limited amount of research, development, and application themselves. This proportion should be relatively small, however—perhaps 10 to 15 percent. The majority of the work should be executed through grants made by the institutes to selected institutions, both public and private.

The Commission recognizes the importance of conducting both basic and directed research. Basic research, in which the investigator is free to formulate his own questions, can lead to far-reaching discoveries which could not be defined in a blueprint for investigation. On the other hand, directed research, in which the questions are clearly structured, can be a powerful tool for achieving specific desired results.

Each institute should establish subsidiary research, development, and application programs, tied in closely with individual institutions and with existing and projected regional centers. The National Institutes of Education and its component institutes should work closely with state educational agencies, especially state departments of education, and with the Education Commission of the States.

To insure maximum effectiveness and influence, the National Institutes of Education should be a strong arm of the Department of Health, Education, and Welfare, reporting directly to the Assistant Secretary for Education* as shown in the following chart.

The National Institutes of Education should be headed by a director with outstanding qualifications appointed by the President and aided in policy making by a small strong top-level Advisory Board, composed of government and nongovernment representatives. Each constituent institute should also be headed by a highly qualified director. Together the Advisory Board and the directors would act as a council to coordinate the work of the N.I.E.

Through its national visibility and stature, the National Institutes of Education should build up educational research, development, and application throughout the nation. Everywhere—in universities and school systems and state departments of education—there are able, dedicated people working on new approaches to solving educational problems. The National Institutes of Education should strengthen promising work now going on, encourage initiative and invention, and support a diversity of approaches to critical problems. In Recommendation #2 we indicate how one of the institutes—the National Institute of Instructional Technology—could accomplish some of these objectives.

Tradition of Federal Research, Development, and Application Leadership

The establishment of a federal institution such as the National Institutes of Education would be entirely in the mainstream of American tradition. There are outstanding precedents for federal action of this magnitude in other fields. For instance:

Agriculture: Since 1862, when President Lincoln signed the Congressional acts

---

*Note: The Commission believes that the federal government's top official for education should be upgraded to the level of Under Secretary at least, and ultimately to a full Secretary, either under the Secretary of Health, Education, and Welfare or as head of a separate new cabinet-level Department of Education.

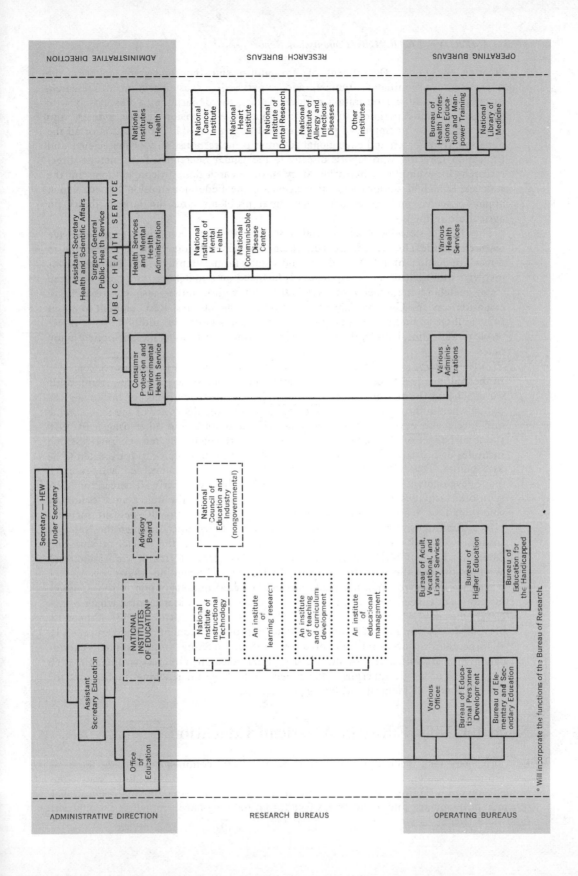

ADMINISTRATIVE DIRECTION

RESEARCH BUREAUS

OPERATING BUREAUS

Secretary — HEW
Under Secretary

Assistant Secretary
Health and Scientific Affairs
Surgeon General
Public Health Service

PUBLIC HEALTH SERVICE

National Institutes of Health

National Cancer Institute

National Heart Institute

National Institute of Dental Research

National Institute of Allergy and Infectious Diseases

Other Institutes

Bureau of Health Professions Education and Manpower Training

National Library of Medicine

Health Services and Mental Health Administration

National Institute of Mental Health

National Communicable Disease Center

Various Health Services

Consumer Protection and Environmental Health Service

Various Administrations

Advisory Board

National Council of Education and Industry (nongovernmental)

NATIONAL INSTITUTES OF EDUCATION*

National Institute of Instructional Technology

An institute of learning research

An institute of teaching and curriculum development

An institute of educational management

Bureau of Adult, Vocational, and Library Services

Bureau of Higher Education

Bureau of Education for the Handicapped

Assistant Secretary Education

Office of Education

Various Offices

Bureau of Educational Personnel Development

Bureau of Elementary and Secondary Education

* Will incorporate the functions of the Bureau of Research.

creating the U. S. Department of Agriculture and the land-grant colleges, the department has initiated, funded, and supervised a vast program of research, development, and demonstration projects. Today, the department works closely with state agricultural experiment stations, the Cooperative Extension Service, industry, and other agencies in a complex of projects related to rural affairs. Coordination of all the department's research and educational activities is the responsibility of the Science and Education Director, who reports directly to the Under Secretary. They include direct research (for example, at Beltsville, Maryland), research done in cooperation with the state experimental stations and other agencies, the Federal Extension Service which applies research findings to day-to-day rural problems, and the largest library on agriculture in the country.

The federal-state-local agricultural research program comprises comprehensive research and development in agriculture and forestry—ranging from basic research to direct application of R&D results to individual farms, families, and business firms involved with agriculture. The program is financed on a matching-fund basis, with the states matching the federal funds allotted and with counties also contributing to extension services. Currently government funds for agricultural R&D amount to about $450 million annually; industry provides an equal amount in addition. As a direct result of agricultural R&D, the productivity of American farmers has multiplied many times.

Health: A large part of the nation's biomedical research and training is concentrated in the National Institutes of Health. Federal funds for these activities grew significantly during the 1950s, as Congress recognized important new prospects for improving the nation's health through research (triggered in part by the discovery of the Salk vaccine and spectacular developments in the new sulfa, antibiotic, and other drugs). By 1970 the total budget of the National Institutes of Health (including ten separate research institutes and certain other responsibilities, notably health manpower) is expected to be $1.5 billion. The National Institutes of Health is primarily concerned with research —not development—and with education in the health field. Nearly 90 percent of NIH-sponsored activities is "extramural," i.e., it is carried out through grants to universities, medical schools, hospitals, clinics, etc. The remaining 10 percent includes NIH's own extensive research activities at Bethesda, Maryland. Although the National Institutes of Health is part of the Public Health Service on the official organization chart, the head of NIH reports directly to the Secretary of Health, Education, and Welfare, through the Assistant Secretary for Health and Scientific Affairs.

NIH-sponsored research has made possible a better understanding of the underlying causes of cancer, heart disease, and other illnesses—an understanding which brings closer the day when these diseases will be successfully cured and, ultimately, prevented. Development of a rubella vaccine, improved treatment of acute leukemia in children, and a successful cure of a rare cancer affecting young women (choriocarcinoma) are but a few of the fruits of NIH research. Other developments, such as progress in the deciphering of the genetic code, have far-reaching implications for the entire field of medical and biological sciences.

Need for New Effort in American Education

Education has long needed a national research effort, commensurate with those in agriculture and health, focused on the improvement of learning and teaching. Now is the prime moment to bring all available resources to bear in strengthening educational research, development, and innovation, which for far too long have commanded insufficient funds and talent.

While many basic questions still remain unanswered or disputed, there are encouraging additions being made to man's understanding of the hows and whys of human learning in all its variations. One important reason is the gradual coming together of research specialists who once operated almost in isolation: new findings from the laboratory studies of human and animal learning, for example, are interacting with findings from actual classrooms.

Today America needs to examine the basic assumptions (too often unexamined) on which schools and colleges operate. If indeed schools are to be humane environments for learning and not mere institutional accumulations, if diplomas and degrees are to be more than mere passes to economic and social acceptance, America's vast decentralized educational "system" must undergo a revision that draws upon the best insights that can be cultivated: from scholars of diverse disciplines, teachers, philosophers, and artists, administrators, citizens generally, and from the ultimate consumer—the student.

In recent years, the federal government has spent increasing amounts for education. Under the Elementary and Secondary Education Act of 1965, for example, about $4 billion has been allocated to upgrade education in deprived areas. But these funds were not invested to get to the roots of education's problems, nor to design a system with more adequate theoretical and technological foundations. The money has been used primarily to repair and extend the present system.

The Commission has concluded that the nation's investment in education must be increased and its thrust changed if America is to resolve its present basic educational and social problems. To be sure, public expenditures on education are nominally accepted as an "investment" in the nation's economic and social future. But the situation today requires that substantial funds for education be allotted for investment more strictly construed: as capital to create an improved system of teaching and learning which will produce more real individual and social achievement for each dollar spent than is done by the present system.

The Commission believes that the problems of teaching and learning could yield to an organized and systematic attack, and that the refinement and imaginative use of instructional technology could contribute signally to the success of that attack. Certainly the solution of education's problems is as critical for the nation's future well-being as is a cure for cancer, heart disease, or stroke, or the development of more efficient techniques for growing and harvesting wheat.

A New Emphasis: Development and Application

Fully as urgent as expanded, sharply focused research is the need to improve the essential follow-through known as development and application. The process of successful innovation entails several stages. First, there is specific development which produces from a new idea a particular program—for teaching reading to children in the early grades, for instance. Second, there is a design-and-proving stage, to test the new program in the schools. Third, training and follow-through enable key people to run broader trials in the schools, and constantly feed back information on problems and discoveries which may modify the program. Finally, there is a transmission of the new program in usable form to interested schools throughout the nation.

There is, of course, seldom so orderly a process as this sequence suggests. The role of creation, of pure *invention,* is all-important in education as in any other science or art. And it would be stultifying if innovation had to wait on solid research results and development procedures. The ideal process that needs support and encouragement is circular: the bright idea, successfully improvised by a teacher, administrator, or student can spur research, as well as the other way around.

It is clear, moreover, that even the best programs of research, development, invention, and application, if they are to have practical, large scale effects, require improved efforts in packaging, disseminating, and evaluating. Therefore, educational improvement could be furthered by concentrating funds and effort on disseminating *outstanding* theoretical and empirical findings in usable form. Increased funds could be applied, for example, to quicker and wider communication of important findings through television, radio, and other new media.

Further Details With Respect to the National Institutes of Education

1. The National Institutes of Education, through its various constituent institutes, should take over the activities of the Office of Education's present Bureau of Research, which include the ten Research and Development Centers and the fifteen Regional Educational Laboratories funded under Title IV of the Elementary and Secondary Education Act of 1965. It should also assume such other educational research, development, and application projects as clearly fall within its purview.*

The recommendation that a new agency absorb the present functions of the Bureau of Research implies no derogation of that hard-pressed organization which in its brief existence has made a marked contribution, quantitatively and qualitatively, to education. Federal support for educational research, however, is still wholly inadequate. The total for 1969 (all of it in the form of grants or contracts) amounts to no more than $125 million, and goes largely for applied research, very little for basic research or for development. Moreover, in the summer of 1969, the research program is in the midst of a cutback.

2. The National Institutes of Education should also be expected to maintain close ties with relevant research and development being conducted in the many federal agencies outside the Department of Health, Education, and Welfare that operate education programs;** also with the American Educational Research Association and with practitioners in other relevant disciplines such as social scientists and engineers.

3. The National Institutes of Education could use the research models in agriculture and health as guides. In its disposition of research funds, for instance, the N.I.E. might well follow the lead of the National Institutes of Health in concentrating research in universities and other research-oriented institutions through grants. In other important matters, however, agricultural research and development might offer a more appropriate model; e.g., with respect to the close collaboration maintained with state and local agencies and the emphasis on development and application as well as basic research.

4. The National Institutes of Education proposed in this report may well be involved in research projects running three to five years or more in length. Annual funding in the ordinary way would limit the effectiveness of such projects. The new organization, therefore, should explore with the Bureau of the Budget the possibility of obtaining

---

*The National Institutes of Education should assume only the research responsibilities now under the Office of Education. Operating programs (see chart, page 43), which now make up the bulk of OE programs, should remain in the Office of Education.

**Among these other agencies are the Atomic Energy Commission, the National Aeronautics and Space Administration, the National Science Foundation, the Office of Economic Opportunity, the Department of Labor, and the armed forces. (The U. S. Office of Education budget in fact, has never amounted to more than one-half of the total federal funds devoted to "education and manpower.") Another relevant private-public enterprise of importance is the program recently established by the Office of Education with the National Academy of Sciences and the National Academy of Education to finance basic research in education.

authority to use "no-year appropriations" for research programs, or forward-funding arrangements (100 percent committed for the first year, two-thirds for the second year, and one-third for the third year) similar to those developed by a number of government agencies including the National Science Foundation, the Atomic Energy Commission, the Environmental Science Services Administration, the National Aeronautics and Space Administration, and the Department of Defense.

Recommendation #2

We Recommend:

A National Institute of Instructional Technology (N.I.I.T.) should be established as a constituent of the proposed National Institutes of Education. The purpose of the N.I.I.T. should be to improve American education at all levels through the use of instructional technology. The focus of the Institute's activities should be on research, development, and application in equipment, instructional materials, and systems, and also in training personnel.

The proposed National Institute of Instructional Technology should strengthen and promote the most promising of the Research and Development Centers and Regional Educational Laboratories (now operating under Title IV of the Elementary and Secondary Education Act of 1965) which are conducting programs involving instructional technology, and should establish such other regional centers as it deems necessary.

The National Institute of Instructional Technology should increase significantly the quality and quantity of the research, development, dissemination, and action programs needed to fulfill instructional technology's potential for advancing learning and teaching.

Like its fellow institutes, the National Institute of Instructional Technology could be a new locus of talent, energy, expertise, and imagination for American education, providing leadership and initiative for efforts from many sources. It should bring together scholars from many disciplines and experts from the various media representing divergent viewpoints, including talented people who have hitherto dedicated themselves primarily to their own professional fields and organizations and to their own communities and institutions.

The influence and impact of the National Institute of Instructional Technology, like the National Institutes of Education as a whole, would derive principally from the stature and performance of the people mobilized, and from the initiative taken in advancing educational improvement. By its use of funds, its development and dissemination of new ideas, and its direction of selected pilot programs to achieve innovation in schools and colleges, the National Institute of Instructional Technology should generate a new, more coherent thrust toward continuing improvement throughout American education. Its work and that of the other institutes should serve as guides for the many programs carried out through the Office of Education—a cooperative way of translating researched, developed, and tested methods and ideas into effective action programs.

In line with the general policies for the proposed National Institutes of Education outlined in Recommendation #1, the National Institute of Instructional Technology should instigate and sustain programs of research, development, and application relating to its responsibility. It should encourage and support regional, state, and local activities, encourage initiative and invention, and provide a diversity of approaches to the critical problems of instruction in the schools and colleges. Of first importance would be the National Institute of Instructional Technology's leadership in finding effective ways to improve and expand the production of educational materials—perhaps through the creation of new production centers that would draw on both public and private resources.*

The Commission cannot emphasize too strongly the importance of "a diversity of approaches." The National Institutes of Education and its constituent institutes should constantly foster *alternative* schemes, in much the same way as systems analysis encourages alternative solutions to an objective that has been established. The problems of education will not be solved by any one approach. The very diversity of human beings and cultural patterns demand diverse approaches. In the past, education has tended to overlook this diversity and has been inclined to proceed on the assumption that everyone should be able to learn in much the same way. We propose, therefore, a decentralized pattern for the programs sponsored and coordinated by the National Institute of Instructional Technology, and we envisage regional clusters of institutions—universities, school systems, state departments of education, production centers—working together on projects of common interest and of national significance.

The Commission strongly endorses the concept and objectives of the Research and Development Centers and Regional Educational Laboratories.** In line with the institutional pattern outlined above, certain centers and laboratories would clearly fall within the scope of the National Institute of Instructional Technology. All the laboratories make some application of technology, with considerable variation in the degree of sophistication of the various programs. A few of the Research and Development Centers, such as Pittsburgh, Johns Hopkins, and Stanford, stress technology. The center at the University of Pittsburgh has been outstanding in combining basic research with regular programs in the local schools. This center and others are in effect providing models and prototypes for further development by the Regional Educational Laboratories.

But underfinancing has been a major handicap in the evolution of these fledgling enterprises, both centers and laboratories, and has slowed down their contribution to education. In comparison with the amount of federal support for major research and development installations in other fields, the federal support for educational research, development, and application must be described as token. The Jet Propulsion Laboratory, sponsored by the National Aeronautics and Space Administration, and the Lawrence Radiation Laboratory, sponsored by the Atomic Energy Commission, each receive 20 percent or more of the total federal obligation for university-administered research and development; no Research and Development Center in education has ever received much more than 1 percent of the total.

The Commission proposes that those laboratories and centers making the most promising advances in the use of instructional technology be funded by the proposed National Institute of Instructional Technology, that the institute be empowered to establish new centers as needed, and that these laboratories and centers be adequately financed, well-directed, competently staffed, and then encouraged to operate with genuine independence. The new centers should, for the most part, conduct multipurpose research, development, and application.*** Exceptions would be R. D. & A. in high-cost experimentation which would necessarily be more highly specialized.

*An example of combined efforts is the Children's Television Workshop, which is scheduled to go on the air in the fall of 1969.

**The Research and Development Centers and Regional Educational Laboratories operate under grants from the U.S. office of Education's Bureau of Research. The R&D Centers, all located within universities, were originally organized to provide basic research, development, and dissemination. Each center aims to bring interdisciplinary talent and resources to focus on a broad problem of particular significance to education and then to design programs to meet it. The Regional Educational Laboratories, on the other hand, were established as an effort to bridge the gap between educational research and practice—in effect, the "application" part of R. D. & A. They were expected to work much more closely with local schools than the Research and Development Centers—to select promising research and development activities, demonstrate their effectiveness, adapt materials and techniques for practical use in the schools, and disseminate their findings.

***The centers could also provide facilities (and possibly funds) for teachers and others with talent and ideas to experiment with the production of instructional materials employing a variety of media.

The National Institute of Instructional Technology should provide a meeting ground for the many organizations concerned with media, such as the Corporation for Public Broadcasting, state agencies including public broadcasting authorities, and the diverse groups with some interest in the technology field.* Although increasing numbers of classrooms make some use of instructional films, television programs, tapes, records, etc., the exponents and practitioners of the various instructional media operate without sufficient contact, coordination, and cross-fertilization. "Media apartheid," as one expert calls it, has helped to subordinate nonprint media to the hegemony of the printed book. Moreover, professional associations and the organization of schools and colleges (for example, the separation of the library, the audiovisual center, the television stations, and the computer facility from one another—even though all of them should be collaborating on instructional programming) have encouraged this separation. Instructional technology needs a central agency with national stature which could function as a base for those outstanding practitioners from each field who want to work with others across media boundaries to apply their knowledge, experience, and insight to the solution of pressing educational problems.

An essential counterpart to the efforts to use technology for more effective instruction is research, development, and application in the techniques for storing and retrieving information in all media. There is need to develop better tools for the analysis of library and information requirements and improved ways of measuring the value of existing systems and services. The Commission, in considering this problem, finds itself in agreement with recent recommendations of the National Advisory Commission on Libraries.** A principal recommendation was for a Federal Institute of Library and Information Science to conduct basic and applied research aimed at using technology to improve library services. The National Institute of Instructional Technology would be a logical location for these functions.

Another highly important feature of the research, development, and application efforts recommended here should be worldwide cooperation in the full utilization of instructional technology. If technology's potential can be thoroughly explored, analyzed, and confirmed in the United States, the results could be adapted to the educational needs of other countries—with particular impact on the developing nations. Also of importance are the lessons the United States could learn from other countries, a number of which are experimenting widely with instructional technology.*** International collaboration could reduce duplication of research, development, and application and speed the advancement of education in the United States and throughout the world.

Major functions and programs envisaged for the National Institute of Instructional Technology are spelled out in further detail in Recommendations #3 through #6, which, together with the details in this recommendation, reflect the following priorities:

- Fundamental research in technology as a total system, both in helping to find answers about the learning and teaching processes and in putting research results into practical application.

- Development of a system by which practicing educators in schools and colleges throughout the country would have ready access to the widest possible range of materials and resources for instruction, in every medium and subject.

*For example, the National Education Association, the American Federation of Teachers, NEA's Department of Audiovisual Instruction, the Joint Council on Educational Telecommunications, the National Association of Educational Broadcasters, the American Association of School Librarians, the Association of College and Research Libraries, the National Audio-Visual Association, the Educational Media Council, the American Council on Education, and the American Library Association.

**In a report to the President of the United States, entitled Library Services for the Nation's Needs, July 1968.

***To cite one example, Japan has been a world leader in the use of instructional television, and should have much to offer in the way of advice, direction, and example.

- Improvement of methods of evaluating the relative effectiveness of various educational resources (human and nonhuman) and their combinations in the learning patterns of individual students.

- Exploration of means for developing high-quality educational materials comparable in sophistication to the machines or equipment now available or about to be available.

- Development and application of improved methods of preparing teachers, administrators, and many different kinds of specialists in the best uses of instructional technology, including access to reliable comparative economic and performance data on hardware, programs, and technological systems.

- Collaboration with industry in exploring ways to develop hardware especially suited to instructional needs.

- Concentration of all the foregoing efforts on helping achieve, through technology, solutions to the nation's most acute educational problems, such as:

    Improving learning in disadvantaged schools, urban and rural; for preschoolers; and for the handicapped.

    Developing the most fruitful approaches to making instruction truly individual.

    Revitalizing liberal arts and professional education and relating higher education more significantly to personal and social experience.

    Developing practical ways for community colleges to meet the diverse and increasing demands being made upon them.

Recommendation #3

We Recommend:

The proposed National Institute of Instructional Technology should take the lead in efforts to identify, organize, and prepare for distribution the high-quality instructional materials, in all media, capable of improving education.

For this purpose, the National Institute of Instructional Technology should consider establishing a center or "library" of educational resources. Among this agency's responsibilities would be: identifying those areas in which there is a shortage of educational software, and making public these findings; assisting school and college libraries to transform themselves into comprehensive learning centers; and stimulating interconnections (among specialized libraries, data banks, schools, and colleges) for comprehensive and efficient access to instructional materials and educational management data.

The improvement of teaching and learning through the use of instructional technology has been impeded less through the lack of equipment than through the lack of high-quality instructional materials designed for use with the equipment. The Commission has learned from people in virtually every field—teachers and educators, as well as experienced producers in film, television, and the computer—that the insufficiency of excellent materials or programs has been a critical and persistent factor in preventing the development of a genuinely effective instructional technology.

Yet there is a considerable amount of potentially useful material in many media which could be made available to education. The chief problem is that there is no effective system by which materials can be identified, organized, and made conveniently available to educators.* Such a system would provide a new wealth of information for the improvement of learning and teaching.

The suggested center or library of educational resources would not be a "library" in the usual sense of a repository of books, magazines, and other printed materials. The most advanced libraries today have begun to expand the usual meaning of "library" by gradually developing into complex information storage and retrieval institutions designed to be much more than a collection of books. The center which the National Institute of Instructional Technology might establish would perform a set of functions quite distinct from collecting books and other instructional materials. It would not itself store the vast amount of relevant resources. Rather, the center would supervise and coordinate a wide range of functions that would include finding, sifting, adapting if necessary, and cataloging materials suitable for educational use. It would provide educators with information about materials in each subject field, for each level of instruction, and in every instructional mode and media. A kindergarten teacher seeking manipulative materials to develop eye-hand coordination, a third-grade teaching team seeking films and audiotapes about the American Indian, a middle-school curriculum supervisor preparing a unit of programmed instruction in mathematics, a high school principal looking into televised courses in Far Eastern culture and history, a college professor desiring to use language-laboratory tapes for teaching introductory Swahili, a graduate university seminar studying the sociology of Latin America, a corporation developing a literacy program for hard-core unemployed—all would be guided by the center to materials relating to their instructional tasks.

Because it would cover all media, all subjects, all levels of education, the center's program would provide a needed synthesis and augmentation of the various national organizations already involved in this field, such as the National Audiovisual Center, the National Instructional Television Center, the Great Plains National Instructional Library, the National Center for Audio Tapes, the National Educational Television Libraries, and the National Medical Audiovisual Center, as well as pertinent collections at the Library of Congress.

This agency should also assist school and college libraries to identify, receive, store, and make available new instructional materials. This would entail their transforming themselves into comprehensive learning centers. Fortunately, many libraries are already far advanced in this reorientation. Further progress should facilitate the development of more flexible, individualized instruction at every level of education.

A central educational resource center would provide educators everywhere with the fruits of "search/find" operations, and might encourage the establishment of working arrangements for exchange of material within educational institutions, libraries, and clearinghouses. These arrangements should be coordinated on a regional basis, with the aim of eventually becoming computer-based.

Exchange of materials between libraries is an old practice. The computer has made it possible to completely revolutionize this process and has made the planning of networks central to the creation of any new national library facilities. In the last decade a number of computer-based storage and retrieval systems, centers for gathering and dispersing technical information in various fields, and cooperative interconnections of learning institutes have taken shape. But there has been no comprehensive attempt to unite these systems, libraries, and data banks to meet the demand for both instructional materials and research informa-

---

This gap is in large part the result of the rudimentary state of research and development in the techniques for handling information transmittal in all media. As noted in Recommendation #2, the National Institute of Instructional Technology should give high priority to a program designed to meet this need.

tion on the process and management of education.* The National Institute of Instructional Technology should take the initiative in exploring possible arrangements for organizing such networks for instructional use.

In the immediate to short-term future, a network could feasibly develop the capability to provide bibliographic information on educational materials and research, indexed conveniently for the inquirer. However, the long-range future presents the possibility, indeed probability, of full-text access to books via computer, as well as instant transmittal of nonprint media. The realization of this potential, however, requires the solution of several very complex problems, among them the development of principles and practices relating to standardization, compatibility, and copyright.

Systematic coverage and analysis of what exists in all instructional media, subjects, and grade levels would yield an invaluable by-product—the identification of gaps in the supply of instructional materials. The National Institute of Instructional Technology could then keep the whole private sector (including producers and distributors of hardware and software for every level and area of education) informed and aware of the schools' needs and priorities. (This would be done in collaboration with the council suggested in Recommendation #6).

Recommendation #4

We Recommend:

The National Institute of Instructional Technology should support demonstration projects designed to improve instruction through the wise exploitation of technology. These projects should be concentrated initially on a few carefully selected communities or individual schools—including urban ghettos, impoverished rural areas, and communities with populations that are predominantly black, Mexican-American, Puerto Rican, or Indian.

The school system of the District of Columbia might be invited to mount the first of such model demonstrations.

The National Institute of Instructional Technology should invite selected schools and communities to participate in demonstration projects and should be responsible for coordinating the use of public and private funds for this purpose. However substantial the amount of money involved, the total number of projects should be relatively small, in order to sustain a high-quality, concentrated effort in each one with a saturation of available resources.

Projects should be designed to achieve maximum visibility and impact, and should initially be keyed to meet severe educational problems. The Commission believes, therefore, that the first and largest demonstration might well be in Washington, D. C. The rationale is clear. While education in the nation's capital should be a model of excellence, this city's schools suffer perhaps more than most city school systems from lack of funds, inadequate

---

Educators are faced with the problem of accessibility with regard to information about the process and management of education. These data must be readily available if they are to attempt to effectively design conditions of learning along "systems" lines. The ERIC system is attempting to collect and make available such information. It is limited by lack of funds as well as by the difficult problem of reproduction of copyrighted materials. The Commission believes that the ERIC system should be strengthened, and that it should be tied into any network plans established by the National Institute of Instructional Technology.

staff and facilities, preponderance of impoverished minority-group students, flight of the middle classes to the suburbs.

While these demonstration projects would specifically try out technology in its various ramifications, each project should be based on a total educational concept. The choice of schools and communities should take account of prospects for eventual self-support. Strong commitment of school and community leaders therefore would be a prerequisite. In some cases the actual administrative and instructional patterns would have to be altered to accommodate the demonstration. The experiment should include not only public schools and community colleges, but also programs for persons now outside the formal educational system—such as preschool children and unemployed, under-employed, and retired adults.

These comprehensive demonstration projects should operate under the continuing guidance of the National Institute of Instructional Technology and its regional affiliates. Purchase of hardware, physical changes to buildings, and preparation of new curricular material should all be closely interwoven, and the impact of these developments might well stimulate even more fundamental changes.

As for demonstrations designed to benefit out-of-school groups, we suggest that private foundations, industry, and educational institutions be urged to supplement federal, state, and local government funding, and in addition, to provide professional and technical aid. Funding and active collaboration could come from a variety of sources, depending on the projects. For instance:

(a) A community agency could develop an educational package in cooperation with a local vocational school, a local television station, local employers, and a nearby university or community college. Citizens could be trained for specific jobs through special counseling and multimedia presentations, including television and programmed texts. The "diploma" would be a job.

(b) A day-care center could augment its usual activities by installing individual learning carrels equipped with imaginative programmed materials for preschool children. Here the children could pursue beginning reading, number concepts, and entertaining introductions to other new worlds—nature, the arts, or certain sciences. Neighborhood housewives, college students, and retired people could, with minimal training, oversee the enterprise without the need for constant attendance of professional teachers.

(c) A variety of distribution media (telephone, television, radio) could reach adult audiences at home. Projects for homemakers and workers could be mounted in subjects as diverse as business arithmetic, health care, and computer programming. Imaginative programs to acquaint the public with the accomplishments and promise of technology in education could prove of great value.

(d) The National Institute of Instructional Technology could help design a Job Corps center that would use instructional technology in depth, taking full advantage of the armed services' experience in job training, and trying out various combinations and sequences to meet each student's individual background, capacities, and interests.

Technology could facilitate distribution, presentation, and feedback. It could also encourage cooperation among several agencies—a critical aspect of any successful project. The National Institute of Instructional Technology's challenge would be to bring schools, universities, industries, social agencies, and individual citizens together in active participation and involvement in the advancement of education.

Recommendation #5

We Recommend:

The National Institute of Instructional Technology should take the initiative in encouraging the development of programs to improve the capacity of educators to make more effective use of instructional technology and programs to train specialists. To this end, the N.I.I.T. should support new programs, based on increased research and development:

(1) To provide administrators and department heads with the knowledge necessary for managing technology effectively;

(2) To educate school and college teachers in the most effective uses of instructional technology and in the differentiated staffing patterns technology properly entails;

(3) To increase the number of qualified specialists such as producers, programmers, and technicians that schools and colleges need if they are to exploit technology fully.

Besides initiating new programs, the National Institute of Instructional Technology should also strengthen and expand the best existing programs for training and employing educational manpower in the wise application of instructional technology.

"Teaching is the only major occupation of man," Peter Drucker wrote recently, "for which we have not yet developed tools that make an average person capable of competence and performance. But education will be changed, because it is headed straight into a major economic crisis. It is not that we cannot afford the high costs of education; we cannot afford its low productivity. We must get results from the tremendous investment we are making."

In order to increase their productivity, the nation's schools and colleges require a larger supply of diversified, highly qualified manpower. They need administrative leaders—college and university presidents, deans of instruction, department heads, school superintendents, and principals as well as state and federal officials, school board members, and college trustees—who fully understand the prospects for improving education through technology.

In addition, the teacher or professor, from kindergarten through graduate, professional, and continuing education, should understand how new media can be employed to make instruction more effective and more responsive to the individual student.

Moreover, supporting specialists and technicians of many types are needed if a mature technology of instruction is to flourish. The qualifications required in these three categories—administrators, teachers, specialists—are distinctive.

Administrators

In the decades ahead, administrators will be required to make many complex decisions which they are not now being prepared to make wisely. The problems faced by the educational manager are changing rapidly. Tomorrow's educational manager will have to be able to handle a variety of responsibilities, many of them outside the walls of the school or college or state education department. He will need a background in education certainly; but he will also need training and experience in the behavioral and social sciences, in finance and management, and in the development of human resources. The thrust of this recommendation is not toward reviving a "cult of efficiency" for education. Schools and colleges are already overcommitted to rigid formulas for efficiency which prescribe class size, block scheduling, departmentalization, credits, etc. Technology must free, not fetter.

Of great importance, then, is concentrated research, development, and application on the special knowledge school and college managers can make effective use of: what tools are required, what methods (of economic analysis, staff recruitment and deployment, community and staff relations) are most efficacious, how the essential data can be acquired, how purposes and accomplishments can be best evaluated, how educational institutions can be staffed for maximum exploitation of television, recordings, projectors of various kinds, programmed instruction, and other kinds of instructional technology—ultimately, how schools and colleges can redesign themselves to educate America's young people most effectively.

The paucity of data even as to the *functions* of administrative manpower in education was recently emphasized by the Office of Education's first report on the state of the education professions, required under the new Educational Professions Development Act. In the matter of instructional technology, the educational manager should understand how to find out what he needs to know about the potentialities and problems of instructional technology, and how to recruit and use the talents of people who can serve in this field effectively. Obviously the school superintendent or university president himself cannot and need not be a sophisticated judge, purchaser, or user of hardware and software. But he should be able to depend on a staff qualified to advise him or to act in these matters. He and his associates should know also which technological applications have proved their worth, and which promising developments are imminent, whether in "older" media such as film or in new ones like the computer.

In instructional technology, as in other crucial aspects of educational management, the immediate need is for programs that will combine down-to-earth experience with formal training in appropriate disciplines. Various graduate schools of education are concerning themselves with this task, but their efforts must be multiplied and reinforced to make any real dent on the day-to-day management of the nation's educational institutions. Schools of business and public administration, architecture, and engineering should also participate. To this end, intensive efforts to establish management-training programs should be mounted by federal agencies in partnership with universities, school systems, state departments of education, and industry.

These management-training programs should command sufficient money to produce a marked improvement in the use of technology and in the way schools are managed. They could take many forms, including summer institutes, continuing seminars, and longer-term university internships and fellowships—all informed by constant feedback from the field.

One educational observer has suggested the creation of a "staff college for higher education executives," adding that top university officials "need both mirrors and windows—so that they can look inward as well as outward." The National Academy for School Executives' advanced seminars, which have devoted particular attention to instructional technology, point the way toward such a program for school administrators.* Clearly, the most promising of these programs now in operation or projected should be supported by the National Institute of Instructional Technology.

Sophisticated, practical *pre*-service management training is also essential. The immediate concentration of funds and ingenuity should, however, be on in-service training, since most administrators, especially in the lower schools, come up through teaching.

Teachers

There is evidence today that school teachers, a traditionally conservative group, are beginning to see the value of using technology for educational purposes. Lois V. Edinger, professor of education at the University of North Carolina, wrote to the Commission:

The National Academy for School Executives is an adjunct of the American Association of School Administrators.

The vast majority of the members of the teaching profession have accepted the fact (or in some cases simply become resigned to it) that education must leave the era of "hand labor" and turn to machines to help increase their productivity. That we must turn to the using of power tools in education to allow teachers to become more effective is a fact accepted by the teaching profession today, albeit with varying degrees of pleasure and readiness.

Dr. Edinger's words are of special significance since she is a recent past president of the National Education Association and undoubtedly expresses the view of many schoolteachers. It appears to be true, however, that most *college* teachers continue to resist the "inroads" of technology.

A central benefit (as well as prerequisite) of the comprehensive application of technology to education will be a more systematic approach to instruction. The role of the teacher needs to be more explicitly defined than ever before. The teacher, therefore, should understand the far-reaching implications of technology in order to function at his individual best as the central element of the total system. The base for this understanding should be laid in the teacher's own education, not just in demonstrations and lectures on technology, but through the actual use of technology in his courses.

Unfortunately, few teacher-training institutions give even passing attention to the role which technology could play in improving the quality of education. Only infrequently does the education of prospective teachers make use of such media of instruction as television, tape recorders, or computers. And the teacher who *does* have exceptional training in technology will be frustrated if the school or college where he begins his teaching career regards technology as a mere accessory.

Once on the job, moreover, teachers are apt to find that daily pressures leave little time to "figure out behavioral objectives" or to experiment with the best tools for meeting those objectives. There is little incentive for the teacher to innovate. And should the teacher decide that he indeed does want to use some new medium, he is faced with the problem of availability and maintenance. At worst, the elementary-school teacher (probably female, and probably "allergic" to machinery) is required, for instance, to manage a 16mm film projector which was designed by a male for nonschool purposes and which needs mechanical expertise for operation and maintenance. Margaret Mead said on this point:

> Teachers will use machines for instruction when they're as easy to use and as foolproof as the washing machine.

In-service training for school teachers, while it may provide the new teacher's first brush with technology at work, is often as unsatisfactory as pre-service training. Both are centered far more on the mechanical "how" of technology rather than on the "why."

The situation was summarized for the Commission by A. W. VanderMeer, dean of Pennsylvania State University's Graduate School of Education, as follows:

> The pre-service preparation of the teacher must be followed by a continuing program of in-service education. It matters little whether these in-service activities are conducted by the universities, by school districts, by professional societies, or by a combination of these. The essential thing is that they be conducted and conducted well. Not only must education follow current graduates into the field, but also the existing instructional personnel presently manning the schools must not be neglected.

> Of particular importance is the use of technology itself in bringing in-service education to the field. Modern extension work is pioneering the use of video- and audio-tapes, conference telephone hook-ups, and other exploitations of instructional technology. Such advanced applications of technology are, unfortunately, in the minority.

Nevertheless, more and better training in itself will not satisfy the diversity of demands on education and educators. A true technology of instruction almost demands a re-ordering of the instructional staff, to take account of individual talents and capabilities among teachers and also of the range of different jobs teachers are asked to do. One answer to this complex problem is differentiated staffing, with which a few schools have begun to experiment.

This new concept was set forth as follows in the Office of Education's first report on the state of the education professions:

> Differentiated staffing is based on carefully prepared definitions of the jobs educators perform, and goes beyond traditional staff allocations according to subject matter and grade level. For example, a differentiated staffing plan developed by Temple City, California, has created a logical hierarchy that includes not only teaching but instructional management, curriculum construction, and the application of research to the improvement of all systems. . . .

> The aims of differentiated staffing can be realized through a number of different methods. Additional positions such as part-time tutors and aides on one hand and educational specialists on the other could be appended to either end of the hierarchy. Organization need not be hierarchical, but can be based on teams of peers. Whatever the method, however, the aim is to permit a variety of people to contribute. The housewife-teacher, for instance, can make her services available on a schedule satisfactory to her, and without hindering the professional advancement of the career-minded teacher. Indeed, the career-minded teacher is stimulated by such a system, which provides not only a hierarchy of more challenging and more significant roles but also allows for promotion and advancement as a teacher instead of solely as an administrator or supervisor.

Even short of fully differentiated staffing, schools and colleges require specialists of many kinds. As the next two sections suggest, the full realization of technology's potential for education calls for an array of staff members who are not teachers. The key figure may ultimately be a versatile and highly trained specialist called an "instructional designer."

Specialists

Throughout American schools the need for talented people who are not specifically trained as teachers is becoming more and more acute. Specialists are needed to develop technology as an integral part of the instructional process. Aides of all kinds are needed to assist teachers in making the best use of technological media and of their own professional capacities. Perhaps most important, scholars in many disciplines and creative people in every area should be contributing their special gifts to the instructional process. "As the field of education assumes new tasks and broader responsibilities," Harold Howe II has written, "there will be a growing need for people with competencies in many areas, from poetry to biochemistry, from plumbing to philosophy, people who might be persuaded to offer their expertise on a full- or part-time basis to the purposes of education."

Technology can achieve its fullest potential in schools and colleges only with technical and paraprofessional support—"media coordinators" serving as advisors on the use of instructional technology, experts on the production and procurement of instructional materials, plus specialists in many different disciplines working with teachers in research and development.

The lack of specialists to facilitate its use in the schools and colleges could well be the Achilles' heel of instructional technology. The urgency for designing machines for easy use in instruction is equaled only by the urgency of having someone available to repair them if they break down. A language laboratory is of little use if it is out of operation for several weeks because chewing gum and bobby pins clog its vital parts. An investment in proper operation and maintenance of equipment is good economy.

Nonprofessional assistants are also needed, especially in the elementary schools. Such tasks as running simple machines, playground duty, and routine clerical duties can be carried out by teacher aides (who may be housewives willing to work part time), thus releasing regular teachers to more adequately employ their professional talents in advancing the quality of instruction.

Planning for the development of instructional technology should include the recruitment of such nonprofessionals. As Professor Robert H. Anderson of the Harvard Graduate School of Education told the Commission: "The emerging concept of auxiliary personnel in education has already created an impressive literature, which has recently begun to focus on the important topic of *training* auxiliary personnel. Not only can technology play an important role in the training of such workers, but it seems increasingly necessary for these people to be familiar with technology as an aspect of their work."

Whether a staff advisor in instructional technology is necessary might be disputed by those who have been discouraged by experiences with the typical audiovisual department of a school or college. It is the exceptional audiovisual department that is integrated into the fabric of the institution—with qualified audiovisual consultants sitting in on courses, sharing in the teaching methods and environment, and then contributing to improvements through technology and otherwise.

Qualified specialists in the production of instructional materials are scarce. Producers, graphic artists, audio technicians, and programmers are but a few of the professionals needed to develop maximum effectiveness in instruction. Lack of expert advice in the production of instructional television programs, for instance, has often produced mediocre results. All too little is known about how to present instructional material over television most effectively. Creative use of the medium has been barely attempted. There is no doubt that the "talking face" has been overdone in instructional television. But even this technique has its usefulness and could be made more effective. Outstanding lecturers who fail to come across over television could improve their performance on the screen with help from skilled professionals.

The scarcity of good programmers for the teaching machine undoubtedly tempered the initial enthusiasm for this device, and may be seriously handicapping current efforts in the various modes of programmed instruction. Training and financial support for production and programming specialists should have top priority.

Instructional Designers

The need for someone to work with teachers in their planning strategy as well as someone to help students in using libraries, data banks, or computers to their best advantage, is apparent. Institutions could combine forces and share the services of one instructional technology advisor, who could also conduct research and development in "instructional design."

Research and development in education are dependent upon the interaction of specialists from many different fields. The meager success of research efforts to date can be attributed in part to the dearth of well-qualified research specialists. If research and development efforts are to be relevant and fruitful, they must enlist the participation of behavioral scientists, subject-matter scholars, engineers, educators, and others. The central figure in this "mix" may well be an instructional designer, whose role Robert Glaser has described as follows:

> It is highly probable that a unique occupational specialty called instructional design will emerge in view of the current level of heightened interaction among educators, behavioral scientists, educational publishers, electronics and computer industries, and R&D organizations in educational technology. This specialty will involve a person or group of persons concerned with the production of educational procedures, materials, and systems.

Instructional designers need to pick off appropriate research and development activities from behavioral science knowledge, and behavioral scientists need to pay attention to the fundamental problems generated from attempts at technology. From this interplay there will emerge a body of pedagogical principles or a technology of instruction that will be fundamental to the task of instructional design.

As educational systems incorporate more of the advances of science and technology into their design, the specialty of instructional design will grow, and there will probably be many different sub-specialties; for example, applied research and development, operational materials design, computer systems, teacher practices, language and linguistics, preschool learning, etc.

Instructional designers in applied research, development, and production capacities will be in increasing demand in the near future. Indeed, at the present time, such persons are rare and eagerly sought.

Recommendation #6

We Recommend:

The National Institute of Instructional Technology should take the lead in bringing businessmen and educators together in a close working relationship to advance the productivity of education through technology.

To this end, the National Institute of Instructional Technology should consult with other interested organizations and develop an appropriate mechanism. A possible course of action, for example, could be the establishment of a National Council of Education and Industry that would focus on how technology can best meet the needs of individual students, teachers, and administrators. A small high-level council of this nature, with representatives from key branches of education and the education industry, could help speed appropriate advances in the design, development, and application of technology to instruction.

The free marketplace for materials and equipment has generated great benefits in education, as in other sectors of American society. However, there is increasing realization today that in the major fields of social service, such as medicine, the operation of the free market must be supplemented by some mechanism to make sure that innovation and diversity are encouraged, quality maintained and enhanced, and the most urgent social goals achieved. Education lags behind other fields in providing help to practitioners in making wise choices among competing products, and in spelling out its precise needs.

Until a decade ago, the "education industry" was virtually synonymous with textbook publishing. Then, as substantial new federal funds became available for the purchase of newer kinds of equipment and materials, publishers began, through acquisition or expansion, to branch out into various areas of instructional technology. But the central fact remains that the school and college budget for equipment and materials is still relatively small.

What is called for is a closer scrutiny of the process by which machines and programs have been developed and marketed. Educators have played little or no part in developing new products. They have not been informed on a regular basis of recent developments, nor has industry devised an adequate process for obtaining their advice and counsel. When new equipment comes on the market, many educators are in the dark about the advantages and disadvantages of the various options offered and are at the mercy of sales propaganda and rhetoric. Thus many purchases made by schools and colleges have been inappropriate and premature. On the other hand, educators themselves have not always demonstrated a realistic understanding of technology's potential for instruction, nor of industry's problems in meeting educational needs.

In general, these conditions obtain today:

- Many technological devices offered to educators are designed mainly for uses other than education; this drawback applies particularly to the computer, which needs distinctive features to be wholly adaptable to education (for example, larger memory capacity, greater simplicity, and better display capabilities).

- Equipment prices are geared to what the *commercial* market can bear; there has been no concerted attempt to bring them down to levels acceptable to education and the taxpayers who support it. Most schools and colleges simply cannot afford needed equipment.

- Many institutions lack equipment they need (e.g., television, computers). Some are overstocked with equipment (e.g., movie projectors, overhead projectors) which is largely unused or seriously underused; in many cases the equipment on hand is fast becoming obsolete and constitutes a serious barrier to the acquisition of new improved devices.

- Instructional material to stoke promising devices is inadequate; new hardware comes to the market years before enough worthwhile programs are ready to meet school and college needs.

- The quality of most of the software that *has* been developed is relatively poor. The problem is insufficient money and talent for the concentrated effort required to produce good materials.

- Material is often limited to use on a machine of one particular make. For example, one company's videotape recorder will not take another company's tapes. Until a solution can be found to the problem of incompatibility of equipment and programs, the effectiveness of instructional technology will be correspondingly retarded.

- As indicated earlier in this report, many technological devices are too complex for teachers to use readily and often. When breakdowns occur, repairmen are not immediately available. Maintenance is a serious problem; lack of funds and manpower often renders equipment unusable.

- Field testing of new devices before they come on the market is minimal. As a result, educators receive little validated evidence on which to base their purchasing decisions.

In short, educators at present who do not suffer from lack of equipment often suffer from having too much obsolete or unused equipment, or the wrong kind of equipment, or equipment with insufficient good software, or incompatible equipment, or equipment too complex for proper maintenance.

A close new working relationship between industry and education should be possible if each group actively demonstrates its willingness to cooperate, to understand the other's problems, and to make necessary compromises.

For this essential cooperation of education and industry to bear fruit, certain changes in attitude and approach are required.

For instance, *industry* must be willing:

- To forego immediate profits, to concentrate on development of equipment and materials for the long run, and to abandon the belief that because a product sells well, it is educationally sound. (Since the market for educational materials is still relatively small, sustained development by industry may well require federal pump priming.)

- To develop intensively a limited number of products which have proven effective for instructional purposes; and to work toward solving the incompatibility problem.

- To work with teachers, administrators, and students in the development and redevelopment of materials and equipment.

Educators, for their part, must be willing:

- To define instructional objectives clearly enough so that materials and equipment can be produced to meet them, and then to use items produced that meet these specifications.

- To help test new devices and to persevere with innovations until they can be properly evaluated.

- To acquire the necessary understanding of technological innovations and develop sound methods for measuring their capabilities.

The Commission believes that a mechanism should be created to initiate and cultivate such a cooperative effort. We therefore recommend that the National Institute of Instructional Technology take the lead in establishing an effective group to carry out these objectives. One mechanism would be a small, strong, high-level national council, with representatives from key branches of education and the education industry. In setting up an appropriate and forceful group of this order, the N.I.I.T. should work with organizations such as the Corporation for Public Broadcasting, the Educational Media Council, the American Textbook Publishers Institute, the Education Commission of the States, the Joint Council on Educational Telecommunications, the American Library Association, state departments of education, the National Association of Educational Broadcasters, and the National Audio-Visual Association. Through constant feedback from the field (teachers, administrators, salesmen, managers), a council of this sort could keep in touch with new and persistent problems and with the most promising lines of product development.

An organization representing education and industry should develop and institute improvements in the design, development, maintenance, and utilization of instructional technology. The functions of such a group would include:

(1) The establishment of standards for instructional equipment.

(2) Concerted action to meet the specific needs of schools and colleges.

(3) The development of practical methods to make equipment and materials compatible.

(4) The establishment of a mechanism—perhaps a clearinghouse—to provide education's managers with comparative operating and economic data on technological instruments and systems designed for administrative as well as instructional purposes.

(5) Initiating or improving laws and regulations affecting instructional technology

(e.g., copyright laws, satellite controls, reduced rates for long-distance educational communication).

(6) Active cooperation with the National Institute of Instructional Technology in devising ways of directing federal and private funds toward the production of high-quality instructional materials.

(7) Exploration of new methods for providing school districts with funds for instructional technology, including the possibility of leasing or renting equipment, or the purchase of equipment on a "pay-as-you-go" basis.

(8) Active cooperation with educational institutions, under National Institute of Instructional Technology leadership, in establishing practical programs to train and retrain the managers of education.

VI.
Note on Appropriations Required

For more than a year the Commission on Instructional Technology has examined technology as it affects or could affect instruction. Our focus throughout the study was to determine how technology could contribute to the improvement of learning in schools and colleges. Our recommendations deal with the major problems to be solved if instructional technology is to fulfill the potential the Commission believes it has for education.

The questions that naturally follow are: How much money is needed? How soon is it needed? What sources should supply it?

For guidance the Commission looked at the research and development carried on in industry, agriculture, and health. Extensive national programs have been in operation for many years in these fields, conducted and financed in partnership with local government, business, universities, health and agricultural agencies, and other organizations. The programs have grown substantially during the past decade:

In *industry*, about 4 percent of net sales is spent on basic research, applied research, and development of research findings by manufacturers performing some research and development activities (that is, approximately $18 billion a year).

In *health*, an amount equivalent to nearly 5 percent of the nation's total expenditures for health services is spent on research (that is, about $2½ billion a year).

In *agriculture*, an amount equivalent to almost 6 percent of the total net income from farming is spent on research, development, and application by government agencies, universities, industry, and local agricultural organizations (that is, about $900 million a year).

In education, however, research expenditures amount to no more than one-fourth of 1 percent of the nation's expenditures for schools, colleges, universities, and other educational enterprises—that is, a total of no more than $125 million a year. A few years ago the ratio was only one-tenth of 1 percent.

By 1980, the Commission believes, educational research, development, and application should reach the proportions already achieved in industry, agriculture, and health—in other words 4 to 6 percent of total expenditures for education. It is essential to take appropriate steps now toward meeting this greatly increased outlay.

Obviously a program of these dimensions must be phased in gradually. Even if all the money which education needs for basic and applied research, development, and the application of important findings to instruction were available immediately, the nation could not at once supply the manpower of appropriate background, training, or experience to put the money to use effectively and wisely. The United States has just begun to apply to education the research, development, and application techniques that have long since proved their worth in other sectors of society. Within the past few years, for example, new Research and Development Centers and Regional Educational Laboratories have made advances in the theory and practice of instruction. It will be necessary to strengthen and expand such advances, building upon them to achieve a more fully effective educational system.

In educational research and development we must learn by doing. As in the space program, there is no other way. The formulation and refinement of new basic theories are essential. But basic research encompasses only part of the total research-and-development effort required. Sustained development and the application of findings to thousands of practical school and college problems are also essential. Moreover, research findings must come to the schools and colleges packaged for practical use.

The Commission has concluded that only the federal government can undertake the major responsibility for the expenditures for basic and applied research, development, and application required in the years immediately ahead. Furthermore, we believe that the minimum initial financing required to carry out the recommendations of this report is approximately $565 million. Of this about $150 million would be required to launch the National Institutes of Education and the National Institute of Instructional Technology. The remaining $415 million would be required for the first full year of operation, including approximately $250 million for the research, development, and application activities of the institutes, $25 million for the center or "library" of educational resources, $100 million for demonstration projects, and $40 million for the training of personnel. The aggregate amount suggested would equal no more than 1 percent of the projected total expenditures for American education in fiscal 1972.

This proposed budget, it should be noted, includes the present research activities of the U.S. Office of Education; it is, however, an *addition* to other authorizations for education programs by government and private agencies. It assumes that existing programs as authorized by Congress and other appropriating bodies would be fully funded, including specifically those provided by the Public Broadcasting Act of 1967 for the construction of educational television and radio stations and for the continued operation of the Corporation for Public Broadcasting.

A.
The Status
of Instructional
Technology Today

The impact of technology on instruction has been small compared with the magnitude of the educational system in the United States as a whole. For example, some 50 million pupils attend class in elementary and secondary schools every day for an average of five hours each. This amounts in the aggregate to a total of 250 million pupil class hours every day, or a grand total of 1,250,000,000 pupil class hours every week from early September to mid-June. A reasonable guess is that in any week not more than 5 percent of the time involves media of instruction other than the teacher, the book, the blackboard, and pictures, charts, and maps hung on the wall. For higher education, the estimates are of the same order. There are many observers who say that a closer estimate would be 1 percent. These low estimates reflect the well-attested fact that even schools that are equipped with technological media may use them little if at all.

> Research indicates that a large part of the existing hardware now in our nation's schools is not being used, or used properly. This has come about partly because the national audio-visual thrust has been toward the acquisition of equipment and materials with very little concern toward the development of programs that increase the proficiency of their utilization.

Ira Polley
Superintendent of Public Instruction
Michigan Department of Education

The Commission had many well-informed specialists prepare reports on the present status of the various technological media used for instructional purposes.* In addition, the staff assembled information on the use of technology from individual institutions, from manufacturers and distributors, and from state and federal government agencies. Briefly, the situation with respect to the major media and their applications is as follows:

1. Audiovisual media**

*A diagnosis of the causes of the current low status of instructional technology will be found in the next appendix.

**For convenience, this account follows the common if unsatisfactory usage that reserves the term "audiovisual media" for the oldest of the newer media such as 16mm and 8mm film and projectors, slides and film strips, telephones, audio tape-recorders, records and record-players, and overhead projectors. These are the "audiovisual aids" that most parents and some teachers think of when the subject of instructional technology is raised.

Today most schools and colleges have some audiovisual equipment. This ranges from two or three record-players in the library and one broken 16mm projector in the auditorium, to an active audio-visual facility with an extensive film library, many well-maintained projectors, and a production unit for slides and transparencies.

The growth of some audiovisual departments in recent years has been dramatic. In 1955, for example, the University of Colorado's film library owned one projector and 1,200 films and had a staff of three people. By 1969, the film library had grown into a regional center, with 2,800 pieces of equipment, between 8,000 and 10,000 films, a computerized film-booking system, and a full-time staff of 45.

The increase in equipment for the nation as a whole has been less dramatic than in this example, but it has been constant. Some estimates on individual types of equipment appear in the next two pages. The table shows the present stock of selected items; the graph shows the trend in expenditures for audiovisual equipment and materials.*

Estimated Number of Items of
Audiovisual Materials and Equipment
Owned by U.S. Public Schools, July 1969

SELECTED EQUIPMENT		SELECTED MATERIALS	
Screens	919,000	Filmstrips	21,700,000
Record Players	698,000		
Earphones	576,000	Still and flat	
Overhead projectors	453,500	pictures	12,400,000
Slide and filmstrip			
projectors	426,000	Disc recordings	7,200,000
Tape recorders	320,000		
16mm projectors	251,000	Overhead trans-	
Learning carrels	171,000	parencies	5,230,000
Slide or filmstrip viewers	163,000	Maps and globes	4,200,000
Reading devices	98,600	2″ × 2″ slides	2,400,000
Opaque projectors	91,600		
Transparency makers	71,200	Tape recordings	2,020,000
8mm projectors	58,600		
35mm slide cameras	27,200	16mm films	1,315,000
Rear screen projectors	22,200		
16mm cameras	14,100	Reading programs	336,000
Drymount presses	11,750		
8mm cameras	7,200	8mm films	104,000
Microprojectors	6,180		

Source: Loran C. Twyford, New York State Education Department, 1969

Note: The total number of public schools operating in 1969 was estimated at 92,500.

The statistics do not by themselves reveal how often the various media are used, nor for what purpose. According to informed opinion, audiovisual media are generally employed intermittently and then only to enrich and supplement the familiar patterns of classroom instruction. For the most part, they merely augment the conventional teaching strategy which has hardly changed for more than a century. "They are used primarily to give data which the reasonably effective teacher could give anyway and/or at least to furnish a mo-

Including, in this case, radio and television.

mentary diversion from business as usual," Wilbur Rippy, curriculum resources specialist at Bank Street College of Education, wrote to the Commission.

Except for the promise of the application of programmed instructional principles to conventional audiovisual production, few innovative breakthroughs have been made to involve the learner actively in learning from audiovisual presentations. Active participation by the learner has been shown to increase learning significantly, yet our audiovisual materials show no signs of recognizing this fact.

William H. Allen, Adjunct
Professor of Education and Cinema
University of Southern California

Expenditures for Audiovisual Equipment and Materials by Elementary and Secondary Schools 1955 to 1970
(with projections to 1975)

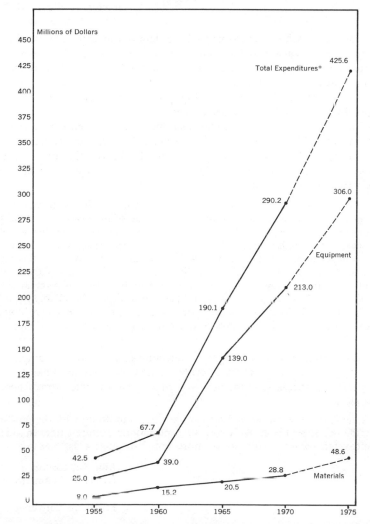

NOTE: Total expenditures include equipment and materials plus other items such as maintenance and general overhead. Totals are probably low but trend is indicative of recent developments. Data do not include computers or programmed textbooks, but do include radio and television.

SOURCE: *U.S. Office of Education*

Overall, it is reasonable to say that despite increasing demands for greater individualization of instruction and for more emphasis on learning rather than teaching, audiovisual technology is seldom used to bring about educational change. It is still predominantly a subsidiary and supplementary element of group-paced, group-prescribed instruction where one teacher faces 20 to 30 students in 45-minute units of time in classrooms comprising around 1,000 square feet of enclosed space.

A miniature self-instructional system using 8mm cartridge films has been developed at San Jose State College and was initially applied in teaching audiovisual techniques. This method has proven that for many "how-to-do-it" and informational topics college students can use media to learn successfully by themselves. The 8mm methods developed for audiovisual production and equipment operation techniques have been extended to teaching the operation of keypunch machines, industrial arts woodshop and craft skills, use of advanced chemistry laboratory equipment, and occupational therapy practices.

> Richard B. Lewis, former
> director, Audiovisual Services
> San Jose State College

In recent years, some schools and colleges have demonstrated the ability of the audiovisual media to liberate teacher and student from the educational lock-step. Audiovisual storerooms that once served only the classroom teacher have been transformed into rich and responsive learning centers for both teachers and students. According to Colonel Howard B. Hitchens, Jr., the traditional audiovisual media have been integrated into the instructional processes at all of the military academies.

Harvard's Project Physics has used audiovisual media to fuse the reality of physics with the requirements of individual students and teachers. Overhead transparencies, 8mm film loops, 16mm films, and laboratory equipment are combined with the live teacher, standard printed materials, and programmed texts in a course which provides maximum flexibility. In the words of Gerald Holton, director of the project:

> It should be possible for a given student to become fully fascinated with the straightforward quantitative content of the discussion of the law of universal gravitation and its consequences in physics; he should be able to pursue this by further reading (as in the *Reader* excerpts on gravity experiments) and/or by doing a Cavendish experiment, or at least getting the data from film. And for this particular student this involvement might be at the expense of the study of the historical background of Newton's work, which in his case might not be of primary interest. But his neighbor, in the same class, should to some degree be allowed (and furnished equally good tools) to have somewhat the reverse experience, as long as he does not slight the minimum physics content which is set out for him in the course.

In a small number of schools, photography and film-making are encouraging an active, participatory type of education. There is evidence that film-making, linked in with film-watching, "speaks" (particularly to the deprived child) in a way that normal book-oriented instruction does not.

> Doing, however, is even more fun than viewing. And doing with the new media is where the sex appeal is at. Kids with still and motion picture cameras, kids with audio and video recorders are having more fun than other kids.

> John M. Culkin, S.J.
> Director, Center for Communications
> Fordham University

2. Television and Radio

Today instructional television fills less than 3 percent of total classroom hours in the elementary and secondary schools of the country's 16 largest cities. In Boston, home of one of the most successful educational television stations, WGBH, the city's 148 elementary schools own only 150 television receivers, with another 50 spread among its 36 junior and senior high schools. Ohio State University's radio station, which helped pioneer the use of radio in schools in the 1930s, was transmitting two programs a week to schools by 1967-68.

One is tempted to say that television courses today are in the McGuffey Reader stage. For nearly half a century educational films have compressed large amounts of pictorial information into ten-minute reels with a narrator "telling it." They break the class routine, then it's over and done without much relation to course or lesson plan.

> Robert B. Hudson
> Senior Vice President
> National Educational Television

Elementary schools are the major audience for open-circuit instructional television (as differentiated from closed-circuit television and 2500 megaHertz). The all-purpose teacher in the self-contained classroom has been willing to get some specialized help, in subjects like music, art, and science, from educational stations. Secondary schools make significantly less use of instructional broadcasting, because of scheduling difficulties and also because secondary schools of any size have such specialists as art and music teachers. Radio and television appear spasmodically in adult (or "continuing") education.

With few exceptions, television is usually simply imposed on long-established curricula and administrative systems. As such, television becomes an addendum, an adjunct, and ultimately an insignificant line item in the school budget. Solid attempts to use the medium effectively for instructional purposes are few.

> Frederick Breitenfeld, Jr.
> Executive Director
> Maryland Center for Public
> Broadcasting

According to a 1967 survey, closed-circuit television was being used at 717 out of 15,581 educational institutions identified as likely television users. Five years earlier, 403 such institutions were found to be using closed-circuit television. One major function of closed-circuit television in colleges is to distribute the normal classroom lecture to overflow students in the crowded first-year and second-year courses. At Michigan State University, for example—one of the largest users of closed-circuit television in higher education—13.3 percent of student credit hours in the freshman and sophomore classes are earned via television.

Generally, television and radio, like older audiovisual materials and devices, are being used to "enrich" but not change traditional education. In most school television the screen time is filled with the face of the studio teacher, who is almost certain not to be one of the great minds working on the frontiers of the subject matter presented. Despite the growth of videotape libraries and regional networks, the dream of shared resources and the widespread exposure to a corps of real master teachers has not been fulfilled. Moreover, the large number of local production units have led to a dissipation of talent and dollars. Underused studios are constant reminders of television's status in American education at the present time.

There have been demonstrations, however, of television and radio used imaginatively and effectively. Some colleges of medicine and dentistry, for example, are realizing one constructive potential of television: image magnification and image transportation. Psychiatrists also find television a useful research tool. A North Texas network is using television with telephone talkback to take postgraduate education from the campus to graduate engineers who have gone out into industry. Low-cost videotape recorders are giving some student teachers the opportunity of watching themselves teach. In a few schools and colleges, television brings *visual* primary source materials to students—live meetings of the Security

Council of the United Nations, for example, or taped presidential press conferences of the past.

In American Samoa, for a number of years, television has been part of—and an enabling agent for—a comprehensive reform of elementary and secondary education, along systems lines. This comprehensive reform included a major overhaul of curriculum, a move away from rote memorization in the classroom, the production of high quality integrated materials in print and nonprint, a complete administrative and logistical reorganization, the construction of new schools, a school lunch program, and systematic in-service training and supervision for the classroom teachers. Television was designed as the core of instruction, part of an overall instructional strategy worked out by teams of specialists.* Samoa contrasts strongly with the highly fragmented organization of schools on the mainland where it is customary for one committee to decide on textbooks, another on television lessons, a third on school architecture, with minimum cooperation and maximum autonomy.

> The scope and limits of educational radio today are clearly indicated by the range of operating budgets available to the medium. Almost 50 percent of the stations operate on budgets of less than $20,000 a year. As might be expected, the educational radio medium is beset with manpower problems. These arise from the obvious budgetary limitations, the lack of salary and career incentives, and the powerful attraction to the young of television, which has overshadowed the aural medium for almost two decades. Moreover, there do not appear to be many managers who function full-time in station operation. Most often the school-connected stations combine station management with other functions, such as teaching, departmental administration, TV management, and so forth.

> Management, staffing, and budget limitations are in the final analysis directly related to school administration attitudes toward the medium. With few exceptions, institutions of higher education do not accord radio the same degree of concern they do other interests, and thus fail to develop it fully as an educational resource.

> *The Hidden Medium: Educational Radio*
> Prepared for National Educational Radio
> by Herman W. Land Associates, 1967

Since 1955, Albany Medical College, through WAMC, has been pioneering the use of two-way radio for the continuing education of doctors. There are now more than a half dozen of these networks in operation across the country. The Wisconsin State Radio Network uses part of its frequency allocation to provide specialized programming for nurses and a French program for high-school students, through a system called multiplexing which permits normal programming to continue undisturbed.

> A typical WAMC two-way radio conference includes an announcer, a studio moderator, the network audience (located at 70 hospitals in a 100,000 square mile area), a moderator at each hospital, and faculty drawn from one or more of 28 medical colleges. The audience in the community hospital is able to follow the presentation with the aid of mimeographed outlines and sets of 35mm slides previously mailed to each hospital.

> At the completion of the "lecture" the community hospital moderator gathers written questions and comments from his associates and alerts the studio moderator, using an electronic alerting system. Replies to the questions are made directly by the faculty. Unanswered questions are mailed to Albany for transmission to the faculty who then mail replies directly to the questioner.

Multiplexing, 2,500 megaHertz television (Instructional Television Fixed Service), community-antenna television arrangements, low-cost recorders, satellites, and Electronic Video

---

* *The report from the new Governor of Samoa, in July 1969, was that the change in the management contract for the Samoan educational program would not affect the achievements described above.*

Recording—all have great potential for education. To date, however, their use and effectiveness have been limited—both in quantity and quality.

The current sum total of all applications of television to instruction has not made any lasting, important, or basic impact on any part of American education.

Detailed arguments supporting the learning effectiveness of televised materials are not needed in this paper. Suffice it to say that there is a veritable mountain of research findings to indicate that people can learn any number of skills from television-facilitated instructional systems.

Television provides the potential of allowing mass-scale educational programs to be carried forward with uniform, basic opportunities and standards for all participants. It can be the facilitating means of mass education in a genuinely democratic age.

The fact that the medium has been seldom used to carry out this important function in no way denies the truth of these assertions.

The National Association of
Educational Broadcasters

3. *Programmed Instruction*
During the second half of the 1950s, programmed instruction, embodied in the teaching machine, enjoyed a short period of enthusiasm which quickly waned. In the words of Susan Meyer Markle, a pioneer and authority in the field, "The impact of programmed instruction on the educational system has been minimal, quantitatively and qualitatively."

One important reason for the decline in the use of programmed instruction was that the teaching machine came onto the market long in advance of the appropriate software. Also according to a 1965 survey of recent programs produced for schools, 40 percent provided no evidence of pretesting, despite the fact that programmed instruction claimed to be the first real application of scientific principles to learning. By 1967, a sampling survey showed that the situation had actually deteriorated—70 percent of the programs had not been prevalidated.

The computer can be an exciting educational tool without requiring tremendous financial investment. Students of every age use it and have a wonderful time with it. For instance, they can try out arithmetic problems on the computer, and it will give answers. Used this way, the computer creates a responsive learning environment and is thus a very powerful system. And the price is not high, because this kind of software is not expensive. If we limit its instructional use to the programming of full courses, however, the fate of the computer could be similar to that of programmed instruction: a good idea that was more or less ruined by poor and premature exploitation.

J. C. R. Licklider, Professor of
Psychology and Electrical
Engineering
Massachusetts Institute of
Technology

Today the sale of programmed instruction materials to education constitutes only a small fraction of the total dollar sales volume for textbooks. However, programmed instruction has had considerably more impact on training programs in the armed services and in industry.

The technology of programmed instruction challenges traditional teaching methods. The teaching machine and the programmed text which has now largely replaced it present the subject or skill to be learned in many small steps, with regular opportunities for the student to make responses and to know immediately if he is correct. The learner moves at his own pace, instead of at the pace of the group, and some programmed materials permit him to branch off on different tracks.

When a study at Michigan State University revealed inefficient use of laboratory time in Advanced Mammalian Physiology, the Instructional Media Center developed a preparatory course in basic laboratory techniques. Audiotapes and slides—supported by programmed texts and 8mm single concept films—are incorporated in a course through which each student can proceed at his own pace prior to entering the action lab. The most notable result of the new system was to reduce the time needed in the regular lab from five hours to four. The hour saved was used for the discussion of experimental results, which before tended to be crowded out by the time taken just to set the experiments up. Student interest and appreciation for the course were greatly improved.

But too often, instead of changing educational procedures in the direction of greater individualization, programmed instruction has become an addendum to conventional educational offerings. Recently, proponents of programmed instruction have redirected the thrust of the movement. According to Douglas Porter of Harvard: "Some educators think of programmed instruction as another 'medium' of instruction, like television or tape. It is not. Programmed instruction is a process for the specification, design, perfection, and validation of instruction, a process which is applicable to all media. The full implication of programmed instruction can be appreciated only when this point is understood."

Programmed instruction thus becomes synonymous with instructional technology in its "systems approach" meaning. "The concept of programmed instruction," according to Robert Glaser of the University of Pittsburgh, "should de-emphasize the present orientation around educational 'media,' e.g., films, television, and language laboratories, and place emphasis upon the process of instruction in which the special advantages of various media can be assessed."

When considered in relation to their proposed intent to truly individualize instruction, the quantity of programmed materials available to the schools is still miniscule. Given the wide range of objectives which school systems might wish to reach and the wide variance in student characteristics, we are a long way from the "well-stocked shelves" that would enable teachers to diagnose and prescribe, as promised by the technology. Small doses of self-paced instruction prove disruptive within the normal lockstep progression, but individualized instruction without appropriate materials also has disadvantages.

Susan Meyer Markle, Head
Programmed Instruction
Office of Instructional Resources
University of Illinois

4. Language Laboratories

Language laboratories began to appear at some of the larger universities in the early 1950s. After 1958, when the passage of the National Defense Education Act provided matching funds for the purchase of such equipment, thousands of schools and colleges in every part of the country began to install it.

However, there was a serious lack of software. The assumption was that the classroom teacher could write the script in her spare time and record the tapes that would be needed. "The results were sometimes disastrous," Elton Hocking, Professor of Modern Language Education, Purdue University, told the Commission. "Lacking the facilities and techniques for successful recording, the high-school teacher produced a soundtrack that was amateurish at best. More important, the content was often merely copied from the textbook, which was never intended for such use."

After a few years, despite the establishment of NDEA Institutes for the training of teachers in the use of the new equipment, the early enthusiasm for language laboratories declined. Interest was reawakened only after the arrival on the market of commercially produced integrated materials which included films and filmstrips along with tapes and textbooks. Although these packages promised to be effective, they were expensive, and many school boards therefore purchased just the book and tape combinations, foregoing the films and filmstrips. Moreover, the teachers, now released from the heavy task of recording tapes, found themselves almost as busy cataloging, bookkeeping, ordering supplies, and arranging for repairs required as the result of breakdowns or vandalism.

Today, after nearly a dozen years of intensive experience, it is clear that language laboratories have realized only a fraction of their educational potential. Moreover, their success is likely to depend to a large extent on comprehensive reform in the method of teaching languages. The traditional grammar-based method is likely to be changed only over a considerable period of time.

> "The language lab as a teaching machine" was a perfectly sound concept of the programmer, but to the public and to many schoolmen it meant that the machine, as such, could teach. Not a few teachers actually feared for their jobs. Today it is common knowledge that the machine can only repeat the program fed into it, and that a good program requires almost infinite care and time to prepare, try out, and revise repeatedly.

> Elton Hocking
> Professor of Modern Language
> Education
> Purdue University

5. The Computer

The computer has three main uses in education: it is a research tool; it is a management tool; and it is a teaching-learning machine.

As a *research and study tool,* especially in higher education, computers have been in use since the mid-1950s. Today faculty and students in many disciplines are increasingly exploiting the computer's power of computation, data processing, problem solving, and simulation. In this usage the computer's function is not to "teach," as it is in computer-assisted instruction (CAI), but to provide the student with new ways of exploring and manipulating the subject matter he is studying and the data at his disposal.

One problem, however, is that computers—both the machines themselves and the skilled manpower they require—are expensive to acquire or lease and to operate. Their use for research and study purposes is concentrated, therefore, in a relatively small number of institutions. The President's Science Advisory Committee, in its 1967 report on *Computers in Higher Education,* noted:

> . . . at some fortunate and forward-looking colleges and universities the educational use of computers is widespread and effective. But this does not apply to the majority, where computing facilities are often absent or inadequate. . . .

Recently the computer has been playing an increasing role in the development of information-retrieval systems for research purposes. Information-retrieval services for educational needs—to date, highly specialized—are beginning to appear. Some examples of research-directed information retrieval are:

1. The National Library of Medicine's Medical Literature Analysis and Retrieval System (MEDLARS), based in Bethesda, Maryland, with various regional stations. MEDLARS indexes the contents of approximately 2,300 biomedical journals published throughout the world and stores bibliographic details on magnetic tape. Doctors and research workers can retrieve bibliographic information both by subscription to bibliographic publications and by computerized demand searches.

2. Chemical Abstracts Service, based in Columbus, Ohio, has been collating and publishing information about chemistry and chemical engineering since 1907. Now becoming increasingly computerized, it has a full-time staff of about a thousand and an annual budget of over $12 million.

3. A consortium of institutions of higher education, with headquarters at the University of Michigan, has developed a computerized system for political-research data.

Educators have already begun to consider the broader applications of computerized information retrieval for schools and colleges. At the higher education level, the Interuniversity Communications Council (EDUCOM) has among its concerns, yet unrealized, information retrieval for research, instructional, and administrative purposes.

Computerized information retrieval could also upgrade the few operations already serving the needs of educational researchers. The Educational Resources Information Center (ERIC), set up by the United States Office of Education and comprising 19 regional centers, is the outstanding example. "ERIC on Line," at the Stanford clearinghouse which concentrates on instructional technology, is an experimental advanced computerized retrieval system that permits searching more than 12,000 documents in the ERIC system and viewing selected abstracts on a cathode-ray screen. ERIC looks forward to further development of computerized services.

The extensive use of computers for *management* purposes in higher education, particularly in larger institutions, is not surprising, considering bulging enrollments and increasing amounts of data to be processed. Administrative uses of the computer vary from the fairly straightforward keeping of scholastic records to the more complex problems of forecasting future building and staff requirements via simulation techniques.

In elementary and secondary schools, the computer's use in administration is less widespread, but growing. New England Education Data Systems (NEEDS), based in Waltham, Massachusetts, provides computer services to help member schools with file creation and maintenance, schedule construction, attendance accounting, test scoring and analysis, and student marks. NEEDS has found that the introduction of computers for such administrative purposes can open the door to instructional uses of the computer.

The computer may prove to be essential for schools wishing to introduce flexible scheduling, with classes of different sizes meeting for different lengths of time. A truly individualized system of instruction, which tracks the student through his own curriculum at his own pace using an appropriate range of different media, will generate—and require—masses of data which must be manipulated if the system is to work.

A few programs are exploring the use of computers to relieve the increasingly heavy burden placed on guidance counselors. The computer can advise a student on course selections as well as on future educational and career decisions. David V. Tiedeman of Harvard University carefully notes that the computer, in itself, can "only help individuals understand their career development. To this end machines are instruments, not masters, in career development."

Computer-assisted *instruction,* although it dominates the headlines, has to date had much less impact on education, both quantitatively and qualitatively, than the other two uses of computers. One of the nation's most publicized CAI systems operates in New York City. Here there are 200 terminals in 16 schools operating at an annual cost of about $1 million a year. At the most, 6,000 children—out of one million children in daily attendance in the city's schools—are getting an average of 10 minutes of CAI in one subject per day.

Despite the claims that the computer is a highly flexible teaching-learning machine, the predominant application thus far of CAI in schools and colleges is for drill and practice. Don D. Bushnell of the Brooks Foundation told the Commission that most such systems do little more than dispense "instruction in a fixed, preprogrammed sequence of graded instructional material . . . designed to perpetuate the standard classroom procedures." The more creative modes of computer-assisted instruction—tutorial, inquiry, and simulation—are used much less frequently.

Lawrence M. Stolurow, director of the Harvard Computer-Aided Instruction Laboratory, observed in a paper prepared for the Committee for Economic Development: "The available software, both computer and educational, is in a very primitive state of development." The lack of an empirically validated theory of learning and teaching has been a major obstacle to the development of computer-assisted instruction. But CAI does hold out the promise of helping to make learning a truly individualized process. In this connection Stolurow warned the Commission not to confuse the present reality of CAI with its potential: "Projections based upon today's systems would have the same degree of fidelity as projections based upon the Wright brothers' first plane would have had for predicting the design of the supersonic transport."

Today, there are fewer than 1,000 computer-assisted instruction terminals serving fewer than 20,000 public-school students. When we subtract from these totals terminals and students involved in limited experimental and demonstration projects, we find that the parameters of operational computer-assisted instruction shrink to less than 500 terminals and 16,000 students.

Until now mathematics drill and practice at the elementary school level accounts for a large percentage of what has been defined as operational computer-assisted instruction.

There has been practically no systematic assessment and evaluation of the effects of the use of computer-assisted instruction where it has been employed. In some cases, CAI installations have not had access, either internally or externally, to personnel qualified to conduct valid evaluations; in other instances, the individuals responsible for CAI have been preoccupied with the myriad problems accompanying the introduction of a highly innovative program and, therefore, have postponed evaluation.

There is an urgent need to deeply involve specialists in learning research from the university community in the systematic assessment and evaluation of present and future computer-assisted instruction applications in the public schools. Federal and state educational funding authorities must assign a higher priority to this need than they have in the past.

The relatively few studies which have been conducted on CAI effectiveness do create a basis for optimism about the eventual contributions of the medium.

Lawrence Parkus
Radio Corporation of America

6. Dial Access

There are an estimated 120 dial-access information-retrieval systems in schools, colleges, and universities across the country, enabling the teacher in the classroom and the individual student in the study carrel to retrieve, by dialing a number, limited amounts of instructional material. (The material is stored centrally and distributed via audio and/or audio-video channels.) For example, the system at Ohio State University, which like many others developed out of a language laboratory, has approximately 400 different reception points at various campus locations.

A dial-access system at Oklahoma Christian College, opened in 1966, has 136 audio channels and one reception point for each of the thousand-plus students on campus. It has enabled substantial revisions of teaching methodology to take place. A major problem in education the disparity in background knowledge which students bring to courses—is being tackled at Oklahoma Christian with special tapes to which any student can listen whenever he wants.

At some institutions, however, the effectiveness of dial-access has been slight. Hardware was developed without appropriate software, teachers were not sufficiently consulted, curricula were not revised to use the new media, and the dial-access equipment, often costing well over a hundred thousand dollars, has been left to gather dust.

7. Games and Simulation

Games and simulation, which can be enacted via a variety of media, have been used quite extensively by the armed services to teach military strategy and to train servicemen in the handling of highly complex electronic equipment. Simulation techniques are also proving popular in business, particularly for management training. In medical education, Hilliard Jason, Director of Medical Research at Michigan State University, told the Commission: "Instructional needs are of such complexity that simulation is likely to become the most important new educational development of the decade."

The Board of Cooperative Educational Services in Yorktown, New York, has developed a game using a computer which permits the student to experience directly the basic principles of a primitive agrarian economy. An IBM 1050/7090 computer system simulates selected elements of the economic functioning of a Sumerian city-state around 3500 B.C. The student sitting at the typewriter terminal is the King, and the computer asks him on the basis of economic reports to decide how to use resources, while trying to keep the population stable and well fed.

Games and simulation are beginning to enter a small number of schools and colleges. A relatively uncomplicated application is driver education. More complicated are games such as those designed by the Educational Development Center in Newton, Massachusetts, for use by elementary and secondary school students in social studies. *Empire,* for example, enables children to gain an understanding of mid-18th century trading patterns by letting them play the roles of New England merchants, Southern planters and admiralty customs men. The student seeks information, uses it actively, makes decisions, and then sees almost immediately the results of his decisions.

B.
The Causes
of Technology's Lack
# of Impact
on American Education

There is hardly a school system or university that does not have one or more film projectors, slide projectors, record players, television sets, or other technological devices and materials. But the actual use of such media for instruction plays a very small part in the nation's total educational effort, and the systematic harnessing of technology to improve learning has been attempted only rarely.

Why has progress been so slow in fulfilling technology's recognized potential for education? What has impeded technology's impact on instruction?

There are many causes. Though most have been touched on in the recommendations and in the text of this report, it seemed useful to summarize them here.

The causes of instructional technology's present low status are so intertwined that it is difficult to separate them. Moreover, the Commission's study has revealed that certain conditions—perhaps the most basic and telling causes of all—are not peculiar to technology *per se* but pervade all American education. The first and most far reaching of these is lack of practical understanding about the process of human learning. Despite recent progress in educational research and development, educators still have few reliable, validated guidelines for choosing one instructional medium over another.

> The degree of ignorance about the process of education is far greater than I had thought. Research results are more meager or more contradictory and progress toward the development of viable theories of learning and instruction is far slower.
>
> Charles E. Silberman, Director
> Carnegie Study of the Education
> of Educators

On a more prosaic level, education suffers from insufficient money. Taxpayer resistance, outmoded sources of support, and rising demands for extended schooling have created major problems for education in general. The hard fact is that only a small fraction of school or university budgets is ever available for *any* form of instructional materials. The implications for instructional technology and other innovations are obvious. Most educational dollars are earmarked for staff salaries, and for new construction and maintenance.

Both inadequate knowledge of the learning process and lack of funds contribute to a third major barrier to needed educational reform. This is the very structure of today's formal education, a pattern of grades, courses, credits, departmentalization—four years of higher education added to twelve years of elementary and secondary education—which affords scant leeway for substantive, effective change in schools and colleges.

Until we stop our futile efforts at minor adaptations of our obsolete egg-crate schools and build a new organizational and administrative structure, we have small prospect for success in gaining the full potential of recent advances in science and technology to dramatically improve learning in our schools and colleges.

> T. H. Bell
> Superintendent of Public
> Instruction, State of Utah

Thoughtful critics of education, within and without the establishment, are becoming convinced that only by radical rearrangement of the prevailing patterns of schooling can education be sharply improved. Some of the chief obstacles to fulfilling the potential of instructional technology reflect, according to these critics, organic defects in the educational system itself.

There is no system to reward the innovator. A system does not exist which gives support (i.e., promotion, salary increase) to those interested in improving instruction. The organization and the institutionalization of education itself have formed the greatest barrier to the use of instructional technology. The research on instructional technology has consistently occurred *within* the system—affected and controlled by the systemization already in existence. This system controls what we may experiment upon, how we may experiment, and how we are to treat the results.

> Richard E. Spencer
> Professor of Educational Psychology
> University of Illinois

Innovations patched on the conventional structure produce indifferent results. No matter how good a programmed text is, for instance, it will find only marginal use in a group-paced school. Broadcast television programs, even with repeats, seldom fit in with standard academic schedules, especially in secondary and higher education. Innovations like programmed instruction and television, it would appear, can effectively improve instruction only as part of an integrated, systematic reconstruction of the curriculum.

A curriculum is a thing in balance that cannot be developed first for content, then for teaching method, then for visual aids, then for some other particular feature.

> Jerome S. Bruner
> Professor of Clinical Psychology
> Harvard University

Within this overall context constraining change, there are a number of more specific reasons for instructional technology's limited progress to date:

1. Indifference or Antipathy toward Using Technology in Education

Many administrators of school districts, colleges of education, universities, or state education departments regard technology, Professor Elton Hocking of Purdue University told the Commission, "as a kind of profanation of the classroom." The term "teaching machine," coined by early programmed-instruction enthusiasts, epitomized the dehumanizing, depersonalizing influence of technology feared by many critics.

Teachers exhibit a "bi-stable" attitude with respect to the use of technology:

> If they haven't used it, or if what they've used has been an irrelevant part of their busy schedules, they're sure they don't have time to use it.

If, on the other hand, they *have* used it, and it has been a coherent part of a full set of learning aids, they say they don't have time *not* to use it.

> Jerrold R. Zacharias
> Professor of Physics
> Massachusetts Institute
> of Technology

2. Poor Programs

Many educators believe that:

The majority of television lessons, instructional films, programmed texts, computer programs for instruction are of poor quality.

Television is often little more than the distribution of a dull lecture.

Many programmed texts are uninteresting, uninspired, and just plain tedious.

Instructional films are unsophisticated and unprofessional in comparison with offerings of the local movie theater or television stations.

Poor software is itself the manifestation of many contributing difficulties: lack of money, lack of trained and imaginative writers, directors, and programmers; and resistance of educators to materials that are foreign to current classroom practice.

Much of "the industry" is still too much outside the thought stream of professional education; there is too much tendency to "think up" films, etc., and then try to merchandise them later. We do not, in saying this, point a derisive finger at the industry. The schools have done far too little to help achieve a unified approach. Nevertheless, the lack of media programs that are genuinely rooted in the schools' concerns remains very serious.

> Fred T. Wilhelms
> Executive Secretary
> The Association for
> Supervision and Curriculum
> Development

3. Inadequate Equipment

Equipment frequently is not good enough to meet the needs of the classrooms. It breaks down, and there is often no provision for immediate repairs. Not until technical equipment in education becomes as foolproof, teacherproof, and childproof as common household appliances will teachers use it everywhere. But today such equipment is characterized by:

- *Poor design*—For years educators have complained about the fact that equipment is poorly designed for their particular needs. So-called daylight screens, for example, in fact require darkened rooms; 16mm film projectors are difficult to operate, heavy to carry around, and expensive; reels of film do become unwound in the classroom.

The hardware is really in a never-never land of great promise and disappointing achievement. The content is usually nonexistent, where used it is irrelevant, and its integration with the rest of the curriculum is haphazard.

> Howard J. Hausman, Head
> Student and Curriculum
> Improvement Section
> National Science Foundation

In part the problem is that educators frequently acquire equipment that is designed primarily for noneducation markets. The equipment does not fit education precisely. For example, one company's decision to limit its new 8mm film cartridge to a four-minute running time was based on home use of 8mm cameras which generally accommodate four minutes of film in each load.

● *Incompatibility*—A videotape recorded on the equipment made by one manufacturer cannot be shown on the equipment made by another. A computer program is usually designed for use on only one computer system.

Our first acquaintance with the videotape recorder brought sharply to our attention the problems related to the fact that there is no compatibility between the products manufactured by one firm and another. Thus software produced with one brand of videotape recorder cannot be utilized on another. This certainly poses a major handicap for those who wish to produce educational software.

> John K. Hemphill, Director
> Far West Laboratory for
> Educational Research and
> Development

● *Obsolescence*—Once purchased, equipment usually has to be kept until it wears out completely. Thus schools and colleges cannot quickly adopt new easy-to-use equipment in place of outmoded hard-to-use equipment which they have on hand.

Considering the current inaccessibility of motion pictures in education, 16mm films might better be likened to manuscripts, chained to monastery reading tables, in which case 8mm might be the book liberated and made ubiquitous by the invention of print with movable type.

> Louis Forsdale, Professor of
> English, Teachers College
> Columbia University

4. Inaccessibility

Neither the existence of good films, television lessons, or programmed courses nor the desire to use them guarantees extensive use. A major problem is accessibility. Expensive film prints are housed in central libraries to be distributed to teachers who have to requisition them months in advance. In many schools (and especially big school systems) the red tape is almost insurmountable. The process is annoying and time-consuming, and alienates many teachers.

Other problems of accessibility include:

● School television producers find it difficult to obtain film footage, stills, or research data on optimal ways of designing programs for the improvement of learning.

● Copyright has made access to much material extremely complex.

During a recent visit to an inner-city school in a large city, it was brought to my attention by the principal and teachers that in order for them to use the equipment available, it would be necessary for the teachers to leave their classrooms unattended while obtaining the use of the equipment. In a situation where free time is not even provided for the teacher to eat lunch, it seems ridiculous to expect them to take the time necessary to actually physically secure the equipment, not to speak of the time necessary to plan for its use in order to be effective.

> Freeman H. Vaughn, Director
> of School Projects
> Industrial Relations Center
> University of Chicago

Instructional technology lacks a well-funded and comprehensive system for disseminating materials, research data on effectiveness, and information about institutions which are making significant uses of technology.

5. Teachers Not Trained in Instructional Technology

Where there are good programs, and access to them is well-organized, the use of materials is often minimal because teachers are inadequately trained to exploit what is available. Most colleges of education do not integrate the basics of instructional technology in their training programs. Most courses at such colleges are taught without recourse to instructional technology. In-service training programs in schools which do use technology exert less influence than they should.

> Regardless of whether a school buys a closed-circuit television system, language lab, science lab, or shop equipment, any pretraining in the operation of the equipment is minimal. The equipment, therefore, in many cases lies idle, waiting for an instructor to learn how to use it and to develop confidence in its usefulness in teaching.

Bruce Boal, President
Hickock Teaching Systems, Inc.

6. Media Specialists Excluded from Central Planning

If media specialists are consulted about curriculum and organization at all, it is usually after key decisions have been made. As a result, schools and colleges usually make little effort to weave new kinds of materials and modes of instruction into the fabric of the institution; generally the best programs utilizing the newer media are tacked on as afterthought or optional "enrichment."

Though many instructional technologists blame this critical flaw on the conservatism of the educational system, there is reason to place some of the responsibility on the innovators themselves. In a recent address to a conference of instructional television specialists, Robert L. Hilliard, chief of the educational broadcasting branch of the Federal Communications Commission, said: "We have been content to bow gracefully away from a direct impact upon the curriculum and to permit a curriculum coordinator to determine exactly what will be televised so that it can 'enrich and supplement'—not change—the present outmoded content and process in learning and teaching."

> What has become normal, unfortunately, for most school communications people is a world full of mad dashes from one crisis to the next. There is seldom time for effective planning and for doing creative work which is the lifeblood of progress. The technological phase of schooling is now mature enough so that it should have its staffing needs met in a businesslike manner. Limited staff is now the most critical item holding up progress in this area.

A. Richard Clark, Director
Educational Communications
Department
Scarsdale (N.Y.) Public Schools

C.
The Cost
and Costing
of Instructional Technology

Introduction

Ten or fifteen years from now schools, colleges, and universities will probably be able to determine how much it costs to teach a child arithmetic, what it costs per unit of instruction to teach in the summer as compared with the winter or to teach at night or on Saturdays as compared with the regular school day, how much it costs per unit of achievement to teach inner-city children as compared with suburban children, what it costs to use instructional television or computer-assisted instruction as a part of the regular teaching process compared with not using these devices.

Today none of these comparisons are possible because the accounting practices of educational institutions do not produce the required data. Present practices are primarily *fiduciary* in nature; that is, their primary purpose is to assure the public that each dollar received is properly accounted for and that each dollar spent has been properly authorized.

Fiduciary accounting systems are used extensively by trust departments of banks and by most government agencies—federal, state, and local. They serve an important function in society. However, the figures derived from such records cannot be used directly for the management of an enterprise, whether a government agency or a school system. The data have to be reprocessed, supplemented, and analyzed, sometimes at great cost and effort, to make them informative, useful, and even understandable to anybody but the keepers of the records. Without this processing or analysis, it is frequently impossible to make direct cost comparisons between school systems, or even to compare one system's costs from one year to the next.

Nor is this problem new. Beardsley Ruml, once chairman of R. H. Macy's in New York and a long-time leader in analyzing educational economics (from the early 1920s to his death in 1960), called it to the attention of the U.S. Office of Education more than a decade ago.

Cost of Instructional Technology

Well aware, then, of the inadequacy and limited comparability of most available economic data in education, the staff of the Commission on Instructional Technology examined a group of reports by experts on the cost and costing of instructional technology. The conclusions were as follows:

1. *Only a small percentage of the annual budget of any school, college, or university is available for instructional materials (including books).*

A paucity of funds is a major obstacle to the introduction of instructional technology. No more than 4 percent of per pupil expenditures in public schools in any year is spent for instructional materials of all types—including textbooks, library books, maps, charts, globes, and laboratory items, as well as the newer media.

Per Pupil Expenditures for Instructional Materials in Public Schools 1967–68 and 1968–69

ITEM	NATIONAL MEDIAN		HIGH QUARTER		TOP TENTH	
	1967–68	1968–69	1967–68	1968–69	1967–68	1968–69
Dollar Expenditures						
Teaching materials	$14.75	$15.08	$18.94	$20.62	$24.98	$27.35
Textbooks	5.10	5.58	7.04	7.67	9.19	9.66
Percentage of total per pupil expenditures						
Teaching materials	3.2%	2.9%	3.8%	3.7%	4.9%	4.7%
Textbooks	1.1%	1.1%	1.4%	1.3%	1.9%	1.7%

Source: School Management, *January 1968 and January 1969*

On the other hand most school systems, colleges, and universities spend more than 60 percent of their operating budget on instructional salaries. When the heavy costs of building construction and maintenance are added, the average school or college has little left over to meet change through technological or other experiments. Commenting on this dilemma, Charles J. Hitch, president of the University of California, told an international conference in Paris (April 1969):

> Changes in academic organization, when a university does want to strike out in a new direction, almost inevitably require that most potent of all social lubricants: lots of money.

This, he went on to say, was not usually available.

2. *The costs of instructional technology vary widely, depending upon the range of equipment and services.*

For example:

- About $700 can buy a 16mm film projector.

- Fifty to sixty thousand dollars can cover the initial cost of a dial-access information system in a college or university, but costs can run into the hundreds of thousands.

- On the average, a closed-circuit television system costs $178,000 to install, and can be operated for $86,000 per year.

- Nine self-instructional units of a physiology course developed and produced at Michigan State University, making use of carrels, audio tapes, slides, 8mm films and programmed texts, cost $40,000.

- The high school physics course produced by the Physical Sciences Study Committee (PSSC) cost $6.5 million.

- The Midwest Program on Airborne Television Instruction cost $18 million for the period 1961-1965.

- A simple televised lecture can be produced for as little as $50 an hour, while a presentation making use of film and other visual materials might cost as much as $6,000 an hour.*

- Computer-assisted instruction of the drill-and-practice variety is likely to cost $27.2 million a year in a school district of 100,000 students. But using the computer more creatively as a sort of tutor puts the price up to $71.8 million.*

These are costs for individual applications. On a nationwide basis, the figures are very large. Booz, Allen and Hamilton (Chicago-based management consultants) concluded that:

If instructional television were installed in the 16,000 public school systems which represent 75 to 80 percent of our elementary and secondary school population, the cost for ITV would be $265 million to $1.5 billion.**

In the spring of 1969, the American Library Association and the National Education Association published a book of guidelines* setting forth standards of equipment and materials required for media programs of good quality and establishing criteria for the media services, resources, and facilities essential in the educational process. Loran C. Twyford, Jr., Chief of the Bureau of Classroom Communications of the New York State Education Department, reviewed the standards and then estimated that if they were fully implemented in one year, the cost would be $38 billion classified in broad categories as follows:

PUBLIC ELEMENTARY AND SECONDARY SCHOOLS	(IN BILLIONS OF DOLLARS)
Equipment	$ 8.0
Materials	16.0
Professional staff	1.0
Supporting staff	1.0
Film rental and television	1.0
Subtotal, public schools	$27.0
Nonpublic schools	4.0
Higher education	7.0
Total	$38.0

*Source: Carter, Clyde N., and Walker, Maurice J. Costs of Installing and Operating Instructional Television and Computer Assisted Instruction in the Public Schools Booz, Allen & Hamilton, Inc, 1968 Prepared for the Committee for Economic Development in 1968 during a study which led to the publication of the report Innovation in Education: New Directions for the American School, Committee for Economic Development, New York, 1968.

**Standards for School Media Programs, American Library Association and National Education Association, Washington, D.C., 1969. The standards presented were prepared by a joint committee of the American Association of School Librarians of the American Library Association and the Department of Audiovisual Instruction of the National Education Association, in cooperation with an advisory board consisting of representatives from 28 professional and civic associations. The publication notes that although the American Association of School Librarians revised its standards in 1960 and the Division of Audiovisual Instruction released standards in 1966, significant social changes, educational developments, and technological innovations made it imperative to bring standards in line with the needs and requirements of today's educational goals.

Twyford calculated that once this investment had been made, it would cost $11 billion per year to operate and maintain a system of instructional technology in the nation's schools, colleges, and universities, including the replacement each year of the equipment and materials becoming worn out or obsolete. S. Barry Morris, Assistant Superintendent for Finance, Fairfax County schools, Virginia, estimated that for a school with 1,000 pupils the annual cost of maintaining and replacing equipment and materials alone would amount to about $42,000 a year or an average of $42 per pupil.

3. *The costs of instructional technology could be reduced in a number of ways.* For example:

   (a) *By increasing the number of students who receive instruction through a particular technology or by increasing the period of time over which the equipment is used.* The cost of operating an instructional television system for 10,000 students may be as much as $250 a year per student; however, if the number of students using television were to rise to 500,000, the cost per student could be as low as $12 a year.*

   If the television system could be operated for more than the usual number of hours in a typical school day, and for more than the usual number of days in a typical school year, then the cost per student could be cut again.

   Richard E. Speagle, professor of finance at Drexel Institute of Technology, observed after analyzing data on the costs of instructional technology submitted to the Commission:

   The annual bill at schools, colleges, and universities for physical facilities, like science and language laboratories, gets folded into total costs without reference to degree and intensity of use.

   In industry, by contrast, inputs of plant and equipment are firmly controlled by a benchmark of performance, "standard costs." These shoot up sharply when the utilization rate falls below a desired percentage of capacity.

   In order, then, to benefit from the economy of large-scale operation, schools, colleges, and universities would have to pool resources. To date, however, cooperative arrangements between educational institutions of the requisite magnitude have not been made. A prime reason appears to be opposition by those teachers who resist any threat to their traditional autonomy.

   (b) *By stepping up the output of products that educators want.*

   (c) *By designing and building instructional machinery specifically for instructional purposes.* Lawrence Parkus of Radio Corporation of America told the Commission that the IBM 1500 system, for example, which is being used for computer-assisted instruction, was originally designed for such tasks as process control of cracking towers in petroleum refineries. Consequently the system incorporates many expensive features not needed in elementary and secondary schools. Some people believe that a computer designed especially to meet school needs might be cheaper than existing or projected commercial models— although the Commission has heard from well-informed sources who believe otherwise.

   The halting growth of computer-assisted instruction in elementary and secondary education has been, above all, a function of the high, indeed exorbitant

---

Based on data from Costs of Installing and Operating Instructional Television and Computer Assisted Instruction in the Public Schools, prepared for the Committee for Economic Development, 1968.

costs of the medium. These costs include hardware, software, and general operating expenses. Until these costs are significantly reduced, it is impossible to predict when, if ever, computer-assisted instruction will be absorbed into the mainstream of the instructional process at the elementary and secondary levels.

* * *

There is a rather widely held belief within the educational community—by those who are involved in computer-assisted research and development as well as those who are users or potential users of the medium—that the advancing state of the art of computer technology will significantly reduce the costs of computers and peripheral equipment. This belief reflects a serious misunderstanding of the computer industry and its major marketing thrust.

* * *

Data processing equipment has, is, and will continue to be designed to serve the needs of extensive and well-endowed commercial and scientific markets. The users in these markets require data processing equipment that possesses extremely sophisticated and complex capabilities. Computer-assisted instruction systems now used in education are created from this equipment which, in many cases, offers capabilities not needed, in other cases lacks capabilities required in education.

* * *

If the potential of computer-assisted instruction is to be realized within a reasonable time, a system must be developed for education which possesses the data processing capabilities peculiarly required by educators and falls in a much lower price range than is possible at present. Federal and state educational funding authorities must supply the initiative for this program of research and development.

Lawrence Parkus
Radio Corporation of America

(d) *By increasing the speed at which a student learns.* If the average student aided by instructional technology could master a given curriculum in less time than with traditional methods, the cost of his education could drop. In some branches of the Air Force, for example, the introduction of programmed instruction has reduced training time by about 30 percent, with the financial savings more than offsetting the development costs of programmed instruction.

In order to achieve these savings, however, educational institutions may have to reorganize themselves. In some cases, for instance, a student able to obtain the objectives of a programmed course more rapidly than the rest of his group cools his heels until the rest of the class catches up.

4. *Most data on the costs of instructional technology lack the necessary scope and depth to help education's managers make policy decisions.* The data are usually subject to many limitations and footnotes, sometimes to a heavy burden of reservations. In some cases the data yield only future models. For these, the range of cost estimates varies widely, depending upon the assumptions.

For example, a model prepared by Booz, Allen and Hamilton assumed:*

A system having (a) a student population of 100,000 in grades one to 12; (b) 152 schools in 24 classrooms each; (c) 30 pupils per elementary class and 25 per secondary class; (d) continuous operation through a six-hour school day for 150 instructional days per school year; and (e) one hour of instruc-

*Prepared for the Committee for Economic Development in 1968 during a study which led to the publication of the report *Innovation in Education: New Directions for the American School*. Committee for Economic Development, New York, 1968.

tion per student per day through television and one hour through computer-assisted instruction.

For this single specific model, cost projections ranged from $800,000 to $4,600,000 a year. Obviously a range of this magnitude—where the top figure is more than five times as large as the bottom figure—rules out the making of a firm policy decision.

5. *The costs of instructional technology cannot be considered in isolation. They must be compared with the costs of other forms of instruction, as well as the real costs to society of an unproductive education system.* The comparative figures needed depend on (or can only be generated by) the kind of cost analysis techniques pioneered recently by business and government, including systems analysis, cost-benefit and cost-effectiveness analysis, and planning-programming-budgeting system (PPBS). A few educational institutions, such as the University of California under President Hitch (a key figure in introducing PPBS into the Department of Defense), Stanford University, Princeton University, and the University of Toronto are experimenting with these techniques, financed partly by grants from the Ford Foundation. And a cost-benefit analysis has been worked out to identify the relative effectiveness of various Job Corps centers.

Notes on techniques of cost analysis:

Systems analysis, a technique for problem solving already used by industry and government (someday it may be used extensively in education) raises three main questions about an organization's activities:

1. What are the objectives to be reached?

2. How can these objectives be reached most efficiently?

3. How do we know when the objectives have been reached?

In developing answers to these questions, the researcher has to consider the organization involved both as a whole and in parts; also the relationship of the various parts. When applied to education, the technique considers the many different components which interact with each other (in a school, for example, such components as students, teachers, parents, buildings, books, technology, lunch programs). Although precise descriptions of the interrelationships are vital to the process, they are, obviously, difficult to obtain.

Cost-benefit and cost-effectiveness analysis are used in the second stage of systems analysis in order to choose among alternatives for reaching the desired objectives. The best alternative is the one which has the highest ratio of benefits to cost. Cost benefit, the broader category, includes cost effectiveness, which may be measured concretely in dollars or valid test scores. In addition, cost benefit includes such aspects as enjoyment or recreation, which may be deeply felt but defy precise quantification.

Planning-Programming-Budgeting System (PPBS) is, in effect, cost-benefit analysis conducted on a big scale. It is a fiscal form of systems analysis designed to assist decision-making.

James G. Miller, vice president of EDUCOM, states the problem which PPBS sets out to answer as follows: "With a given level of resources available, the task of an educational administrator is to select the policies, people, facilities, and equipment that will give the students the 'best and biggest education per buck.'"

Richard E. Speagle
Drexel Institute of
Technology

Until now the results of cost-analysis techniques at educational institutions have been fairly crude. The reasons are not hard to find. To be successful these techniques require far more knowledge about the process of education than is available today. For example, what are the specific objectives of education? of teaching particular subjects or particular skills? What input or volume of resources applied to a learning situation causes which output? which benefits? What is the relationship to teaching and learning of nonschool factors (as, for instance, how much does diet affect learning ability)?

In writing about these matters, Richard Hooper, Harkness Fellow studying educational technology in the United States, told the Commission that the acquisition of objective data about the costs and benefits of various forms of instructional technology would require a "great will to do the job," this to accompany a vastly increased research program. Even granting that such effort could be mounted, moreover, Hooper noted that education, essentially a human process, would always defy measurement. He added:

> If analytical techniques (similar to those used in industry which deals in definable products and profit objectives) are applied uncreatively, they might drive out the moments of spontaneity, the intuitive idea, and the unpredictability of human relationships.

> The benefits of education which can be given a dollar value (for example, students' earning power in later life) should not be overemphasized at the expense of benefits which resist economic analysis.

D.
Instructional Technology
and the Poor

Can technology help to meet what many regard as the most pressing problem in education today: the needs of the poor—in the central cities, in depressed rural areas, on Indian reservations.

Not surprisingly, there is very little evidence at present on which to base a sound conclusion. Most of the experimentation with instructional technology has been in the more affluent school systems. It is hard to find money for teaching machines and television sets in a school which lacks paper and pencils, decent lighting, adequate plumbing, or even minimum maintenance and safety provisions.

But based on what little evidence does exist, and on the judgments offered to the Commission by educators, specialists, and students themselves, it does seem that technology, wisely and comprehensively used, could help greatly to upgrade the education of the poor. If so, the investment required should surely assume high priority on the nation's list of unfinished business.

This section highlights the magnitude of the problem and a few of its salient features, and then presents positive and negative views on instructional technology's potential role in reaching some solutions.

The Magnitude of the Problem

Some of the inequities in the nation's educational system stem directly from geography, some from the way schools are financed. Other are the bitter heritage of poor and minority groups—blacks, Puerto Ricans, Mexican-Americans, Indians, the rural poor, and migrants to the city.

One major obstacle to fulfilling America's commitment to universal public education and equality of educational opportunity is the haphazard pattern of support for education across the nation. Some school districts spend more than $1,500 per year per pupil while others spend less than $400. These figures are not necessarily an indication of a community's *effort* to support their schools. The district paying $400, for instance, might be taxing itself two or three times more per dollar earned than the richer district paying

$1,500. Moreover, since the bulk of revenue going to schools is drawn from local property taxes (about 52 percent nationally) those communities with the most valuable (that is, taxable) properties fare much better than the poorer communities.

> This grant of unequal power to tax is the central fact of life in school finance, and if taken by itself implies a public policy that the rich deserve better educational services than the poor.
>
> National Committee
> for Support of the
> Public Schools

Inequities in educational opportunity penalize millions of American children. In attempting to better the lot of children thus penalized, educators, technologists, and social reformers should consider a number of special factors.

• *The Rural Poor*—There are 14 million rural poor in America. (There would be more if so many hadn't moved to the cities.) Low salaries, coupled with the drawbacks many teachers find in small-town life, make it difficult for rural schools to attract and hold qualified teachers. The percentage of uncertified teachers in rural areas is twice as high as it is in metropolitan areas.

In recent years there has been a considerable amount of consolidation of small school districts—enabling schools to have better facilities and staff—but many rural schools are still ill-equipped, some with outdoor privies, some without running water. And today there are still about 10,000 one-room schools in this country. Schools lacking basic necessities (and even many which have them) naturally lag far behind in more sophisticated equipment —language and science laboratories, etc.

• *American Indians*—In the United States about 600,000 people belong to more than 300 different Indian tribes. Almost half leave school before completing high school, and 75 percent live on incomes under $3,000.

> At one elementary school for Indian children a highly elaborate teaching system was set up under the direction of a private company. Daily tests were administered on the concepts that had been taught in each subject area. Test results were processed by a computer and a printout of the conceptual areas in which each child was deficient was given to teachers before the beginning of school the next day.
>
> At the same time, several hundred films had been catalogued according to the concepts they presented. The computer searched out the films which corresponded to the areas in which most of the students appeared deficient. The relevant films were transmitted by closed-circuit TV throughout the school. Teachers could make the choice as to whether they wished their class to view a film, which film, and when.
>
> The elaborate program was discontinued the next year much to the relief of students and teachers. The term "concept" had not been sufficiently defined; many of the films which were to teach specific "concepts" actually were irrelevant to the teachers' purposes; or the film took much too long to achieve what the teacher could do alone in a matter of minutes. Observers reported that toward the end of the school year most teachers left their TV receivers turned off all day long.
>
> Vincent P. Kelly
> Bureau of Indian Affairs

Most Indian children enter school handicapped by impoverished backgrounds and also by a serious language problem. At a school on one large reservation, for example, 95 percent of the six-year-olds regularly begin school speaking no English at all.

The educational needs of American Indians are not too different from those of other minority groups: more and better teachers; teachers who understand and respect them; a curriculum which is relevant to Indian life, history, and culture. But perhaps most pressing is the Indians' need for active participation in their children's education, and control over their own schools.

● *Mexican-Americans*—One-sixth of the school-age population in the five southwestern states is Spanish-speaking. In 1960, in California alone, about half the population of Spanish-speaking 14-year-olds and over had not gone beyond the eighth grade. Here again the language problem is fundamental.

> Ironically the child who enters school with a language deficiency and the cultural deprivation of long-continued poverty is often made unbearably aware of his disadvantages. School is supposed to help him solve these problems; instead it convinces him that they are beyond solution.
>
> Herschel T. Manuel
> *Spanish Speaking Children*
> *of the Southwest,*
> *Their Education and*
> *the Public Welfare*

In 1965 the National Education Association asked a group of Tucson, Arizona, teachers to study the education of Spanish-speaking people in the Southwest. The results of the survey, published in a book called *The Invisible Minority,* were summed up thus: "Is there something inherent in our system of public schooling that impedes the education of the Mexican-American child—that indeed, drives him to drop out? And the answer, unhappily, must be yes."

● *Urban Ghettos*—The most concentrated, dangerous problem in American education today lies in the ghettos of our big cities. The schools there have been overwhelmed by difficulties, and lack the capacity to master them.

Urban schools have not succeeded in providing the vast majority of black, Mexican-American, and Puerto Rican children with education that might help overcome the effects of discrimination and poverty. The Coleman report* revealed that black students fall further behind whites for each year of school completed. In the metropolitan Northeast, for example, black students on the average begin the first grade with somewhat lower scores on standard achievement tests than white students, lag about 1.6 grades behind by the sixth grade, and have fallen 3.3 grades behind by the twelfth grade. One result is that many more black than white students drop out of school. In the metropolitan North and West, black students are more than three times as likely as white students to drop out of school by age 16-17.

> An official report on the educational system in Newark, New Jersey, puts the picture in statistical terms:
>
> ● One-half of secondary pupils are or will be functionally illiterate when they complete their high school education.
>
> ● In grade seven, Newark's average on the Stanford arithmetic test was 5.1 compared to the national norm of 7.2.
>
> ● The dropout rate from 1962–1966 (cumulative) was 32 percent.
>
> ● The public school system is $250 million behind in capital construction, yet the city and school board have reached legal bonding limits.

*James S. Coleman, et al., Equality of Educational Opportunity, U.S. Office of Education, 1966.

- 30 of the 75 buildings were constructed before 1900; 44 are more than 50 years old.

- 35 of the 50 elementary schools are operating at from 101 to 151 percent of capacity.

- 23 percent of the children leave Newark's system each year for suburban or parochial schools; they are replaced by southern Negro immigrants and Puerto Ricans from New York City.

> *Report for Action*
> Governor's Select Commission
> on Civil Disorder
> State of New Jersey,
> February, 1968

To make matters worse, the economic cards are stacked against those blacks who do persist through school and college. According to a recent Census Bureau report, black college graduates earn only 74 percent as much as white college graduates, and their median income is only $13 more per year than that of whites who never went beyond high school.

Present Obstacles

These problems will not yield to any panacea. When America finally began to recognize the state of ghetto education a few years ago, the prevailing view was that once certain handicaps were surmounted, the disadvantaged child could then benefit from the standard school fare designed for middle-class white youngsters. Based on this approach, preschool programs have provided needed health and psychological services, as well as some of the social experiences common to most middle-class homes or nursery schools. But the spurts of measurable growth thus achieved and the momentum begun in such programs are imperiled once children move into public school. Studies now suggest that "compensatory" education must begin in infancy or shortly thereafter.

As for secondary schooling, many educators have now concluded that mere "enrichment"—exposure to experiences commonplace among middle-class youngsters—is unavailing in the struggle to hold the interest of the ghetto adolescent. As with the youngest children, a quite distinctive program appears essential, including powerful components of ethnic culture and projects that really mean something to the students.

> Only in the American public-school system is the Indian still roaming the plains in search of bison, the black still on the plantation, and Africa still a dark continent.

> Ben A. Watford, Student
> Graduate School of Education
> Long Island University, N.Y.

Bernard E. Donovan, former superintendent of New York City Schools, recently defended the schools as "still doing exceptionally well those things they have always done well"—that is, educating the majority of middle-class white children. But, he said, "deficiencies lie in the system's difficulty of coping with a new and massive group of seriously disadvantaged children. . . . Unfortunately we, in addition to every other large city in the nation, have not been able to marshal effectively our own and all the other forces of society which must be brought together to solve this problem."

The failure of schools to cultivate the most basic skills of reading and writing is particularly critical. David X. Spencer, a black community leader and the elected chairman of the Governing Board in East Harlem's I.S. 201 Complex, put it plainly to a white reporter: "I don't care what your hangups or my hangups are. We can get along as long as my kid is learning to read and write."

The sheer complexity of the problem of ghetto education precludes a technological or any other "fix." A noted black psychologist, Dr. James P. Comer of the Yale Child Study Center, told the Commission:

> Instructional technology introduced into a school or system operating at a "survival level" can be another burden for administrative and teaching personnel. Increasing the vocabulary of a child through instructional equipment will usually be of limited value in a chaotic system not capable of producing or sustaining a learning environment. All too often, help for the inner-city school has been an input of new ideas, people, programs, etc., without systematic attention to the critical aspects of basic school programs.

> Unlike the good football teams which, when showing signs of slipping, revert to fundamental patterns of blocking, tackling, and passing, schools have gone for the razzle-dazzle plays. Cultural enrichment, ethnic relevance, new technology, fancy new buildings, and the like have been the response to the crisis in inner-city education. The principal of one inner-city school recently counted twelve new program inputs in his school within three years, all now abandoned, none carefully evaluated, with little apparent impact on the youngsters.

In some respects, resistance to the introduction of technology into ghetto schools resembles the resistance encountered even in wealthy suburban school systems. Some educators and citizens feel that instructional technology would merely serve to distract attention from basic problems; in the case of the ghetto—control, governance, financing. And some critics believe instructional technology may even have positive disadvantages. In this view, the slum child's prime need is a continuing close relationship with his teacher; he may react adversely to the intervention of impersonal technology.

In reviewing for the Commission the situation in sixteen cities Alva R. Dittrick, of the Research Council of the Great Cities Program for School Improvement, reported a number of promising technological experiments, but summed up overall progress as follows:

> At the present time, a direct assessment of the impact of instructional technology on making learning more relevant for ghetto children cannot be made adequately. Operational situations simply do not exist in which large-scale coordinated use of instructional technology is being applied to classroom situations.

> Isolated success stories and promising practices related to the use of specific machines or programmed instructional materials can be identified. For the most part, they are singular instances without consistent application as a regular integral part of daily instructional activities. At this point in time, the application of instructional technology must be considered to be in a trial-and-error, exploratory period.

There is, then, need for sustained and well-financed research and development programs which could point the way toward effective and comprehensive use of technology in ghetto schools.

The State of the Art

What *has* been learned from the limited experience to date in using technology to enhance learning for the children of poverty? Three chief points were stressed by the experts whom the Commission consulted:

> 1) Instructional technology should put the student in an active, independent learning role, in contrast to conventional classroom procedure which requires him

to spend most of his time passively sitting and being talked at. There should be ample opportunity for students to actually touch and use equipment themselves in order to gain a sense of mastery.

2) To be effective, instructional technology must be responsive to the people it is designed to serve. There is a fear, for instance, that since ghetto schools have received the short end of the stick in education generally, they are destined to receive only the most pedestrian, shortsighted, and harmful applications of technology. In the design and use of hardware, therefore, and even more in the concept and production of programs, ghetto residents—students and adults—should have an important voice.

3) Instructional technology should be used comprehensively. Merely introducing a film or a record from time to time will not make any significant impact in the ghetto (or any other) school. Only through a coordinated and intensive use of a broad repertoire of new media—including the most effective use of good teachers—can a significantly better environment for learning be created.

- In the St. Louis School System emphasis is being placed on speech improvement in inner-city schools through the use of tapes, tape recordings, and radio lessons.

- The Baltimore School System has developed closed-circuit television instruction in math for selected children in junior highs with large concentrations of disadvantaged children. Longitudinal studies are being made to determine effectiveness of this technique over conventional approaches. A similar study is being conducted in senior highs with experimental and control groups.

- The Los Angeles Public School System has developed and is evaluating instructional programs designed to improve oral English of Negro and Mexican-American children, using various media including recorders and auto-tutors.

- In San Diego junior highs, electronic classrooms have been organized to teach foreign languages. Closed-circuit television is being used to transmit 75 systematically prepared tape lessons to facilitate teaching English as a second language.

- The Cleveland Public Schools are studying the effect of programmed instructional materials on development of basic reading skills, in an attempt to identify successful approaches with children in six inner-city schools.

- The New York Public Schools' "More Effective Schools Program" has made abundant quantities of equipment and instructional materials available to teachers. The effects of mechanical facilitators such as overhead projectors, film cartridges, film libraries, and teaching machines are being studied.

- The Philadelphia schools have developed a Language Arts Communication Media Program. Students are provided with opportunities to employ communication media such as motion pictures, still photography, and tape recorders to extend their understanding and appreciation of literature and competence in spoken and written expression. Teachers are trained in techniques necessary to implement the program. Teachers and students work with various types of equipment. Much individualized instruction is required.

- The Boston School System has developed an Interdisciplinary Slide/Film Program. This material was created by ninth-grade students. *The Concept of The Hero* was developed in an interdisciplinary context making use of a slide/tape presentation.

Alva R. Dittrick
Research Council, Great Cities
Program on School Improvement

Today, if only in a small way, instructional technology is helping teachers to establish new educational contact with poor children. Where with traditional techniques children have failed to reach a satisfactory level of achievement, new approaches—such as talking typewriters and other programs and equipment specifically designed to improve reading instruction—are offering fresh alternatives and options. Materials and machines are creating environments that challenge children to respond as they have not in the past.

An important element in altering the educational environment which various forces of instructional technology can provide is a reward system that evokes the child's intrinsic drive for competence. Programmed instruction, for instance, can enable the child to grasp a relationship or an idea and thereby generate enthusiasm for further learning.

Hopes for the Future

Limited as it is, experience to date suggests that technology could help solve major instructional problems of schools in districts serving poor and minority-group students. Cameras and recorders, for example, help to dilute the ororverbalism of schools and relate education dramatically to the students' out-of-school life. These and other media foster original expression and help to make learning more individual and effective. On the basis of results thus far, many hold high hopes for technology's potential effectiveness in ghetto and other disadvantaged schools. Technology would at least replace incompetent or unsympathetic classroom teachers for some of the time. Too often teachers in ghetto schools disapprove of students' styles of behavior or speech, and sometimes, knowingly or not, of their color. A teacher's belief that children are not capable of learning can become a self-fulfilling prophecy.

Technology, properly used, could sidestep many of these problems. A teaching machine or talking typewriter is infinitely patient and adaptable to a child's pace or needs, and is not offended by his dress or speech. A film or language tape can provide information and drill unaccompanied by censure and irritation. In particular, instructional technology could prove invaluable in facilitating what many feel to be the most acute problem of all—learning to read. Programmed instruction and the computer with its capacity for endless repetition are likely reading tutors for the ghetto child, as experiments are beginning to demonstrate.

Technology can serve as a powerful creative tool for all kinds of students, but most of all perhaps for the underprivileged. In Philadelphia, a group of young gang members and former delinquents formed a movie production company which provided not only emotional and artistic satisfaction but which also vastly expanded their perception, understanding, and pocketbooks. In many large cities ghetto youth, provided with cameras by various film companies, have felt whole new horizons open out before them.

Putting all these pieces together, some observers see in instructional technology the promise of developing a comprehensive, potent teaching strategy which could be uniquely effective with deprived and minority-group youngsters. It could actively engage them in the learning process through all their senses and modes of awareness; it could adjust to the individual learning style of each child; it could bring material of relevance and interest into the school; it could filter out the antagonism and indifference of some teachers; it could open the school to the media-rich environment. Such a comprehensive system of instruction is admittedly visionary, but experience to date is hardly an adequate guide to future possibilities.

E.
Technology
and the Education
of the Handicapped

Toward the end of its study, the Commission on Instructional Technology noted that the Congress was considering legislation for the establishment of a National Center on Educational Media and Materials for the Handicapped.

This center is expected to provide a comprehensive program for developing instructional media and materials for use in educational programs for the handicapped; adapting instructional media and materials now in use for the handicapped; and familiarizing and training teachers of the handicapped to use the new educational media and materials available.

When the congressional committees responsible for the legislation reported out the bills providing for the establishment of the center (in mid-1969), they observed that although the federal government has been committed for nearly a decade to programs for training teachers for handicapped children, there are still far too few teachers available. The testimony presented to the committees showed that:

- The Department of Health, Education, and Welfare estimates that more than 300,000 teachers, speech pathologists, audiologists, and other specialists are needed at the present time to work with handicapped children. Only 75,000 to 80,000 teachers and specialists are now available for those children.

- Only 2 million of the 5½ million handicapped children needing special education services are receiving them.

- Even if funds were available it would not be possible in the near future to educate and train a sufficient number of teachers and specialists for handicapped children. The problem is that a sufficient number of trained persons who can train teachers of the handicapped does not exist.

- Many applications of communications technology can be made to the special problems of the handicapped. For example, educational television, commercial radio and television, and computer-assisted instruction may help solve teacher shortages and provide educational programs to those handicapped children not able to attend a special school. The potential of these developments has yet to be carefully analyzed.

- The Office of Education has been supporting 14 regional Instructional Materials Centers. These centers have been so successful in demonstrating the usefulness of instructional materials in the teaching of handicapped children that states and local communities, using local sources of funding, have established more than 80 associate centers to distribute these materials.

- There is a need for a national center which will coordinate the various aspects of a comprehensive media and materials research, development, and delivery system for making instructional media available to all handicapped children.

Interdisciplinary, collaborative research is a must in the study and investigation of the needs of the mentally, physically, and emotionally handicapped in any state program. In order to give depth and breadth of understanding to the concepts which underlie the principles of special education and rehabilitation, it is necessary for workers in the fields of psychology, sociology, and medicine to combine their knowledges in conducting research for physically and mentally ill children and adults.

Research findings, in order to be of some value, must be made readily available to practitioners. These include workers on all levels as well as professional educators, supervisors and administrators, employers, families, and the general public.

Peter J. Salmon, Chairman
Ad Hoc Committee on Education
and Training of the Handicapped

The Commission on Instructional Technology noted as its report was about to be completed that both the findings and the recommendations by the congressional committees were consistent with those the Commission has incorporated into other sections of this report.

F.
The Establishment
of the Commission
on Instructional Technology
and the Conduct
of Its Study

Establishment of the Commission

On November 7, 1967, before 500 educators and broadcasters and a battery of television cameras, the Public Broadcasting Act became law. Created thereby was the Corporation for Public Broadcasting, a quasi-governmental body designed to rally and focus support for noncommercial television and radio.

In signing the act into law, the President said:

> Noncommercial television can bring its audiences the excitement of excellence in every field.

> A vital and self-sufficient noncommercial television system will not only instruct, but inspire and uplift our people.

The need for the Corporation has been described some months earlier by the Carnegie Commission on Educational Television, a committee of educators and civic leaders established and privately financed as a public service by the Carnegie Corporation of New York. Although the Carnegie Commission had excluded from its study the formal instructional aspects of television and radio, it had emphasized their potential importance, and recommended a study of the instructional uses of these and other technological media. The Public Broadcasting Act provided for this study, but the title involved did not receive an appropriation from Congress.

In March, 1968, the Secretary of Health, Education and Welfare appointed a nine-member Commission on Instructional Technology and asked the Office of Education to allocate the needed funds for its activities. On April 22, 1968, the Commission met with the U.S. Commissioner of Education to discuss the scope of its assignment.

The Commissioner provided a broad mandate for the study by saying:

> The scope of the Commission's work should be wide-ranging. Every aspect of instructional technology and every problem which may arise in its development should be included.

He then went on to say:

> The independence of this Commission must be maintained. The Commission is not an adjunct of the U.S. Office of Education. Therefore, except for this initial

meeting, neither the Commissioner of Education nor any member of his staff will take part in the Commission's activities, unless asked specifically for information.

In July 1968, the Commissioner further described the rationale for the assignment to the Commission when he said at a national convention:

> We have reached the point where we have simply got to come up with a more orderly, informed way of taking advantage of all that the new technology has to offer.
>
> The new educational technology holds no more exciting prospect for American education than the possibility of providing—on a scale and to a standard far beyond our grasp—an educational system able to respond to the unique needs and abilities of the individual learner.
>
> One problem is: how do we do this economically, at a price both industry and educators can afford?
>
> Even more important: how do we design and develop this technology so that it meets the needs of both the individual student and the educational system as a whole?
>
> These are questions that none of us—in education, in industry, in government—can answer except by asking them of each other, over and over and over again.

How the Study Proceeded

At the April meeting the Commission on Instructional Technology selected the Academy for Educational Development, a nonprofit educational research and consulting firm, to undertake the necessary staff work. The Commission and the staff then proceeded, in the light of the broad mandate for the study, to:

- Examine the whole gamut of instructional technology—old, new, and future; printed, mechanical, and electronic; automated and cybernated; from books to computers, from carrels to learning centers, from overhead projectors to satellite transmission; from preschool to graduate school.

- Study instructional technology as a whole, as a system greater than the sum of the various media.

- Consider the many critical questions raised by the application of technology to education.

- Weigh technology's potential toward alleviating the urgent problems now confronting America's schools and colleges.

- Examine the federal role, past and potential, in educational technology.

The Commission invited observations and opinions from a broad sample of the educational community, business and industry serving education, and other institutions, individuals, government agencies, and associations interested in education or technology. In addition, invitations to communicate with the Commission were placed in trade and professional publications.

Simultaneously, a series of questions were drawn up that were designed to probe broad policy matters as well as technical details and specific uses of instructional technology, in order to obtain expert information and opinion on every phase of the Commission's mandate. The Commission arranged for the preparation of more than 150 papers from "establishment" representatives as well as mavericks, from scholars, politicians, social critics, and generalists as well as from specialists and practitioners.

Commission meetings were convened at various places throughout the country in order to permit visits to be made to a variety of projects (in public schools, universities, the armed services, industry, the Job Corps, etc.). The meetings often included discussions with theorists and practitioners in instructional technology.

The Commission also participated in a number of seminars arranged to elicit a range of views and experience in different aspects of instructional technology. For example:

- A seminar to explore communications satellites and their implications for instructional technology, which included representatives of the National Aeronautics and Space Administration, the National Association of Educational Broadcasters, the Federal Communications Commission, National Educational Television, the U.S. Office of Education, the President's Task Force on Communications Policy, and the Joint Council on Educational Telecommunications.

- A seminar to explore developments in instructional television, which included network, ETV station, and school people, as well as representatives from such associations as the National Association of Educational Broadcasters, the Joint Council on Educational Telecommunications, and the National Education Association.

- A seminar to probe student reaction to instructional technology (both pro and con); participants were twenty high-school and college students, all of whom had had varied experience with technological media.*

- A seminar with fifteen elementary-school and high-school teachers of varying background and experience in instructional technology.

- A number of seminars with technology specialists, and with representatives of educational and industrial associations concerned with technology.

Meantime, staff members and special consultants conducted interviews and field trips, and prepared reports on a wide variety of projects and organizations involved with instructional technology. Included were military installations, museums, and business organizations, as well as programs and activities conducted by schools, colleges, and universities.

The staff also searched out and catalogued a library of relevant materials, both published and unpublished. Selections from this material as well as the reports prepared especially for the study were reviewed by the Commission.

Finally, liaison was established with departments and agencies of the federal government concerned with instructional technology, with Congressional bodies, and with quasi-governmental organizations.**

The Commission was gratified by the interest manifested in its work. Scores of distinguished people—scholars, technicians, practicing schoolmen, reformers, and others—prepared papers or granted interviews. Hundreds of thoughtful letters came in response to the Commission's invitation. They came from industry; from superintendents and staff members of big school systems such as Detroit, Chicago, and New York, and from dozens of smaller places; from nearly every state office of education; from the deans of educa-

The student seminar was co-sponsored by the Institute for Development of Educational Activities, Inc. (I/D/E/A), an affiliate of the Charles F. Kettering Foundation.

**Including the Federal Communications Commission; the Corporation for Public Broadcasting; officials in the U.S. Office of Education charged with administering such legislation as the Educational Professions Development Act (which provides grants to help solve the critical shortage of education personnel and to improve their training), the National Defense Education Act (which provides grants and loans for the acquisition of certain kinds of equipment), Title I of the Public Broadcasting Act (which provides federal financial assistance for noncommercial educational radio and television broadcast facilities), the Higher Education Act (which provides funds to institutions of higher education for the acquisition of television, laboratory, and other special equipment), and the Higher Education Facilities Act (which provides grants and loans for construction and improvement of facilities); and sponsors of such proposed legislation as the Educational Technology Act of 1969.*

tion of leading universities; from college deans, department heads, and professors in many specialities, including computer science, behavioral research, medicine, engineering, instructional resources, communications and television.

Through all these varied means, the Commission was enabled to arrive at a realistic picture of instructional technology as it exists today in the United States, to assess its values, and to form a responsible judgment on its probable future.

G.

Papers Requested by The Commission on Instructional Technology

ALTER, CHESTER M.
    The Potential of Technological Instruction for the Less Affluent College
ANDERSON, ROBERT H.
    Changes Necessary in the Organizational Patterns and Administrative Procedures of
        Schools and Colleges in Order for New Techniques to Effectively Improve Instruction
BAIR, GEORGE E.
    The Promise that Technology Holds for Education
BAZEMORE, A. W., and SILVERZWEIG, STANLEY
    Toward a Learning Technology for the Inner City Schools
BEAMISH, ERIC E.
    Educational Technology and the Preparation of Teachers
    The Instructional Technologist and Some Recommendations for his Professional
        Preparation
BECKWITH, HUGH
    Innovation in Industry that Appears Likely to Affect Instructional Technology During
        the Next Ten Years
BELL, T. H.
    Changes that will be Necessary in the Organizational Patterns and Administrative
        Procedures of Schools and Colleges in Order for New Technologies to Effectively
        Improve Education
BELZER, JACK
    Patterns for Development of Education in Information Science
BITZER, DONALD L., and SKAPERDAS, D.
    The Design of an Economically Viable Large-Scale Computer-Based Education System
BLAISDELL, W. M.
    Instructional Media Activities in USOE Research and Development Centers
BOLVIN, JOHN O.
    The New Technology and Its Implications for Organizational and Administrative
        Changes
BORD, NANCY A.
    Application of Cost Analyses to Instructional Technology

BREITENFELD, FREDERICK, JR.
Instructional Television: The State of the Art
BRIGHT, R. LOUIS
Should Educators Generate Specifications for the Purchase of Equipment?
BROWN, B. FRANK
Instructional Technology and the Student: The State of the Art
BUSHNELL, DON D.
Introducing the Docile Technology in Memoriam of CAI.
CARROLL, JOHN B.
The Role of Measurement and Evaluation in Educational Technology
COGAN, EUGENE A.
The Use of Systems Analysis in Introducing Educational Technology into Schools
COLEMAN, JAMES S.
The Role of Modern Technology in Relation to Simulation and Games for Learning
COMER, JAMES P.
Technology and the Inner City School
CONGREVE, WILLARD J.
Possibilities in the Use of Technology for the Education of Underprivileged Children
CRIM, ALONZO A.
Use of Technology to Improve the Pre-service and In-service Training of Teachers
Who Work with Ghetto Children
DAVIES, DON
Training Personnel for Roles in Instructional Technology
DAVIS, ROBERT B.
Past Practices and Likely Prospects for the Use of Technological Devices in Relation
to School Mathematics
DE LONE, RICHARD H.
Sketching a Context for Instructional Technology
DEMPSEY, REV. MICHAEL J.
Some Reflections Upon the Relationships Between the Restructuring of Schools and
Communications Technology
DIETRICH, JOHN E., and JOHNSON, F. CRAIG
Cost Analysis of Instructional Technology
Changes in Administrative Organization Required for the Introduction of Appropriate
Educational Technology
DITTRICK, ALVA R.
Developing Relevant Education Through Instructional Technology
EDINGER, LOIS V.
Educational Technology and the Teaching Profession
EVANS, RUPERT N.; SREDLE, HENRY; CARSS, BRIAN, and WALKER, ROBERT W.
Instructional Technology and Vocational Education
FADIMAN, CLIFTON
A Practitioner's Notes
FINLEY, ROBERT M.
Changes in Patterns of School Organization, Management, Staffing, Facilities, and
Finance are Required if Technology is to be Effective in Improving Instruction
FLORY, JOHN
Films for Learning
FORSDALE, LOUIS
8mm Film in Education, Status and Prospects—1968
FORSYTHE, RICHARD O.
Instructional Radio: Its Broad Capabilities as an Educational Delivery System

FREDETTE, ALBERT P.
The State of the Art Relative to the Use of Radio in Medical Education
FRIEDENBERG, EDGAR Z.
Effects of the Technological Mystique on Schooling
FUND FOR MEDIA RESEARCH
Survey on Industry's Use of Technology for Education and Training
Use of Instructional Technology by the Job Corps and Peace Corps
The small formats
GABLE, MARTHA A.
Instructional Television and its Relation to Other Forms of Educational Technology
to Serve Needs in Urban Areas
GINTHER, JOHN R.
Technology, Philosophy, and Education
GLASER, ROBERT, and GOW, J. STEELE, JR.
Comments on the Proposal by CED to Create a Commission on Research, Innovation,
and Evaluation in Education
GODFREY, ELEANOR P.
Availability and Use of Instructional Media
GOODLAD, JOHN I.
Education and Technology
GREEN, ALAN C.
Instructional Technology and School Buildings—Influences, Conflicts, and Guidance
GREEN, ROBERT L., and THOMAS, RICHARD
Racism and Attitude Change: The Role of Mass Media and Instructional Technology
GREENHILL, LESLIE P.
The Expanding Usage of Instructional Technology in Japan
GROVE, RICHARD
Increasing the Educational Effectiveness of Museum Exhibitions through Applications
of Instructional Media
HAMMEREL, MARY ANN, and LAIDLAW, WILLIAM J.
Instructional Technology and the Job Corps Curriculum
HAROLD, JOHN W.
The use of Technology as a Strategy for Crossing Language and Cultural Barriers
HEATHERS, GLEN
Educational Philosophy and Educational Technology
HITCHENS, HOWARD B., JR.
Instructional Technology in the Armed Forces:
Part I. Precommissioning and Professional Training
Part II. Technical Training
Part III. Opinion, Trends, and Outlook for the Future
HOCKING, ELTON
Technology in Foreign Language Teaching
HOOPER, RICHARD
Observations on the Use of Instructional Technology at 20 Important Educational
Institutions in the U.S.
HUDSON, ROBERT B.
The School Broadcasting System in Japan
HUGHES, THOMAS P.
Some Problems of Technological Innovation
HULL, RICHARD B.
Random Audio and Video Access Information Retrieval Systems

HYER, ANNA L.
Activities of the National Council for Educational Technology in Great Britain
JAMESON, SPENSER, and IANNI, FRANCIS A. J.
The Reading Process and Processed Reading
JASON, HILLIARD
Instructional Technology in Medical Education
JENNINGS, FRANK G.
The Prospect for the "Book" as an Educational Medium
JOHNSON, HARRY ALLEYN
The Promises of Educational Technology in Ghetto Schools
KELLY, VINCENT P.
Instructional Technology and the Education of American Indian Children
KENT, ALLEN
Information Science: Media Implications of the New Means of Information Organization
KEPPEL, FRANCIS, and CORNOG, MICHAEL L.
Evaluation and Measurement of Instructional Technology
KIESLING, HERBERT J.
On the Economic Analysis of Educational Technology
KOMOSKI, P. KENNETH
Toward the Development of Effective Instructional Technology for American Education
KOZOL, JONATHAN
Prospects and Problems in Using Instructional Technology to Meet the Needs of Negro Children in the Big-City Ghettos
KROPP, R. P.
What is the Role of Measurement and Evaluation in Technology?
KURLAND, NORMAN D.
Educational Technology in New York State—Theory, Practice, and the Future
LANGE, PHIL C.
The Teaching-Learning Process and Instructional Technology
LEITMAN, ALLAN
The Public School: Agent of Community Education
LEVIN, HENRY M.
Cost Effectiveness Evaluation on Instructional Technology: The Problems
LIEBERMAN, JAMES
Instructional Media in the Biomedical Fields
LOCKE, ROBERT W., and ENGLER, DAVID
Instructional Technology: The Capabilities of Industry to Help Solve Educational Problems
LYONS, CHARLES A., JR.
How Can Instructional Technology Help Solve the Problems of the Less Affluent Small Colleges?
MARKLE, SUSAN MEYER
Programming and Programmed Instruction
MARTIN, JOHN HENRY
Technology and the Education of the Disadvantaged
MARTINSON, JOHN L., and MILLER, DAVID C.
Educational Technology and Future of the Book
MARX, LEO
Notes for a Humanist Critique of Technological Innovation in Teaching
MASON, WARD S.
Instructional Media in USOE Research and Development Centers: How the work of the R&D Centers relates to instructional technology and plans for the future

MASTON, ROBERT E.
Instructional Technology and Language Learning
McCAFFREY, AUSTIN
The Prospect for the "Book" as an Educational Medium in an Era of New Technological Developments
MEAD, MARGARET
Age Discrepancies in the Understanding and Use of Modern Technology Especially in the Mass Media, or How Parents and Teachers Fail to Tune in on the Children's Media Environment
MEANEY, JOHN W.
The Multimedia Age
MESTHENE, EMMANUEL G.
Instructional Technology and the Purposes of Education
MILLER, ARTHUR R.
The Invasion of Privacy and Instructional Technology
MILLER GEORGE E., and HARLESS, WILLIAM F.
Instructional Technology and Continuing Medical Education.
MILLER, JAMES G.
The Nature of Living Systems
The Living Systems Involved in the Educational Process
A Suggested Ten-Year Phased Program for Developing, Evaluating, and Implementing Instructional Technologies
Deciding Whether and How to Use Educational Technology in the Light of Cost-Effectiveness Evaluation
MILLER, JAMES G., and RATH, GUSTAVE J.
Priority Determination and Resource Allocation by Planning-Programming-Budgeting and Cost-Effectiveness Analysis in Educational Systems
MINEAR, LEON P.
Reinforcing Teacher Education through Exposure to the New Educational Technology
MORGAN, ROBERT M.
Instructional Technology in Vocational Training
NATIONAL ASSOCIATION OF EDUCATIONAL BROADCASTERS
Television-in-Instruction: The State of the Art
Observations on Instructional Television and Instructional Technology
NELSON, LESTER W.
Some Alternative Approaches to the Establishment of A National Effort in Research, Innovation, and Evaluation in Educational Technology
NORTH, R. STAFFORD
Dial-Access as an Instructional Medium
NYGREN, CAROLYN
Combining the Insights of Linguistics and Educational Technology to Teach Language in the Black Community
PARKUS, LAWRENCE
Computer Assisted Instruction in Elementary/Secondary Education: The State of the Art
PODSHADLEY, DALE W.
Instructional Technology in Dentistry
POSTMAN, NEIL
Curriculum Change and Technology
RAINSBERRY, F. B.
Educational TV in Canada

RANKIN, JOHN H.
> Production Problems Involved in Producing Art Courses to be Taught Utilizing the Latest Developments in Technology

RIPPY, WILBUR
> The Technics and Techniques of Educational Technology

ROSENFIELD, HARRY N.
> Major Problems of Copyright Law as Viewed by the Ad Hoc Committee on Copyright Law Revision

RUMMLER, GEARY A.
> What is Programmed Learning?

RYAN, KEVIN
> Teacher Training in Instructional Technology

SAETTLER, PAUL
> Lessons for Education Drawn from a Study of the Effects of New Technologies in Various Areas of Society

SAND, OLE, and McCLURE, ROBERT
> Instructional Technology and Curriculum Change

SCHULLER, CHARLES F.
> Production Facilities Needed in Order for a University to Adequately Satisfy its Instructional Technology Requirements

SCHURE, ALEXANDER
> Technological Systems for Education which Adapt Technology to People

SELDEN, DAVID, and BHAERMAN, ROBERT
> Instructional Technology and the Teaching Profession

SINGER, IRA J.
> At Will and At Once—The Audio-Video Dial Access Information Retrieval System

SIZER, THEODORE, and KIRP, DAVID L.
> Technology and Education: Who Controls?

SMITH, KARL U.
> Recommendations Regarding Further Emphasis in Educational Technology as Based on Behavioral Cybernetic Projections

SMITH, MARY HOWARD
> Cooperative Planning and Production: Problems, Pitfalls, and Privileges

SMITH, ROBERT G. JR.
> The Media Manufacturer and the Educator

SPEAGLE, RICHARD E.
> Cost Estimates of Major Instructional Technologies
> Cost Benefits: A Buyer's Guide for Instructional Technology
> Systems Analysis in Education

SPENCER, DAVID X.
> New Machines and New Methods for New Education

SPENCER, RICHARD E.
> The Role of Measurement and Evaluation in Instructional Technology

STAHR, ELVIS J. and CLARK, DAVID L.
> Establishment of a National Study Commission on Research, Evaluation, and Innovation in Education

STARKWEATHER, JOHN A.
> Adaptive Machine Aids to Learning

STONE, C. WALTER
> Some Reflections and Recommendations Concerning the Chief Problem of Instructional Technology Application—Access

STONE, SONJA H., and JONES, LEANDER
Instructional Technology and the Inner City
STREET, DAVID
New Instructional Technologies and the Teaching Profession
SWANSON, DON R.
Education and the Communication of Scientific Information
SWANSON, J. CHESTER
Instructional Technology in Service to Vocational Technical Education
THORNTON, BASIL
The Instructional Media in Italy
VANDERMEER, A. W.
How Teachers and Administrators Can be Given a Better Indoctrination on the Potentialities and Uses of Instructional Technology
WAGNER, ROBERT W.
The Generation of Images: A State-of-the-Art Report on Sixteen-Millimeter Film
WEINBERG, MEYER
Instructional Technology and the Disadvantaged Child
WENTWORTH, JOHN W.
Cable Television and Education
WILSON, JOHN D.
The Idea of Living-Learning: Innovations in the Academic Use of Residential Facilities
WINSLOW, KEN
The Adoption by Education of Videotape Techniques for the Creation and Use of Instructional Materials and the Development of Sources for the Inter-Institutional Distribution of Prerecorded Videotape Materials
WITHROW, FRANK B. JR. and GOUGH, JOHN A.
Instructional Technology for the Handicapped
WOLFE, ARTHUR B.
The Combination of Instructional Technology with Technological Instruction

II.

Papers Submitted to the Commission on Instructional Technology for Information

ADELSON, MARVIN
>   Decisions, Decisions, Decisions: Is Education Important Enough? The Technology of Forecasting and the Forecasting of Technology Educational Ends and Innovational Means

ALL, STEPHEN A.
>   Suggestions and Possible Solutions for Some of the Problems of ITV in the Great Cities

ALLEN, WILLIAM H.
>   Audiovisual Instruction: The State of the Art

ALTER, HENRY C.
>   Of Messages and Media: Teaching and Learning by Public Television

BARUCH, JORDAN J.
>   The Extended Use of Public Broadcasting Facilities

BENSON, CHARLES S.
>   The Application of Economic Reasoning to Resource Allocations in Education

BITZER, DONALD L.
>   Some Pedagogical and Engineering Design Aspects of Computer-Based Education

BOOCOCK, SARANE S.
>   Restructuring the Education System for Advantageous Use of Instructional Technology

BOWER, RICHARD S
>   Computer Time-Sharing and the Teaching of Economics

BUNDERSON, C. VICTOR
>   The Computer and Instructional Design

BURRIS, RUSSELL W.
>   Major Areas of Emphasis for Instructional Engineering

BUSH, ROBERT N.
>   New Directions for Research and Development in Teacher Education

CARPENTER, C. R.
>   Abstracts of Seminar Discussions on Quality Factors in Instructional Materials [1]
>   Educational Media Production System for the Southern Region
>   Quality Factors of Media and Conditions of Learning [1]

[1] USOE commissioned project for the Commission on Instructional Technology.

Summary: A Constructive Critique of Educational Technology
Teleinstruction and Individualized Learning
Toward A Developed Technology of Instruction—1980
CARTER, CLYDE N., and WALKER, MAURICE J.
  Costs of Installing and Operating Instructional Television and Computer Assisted
    Instruction in Public Schools
CHASE, FRANCIS S.
  Educational Research and Development: Promise or Mirage?
  Problems of Autonomy and Accountability in Government Contracts for Research and
    Development in Education
CHU, GODWIN G., and SCHRAMM, WILBUR
  Learning by Television[2]
COULSON, JOHN E.
  Computer-Assisted Instruction and Its Potential for Individualizing Instruction
DEIGHTON, LEE C.
  Instruments of Instruction: The Book Plus the New Media
ELLIS, ALLAN B., and TIEDEMAN, DAVID V.
  Can a Machine Counsel?
FERRAGALLO, ROGER J., and HOMITZ, WALLACE T.
  Proposal to Investigate the Effectiveness of Controlled Manipulation of Classroom
    Environments in the Teaching of Junior College Subjects
FERRY, W. H.
  Tonic and Toxic Technology
GAGNÉ, ROBERT M.
  Learning Theory, Educational Media and Individualized Instruction
GENERAL LEARNING CORPORATION, EDUCATIONAL SERVICES DIVISION
  Cost Study of Educational Media Systems and Their Equipment Components[1]
    Part I: Guidelines for Determining Costs of Media Systems
    Part II: Technical Report
    Part III: Supplementary Report: Computer Assisted Instruction
GLASER, ROBERT
  Educational Technology—The Design and Programming of Instruction
GOODLAD, JOHN I.
  Thought, Invention, and Research in the Advancement of Education
GREENE, HUGH
  Instructional Technology in the Context of Educational Theories
HADDON, ALEXANDER M.
  A Low-level Technical Systems Design for Programmed Instruction
HENDERSON, JOHN
  The Audio-recorded Tutorial Method of Assisting Students in Specific Problem-solving
    Difficulties
HILGARD, ERNEST R.
  The Psychological Heuristics of Learning
HOBAN, CHARLES F.
  The Concept of Instruction as a System within Which to Approach Instructional
    Technology
HUDSON, ROBERT B.
  The Future of Educational Television
HUNTER, WALTER E.
  Using Automation for Instruction

[2] *USOE commissioned project for the Commission on Instructional Technology.*

JACKSON, PHILIP W.
   The Teacher and the Machine: Observations on the Impact of Educational Technology
JAMES, H. THOMAS
   Financing More Effective Education
JERMAN, MAX
   Characteristics of Computer Assisted Instruction from an Author's Viewpoint
JOYCE, BRUCE R., and JOYCE, ELIZABETH H.
   Data Banks for Children
   The Principal and His Staff: The Multiple Systems Approach to Curriculum
KANTNER, HAROLD H.
   Telecommunication Tools for Schools: Opportune Policy Soon?
KELLEY, ALLEN C.
   The Economics of Teaching and the Role of the Teaching Information Processing
      System
KENT, WILLIAM P. AND ASSOCIATES, SYSTEM DEVELOPMENT CORPORATION
   Feasibility of Using an Experimental Laboratory for Identifying Classroom Multi-
      Media Problems and Requirements[3]
KOPSTEIN, FELIX F., and SEIDEL, ROBERT J.
   Computer-Administered Instruction Versus Traditionally Administered Instruction:
      Economics
KRATHWOHL, DAVID R.
   Proposal for Development of National Institutes of Education in the Department of
      Health, Education, and Welfare
LANIER, VINCENT
   The Teaching of Art as Social Revolution
LESSINGER, LEON
   Educational Stability in an Unstable Technical Society
McMURRIN, STERLING M.
   Technology and Education: A Consideration of Ends and Means
MEIERHENRY, W. C.
   Whither Instructional Technology?
MEISLER, RICHARD
   Technologies for Learning
MINOR, FRANK J., MYERS, ROGER A., and SUPER, DONALD E.
   An Experimental Computer-Based Educational and Occupational Orientation System
      for Counseling
MORRIS, ALBERT J., and GRACE, DONALD J.
   Conceptual Design of a Television System for Continuing Education
NATIONAL ASSOCIATION OF EDUCATIONAL BROADCASTERS
   Proposal for Electronically-Facilitated Educational Parks in Harlem
RAO, PENNA LAKSHMIKANTH
   Broadcast Satellite System for India
RATH, GUSTAVE J.
   Models, Means and Measurement in Education
RICHARDS, P. H.
   The New System of Education Needed in Today's Technological Age
RUTHERFORD, WILLIAM L.
   Proposal for a National Instructional Materials Center
SCHRAGER, PHILLIP E.
   Line of Sight: A Communications Feasibility Study

---

[3] *USOE commissioned project for the Commission on Instructional Technology.*

SEIDEL, ROBERT J.
  The Copernican Revolution in Education/Training
SIMMONS, ROBERT F.
  Linguistic Analysis of Constructed Student Responses in Computer Assisted Instruction
SMALLWOOD, RICHARD D.
  Optimum Policy Regions for Computer-Directed Teaching Systems
SMITH, DONALD K.
  Federal Support for University-Based Programs of Instructional Research and Development
STOLUROW, L. M.
  Computer Assisted Instruction
STRINER, HERBERT E.
  Counselling: A New Process in a Dynamic Economy
SUPPES, PATRICK and MORNINGSTAR, MONA
  Four Programs in Computer-Assisted Instruction
TAYLOR, JOHN W.
  The Effect of Modern Technology in Education
TIEDEMAN, DAVID V.
  Can a Machine Develop a Career?
  The Information System for Vocational Decisions: Description, Subsequent Development, and Implications
TWYFORD, LORAN C.
  Proposed Federal Legislation and Suggested Guidelines in Educational Technology
TYLER, RALPH W.
  The Problems and Possibilities of Educational Evaluation
  Evaluation: The Ultimate Reality
UTTAL, WILLIAM R.
  A Generative Computer Teaching Machine Project
WAGNER, RICHARD V., LYBRAND, WILLIAM A., and REZNICK, WAYNE M.
  A Study of Systematic Resistance to Utilization of ITV in Public School Systems[1]
  Problems Public Schools Face in Increasing Utilization of Instructional Television[4]
WAGNER, ROBERT W.
  Modular Design for a Series of Films on Communication Theory and the New Educational Media for Use in Teacher Education
WATSON, PAUL G.
  A Model for the Selection of Instructional Strategies and the Design of Efficient Learning Systems
WESTIN, ALAN F.
  Out of Crisis, Opportunity: A New Instructional Format for American Universities
WGBH-ETV STAFF, BOSTON
  Demonstrating Instructional Television's Potential Role in Education
WOOD, DONALD N.
  The Future Role of Educational Media in Hawaii

---

[4] *USOE commissioned project for the Commission on Instructional Technology.*

H.

Sources of the References in the Report of the Commission on Instructional Technology[1]

SUMMARY

Page 11: Nixon, President Richard M. "Statement on Education," October 21, 1968.

I: Focus on Learning

Page 13: Finch, Robert H. *New York Times Magazine*, April 6, 1969, p. 87.

Page 14: Silberman, Charles E., "Progress Report of the Carnegie Study of the Education of Educators," January 1968.

Page 15: Higgins, Dick, *foew&omBwhnw*, New York, Something Else Press, Inc., 1969, p. 217.

Page 16: Suchman, J. Richard. Memorandum to the Commission on Instructional Technology, August 1968.

Page 17: Smith, B. Othanel, in collaboration with Saul B. Cohen and Arthur Pearl, *Teachers for the Real World*, Washington, D.C., American Association of Colleges for Teacher Education, 1969, p. 9.

Page 17: Finley, Robert M. Paper prepared for the Commission on Instructional Technology, February 1969.

Page 18: Mead, Margaret. Paper prepared for the Commission on Instructional Technology, November 1968.

Page 18: McLuhan, Marshall, *The McLuhan DEW-LINE*, V. 1, no. 6, December 1968, p. 1.

Page 19: Caffrey, John. Letter to the Commission on Instructional Technology, August 1968.

II Instructional Technology Today

Page 21: Kurland, Norman D. Paper prepared for the Commission of Instructional Technology, October 1968.

Page 22: Snider, Robert C., "Technology and the School: Promises, Promises," *American School Board Journal*, September 1969.

Page 22: Oettinger, Anthony G., *Run, Computer, Run*, Cambridge, Massachusetts, Harvard University Press, 1969, statement on book jacket.

[1] *Materials set off in dashes not otherwise credited were assembled by members of the staff.*

Page 23: Mesthene, Emmanuel G. Paper prepared for the Commission on Instructional Technology, January 1969.

Page 23: Wagner, Robert W. Paper prepared for the Commission on Instructional Technology, February 1969.

Page 23: Schramm, Wilbur, address before the American Psychological Association, September 1967.

Page 24: Meaney, John W. Paper prepared for the Commission on Instructional Technology, November 1968.

Page 24: Minow, Newton N. Conversation with staff of the Commission on Instructional Technology, July 1969.

Page 25: Ofiesh, Gabriel D., "The Failure of Educational Television," *Educational/Instructional Broadcasting,* v. 1 no. 3, June–July 1968.

Page 25: Lange, Phil C. Conversation with staff of Commission on Instructional Technology, May 1969.

Page 25: Dietrich, John E. and F. Craig Johnson. Paper prepared for the Commission on Instructional Technology, October 1968.

Page 26: Spencer, Richard E. Paper prepared for the Commission on Instructional Technology, November 1968.

Page 26: Rourke, Francis E., and Glenn E. Brooks, *The Managerial Revolution in Higher Education,* Baltimore, Maryland, Johns Hopkins Press, 1966, p. 18.

Page 27: Harris, Louis and Associates, Inc., "The Life Poll: Crisis in the High Schools," *Life Magazine,* v. 66, no. 19, May 16, 1969, p. 30.

Page 27: Smith, Mortimer. Letter to the Commission on Instructional Technology, August 1968.

Page 27: Nixon, President Richard M. Statement from the White House, May 29, 1969.

III: Instructional Technology Tomorrow

Page 29: Suppes, Patrick, "The Uses of Computers in Education," *Scientific American,* September 1966, p. 207.

Page 29: Beckwith, Hugh F. Paper prepared for the Commission on Instructional Technology, January 1969.

Page 29: "The Chemistry of Learning," Occasional Paper, Institute for Development of Educational Activities, Inc., January 1967.

Page 30: Miller, James G., "Potentialities of a Multi-Media Inter-University Educational Network," *Ciba Foundation Symposium on Communication in Science: Documentation and Automation,* 1967, 235.

Page 30: Thorndike, Edward L., *Education,* New York, The Macmillan Company, 1912, p. 167.

Page 31: Riesman, David, Letters to the Commission on Instructional Technology, July 1968 and July 1969.

Page 32: Hitchens, Lt. Col. Howard B. Paper prepared for the Commission on Instructional Technology, January 1969.

Page 33: Postlethwaite, S. N., "Audio-Tutoring, A Practical Solution for Independent Study," *Medical and Biological Illustration,* v. 15, July 1965, p. 184.

Page 34: Foster, Marcus, quoted in paper prepared for the Commission on Instructional Technology by Martha A. Gable, December 1968.

Page 34: Whitehead, A. N., *The Aims of Education and Other Essays,* New York, The Macmillan Company, 1959, p. 79.

Page 35: Clarke, Richard. Participant, Commission on Instructional Technology Student Seminar, February 11, 1969.

Page 35: Cohen, Wilburn, J., conversation with staff of the Commission on Instructional Technology, July 1969.

IV: To Improve Learning

Page 37: Allen, James E., Jr., "Strengthening Educational Research and Development." Remarks at Conference on American Education, National Network of Regional Educational Laboratories, Washington, D.C., July 1969.

Page 38: Prepared by the U.S. Office of Education for an address by Harold Howe II before the American Management Association's First Practicum in Educational Technology, New York City, August 9, 1966.

Page 38: Committee for Economic Development, *Innovation in Education: New Directions for the American School,* Statement by the Research and Policy Committee, July 1968, p. 28.

Page 38: Locke, Robert W. and David Engler. Paper prepared for the Commission on Instructional Technology, October 1968.

Pages 38–39: Howe, Harold II, reproduced with permission from *Technology in Education,* ©National School Public Relations Association U.S.A. Special Report, 1967, p. 22–23.

Page 39: Allen, Dwight W. Letter to the Commission on Instructional Technology, August 1968.

Page 39: Harley, William G. Memorandum to the Commission on Instructional Technology, April 1969.

Page 39: Gardner, John W. Conversation with staff of the Commission on Instructional Technology, July 1969.

V: Recommendations

Page 54: Drucker, Peter F., *The Age of Discontinuity,* New York, Harper & Row Publishers, Inc., 1968, pp. 334, 338.

Page 55: Edinger, Lois V. Paper prepared for the Commission on Instructional Technology, November 1968.

Page 56: Mead, Margaret. Paper prepared for the Commission on Instructional Technology, November 1968.

Page 56: VanderMeer, A. W. Paper prepared for Commission on Instructional Technology, October 1968.

Page 57: Howe, Harold II, *The People Who Serve Education,* A Report on the State of the Education Professions, OE–10059, December 1968, pp. 13–14.

Page 57: Howe, Harold II, *ibid.,* p. 10.

Page 58: Anderson, Robert H. Paper prepared for the Commission on Instructional Technology, February 1969.

Page 58: Glaser, Robert, "The Design and Programming of Instruction," *The Schools and the Challenge of Innovation,* Supplementary Paper No. 28, New York, Committee for Economic Development, 1969, pp. 174–5.

APPENDIX A

Page 65: Polley, Ira. Letter to the Commission on Instructional Technology, July 1968.

Page 66: Twyford, Loran C., Statistical Sheet "Educational Technology in Elementary and Secondary Public Schools with Amounts Required to Attain Standards," New York, June 10, 1969.

Pages 66–67: Rippy, Wilbur. Paper prepared for the Commission on Instructional Technology, February 1969.

Page 67: Allen, William H., "Audiovisual Instruction," *The Schools and the Challenge of Innovation,* Supplementary Paper No. 28, New York, Committee for Economic Development, 1969, p. 226.

Page 67: Phillips, Harry L. and Patricia Spross. Memorandum to the Commission on Instructional Technology, Office of Education, Division of State Agency Cooperation, March 1969.

Page 68: Lewis, Richard B., "Self-Instruction in Audiovisual Equipment Operation, San Jose State College," *New Media and College Teaching,* James W. Thornton, Jr. and James W. Brown, Department of Audiovisual Instruction, National Education Association, 1968, p. 46.

Page 68: Hitchens, Lt. Col. Howard B. Paper prepared for the Commission on Instructional Technology, January 1969.

Page 68: Holton, Gerald, "Project Physics. A Report on Its Aims and Current Status," *The Physics Teacher,* v. 5, no. 5, May 1967, pp. 209–211.

Page 68: Culkin, John M., S. J., "For Kids, Doing is More Fun Than Viewing," *New York Times,* July 28, 1968.

Page 69: Hudson, Robert B., "The Future of Educational Television," Paper presented at Stanford University, April 1968.

Page 69: Breitenfeld, Frederick, Jr. Paper prepared for the Commission on Instructional Technology, November 1968.

Page 70: Herman W. Land Associates, Inc., *The Hidden Medium: Educational Radio,* prepared for National Educational Radio, April 1967, pp. I–5, I–8, I–13.

Page 71: National Association of Educational Broadcasters. Paper prepared for the Commission on Instructional Technology, October 1968.

Page 71: Markle, Susan Meyer, "Programming and Programmed Instruction," Pre-publication draft, September 1968, *Macmillan Encyclopedia of Education,* © The Macmillan Company, New York.

Page 71: Licklider, J. C. R. Interview with staff of the Commission on Instructional Technology, November 1968.

Page 72: Porter, Douglas. Interview with staff of the Commission on Instructional Technology, October 1968.

Page 72: Glaser, Robert, "The Design and Programming of Instruction," *The Schools and the Challenge of Innovation,* Supplementary Paper No. 28, New York, Committee for Economic Development, 1969, p. 166.

Page 72: Markle, Susan Meyer, *op. cit.*

Pages 72–73: Hocking, Elton. Paper prepared for the Commission on Instructional Technology, January 1969.

Page 73: *Computers in Higher Education.* Report of the President's Science Advisory Committee, February 1967, p. 2.

Page 74: Tiedeman, David V., "Can A Machine Develop A Career? A Statement About the Processes of Exploration and Commitment in Career Development," paper prepared under Office of Education grant, July 1968.

Pages 74–75: Bushnell, Don D. Paper prepared for the Commission on Instructional Technology, January 1969.

Page 75: Stolurow, Lawrence M., "Computer-Assisted Instruction." *The Schools and the Challenge of Innovation,* Supplementary Paper No. 28, New York, Committee for Economic Development, 1969, p. 273.

Page 75: Parkus, Lawrence. Paper prepared for the Commission on Instructional Technology, February 1969.

Page 76: Jason, Hilliard. Paper prepared for the Commission on Instructional Technology, December 1968.

APPENDIX B

Page 77: Silberman, Charles E., "Progress Report of the Carnegie Study of the Education of Educators," January 1968.

Page 78: Bell, T. H. Paper prepared for the Commission on Instructional Technology, October 1968.

Page 78: Spencer, Richard E. Paper prepared for the Commission on Instructional Technology, November 1968.

Page 78: Bruner, Jerome S., *Toward a Theory of Instruction,* Cambridge, Massachusetts, The Belknap Press of Harvard University Press, 1966, p. 164.

Page 78: Hocking, Elton. Paper prepared for the Commission on Instructional Technology, October 1968.

Pages 78 79: Zacharias, Jerrold R. Interview with staff of the Commission on Instructional Technology, December 1968.

Page 79: Wilhelms, Fred T. Memorandum to the Commission on Instructional Technology, October 1968.

Page 79: Hausman, Howard J. Letter to the Commission on Instructional Technology, July 1968.

Page 80: Hemphill, John K. Letter to the Commission on Instructional Technology, August 1968.

Page 80: Forsdale, Louis. Paper prepared for the Commission on Instructional Technology, November 1968.

Page 80: Vaughn, Freeman H. Letter to the Commission on Instructional Technology, October 1968.

Page 81: Boal, Bruce. Letter to the Commission on Instructional Technology, September 1968.

Page 81: Hilliard, Robert L. Address to the Fifth Annual ITV Conference of the National Association of Educational Broadcasters, New York City, April 1967.

Page 81: Clark, A. Richard. Letter to the Commission on Instructional Technology, August 1968.

APPENDIX C

Page 83: Ruml, Beardsley, in connection with the preparation of *Memo to a College Trustee,* New York, McGraw-Hill, 1959.

Page 84: *School Management,* January 1968, pp. 124 and 126, January 1969, p. 85.

Page 84: Hitch, Charles J., "Rationality Under Stress in Higher Education," paper given at conference of Organization for Economic Cooperation and Development, Paris, April 1969.

Page 85: Twyford, Loran C., Jr., Statistical Sheet, "Implementing the Standards," New York, June 10, 1969.

Page 86: Morris, S. Barry, "Estimated Annual Cost of Maintaining the Recommended Collection," Fairfax County, Virginia, developed in response to American Library Association-National Education Association publication, *Standards of School Media Programs,* 1969.

Page 86: Speagle, Richard E. Paper prepared for the Commission on Instructional Technology, April 1969.

Page 87: Parkus, Lawrence. Paper prepared for the Commission on Instructional Technology, February 1969.

Page 88: Speagle, Richard E., *op. cit.*

Page 89: Hooper, Richard. Paper prepared for the Commission on Instructional Technology, April 1969.

APPENDIX D

Page 92: Brochure, National Committee for Support of the Public Schools, 1968.

Page 92: Kelly, Vincent P. Paper prepared for the Commission on Instructional Technology, April 1969.

Page 93: Manuel, Herschel T., *Spanish Speaking Children of the Southwest, Their Education and the Public Welfare,* Austin, Texas, University of Texas Press, 1965.

Page 93: National Education Association, *The Invisible Minority* Washington, 1966, p. 7.

Pages 93–94: *Report for Action.* Governor's Select Commission on Civil Disorder, State of New Jersey, February 1968.

Page 94: Watford, Ben A., "Racism in Suburban Schools," *Changing Education,* v. IV, no. 1, Spring 1969, p. 48.

Page 94: Donovan, Bernard E., *New York Times,* March 5, 1969.

Pages 94–95: Spencer, David X., *Washington Post,* January, 1969.

Page 95: Comer, James P. Paper prepared for the Commission on Instructional Technology, November 1968.

Page 95: Dittrick, Alva R. Paper prepared for the Commission on Instructional Technology, December 1968.

Page 96: Dittrick, Alva R., *ibid.*

APPENDIX E

Pages 99–100: Salmon, Peter J., for the panel submitting views at the hearings before the Ad Hoc Subcommittee on the Handicapped of the Committee on Education and Labor, House of Representatives, New York, December 19 and 20, 1966, p. 1066.

APPENDIX F

Page 101: Press Conference, November 7, 1967.

Pages 101–102: Minutes, first meeting of the Commission on Instructional Technology, April 22, 1968.

Pages 101–102: Howe, Harold II, Address, "Profits, Principles, and Educational Technology," before the annual convention of the National Audio-Visual Association, Washington, D.C., July 13, 1968.

PART TWO

Instructional Technology: Selected Working Papers on *The State of the Art*

1.
Patterns for Development of Education in Information Science

by JACK BELZER
Associate Director
Knowledge Availability Systems Center
University of Pittsburgh

Introduction

The world has moved from the industrial revolution to mass production to the development of the computer and is now undergoing an information revolution. Our society is becoming more dependent on information each day. Industry and commerce in our competitive society is information dependent. Management, as Jay Forrester defines it, is the process of converting information into action. The conversion process is defined as decision making, and the success or failure of a management decision is a function of the pertinency of information selected for that decision, out of a large number of sources or a large file. Research and development is built on the work of and in cooperation with others and is possible only when unrestricted communication among colleagues and peers exists. This implies selection of information out of a large volume of current publications where progress and results of research and development are reported by or for each scientist engaged in such activities. To keep scientists informed of peripheral activities from other disciplines which are of interest to them complicates the information problems. Command and control systems and logistics are information systems on which the military depends, and our political and socio-economic culture to be responsive to its needs is information dependent. Information today has a tendency to complicate our society because more information exist, larger volumes of information can be communicated more rapidly, and the response time to information is becoming shorter. Information science as a discipline is an outgrowth of this.

During the past decade, the scope of information science has been evolving into a broader but better defined area of specialization. The profession of information science deals with many aspects of information. It deals with its properties, origination, organization, manipulation, structure, control and use of information. It is concerned with information systems, their designs, operation, evaluation and with the systems components. It cuts across such disciplines as logic, behavioral sciences, cybernetics, communication theory, languages (both natural and artificial), machine translation and pure and applied mathematics. It interacts strongly with the development in the new technologies of computers, automation, microimaging, storage and retrieval, and communication, transmission and displays of information. The professional practice concerned with information has been placing new demands on the personnel dealing with the problems of information.

Information Science Environment

The term information science means different things to different people; and rather than giving a formal definition of "information science", it would be more useful to present several points to view. Curriculum 68[2], the report of the ACM Curriculum Committee on Computer Science, points out that there was sentiment among their members to call their discipline "information science". This point of view would make the total information science program strongly numerical analysis and computer oriented. Another school of thought is information science oriented in the pure sense. It is concerned primarily with the theoretical aspects of information and with the methodology for dealing with it. Mathematics and logic are the basis on 'which the science is built, but it has also information engineering aspects. It is also concerned with the design and performance of information systems, both operational and experimental. There are schools whose information science programs are oriented in this direction either with or without the emphasis on the literature or library problems. Many of the academic programs in information science are subject oriented, such as Biomedical, Management information systems, and Library and Information Retrieval systems.[3] The last named has been receiving the greatest impetus, with the possible exception of "computer science" programs. "Library and Information Science" schools have been the most active in providing academic training in information science. Computer science programs train students in all aspects of computer science and technology, and occasionally an individual expands his horizons to the information field. Where many computer science programs offer undergraduate curricula to provide students with tools for dealing with problems in other disciplines, the library and information science programs are professional in scope and offer graduate programs only. The emphasis is on dealing with recorded knowledge closely akin to the library problem.

The major educational programs in information science today are library oriented, and most of them are either part of a library school or reside side by side with one. At the same time, one of the major problems in our cultural, scientific, and economic society which requires attention is the library and information problem. The proliferation of published materials, the storage, retrieval, dissemination and communication of recorded knowledge can retard our cultural progress, curtail scientific advancement, and drive us to economic disaster. Industry, government, and academic and research institutions are faced with this problem, and professionally trained people in information science who can deal with these problems are in great demand. The library schools in updating their own programs to meet the new demands placed on them and responding to the new technology have been forced to move in the direction of information science. To expand their programs to information science, it became necessary for these schools to define and perhaps isolate that knowledge competence which would be needed for professional practice in information science.

Several Conferences on Education

There are many factors which contributed to the development of education in information science. As the field was evolving several conferences were held on education in information science. A brief review of a few of these will shed light on the progress made in the education field for information science.

The first significant conferences relating to education in information science were held at Georgia Institute of Technology, Oct. 12-13, 1961 and April 12-13, 1962.[4] One of the outcomes of these conferences was a definition of "information science," and whether one agrees with this definition or not, it created a starting point, a foundation to build on, or a point of departure.

The science that investigates the properties and behavior of information, the forces governing the flow of information, and the means of processing information for optimum accessibility and usability. The processes include the origination, dissemination, collection, organization, storage, retrieval, interpretation, and use of information. The field is derived from or related to mathematics, logic, linguistics, psychology, computer technology, operations research, the graphic arts, communications, library science, management, and some other fields.

Another contribution resulting from these conferences was the creation of the School of Information Science at Georgia Tech, the host institution, and the Division of the Information Sciences at Lehigh University, neither of which has a library school.

During September 7-10, 1965, The American Documentation Institute, under the sponsorship of the Office of Education, held a conference at Airlie House at Warrenton, Virginia, on Education for Information Science.[5] Of 55 attendees less than one third were academicians. They were less concerned with education of documentalists and information scientists than they were with the effort of defining the field. This was true of the many excellent formal papers presented as well as the discussions which took place between the presentation of papers. Several recommendations concerning educational aspects of information science resulted from this conference. Among these were:

1. The need exists to acquaint librarians with message processing by computers and its mathematical base, and computer experts should be acquainted with the human being as an information processor.

2. Many diversified information science programs are taking shape. They have difficulty in defining educational requirements especially for those who handle information at the least complicated level and the programs lack a "core" of subjects.

3. PhD programs were described and discussed which indicated a lack of planning adequate curricula for these programs.

4. The concepts of the content and the elements that comprise them should be well defined for the fields of documentation, information science and computer science. Education in these fields must prepare its professionals to define problems in precise algorithmic and machine tractable terms.

5. Students should be taught to apply available technology to existing problems rather than wait for the ultimate systems to be developed.

The conference chairman L. B. Heilprin summarized the conference's accomplishments as follows:

1. The field of information science consists of theory, as a pure science, and it also consists of the application of the science to the solution of the information problems.

2. Information science is concerned with stored or recorded messages, their creation, propagation and use; the user is a component of the system which constrain it as a result of his physical, psychological and psychophysical limitations.

3. Clarification with regard to contributions made by schools of library science and computer science towards his education.

The International Conference on Education for Scientific Information Work, sponsored by the International Federation for Documentation, (FID)[6] was held at the Queen Elizabeth College, London, April 3-7, 1967. It was a most comprehensive program of its kind. Thirty-three papers were presented at the conference and with a very few exceptions they all related to the library oriented information field. Most papers related to the author's ongoing programs in his own institution where some goals for the future were discussed. V. Slamecka and P. Zunde from Georgia Tech[7] presented a generalized model for developing educational programs.

The program   P = f(G,L,E,S,R)
Where P = structure of an educational program
       G = a set of educational goals
       L = characteristics of a set of learners
       E = a given educational system
       S = a subject of knowledge relevant to P
       R = environmental factors

   The intent of this model is to indicate a vigorous approach to the design of educational programs. The available financial resources both private and public are aimed at the goals which relate to the educational system and the educational program. These are aimed at a learner which produces professional and intellectual resources. The learners interact with the program and the resultant resources interact with the goals as well as the original resources which support these programs financially. This in a way closes the loop and the feedback process keeps the program dynamic. The model was applied to Georgia Tech's own program by means of which it was possible to identify the substantive knowledge required for information science. It is composed of three areas, namely, the theoretical which consists of modern algebra, mathematical logic, structural linguistics, general systems theory, and communication theory. The engineering area consists of techniques of information control, bionics (including control and man-machine systems) information systems design, computer systems design, and operations research. The third area consists of electives which enriches the program in computer techniques and applications, optimization theory, etc. or management or industrial engineering.

   The one significant feature of this conference was that the diversity of views and the spectrum of what constituted the field was great indeed. The professionals in this field were referred to or identified as "information scientists", "documentalists", "information engineers", "scientific librarians", "industrial librarians", "scientific information specialists" etc. In many instances reference was made to them as literature searchers, literature advisors, research workers, special librarians and so on. Another inconsistency existed because no distinction was made between short courses and courses offered for academic credit. The distinction to be made here is between training and education.

   During September 25-28, 1968, the Curriculum Committee of the American Society for Information Science (ASIS) met at the University of Pittsburgh for the purpose of developing methodology and/or guidelines for structuring and evaluating curricula and information science. In attendance were nineteen members, nine of whom were deans or directors of library and information science schools or centers in all representing seventeen institutions with major programs in information science. Represented on this committee were all of the points of view discussed later on under "Educational Objectives". Although a report of this conference has not yet been issued, a preview of its major accomplishment would serve well here.

   After considerable deliberation by the total group with diversified points of view and a spectrum of interests it was rewarding to find that a substantial amount of agreement and understanding was reached among the members in terms of what constitutes the field of information science and in terms of goals and objectives of information science programs. Two factors account for the agreement that was possible at the conference. One is that before any attempt was made to identify programs and/or curricula, career opportunities were examined. This led to the identification of the professional practice in the field. As soon as an understanding was reached on this score it was possible to visualize graduates in information science assuming positions in our society. Once it was possible to identify the types of positions these graduates would fill, it was also possible to define the existing knowledge required for each. The second factor is a reflection of the maturity of the field itself. The discipline of information science and the function it performs in our economic structure is better understood. This kind of understanding brings several points of view closer together thus minimizing their differences. It was obvious however that the special interests and the environment of the individual institutions represented were sufficiently different in nature that to meet the objectives of each, different levels of courses were needed. To accomplish this, the committee broke up into three naturally forming groups, the library schools, the library and information science schools and the information science schools. The individual members joined that group to which they had the greatest affinity.

The Library Schools were concerned primarily with revising some of their traditional courses making them information science oriented, and introducing several new courses to provide an integrated library and information science curriculum. Under the basic assumptions that their concern is with recorded information and with handling documents, information and data, their core curriculum included:

1. Information Resources
2. Organization of Information for Use—Theory and Implementation
3. Communication Media
4. Management of Libraries and Information Organization
5. Technical Processes—Manual and Mechanized
   (including acquisitions, circulation, serial records, and cataloging.)

The next level of courses recommended by this group were:

1. Information Technology
2. Computer Application in Information Systems
3. Information Storage and Retrieval
4. Systems Analysis and Design
5. Information Systems Administration

The program would provide traditional library specialization in school, public, academic, special libraries, and information science.

The Information Science Schools were concerned mainly with the theoretical aspects of information and with the methodology for dealing with it. It saw graduates of its programs, primarily as PhD's, practicing the profession in academic pursuits and conducting research. The educational goals were defined on this basis, and its recommendations for the substantive knowledge required were segmented essentially into four areas: 1) Methodology, which included all basic science such as mathematics, statistics, operations research, logic, etc.; 2) Behavioral, which deals with topics in human information processing and cognitive theory; 3) Technology, which is concerned with information presentation and transmission and computer aspects of information; and 4) Engineering, with systems analysis, linguistics, operational analysis, etc.

A curriculum in information science responsible to this group's programs falls into three levels, that of beginning graduate, graduate, and advanced graduate courses. A sample of courses at each level follows realizing that variations from school to school exist.

Beginning Graduate Level

1. Algorithmic languages
2. Data processing
3. Introduction to programming
4. Introduction to information theory

5. Introductory linguistics (philosophy of languages)
6. Numerical analysis
7. Statistical computations

Graduate Level

1. Computer design and organization
2. Computer systems
3. Information storage and retrieval
4. Processing of natural and artificial languages
5. Programming language design
6. Simulation Techniques
7. (Statistical computations)
8. Systems analysis

Advanced Graduate Level

1. Advanced numerical analysis
2. Automata theory and finite-state machines
3. Computational linguistics
4. Graph theory
5. Man-machine communication
6. Research methods in information science
7. Theoretical foundations of information science

The three levels of courses relate to theory, application and systems.

The Library and Information Science Schools related their concern to input, output, and use of information. Input deals with acquisitions, analysis, control of vocabulary, recording results of analysis, and storage of information. Output or dissemination is concerned with identification and analysis of requirements, processing, and delivery of information materials. Use relates to the application of the service in a specialized situation unrelated to the service. Rather than enumerating the specific course content in its curriculum, this group developed a model to serve as a methodology for the evaluation and development of curricula in information science. The concern of maintaining a proper balance between library and information science and a balance between theoretical and practical content prompted this approach. The model considers four levels for curriculum evaluation, 1) context, 2) types of position for which the program is intended, 3) exit knowledge or substantive competence, and 4) courses and course content. By context is meant the formal institution for communication of recorded data. The variables are kind of institution, media of recording, environment (government, industry, university, etc.) and scope. Types of position fall into three categories, the academic and research, the integrative position bridging the gap between traditional approaches to information handling and the new technology including systems design, and the administrative and operational or functional positions. Exit knowledge or substantive competence defines general areas in which competence is either useful or required.

Evaluation of course content or substantive competence in specific areas as they relate to the types of position is possible by developing a scale which is a measure of the relatedness. A scale of 0 to 3 was suggested as follows:

0 = completely unrelated
1 = peripherally useful; for background information
2 = useful; knowledge of subject matter is important
3 = important to the practice of profession; in depth knowledge is required.

This model has not been tested and it is conceivable that it will have to go through several modifications before it will be accepted as the mechanism for the evaluation and development of curricula in information science. The methodology, however, appears to be sound and it was adopted for this purpose by the American Society for Information Science (ASIS) Curriculum Committee. The Curriculum Committee for ASIS has as its task for 1968-69, the evaluation and analysis of existing curricula or individual courses on some comparative basis. Hopefully several subject areas within the scope of information science will be identified and courses with syllabi within each suggested.

Educational Objectives

The educational objectives of a graduate program are to prepare students for professional practice in the application of information science and for research in the field. A practitioner must acquire certain skills for the practice of his profession, but he must also possess a foundation with a strong theoretical base to enable him to adapt himself to the environment of a dynamic and ever-changing new technology applicable to the solution of problems of information. The educational objectives in information science should therefore focus on three broad but major areas: (1) theory concerning information, its environment and its relationship to information systems; (2) information systems, design testing and evaluation; and (3) information services.

Theory concerning information should be the basis for explaining the environment for information systems and the analysis of problems relating to them. It would deal with the methodology for developing models and simulation techniques for testing and evaluation of alternative approaches to systems design. It should contribute to the understanding of the principles and methods for processing of information. Properties of systems, properties of arrays and symbols which come from their organizational structural properties, and properties of information should be its concern.

Information systems deals with the design and testing of systems for a specific purpose of usage in handling information. The collection, reduction, organization, storage, transmission and dissemination are components to be dealt with and must be integrated into a system. It is concerned with man-machine interaction and examines information processing systems, management information system, information storage and retrieval systems, and computer systems.

Information service is concerned with providing service to many users of information centers. The understanding of the various service functions and the environment in which they can be provided is most essential. The knowledge and understanding of administration of information centers focusing on information resources, the cultural attitudes towards information and education of the user group and the influence of technological development.

It is of interest that these three areas to which academic programs should address themselves are also job oriented. Career opportunities in information science exist on all three levels. The first category is aimed at individuals who are pursuing PhD programs and whose major career interests are geared toward an academe and/or research. The second is engineering oriented, whose on the job responsibilities are to design, implement, maintain, and update information systems. The third category is for people whose career interests lie in the direction of management and administration of information centers. Obviously, no matter what career one wishes to pursue, his education and training must be a composite for all three areas with a variation in emphasis for each.

Curriculum Development

Schools which offer programs in information science also have a tendency to fall into three categories similar to those described under Educational Objectives. One of these is the library school which finds that its program must meet the new challenges of the present day technology. The type of professional services which are needed today, especially in areas where research and development activity is being pursued, have been undergoing dynamic changes, and library school graduates must be trained for these careers. Library school curricula are being expanded to meet the new demands and this in turn begins to give them the flavor of information science.

Another category consists of the Library and Information Science Schools which recognized this problem several years ago and are now established to provide an education which more adequately meets the new challenge. These schools generally see a continuum in the library and information science and as a result of their experiences have developed strong programs where the relation of the new technology of microimaging, computer science, and systems, are integrated into the total program of information transfer. The third group developed its program in information science in an engineering or pure science environment and treats the field from a somewhat different point of view. It too is concerned with the problem of recorded knowledge but views transfer of knowledge as an important application in the field. In all programs substantive knowledge in mathematics and statistics, computer science, linguistics, economics and cost analysis, system design and engineering, behavioral science, and librarianship are recognized. The emphasis and the depth with which they are pursued at the various institutions are the variables which differentiate one program from another.

In developing curricula in information science, the Library School normally provides an introductory course which introduces the student to the new technology and its impact on information services. A sample introductory survey course of this kind would discuss the functions of information systems, as they relate to mechanization or automation. Beginning with acquisitions, to analysis, indexing and vocabulary control, recording of information, storage and retrieval, display, evaluation, and dissemination and/or transmission of information, each of these functions is related to the new technology. The student here becomes acquainted with marginal-hole cards, unit record punched card methods, optical coincidence or peekaboo systems, microimaging, and general computer methods. The intellectual transformation from classical librarianship to the so-called documentation methods begin to take place in this classroom. It must therefore introduce such topics as developing search strategies relating to various types of files, coding techniques, and search methodology and discuss measures and criteria for the evaluation of user satisfaction. The school would do well if it required this knowledge of the student for admission to the graduate program.

Beyond this in subsequent course work such topics as "Information Systems Organization and Design"; "Introduction to Computers", and their relationship to peripherals and methods for programming; "Computer Applications" usually relating to problems of information retrieval, dissemination of information, automatic indexing, production of surrogates, and automation of library functions; "Special Tools" microforms, audiovisual facilities, duplicating and copying. As a general rule, these courses are on an introductory level either offered toward a MLS degree or imbedded in an MLS program. Much of this knowledge could also be acquired on an undergraduate level.

The Library and Information Science Schools at present dominate the library oriented field in information science. Although, in most instances, they took an empirical approach in developing their programs they have an integrated program which fills a very important need in our society. Their experience over the last several years gave these schools an opportunity to develop a competent faculty from both their own school or department and existing talent elsewhere within the University. These programs have acquired the sophistication which exists in other disciplines in that they provide several levels of competency in each cognate area within the program. For example, a student can take several courses in computer science, each being a prerequisite for the following one, or he can take them in systems analysis, statistics or linguistics depending on his interest. This type of depth is non-existent in the library schools discussed earlier. Schools in this category have been building upon their master's program and several now have advanced degree programs leading towards a PhD. The advanced program demanded curricula in depth training in specific areas. Similarly building a curriculum where substantive competence in specific areas was possible paved the way for the advanced programs leading toward the PhD programs in information science. Most of the schools in this category still offer degrees in library science in spite of their substantive curricula in information science. A very few offer degrees in information science. One library school, for example, offers a MLS degree where electives in information science are possible, however the school also offers a MS degree in information science. The tendency to offer MS degrees in information science along side of MLS degrees will probably grow because a demand for information scientists exists now and will continue to grow. In a masters program a student is limited to the number of credits he can take if he wishes to complete his education in a reasonable time. If the degree is in library science he is usually required to take a specified set of courses in a traditional library science curriculum which constitutes the core. This obviously limits the strength which one can acquire in information science. The assumption is that if the degree is an MS in information science then the student is not obligated to take the total core program in traditional librarianship. He can therefore concentrate his efforts in his major field of interest to a greater depth. As a rule, the schools in this category offer courses in each of the several general headings which can be identified as information retrieval and documentation theory and systems, computer operation, mathematics of a special kind and statistics, and linguistics. No single school offers enough courses in depth in all of these areas for a student to develop proficiency on a professional level in a masters degree program. Those schools which have a PhD program in information science rely heavily on cognate areas in conjunction with other schools or departments at their Universities and thereby manage to fill this need. An alternative to offering an MS degree in place of the MLS, is to revise the curriculum in the core program in such a way as to include the new science and technology in the traditional courses.

In the third category are schools or departments in information science completely independent of library schools. From this group are excluded the computer science and/or computer and information science departments whose programs are strongly computer science oriented. Although a great deal of commonality in the two programs exists, there are distinct and important differences. Even at points of commonality the emphasis in each is different. The materials which constitute the major thrust in information science are often considered peripheral to computer science. The schools which fall into this third category generally interpret information science as a discipline of a scientific nature in which mathematics and logic are the theoretical arm, and design and operation of information systems are its applied arm. They attempt to develop curricula to meet these two objectives. However different schools accomplish these objectives differently. It is reasonable to assume that the environment in which these programs or departments were developed influences their orientation. The environment is a function of such variables as the research interests of the faculty, conflict of interest or overlap with programs in other departments, and goals they are trying to achieve in complementing other programs at the institution. Sometimes these variables tend to influence the program in the direction of theoretical aspects of information and sometimes in the direction of professional training for the design and evaluation of information systems. In schools where the program encompasses both aspects, electives in the curriculum exist whereby the student can develop an option which represents his personal interests and desires. These programs are well structured and the student is required to take a specified set of courses as his core with additional courses which develop the required competency in his selected option. The areas in which substantive knowledge encompasses these programs are:

1. Mathematics, statistics and symbolic logic.

2. Theory of information and systems which cover topics in computer systems, management information and information storage and retrieval systems, and man-machine interaction.

3. Simulation and modeling including topics in self-organizing systems, Turing machines and theory of automata, artificial intelligence and pattern recognition, and compatability and unsolvability.

4. Mathematical linguistics, theory of grammars, artificial languages, and machine translation.

To offer courses in all of these areas and to provide in-depth competency in each would require a faculty of a size and scope which few departments in information science could afford. It is much easier to provide introductory courses in each where the enrollment is substantial in size. It is not so when courses at all levels have to be made available. For this reason these courses are not necessarily offered by the department of information science. They may exist in other departments and cross-listing of courses among departments is a mechanism used to make the most out of the existing talent at an institution.

One area to which little attention has been given here is the computer science, or computer and information science as some departments call themselves. Because computers have made one of the major contributions to the field of information science many regard it as the information science discipline. There are aspects of computer science which relate directly to information science and no information science program is complete without it. But the major concern and the emphasis placed on the various aspects in computer science differ drastically from that of information science. A prime consideration must be given to the fact that computers as such are now a part of our every day life. One can hardly mention an area where application of computers does not exist, and the limits are almost boundless. Computer science curricula therefore must train students in the use of computers in order for them to be able to utilize computers in the solution of problems in other disciplines. To provide students with this tool, undergraduate computer science programs are taken for granted in many institutions and they are the mainstays of their computer science programs. Graduate programs are being structured upon the undergraduate curriculum, and this too is important because frontiers in the computer field are being extended, and further extensions are of the essence. Time sharing, real time problems, communications with computers both in transmission and linguistics, newer and better monitors and executives for automatic communication with users are the variables which influence the rate at which frontiers in the field can be extended. The Curriculum Committee on Computer Science for the Association for Computing Machinery (ACM)[2] has subdivided computer science into three major divisions: "information structures and processes," "information processing systems," and "methodologies." This structure, in format, is similar to that of information science; however the course content in each varies substantially. Both sciences consider the mathematical, and the physical and engineering sciences as related areas, but the emphasis in each varies significantly. For example computer design, organization, and structure, and computer operating systems are vital to the computer science programs; so is numerical analysis. These are of interest to the information science discipline but they relate to it peripherally only. On the other hand information retrieval systems including indexing and classification, statistical techniques, automatic indexing, and search strategies are essential to information science but relate minimally to computer science.

Availability of
Educational Programs in Information Science

In schools where Information Science is offered not as a separate discipline, but as a part of another curriculum, most of them occur as part of the Library Science department or school. Other departments involved, in individual cases, are Computer Sciences, Electrical Engineering, Psychology, Business Administration, Public Administration and Liberal Arts.

The accreditation of library schools is made by the American Library Association (ALA) and a list of the accredited schools with the courses they offer appears in Journal of Education for Librarianship.[8] The analysis of the course content in these programs which are information science oriented is the task of the Curriculum Committee of the ASIS for 1968-1969 and therefore is not now available. Among the non-Library School educational programs in information science, there appears to be no firmly established opinion of exactly where information science belongs within a university framework. For this reason an additional list of schools with such programs is available in a report of the Biological Sciences Communications Project of George Washington University[3].

Conclusion

What is the relation of curricula in information science to instructional technology? The technology relevant to information science consists of computers in general, computers in a time-sharing environment, real time systems and telecommunication networks for remote access to the system. Conversational type languages and CRT displays establish the proper man-machine communication. The important extension of this technology is to provide a common framework for remote access, and to establish a system whereby each participant has an immediate personal contact with the network. Several regional networks are in existence now, and with time they will provide the experience necessary for the larger systems. Triangle Universities Computation Center, (TUCC), is a network tying in the University of North Carolina, Duke, and North Carolina State. They share the costs in order to share their resources through the computer network. The North Carolina network has been extended to include other institutions in the state. The North Carolina Computer Center Orientation Project, (NCCOP), is associated with TUCC and buys remote computer service from the Center which is made available through dial-up teletype.

The library's traditional role in the educational process has not been diminished. The new demands which are being placed on the profession have become so great that it no longer is able to meet them in a traditional manner. At the same time the technology for processing information is being advanced at a rapid rate. The marriage between the two has made it possible to provide educators with materials they need for research in the educational process. This marriage did not come easily. The adaptation of the new technology required the development of new concepts and information storage and retrieval was one of the major by-products. The integration of the new technology into the framework of meeting the new demands for information services required talents from many disciplines. Information science was the culmination of this interdisciplinary effort. However other by-products of this effort resulted in important contributions to the instructional technology. For example, in a time-sharing environment, tutorials are being developed in order to permit users of information direct access to files for seeking the literature relevant to their special needs. Where tutorials exist, users at a console are required to identify themselves and state their business. From there, the tutorials take over and lead the users to the final conclusion of their search needs. Not only is this a new approach to teaching methodology in the documentation and information science discipline, but it exerts an influence on teaching methodology in other areas. Computer aided instruction (CAI) which is being developed aside from this, shares in the advances made by research and experimentation in the information science area. The proposed Educational Information Network (EIN) which is being designed by a task force of EDUCOM will permit an exchange of computational resources on a national scale. The Practice Oriented Information System Experiment (POISE) has been set up by EDUCOM to provide a base of knowledge, techniques, and experience to be applied to the development and construction of computer-based information systems. The initial endeavor will be towards providing direct access to bibliographic information from a number of diverse data bases to users at remote locations. This has the potential for creating banks of the most expertly prepared educational materials which can be shared by schools everywhere.

REFERENCES

1. Jay W. Forrester. *Managerial Decision Making.* Computers and the World of the Future. MIT Press, 1962.

2. A Report of the ACM Curriculum Committee on Computer Science. Curriculum 68, *Communications of the ACM.* V. 11, No. 3, March, 1968.

3. Marilyn C. Bracken and Charles W. Shilling. "Survey of Practical Training in Information Science." *Biological Science Communications Project.* George Washington University, April, 1967.

4. Robert S. Taylor. "Professional Aspects of Information Science and Technology." *Annual Review of Information Science and Technology.* V. 1, John Wiley Sons, Inc., 1966.

5. Harold S. Wooster. Airlie House Conference. *Encyclopedia of Library and Information Science.* V. 1, Marcel Dekker, Inc., 1968.

6. International Conference on Education for Scientific Information Work. *Proceedings.* Queen Elizabeth College, London, FID, The Hague, September 1967.

7. V. Slamecka and P. Zunde. "An Application of a Preliminary Model for the Design of Educational Programs International Conference on Education for Scientific Information Work." *Proceedings.* Queen Elizabeth College, London, FID, The Hague, September 1967, p. 47-55.

8. Journal of Education for Librarianship. *The Association of American Library Schools.* V. 8, No. 3, Winter, 1968.

2.

Instructional Television
The State of the Art

by FREDERICK BREITENFELD, JR.
Executive Director
Maryland Center for Public Broadcasting

Foreword

This paper is divided into four sections in an attempt to isolate a variety of overlapping issues under the headline, "Instructional Television." Section I concerns the various distribution systems and pieces of machinery available to educators and in use across the country. Section II addresses itself to the larger question of television in *education,* and the third section amounts to a comment on organizational patterns in education and their inherent ability to assimilate television systems. Section IV is a collection of case studies, as they were submitted recently to the National Association of Educational Broadcasters.

Any attempt at a statement of the "state of the art" becomes, sooner or later, an editorial comment. So it is with this submission. The opinions, as they are rendered in the text, do not necessarily represent those of ITV practitioners or other educators.

Recommendations

I. Toward the Wired City

With a combination of public and private money made available, an American city with classic urban problems could be wired for multi-channel closed circuit operation. Instructional services could be provided for schools, municipal agencies, industry and other entities, and the entire project could become a showcase for the effective use of television in education.

II. Toward the Enlightened School System

Architects designing schools deserve assistance in providing flexibility for television. A national project, in cooperation with AIA, could be mounted toward this end. Similarly, through the American Association of School Administrators, an informational service on television systems and curricula could be established for a continuing flow of "state-of-the-art" facts.

Public and private assistance is required to equip schools with equipment for internal television distribution systems and, where appropriate, recorders and production facilities.

Developing school districts should be encouraged with public and private aid to establish new administrative structures that are appropriate for the use of television.

Demonstration vans and traveling TV advisory services, as now funded in part by Title III of the Elementary and Secondary Education Act, should be further developed and supported on local and regional bases.

III. Toward an Improved Educational Product

Colleges training teachers and administrators must be urged to change curricula to include proper emphasis on the use of television in classrooms. Separate curricula should be developed for ITV specialists.

The production and distribution of superior ITV packages must be encouraged with public and private money. Toward this end, aid might well be given to existing ITV libraries and program services.

IV. Toward Technical Compatibility

Standardization of video recorders and attendant machinery must be urged through professional engineering associations and manufacturers.

I. Technical

There are basically three ways to distribute television signals. They are used in combination and singly, depending upon specific circumstances. The three are closed circuit television, 2500 mc operation, and broadcast television.

Closed circuit television is sometimes called "wired" television, though this name is not altogether accurate. CCTV amounts fundamentally to cameras and recorders and film projectors at one end of a system, television screens at the other end and coaxial cable or microwave links between them. Many schools, universities and industries own closed circuit systems that involve such sources and reception points. As buildings are wired for television origination, distribution and reception, the term "CCTV" is applied.

A closed-circuit distribution system can also include only an antenna, attendant transformers, other hardware, cables and the usual reception points. Here, the origination of the signal can take place beyond the building, and the antenna itself acts as the source of signal for the system. This is also called "closed-circuit," though it is more accurately a simple "internal distribution" system. Thousands of schools are participating in television projects with only basic reception capability and internal distribution systems. As a group of buildings might be interconnected within the same CCTV system, the coaxial cables can be placed underground, or permission may be granted by the Federal Communications Commission for the institution to operate "point-to-point" broadcasting systems. This involves the use of extremely high frequency (microwave), broadcast and reception links, with specific routes for the signals. The telephone company provides both wired and microwave interconnection services.

Decisions are usually made by technically qualified consultants and engineers regarding the best possible means of signal distribution within closed circuit systems. The decisions are based upon the primary purpose of the system, topography, the desire of a local telephone company to carry signals, and the presence of educational television production facilities or stations in the area.

Thus, a closed-circuit system can amount to a distribution system within a building, wired interconnection among buildings and microwave links. "CCTV" refers to the simple reception and distribution of a signal, or it can include signal preparation and production within local studios.

In some instances, entire states are interconnected through closed-circuit television systems. In South Carolina, for instance, the majority of public schools are interconnected on a state-wide basis. The legislature appropriates money for the ETV operation, and the telephone company provides network facilities. Distribution systems are built into each school.

In Delaware, another example, the entire State is interconnected in much the same way. The State Center for Educational Television is located at Dover, and signals are distributed to all schools, which in turn have their own distribution systems. Another extensive closed-circuit system is the well-known installation in Washington County, Maryland, with studios at Hagerstown. Here, a collection of county schools is bonded with television interconnection, again through services provided by the telephone company.

One great advantage of wired systems is that more than one signal can be carried through the same cable. Thus, the South Carolina, Delaware and Hagerstown installations provide many channels for each school. Within schools, the same is true, assuming that "RF" distribution systems are incorporated.

Closed circuit television is used by the military, by industry, by schools and by colleges, as well as by hospitals and municipal agencies. Since no federal permission is required to operate a CCTV system, at least if a microwave link is not included, there is no precise knowledge as to how many systems exist. Estimates are that there are well over one thousand closed circuit installations, complete with studios, across the country and many think that there are probably twice that number. Assuredly, there are thousands of schools with simple reception and distribution capabilities, *though we have barely started in equipping classrooms with receivers.*

The campus-wide closed circuit system at Ohio University is an example of installations at colleges and universities; there are scores of others. These are totally intramural systems, owned and operated by and for the local institutions, though there are examples of inter-institutional cooperation within states, such as New York, and even among states, such as television projects now being considered by the Southern Regional Education Board. These systems allow for taped lectures to be distributed to screens viewed by small groups of students. Technically, the systems are quite successful, since simple transportation of a moving image from one place to another via television is quite common.

In a growing number of areas, commercial entrepreneurs establish community-wide distribution systems called "Community Antenna Television" or CATV. There are close to two thousand such systems, some providing service to very wide areas, such as a CATV serving northern Michigan. Very often, these cable systems provide free distribution for school boards, universities or other agencies. This could well be one of the most important distribution means for instructional television signals in the future, though it might not be apparent at present, at least as measured by usage.

If special frequencies were set aside for use by satellites, then an extension of the microwave idea could include interconnection across entire countries. Satellite-to-school reception is not something to which we can look forward in the near future, however, and nationwide interconnection of this sort would probably involve placement of regional "ground stations." This would mean that statewide and even regional distribution would still be required.

A second method of signal distribution is a low-power broadcast technique requiring a license granted by the Federal Communications Commission. This is *"2500 mc."*

The segment of the electromagnetic spectrum between 2500 and 2690 megacycles has been set aside by the FCC for the exclusive use of educators. The band of frequencies has become known by a number of names such as "2500 mc," "2500 megaHertz," (2500 mHz), and "2.5 gigaHertz," (2.5 gHz), or, as the FCC refers to it, "Instructional Television Fixed Service" (ITFS).

A television picture, with accompanying sound and technical signals, requires a band width of six megacycles. Therefore, between 2500 and 2690 megacycles, there lie a maximum of 190/6 or 31 possible channels. The FCC has regulated the 2500 mc band in such a way that applications for channels are submitted in groups of four.

ITFS systems, therefore, provide for simultaneous broadcasting, by a single licensee, of more than one signal.

A 2500 mc signal generally has a coverage radius of from 8 to 25 miles, depending upon topography. Usually, an entire school system can be covered with such a system. Schools receiving 2500 mc signals use special antennas and ordinary intramural distribution systems, with "down-converters" to allow classroom monitors to receive the signals.

The Federal Communications Commission has encouraged school systems to investigate the potential of this specially reserved frequency band.

During the final quarter of 1968, close to one hundred ITFS construction permits had been granted by the Commission, with approximately twenty-five permits pending. Almost sixty 2500 mc systems are now on the air, using a total of one hundred and twenty-eight channels, an average of something more than two channels per licensee.

The chief of the Educational Broadcasting Branch of the FCC has commented that the growth in 2500 mc applicants and licensees has taken a strong turn. He has indicated that the number of school systems involved in this type of signal distribution is likely to increase quite rapidly in the near future.

There are any number of uses to which a 2500 mc system might be put. For instance, training for firemen, policemen, clerks and other municipal employees could take place with this type of system. Industries could take advantage of the 2500 mc potential, and institutions of higher education could also participate. The problem is one of equipping the reception points with proper antennas, distribution systems and monitors, and in convincing various administrators that the service is worth an initial investment and commitment.

The idea that more local agencies than a single school system might use a 2500 mc system has given rise to a new and fascinating concept. The idea of a "single licensee" for all noncommercial broadcasting in a market has been proposed, and the Federal Communications Commission—along with many others in the field—is now considering the possibility.

The suggestion is that a noncommercial broadcast station, a municipal production facility or a school system might be given FCC permission for eight, twelve, sixteen or even more channels in a single market. In this way, the instructional needs of a wide variety of populations could be served through a central television production and distribution facility. WVIZ, the noncommercial broadcast licensee in Cleveland, has applied, as a "single licensee," for sixteen channels in the 2500 mc band, with the understanding that the system would be used in conjunction with a large group of industrial, municipal and educational agencies.

It may be that this new idea in local instructional service will become the cornerstone for instructional television in this country. If a municipality can centralize its instructional television production and distribution facilities, and still have the freedom to make use of broadcasting, 2500 mc channels and even closed circuit installations, the variety of services that could be provided is staggering, and the quality of the lessons themselves could assuredly be higher than if each agency went on developing and producing its own internal training projects.

Television signals are also distributed, on a one-single-per-licensee basis, by commercial and noncommercial *broadcasting stations*. These signals are received at schools and universities with ordinary antennas, and are then fed into internal distribution systems within buildings or campuses.

Many commercial stations in the country have provided free air time for school systems. In Baltimore, for instance, instructional television has been part of the city's Board of Education since 1948, and commercial stations in the area provide production spaces and air time. (In that city, barely one fifth of the public classrooms, however, are equipped with television receivers.) Special note should be made of the cooperation and generosity of the commercial broadcasting establishment over the years in providing all kinds of help for ITV practitioners.

More commonly, noncommercial, educational, or public TV stations provide instructional services for schools in their coverage areas. These stations are owned by private corporations, by school systems, by colleges and universities, and by state authorities. In many cases financial arrangements are made between stations and school systems in an area and it is not uncommon to find a school system paying something like two dollars per student per year for instructional television services. These contractual agreements have provided many noncommercial television stations with up to a third of their annual incomes.

The number of noncommercial, educational—or public—television stations on the air is growing each month, with more than one hundred seventy-five stations on the air in early 1969.

This "broadcast" signal is the most commonly understood means of television distribution. The details of public broadcasting as a national instrumentality and as a group of local stations, however, have been covered in other documents.

School officials often ask what it "costs" to use or to build ITV systems. The question has no answer without specific sets of circumstances. In some cases a school will simply receive a signal and distribute it within its own walls. In this case, the antenna will cost from $50 to $200, and receiver costs will vary from $100 to $400 depending upon quality and the ubiquitous color-or-monochrome decision. In wiring buildings, a "per drop" cost estimate is common. If enough reception points are to be built into a system, then a $35 to $50 "per drop" charge is probably appropriate. This means that if a building is to include a television distribution system for forty rooms, then the cost of wiring the building, excluding antenna and monitors, will be forty times the local "per drop" charge, as estimated by technical consultants.

Beyond simple distribution systems, however, types and costs of equipment continue to change and to confound educators. Once a school, a school system or a university decides to include a recording or simple playback capability in its system, for instance, new decisions must be made.

Virtually all broadcast stations, both commercial and noncommercial, use video tape recorders of the highest quality. These require video tape two inches wide, and the machines are called "quadrature" recorders. All quadrature recorders are compatible, which allows for total interchange of tapes among broadcast stations. Still, they cost from $50,000 to $100,000 each, and this is generally well beyond the budget limit that a school system might have for a single recorder.

Less expensive tape recorders (as low as $500), make use of a different scanning technique in recording and playback, and these are called "slant track" or "helical scan" recorders. The tapes required by these machines are of varying widths, and this important factor is only one of several contributing to the tragedy that *slant track machines are basically*

MAKE	WIDTH OF TAPE	TYPE NO.	COUNTRY OF MANU- FACTURE	USE FOR WHICH DESIGNED	NO. OF HEADS	HEAD SPEED RPM	WRITING SPEED INS/SEC	FR R SP
Ampex	2	VR100C	U.S.A.	Broadcast	4	14,400	approx. 1,500	4.5
Ampex	2	VR1100C	U.S.A.	Broadcast	4	14,400	1,500	4
Ampex	2	VR2000	U.S.A.	Colour Broadcast	4	14,400	1,500	4.2
Ampex	2	VR660	U.S.A.	Portable Broadcast	2 @ 180 deg	1,800	650	3
Ampex	2	VR1500	U.S.A.	CCTV	2 @ 180	1,800		3
Sony	2	BV 100 BV120	Japan	Broadcast	1 Video 1 Sync			3.4
RCA	2	VR6000	U.S.A.	Broadcast	4	14,400	1,500	
Dage Navico	1	DV 300	Japan	CCTV	2	1,800	833	Ap 4
Ampex	1	VR7000	U.S.A.	CCTV	1	3,600	1,000	3.5
Sony	1	EV200	Japan	CCTV	2 @ 180		550	3.2
Philips	1	EL3400	Holland	CCTV	1	3,600	930	2.5
Precision instruments	1	P13V P14V	U.S.A.	CCTV	2 @ 180	1,800		3.5
Ampex	1		U.S.A.	Home T.V.	1	3,600		2.2
Sony	½	Video- corder	Japan	Home T.V.	2			1.5
Concord	½	VTR 600	U.S.A.	Home T.V.	2			1.5
Pana- sonic	½	Tape A Vision	U.S.A.	Home T.V.	2			1.5
Wollen- sak	½		U.S.A.		2			1.5

Reprinted with permission of SCHOOL PROGRESS, A MacLean-Hunter Publication, Toron

TAPE INTER- CHANGE ON SAME MODEL	TAPE SPEED IN./SEC.	LENGTH OF PLAYING TIME	SIGNAL TO NOISE	STILL FRAME	EXTRAS, BENEFITS, ETC.	PORT- ABLE	WEIGHT LBS.	EDUCA- TIONAL PRICE $
yes, also w/other models	15	96 min. 14" Reel	42 db	No	Automatic & Vert. Electronic edit	No	1,900	
Yes, and w/o. mods.	15/7½	96/192 min.		No	Transistorized Electronic edit	No	800	40,500.
Yes, and w/o. mod.	15/7½	96/192 min.		No	As for VR1000C plus colour	No		approx. 70,000.
Yes	3-7	5 hrs. 12½ R	40	Yes	2nd Audio Track simple electronic edit	Yes	100	approx. 9,000.
Yes	3-7	64 min. 8" R	40	Yes	2nd Audio Track	Yes	120	
Yes	4.25	84 min.		Yes	Slow Motion	No		
Yes, and w/o. mod.	15	96 min. 14" Reel		No		No		
Yes	5.91	63 min.	38	Yes	Slow Motion Audio Amp. & Spkr.	Yes	147	approx. 8,500.
Yes	9.6	63 min.	42	Yes	Audio Amp. & Spkr. RF Out	Yes	100	3,505.
Yes	7.75	63 min. 8" Reel		Yes	2nd Audio Track Slow Motion	Yes	70	.4,250
Possible	9.0	45 min.		No	RF In RF Out	Yes		2,850.
Yes	7.5 0-85	96 85		Yes	Variable Speed	Yes	75	9,462. 12,490.
Possible	9.6	63 min.						approx. 1,600.
No	7.5	30 or 60 min.						approx. 500.
No	12	40		Yes				approx. 500.
No	12	40		Yes				approx. 1,500.
Possible	7.5							approx. 1,600.

incompatible with one another. Of course, single manufacturers now guarantee that their own machines are compatible, *but there remain no industry-wide standards for compatibility among slant track video recorders.*

This means that it is possible for an entire school system to equip itself with helical scan recorders that are either incompatible with one another or, at best, unable to play tapes recorded on other machines in other geographic areas. A "dubbing" process is possible in transferring from one type of tape to another, but this simply provides a delay and a financial burden.

Page 142 of this report shows comparisons of a number of recorders now available. There are others, to be sure, but the important point in discussing the state of the art is that compatibility of video tape recorders remains a serious impediment to regional and national cooperation among institutions. Efforts have been made within various associations to establish technical standards for recorders. Such standards could easily be drawn, and their universal use could virtually eliminate the incompatibility problem. Still, with manufacturers across the globe distributing video equipment for varieties of purposes, it does not seem likely that the industry will settle the question itself. Instead, county, state, and even national education agencies might have to develop standards for compatibility, distributing them as widely as possible among potential customers in education.

As schools and colleges move toward the actual production of instructional television series, they must purchase studio equipment. Here again, the field is confusing. Without a "systems" approach, the educator is forced to make decisions that go far beyond one fiscal year in impact.

Television cameras are defined in two ways. First, of course, they are either black-white cameras, or they are capable of reproducing color. Beyond that, television cameras are identified by the type of pick-up, or light sensitive, tubes they use.

Cameras generally regarded as providing "broadcast quality" pictures (that is, cameras used in conjunction with quadrature recorders at broadcast stations), use *image orthicon* tubes or *plumbicon* tubes. Cameras with these tubes as their hearts are generally more expensive, larger, and operate surprisingly well under low light levels. Cameras used most frequently in industrial television systems, instructional closed circuit systems, many ITFS systems and other non-broadcast installations incorporate *vidicon* tubes. These cameras are smaller, easier to operate, and provide perfectly satisfactory pictures for general use. Black-and-white vidicon cameras can be purchased for as little as $300, though these are not suitable for most instructional purposes. *Image orthicon* cameras begin at about $12,000 and most broadcast facilities purchase cameras that cost $40,000 or more. Descriptions of cameras are included on page 145.

The state of the art in instructional television, then, includes many possible studio packages involving cameras of varying qualities and prices.

Color television is becoming quite common in the broadcast industry. In fact, most noncommercial television stations are either converted to color or planning for it. (Purchasing a broadcast quality black-and-white camera at this time is actually quite difficult!) In instructional settings, though, black-and-white systems persist. With color systems generally costing at least twice as much as comparable monochrome installations, and with maintenance costs being much higher for color, educational institutions seem to continue to build black-and-white systems.

The total costs involved in instructional television are estimated in a variety of ways. Some prefer to discuss simple capital and operating expenditures for television installations, and others insist that a "per-student" cost is the proper foundation for cost estimates. To confound the issue further, the varying types and qualities of recorders, cameras and other pieces of equipment make precise figures almost impossible to report. However, cost estimates are usually easy to project with given circumstances and systems.

LENS ANGULAR FIELD OF VIEW TABLE

LENS FOCAL LENGTH IN MM	HORIZONTAL ANGLE APPROX.	VERTICAL ANGLE APPROX.	WITH THE CAMERA WIDTH OF VIEW	12 FT. FROM SUBJECT HEIGHT OF VIEW
12.5		45°	12'	9'
25	30°	22.5°	6'	4'6"
50	15°	11.25°	3'	2'3"
75	11.25°	8.5°	2'3"	1'8¼"
100	7.5°	5.75°	1'6"	1'1½"
150	5.75°	4.25°	1'1½"	10"
200	3.25°	2.5°	9"	6¾"

PRICE RANGE (EDUCATIONAL)	SOME OR ALL OF THE FEATURES	RESOLUTION	USES
Up to $500	Non-professional cameras Random sync, oscillator controlled	200 to 400 lines	Home TV Some Industrial application.
$500 to $1,000	Industrial sync, crystal controlled Some variable adjustments Full scan protection Automatic Target	400 to 650 lines	Many Industrial applications. Static views, timetables, etc. Many general closed circuit TV uses, where small detail is not required.
$1,000 to $2,500	2:1 interlace or EIA sync May be internal or external sync drive All variable adjustments Some adjustments remotely controlled 3 or 4 lens turret Scan protection Automatic Target often for 4000:1 light variation Tally lights Plug in circuit boards and sub-assemblies	650 to 800 lines	Closed circuit TV Used for detailed work. Slides, books, photographs, microscopes, etc. can be used singly or in systems of 2, 3, or 4 cameras. Can be used in remote locations and remotely controlled. With small modifications may be used in film chains. Used where a clear sharp picture is required.
$2,000 to $5,000	Full EIA sync. Internal or external or both Viewfinder types All variable adjustments Some adjustments remotely controlled 3 or 4 lens turret Scan protection Automatic Target Tally lights Plug in circuit boards and sub-assemblies Intercom systems using camera headsets	650 to 800 lines	As above, plus the use of Viewfinder in studios, laboratories, arenas, theatres. Any time any artistic camerawork is required, using a cameraman.

Chart above lists various types of television cameras as a guide to price range, features and uses.

Reprinted with permission of SCHOOL PROGRESS, A MacLean-Hunter Publication, Toronto.

Types of monitors now available

COMMON TYPES AVAILABLE	EXAMPLE	MODEL NO.	APPROXIMATE COST EDUCATIONAL
Video, high quality in metal cases	Conrac 23″	CVA23C	$444.00
Classroom type, for video, VHF and UHF	Admiral 23″	E55YU	239.00
Classroom type for VHF and UHF	Admiral 23″	E55U	220.97
Classroom type for VHF only	R.C.A. 23″	TE3543	213.95

(A factory installed video input modification is available for the TE3543 at $30 extra)

Conclusion

The state of the art, as far as technical capability in ITV is concerned, is advanced and still improving. We are capable of transmitting TV pictures over long distances with accuracy, using a variety of possible systems and combinations. Costs are dropping as new circuitry and modes are developed. Among educators, however, knowledge of the technical "state of the art" is generally lacking. Our technical prowess in ITV is much more advanced than our educational, social and political abilities.

II. Educational

Any discussion about *instructional television,* except one concerned solely with hardware, must logically become a discussion about *instruction.* The general, public state of the art in instruction is just about what it was fifty years ago: crude, static, ponderous, administered through hopeless bureaucratic entanglements, and generally oriented toward *teaching* rather than toward *learning.*

No reasonable definition of "instructional television" seems possible, except in lofty and unmanageable terms. Beyond that, the very function of television in instruction varies with every application, so an attempt to define it through what it does is also disappointing. ITV has been called "a teaching tool" and "an aid to teaching," but both of these imply that the medium is something to be added to present modes of instruction. This is an important factor in the state of the art: ITV is regarded in many areas strictly as a *supplement.* However, the medium can be employed successfully as the prime distributive belt in instruction, as on American Samoa. The point is that the state of the art is so primitive that the *supplement* versus *core* argument is still being waged, just as if it had meaning.

Estimates of those exposed to television in classrooms vary between one-fifth and one-half of our student population. A recent study conducted by the Morse Communications Research Center of Brandeis University and National Instructional Television Center (previously National Center for School and College Television), concentrated on programming trends among the nation's ETV stations. About a third of all material aired by the noncommercial licensees, according to the report, is designed specifically for school audiences. Of this programming, almost a third comes from regional or national sources.

The numbers and types of instructional programs being produced, used and distributed are so many and so varied that the *Compendium of Televised Education* is published by Michigan State University, as compiled and edited by Lawrence E. McKune. This vital document has been brought up-to-date more than a dozen times, and the listings—the good with the not-so-good—continue to grow.

Many installations, such as the ones in Hagerstown and South Carolina, produce most of their own television material. The many military installations using television for training also concentrate on locally produced material as do most universities employing the medium. There is a lot of seminar talk about "sharing resources," and television can certainly make this possible. Still, many institutions and agencies consider their needs unique, and widespread interconnection and commitment are not to be found.

Scores of ITV systems, however, use material produced elsewhere, usually at broadcasting stations, which serve large numbers of schools and school systems. Several regional and national libraries have been established as distribution agents for these series. The Eastern Educational Network, for example, of which almost two dozen stations are affiliates, distributes ITV programming among its members, and even to customers beyond the northeast.

Other libraries, such as the Great Plains Instructional Television Library and National Instructional Television, exist across the country and are growing, however slowly. The fear of "nationalized" curricula is as it must have been when textbooks were first published and distributed, but this feeble objection to centralized production services will probably disappear.

Whatever the distribution means, and whatever the institutions or schools involved, the administrative and educational procedure is usually the same. A "teacher's guide" is developed and distributed by the television agency to all classrooms in which a specific television series or lesson is to be received. The document contains suggested "pre-telecast" activities, a description of the televised segment, and suggestions for "post-telecast" activities. These guides are duplicated by a variety of processes, depending upon local budgets and commitment, and they range from the pitifully amateurish to the professional.

Assumedly, the classroom teacher studies his guide, arranges his schedule to include the television segment (contrary to what many believe, a televised lesson usually amounts only to a segment of a class period), and proceeds with the planned lesson. Unfortunately, many teachers are reluctant to become involved, and they demonstrate this by leaving the room while the television set is on, by paying no attention to the lesson as it might be relevant to activities in the classroom and by implying a negative attitude to the students. This is far more prevalent than might be inferred from scattered reports of ITV "successes." This lack of involvement on the part of classroom teachers is probably one of the most significant properties of instructional television.

Where a school or university receives the signal of a broadcast station, or any signal over which it does not have full control, the problem of scheduling becomes critical. If tenth grade mathematics is to be offered at 11:00 a.m., for instance, fitting it simply into one large high school would be quite an achievement, but arranging an entire school system for it would be an administrative miracle. Under present circumstances, then, the school with its own recording and playback ability has a distinct advantage, especially if it has the internal ability to distribute more than one signal at a time. As it happens, very few schools are so equipped, and only a small percentage of our nation's classrooms are capable of receiving and showing television pictures. Therefore, as we design "production centers" and other centralized ITV establishments, we become part of the educational establishment that tends to forget that the drama's leading character is the student. The "software" know-how, as in education *without* technology, is missing.

With very few exceptions, television is usually simply dumped on established curricula and administrative systems. As such, it becomes an addendum, an adjunct, and ultimately an insignificant line item in the annual budget. Solid attempts to use the medium effectively are few. Television has simply not caught the fancy of those who make big educational decisions.

The exemplary cases, however, should not go unnoticed. In Chicago, it is possible to earn a junior college degree with broadcast television—into the home—as a principle means of instruction. In South Carolina, at the United States Air Force Academy and at scores of other establishments, television is accepted as part of the instructional patterns. Generally, however, these systems become exemplary only because there are so few in which the medium has made any positive impact at all.

What is happening to students exposed to television remains fundamentally as mysterious as what is happening to them through books, field trips, overhead projections and efforts of teachers in classrooms. The question always becomes one concerning *education* and not one concerning a *medium*. Television does not teach; teachers teach.

Still, "Can television teach?" is the question that has been asked since the medium first appeared in classrooms. The answer is no, of course, just as a megaphone can't teach, but the apparent need to deal with the question continually demonstrates the basic attitude with which educators approach television. The research done by graduate students, psychologists, government agencies, and teachers continues to abound, with much the same design. One group is taught through television, and another group is taught by what are somehow called "traditional" methods. There are variations, to be sure, but the same basic research has been done hundreds of times, with various peripheral questions shifted to become paramount. We continue to set up controlled circumstances and then to measure, however crudely, which lenses, which graphics and which program formats "teach" more than others.

The Institute for Communication Research, at Stanford University, has published a document by Godwin C. Chu and Wilbur Schramm called, "Learning From Television: What The Research Says." It is a compilation of the investigations that have been taking place for years. The authors suggest that many statements can now be considered valid:

- Given favorable conditions, children learn efficiently from instructional television.

- So far as we can tell from present evidence, television can be used efficiently to teach any subject matter where one-way communication will contribute to learning.

- Television is more effective as a tool for learning when used in a suitable context of learning activities at the receiving end.

- Television is more likely to be an efficient part of an educational system when it is applied to an educational problem of sufficient magnitude to call forth broad support.

- Television is more likely to be an efficient tool of learning if it is planned and organized efficiently.

- Where learning of perceptual-motor skills is required, a subjective angle presentation on television will tend to be more effective than an objective angle presentation.

- Attention-gaining clues that are irrelevant to subject matter will most probably have a negative effect on learning from instructional television.

- There is no consistent evidence to suggest that either humor or animation significantly contributes to learning from instructional television.

- Subtitles tend to improve learning from instructional television, particularly when the original program is not well organized.

- Inserting questions in a television program does not seem to improve learning, but giving the students a rest pause does.

- Whether a television program is used to begin or to end a daily lesson by the classroom teacher makes no difference in learning.

- Repeated showings of a television program will result in more learning, up to a point. But teacher-directed follow-up, where available, is more effective than a second showing of the same program.

- If saving time is important, a television program can probably be shortened and still achieve the minimum requirement of teaching.

- There is no clear evidence to suggest whether eye-contact in television instruction will affect the amount of learning.

- Problem-solving instruction on television is more effective than lecturing where the materials taught involve solving of a problem.

- The students are likely to acquire the same amount of learning from instructional television whether the materials are presented as a lecture, or in an interview, or in a panel discussion.

- Where accurate perception of images is an important part of learning, wide viewing angles and long distance will interfere with learning from instructional television.

- Adequate attention provided by the classroom teacher will, in most cases at least, remedy the adverse effect due to a wide viewing angle.

- Noise will reduce the effectiveness of learning from film and television so far as part of the learning comes from the auditory medium.

- Instructional television appears to be equally effective with small and large viewing groups.

- Instructional television may or may not be more effective with homogeneously grouped students, depending on other factors in the learning situation.

- Whether instructional television can teach students who view at home as effectively as students in the classroom seems to depend on other conditions.

These are less than half of the conclusions presented by the authors, but the list seems adequate to show the level of research in ITV.

There is still some doubt as to whether ITV is an academic and professional "specialty." To some, an instructional television producer must possess certain basic television skills, but he must, more importantly, have "educational" qualifications. Thus, the ideal ITV executive is an ex-teacher, a person with educational credentials and someone who understands the establishment. To others, the ITV producer is the best that television can offer: a person with the skills of articulate communication, and superlative experience in television.

Regardless of whether an ITV professional is more *I* than he is *TV,* there remains virtually no specific training ground for these professionals. Colleges and universities continue to offer traditional education courses, and many of them have turned to "communication arts" as important, but the idea of instructional television as a field in itself is not prevalent among universities. Therefore, people continue to move into instructional television via back alleys and windows. Instructional television, if it is indeed a field of its own at all, attracts commercial broadcasters, classroom teachers, school administrators and advertising managers. There is no universal front door. The title given to such people is usually "TV Utilization Specialist," or something related. Their duties vary from selling television services to writing teachers' guides.

A much more critical vacuum exists, however, if television is to have an impact on education. The colleges and universities dedicated in one way or another to the training of teachers tend to use the same curricula that seemed appropriate decades ago. The young, fresh graduate of a teacher-training institution is usually painfully ignorant about educational technology in general, and instructional television specifically. As thousands of new teachers move into classrooms, their attitudes are no different from those of their older and more experienced colleagues. There is no widespread attempt to train classroom teachers in the use of television, and this means that we have, at any given point, just about one hundred percent of the classroom teachers to train. This item alone contributes heavily to a rather disappointing state of the art.

Conclusion

Instructional television has made little impact on American Education. Commitment to the use of television is generally lacking on the part of administrators and teachers. While individual systems can claim some success, the simple imposition of television on traditional administrative and educational structures is usually disappointing. The medium itself cannot be blamed, however; the major reforms necessary are much more basic than any single medium. Our educational structure resembles the structures of our most decrepit urban sections, and massive renewal projects are necessary.

PROMINENT SOURCES OF PRE-RECORDED VIDEOTAPE MATERIALS*

Advanced Management Research, Inc.
1604 Walnut Street
Philadelphia, Pennsylvania 19103

Courses for executives in business and industry.

Manager
Ampex Tape Exchange
2201 Lunt Avenue
Elk Grove Village, Illinois 60007

An exchange and distribution service for instructional and training courses and modules.

Director
California Medical Television Network
Continuing Education in Medicine
University of California Extension
10962 Le Conte
Los Angeles, California 90024

Postgraduate level modules covering many medical topics available to recognized medical agencies.

Center for Instructional Television
Eastern Education Network
575 Technology Square
Cambridge, Massachusetts 02139

Instructional courses available to schools and educational television stations within the Eastern Network area.

Programming Counselor
Great Plains National
    Instructional Television Library
University of Nebraska
Lincoln, Nebraska 68508

Instructional courses and supplementary materials available to recognized educational institutions. Cover pre-school through college level.

Director of Broadcast Services
Midwest Program on Airborne
    Television Instruction, Inc.
Memorial Center, Purdue University
Lafayette, Indiana 47902

Instructional courses and supplementary materials available to recognized educational institutions. Cover pre-school through college level.

As reported by Ken Winslow in Educational/ Instructional Broadcasting, Volume 1, Number 4, September-October, 1968.

Modern Talking Picture Service
1212 Avenue of the Americas
New York, New York 10036

Portions of existing library of
free-loan 16mm titles now
available on videotape.

Director of Field Services
National Center for School
   and College Television
Box A
Bloomington, Indiana 47401

Instructional courses and supplementary materials available
to recognized educational institutions. Cover pre-school
through college level.

Director of Network Affairs
Network for Continuing Medical Education
342 Madison Avenue
New York, New York 10017

Postgraduate level modules
covering many medical topics
available to recognized medical
agencies.

Director of Instructional Television
Western Video Industries
1541 North Vine Street
Los Angeles, California 90028

Instructional courses and supplementary materials available
to recognized educational institutions. Cover pre-school
through college level.

Also contact: Educational Television Stations and Regional Instructional Television Authorities and
major Colleges and Universities.

III. Political

The word political often connotes some kind of evil, but it is used here simply to describe
relationships among people. The state of the art in education—and therefore in instructional
television—is basically a function of the arrangements that exist among institutions, agencies
and ultimately individuals.

The National Instructional Television Center has estimated that at least $12,000,000 a
year are spent on school television. This money is used to operate machinery representing
capital investments of approximately $250,000,000. These figures are impressive, but not in
comparison with statistics describing the entire education enterprise in the country.

The size of the educational establishment, according to latest available estimates from the
U.S. Office of Education and the National Educational Association, is staggering. There are
more than 122,000 institutions of education, including elementary and secondary schools,
junior colleges, colleges and universities. There are almost 22,000 separate school districts in
the nation. There are more than 2½ million teachers at all levels, supervised by more than
210,000 administrators. The total number of students enrolled in the country is close to
58,000,000, and the total educational cost in the country is estimated at slightly more than
$58,000,000,000 per year. These figures exclude military training, and other municipal or
private instructional projects, so even these remarkable totals are probably something less
than the truth.

The world of ITV is only a tiny part of the educational galaxy, which in itself is a comment on the state of the art.

As mentioned briefly in the preceding section, the "ITV specialist" often has the problem
of being neither fish nor fowl. His training is usually his experience, and his formal study
has usually been in education *or* in broadcasting. Those in commercial or noncommercial
broadcasting tend to regard him as a representative of the educational establishment, and
those in administrative or teaching positions look upon the same man as a weird sort of
broadcaster. Glamour goes to the broadcaster, and the educator claims dignity. ITV personnel sometimes feel that this situation leaves them very little, and "second-class citizenship"
is often the cry. In some cases it is deserved.

The problem seems to be that the medium itself doesn't fit within present administrative and organizational structures, and so the people representing the medium feel the rejection on professional and even personal grounds.

The usual public school system, for instance, has at its highest level an elected body. These members of the Board of Education are justifiably interested in the best possible education for their youngsters at the least possible cost. They listen and decide in much the same fashion that our legislators do, relying on their own common sense and their knowledge of the wishes of their constituents. The superintendent, whom the Board hires, is the chief executive officer of the school system, and he is charged with providing the type of educational system that the Board desires. The superintendent is, in every possible way, under the control of the Board of Education, and if he pleases nobody else, he does what his collective boss requires.

The superintendent, in turn, hires an array of associate and assistant superintendents. One works in curriculum; another, in administration; a third in instructional services. Sometimes the list grows to well over half a dozen. Each of these public officials has his own staff; overlapping responsibilities and petty jealousies are as common as in any other enterprise.

Usually, an "audiovisual supervisor" is a member of one of the staffs. His placement on the tragic pyramid is not very high, but he takes his responsibilities very seriously, as he attempts first to keep his inventory of equipment up-to-date, and then to convince teachers that some tools are quite effective in learning.

As instructional television appears, it is usually the audiovisual supervisor who receives the "coordinating" assignment. If he does not receive it, and "AV" becomes separate from "TV," then he feels slighted, perhaps justifiably. In any case, the responsibility for television has often gone to school officials too far down in the administrative structure for any kind of massive action, and where it has gone to an existing audiovisual service, the result has been internal political strife.

The concept of a "learning resources center" is growing more popular among the larger and more sophisticated school systems. Here, the audiovisual supervisor has become an "educational technologist," and his bailiwick includes promoting the use of computer assisted instruction, dial-access and other modern ideas. A school system with such a center usually places its director higher on the administrative ladder than the "audiovisual" predecessor, and instructional television—and sometimes even libraries—become part of this centralized effort. Even if the center is placed at the associate superintendent level, however, there are still internal pressures brought by other assistant or associate superintendents to keep the learning resources center a small, non-threatening empire.

It seems that most school systems simply cannot house divisions of television, or centers for technology, or learning resources branches. *The reason is that the approach is through media, at the convenience of current administrative patterns.*

If an approach were made through *learning*, then choices of techniques and media would become common decisions for *all* administrators, teachers and organizational divisions.

The same problem seems to occur at the state level. State Departments of Education are simply not organized to handle state-wide television systems. As a new "Division of Instructional Television" is created, and placed beneath an associate superintendent for instructional services, the illusion is created that all technology—and television in particular—should be regarded as another organizational branch or division. (On American Samoa, as a contrary example, the decision was made that the entire educational system would take advantage of the distribution ability of television. The result is that administrators, division chiefs, associate superintendents and teachers accept the medium as basic to the system.)

Disappointments in instructional television occur most frequently as the new technical system is imposed upon older administrative patterns. It is likely that widespread and effective ITV will be known only as boards and administrators are willing to make necessary adjustments in staff, budgeting, curriculum development and overall commitment.

The placement of instructional television in existing organizational patterns can also result in hostility between traditional academic disciplines and the television experts. A well known new university in the South was founded only a few years ago with heavy publicity announcing that the school would be "media oriented," and that television would play a major part in academic life. Unfortunately, it seems that little attempt was made to convince the faculty that the new electronic techniques were worthwhile, and it was only a few years before major administrative shifts were made and the "media center" became something less than pivotal in the academic program. The error seems to be in placing the technologist in the role of "witch doctor," and in establishing his activities as another department or division. The polarization that ultimately results has at one end the radical who claims that a medium is all that is necessary to right the many wrongs in instruction and at the other end, the traditionalist who claims that the idea of using television in any instruction at all is poppycock.

The various disagreements that become so fiery in local situations are less discernible through national organizations, since the jealousies become institutional rather than personal. Still, as a variety of educational and professional organizations progress, their efforts in television seem to remain somewhat separate and distinct. This could well be a sign of health, since we usually give homage to the concept of "pluralism," but it also provides for duplication and wasted effort in an area already marked by piecemeal and sporadic successes.

Conclusion

We have tended to approach ITV as a medium, as "another tool," and we have generally tried to impose it on existing organizational and administrative structures. This had led, time and again, to disappointment. Where television has proven most successful in instructional settings, it has been because there was a definite need to use the medium, and because administrators, teachers and students have been arranged accordingly.

> Note: The installations and services described in Part IV were chosen by the National Association of Educational Broadcasters as examples of instructional uses of radio and television.
> Though they have been edited, they were originally written by the agencies concerned, so they do not necessarily stress difficulties or disappointments.

I. New Hanover County, North Carolina

TV KINDERGARTEN

The public schools of New Hanover County, North Carolina, are now using a commercially-owned CATV system to make possible the regular operation of a large-scale kindergarten program for pre-school youngsters living in the county's high population Wilmington area. The children are brought together each day in one of a dozen "community centers" scattered about this metropolitan area. The centers are conveniently-sized, multi-purpose activity rooms located in churches, recreation halls and the like—spaces "loaned" the schools by various private and public agencies. Each such center is managed by a part-time, para-professional kindergarten leader, usually a mother from the immediate neighborhood who is paid a "tiny annual fee" to oversee the morning-long sessions being conducted for twenty-or-so-youngsters.

The centers are equipped with television receivers, wired into the local CATV network, and a few basic activity "toys" which are useful in creative play. There is no elaborate learning apparatus of any sort.

Each day's session begins with a special forty-five minute television lesson designed by a professional kindergarten specialist hired by the school system. Following the televised segment, the para-professional carries forward some carefully structured reinforcement activities built on the specific content of the electronic lesson element. Coordination for these related activities is made possible by a detailed printed guide distributed to local leaders and by regular meetings conducted for the leaders by the studio teacher herself.

In the opinion of the New Hanover school officials, the program is successful in meeting its "school readiness" objectives.

II. Des Moines, Iowa Public Schools

CORRELATING INSTRUCTIONAL MATERIALS
BY RADIO-TELEVISION-FILM

In Des Moines, Iowa, KDPS-TV currently presents thirty-seven different courses, most of which are designed as complementary teaching resources for the elementary and secondary programs of instruction throughout Des Moines, the county schools, and neighboring counties.

Basically, the major part of the instruction provided through KDPS-TV is required for use by all teachers at the grade level of the lessons, unless there is some special reason for an exemption. Such a requirement has been successful in establishing more uniform levels of instruction and has resulted in more regular responses from teachers concerning the effectiveness and suitability of the lessons. Lessons are not necessarily scheduled daily. They may appear once a month, or three times a week, depending on their purpose.

In conjunction with the companion FM station, it has been possible to provide supplementary, reinforcing instruction that is directly related to the television and classroom lessons. (For example, conversational Spanish on the radio employs the same vocabulary as the television lessons, but with new sentences and a different format.)

Beyond this, KDPS-TV has inaugurated a daily afternoon series for children featuring films from major educational film suppliers that are *curriculum-coordinated with the week's work* in all basic subjects. This provides home viewing assignments and through a teacher-host who moderates the 90-minute afternoon program, suggestions are made for additional activities.

III. Washington County Public Schools
Hagerstown, Maryland

AN EARLY EFFORT TO UTILIZE TELEVISION
AS THE CORE OF INSTRUCTION

For the last twelve years, the Washington County School Board has been able to provide students improved instruction through the use of a six-channel, closed-circuit, County-wide television system. It is used not as a secondary source of information, but as the core for most of the instruction within the school system. The success of the Hagerstown Project can be measured by test results and in the attitudes of administrators, teachers, and students.

In 1956, the district needed many more teachers with more specialized training, as well as new facilities throughout the 465 square mile district to meet the anticipated enrollment increase of 10,000 students in a two-year period. The school board elected to make the maximum use of television in meeting their problems, and a proposal was presented to the Ford Foundation's Fund for the Advancement of Education for support.

Faced with the expiration of initial project funds in 1961, the school district had to decide whether to continue the use of television. Seventy two percent of the teachers then agreed that television was an important part of the system and should be retained. Students felt they had learned more by television than by conventional means, and the school board found that television utilization provided a good education for less than the average per student cost elsewhere in the State.

Today, Washington County children cannot imagine school without television, and teachers feel that the schools would be severely handicapped without television providing a core of the instruction.

IV. The Educational Television Association of Metropolitan Cleveland

AN EDUCATIONAL COMMUNITY'S COOPERATIVE USE OF FACILITIES AND PERSONNEL

The Educational Television Association of Metropolitan Cleveland operates an educational TV station (WVIZ) on Channel 25, and has also accepted a leadership role in more effective allocation of Instructional Television Fixed Service channels. It recognized that the inadequate number of channels for the potential number of users throughout Cleveland, the inadequate number of professional personnel available, and high costs would all be inhibiting factors in developing useful ITFS programs. The Association is now attempting to serve as a coordinating administrative unit and as a cooperating production center for all educational interests in Cleveland.

It is premature to report on the outcome of this effort, since it is only now being developed. However, this action by the licensee of an educational television station represents a new approach to the integration of often competing hardware transmission systems. As currently developed, each party to the agreement is guaranteed 40 hours per week on a channel that its schools can receive; but the channel is not licensed to such user. Rather, it is rented on a guaranteed basis, and those users requiring more time can apply for it.

Materials can be produced locally through the production facilities of the Association, or rented from libraries or other learning groups; only technical standards must be met, and the user can determine whatever material he wishes to use. It is anticipated that common needs will lead to the shared production and use of lessons designed and televised under these arrangements.

V. The Diocese of Brooklyn, New York

IMPROVED INSTRUCTION THROUGH ITFS

The Diocese of Brooklyn is developing a system-wide television facility to improve instruction in grades 1–12. Four Instructional Television Fixed Service channels are used to reach 212 school locations.

The Brooklyn system will soon be capable of interconnection with a new Instructional Television Communications Center in the Bronx, thereby affording an opportunity to develop instructional material cooperatively and to share the costs as well as the educational benefits. The present Brooklyn facility is used not only for schools, but also for adult education programs.

Currently, between 30 and 35 different series of lessons are distributed weekly; approximately 50% are obtained from instructional television libraries or exchange arrangements with other schools. Eight to ten new series are produced locally each year. The lessons are designed for in service teacher education programs, as well as for student use.

The Brooklyn program has not begun on a massive scale, although its current operation allows for improved instruction in a variety of different teaching areas, most of which are identified by the teachers themselves.

VI. KBPS, Portland, Oregon

IN-SCHOOL USE OF EDUCATIONAL AM
TO REACH THE DISADVANTAGED

KBPS, the only educational *AM* radio station in the United States, has been broadcasting to the Public Schools of Portland, Oregon for 45 years. Begun as a challenge for the engineering department of a technical high school, KBPS has developed over 100 series of programs for in-school use.

In 1967, with the help of a federal grant, the station created several series for disadvantaged children. One of these series, called "Teen Time," was broadcast in the poorer areas of the school district. Students in these schools telephoned in questions to a rotating panel of other teenagers. While low-key, this format gave these children a chance to participate in public events. Adults were not involved.

Another series was put together using books about individuals who had been challenged in life with different handicaps and who overcame them. The stories were adapted for radio by leading writers and dramatized for juveniles.

Following this series, the station allowed the disadvantaged children to broadcast their own creative writing.

The station is working on a weekly newscast directed at primary school children. This series will cover mainly community events, although national and international news will be mentioned. All programs are primarily prepared by teachers.

VII. South Carolina Educational Television Center Columbia, South Carolina

MULTI-CHANNEL ACCESSIBILITY TO TELEVISED RESOURCES

South Carolina operates a closed-circuit television system capable of accommodating six channels simultaneously, and three broadcast television stations. Together, this gives the Center a capability of reaching 95% of the student population.

The Center has been operating for eight years. Respecting concerns about local control, teacher responsibility, and jurisdictional prerogatives of the State Educational Department, the Center and its system is increasingly seen as the means by which curriculum reform can be effected on a regular basis. It is gradually becoming more than an adjunct to the schools, and it has assumed the major instructional content responsibility for arithmetic and mathematics from grades 4-12, and physical sciences in the high school program. Each year the role of the Center in providing this central instructional responsibility is applied to new areas of the curriculum.

Beyond its regular instructional programs in the schools, the educational television system in South Carolina has been used for direct professional instruction and training for doctors, state employees, law enforcement officers, food handlers, and industrial supervisors. A special corporation, the Educational Resources Foundation, has been established to design instructional training materials which are implemented statewide through the South Carolina Educational Television Center.

The annual operating budget of the Center is $3 million.

VIII. American Samoa

COOPERATIVE INSTRUCTION BY TELEVISION:
A MODEL FOR DEVELOPING AREAS

The education system of American Samoa has undergone a comprehensive change in instructional design, instructional effectiveness, and economic efficiency as a result of the deliberate application of advanced television technology.

By using six broadcast channels it is possible to reach all the schools in Samoa, even though several are 60-70 miles across the ocean. The six channels provide for a flexible schedule for the classrooms. In an average week, 170 lessons are produced by the Department of Education, representing nearly 60 hours of air time and almost 200 hours of studio time. Additional use of the facilities for evening broadcasts to adults means nearly 100 hours of programming are transmitted each week.

The television system in Samoa has given the education program the capability for being immediately responsive to changing needs in the classroom. New content, new teaching strategies, or remedial lessons can be diffused throughout the system immediately, without having to wait for the training of a new generation of teachers, or the retraining of the present ones.

The Samoan system spends under $500 per child per year for operation. Within this budget all curriculum materials are planned, developed, written, and printed; the television system is supported; transportation, teaching personnel, school lunch programs, and support services are provided. As student enrollment increases, the system will be able to reduce unit cost of instruction.

IX. Chicago Television College

CREDIT COURSES FOR OFF-CAMPUS STUDENTS

Since 1956 the more popular courses available at the fifty year old Chicago Junior College have been offered by television. To date over 1500 television students have *completed* degrees, and over 120,000 TV students have registered for courses. Originally begun with the help of the Ford Foundation, Television College has been able to keep investment costs down by leasing offices, studios, and broadcast time from Chicago's ETV station, WTTW. Since the winter of 1960 the cost of television instruction has fallen below the cost of conventional instruction on campus. Today the cost of a credit hour on TV is $23.43 as compared to $37.21 on campus.

The students who attend are for the most part physically handicapped, mothers with children at home, men who must work all day, and other groups normally isolated from conventional education. (Last year twenty-nine convicts in state prisons earned the Associate in Arts degree.) Through the use of telephone conferences held twice a week, counseling services, optional meetings on campus, and the availability of audio tapes of previous lectures, the system has proven flexible enough to serve these divergent groups.

Over the last ten years the television courses have included: Art, Biology, Business, Data Processing, Education, English, Humanities, Mathematics, Modern Language, Music, Physical Sciences, Social Sciences, and Speech.

X. The Pennsylvania State University

PROFESSORS REACH BRANCH-CAMPUSES BY TELEVISION

The Pennsylvania State University has a full range of television production facilities, including six studios on the main campus. Of the 19 branch-campuses of the University, 14 are served by mailing videotaped materials, 1 by one-way microwave system, and another by a two-way microwave system. Twenty-eight courses are available to these campuses, some such as meteorology and art history taught by University Park specialists who could not be available on local campuses to teach in conventional classes.

Televised instructional materials are produced by the Division of Instructional Services, responsible for all resident instruction activity. The Division's television production facilities are closely aligned with other academic services that report directly to the Vice President for Resident Instruction. The University broadcast facility (WPSX-TV) is concerned academically only with continuing educational programs, and while the two television production units cooperate when appropriate on project design and materials, they are not otherwise related administratively.

Comparable systems for using TV to assist higher education are developing at Michigan State University, the University of Delaware, Florida Atlantic University and elsewhere.

XI. Albany Medical College

CONTINUED EDUCATION BY FM AND
SHORT-WAVE RADIO

The Albany Medical College, through its educational FM station, WAMU-FM, has developed a unique scheme for effective and economical post-graduate medical education and training.

The Division of Continuing Education uses the educational FM station 7 hours per week, to present lectures or discussions on new developments in medicine; physicians can participate directly in the discussions if they are at listening/viewing centers in hospitals which are connected by short-wave radio or direct telephone circuits to the medical college's station in Albany. *Viewing* is arranged by advance preparation and distribution of slides to the hospital centers; they are displayed on cue from the radio lectures. Physicians not able to be at the Center can share in the total program by listening to WAMC-FM on radios in their homes, offices, or automobiles. The technical systems used by the Albany Medical College are flexible enough to allow for multiple origination points selected for professional priorities; faculty from more than 26 medical colleges contribute to the lectures and presentations.

WAMC-FM is used by the Albany Medical College for general educational and cultural broadcasts over 60 hours per week, beyond the time used for the professional medical broadcasts.

XII. GENESYS, University of Florida Engineering College Gainesville, Florida

GRADUATE COURSES AVAILABLE TO WORKING ENGINEERS

GENESYS (Graduate Engineering Education System) joins aerospace installations with the University of Florida Engineering College, Gainesville. The system allows on-the-job scientists and engineers, who cannot meet in campus classes, to continue advanced degree work by participation on a two-way basis—that is, video and audio feed-out with audio feed-back.

University staff professors teach approximately 50 courses in Industrial, Electrical and Aerospace Engineering from small television studios in Gainesville, Daytona, Port Canaveral, and Orlando. Each of the four major TV locations can broadcast to the others;

library and study facilities are available at all seven receiving locations; professors try to visit students several times during the course.

Students (as few as two, or as many as fifteen) view the lectures with an opportunity to interrupt the lesson for clarification or to ask questions following. The audio feed-back system allows everyone to hear discussion on the lecture and on homework. All telecasts are live.

In addition to the regular course offerings, short, non-credit courses are given on Saturday mornings when the system is free. During the normal school period, facilities are used approximately 45 hours a week.

XIII. Center for Mass Communication Research
University of Denver, Colorado

TELEVISION UTILIZED FOR "SOCIALIZATION" OF MINORITY GROUPS
The Center for Mass Communication Research, University of Denver, has prepared a series of special television programs for minority groups through the facilities of the local educational station, KRMA-TV. The eight half-hour informational programs presented in the popular "soap-opera" format are intended to aid Negroes and Spanish-surnames. "Our Kind of World" was presented through the lives of two families living next to each other, one Negro and the other of Spanish-surname.

A sample of approximately 600 people was selected from a public housing project to research the needs and to test techniques. Topics chosen include: family health, buying and preparation of nutritional foods, family finances, job-seeking, social responsibilities in the community, and consumer behavior. A follow-up testing showed that the informational level of those watching was raised in all subjects but family financing.

The series was found to be realistic, believable, and informative. Professional and semi-professional actors from the two minority groups were employed. The Denver University Center for Mass Communications is currently researching a program of wider scope for the Los Angeles educational television station (KCET). This program series plans 14 weeks of day-time serials aimed at the Mexican-American population.

XIV. Fort Monmouth, New Jersey

CCTV PROVIDES UNIFORM, TECHNICAL TRAINING ON A MASS SCALE FOR U.S. ARMY
The U.S. Signal Corps School at Fort Monmouth, New Jersey, makes heavy use of closed-circuit television to facilitate the training of several thousand men annually in basic technical courses in the electronics and communications area. The facilities, scattered throughout the military post, are equipped with an elaborate network of audio-video channels. Instructional and informational programming originates in a well-equipped studio complex located in the headquarters section.

Without use of regular television presentation, the mass scale of course operations would be practically impossible to realize with the kind of responsive control and efficient coordination needed. In the opinion of school administrators, civilian and military, television is helping to make possible uniform, articulated courses-of-study which can be modified and improved school-wide on a truly comprehensive basis.

XV. North American Aviation, California

CCTV PROVIDES EFFICIENT TRAINING AND OPERATIONAL COMMUNICATIONS FOR INDUSTRY

When North American Aviation was awarded two large Apollo Spacecraft contracts in 1961, closed-circuit television was introduced to carry the major burden of training. An average day at the Downy, California plant might now start at 8:45 a.m. with a 23-minute training program entitled "Apollo Sequential Systems," transmitted to 25 of the 500 in-plant viewing locations. Next, perhaps "Accounting for Labor Costs," "Aircraft Wire Harness Fires," or "Configuration Management" would be selectively shown at appropriate on-the-job viewing locations. Today the 11,000 sq. ft. facility remains busy most of the time producing programs shown around the clock.

Management communication is also facilitated by television when everyday at 4 p.m. a news report is transmitted to top management about the day-to-day operation. Topics include important developments, major problems, proposals, new contracts—all supported by charts, film clips, and video tape inserts displayed in combination with a two-way audio system that allows a briefing to become a conference.

North American does not have a full cost break down on the closed-circuit television facility, as it is considered a vital part of the company rather than an adjunct. It is known that under the Apollo contract the cost for training 1,000 workers in a specific subject was $0.55 per worker by CCTV as compared to $2.25 per person by regular methods.

3.

Introducing the
Docile Technology
In Memoriam of CAI

by *DON D. BUSHNELL*
President
Communications Foundation
Santa Barbara, California

"We're going to limp along in this country from one creaking innovation to the next on an incomparably, incompetent pathway to big brother norms and mice standard mediocrity until we take a divergent road in education. And that road is marked by an absence of competitiveness and compulsion . . . What we have to have are generous and unbuttoned classrooms and many, many styles of living and learning, without universal checkpoints to measure us . . ."

Dan Pinck[1]

The general alarm that establishment education is not working with the slum child generally causes us to overlook the fact that it has not worked with many suburban white students either. The safe and sane technologies that have entered the educational market place over the last few years have been less than a match for those hallowed classroom traditions of our WASP ancestry:

(1) The tradition of authoritarianism dampens or destroys the student's innate drive toward learning and self-determination. The authoritarian posture of our educational system requires that student energies be directed at slavishly fulfilling tasks set by the system rather than by the students themselves.

(2) The tradition of passivity is extant in the schools. There is little requirement for the student to risk himself or to become even actively involved. Discipline is too often the principle and only concern of the instructor. Eventually the "undisciplined" leadership turns off and drops out.

(3) The tradition of "no controversy" in our schools—supporting the pretense that all life is good and simple and that controversy is somehow unwholesome—is current among educators. The great majority of schools will simply not recognize conflict and hence, in my opinion, fail to interest the student or prepare him for an honest encounter with the real world.

(4) The schools are word bound, little use is made of a physical or visual mode of learning.

(5) The inordinate dependency on competition as the one and only strategy for motivation stifles the innate joy of learning.

These are time-honored conventions that sap the strength from most educational innovations. Much of the new electronic technology that has been readied for use in the classroom merely furthers these traditions, and unless we unbutton our thinking, computer assisted instruction (CAI) as currently applied will be no exception.

During the sixties, computer technology has reached a high level of acceptance into the educational system, both at the universities and in the public schools. With the marriage of the teaching machine and the flexible and "inhumanly patient" digital computer, CAI was given birth. The offspring inevitably caught the eye of the innovators who were beginning to despair of programmed instruction as the panacea for all educational ills. Numerous magazines, including the in-house *American Education* at HEW, saw CAI as a teacher surrogate. The CAI system will reportedly "never get tired . . . allow the individual to proceed at his own pace . . . make possible a daily tracking system in which a youngster moves up or down each day after each lesson . . . ensure the acquisition of basic skills for children of educationally deprived backgrounds . . . and provide a complete, instantly available record of each child's achievement and furnish information for course modification."[2] With this siren song offered up by the U.S. Office of Education, it is not surprising that many big city schools sought to tap into federal funds, and placate restless natives by bringing the most modern of all technologies into their classrooms. The history of these past applications has been chronicled for all to see.[3]

My quarrel with CAI, documented in subsequent pages, is not basically with factors of economics, standardization, or the lack of compilers and appropriate CAI languages, or even the paucity of curriculum, but with the simple fact that CAI perpetuates those traditions of education that have brought us to the present policy of brinkmanship that can lead only to disaster.

Consider the tradition of passivity for a moment. CAI, as it now stands, perpetuates this custom from a time when children were seen and not heard. If the learner's own interests and talents are stifled by machine-directed learning or the imposed demands of the system, the results may be facts temporarily stored, but at the cost of knowledge becoming irrelevant and curiosity being destroyed. The role of the teacher or teaching machine is to establish a balance between (1) a structured program and (2) the individual student's innate desire to explore areas of his own interest. As a rule of thumb, it is perhaps better to offer opportunities or resources that the student cares about than the particular body of information that the teacher happens to know. At the very least, and no matter the discipline, if a student is allowed to ask questions that matter to him, he soon learns the habit of self-generating inquiry. Certainly active involvement or a willingness to risk himself in the process of change can't be expected in a system that is busy inculcating passivity and compliance.

The use of CAI in most applied programs could be characterized as machine-directed learning. The system dispenses instruction in a fixed, pre-programmed sequence of graded instructional material. Control of the instructional process lies with the machine and not with the student. The programmer-author develops an explicit a priori model of instructional needs for all hypothetical learners and attempts to program instructional sequences that are tailored to these various needs. In fact, not enough is known about the human learning process to prescribe a specific model for organizing or programming a number of alternative learning experiences; therefore, CAI has had to proceed on a trial and error basis. Unfortunately, the programmer-author almost exclusively uses answers to multiple choice questions as his criteria for instructional sequences that work or don't work. Rarely is the student asked directly why he made an error or what particular misconceptions he might be laboring under. Horn[4] raised the question of what errors in instructional programming can be discovered by diagnostic or criterion testing alone. He concludes that twenty-four of twenty-seven listed kinds of errors are not easily discovered through testing, and recommends interview of individual learners as a supplemental technique in materials development.

Contrasted with the CAI form of machine-directivity is machine-docility: a docile teaching system (under computer or human control) with perform operations *only* on the basis of student requests. It gives rapid and responsive acquiescence to the wishes of the learner. In this learner-directed mode of operation, the computer becomes the key to information retrieval from a vast knowledge bank of resource materials, or the students could apply themselves to a variety of complex projects in an ever widening range of disciplines. In the process, they could gain an understanding of the nature of problem solving and the variety of approaches open to solutions.

Some practical applications of machine-docility can be found in the work of Kemeny at Dartmouth, Jesse Richardson in Massachusetts, and Glen Culler at the University of California at Santa Barbara. In each instance, the computer's function is that of a rapid calculator letting the student "do his own thing." Here the machine is docile, not the student. And when the technology is used appropriately and uniquely for its particular capabilities, the student can study subject matters heretofore beyond his reach.

In Memoriam of CAI

The thesis of this paper is that projects and programs involving instructional technology must place the learner in a key position of high involvement and self-directedness. To "turn on" the disenchanted, we need to engage him as an active participant in the real world: in the sciences, the arts, the community, the outdoor world, business and industry. By giving him the tools to become involved—i.e., the technology of the trades—we can succeed where other methodologies have failed: any functional system which allows for or actively solicits "hands on" experience will give the learner a sense of "nowness" that most educational experiences lack. Combining newly learned skills with the tools of the modern world gives an immediate opportunity to put these skills into practice. This fact, plus the promise of large rewards, makes learning relevant and exciting, and entrusts the learning to the student himself. This is what instructional technology should be all about, from the motion picture camera to the digital computer.

The history of technology in education is a history of great expectations and student disappointments. Where the technology has been placed in the hands of the learner—in the machine shop or the open computer shop—the promise has been fulfilled. Where it has been "screwed to the floor or locked in a booth"[5] the student has not had the opportunity to become engaged. The older generation is inclined to think of instructional hardware as a means for dispensing *their* information which is in turn to be digested by students. Students, on the other hand, recognize the hardware for what it is—a part of the new information environment of electronically processed data and experience. Take the technology away from the student and he will have lost one of the best means for involvement and for relating "the educational scene to the mythic world of electronics and circuitry", to use McLuhan's words.[6]

Is the technology used to create an environment of involvement? This should be the first step in the evaluation of a CAI program. Involvement here is not defined as simply pressing typewriter keys in response to a controlled stimulus. Involvement with a central computer should require learning a simplified I/O language, probably an on-line mathematical language directed toward problem solving or mathematical analysis. The student should then be required to prepare a computer program to solve a simple mathematical problem.

At the end of this short indoctrination, the student is ready to tackle problems appropriate to his course work. He is also free to use the computer for independent projects of any sort or even for his own entertainment. This kind of involvement helps the student gain a realistic assessment and attitude toward cybernetic systems. Direct participation in the technology is a means of conquering the fear that the student might have when confronting new forms of electronic education. Once the barriers are broken down, and the student is sufficiently skilled to directly approach a subject area using the technology as a tool, the "turn on" between student and machine is a matter of course.

How does CAI stack up against the criteria of involvement? To answer this question adequately, I should like to distinguish among three different aspects of CAI systems paraphrasing a statement made by Ed Adams—Research Director of CAI at IBM—at a recent Project ARISTOTLE Symposium.[7] He refers to (1) *content,* (2) *structure,* and (3) *mediation.* Dr. Adams defines *content* as the corpus of information in a course; *structure* refers to the problems of sequencing learning experiences, or the strategy of building a complex of basic skills; *mediation* involves the process of communication with the student, the hardware system, the programming language the media forms, and human factoring of the interface between student and machine. Dr. Adams contends that a successful CAI program must succeed in each of these three aspects, stressing the point, however, that if the learning program is to be deemed successful *as CAI,* "the computer's function should be *essential* to realize some important instructional value." In other words, if you can fulfill the computer's function in any other fashion, then the computer should probably not be a part of the system: its role can probably be taken over by some less expensive form of technology, if technology is really needed.

Content Mediated by CAI Systems:
Publishers and Sponsored Research

A major obstacle to the implementation of even the most rudimentary forms of CAI has been the lack of curriculum material appropriate to the power of the mediating system. The public schools rely heavily upon the educational publishers and the manufacturers of multimedia instructional materials to produce the bulk of software packages. The educational publisher, on the other hand, looks at his market place with an eye to sales and can be counted on to prepare subject matters that are simply an adjunct to traditional classroom practices. Furthermore, textbook publishers employ few people who are skilled in automated communications systems: they end up producing lessons for CAI that are more appropriate to book form.

There are some lesson designers who use existing CAI systems to prepare and test new course material and find themselves locked into formats that frequently are not right for the subject matter under development.[8] Because of the particular configurations of most CAI systems, either experimental or commercial, these authors must necessarily avoid untried techniques and depend almost exclusively on programmed instruction formats. These researchers/authors fail to utilize the computer's unique potential in executing their curriculum programs. For this reason, and those given above, it is recommended that projects aimed at the development of CAI materials should be initiated for the explicit purpose of exploiting the computational or simulation powers of the computer for computer-mediated learning experiences, that is, experiences which a printed, linear text could not offer, or any other media system could purvey.

It has been suggested by computer manufactuers that the computer industry itself will supply curriculum materials. With the possible exception of RCA, this suggestion has not borne much fruit. IBM, which bought Science Research Associates, Incorporated in 1964, has had a recognized capability in this direction, but has not yet demonstrated its abilities to produce. When IBM introduced the 1500 CAI System, they announced:

> "Preliminary versions of course materials that educators may use with the new instructional system are being developed by Science Research Associates, Incorporated, an IBM subsidiary. Course materials are in algebra, computer science, German, and statistics. SRA is also developing supplementary materials that allow the student to use the system to solve problems and perform simulated experiments in the study of physics, chemistry, biology, general sciences, and the social sciences."[9]

To date, SRA has not produced any CAI courses and the future is clouded as to whether they will even retain their exclusive status as IBM's purveyor of instructional materials. RCA, on the other hand, does show some promise of producing, through Random House and Harcourt Brace Jovanovich, supplementary materials for use with existing curriculum packages. The problem that some industry people seem to be having with publishers is that the publisher recognizes that if they enter the market place at this early juncture married to a particular system, they may be limiting their future sales.

Another strategy—that teachers produce their own CAI materials—has received much greater support from those districts actually placing CAI on line for student instruction. The Brooks Foundation made the following recommendation to the School District of Philadelphia as part of its findings after a year's system study:

> "A serious lack of instructional materials is the major problem facing a school district that plans to implement an individualized education program. The administration of the School District of Philadelphia will need to recognize this lack, and to tap resources in many parts of the country. In this regard, recommendations have been made for the establishment of *a central library of computer-ready instructional programs* in the District.

> ". . . Even with the establishment of a central library for its use the District will have to develop and validate instruction resources of its own. Recognizing the immensity of the programming task required for the introduction of CAI systems into the School District, the District must start to train instructional programmers. Because the skills required for instructional programming are difficult to identify and to impart, it should be expected that only three out of ten teachers will develop into good programmers.

> ". . . But the involvement of experienced teachers in the materials production program has major advantages:

> (1) Teachers who have become programmers are more likely to accept and utilize the CAI system when it is introduced into their school.

> (2) Years of experience with many approaches to conventional instruction will help teachers generate the numerous alternative approaches to the subject matter that are needed in an individualized program of study.

> (3) A certain face validity for the material is gained where teachers know that other experienced educators have had a hand in its production."[10]

In looking back at this recommendation of some two years ago, it seems now that the Foundation was naive in assuming that the teachers could produce anything approaching the variety of experiences needed to truly adapt to the styles of learning of the individual student. They also suffer from the same unfamiliarity with the potential or power of automated instructional systems that commercial textbook publishers have in the past.

Summary

As long as CAI materials are limited to modes of instruction characterized by machine-directivity, they will not bring about the student involvement that is so desperately needed in the "buttoned-up" classroom. Rather, the time-shared CAI console should be used as a problem-solving tool for the student. This advantage, limited as it may now seem, will eventually enable the learner to undertake subject matters heretofore considered impossible in the classroom. Subjects that had been taught only at the college and university level could be approached in the secondary schools. For example, the launching and control of satellites, the study of the chemistry of genetics, the modelling of voter behavior, the analysis of creative writing styles, the composition of electronic music, the engagement in bargaining games—all become possible with the time-shared console. Systems are being designed so that students have direct access to primary sources of knowledge. From here it is not a big step to training in information management and decision-making, or for recognizing patterns in a vast data base. *The computer becomes the ideal tool for experimentation in new subject matter and for giving the student an early experience with the tools that can involve him directly in a future world of electronically processed information and data.*

Computer Sequenced Learning Experiences

Using Ed Adams statement, "clear identification of the *computer added value* should be the first step in evaluation of a CAI program"[11] the matter of structuring or sequencing learning experiences by computer takes on a new focus. In the halcyon era of CAI, it was rather glibly claimed by this author that "responsiveness to student learning behavior can be achieved by branching the student forward, laterally, or backward through subject materials . . . for the following reasons:

"(1) Characteristics of student response—the promptness and/or definitiveness of his reply.

"(2) Nature of response—was it right or wrong, what specific errors were committed by the student?

"(3) History of student learning behavior—his previous response pattern, problem areas, and reading rate.

"(4) Relevant student personal data—his IQ, sex, personality, aptitude.

"(5) Nature of subject matter.

"(6) Degree of student motivation.

"(7) Student-generated requests for rerouting."[12]

Certainly, if all of these factors were to be considered in determining the particular sequence of instructional materials for a given student at a given moment, the computer added value to CAI programs would be obvious. The computer is the only system that can carry out this kind of bookkeeping activity and monitor many students at the same time. But the question must be raised: how do the above listed criteria specifically affect the structure or sequence of learning experiences? The state of the science of learning being what it is, educational researchers have not devised a satisfactory strategy for the practitioners to lay hold of. The tool is willing, so to speak, but the body of knowledge is weak.

The programming of learning experiences can depend on "expert opinion" as it has in the past, or upon a theoretical structure based upon empirical research. Some would argue, as Karl Zinn does, "that the research tool must exist first before empirical data can be collected." But the research can't be conducted unless the significant variables are already known. Fortunately, a number of issues are already emerging from the research on programmed instruction. They all have some bearing on the factors relating to sequencing.

The three most general categories of variables are: "(1) content variables, arising from the structure of knowledge or the nature of the world; (2) instruction variables, arising from the method of instruction or the behavior of the instructor; and (3) inquiry variable arising from the behavior and characteristics of the learner."[13] These three variables, suggested by I. A. Richards, are not new by any means, but they will become more explicit and differentiated as the learning process is objectified so that it will be mediable by computer.

"*Content variables.* These involve differences among familiar areas such as reading, mathematics, spelling, or music, or across such relatively unfamiliar categories as semantic, symbolic, figural (space, time, motion), and behavioral (social). I. A. Richards, for example, proposes a computer-based method for teaching reading and typing simultaneously to backward or underprivileged pupils, or to first graders or even pre-schoolers. The development of programs for such instruction is bringing to light certain interdependencies between literal notation (alphabetics or phonics), syntax, and meaning that are intrinsic to the subject of reading instruction. Richards recommends an approach that appears to combine the advantages of pure phonics and the word-gestalt methods while avoiding the outstanding disadvantages of both, such as rote drill in phonics and excessive redundancy in the word-gestalt method. While the objectives of this research may be to produce better methods of instruction, immediate rewards are forthcoming in a better understanding of the structure of knowledge itself in a particular area whose importance can hardly be overstated.

"*Instruction variables.* These include sequence or order effects, size of units or steps, nature of reinforcement (positive or negative, simple or complex, intrinsic or extrinsic), frequency or regularity of extrinsic reinforcement, the whole area of teacher characteristics, and many other aspects of instruction that are relatively familiar. Not so familiar are instruction variables arising from the presence of the computer in the role of the teacher. The degree of program docility, as mentioned earlier, is a variable representing the degree to which the learner can direct the learning process, even into channels that the average teacher might reject as irrelevant or at least unscheduled.

"A whole family of instruction variables will have to be isolated in the effort to realize the computer's potential for on-line or short-lag modification of instruction to suit the needs of the learner. Essentially, this means that learners will encounter difficulties that are to varying degrees unexpected; the difficulties may be unique, rare, infrequent, or common. Common difficulties will be anticipated by branching sequences in instructional programs.

"A method of instructional materials development referred to as iterative (cyclical) tutorial revision promises to provide a data bank or library of common problems experienced by students in learning with textual materials. This methodology is the result of two years of experimentation in a slum high school in North Philadelphia by the Brooks Foundation.[15] Tables of frequency of occurrence of these problems have been constructed, and the more frequent problems could be anticipated in automated programs. Infrequent problems would require the intervention of a human teacher who was monitoring the learning process or who called in to help by the computer program itself when unanticipated responses were given by the learner. The teacher might then request from the data bank a list of alternate instructional tactics and select one or more for presentation to the student. Rare or unique difficulties would signify either a special disqualifying characteristic on the part of the learner or, alternatively, a conceptual approach to the material completely overlooked by the instructional programmers and curriculum developers. The discovery of such an omission would be a significant and valuable event and would call for a curriculum conference including the most expert personnel; it has even been suggested that the instructional computer center might have "hot lines" to various university resources around the country who would be called in automatically to contribute to the solution of rare problems.

"*Learner variables.* The familiar concerns with aptitude, achievement, and interests are not diminished in our search for significant variables related to automated sequencing, but they will be supplemented by growing attention to new kinds of variables.

"It seems likely that the measurement of temperamental variables must develop rapidly, as the ease of massive complex data analysis begins to show important relationships with instructional variables. Such relationships have been very elusive in the past, but some investigators believe that they are both real and important in the educational process. The question, for example, of whether a student's preferred style of learning, active or passive, is dependent on inherited components of temperament, on learning during infancy or the pre-school years, or on learning during early school years has vast implications for instruction. For the educator, the essential question is: what can we change through instruction, and what are the givens, to which instruction must be adapted? The successful individualization of instruction depends heavily on the answers to such questions.

"In general, and especially among special school populations, such as the disadvantaged, the use of non-behavioral variables is important. Family background, neighborhood conditions, information in social agencies, from police to welfare, all have great potential value for research, both evaluative and theoretical, and for administrative planning.

"The study of motivational variables and blockage of learning is important for individual adjustment of instructional items and in studies of special populations that may have attitudinal or emotional handicaps . . . Computer-assisted instruction programs can be alerted likewise, so that teacher help can be requested immediately when signs of behavior disorganization appear, or when students thought to have emotional or motivational problems are being machine-instructed. Special programs can be devised to hold attention and minimize threat in the instruction of these disadvantaged students."[14]

Summary

The early promise of CAI was that it would give the learner rapid access to a body of information organized to his particular style of learning. Somehow we lost the way, probably due more to the paucity of programming strategies—based on a rigid, linear, step-by-step model—than to any other single cause. *A prime need for advancing the state of the art for CAI is to develop programming strategies that permit the learner to explore and manipulate a corpus of information in a manner of his own choosing while simultaneously giving feedback that increasingly develops the student's power to search and to learn on his own.*

There is a clear need to continue the process of research into the variables that relate to the organization of a body of knowledge for easy access and productive learning; content, instructional methods, and inquiry practices should constitute a challenge for quite some time.

Communication Between Student and Machine— The Mediation Process

Applied CAI, as already emphasized, primarily is an automated means of dispensing information in the drill and practice mode of instruction. Students type answers to a string of spelling or word lists or select multiple choice answers to math problems in a paced presentation. The computer matches these responses with a string of correct answers stored in its memory. The pedagogical model here is the standard teacher operation of test and retest in a fully programmed atmosphere in which all conditions of the stimulus and response cycle are anticipated (or thought to have been anticipated) by the programmer or instructor.

As David Stansfield states in a recent article in *Educational Technology*, "the chief weakness of any type of automated instruction is that it cannot cater to unanticipated responses from the student. If the student, quite reasonably, responds to the question, "What do cars run on?" with the word "roads" or "wheels" or even "faith" or "credit" (instead of "petroleum") or whatever it is, all the computer will be able to say is "Your answer is wrong, try again."[16]

The computer could be programmed with every possible response the student might be anticipated to make, but this would use up memory in short order. The basic point here is that the drill and practice mode of instruction is not a good use of CAI's potential. Even if the arguments that bookkeeping and releasing the teacher for more appropriate functions are proffered, this outmoted form of pedagogy is not appropriate to a cybernetic system. Better the memory drum or the flash card. And, for all that, how is the teacher expected to use all the data generated by these drill and practice sessions when he hasn't the time or the skills to digest the data he has already for improving his classroom procedures? The teacher could justifiably resent picking up a mountain of data where the computer left off.

Zinn comments that if, in this mode, economic criteria are important, users of computer-based drill exercises should also consider alternative ways of achieving their objectives for student learning. Skills might be acquired more efficiently through paper-and-pencil exercises, or more pleasantly through interaction with other students, or more efficiently as side benefits of more complicated problem solving tasks aided by the computer.[17]

Beyond drill and practice applications, tutorial interactions between computer and student are basically of a programmed instructional nature. That is, the programmer has devised a computer program which in turn controls a pre-determined sequence of instructional material. By adding a computer to a programmed instruction course, the programmer theoretically gains the advantages of allowing for (a) constructed responses by the students; (b) variable sequencing of instructional materials (tailoring the sequences to a variety of student needs); and (c) easily computed statistical information on how well the students are learning, how effective the instructional routines are as teaching tools, et cetera. We have already seen how difficult it is to put these advantages into practice. In reality, this CAI mode has little to recommend beyond its value as a teaching machine except perhaps the pinball effects of the simulated conversation between the student and the machine (see the language interaction in the appended illustrations).

Consideration of the mechanics of communication between learner and machine falls into two general areas: (1) the "interface" between student input and machine output and (2) the language of the communication. Of the two areas, interface problems are the most easily solved as they are basically of an engineering nature.

An almost universal practice with CAI systems is to tediously type out the content material and then to follow this presentation with a long multiple choice question that calls for a one digit response. Perhaps one of the reasons that use of the time-shared computer in a problem solving or inquiry mode is so successful is that the computer and student or mathematician are in constant interaction. The laborious process of typing out long linear sequences of words is circumvented by the use of abbreviated terms that cause complete cycles of computation to occur. Tedious typing is avoided, but more importantly, there is an opportunity for frequent give and take between the inquirer and machine that approaches genuine dialogue. So arresting is this dialogue that a recurring phenomena among those who have a console in their office or study area is the "computer-bum syndrome." The intensity of interaction between student and machine causes some highly motivated learners to go without food and sleep while trying to resolve a particular analysis or debug a program. The interaction becomes everything and the basic needs are overcome by the responsive system.

The limitations of the alphanumerical typewriter as currently applied to common CAI systems is not the only engineering problem related to this mode of automated instruction. Educators attempting to match their instructional needs against the characteristics of a particular CAI system must analyze input/output capabilities of the system against the kinds of media to be used in the instruction and the kinds of responses it may be necessary for the learner to make. Listings of some representative examples of both media and response problems can be found in James Rogers' article in the September issue of *Datamation:* [18]

"(1) *Kinds of material to be displayed to the learner.*

   (a) **Text:** in teaching foreign languages, we may wish to display text including special alphabetic characters; in teaching mathematics, chemistry, and logic, we require special symbols, signs, subscripts, et cetera, for displaying equations, formulas and expressions.

   (b) **Audio:** we may want to play back recordings of spoken messages in teaching communication skills, languages or basal reading; and recordings of instruments in teaching music appreciation.

   (c) **Graphics:** we may wish to display maps in teaching history; motion pictures in engineering or science; still photographs in medicine or art; circuit diagrams in electricity; graphs in mathematics or statistics; engineering drawings in blueprint reading; cardiograms in medical diagnosis; and so forth.

"(2) *Kinds of responses to be required of the learner.*

The terminal behavior specifications (i.e., the teaching objectives of the course, stated in terms of observable changes in the learner's behavior) for courses in various subjects might include the following items:

   (a) State the expression for the area under the curve.
   (b) Translate the above sentence into Russian.
   (c) Fill in the missing parts of the following table.
   (d) Point to the antibodies in the microphotograph.
   (e) Outline the temperate zone on the map.
   (f) Complete the circuit diagram.
   (g) Describe a relationship.
   (h) Define a concept.
   (i) Explain how something works.
   (j) Summarize the speaker's remarks orally."

In addition to the problem of supplying special type fonts or requiring graphic input capabilities, the nature of a student's constructed response is limited by the constraints of the CAI language and/or the techniques available for handling the problem of meaning. As with the varying responses to the question "What do cars run on?" constructed sentences of any significant number or length can have an almost infinite variety of word combinations, and it is difficult to compare the student's response to that stored in the computer's memory. Far too many of the CAI languages that program authors are required to use do not even permit acceptance of misspelled words, incorrect punctuation, or key word synonyms.

Because CAI languages represent an entire subject matter in themselves, they will be given short shift here. Zinn[19] lists over twenty author-languages being used in CAI systems. Of these, all but the machine language programs fall into essentially three categories: (1)

CAI author-languages; (2) compiler languages; and (3) interactive computing and display languages. The first category represents those languages that are usually identified with most CAI systems (coursewriter, dialog, planet) and are designed to facilitate the construction of linear sequences of instructional materials and the control and sequencing of instructional items for the student. The prime limitation of most of these languages are that they do not permit genuine interaction with the computer to solve problems. This capability for interactive computing and retrieval or to retrieve data is a prime prerequisite for the kind of computer aided learning which has been defined throughout this paper as the only form of CAI worth its educational salt. CAI languages are designed to perpetuate the standard classroom procedures of student monitoring, teacher directivity, passive learning, and frequent testing. Conventional compilers and interactive computer languages on the other hand permit great flexibility in problem solving behavior, allow the learner to monitor his own program, and most importantly, make it possible for him to interact with the computer as a computing machine and as a rapid data retriever and symbol manipulator. In other words, the computer in the hands of the user who is conversant with the general purpose or even special purpose compiler languages, can use this most powerful of intellectual aids in a manner entirely appropriate to its limitations and its unique capabilities.

Summary

If a search were launched for the ideal interactive computer system applied to on-going learning activities, Kiewit Computation Center at Dartmouth would be well up in the running. As described by Tom Kurtz, Director of the Center,[20] the use of the computer in secondary and even elementary education follows the earlier pattern set at Dartmouth. After a relatively short indoctrination course in which the students learn BASIC, a simple compiler language, students as far down as the seventh grade level use the time-shared system in almost all their science and math courses. In some eighteen private and secondary schools the full-time availability of time-shared computing enhances most of the student's formal course work, even without major curriculum changes. Reportedly on the Dartmouth campus itself, the ability to have access to an interactive computer system has brought about radical changes virtually in all courses that deal with quantitative data. In the sciences, in the study of social data and courses in design engineering, business school, and the physical sciences, both students and faculty learn to use the computer as a matter of course.

The only problem today is that this kind of interactive system application is being overshadowed in many ways by conventional forms of programmed CAI. It is probably true that CAI applications are more easily understood because they don't require any sophistication in mathematical processes, but because the educators lack the facility to learn anew, it doesn't mean that student can't be more flexible.

In the design of hardware systems for CAI, there has been much discussion of multiple media capacities of the terminal devices. We have seen that for some course work a graphic of CRT display is almost essential. But if a priority were to be established on the design of hardware systems for a large number of schools, those that permitted genuine interactive or problem solving usages through inexpensive or economical ties to a few central computer systems would have to receive prime funding.

Appendix

Reduction of Teacher's Bookkeeping Tasks

It has been pointed out that the teacher spends a third of his time in the classroom not teaching. He acts as host, clerk, librarian, counselor, housekeeper, policeman, data processor, and test grader and analyzer. Such time-consuming paperwork can be automated: a few school districts and two research centers are exploring the automation of various aspects. In Bellingham, Washington, for example, teachers report attendance by using a data-phone. The automated classroom at the System Development Corporation makes it possible for the instructor to collect test data automatically by means of the individual keyboard units at each student's desk, which are used to answer study questions and test items, or the use of an optical scanner which reads both typed and handwritten data. Scores are fed back to the teacher with both group and individual analysis handled by a time-shared digital computer. This feedback is received through a print-out device connected to the computer or through a TV display in the classroom. Even the student in his individual study carrel or working at a computer-based typewriter station can get immediate feedback on his test scores as well as appropriate normative data showing how he relates to students of similar ability and placement in the program.

Unquestionably, one of the most time-consuming activities of teachers in secondary schools is that of grading written compositions. The instructor faced with a typical student load of 130 to 150 students, producing essays once a week, has time to do little more than scan a paper, assign a grade, and write an innocuous comment in the margin. A computer at the University of Connecticut has been programmed with the data required for the grading of content errors, leaving the teacher free to study the creative aspect of the essay. By researching the kind of information which can be automatically gleaned from written essays—errors in spelling and punctuation solecisms, distinctive vocabulary, style, et cetera—combinations of data have been sought which have high correlation with the evaluation of competent human judges. Researchers on Project Essay Grade report to date that when the computer is used to make evaluations of essays on the basis of quantitative elements, a correlation with human judging can be achieved at a level significantly higher than that which could occur by chance. Investigators are currently working on the problem of machine response to what the student is writing about and his scheme of organization. A computer-stored thesaurus is used to make comparisons with the student's selection of words and phrases. For determination of a student's mode of organization, the detection of such key words as "first, then, at that point, finally" helps suggest chronological organization. Words such as "consequently, therefore, inevitably, result" could indicate preoccupation with cause and effect. Such lists are currently being used to confirm grading through application to student's essays which have already been judged by skilled graders.

Physical and Psychological Needs of Students in the Educational Facility

New computer-based simulation techniques should be of vital interest to those planning the educational facility.

At Indiana University, Purdue University, and at the St. Louis Junior College District, simulation techniques are being used to forecast future building and staff requirements under varying academic conditions. Scheduling, staff, and space are interrelated, for the manner in which the schedule is constructed determines, in part, the need for classrooms and laboratories. The development of a computer operated program or model at Purdue demonstrates the ease and simplicity with which the computer can facilitate the making of repeated calculations, summarizations, and reports of facility requirements by years (or terms) for varying programs, course requirements, student enrollments, and types of facilities.

Facility planning conventionally places greater emphasis upon the physical functions of a school building and the physical requirements of its users than upon the users' psychological needs. In a meaningful educational program, the student must develop certain social skills, acquire favorable attitudes toward learning and must be able to experience the integration of a wide range of learning activities. A student's success in these areas depends to a large extent upon his relations to other students, to teachers, and to the physical plant itself. The psychological needs of the student can best be met when requirements are taken into account from the beginning in the design of schools.

Informal learning experiences can help reinforce the skills and attitudes mentioned above. Such informal activities as brief conversations between teachers and students in the hallways, perusal of an exhibit or bulletin board, a casual review of games or plays in rehearsal have been identified and built into computer models to insure that architectural design will help to promote the satisfaction of cognitive and psychological needs. At George Washington University the psychology of architecture is becoming a new subdiscipline in the planning of educational and industrial facilities. A primary concern is with the "mix" of people that can be produced by planning a variety of informal learning situations, and "nodes" (small areas where two or three people may meet), and "zones" (large areas or territories in which people congregate). The use of a computer is making it easier for the architect to consider the mix, routes, nodes and zones that will support the informal learning experiences. While it is clear that a relationship exists between architecture and psychological dispositions, the nature of a relationship and its effect upon learning is obscure. A study in terms appropriate to both architecture and the social sciences is needed. The computer might be employed for simulation and exploration of relevant variables so that the design of the educational facility will augment the effectiveness of its formalized program.

Scheduling the Non-Graded Continuous Progress School Program

Given the premise that students in the educational facility will no longer be herded in permanent packages of twenty to thirty, but will instead move back and forth within a fluid, larger setting that allows for independent study, small group work of many types, and various larger class activities, the administration will be hard pressed to keep track of each youngster's progress, and at the same time to organize the overall program around topics or themes with relevance for everyone. Flexible scheduling techniques offer the solution to this problem. It is widely held among educators that the flexible schedule increases the possibilities of innovation many-fold and, of course, scheduling involves a great many parameters whose experimental manipulation is indispensable to the development of educational methodology.

Among possible scheduling variations are: even period exchange, period augmentation, sequence rotation, compressed or expanded rotation, variable period length, and combinations of these. Grouping practices may involve size of group, grouping for ability, and grouping for motivation. Sections may be scheduled horizontally or vertically. Subjects may be integrated in various patterns. When carrying scheduling to the ultimate degree, each individual may have a unique schedule and, moreover, his schedule may respond to his progress, so that it is not only unique but variable.

Every element in the dynamic system of the school is affected by any change in any of these parameters. With full computer support, the school can engage in wholly new approaches with little drudgery and waste of resources.

The last three years have seen widespread tests of two families of computer programs for building master schedules: Robert Holz's General Academic Simulation Programs (GASP), first developed to schedule the Massachusetts Institute of Technology, and the Stanford School Scheduling System (SSSS or S⁴) devised by Robert Oakland and others at Stanford University's School of Education. The two approaches that led to GASP and SSSS may be distinguished as heuristic versus algorithmic, or pragmatic versus theoretical. These distinctions are somewhat artificial and inaccurate, but they reflect the fact that GASP involves producing twenty to thirty successive master schedules, each improved by human judgments of the previous schedule; while SSSS generates schedules from a more complete set of mathematical proposition concerning the nature of the scheduling problem and requires only a few repetitions to achieve its final solution.

Advantages and disadvantages exist on both sides in the present state of the art, though further development will undoubtedly reduce them to the vanishing point. It appears that the heuristic and algorithmic approaches will gradually converge, so that the former becomes more elegant, more related to theory and less costly, while the latter becomes more articulated, more flexible and more responsive to hard realities. The non-graded program of the educational facility may be the ultimate test.

Simulation and Gaming:
New Tools for the Disadvantaged Learner

Simulation and gaming are evolving computer applications which can provide particularly relevant instructional approaches to disenchanted youth. The greatest problem with these students is motivation; they are discouraged or hostile, or they just do not see the immediate relevancy of public school education to the lives they expect to lead. Nevertheless, these young people have motives. They like the approval of their peers, they like to compete in situations where they can win, they like to succeed. They like to talk about and participate in things that seem relevant to their own lives. They like to be in a situation where discipline does not seem to come from outside or from older authorities or from members of social groups of whom they are suspicious.

In connection with this type of student, games offer the following benefits:

(1) They can include competition among teams or between individual player and computer to any desired degree, a condition that tends to increase interest to the point of enthusiasm.

(2) They are student-centered and do not involve direction by an authority figure who might be resented.

(3) The teacher acts as an ally of the student, helping him to play the game so as to have the best chance of winning, just as a football coach is primarily an aide to winning the game and secondarily an instructor.

(4) Approval is largely or wholly from teammates, who are peers.

(5) Discipline does not need to be enforced from outside in gaming situations. Discipline is self-imposed by having to play by the rules and the necessity for team cooperation.

(6) If appropriate, real rewards, such as money, may be given for success in playing.

(7) The games may present any problem area, from those of strictly intellectual or mechanical content to those involving inter-personal relations. A game called the Family Game has a great deal in common with family counselling,

and could have a therapeutic effect on students whose family relationships are disturbed to some degree, as indeed many may be expected to be.

(8) A great deal of factual knowledge can be learned while playing the game, as well as from the requirement to marshall one's facts before entering the fray.

The Sumerian Economic Game has been developed at the Board of Cooperative Educational Services in Yorktown, New York. A set of programs have been written to permit a student to experience directly the basic principles of primitive agrarian economy. An IBM 1050/7090 computer system simulates selected elements of the economic functioning of a Sumerian city/state of 3500 B.C.

Each student takes the role of the king of ancient Sumer. Through interaction with the typewriter computer system, he begins playing the game. The following print-out is a typical portion of the simulated game showing the typewriter print-outs and the student's responses:

Imagine that you have just been made King of Lagash, a city/state of Sumer in our year 3500 B.C. Twice yearly your royal steward will report to you the economic condition of the kingdom. Guided by these reports, you will decide the use of your resources (symbolized by grain), trying to keep your population stable and well fed.

Initial economic report made to you, the new King of Lagash, by humble steward:

Total population:	500
Net harvest, bushels:	5,000
Total farm land, acres:	2,000
Land now under cultivation, acres:	500

You must now decide how to use your resources.

How many bushels of new grain do you want placed in storage?

STUDENT RESPONSE: 100

The quantity of food the people received last season was satisfactory.

Expected gross harvest (based on planting):	7,920
Disaster crop losses this season:	
Net harvest, bushels:	7,920
Initial inventory:	100
Removed from inventory:	−100
Loss by spoilage:	none
Disaster inventory losses this season:	1,000
Final inventory:	1,000

You must now decide how to use your resources.

In the storehouse there are 1,000 bushels of grain one period old. How many bushels of this grain do you want taken out?

STUDENT RESPONSE: 1,000

How many bushels of new grain do you want placed in storage?

STUDENT RESPONSE: 3

Entry error. Please review instructions and try again.

STUDENT RESPONSE: 2,500

In the Career Game, now being prepared for computer mediation and developed in the Department of Social Relations at John Hopkins University, teams of girls are given information about a fictitious but realistic girl of seventeen. The players must decide what her life goals shall be, indicating the relative importance to her of marriage, children, an occupation, personal development, and the family standard of living. They then must decide about specific opportunities to fulfill these goals: when and whom to marry, how soon to have a child, how many children, whether to get a job, what kind of job to try for, whether to get additional education, and so on. In making these decisions, the players get help from various resources, ranging from a table showing them how much time certain activities take to extensive information about training requirements, competition, and recompense for various occupations.

After each set of decisions, the players get back results indicating how well the woman is doing at achieving her goals and introducing certain events (whose occurrence is based on statistical tables), such as the birth of a child or success or failure at getting a certain job. A game may include ten decision periods, which take the woman to age fifty.

Games developed at John Hopkins University, Western Behavioral Science Institute, Brooks Foundation, and the IBM Corporation, run the gamut from democracy games— legislative, designed to show the dependence of a legislator's re-election upon his ability to satisfy the desires of his constituents—a family game, and games to impart specifics of scientific subject matter.

REFERENCES

1. Dan Pinck. As quoted in *The Village Voice,* Nat Hentoffs' column. December 28, 1968.

2. Louis Hausman. "The ABC's of CAI." *American Education.* U.S. Printing Office, Catalog Number FS 5.210:10050. November, 1967.

3. *Notes and Working Papers Concerning the Administration of Programs Authorized Under Title III, ESEA 1965.* Prepared for the Subcommittee on Education of the Committee on Labor and Public Welfare/United States Senate. U.S. Government Printing Office. April, 1967.

   Datamation. September, 1968, Volume 14, Number 9.

   PACE: Catalyst for Change. Report Number 6 of the Second National Study of PACE. November 29, 1968.

   C. A. Riedesel and M. N. Suydam. "Computer-Assisted Instruction: Implications for Teacher Education." *The Arithmetic Teacher.* January, 1967, Volume 14, Number 1, pages 24–29.

4. R. E. Horn. "What Programming Errors Can Be Discovered by Student Testing?" *Programmed Instruction.* 1964, 4 (2).

5. Anthony Schillaci. "The Now Movie." *Saturday Review.* December 28, 1968.

6. Marshall McLuhan. *Understanding Media.*

7. E. N. Adams. In *Proceedings of the First Annual ARISTOTLE Symposium.* December 6 and 7, 1967, Washington, D.C. National Security Industrial Association, 1968.

8. James L. Rogers. "Current Problems in CAI." *Datamation.* September, 1968, Volume 14, Number 9, pages 28–33.

9. International Business Machines Processing Division *press release.* March 31, 1966, page 2.

10. Brooks Foundation. *The Computer and Educational Progress in the School District of Philadelphia.* 1967.

11. E. N. Adams. In *Proceedings of the First Annual ARISTOTLE Symposium.* December 6 and 7, 1967, Washington, D.C. National Security Industrial Association, 1968.

12. Don D. Bushnell. *The Computer as an Instructional Tool: A Summary.* System Development Corporation, SP-1554. February 13, 1964.

13. I. A. Richards. In *The Computer in American Education,* (Don D. Bushnell and Dwight Allen, Editors). John Wiley and Sons, 1967, pages xvii–xxvii.

14. Richard de Mille. *In Notes and Working Papers Concerning the Administration of Programs Authorized Under Title III, ESEA, 1965.* Prepared for the Subcommittee on Education of the Committee on Labor and Public Welfare/United States Senate. U.S. Government Printing Office. April, 1967, pages 356–359.

15. Brooks Foundation (under U.S. Office of Education contract). *The Validation of Educational Systems Packages for Occupational Training of Depressed Area Students.*

16. David Stansfield. "The Computer and Education." *Educational Technology.* May 30, 1968, Volume 8, Number 10, pages 3–8.

17. Karl L. Zinn. "Instructional Uses of Interactive Computer Systems." *Datamation.* September, 1968, Volume 14, Number 9, pages 22–27.

18. James L. Rogers. "Current Problems in CAI." *Datamation.* September, 1968, Volume 14, Number 9, pages 28–33.

19. Karl L. Zinn. "Instructional Uses of Interactive Computer Systems." *Datamation.* September, 1968, Volume 14, Number 9, pages 22–27.

20. Thomas E. Kurtz. "The T-Computer: Its Role in Education." In *Proceedings of the First Annual ARISTOTLE Symposium.* December 6 and 7, 1968, Washington, D.C. National Security Industrial Association, 1968.

4.

Learning from Television: What the Research Says

by GODWIN G. CHU and WILBUR SCHRAMM

Director
Institute for Communication Research
Stanford Univ.

Assoc. Prof.
Sociology
Univ. of Canada

Summary of Major Observations from the Report

The report, "Learning from Television: What the Research Says," is the result of a study conducted in 1967 by the Institute for Communication Research, Stanford University, for the U. S. Office of Education under contract number 2 EFC 708 94. Only the summary of major observations from the report is included in this volume inasmuch as space limitations prevented the reprinting of the entire 213-page document.

Outline Summary

I.   Do pupils learn from television?

    1.   Given favorable conditions, children learn efficiently from instructional television.
    2.   By and large, instructional television can more easily be used effectively for primary and secondary school students than for college students.
    3.   So far as we can tell from present evidence, television can be used efficiently to teach any subject matter where one-way communication will contribute to learning.

II.   What have we learned about the efficient use of instructional television in a school system?

    4.   Television is most effective as a tool for learning when used in a suitable context of learning activities at the receiving end.
    5.   Television is more likely to be an efficient part of an educational system when it is applied to an educational problem of sufficient magnitude to call forth broad support.
    6.   Television is more likely to be an efficient tool of learning if it is planned and organized efficiently.

III.   What have we learned about the treatment, situation, and pupil variables?

    7.   There is no evidence to suggest that either visual magnification or large-size screen will improve learning from television in general.

8. There is insufficient evidence to suggest that color will improve learning from film or television.

9. Where learning of perceptual-motor skills is required, a subjective angle presentation on television will tend to be more effective than an objective angle presentation.

10. There is no clear evidence on the kind of variations in production techniques that significantly contribute to learning from instructional television. However, students will learn better when the visuals are presented in a continuous order and carefully planned both by the television team and the studio teacher.

11. Attention-gaining cues that are irrelevant to the subject matter will most probably have a negative effect on learning from instructional television.

12. There is no consistent evidence to suggest that either humor or animation significantly contributes to learning from instructional television.

13. Subtitles tend to improve learning from instructional television, particularly when the original program is not well organized.

14. There is insufficient evidence to suggest that dramatic presentation will result in more learning than will expository presentation in instructional television.

15. Inserting questions in a television program does not seem to improve learning, but giving the students a rest pause does.

16. Whether a television program is used to begin or to end a daily lesson by the classroom teacher makes no difference in learning.

17. Repeated showings of a television program will result in more learning, up to a point. But a teacher-directed follow-up, where available, is more effective than a second showing of the same program.

18. If saving time is important, a television program can probably be shortened and still achieve the minimum requirement of teaching.

19. There is no clear evidence to suggest whether eye-contact in television instruction will affect the amount of learning.

20. Problem-solving instruction on television is more effective than lecturing where the materials taught involve the solving of a problem.

21. The students are likely to acquire the same amount of learning from instructional television whether the materials are presented as a lecture, or in an interview, or in a panel discussion.

22. Where accurate perception of images is an important part of learning, wide viewing angle and long distance will interfere with learning from instructional television.

23. Adequate attention provided by the classroom teacher will, in most cases at least, remedy the adverse effect due to a wide viewing angle.

24. Noise will reduce the effectiveness of learning from film and television so far as part of the learning comes from the auditory medium.

25. Instructional television appears to be equally effective with small and large viewing groups.

26. Instructional television may or may not be more effective with homogeneously grouped students, depending on other factors in the learning situation.

27. Whether instructional television can teach students who view at home as effectively as students in the classroom seems to depend on other conditions.

28. At the college level, permissive attendance does not seem, by itself, to reduce the effectiveness of instructional television.

29. Students will learn more from instructional television under motivated conditions than under unmotivated conditions.

30. Learning from television by the students does not seem necessarily to be handicapped by the lack of prompt feedback to the instructor.

31. Showing, testing, revising an instructional television program will help substitute

for lack of live feedback to the teacher and make for more learning by the students.

32. The lack of opportunity for students to raise questions and participate in free discussion would seem to reduce the effectiveness of learning from instructional television, particularly if the students are fairly advanced or the material is relatively complicated.

33. If a student being taught by instructional television can be given immediate knowledge of whether he has responded correctly, he will learn more.

34. Students taught by television tend to miss the personal teacher-student contact, but there is insufficient evidence to suggest that the lack of such contact will impair learning from instructional television.

35. Practice, whether by overt or covert response, will improve learning from instructional television if the practice is appropriate to the learning task, and if the practice does not constitute an interference.

36. Note-taking while viewing instructional television is likely to interfere with learning if time for it is not provided in the telecast.

IV. Attitudes toward instructional television.

37. Teachers and pupils are more favorable toward the use of instructional television in elementary school than in secondary school and college.

38. Administrators are more likely to be favorable toward instructional television than are teachers.

39. Voluntary home students of televised college classes tend to be more favorable toward learning by television than are the students who take these same televised courses in the classroom.

40. At the college level, students tend to prefer small discussion classes to television classes, television classes to large lecture classes.

41. There is evidence of a Hawthorne effect among students beginning to use instructional television, but no firm evidence that attitudes toward the medium necessarily improve or worsen with time.

42. Favorable attitudes are distributed widely enough among different televised courses to cast doubt on the assumption that some academic subjects, per se, may be disliked as material for instructional television.

43. Liking instructional television is not always correlated with learning from it.

44. Among the factors that determine teachers' attitudes toward instructional television are (a) how they perceive the degree of threat to the classroom; (b) how they estimate the likelihood of mechanized instruction replacing direct contact with students; (c) how they estimate the effectiveness of instructional television; (d) the difficulties they see in the way of using modern techniques; (e) how conservative they are, and whether they trust or distrust experimentation.

45. Among the factors that determine pupils' attitudes toward instructional television are (a) how much contact they think they will have with a teacher; (b) how they compare the relative abilities of the studio and classroom teachers; (c) whether they find instructional television boring or interesting; (d) the nature of the televised programs they have seen; (e) the conditions of viewing.

V. Learning from television in developing regions.

46. There is no evidence to lead us to believe that children learn any less efficiently from television in developing countries than elsewhere.

47. Under suitable conditions, television has been shown to be capable of highly motivating learning in developing regions.

48. Illiterate people need to learn certain pictorial conventions. There is some evidence suggesting that these conventions are not hard to learn.
49. When media are introduced for upgrading the level of instruction, then it has proved very important to train teachers in their proper use and to keep in close touch with them.
50. Resistance to television and other media is likely to be no less in developing countries, but the size and urgency of the problems are likely to provide greater incentive for overcoming it.
51. Feedback from the classroom teacher to the studio teacher will be helpful to effective use of the media.
52. There is ample evidence that the new media, particularly television, are effective for in-service training of teachers for developing regions.

VI. Learning from television: Learning from other media.

53. Given favorable conditions, pupils can learn from any instructional media that are now available.
54. There appears to be little if any difference between learning from television and learning from film, if the two media are used the same way.
55. Television and radio have certain advantages over films in flexibility and deliverability.
56. Radio is less expensive than television; economy of scale usually governs cost comparisons of television and film.
57. More complete control of film by the classroom teacher gives it a potential advantage over television.
58. The use of visual images will improve learning of manual tasks, as well as other learning where visual images can facilitate the association process. Otherwise, visual images may cause distraction and interfere with learning.
59. There is some evidence to suggest that moving visual images will improve learning if the continuity of action is an essential part of the learning task.
60. Student response is effectively controlled by programmed methods, regardless of the instructional medium.

5.

The Role of Modern Technology in Relation to Simulation and Games for Learning

by JAMES S. COLEMAN
Professor of Social Relations
Johns Hopkins University

The use of simulation and games for learning at all levels of school has grown rapidly in only a few years. Yet there is a lack of clarity about what such activities are intended to do, about how they are best used, and even about what precisely they are. I will provide some answers to each of these questions, beginning with the last.

Simulation

Simulation and games are related but not identical activities. Both simulations that are not games and games that are not simulations are used for instructional purposes, along with simulation games. A simulation activity, as the term is used in instruction, is a re-creation of some aspect of reality in which students participate as part of the simulation of reality. Simulations differ from laboratory work in physics, chemistry, or other sciences in that the system of activities about which students learn involves them directly as participants, and not as external scientific observers.

Simulations ordinarily involve interaction between different individuals in various roles, but they need not do so. For example, simulated flight in a Link Trainer, or simulated driving in a driver-training simulator involves only the activities of the single student in a mechanically simulated environment. Or a simulation that is widely used for management training, known as the "in-basket" simulation, involves only a single participant in a simulated environment consisting of letters to answer. He has just taken over a new managerial job, and must answer the letters, involving minor and major problems, left by his predecessor. And there are computer simulations such as the "Sumerian game," a simple simulation of economic resource allocation, in which the computer provides information constituting the environment being simulated, and a single individual interacts with this environment by making decisions and transmitting these to the computer.

Single-person simulations, as in the examples given above, are not typical. Most simulations involve a number of persons in roles that require their interaction. Simulation as a learning activity has some of the aspects of the theater, and some aspects of role-playing. It ordinarily involves a setting in which the participants have specified roles; but it differs from the theater in that the actions are spontaneous rather than pre-determined, and it differs from role-playing in that although the actions are spontaneous, the rules under which action takes place are more fully specified than in role-playing.

A simulation always involves a *simulated environment* within which each player acts. Sometimes this environment consists wholly of the other players and the rules of the game; sometimes it is incorporated in a computer or other electronic device, or in written materials, as in the examples above. A simulation also involves rules of action, which specify the kinds of action which each player may carry out. Finally it includes a specification of what the *goals* of each player are, either in very specific terms or in general terms.

It is the last point that differentiates simulations that are games from simulations that are not. The most useful distinction between game-simulations and non-game simulations is in the specification of what constitutes success. In a game, success is well-defined, and there are one or more winners to the game. In a non-game simulation, at the end of the exercise, each participant is in a given position or condition, but there is no explicit comparison of these to determine winners.

Some simulations, in which participants have a single score at the end of the exercise, may be played either as a game or as a non-game simulation. For example, in the Life-Career game, a player at the end of the game has a score, which can be compared to that of other players, or can merely be regarded as his final position, if he is playing alone. Some simulations, however, such as a number of simulations of international relations, or the in-basket simulation described earlier, have no final score at all, and the simulation is regarded as an exercise, in which the relative quality of play by different participants is only loosely evaluated, or perhaps is scored as an exercise by an external evaluator, but is not intrinsically structured as a contest.

This discussion of simulation suggests that simulations are directly analogous in the social and behavioral sciences to laboratory work in the natural sciences. In both cases, the simulation or laboratory involves actually setting up a system of behavior, in contrast to having it described in print or in films or through some other medium of information transmission. The critical difference between the laboratory and the simulation is the role of the student relative to the system of behavior he is studying. In the natural sciences, he must be an external observer and experimenter with regard to the physical, chemical, or biological system of behavior he is studying. In the social and behavioral sciences, the systems of action he studies involve individuals like himself in various institutional settings. Through simulations, he studies this system of action through his own participation in it.*

Games

Games as used in schools include simulation games, but are not limited to them. Some of the most widely used of the new educational games are games of logic, or mathematical games, such as Wff-n-Proof and Equations. Other games, in the social sciences as well as in humanities, mathematics, and the physical sciences, are modifications of drills so as to make a game out of the drill. The classic learning game in American schools is a drill game, the spelling bee.

Despite the fact that games are much broader than simulation games, the essential characteristics of a game have some similarity to the characteristics of a simulation. A game first of all involves *action* on the part of the student, like simulations but unlike many instruc-

---

*It is possible in the social sciences for non-simulation activities to be carried out in which the student is an observer or experimenter, and which directly parallel laboratory work in natural sciences. A neighborhood survey involving interviews is such a laboratory activity, as is the use of census materials for statistical analysis. The curriculum under construction by the American Sociological Association under the title of Sociological Resources for Secondary Schools consists of a set of laboratory activities of this type.

tional techniques. It has goals for the players, which define the winning of a game. Finally, it has *rules of action,* which both determine sequence of activities and fix constraints upon the actions of each player, defining what is legitimate action within the rules, and what is not. Unlike a simulation that is not a game, and unlike most other instructional techniques, games are self-initiating and self-sustaining. The enjoyment an individual experiences from a game is such that he will play it quite independently of any desire to learn. The learning occurs as a by-product of the game-playing activity, and need not be a goal at all. An individual does not play chess *in order to learn* something; he learns to play chess *in order to play* the game. The interest is in playing the game, and possibly in winning, not in learning.

These characteristics of a game give it great similarity to the characteristics of social life generally. There has, in fact, been speculation by philosophers concerning the similarities and differences between life and a game, as well as work by psychiatrists describing many activities of life in interpersonal situations as games. It is natural, then, that many simulations, designed to mirror some aspect of social life, are cast as games.

Purely for purposes of definition, then, simulations and games may be defined by these characteristics.

	simulation	game
active participation	X	X
rules governing play	X (loose or precise)	X (precise)
goals of players given	X (loose or precise)	X (precise)
definition of winning and losing		X
abstraction from life activities	X	

Those activities that have both the properties of a game and the properties of a simulation may be termed simulation games.

Assumptions About Learning in the Use of Simulations and Games

The use of simulations and games implies some general perspectives about how people learn. Certain of these perspectives are common to both games and simulations, and some are specific to one or the other. Both share the perspective that learning occurs best by active participation of the learner. The implication is that people learn not by being taught, but by acting, and then learning from the consequences of that action. The further implication of this is quite strong: that variations in learning are less dependent on variations in the quality of the teacher than upon the way in which the activity of learning is structured, in particular upon the kinds of actions the learners take and the kinds of feedback they get from these actions.

Both games and simulations imply a sequence of learning in which conceptual learning, or understanding, follows ability to perform rather than preceding it. Much school activity uses the reverse sequence: conceptual learning, which occurs mostly through transmission of information from teacher or books, is attempted first, and performance is seen to derive from that understanding. In a simulation or a game, a student may learn to perform very well in a given decision-making capacity, yet not be able to verbalize what elements go into his action. In learning the same material from books, a student may be able to describe what elements should go into a given decision, but not be able to make such a decision correctly.

Games and simulations as learning environments also imply that for a person to learn principally through another person in the role of "teacher" may induce severe distortions of the learning process, particularly in a classroom with other children. The teacher has a certain relation to the class as a whole, and to individual children in that class. Each child has a relation to the class as a whole and to the teacher. Depending on these relations, certain children may be particularly induced to learn wholly because of the interpersonal relations while the learning of others may be inhibited for interpersonal reasons. From the perspective of games, one may regard the classroom situation as a multi-person game among the teacher and various groups of students and individual students, a game in which success for some players may not involve learning at all, or may even be facilitated by rejection of learning. The use of games and simulations constructed for the purpose of learning assumes that it is better to establish explicit role relations such that performance in the role requires learning.

Besides the content that may be learned from participation in a game or simulation, exponents of game-learning argue that a certain principle or attitude or belief is learned as well. The principal or attitude or belief may be described as a belief in the predictability and responsiveness of one's environment, a belief that arises by learning through the responses of an environment. This belief in "control of environment" or "efficacy" or "responsiveness of environment" has been found to be highly related to measures of ability and school achievement. The use of games or simulations is designed to strengthen such beliefs, through the very mode by which learning occurs: his action and the contingent response of those in his environment. The aim is for learning to occur through the construction of simulated environments or game structures that are in fact responsive to his actions, with his success contingent upon his actions.

The use of simulations for learning involves specific assumptions about the kinds of things it is necessary to learn in social studies, and how they may best be learned. The general thesis is that the adult world will involve types of interactions and activities much more complex than those he presently faces, and he can best learn about these through simulating the activities before he confronts the real ones. In particular, the adult world is far more role-segmented than a child's or adolescent's world, and is much more impersonal, involving a higher proportion of interactions with institutions and organizations than he ever confronts as a child or adolescent. Through simulations, the child or adolescent experiences these complexities in trial form before confronting them in real life, and thereby is better prepared to cope with them in real life.

In addition, simulations often place an individual in a role he will never inhabit in real life: a role in a simulation of an historical episode, or a role as a Congressman or labor negotiator or business owner. The thesis behind such simulations is that they allow the child, and subsequently the adult, to understand the functioning of aspects of society from a perspective other than his own, to comprehend what he would otherwise see as inexplicable actions on the part of persons far distant from him.

Thus simulations are designed to provide a means for exploring the complexities of society in relative security, small segments at a time, as a means of improving one's subsequent performance in it and understanding of it. Simulations are designed to extend the natural mode of learning by experience, which is the principal way one learns outside school, beyond the direct experiences the child, or even the adult, is likely to have. They represent a natural extension of Dewey's ideas about learning in close conjunction with the community and with life. They differ from Dewey's ideas in that Dewey's conception of the community was a close interpersonal environment. Social simulations as currently being developed and used are based upon a conception of society as composed of complex institutions, and of life as including activity in the framework of such institutions, and including interactions with impersonal organizations as well as persons.

In addition to the common learning assumptions of games and simulations, a principle underlies the use of games, somewhat as follows: learning is appropriately a by-product of activity directed to another goal. One is seldom motivated to learn merely for learning's sake alone, nor is there any reason to be. Outside school, in natural learning environments, one learns because he wants to succeed or accomplish some action in that environment. In the artificial learning situation of the school, he learns in order to get good grades, to please his parents, and to escape failure in school. In games and simulations, he learns, much as in the natural learning environment, in order to succeed at his goal in the simulation or the game, a goal that is more intrinsically connected to the learning than are the grades which are often his goal in school.

With this general orientation, the usual question about "motivation to learn" is inappropriate. Motivation to learn is intrinsic, deriving from motivation to succeed in the game. The only problem of learning is a problem of facilitating or aiding the players to learn that for which the game structure itself, substituting for the real life structure in natural learning environments, motivates them.

If this general aim is to be realized, it is evident that those things it is desired to learn must be necessary to the play of the game. Since the principal aim of a player is success in the game, then the player will bypass or neglect those matters that in a more exploratory mood he might have stopped to examine. It may well be that the play of the game will increase his general level of interest in those matters on which the game focuses, leading him to subsequently explore them (as, for example, the game of baseball develops among former players an intense interest in a variety of ancillary details, statistics, and rituals). But this extension of interest and learning is a secondary effect rather than a necessary consequence of play.

Questions and Problems in the Use of Games and Simulations in Learning

The preceding section indicated the general assumptions behind the use of games and simulations for learning, but it said nothing about the unresolved questions and problems involved in their use.

What do games and simulations actually teach? The simple answer to the question of what games and simulations that have been designed for learning actually teach is that the evidence is very unclear. There are a few examples of quite spectacular gains from the use of non-simulation games and drill games. Also, there have been comments by observers describing spectacular changes in interest levels in the use of simulation games, as in the following extract from a letter written by a teacher in an Indian school.

> Thank you for forwarding your games; Game of Democracy and Life Careers. You requested that we report how the games worked in the Sioux culture.

> The results were astounding. Boys who had dropped out of high school the year before patiently went through the long explanation of how to play and then threw themselves into the game. One even asked if he could stay after school to continue the game (even though this same day he had earlier spoken about dropping out of school). Kids who I had never observed smiling suddenly lit up as they bargained with their classmates.

Apart from such testimonials, and the enthusiasm of game designers, quantitative evidence of *information learned* shows some learning in some experiments, but far from universal and instant success. The near-universal success has rather been in *motivation* and general enthusiasm of students and teachers, as exemplified by the above quotation.

There is a serious problem in testing the effectiveness of games and simulations as learning environments, due to one fact: as described earlier, games and simulations attempt to induce performance learning as distinct from conceptual learning. Yet most testing in schools (except in mathematics, where testing ordinarily involves problem-solving), is testing of conceptual learning, as exhibited by the ability to answer specific questions. Such tests are not necessarily good measures of performance learning, though they are good tests of the conceptual learning that occurs with most instructional methods in schools.

Most of the testing of effectiveness of games and simulations for learning has attempted to make use of paper and pencil tests of conceptual learning or knowledge. In doing this, a number of problems have arisen. First, as is true in social studies generally, there has been lack of clarity about what the game or simulation is designed to teach. Secondly, it is unclear how to translate the performance learning aims of games and simulations to conceptual learning tests. For example, in a consumer economics game, the aim is to improve the player's ability to use credit wisely. But the test that would ordinarily be used is a test of knowledge about use of credit. Obviously, if this knowledge is taught directly, through traditional methods, and students are sufficiently motivated to absorb the information presented, the traditional methods will be more efficient in transmitting the knowledge required to answer the test questions. What is required for testing is a simulation itself, which requires performance in a problem-solving situation.

The question of whether games and simulations teach *values* or *facts* depends very much on how the game or simulation is constructed. In every game or simulation, the rules define the structure of relations, and in some cases they also define the returns contingent on particular actions. Values of the game designer may very well be reflected in these rules, and the game or simulation thus teach the values of the designer. While some arbitrary decisions in scoring must in any case be made, the arbitrariness is greatly reduced if the designer has carried out careful research on the constraints inherent in each role being simulated.

A few simulations in which this has not been done appear designed principally to demonstrate who are the "good guys" and who are the "bad guys." In addition, some simulations with very little structure beyond the definition of particular roles may simply constitute a framework for the participants to act out their own values. These simulations appear to be of little aid in teaching, for rather than giving the participants a *new* perspective on reality, they merely reinforce the participants' existing perspectives. They appear to destroy one of the principal virtues of games and simulation, which is to show that simple judgments which divide reality into "good guys" and "bad guys" are often mistaken. In fact, it may be that one of the rough indicators of a good game or simulation in social science is that insofar as it does affect values, it reduces value consensus among the set of players rather than increases it, strengthening minority positions within the set of players relative to those held by the majority, through the diversity of perspectives it generates.

There are several criteria for helping to insure that a game or simulation does not simply teach the designer's values. One is that the rules and other conditions confronting each player should *not* include anything about the personality of the player, but only the conditions, internal and external, that confront him as an actor. The player must be free to choose his own course of action within the set of constraints imposed by the game. The rules of the game tell him what his interests as a player are, and what he cannot do, but he himself determines how to act in pursuit of those interests. If the constraints themselves are grossly biased and are a caricature of reality, this is often evident simply from a reading of the rules.

A second and related criterion which the game designer himself can apply, is that each role be treated "from the inside," so to speak, that is, sympathetically. It is much as in the design of a novel or a play: each character in a good novel should be motivated, not merely a stooge to serve the author's purposes.*

Several points concerning what games and simulations teach have become clear in their use to date. These are:

1. Games and simulations elicit far more involvement and effort, over extended periods of time, than do most other modes of learning. The increase in effort appears not to be merely a Hawthorne or novelty effect, but to inhere in the competition to succeed or to improve one's relative position—the same motivation that leads people to play games on their own for no purpose other than pleasure.

2. Games and simulations constitute especially intensive experiences compared to most school activities. Players who have played a learning game or simulation often remember it much later, after most other school activities are forgotten. This intensity may be a consequence of the interpersonal involvement which arises in play, but it also may result from the intensity of concentration and attention focus that occurs during play. The latter is suggested by the fact that hard-fought play of games like chess, in which unstructured interpersonal interaction is severely limited, is also vividly remembered by the players.

3. The mere play of a learning game or simulation without discussion may teach little or nothing. Observation indicates that though play of a game sometimes stimulates the player to think, some players simply play mindlessly, with little attempt to gain insight from play. Such players appear to require discussion in order to grasp the fact that one can use the experience of play to gain insights about better play. (This "mindless" play on the part of some players, which can be changed through discussion, may offer a way of studying why some persons do not learn from experience in real life—for it is quite clear from observation that depending on the attitude with which one approaches a game, he may learn much or almost nothing from the experience of playing it.)

4. The use of a game context for information drills is very effective for learning the information contained in the drills, apparently because of the effort that games induce.

5. The extended play of some games of logic and mathematics does improve performance in mathematical or logical tasks.

6. Games and simulations employ different sets of motivations than instructional methods which involve teaching. This is evident in the fact that children regarded as slow learners, unmotivated, and disadvantaged, are as highly motivated in games and simulations as are those who are ordinarily high performers in school. It is also evident in observations that persons who are outstanding or become leaders in simulations and games are often not those who are the highest performers in school. This result indicates that games and simulations may be especially valuable for learning among disadvantaged children.

The source of this difference between methods of instruction that involve teaching and games and simulations may lie in either of two structural differences: first, the fact that the social organization of the classroom with games and simulations does not depend on a teacher-student relation, and is very different from the teacher-oriented

---

*In a novel or a play, it may be necessary, to prevent extreme complexity, that some actions are unmotivated and carried out by "wooden" or "two-dimensional" characters. Corresponding to this in simulation games are actions that are not carried out by players, but are hypothetically carried out by others outside the game, and are part of the rules: the outcome of a chance card, a spinner, or a fixed rule. For example, in a legislative game, the players are legislators. Their actions are part of the game, but their constituents' actions (in voting for or against them) are determined through the rules, together with the distribution of cards representing constituents.

classroom. Second, learning occurs through performance and activity, from which conceptual principles are inferred, rather than by a direct conceptual transfer from teacher to student. If the poor performance of a student in present school activities is because he learns more through action and less through direct intellectual digestion of abstract information, then he can be expected to learn better through games and simulations.

7. The amount of chance in a game is quite important for the amount of learning to be derived from it. If a game is pure chance, as in gambling casinos, obviously there is nothing to be learned beyond the mechanics of play. If a game contains no chance, then ordinarily players must be very carefully matched in order to equalize the opportunity to win. (One exception to this point may be some social simulation games involving much interaction of a cooperative as well as competitive sort among players. The chance element involved in such interaction may substitute for formal chance mechanisms in play.)

Thus in games used explicitly for learning, the amount of chance should be at some intermediate level, enough to encourage learning of skill at play, but not enough to discourage play between players of unequal strength.

How Are Games and Simulations Best Used for Learning?

Some learning games, such as certain mathematical games, are played quickly, and can be played over and over by the same players. At the other extreme, some simulations, best exemplified by some of the international relations simulations, are very elaborate to stage, are ordinarily played only once by a given group of participants, and may last several days running.

These are constraints imposed by the particular games and simulations themselves. But apart from these constraints, most games and simulations may be used in a variety of ways, in the classroom and as extracurricular activities. In order to obtain an idea of the conditions most conducive to learning through games, it is useful to distinguish different types of learning or types of change in individuals that can take place through the use of games and simulations.

1. The first and most universal learning that takes place is learning of the rules of the game, including the structure of action. This learning is necessary in order to play, and thus is intrinsic to play of the game or simulation. In some simulations, the rules of play are themselves complex, and represent some facet of reality. For example, some realistic legislative simulations have included as part of the rules the rules and procedures of the U.S. Congress. The learning of these rules themselves is one of the goals of the simulation.

In some cases, the rule-learning is explicitly recognized through creating different *levels* of the same game, which differ in the complexity of their rules. At the first level, the rules embody certain social, economic, or political processes (or in mathematical games, certain mathematical operations). At higher levels, the increasingly complex rules show a more complex set of processes or operations.

Rule-learning, it should be noted, is learning that occurs in part prior to the play of the game itself, and in part during play, through trial and error. Because much rule-learning takes place before the game, it is important to so structure learning games that play can occur with a minimum of rule-learning. This may be accomplished by having the game playable at several levels, with the first levels requiring very little prior rule-learning.

2. A second kind of learning is the learning of behavior strategies in unfamiliar cir-

cumstances. Such learning, whether or not it generalizes to behavior strategies in general, develops the behavior strategies in areas of life simulated by the game. This kind of learning is the learning that many simulation games are designed to teach. The aim is to give a player an understanding of, and experience with, the behavioral alternatives that would confront him in real life in the role that he occupies in the game. This learning can range from very explicit behavior strategies to a much more intangible way of looking at a set of events from a new perspective.

It is because of this kind of learning that simulation games ordinarily deal with future activities the individual will face (such as a life career game, which gives experience with the kinds of career decisions to be faced in the future), or with activities involving complex institutions that he might otherwise never gain insight into.

3. A third kind of learning that game and simulation designers often aim to bring about is an increased knowledge of actual detail of one's social environment. Some games and simulations are rich in the realism of the setting, and this richness becomes a part of the experience of the player. Not all games and simulations attempt to re-create the factual details of reality, but for those that do (which include simulations of historical events), the aim is to bring that richness into the player's experience.

4. A fourth learning aim of some games is the aim of developing a general sense of behavior strategies, that is, of setting a goal and devising the most efficient means for realizing it. A number of game developers argue, as indicated earlier, that the play of simulation games induces a young person to believe that his environment is responsive to his efforts. There are some strong indications from other research that such a belief is highly related to learning skill. Thus these game developers argue that the responsive environments that games provide will help develop such a belief and thereby improve general learning ability.

5. A general kind of learning about cooperation and competition, about give and take, takes place in many social simulation games. Social processes in reality and in the simulation games involve competition through cooperation, transactions of mutual benefit to both parties, acceptance of temporary disadvantage in the hope of future benefit, and other activities that are neither pure gain nor pure loss. Learning these social processes does not automatically occur to young people in the artificial role of student. In the past, a greater learning of them occurred when children were a more functional and productive part of a household economy, when their roles were not restricted to those of "student" and "adolescent."

In determining how best to use games or simulations to bring about one or more of the types of learning described above, it is useful to recognize a general principle: that one of the major reasons games teach is the intensity of concentration they induce. Thus any use of games that discourages this intensity of concentration for some or all participants will not likely result in much learning. One of the most widespread current uses of games is a use of this sort, in the regular classroom as an adjunct to the regular curriculum. When used as an adjunct to the regular curriculum, a game or simulation is ordinarily played as an interlude to usual classroom activities, followed by a discussion of the game. Such use has the severe limitation that the game may be regarded as an interlude to the "work" of learning itself, so that the only learning which occurs is that necessary for a casual play of the game, principally the rules of the game.

Even when not used as a mere adjunct to the curriculum, a frequent use of games or simulations is play only once or twice by a class or other group. When played once or twice, there is little incentive for learning behavior strategies, and often a general confusion about the relation between one's action and the results of that action. A common result after a single play of a game is that some players understand well what went on, and are ready to begin developing strategy, while others are totally confused. Learning of types 2 and 4 described above appears unlikely to occur under such conditions of play.

It seems clear that for maximum benefit, a game or simulation should be the object of sustained and serious play. This may occur either in the curriculum itself or in extracurricular activities. In either case, but particularly in extracurricular play (such as in tournaments or interscholastic play) there is an inherent conflict between the need to continually extend the game to higher levels to broaden learning of types 1 and 3 and the need to fix on a single set of rules for competitive play to enhance learning of types 2 and 4.

Another question about the best use of games and simulations for learning is in the role of modern technology, such as computers, in relation to games. Computer games exist, best exemplified by computer management games used in some business schools, but including also a few games at the high school and elementary school level. Several points emerge from the use to date, some encouraging to the combination of computers and simulations or games, and some discouraging.

First, the computer can constitute a very flexible responsive logical environment, and it is the essence of simulation games that they involve simulated responsive environments. But second, when the computer is used as a substitute for other players in a *social* environment, much of the instructiveness of that environment is lost. Where the number of other players would be too large to feasibly enter the play of a game (as consumers in a management game, or voters in an election campaign management game), then the computer may usefully take their place; when this is not so, the computer is ordinarily more hindrance than aid.

Altogether, it is very likely that computers and allied technical aids will come to play a valuable but limited role in augmenting the environments that simulations and games provide. The more rich in factual information the game or simulation, the more useful the computer is, in serving up that information. And as input-output media for computers develop, the environments provided by the computer will become more usable in games and simulations. Nevertheless, it is easy, in speculation on the technological marvels of the future, to overestimate the role that such technology will play in simulations and games. Just as the invention of moving pictures enlarged the possibilities for drama, but the possibilities are realized only with a structurally sound screenplay, technological innovations will enlarge the possibilities for games and simulations, but the possibilities will be realized only with structurally sound games and simulations.

A bibliography of groups engaged in the development of simulation games, and of simulation games that have been developed is reproduced below. Both parts of the bibliography are taken from William Nesbitt, *Simulation Games for the Social Studies Classroom,* Foreign Policy Association, New York, 1968.

BIBLIOGRAPHY

Resource Persons and Organizations:

Abt Associates, Inc.
55 Wheeler Street
Cambridge, Massachusetts 02138

Game designers for many educational, business and governmental organizations.

Academic Game Director
Nova High School
3600 Southwest 70th Street
Fort Lauderdale, Florida 33314

Nova High School has been a center for the development and use of TRADE AND DEVELOP and others. Sponsors the Academic Olympics.

The Didactic Game Company
Box 500
Westbury, New York 11590

Designers of games for education, business, and industry.

Foreign Policy Association School Services
H. Thomas Collins, Regional Director
345 East 46th Street
New York, New York 10017

Developed DANGEROUS PARALLEL with Abt Associates. FPA has also been working on simulations with large groups through television.

Interact
P.O. Box 262
Lakeside, California 92040

Two teachers, Paul DeKock and Dave Yount, have organized Interact to produce and disseminate simulation games, such as DISUNIA and SUNSHINE.

Academic Games Project
Center for the Study of Social Organization of Schools
The Johns Hopkins University
3505 N. Charles Street
Baltimore, Maryland 21218

The Johns Hopkins groups have developed a number of educational games, including THE GAME OF DEMOCRACY, PARENT-CHILD, and POOR PEOPLE's CHOICE.

Joint Council on Economic Education
1212 Avenue of the Americas
New York, New York 10036

Have been working extensively with economic simulation games. Bibliography available.

Urban Systems Simulations
Washington Center for Metropolitan Studies
1717 Massachusetts Avenue, N.W.
Washington, D.C. 20036

Designers of such games as REGION and CITY.1. The Gaming Newsletter, sponsored by the National Gaming Council, may be ordered from the Washington Center for Metropolitan Studies at $4.50 for 4 to 6 issues per year.

Project SIMILE
Western Behavioral Sciences Institute
1150 Silverado
La Jolla, California 92037

WBSI has designed such games as CRISIS, NAPOLI and PLANS. Their Occasional Newsletter on developments in simulation may be ordered for $5.00 per year.

Some Simulation Games:

CARIBOU HUNTING (5th Grade)

A board game (map) simulating some of the difficulties Eskimos experience in hunting caribou. Presently available only within trial teaching edition of "Man—A Course of Study," a 5th grade course. This social studies course expected to be published commercially in 1969-1970. For information about the course, write Librarian, Education Development Center, Inc., 15 Mifflin Place, Cambridge, Mass. 02138.

CITY 1 (Senior High-Adult)

Involves various social, economic and political relationships in a simulated urban center and its three suburbs and includes an integration of systemic and role-playing approaches. For information write Peter House, Director, Urban Systems Simulations, The Washington Center for Metropolitan Studies, 1717 Massachusetts Avenue, N.W., Washington, D.C. 20036.

CONSUMER (Senior High-Adult)

Designed to teach something about the problems and economics of installment buying. Information available from Academic Games Project, Center for the Study of Social Organization of Schools, The Johns Hopkins University, 3505 N. Charles St., Baltimore, Md. 21218. Available 1969. (1st edition out of print.)

CRISIS (Senior High-Adult)

A simulation of an international crisis over a mining area of vast importance to the world. Available from Project SIMILE, Western Behavioral Sciences Institute, 1150 Silverado, La Jolla, California 92037.

DANGEROUS PARALLEL (Senior High-Adult)

A simulation in which students play ministerial roles for six fictionalized countries facing a situation approximating that which led to the Korean war. A principal objective is to teach students about some of the factors involved in foreign policy decision-making. Available in the spring of 1969 from Scott-Foresman and Co. (Att: Mrs. Mariette Stieg), 1900 E. Lake Ave., Glenview, Ill. 60025.

DEMOCRACY (Junior High-Senior High)

Simulates some aspects of the legislative process of the United States Congress. Available from Academic Games Project. (See Consumer.)

DISASTER (Junior High-Adult)

Simulates some problems faced by individuals when a community is hit by a localized natural disaster. Information available from Academic Games Project. (See Consumer.) Available, 1969. (1st edition out of print.)

DISUNIA (Junior High-Senior High)

Students attempt to cope with problems of the kind Americans faced in the period 1781-1789 through divisions on a new planet in the year 2087. Available from Interact, P.O. Box 262, Lakeside, California 92040.

DIVISION (Junior High-Senior High)

A simulation of various problems facing Americans in the 1850's, including slavery. Available from Interact. (See Disunia.)

ECONOMIC DECISION GAMES (Senior High)

A series of eight games with teachers' guide, in which students are involved in analyzing and solving economic problems. The series includes: THE MARKET, THE FIRM, COLLECTIVE BARGAINING, THE COMMUNITY, SCARCITY AND ALLOCATION, BANKING, THE NATIONAL ECONOMY and INTERNATIONAL TRADE. Available from Science Research Associates, Inc., 259 East Erie Street, Chicago, Illinois 60611.

ECONOMIC SYSTEM (Junior High-Senior High)

A simulation of the interrelationship of various elements in the economic system, including manufacturers, workers and farmers who try to advance their economic positions. Information available from Academic Games Project. (See Consumer.) Available 1969. (1st edition out of print.)

THE GAME OF EMPIRE (Junior High)

A game modeled on mercantilism and economic factors involved in British subjects becoming Americans. Presently available only within trial teaching edition of "From Subject to Citizen," an 8th grade social studies course. Course expected to be commercially published in 1969-70. For information about the course, write Education Development Center. (See Caribou Hunting.)

FARMING (Senior High)

Players assume the role of a farmer in Kansas during three different periods in American history, beginning in 1888. Available only as part of a unit on "Agriculture and Manufacturing" from the High School Geography Project, P.O. Box 1095, Boulder, Colorado 80302.

INTER-NATION SIMULATION (Senior High-Adult)

A simulation of international relations, including the interrelationship of domestic and foreign policy. This school version of the original Northwestern University INTER-NATION SIMULATION is available from Science Research Associates. (See Economic Decision Games.)

LIFE CAREER (Junior High-Adult)

A simulation of certain features of the labor market, the "education market" and the "marriage market" in which players work with a fictitious person, alloting his time and activities among school, studying, a job, family responsibilities and lesirue time. Write Academic Games Project. (See Consumer.)

MARKET GAME (Upper Junior High-Senior High)

Simulates aspects of the free market process. Part of Comparative Economic Systems, Holt Social Studies Curriculum, Edwin Fenton, editor, Holt, Rinehart and Winston, Inc. 383 Madison Avenue, New York, New York 10017.

NAPOLI (Junior High-Adult)

A simulation of the legislative process and its interrelationship with parties. Available from Western Behavioral Sciences Institute. (See Crisis.)

PANIC (Junior High-Senior High)

Students play the roles of members of economic pressure groups in the United States in the period 1920-40. Available from Interact. (See Disunia.)

PARENT-CHILD (Junior High-Adult)

Simulates interrelationship of parent and child as they bargain over the limits of permissible behavior and attempt to achieve maximum satisfaction. Write Academic Games Project. (See Consumer.)

PLANS (Senior High-Adult)

Players assume the roles of members of interest groups who try to use influence and produce change in American society. Available from Western Behavioral Sciences Institute. (See Crisis.)

POINT ROBERTS (Senior High)

Students play roles of Canadians and Americans in a simulation that approximates the way in which a boundary dispute might arise and be settled. Available in September 1969 as a part of a unit on Political Geography from the High School Geography Project. (See Farming.)

POOR PEOPLE'S CHOICE (Formerly GHETTO- Junior High-Adult)

Simulates economic and social mobility in a poor inner city neighborhood; also simulates the interaction of the neighborhood and the individual. Will be available in 1969. For information write Academic Games Project. (See Consumer.)

REGION (Senior High-Adult)

Through economic and political decisions and inter-team conflicts and compromises, participants obtain an interdisciplinary view of the problems of a growing urban region. For information write Urban Systems Simulations. (See City 1.)

SEAL HUNTING (5th Grade)

A board game simulating some Eskimo strategies for securing enough seals. These include sharing patterns as well as technological strategies. Presently available only within trial teaching edition of "Man: A Course of Study," from Education Development Center. (See Caribou Hunting.)

SIERRA LEONE (Elementary)

An experimental, computer-based game in which the student assumes the role of an American economic adviser attempting to improve various aspects of the economy in different parts of the country. This game is being experimented with at the Board of Cooperative Educational Services (BOCES), Westchester County, Yorktown Heights, New York 10598, and is demonstrated by appointment.

SIMULATION: THE DECISION-MAKING MODEL (Senior High)

Students play the role of decision-makers for five hypothetical countries with a wide range of resources and seek to improve their nation's domestic and international position. Developed by and available from the World Affairs Council of Philadelphia, John Wanamaker's Store, 13th and Market Streets, Philadelphia, Pa. 19107.

THE SUMERIAN GAME (Elementary)

An experimental computer-based game in which a player assumes the role of ruler of Sumeria (an agricultural economy) and must improve the lot of his people by making decisions. (See Sierra Leone for address.)

SUNSHINE (Elementary-Senior High)

Students become members of different races in a mythical city and face various urban problems, including segregation. Available from Interact. (See Disunia.)

TRADE AND DEVELOP

Simulates the processes of international trade and economic development as players make decisions about production, trade and investment. Will be available in 1969. For information write Academic Games Project. (See Consumer.)

6.

Computer-Assisted Instruction and Its Potential for Individualizing Instruction

by *JOHN E. COULSON*
Asst. Manager
Education Systems Dept.
System Development Corp.
Santa Monica, Calif.

Picture a college student of 1975, arriving at his study center in the morning and immediately sitting in front of a sophisticated console complete with tape recorder and earphones, slide and motion picture projectors, a television screen, a keyboard, and an electronic pen allowing free-hand student responses. This console, along with thousands of others on the campus, is connected to and controlled by a large central computer. The student receives instruction by means of multi-media presentations, and uses a variety of response modes to answer questions about the content material. The computer evaluates all responses and provides immediate corrective feedback. When the student needs further information to help him solve a problem he communicates through the computer with a comprehensive automated library, typing his questions in normal English format and receiving immediate answers. He works entirely at his own pace and may see an entirely different sequence of material than any other student. With appropriate breaks for coffee and lunch, the student works in this individual manner until he is ready to go home in the afternoon.

The system just described is technologically feasible today. But does it represent a likely picture of college life in 1975? I believe not, for at least two important reasons:

The first reason is purely economic. For the next 10 years, at least, it would almost certainly be prohibitively expensive for every student to receive a major part of each day's instruction in a direct, individual dialogue with a computer. I will discuss some of the economic considerations of computer-aided instruction in a later section of this paper.

But a more important reason, I believe, is that an education based exclusively or predominantly on a closed-system, man-computer dialogue would be terribly sterile in several important respects, no matter how efficiently the students might acquire content skills. Such a system, in fact, would increase an already unfortunate tendency for education to divorce itself from such important skills as the ability to interact effectively with other humans, to communicate the results of one's labors to others, and to exchange ideas in attempts to solve shared problems.

The reservations that I have expressed thus far do not mean that I believe computers are

Note: This paper was prepared for a series of faculty seminars sponsored by Bucknell University and the Office of Education, Lewisburg, Pennsylvania, March 28-29, 1968.

useless in instruction. On the contrary, I hope to make it clear in this paper that computers will probably play a major role throughout college education within 10 to 20 years. But to understand the potential impact of computer technology on higher education, we need to stop thinking of the computer simply as another audio-visual aid, a desk calculator, or a glorified teaching machine, and begin to appreciate its capabilities as a general-purpose information-processing system. And when we speak of the role of computer-aided instruction in individualizing college instruction, we must clearly define what we mean by individualized instruction, and what techniques we subsume under the label, "computer-aided instruction."

Individualized vs. Individual Instruction

Toward this end, I should first like to make a distinction between "individualized instruction" and "individual instruction." Individual instruction implies that the student is moving entirely independently, with little or no interaction with his fellow students. Such instruction cannot, in itself, provide a total education although it may do an excellent job of teaching certain skills. Other, equally important skills require group interaction.

Individualized instruction, as distinguished from individual instruction, means that the mode, content, and sequence of instruction are tailored to the individual's needs at any moment in time; it does not necessarily mean that he studies by himself although he may in particular circumstances. Thus in a single lesson a student might spend part of his time in self-study (e.g., with a programmed textbook), part of his time watching a film in a large auditorium, and part in a group discussion, yet the entire lesson sequence might be highly individualized.

To insure that each student receives a sequence of instructional experiences that provides effective individualized instruction, a college or other educational institution must have, in addition to its staff, at least three major resources: A large pool of teaching materials designed to produce specified types of behavior; a monitoring and evaluation system to provide continuous assessment of individual performance; and a decision and control mechanism for matching the instruction to the individual needs. The typical college today lacks all three of these resources. There are many textbooks and teaching aids available to augment the instructor's lectures, but these are too often designed to cover a certain amount of content area rather than to produce specified student behaviors. Student assessment is usually piece-meal, haphazard, and infrequent, and consequently has little impact on the instruction. The instructor spends most of his time lecturing, or doing his own research, and has little opportunity to assign different students to different learning modes according to their assessed needs. Thus the lockstep system so common in the public schools often prevails in higher education as well. College students may select their courses cafeteria-style, but once they are in a course they will probably all get the "blue-plate special."

Some small colleges and universities, such as Bucknell, are fortunate to have small student/teacher ratios, and can individualize instruction to a considerably greater extent than the large schools. Even here, however, there is a definite limit to the capacity of any manual bookkeeping system for tracking students who are moving independently, and for seeing that each student is in the right location at the right time, with the right teaching materials, and working in the optimal learning mode. Our research at SDC suggests that, ideally, it should be possible to individually assess and reassign each student to a different learning mode as many as 20 or 30 times a day. In the great majority of colleges and universities, at least, the sheer immensity of the bookkeeping required for such individualized instruction would make it essential that some form of automatic data-processing assistance be provided.

A modern computer has characteristics that closely parallel those needed in any educational system that wishes to provide highly individualized instruction. First, it has a very large memory capacity that can be used to store instructional content material or, under certain conditions, to generate such material. When the material is stored externally, as in reference books, films, etc., the computer can maintain records of the location and nature of the material for subsequent referral. The computer can also store extensive information about classrooms, faculty, teaching aids of all descriptions, and other school resources, as well as data on all students in the college.

Second, the computer can perform complex analyses of student responses inserted by keyboard, punched cards, electronic pen, or other techniques into the computer. It can operate so rapidly in this activity that large numbers of students can be individually assessed many times each day.

Finally, the computer can make decisions based on the assessments of student performance, matching resources to individual student needs. One such decision might be for the computer to present lesson materials directly to the student in a tutorial mode. Other possible decisions might be to refer the student to a particular section of a textbook, to have him try a certain chemistry experiment in the lab, to seek consultation from an instructor, or to join a group discussion being conducted in a particular classroom. Whenever the student completed the assigned activity, he might be reassessed for assignment to a different activity. In the case of the chemistry experiment, for example, he might be required to insert the results of his experiment before he progresses further in his work.

Computer-Assisted Instruction

Consideration of these computer capabilities brings us to a definition of the second key term in the title of this paper: "computer-assisted instruction." I view computer-assisted instruction as including anything a computer can do to help individualize and improve instruction. Thus the term encompasses not only the direct tutorial dialogue between computer and students, but also automated data-management aids to help instructors and administrators design curricula, monitor student performance, and manage classroom instruction.

In 1966, according to a report recently published by the American Council on Education, almost 600 American colleges, or approximately 30 percent of the total, had acquired at least one computer (Caffrey & Mosmann, 1967). The report estimates that, by 1970, more than half of all colleges and universities will have one or more computers. However, only a very small percentage of these machines are used for any purpose directly connected with instruction. Probably 95 percent of the on-campus computer time is used for routine processing of administrative records, payroll and budget calculations, attendance records, and similar activities. These are all important functions that help a college justify the expense of computers and associated machinery, but they fall outside the area of this paper's concern.

Five general applications are found for the remaining campus computer time, the five percent or so devoted to instructional assistance. These include the computer's use as: (1) a problem-solving tool for students; (2) a tutorial teaching device; (3) an automated library or information-retrieval system; (4) a classroom information system for instructors; and (5) a data-management aid for staff and administration in instructional planning. Each of these applications is discussed below, with examples based on actual or proposed projects.

The Computer as a Problem-Solving Tool

Among the computer applications fitting more directly under the heading of computer-assisted instruction, probably the most common, and certainly one of the earliest, is the computer's use as a problem-solving tool for the students. A primary example is the engineering student's use of a computer to solve mathematical problems in designing, let us say, a concrete wall that must withstand certain specified stresses. In such an application the computer serves much the same function as a slide rule or a desk calculator. The computer has one significant advantage as a pedagogical tool, however, aside from its greater power and speed. Before the student can make the computer solve his mathematical problem, he must analyze the problem and explicitly formulate its solution as a series of discrete, operationally defined steps corresponding to the computer's repertoire of operations. In performing the requisite analysis and logically ordering the computer's operations, the student often gains a much better understanding of the original problem, and is better prepared to solve subsequent problems of a similar nature.

A special instance of the computer's application as a problem-solving tool is its use to teach students about computers and computer programming. Here the computer becomes the subject of, as well as the instrument for, instruction. Again citing the report of the American Council on Education, doctorates in computer science are offered at 15 universities in the United States and masters degrees at more than 30. In a far larger number of institutions, separate courses on computer design and programming are offered within the programs of the departments of mathematics, engineering, and other related disciplines. In these courses, an attempt is usually made to have students learn about the computer by using the computer, for example, by programming it to perform certain tasks. Frequently computers used for this purpose operate under an executive program containing a variety of diagnostic routines. When a student attempts to insert his own program he receives feedback messages telling him what kinds of errors his program contains.

The Computer as a Teaching Machine

More recently, computers have been used as sophisticated teaching machines. This is the application most popularly identified with the term, "computer-assisted instruction." In this mode a computer interacts tutorially with a student so that he moves through the course material at a rate and in a sequence determined by his responses to questions contained in the material. Some of the larger computer-based systems operate under a time-sharing program, which means that the same computer can give individualized instruction to many different students concurrently. In actuality the computer processes the students in turn, rather than simultaneously, but because of its great operating speed the computer can cycle through all the students so rapidly that no individual experiences any significant delay between inserting a response and receiving feedback from the machine.

The present paper is not primarily concerned with the history of computer-based tutorial instruction, but for those readers who wish to trace some of the earliest developments in this field, descriptions of practically all the original computer-aided instruction projects can be found in the proceedings of a 1961 "Conference on Programmed Learning and Computer-Based Instruction," jointly sponsored by the Office of Naval Research and System Development Corporation (Coulson, 1962). These early projects included work at International Business Machines, the University of Illinois, System Development Corporation, and Bolt Beranek and Newman. Listings and brief abstracts of more current computer-assisted instruction projects are being maintained by Karl L. Zinn at the University of Michigan, and by ENTELEK Incorporated, Newburyport, Massachusetts.

It is difficult to get any precise figures on the number of projects in this country presently using computers as tutorial teaching devices. In such a rapidly developing field new projects are started almost every month, and occasionally a project silently disappears. A reasonable total figure might be 30 or 35, with perhaps 20 of these located in various colleges and universities. Some of the projects are sponsored by computer manufacturers hoping to develop new educational markets for their products. The majority of projects are conducted as learning research laboratories or as experimental prototypes by universities and independent research institutions. There are probably fewer than half a dozen projects in which computer-based tutorial instruction is used as a routine part of a regular instructional program.

Computer-based tutorial systems come in a wide variety of sizes and shapes, but practically all have at least six major components: the computer; one or more terminals through which the computer and the students interact with each other; communication lines between computer and terminals; sequences of computer commands, called "programs," that control the actions of the computer; the instructional content; and the students themselves. Each of these components is discussed below, with illustrative examples given from actual computer-based tutorial systems.

The Computer. The computer evaluates all student responses, assesses each student's immediate learning needs, and controls the presentation of lesson-material to the students. With perhaps one or two exceptions, all computers presently used for computer-assisted instruction are general-purpose machines originally designed for scientific or business applications. Like most general-purpose devices, they are quite versatile but are not ideally designed for any single type of operation. In the future, as the educational market grows, we may begin to see computers built specifically for educational purposes. Such computers might place less emphasis than most present-day machines on prodigious speed and calculation capabilities, and more emphasis on memory capacity, economy, and simplicity of operation.

Current computer-assisted teaching projects use computers of several different makes, including IBM, GE, RCA, Philco-Ford, and Control Data Corporation. IBM machines are in most common use, probably because of the greater number of these machines already on campus. The machines range greatly in size, speed, and cost. As a rough estimate of the price range, some of the smallest computers used for instruction cost around $80,000, while the larger machines run from two to three million dollars. Generally speaking, the larger computers, operating under a time-sharing system, can handle more students at the same time (theoretically a thousand or more for some of the largest machines although most systems currently handle only 20 to 50 students). They can also give more immediate feedback to the students, store more complete performance records on each student, perform a more complex analysis of responses, and provide more alternative lesson sequences to students who demonstrate varying levels of mastery. It must be kept in mind, however, that clever programmers can make even a small computer behave impressively, and poor programmers can waste most of a large machine's capability.

Terminals. A computer cannot effectively interact directly with the outside world. It is useless without input/output terminals to receive and transmit information. Most commonly, of course, the computer's outside world is represented by the humans using the machine.

As with the computers themselves, terminals are produced by numerous manufacturers and in a large variety of forms. Because of the highly interactive nature of computer-based tutorial instruction, a two-way communication device such as a teletypewriter is commonly used rather than a printing machine or other one-way device. Under computer control the teletypewriter can type instructions, diagnostic questions, and feedback messages to the student. The student, in turn, can use the teletypewriter keyboard to insert his responses to the computer's questions. Two other advantages of the teletypewriter are that it is less expensive than most other types of terminals, and it is more easily connected at sites remote from the computer. SDC's computer in Santa Monica, for example, is connected to teletypewriters in Massachusetts, New Jersey, Washington, and Ohio.

Despite the economy and convenience of the teletypewriter, it is a very noisy and slow device. Furthermore, there are some instructional situations that require more display capability, as in the presentation of graphic or pictorial material. With suitable engineering and programming, any type of presentation device can be controlled by a computer. One of the earliest systems developed by SDC used a random-access slide projector that could display up to 600 slides in any sequence directed by the computer (Coulson, 1962). The PLATO system developed by the Coordinated Science Laboratory at the University of Illinois displays material through closed-circuit television (Braunfeld, 1964). Two separate video pictures are superimposed on the student's TV screen. The televised problem frame contains spaces for the student's answers. When the student inserts his responses through a keyset, they automatically appear in the answer spaces.

In some learning situations it is very important that the student learn the relationships between symbolic and graphic information, as in the representation of mathematical functions. Licklider and Clark (1962) reported on an experimental computer-based instructional system in which the student could vary the coefficients of an equation and observe corresponding changes in the graph displayed on an oscilloscope screen. Alternatively, the student could sketch a graph on the screen, using an electric stylus, and then see the best-fitting function, along with its equation.

Auditory material must often be presented in teaching foreign languages, or in giving directions to young children. Several systems have been developed to provide random access to recorded messages, so that a computer can select them in any sequence judged to meet the learning needs of a student. IBM's 1500 Instructional System, for example, includes a computer-controlled tape recorder in addition to a slide projector and a cathode ray tube display. A similar random-access audio unit built by Westinghouse is used in an experimental teaching system at the University of Pittsburgh (Ragsdale, 1966).

Considerable variety is also seen in the devices used by students to indicate their responses to questions in the computer-controlled lesson sequences. Such devices must allow rapid student-computer interactions, and in most instances this rules out the more conventional computer input channels such as magnetic tapes and punched cards. The most common input device for computer-assisted instruction is the teletypewriter keyboard or other variety of keyset permitting constructed verbal responses. With such a device the student may give multiple-choice answers or short fill-in responses, or even write essays.

When graphic displays are provided on cathode ray tubes, it is often useful to allow students to specify certain areas on this display. For example, a geography student might be shown an outline of a hypothetical continent, and asked to locate the best sites for founding an industrial community. This can be accomplished through a light pen, which the student points at the cathode ray tube display to specify a point or area to the computer.

Another type of graphic input device, called the RAND Tablet, consists of a grid of extremely thin copper wires providing a surface that can be written on with an electric stylus. Using such a device the student can specify areas, draw lines, or even print letters and numbers that can be recognized by an appropriate programmed computer. We are currently experimenting at SDC with a RAND Tablet on which we are projecting images from a cathode ray tube. In this way we can superimpose stimulus and response material on the same surface.

At the University of Pittsburgh, a "touch-sensitive display" allows the computer to detect where a student touches the projection screen with his finger or a pointer (Ragsdale, 1966). Another device under development at Pittsburgh, the "manipulation board," detects the placement of objects, such as blocks, that the student might be asked to arrange in some pattern. The manipulation board and the touch-sensitive display are particularly useful for instruction of young children or mentally retarded students who might have difficulty operating a keyboard.

Communication Lines. Normally the communication lines might be subsumed under the discussion of the terminals themselves. I have broken them out as a separate item, however, because there are some very critical problems in linking computer and terminals that are almost always overlooked in general discussions of computer-assisted instruction.

The simplest type of terminal in common use today, the teletypewriter, can be linked to the computer by a standard telephone line. The installation charge for the teletypewriter is not very high, and the monthly rental is not prohibitive for most users, but the line charges themselves can be extremely costly if the terminals are located many miles from the computer. An hour of line use for computer-assisted instruction will cost the same as a conventional telephone conversation of the same duration and distance. Even at short distances, this could add up pretty fast if hundreds of terminals were being used several hours every day. Thus the communication costs must be a major consideration in any plans for a centralized system in which a single computer is intended to service many schools or campuses over a broad geographic area.

The communication costs are increased many times when terminals are used that require a high density of data transmission. This is true, for example, of many graphic display devices which must be connected to the computer by special high-speed data lines or microwave circuits. Aside from the costs, the use of such terminals also makes the problem of transmission reliability more acute.

Programs. In most computer-based tutorial applications two types of computer programs are required. One type of program is specific to a particular lesson; it contains all the directions to the computer for sequencing the lesson material, evaluating responses, and giving feedback in that lesson. The other type is the control program under which the lesson program is executed. It contains general commands, for example, about how control is to be passed from the student to the computer, and back again.

A lesson program contains the pedagogic strategies for the lesson. Our own experience indicates that the strategy cannot be standardized or stereotyped; it must be tailored to the subject matter covered by the particular lesson and may, in fact, change several times during the lesson. In other words, you cannot establish a rigid pattern and say, for example, that every new topic must be introduced by an instructional frame defining the new concept, followed by three examples illustrating and elaborating on the definition, followed by two question-frames requiring the student to demonstrate mastery of the concept. Such an arbitrary rubric may lend an aura of scientific rigor, but it will inevitably fail the test of practical utility. In the present state of the art, there is no substitute for empirically determining what lesson sequence will be most effective for each topic.

Commonly, an attempt is made to accommodate individual differences among students by means of a branching structure with alternative sequences of lesson material for each topic. On a given topic, one sequence may provide only the bare essential facts; a lower level sequence on that same topic may provide more redundancy and more concrete examples; and a third sequence may give still more practice and repetition, and may phrase the information in shorter, less grammatically complex sentences. Thus a bright student performing well on the material might move rapidly from one topic to the next, seeing relatively few instructional frames and always being kept at the more concise level of exposition, while a slower student might be dropped to successively lower, and more redundant levels in the program until he shows mastery of each topic. Our work with such sequences at SDC indicates that mere repetition or rephrasing of a concept in simpler terms is not adequate. If a student does not learn from one sequence, he should be given a new sequence that takes an entirely different approach to the topic. For example, if the original sequence takes a deductive approach, presenting a rule or principle and then giving examples, the remedial sequence might take an inductive approach, in which the student induces the principle from a series of concrete examples and applications.

A number of different response characteristics can be taken into account in the computer's branching decisions. For example, the decision may be based on a detailed analysis of a single response, where the nature of the student's error suggests a particular misunderstanding that may be eliminated by a particular remedial sequence. Or, branching may be based on error counts accumulated over a number of instructional frames. If a student makes fewer than two errors out of eight questions on a topic, for instance, this might cause the program to branch ahead to a new topic; two to four errors might cause it to present a brief remedial sequence; and more than four errors might lead to the student's being started over on the topic, with less complex material.

Other response measures sometimes used in the branching decisions include response latency, and the student's own expression of confidence in his understanding of a topic. Both of these measures, however, are of somewhat uncertain value, being difficult to calibrate because of the great degree of variability from one student to another, and even within the individual student from one content area to another.

The control program, which may actually consist of several interrelated programs, controls the insertion of lesson-specific programs into the computer. It also governs the overall execution of the lesson programs when the lessons are presented to students. In some computer-based teaching systems the lesson author first prepares his lesson information in flow charts showing the lesson sequence and branching instructions. This information is later transcribed onto coding sheets, then punched onto cards, and finally read into the computer. Such a system can be cumbersome. The lesson author has little direct control over the actual insertion of his material, and he must wait at least several hours, and usually a day or more, before he sees his lesson as compiled and executed by the computer. The delay and partial loss of control frequently encourage the author to prepare long lesson sequences before he attempts to get them into the computer. Because he then has a sizeable investment of effort in the long sequence, he may be reluctant to make any basic changes in it even if he detects flaws when it is "played back" to him by the computer, or even if the students' performance later reveals gross inadequacies in the material.

An alternative approach is to build into the control program the capability for the lesson author to insert his instructional sequence directly into the computer, through a teletypewriter or similar device. This "on-line" capability is provided by IBM's COURSEWRITER (Grubb, 1967) and SDC's PLANIT (Feingold, 1967).

In the "lesson construct" mode, PLANIT allows an author to specify the lesson content, the feedback messages, and the branching decision structure. In the "execute" mode, he can see any part or all of the lesson "played back" to him just as it would be presented to a student. In the "edit" mode, the author can insert new instructional frames at any point in the sequence, or delete or modify existing frames. He can switch immediately from any mode to any other to facilitate trials and revisions of small segments of a lesson.

PLANIT is designed to meet two requirements. The first is to give the lesson author a great deal of flexibility in the types of material he can prepare, and to minimize constraints on the types of responses that can be made by the student. The second requirement is to make the computer-assisted tutorial system user oriented. That is, both author and student should be able to communicate with the system without being computer specialists or spending a long time learning a new code.

To meet the need for flexibility, PLANIT provides many different options to the lesson author in the types of frames he can construct, and in the rules he can insert for sequencing those frames. For example, multiple-choice frames, constructed-response frames, and mathematical problem frames can be assembled in any sequence; there are no standard patterns to be followed. Either author or student can make use of a wide variety of mathematical and statistical subroutines. An author preparing a sequence of mathematical problems need not evaluate the problems for numerical solutions himself, but can merely specify the formulas which the computer can apply to check a student's response.

PLANIT also permits flexibility in the form of the student's responses. When the PHONETIC option in PLANIT is used by the lesson author, for example, a student's constructed response will be accepted as correct despite misspellings if it is phonetically equivalent to any answer previously designated as correct by the lesson author. Thus under the PHONETIC mode, "teechur" would be an acceptable approximation of "teacher."

Similarly, the KEYWORD option causes PLANIT to search for a designated set of words in the student's response. Under the KEYWORD mode, the lesson author might specify "John Kennedy" as the correct answer to a question and PLANIT would accept as correct the response, "I believe it was John F. Kennedy."

Finally, the FORMULA option gives the student credit for his answer if it is one of a subset of expressions algebraically equivalent to any of the designated "correct" responses. For example, the expression, $6(\frac{N}{4})$ would be accepted in place of the expression, $\frac{6N}{24}$.

The PHONETIC, KEYWORD and FORMULA options can be used in any combination selected by the lesson author, with different options for different items in the lesson sequence, if desired.

All of the options available to the lesson author increase his degrees of freedom, but also tend to complicate his task of constructing lesson sequences. To minimize possible confusion, and to make PLANIT a practical tool for the nonprogrammer, we have built the "lesson construct" mode, as well as the "execute" mode, in the form of a two-way dialogue between human and computer. The computer, through a teletypewriter, prints brief messages at each point in the lesson-construction process where the lesson author must provide information. These messages tell the author what type of information is needed before the computer can proceed with the lesson compilation. In the construction of a fill-in type question frame, for example, the computer asks the lesson author to specify the text of the question. After the author has typed the question, the computer asks him to specify all possible answers, correct or incorrect, that he wants the computer to treat in some special way. After the lesson author lists the answers, the computer asks him to specify the actions to be taken for each anticipated response. Depending on the student's response, the author may instruct the computer to tell the student to try again, to give the student a feedback message confirming his response or correcting his error, or to skip him backwards or forwards to some other segment of the lesson sequence. The author can also specify actions to be taken if the student gives an unanticipated wrong answer.

Content Material.   There seems to be a popular misconception that, if you use a large computer and an elaborate branching structure with many alternative lesson sequences, you can be somewhat casual about the preparation of the content material itself. Nothing could be further from the truth. If anything, more time and effort must go into the development of lesson materials for a computer-based teaching system than for a programmed textbook or a simple teaching machine. Although practically anyone can write lesson sequences at a high rate, the development of effective material is many times slower. At one point in our research at SDC, we estimated that it took two man-years to develop 20-hours worth of material. One reason for this slow rate is that in computer-assisted instruction, not only the main sequence, but all the auxiliary branching sequences and remedial loops as well must be carefully tested and revised to ensure that each sequence does the job for which it was designed. This means, first, determining that there is a sufficiently sensitive diagnostic measure of the student's strengths and weaknesses at each point in the lesson sequence, and second, making certain that each remedial loop remedies whatever learning deficiency has been detected. Otherwise, as we have unfortunately found in some of our own research, a student may be directed through two or three remedial sequences and still perform poorly on a posttraining criterion test.

Careful preparation of lesson material does not necessarily require exposing the material to large numbers of students. It does mean working intensively with small lesson segments and individual students, testing and revising each segment until it achieves its objectives. We have found that more can be learned by working very closely with 15 or 20 students, one at a time, observing the details of their behavior, than by simply studying statistical summaries of the responses of several hundred students.

Students.   The students we have worked with and those we have heard about, regardless of grade level, have not been awed, frightened or intimidated by their experiences with computer-assisted instruction. However cleverly we may program the computer, every student soon sees it for what it is: another learning tool, like a textbook or slide rule. And like other learning tools, the computer and its various appendages are viewed as things to be manipulated to the students' own advantage. Some forms of manipulation are less adaptive than others, as when one of our younger students unscrewed the bulbs from several display boxes, but in general we try to encourage the student's feeling that the computer and the input/output terminal are there to help in some learning task, not to make life difficult for him.

Initially, almost all students exhibit a "pinball machine" effect, that is, a motivational lift resulting from the novelty and the automation of the equipment. This effect cannot be expected to have permanence, however; the content material must have intrinsic interest beyond the mechanical gadgetry. One of the most difficult tasks in the development of lesson material is to present information efficiently and economically, yet maintain student interest and curiosity. In some instances motivation appears to be enhanced by the insertion of peripheral comments having no direct relevance to the learning objectives of the particular lesson.

Automated Library and Information-Retrieval Systems

For a number of years computers have seen increasing use, especially in some of the larger universities, for automated handling of certain library functions such as indexing and classification, abstracting, and cataloging. These are basically bookkeeping chores, and though such computer applications save time and reduce clerical effort, they do not solve the basic problem of bringing students in closer contact with the information they should have. Typically, students today must walk to a separate building to obtain library materials, and then they must fill out forms and wait some appreciable time before they receive the material. If they find that the initial materials do not answer their questions, they must wait again before they can see a new set of materials. This obstacle between students and library information has an inhibitory effect on the entire process of student inquiry. It means that, in the more crowded colleges, at least, most students do not seek new information on their own initiative; they search only as far as they must to meet specific requirements levied by the instructor. Or, if the students do any voluntary study in the library, they tend to perceive this activity as quite separate and distinct from the classroom instruction.

What appears to be needed is a method of reducing the obstacles between students and information, and of bringing classroom learning and inquiry together as one integrated process. An important step in this direction is to eliminate the information middle-man, and to give students direct access to a wide variety of reference material. This, I would assume, should be one goal of the dial access information system at Bucknell University.

To take full advantage of improved information-retrieval systems such as the dial access system, changes are needed in the classroom instruction so that inquiry and retrieval activities are an integral part of the instruction. The instruction may present factual problems requiring the students to retrieve specific pieces of information, or it might contain open-ended, discussion-type problems stimulating the students to browse more widely through reference materials so as to gain a broader perspective and more angles of approach on the problems.

The language used between student and computer is another important factor in the effectiveness of computer-based inquiry systems. SDC has been working for several years on a natural-language information-retrieval system that allows a student or other user to ask questions of a computer in his own words. The system uses a computer program, called SYNTHEX (Simmons, 1967), that performs a syntactic analysis of the questions and responds to them by typing out relevant statements from a library of statements in memory. Experiments with SYNTHEX, using the Golden Book Encyclopedia as a data base, have demonstrated the technological feasibility of this question-answering approach, but much more work is needed to make it a practical tool for education.

The Computer as a Classroom Information System for Teachers

Where it is not practical or desirable to have a computer interact directly with students, it can be used as an information system to aid teachers in the individual monitoring and management of student progress. The Instructional Management System (IMS), developed by System Development Corporation, and currently being used experimentally in two California schools, provides such capabilities. Other systems, designed for similar purposes, include the Individually Prescribed Instruction (IPI) system developed by the university of Pittsburgh, and the Program for Learning in Accordance with Needs (PLAN), developed jointly by the American Institute for Research and Westinghouse Learning Corporation.

IMS is a technological tool—a combination of materials, equipment and procedures designed to give teachers both diagnostic and prescriptive information about individual children or groups of children in the classrooms. A computer maintains a pupil data base containing background information and current performance data for each pupil. It also stores information about available seatwork and other exercise materials relevant to each specific learning objective. As the pupils complete each instructional unit, they are given diagnostic tests on machine-readable answer sheets. These tests are not the conventional type of global assessment test; they are designed to give precise evaluations of performance on individual learning objectives defined in terms of the desired pupil behaviors. Test results are used to update the pupil performance records, and on the day after each test the teacher receives machine-prepared summaries showing the pupils' progress and indicating which pupils performed poorly on which tasks. The summary also suggests alternative instructional materials or teaching techniques that the teacher might use for pupils with specific weaknesses. Through a teletypewriter terminal, teachers and administrators can query the computer's data base for summarized or detailed information about individuals or groups of pupils.

IMS is designed to operate initially in the context of a conventional classroom organization, in which groups of pupils move at the same pace with little opportunity for individualized instruction. However, it is anticipated that, through its capability for presenting diagnostic and prescriptive information on an individual basis, IMS will help schools to move toward a more flexible continuous-progress mode of operation. IMS also appears to offer a better chance for economically practical application in public schools than direct computer-assisted instruction of students, at least for the next five or ten years.

Future plans for IMS include the enhancement of both its diagnostic and prescriptive capabilities. Although diagnosis is presently restricted to simple percentage scores on multiple-choice questions, it is quite possible to incorporate other, more complex types of evaluation. In the more advanced grades, for example, the computer might be used to grade essay material. Such a capability has already been developed at the University of Connecticut and applied experimentally to the grading of English essays (Page, 1966). Preliminary results suggest that computers are capable of relatively complex analyses in evaluating discursive responses, and may approach the level of evaluative sophistication of the typical high school teacher. More study will be needed to determine whether such computer applications are of practical utility in the schools.

On the prescriptive side, we plan to explore the possible uses of a computer to increase the quantity and variety of instructional material available to teachers to remedy learning deficiencies detected by IMS. One type of computer program that we hope to develop will describe the characteristics of lesson sequences that need to be written or adapted to fill gaps in the existing material. For example, based on an analysis of student response profiles, the computer might print a message saying, "More than 30 percent of the students show inadequate mastery of transposition rules in algebra. A new lesson segment is needed with the following sequence of instruction: (1) drill work on arithmetic operations; (2) review of rules of transposition; and (3) drill work on application of transposition rules."

Another computer program that we will be working on over the next few years will actually assemble lesson sequences, drawing from a pool of instructional frames generated by human authors. To accomplish this we will have to give the computer not only the pool of frames, but a set of descriptor values for each frame, and a set of rules telling the computer how to draw samples of frames according to their descriptor values, and how to sequence the frames to meet specific learning needs revealed by the performance profiles.

Finally, under certain conditions it is possible to program the computer to construct its own frames as well as to sequence the frames. For example, it is extremely simple to have a computer generate any desired quantity of addition problems, using different combinations of numbers.

In coming years we hope to extend our application of IMS to other grade levels. Although our current work has been exclusively at the public school level, I believe that, with suitable adaptations, it could be an extremely useful tool for higher education as well.

Administrative Data-Management Systems

Since the ultimate purpose of schools and universities is to teach, it seems reasonable that teaching effectiveness, as measured by student performance, should be an important factor in management decisions at the top administrative level of those institutions. Ironically, information about learning progress is rarely considered in the major policy decisions of the typical school or university. These decisions are based largely on economic or political considerations, or are forced by the sheer logistics of trying to keep a rapidly growing number of students busy and out of trouble. The rare exception, when the administrator becomes seriously concerned with student performance, is when they do poorly on some standardized test relative to other institutions, especially if the results are widely publicized.

We are attempting at SDC to develop procedures that will help administrators use student performance data in their administrative decisions. We feel that the use of such data should not be a chance occurrence, but a regular part of the administrative routine. Three things are needed before this goal can be accomplished: (1) The college or school district must have clear-cut, operational objectives with assigned priorities, and at least some of these objectives must be defined in terms of student performance; (2) administrators must have baseline data on student performance in different subject areas, so that they have some relative basis on which to set performance standards; and (3) they must have ready access to information about current performance. This information should not be in the form of large quantities of raw, unmanageable data, but in brief summaries tailored to the administrator's needs.

Some progress is being made toward meeting these three requirements. A number of colleges and universities have recently started efforts to define their objectives more operationally and to set some type of performance standards. This trend is further encouraged by the growth of programmed instruction and by the application of systems analysis techniques in education, as both of these methods place heavy emphasis on the definition of objectives and performance measures.

To aid in the need for better performance data, SDC is developing a computer-based data-management system designed to provide administrators with accurate, up-to-date student performance summaries, along with budget and personnel data. This system, called SPLAN (Krebs & Yett, 1966), allows administrators to query the computer's data base through a teletypewriter in the administrative office. The project is still in its early exploratory stages, but in one small school district where we are currently working with SPLAN, we have seen the superintendent and his staff begin to include student performance as an agenda item in their regular staff meetings. Perhaps it is not too far-fetched to envision the day when all colleges, universities, and districts will base their budget and personnel allocations at least partially on the students' performance in different subject areas, with greater resource being assigned to areas where performance is deficient.

BIBLIOGRAPHY

Braunfeld, P. G. "Problems and prospects of teaching with a computer." *Journal of Educational Psychology, 55*(4), August 1964. 201-211.

Caffrey, J., and C. J. Mosmann. "Computers on campus." American Council on Education, Washington, D.C., 1967. 207 pp.

Coulson, J. E. (Ed.) *Programmed Learning and Computer-Based Instruction.* New York: John Wiley and Sons, Inc., 1962. 291 pp.

Feingold, S. L. "PLANIT: A flexible language designed for computer-human interaction." System Development Corporation, Santa Monica, California. SP-2840, October 11, 1967. 18 pp.

Grubb, R. E. "Learner-controlled statistics." International Business Machines Corporation, Los Gatos, California. April 5, 1967. 10 pp.

Krebs, L. T., and F. A. Yett. "Brief description of SPLAN." System Development Corporation, Santa Monica, California. SP-2657, November 14, 1966. 5 pp.

Licklider, J. C. R., and W. E. Clark. "On-line man-computer communication." *Proc. Am. Fed. Inform. Process. Soc., 21*(133), 1962.

Page, E. B. "The imminence of . . . grading essays by computer." *Phi Delta Kappan,* January 1966.

Ragsdale, R. G. "The Learning Research and Development Center's computer assisted laboratory." Learning Research and Development Center, University of Pittsburgh, 1966. 4 pp.

Simmons, R. F. "Answering English questions by computer." In H. Borko (Ed.) *Automated Language Processing.* New York: John Wiley and Sons, Inc., 1967.

7.

Films for Learning*

Some Observations on the Present, Past, and Future Role of the Educational Motion Picture

By *JOHN FLORY*
Consultant
Motion Picture & Education
Markets Div.
Eastman Kodak Co.

What This Report Is All About:

When we talk about film in the classroom today, we are really talking about a paradox. On the one hand, there have been tremendous developments in motion pictures:

- A new, compact film format

- Shortfilms that deal creatively with single concepts

- Cartridge-loading projectors

- Widespread availability of color film at low cost

- Easy-to-use movie cameras

- And, screens that work without dimming the room lights

On the other hand, educators who have studied the use of A-V materials in the classroom today, tell us:

". . . the so-called educational revolution in America's schools (is) in the skies . . . There is little use of film, filmstrips, tapes, and other instructional aids."

It appears on the surface to be a stagnant situation. Film has been proved to be an effective teaching tool, offering motion, color, sound, accessibility, and "creatibility." Yet teachers are still clinging to the old lecture methods for the bulk of their instruction. The reasons for this resistance to film are complex—stemming perhaps from early experience with complicated projectors, "red tape" scheduling procedures for film and equipment, sketchy catalogues, and even the old axiom that "teachers teach as they themselves are taught"—i.e., *without* film. The overall picture looks bleak, but there are some bright spots—teachers and students in classrooms around the country who are doing exciting things with the film medium. For example:

This paper is published with the permission of Eastman Kodak Company © 1968.

- There are 250 teachers in Chicago's poverty areas who have been equipped with cameras and film to record their students' field trips to such "institutions" as the fire station . . . the airport . . . and the police headquarters. Through these films, the youngsters can re-live and re-tell their experiences . . . can begin to adjust to a heretofore alien, adult world.

- There's Douglas MacArthur High School in Saginaw, Michigan, with its two Multi-Media Learning Centers. Here, eighty students and four team teachers have access, at the same time, to a variety of facilities: commercially produced films, slides, tapes, records, and educational TV broadcasts.

- There's the Sobrante Elementary School in the "curfew" district of Oakland, California. Since the librarians began putting films, tapes, and records right alongside books, the use of the library has increased tenfold. As the principal says, "Youngsters with marginal reading skills now find that the library is the place to watch films or listen to tapes and records . . . And they can produce reports on what they see and hear, rather than what they read."

- There's the social studies teacher in Ossining, N.Y., with her students who's been making films for several years—"to show my classes, in their own idiom, a point I want to emphasize."

Film is the medium of the "now" generation. Some experts contend that today's teen-agers spend ten times as many hours in looking and listening to film and TV as they do in reading the printed word. And somehow they manage to sandwich in all those hours outside the schoolroom, because it's fairly certain that the majority of students aren't seeing many films between 8 a.m. and 3 p.m. each day!

Film, it turns out, is also a compatible medium—it gets along well with computers, TV, and even textbooks, which are now being published with coordinate motion pictures. Furthermore, the systems approach to education—the development of carefully produced materials in every subject area, utilizing all the technology at our disposal—holds a vital key for the future.

But what's even more significant is that the film medium itself is here *today*. Its low cost, clear picture resolution, capability for bringing the outside world inside the classroom—all this is available now to help us meet the staggering problems of mass education in the United States.

Here, then, is a closeup view of the fascinating world of the educational film, from the earliest days of the "silents" at the turn of the century, to the advances of today—with behind-the-scenes examples of what's really happening with pilot programs in film in the schools.

And, finally, we take a look at tomorrow: beginning with the goal of a film library for every classroom in the country, and closing with our recommendations for the development of an integrated systems approach—to put 20th-century technology to work in the educational process.

Diana is black, 16 years old, and angry. The reasons for her anger are complex, stemming from a tangled home life with a father who is a jazz musician, and her own long-standing problems in school.[1]

At one time or another, she's been rebellious, uncooperative and a perennial runaway.

In the past few months, however, there's been a tremendous improvement in Diana's behavior and outlook. What happened?

The key development, it seems is that the principal of her school obtained a new, easy-to-use movie camera. He sold Diana on the idea of "telling it like it is" by making her own film about what it's like to be a teen-ager today.

Under the guidance of a teacher who had film experience, Diana created a script, recruited other students as her "cast," and put together a 20-minute production that was described by a faculty member as "one of the most imaginative and sensitive films I've ever seen." The film has made her a celebrity among her classmates and has earned her an "A" rating—her first!—from the English teacher, who accepted the film as a term project in lieu of a written paper.

An isolated example of what film can do in education? Yes and no. Yes, in terms of what's actually happening in most classrooms in the U.S. today; no, in terms of the potential of the film medium itself.

Today's Classroom

Let's look for a moment at the ubiquitous classroom that everybody talks about. If you were a full-time teacher today, chances are very good that you'd find yourself faced with:

- 45 students in a classroom designed for 30.

- Textbook materials that were published five years ago and are already out of date because of the phenomenal growth of information.

- Increasing clamor on the part of supervisors, parents, and professional journals to devise "individualized instruction" for each of the 45 youngsters in the class.

Multiply these problems by 2 million such classrooms and add in the poverty and alienation of the inner cities and the rural areas; the worn-out school buildings that are health traps and fire traps; and the awful fact that 8% (about 160,000) experienced public school teachers give up their profession each year, taking their skills and talents out of the classroom.[2]

It's readily apparent that the problems of education today *are* so immense that they boggle the imagination. That doesn't mean, however, that we view the situation with alarm and then give up.

A Chinese philosopher said that a journey of a thousand miles begins with but a single step. We can apply the same reasoning to our search for solutions to the problems in education: Film is *not* a panacea for all the ills in the classroom, but it does offer some important steps in meeting the vital and basic needs in the teaching-learning situation.

Teaching and Learning

The teaching-learning situation—that sounds like a phrase in "education-ese" calculated to anaesthetize all but the most ardent readers. And yet, that's really what education is all about. The emphasis, these days, is on getting the learner to learn—getting the message across—using whatever teaching devices are necessary to do the job best.

At this point, I suggest we look beyond the educational scene for a moment to another industry that depends for its very life-blood on "getting the message across": the world of advertising. There can be no doubt about Madison Avenue's effectiveness.

In fact, the awesome power of advertising was made crystal-clear to me the other day when I made a rare excursion into a supermarket. On three different occasions, I watched with amusement and astonishment as toddlers ticked off the advantages, as well as the musical slogans, of one brand of cereal or candy over the choices their mothers had put in the shopping cart. The kids won. Clearly, the message had gotten across to these children. But how? They can't read or write or clip coupons or box-tops. The answer, of course, is that they got the message through the filmed commercials they see daily on television.

These 50-second mini-films offer children the excitement of motion; sound; and, in more and more homes, color. The film attracts the child's attention and never lets go, while at the same time, it directs the youngster to "ask Mommie to get Hum-Dum cereal for you at the food store today." And little Johnny or Susie does just that, as I can testify from my own observations!

Stimulus-Response

In reality, what we've been describing from the world of advertising is the classic stimulus-response-reward pattern that psychology professors have been lecturing about for decades. The advertiser, who must make sure his potential customers *learn* to want and buy his product, has found that he can reach people through the motion-color-and-sound of film. And the amazing thing is that he can get his film message across to any age group—from 2 to 92.

Now let's return to our focal point of interest—film in the world of education. What do we find when we pry open the school-room door today? Most likely, the teacher will be lecturing at the front of the class and the only "audiovisual devices" on hand will be the bulletin board and the blackboard.

Hard to believe? Listen to a report by John I. Goodlad at a recent Washington symposium on education: [3]

> I began to suspect that much of the so-called educational revolution in America's schools was in the skies. The instructional process in the classroom was characterized by much talking, with the teacher by far the dominant participant. There was little child-to-child interaction and relatively little use of films, filmstrips, tapes, and other instructional aids.

Dr. Goodlad concludes that neither teachers nor children seemed enthusiastically involved in their tasks.

The California educator, William H. Allen, points out:

> "In today's schools, the educational media are not treated as integral parts of the instructional process. They are superimposed on an existing pattern of teaching and administration." [4]

> "Practicing educators," says Dr. Allen, have not created a favorable climate for innovation."

That seems to take us full-circle, doesn't it?

- We have severe problems in the educational world: Exploding student populations; mushrooming stores of information, bursting upon an already-crowded curriculum; increased emphasis on the need to individualize instruction for each student.

- We have surveys and reports from both within and outside the "educational establishment" that tell us how we're missing the mark in meeting these problems.

- We have a dozen or more major teaching resources, products of 20th century technology, that we could use now to improve our efficiency and output in the classroom. Yet, we seem unable to let go of the traditional concept of Mark Hopkins, the master tutor, on one end of the log, lecturing to the student(s) on the other end.

Finally, among these teaching resources we have the proven performance of film as a means of getting the message across. In commenting on the use of film, Warren S. Williams of the University of Rochester has written: [5]

> The sound movie projector and accompanying library of films are effective teacher aids. A number of researchers investigated the classroom use of movies and the majority concluded that correct use of this audiovisual aid improved learning.

Furthermore, experts tell us that the "eye outranks all other sensory organs put together as a pathway to the brain. When you couple to this the sense of hearing, it is no wonder that the sound motion picture is a potent tool for persuasion . . ."[6] "A good film, used on appropriate subject matter, can teach students twice as much. Retention is high."[7]

The Business of Education

Our own experience with massive educational programs in the industrial and business setting substantiates the effectiveness of film in the "classroom." At the Eastman Kodak Company a total of 35,000 people participate in some sort of formal learning every year. These efforts—which, together with less formal training on the job, account for at least 10% of the company's annual paid time—range from courses to upgrade manual skills to seminars on problem-solving and corporate management for the executive staff.

Furthermore, because of the "manpower investment" that Kodak makes in education each year, we are eager to find and use the tools that get the message across most effectively. One of the Kodak training departments,[8] for example, has built a substantial library of films, each about two minutes long, on the common personnel problems that range from the use of the suggestion system to on-the-job evidence of an employee's severe emotional problems. These simple productions, shot in the company's plants and offices with employees as "actors," present open-ended situations that are used as the focal point for discussion. We have found that this material can be presented much more effectively and efficiently on film than in written or verbal form. As one seminar leader put it:

> "The reality of the films provides a direct challenge to the new supervisors. They can see the action for themselves—how an employee looked, what he said, his gestures. It's almost impossible to capture these nuances in words; yet, they are important factors for the supervisor to gain insight into the problem being studied."

This commitment to education has also led the company to establish a series of Marketing Education Centers planned for four major cities. These facilities are designed not only for educating Kodak employees and dealers, but also for observing the effectiveness of new techniques and devices that might be useful elsewhere in the field of education.

In the recently completed center in Atlanta, Georgia, for instance, a computer and photo-assisted learning unit, which employs a text with super 8 motion pictures and 2″ × 2″ slides, is already installed and in use. What we gain from this experience, teaming films and slides with a computer, may be of future value in the schoolroom.

The point is that business and education have much to give to—and gain from—each other. The knowledge industry, growing at 2½ times the rate of the national economy, is a vast new market for companies that can listen to what educators want and come up with the products that meet these needs.

At the same time, industry is the major customer for the product that the schools turn out, i.e., educated men and women. As one of old Henry Ford's right-hand men once wrote:

> "We at Ford Motor Company rarely select a man entirely for what he knows. It is his capacity to learn, particularly the capacity to learn that about which he knows nothing."

In the final analysis, then, the goals of education and the needs of industry are the same: creative, self-reliant people. It's imperative, in my opinion, that we nurture this partnership, share our insights, and search together for the most effective ways to teach people to learn.

Capsule Case Histories

If we turn back now to our discussion of what happens with audiovisuals in the schoolroom, we find ourselves facing a bleak picture as described by observers of the educational scene: a talking teacher; little use of A-V materials; burgeoning problems in class size and curriculum.

Fortunately, we don't have to stop here. We can pry open some other classroom doors around the country to give you an exciting glimpse into what does happen when innovative teachers apply their talents to the learning potential of film.

- Take the Douglas MacArthur High School in Saginaw, Michigan, with its two Multi-Media Learning Centers. Eighty students and four team teachers can use these facilities at one time: 16mm motion pictures, slides, tapes, TV, and overhead projectors.

  In describing the Learning Centers, one school administrator says: "Teachers can be more creative and imaginative in their approach . . . (with) a wealth of audiovisual materials readily available. Equally important, this team-teaching approach gives four different teachers an opportunity to reach the students."[9]

- The Granite School District, near Salt Lake City, Utah, has set up a Media Center to train teachers to produce and use audiovisuals in their classrooms.[10] Open evenings, week-ends, and summers, the Center is usually filled to capacity by some 60 teachers. They preview films, work with technical staff on the final touches of a motion picture they produced themselves, or learn how to use any of the A-V equipment on hand.

- In Chicago, some 250 teachers at schools in the city's culturally deprived areas[11] now have movie cameras, projectors and raw-stock film. They are encouraged to plan field trips with their classes and to record their experiences on film. Later, the youngsters write and narrate the commentary for the productions.

  "The emphasis for these trips," explains one administrator,[12] "is on the 'institutions of society: the fire station, the police department, the airport. Once these kids have seen these places from the inside and have sorted out their impressions to make a film record of their trip, they no longer regard policemen and firemen and other authority figures as mysterious and alien. They develop a strong sense of participation."

- Or look over the shoulder of a co-ed in the computer programming class at San Jose College in California.[13] She's missed several sessions and now she's having trouble operating the key-punch machine. Meanwhile, the teacher is busy with a group doing more advanced work.

  What happens? The girl picks out a shortfilm[14] from a file in the study carrel at one side of the room. She reviews the film, which was made by the course instructor, finds out what she's doing wrong, and returns to operate the machine successfully. When the teacher comes to her, she's ready to go on to the next step instead of reviewing the last.

- The Sobrante Elementary School, in the heart of the "curfew" district in Oakland, California, puts films, tapes, and records alongside books on its library shelves. The principal[15] reports that the use of the library has increased by at least ten times. He adds:

  "Youngsters who have reached the sixth grade with marginal reading skills now find that the library is the place where they can watch films or listen to tapes and records. They can produce reports on what they see and hear, rather than what they've read . . . Once they begin to taste success with language skills, then we can begin to reach them, to teach them other things."

- With the realization of what film can do, there has been a new look at the classroom where the film will be shown.

  "There's an entire new approach to the construction of the educational plant," reports the director of the Audio-Visual Center at Western Michigan University.[16] "When new building committees are formed throughout the state, they include a representative of our organization. As a result, new schools have classrooms with built-in screens; the rooms can easily be darkened; there are proper electrical outlets; and there are facilities for storing projectors and films."

- At an elementary school in Ossining, N.Y., a social studies teacher began working with sixth and eighth graders several years ago in the production of films that make the most of the teacher's and students' time.[17]

  "The key word is accessibility," she explains. "When I get hung up in explaining a point in geography or history, I can now say 'Look here,' pop into the projector a film that these or some previous students have helped me make, and show the class in their own idiom exactly what I mean."

Today's Idiom

The teacher put her finger on it, didn't she? She wants to *show* the students *in their own idiom.* Visual media today are not super-imposed on the lives of children. They are a part of these youngsters' everyday experience. As one example, more than half the audiences in movie theatres today are 14-24 years old. As Merle Steir, an independent film producer, has commented:[18]

  "Film is the medium of the Now Generation. At Expo 67's Youth Pavilion; in 100 college degree programs; in 1200 college film societies; anywhere that youth gathers, film is happening."

Or to quote Dr. Williams of the University of Rochester once more:[19]

  "Movies are not only more effective than other means of instruction but are also preferred by many students. D. W. Redemsky distributed questionnaires at Michigan State University to determine student attitudes about the classroom utilization of films. Although Redemsky studied college students, some of his findings are important to lower level teacher.

  "Most of the students questioned had a positive attitude not only toward the showing of films, but also any discussion which followed."

Even with this realization of the integral nature of film in the lives of today's youngsters, we still read and hear about motion pictures as an "audiovisual aid" in the classroom —a kind of extra resource that's tacked onto the regular course work. There's an executive in my company who would like to get rid of the term "visual aids" altogether.

  "The term itself seems to carry over from the past,"[20] "It's like first aid . . .

rather than an integral part of the learning process. Visual media are not 'aids' to anything; they are 'ways to discovery.' "

What Film Offers

At this point, it becomes fairly obvious that film *is* a valuable classroom tool. Film offers:

MOTION
The image can record and illuminate the live action of a person or the microscopic twitches of a paramecium. Film can be used to "break-up" a complicated maneuver and make it understandable, via slow motion or animation. Motion pictures can "grab" the learner and hold his attention, presenting him with a constantly changing scene. "The motion picture is the way *par excellence* of presenting visual cues."[21]

COLOR
Similarly, film offers motion pictures *in color,* adding greatly to the dimension of realism for the learner. The importance of these color cues, moreover, may range from merely strengthening the visual excitement of the image to the crucial color differentiation to be observed in a filmed laboratory experiment.

SOUND
With its own sound track, a film can become a self-contained teaching unit, presenting the student with complete visual and verbal instructions for a complicated manual skill or enlarging his scope of experience with the sights and sounds of a major space shot.

FLEXIBILITY
Depending on how it's projected, the same film can be viewed on a screen large enough for 50 people or small enough for an individual study carrel.

Film can be used anywhere—classroom, auditorium, library viewing station, study hall, in the home. The introduction of a new Ektalite high-brightness screen has nullified the need to darken a room in order to show motion pictures today.* It offers: (1) Evenly bright images as seen from any viewing position over a moderately wide horizontal and moderately narrow vertical angle. (2) Image brightnesses six or more times as great as with screens now in general use (for the same image size and projector output). (3) Almost total rejection of stray light falling on the screen from outside normal viewing positions—permitting excellent image contrast and color saturation, even in brightly lighted areas. (4) A reflecting surface which should last indefinitely with reasonable care.

---

*Kodak introduced this new projection surface in 1967. The screen—which is now available in 40″ × 40″ size suitable for class and conference rooms—is actually a reflecting surface of specially treated aluminum foil.

Film lends itself to use with other media, e.g., TV, computers, and even textbooks which are beginning now to offer coordinated motion pictures for each chapter.

UNIVERSALITY

The film gauges—35mm, 16mm, super 8mm—are standard the world over. That's one reason why the major TV networks have chosen film as the prime distribution medium for their program materials, both in this country and abroad. This advantage, coupled with the flexibility and low cost in shooting and editing film, has meant that 80% of the prime TV network time emanates from the motion picture medium.[22] In addition, film represents 75% of the program source for day-time broadcasts and independent stations.

When the importance of the event warrants real immediacy (such as a space shot, presidential campaign, major sporting event), then the networks go to live broadcasts or sometimes to videotape.

ACCESSIBILITY

A teacher who has a projector and library of films in her classroom has quick and easy access to motion pictures as a learning resource. Furthermore, she can project a film whenever the class is ready for it, *not* at some pre-scheduled broadcast time. She also has the option of *repeating* the film for the entire class or selected students.

"CREATIBILITY"

Just as a teacher can write an original poem for an English class or suggest a new analysis of current events for a course in political science, so today, the instructor himself can produce a film to show a lab experiment or the results of a field trip or even the classroom activities of his students. And students, too, are making their own films:

> "One can hardly attend a public event—be it a football game, a rock concert, a yacht club regatta, or a street fair in a slum—without encountering young people taking light readings, staging vignettes, and checking lens angles."[23]

RECENT DEVELOPMENTS

Teachers are beginning to realize that films, in addition to conveying large chunks of information effectively, can also serve as vehicles for specific drill and testing. A film, for example, is tireless in presenting the slow learner with repeated drill in such areas as multiplication tables or word syllabication. Films for classroom use are being built with several "stopping points," with discussion questions presented by the narrator to probe students' reactions to what they've just seen.

Some educational films are also constructed today with a test for a climax instead of the traditional "Hollywood" fade-out. In addition, filmed segments can provide more challenging exams than older, written-type tests in such fields as biology, medicine, art, and even advanced psychology, where students can be presented with a realistic clinical "case" on film.

Resistance to Film

We've been talking in general terms about what film can do. If we are saying, on the one hand, that film is such a significant educational tool then why are we also saying that many teachers aren't using it as anything but an auxiliary resource? It's an important question, and the roots of the answer lie in many directions.

A major stumbling block to film use has been the central storage and scheduling systems in some schools. A teacher had to go through laborious procedures to get the film she wanted, often ordering the print weeks in advance with no guarantee it would be delivered when her lesson plan called for it.

Film catalogues have often been difficult to use, with sketchy information provided on the content of individual pictures. While no catalogue can serve as a complete guide to the value of a film for a particular learning situation, better descriptive material could ease the problem in which many teachers have been faced with the choice of "taking a chance" on a film whose title sounded good or spending hours in previewing sessions.

Many of the older type educational films tried to be "all things to all learners"—which meant that a production that was ostensibly on the topic usually dragged in material that was far afield of the unit under class study. The object was to cram dozens of concepts into a twenty-minute film.

And, finally, there is the whole, complex cycle of teachers teaching as they were taught. In other words, teacher-training colleges employ professors who lecture their students. Then, these students, as teachers in their own right, continue the tradition by lecturing their own classes, and we are back again to Mark Hopkins and the log!

Of course, as far as film is concerned, teacher training institutions have faced the same problems that have confronted other areas of education over the years: a limited number of commercially available motion picture titles in the specialized subject areas; restricted budgets for purchase or rental of A-V supplies; complicated projection equipment and scheduling requirements.

Here is a critical area, it seems to me, where Federal support could break this dulling "lecture cycle." The teacher training institutions should be the centers for research into *new* ways of teaching teachers to teach, including exploration and creation of resources in film. Today's classroom teacher should be exposed to the best and most efficient methods of education during his own undergraduate years. Then, as experience has shown, he will be likely to apply these same innovative techniques in his professional approach to the learning problems he encounters as a teacher in his own right.

While we have explored teachers' resistance to using film in the classroom, we should underscore the fact that things are changing. Films and film equipment have become easier to use with the development of cartridge-loading cameras and projectors. Schools are recognizing the need to get films out of locked vaults and into the individual classroom. And new film formats are changing our ideas about what a motion picture, a screen, and a projector "must" look like.

Fascinating Film

Film has a fascinating history, and from its very inception, it's been an educational medium.

It was Thomas Edison himself—a key pioneer in the motion picture—who envisioned his discovery as a great educational tool in the 1890's. His prediction, however, has been a long time in coming to fruition.

For one thing, the earliest film stock was made on a nitrate base. It was highly flammable and could only be shown in fireproof projection booths. Hardly the kind of accessibility that educators are demanding today! A major breakthrough came in 1908 when Kodak manufactured its first non-flammable film using safety cellulose-acetate base. Although this film gradually replaced the highly flammable cellulose-nitrate type in educational situations, it did not become commercially successful until 1923. That same year (1923), 16mm reversal "safety" film was introduced and was supplemented by 16mm safety-base, positive film; a decade later, sound was added to 16mm and we were in the era of the "talkies."

Over the years there have been some noteworthy films sponsored by business firms with the classroom in mind. A pioneer series was the Ford Motor Company's, "Ford Educational Weekly" (1916-1920). With the guidance of William M. Gregory, Director (1910 to 1945) of the Educational Museum of the Cleveland Public Schools, this program—circa 1920-25 known as, "The Ford Educational Library"—provided curriculum-oriented motion pictures and accompanying teacher guides to many, many hundreds of schools on such subjects as agriculture, civics, industrial and regional geography, history, nature study, health, and other topics.[24]

The Rockefeller Foundation's General Education Board focused attention on the academic community as an educational film producer in 1938 with a $125,000 grant to the University of Minnesota. The project is chiefly remembered for having established a professional 35mm production unit which produced an epic on the history and problems of the State of Minnesota. This experiment inspired a number of other universities at a later date to plan and produce their own films.[25]

Yale was another institution of higher education that took an even earlier interest in the motion picture medium. In 1923-24, its Yale University Press produced "The Chronicles of America Photoplays," a series of history films that were subsequently shown in thousands of classrooms. Great effort was expended in trying to make the costumes and settings meticulously accurate.[26]

One of the largest ventures in the early days of educational film was the Eastman Teaching Films, Inc.—some 300 titles in many areas of the curriculum. Orders for prints of several of these productions topped the 2800 mark! The series grew out of a massive study of film in the classroom that was financed by the Eastman Kodak Company. It all began in February, 1926, when George Eastman announced that during the preceding three years his company had conducted a survey of the whole field of teaching films. The survey showed in substance the following: [27]

1. That few pictures adapted to classroom use had been produced.

2. That the cost of equipment and films had made the use of films as regular classroom instrumentalities prohibitive.

3. That large capital investment would be required to produce films on a scale adequate to school needs.

4. That adequate experiments had not been made in the practical use of films in classroom work to establish their value as aids to teaching.

5. That school authorities would not be justified in making the expenditures required for film service until adequate experiments were made and the value of films as teaching aids definitely determined.

Mr. Eastman also announced[28] that the Eastman Kodak Company had decided to undertake a practical experiment in the use of films in the schools to study the following questions:

1. Can films be produced which are correlated with standard courses of study?

2. Can the teaching value of these films, when used to supplement the usual pedagogical devices of the teacher in the classroom, be measured?

3. Is the educational value of the contributions of the films sufficient to justify the expenditure required to make them a regular part of the equipment of the schools?

The two men who conducted the study—leading professors at Columbia's Teachers College and the University of Chicago, respectively—were Drs. Ben D. Wood and Frank N. Freeman. When they published their findings, here's what they had to say:

". . . under the conditions which were obtained in this experiment, which probably reflect normal school conditions reasonably well, the use of the films materially increased the effectiveness of instruction."[29]

"If the motion picture film is to be of maximum service in instruction it should form an integral and regular part of the curriculum and of classroom work."[30]

"Usefulness of the films will be seriously limited if they demand that all teachers who use them follow a rigidly uniform course of study. The films should be so flexible that they can be incorporated into a variety of different courses."[31]

"We believe that the Eastman teaching film experiment has uncovered only a small part of the film contributions, but that the demonstrated contributions amply justify the extensive use of films of this type in our schools."[32]

The results were so overwhelmingly in favor of films that the Company decided to continue the work. The experiment had started with 10 geography and 10 general science productions used with 11,000 school children in 12 cities. Over the next 15 years (1928-44), Kodak prepared 300 films in a wide range of subject areas, which were distributed to thousands of classrooms across the U.S. and in 30 foreign countries.

In the more recent days of high priority military training, films have played a vital role. As Major General H. C. Ingles, the Chief Signal Officer—United States Army, declared in 1945:

"Among the major problems confronting the Army at the outbreak of war was the task of getting the message of military techniques to the millions of troops being trained in all branches of the Service. The use of training films took on magnitude during World War II and constituted a real factor in military operations by reducing the time required for converting a civilian into a skilled soldier capable of taking care of himself in the field."[33]

Likewise, the sister service, the Navy, attested to the efficacy of the motion picture in a 1945 report by Rear Admiral D. C. Ramsey, USN, Chief, Bureau of Aeronautics:

". . . it has been recognized that training films as used in the Navy's effective training program contributed in a very large measure to building the most powerful fighting force afloat."[34]

A captured German commander confirmed this evaluation when he admitted that the Nazis had grossly miscalculated how rapidly the U.S. could build its armed services out of civilians. He said:

"The American military made use of film on a scale that we never dreamed possible."

If we return once more to motion pictures in the elementary and secondary school classroom, we find that 16mm has been the dominant format used in education. In fact, a recent survey[35] shows that school systems own only enough 16mm projectors and films to place two projectors and twelve prints in each school in the country. Obviously, this "hardware and software" is not evenly distributed around the U.S., and even these totals fall far short of the guidelines recommended by DAVI (Department of Audiovisual Instruction, National Education Association)[36] for at least one super 8 projector and approximately 50 super 8 prints at each teaching station (classroom).

But an interesting trend has been taking place in education . . . a trend that has placed new demands on film. We've mentioned it before: a shift in accent from *teaching* to *learning.* This new approach calls for shorter films that teachers and students can use anytime, anywhere, in any way. With this approach, we've added a new term to the lexicon of film: super 8.

The Super 8 Story

Although we talk a great deal about super 8, it might be helpful to review some basic facts about the format of this new medium, which has been termed the economical, "paperback book-type breakthrough" of films.

Basically, super 8 film offers a *larger and brighter* picture area than traditional "cine" 8mm. Because of improvements in design, each frame of super 8 is 50% larger than cine 8, which means a bigger screen image. In addition, the larger frame allows more light to pass from the projector through the film, making for a brighter and sharper picture.

At the same time, super 8 also offers the compact film size that teachers want for ease of storage and portability. For example, you can store 1320 100-foot reels of super 8 (in cartridges) in a steel 71″ × 35″ × 16½″ standard-size film cabinet. That would add up to about 110 hours of continuous-viewing—*more* than enough film to "saturate" the average 5-day-a-week, major subject class for an entire school year! The compact format also means *economy* in film and projector costs, and super 8 color prints are available at little more cost than black and white. Manifestly, there is economy in shipping a super 8 print rather than its 16mm counterpart.

The image from super 8 is not only clearer and brighter but the sound system is also superior. At the present time, there are two methods used for soundtracks: optical and magnetic. Traditionally, optical has been the sound system for 16mm film; however, the new direction of super 8 film has emphasized the excellent properties of magnetic for its use with this flexible motion picture system.

Magnetic Sound Advantages:

1. Good quality magnetic sound is easier to obtain, easier for a lab to process, and requires less complicated projection equipment.

2. For the same reasons, magnetic sound is the choice for home projectors, thus increasing the compatibility of school and home visual resources.

3. Soundtracks can be readily changed to suit a specific audience.

4. Magnetic prints, in classroom and laboratory tests, last up to four times as long as optical prints because the film rides through the projector on the tiny tape soundtracks. As a result, the film surfaces do not rub against each other, and there is less chance for damage to the emulsion.

The Cartridge Question

This brings us, finally, to the method of packaging and projecting super 8 film: the closed-loop cartridge and the reel-to-reel design. It is evident that the public wants projectors that offer the ease of cartridge loading. While the initial cartridge design on the market was the continuous, or closed, loop, it is clear now that, in the educational setting, the so-called reel-to-reel system offers more advantages.

Advantages of Reel-to-Reel:

1. Easy to snap regular film reel into cartridge.

2. Fast forward, reverse, and rewind capabilities.

3. Easy to project, repeat, or review any desired segment of the film.

4. Lower initial cost of reel-to-reel cartridge.

5. Automatic re-wind of film to heads-out position, assuring next user of seeing the production from the beginning.

6. Film can be removed from reel by local A-V coordinator for cleaning, editing, splicing.

7. Cartridge provides convenient labelling and storage container.

8. Reel can be easily removed from cartridge for use on home projectors, adding the dimension of compatibility for home and school visual resources.

After much research and study in an effort to assess the film system that offers the most advantages in the educational setting, the Eastman Kodak Company has decided to incorporate magnetic sound and the reel-to-reel cartridge in its super 8 film system. In June, 1969, Kodak will introduce its cartridge design for 50- and 100-foot capacity super 8 reels. Later, 220-and 400-foot cartridges will be available. Furthermore, the company has shared the design plans with a wide cross-section of other manufacturers both here and abroad in an effort to foster interchangeability of "software."

Systems Approach

Now that we have looked at film as an entity, we must also explore film as one of the most flexible modules in a coordinated group of learning resources. What we're talking about, of course, is the Systems Approach. We feel, naturally, that the photographic system—16mm and super 8 cameras, films, and projectors—is going to have an increasingly important place in the educational setting. But too much enthusiasm for the superiority of one medium can mask its potential for use *with* other approaches.

Film, for example, is essentially a storage medium. And we generally think of projection as the means of access to what is stored on it. But coupled with the computer for retrieving information and the electron for transporting it, film capable of storing a billion bits of information per square inch is something else again! Combine the realism and impact inherent in the film image with recorded sound and the computer's infallible memory and endless patience, and you have a system that can meet the challenge of recognizing and coping with individual differences among children.

In the same vein, films can be incorporated into broadcasts on educational TV and we can envision a time when 30 or more electronic channels could service every learner in the classroom with films, computer-programmed courses, and video-tape beamed on individual TV screens at the pace set by the individual student.

At present, the compatibility of film and educational TV has not been fully explored. A major factor in this dilemma is budget. Even though film is an economical visual medium, effective motion pictures, to be used on a broad scale, *cannot* be produced for the $250 we now spend on an average half-hour of educational TV. The film industry, aware of this difficulty, is constantly searching for new technical developments to cut further the cost of motion picture production. Recent improvements, such as front screen projection; new editing and dubbing systems; lightweight and less expensive camera, sound, and lighting equipment; and new shooting techniques offer partial solutions. At some point, however, the Federal Government should try to stimulate greater and more effective use of specially designed motion pictures as a prime source for educational television programming.

In dealing with the immediate needs of education, however, we run into problems when we examine the present "state of the art" of the electronic marvels at our disposal. It is prohibitively expensive to provide a few, let alone 30, TV screens and transmission channels with the color and high picture resolution available already via film and the projector. Similarly, computer outlets are costly, and because today's "electronic brains" can remember only words and numbers—not pictures—it is still necessary to integrate the projected image into the system if we are going to offer the visual dimension to the learner.

What is here right now is the Kodak Ektagraphic MFS-8 Projector. This machine will project individual still frames of a super 8 motion picture for as long as the user wishes. Or press a button, and the projector shows the film at normal movie speed. The dimension of sound is available through a coordinated cassette tape recorder with a binaural track. This means that in the very near future, we can program learning situations in which a computer can present the student with written and verbal information and through an electronic signal, trigger the action of the MFS projector to show either "still" or "motion" pictures.

On a more modest scale, the projector itself can be used today in the average classroom to meet visual learning needs at relatively little expense. A single 50-foot roll of super 8 movie film contains as many separate still pictures as would a 3,600 frame filmstrip.

When we come right down to it, some teachers, for years, have been combining different kinds of materials—films, filmstrips, still pictures, models—to meet their teaching goals. These are instructional systems at the simplest level. Yet, the fact that educators have been obliged to develop their own "systems of instruction" points up the need for a more comprehensive attack on the problem. Now commercial producers are beginning to do systematically what teachers have done informally—"package" related materials for specific curricular areas.

As an outstanding example, take the Physical Science Study Committee's approach to teaching high school physics. Here, millions of dollars have been spent to produce materials, but only after a thorough study of the needs of physics teaching in certain types of high schools. The Committee of experts has supervised the production of more than 80 films; dozens of paperback books; and laboratory apparatus. It's all happening around a central concept—a point of view—as to what the content of high school physics should be. Possibly the key to its success is the fact that it was planned and that there was a reason for everything that was produced.

If we are going to make the systems approach work, we need four things:

1. Centralized planning

2. The involvement of people who are *not* now working side-by-side—curriculum specialists, AV experts, book publishers, equipment manufacturers.

3. Access to top scholars and content specialists.

4. Highly qualified classroom teachers to bring their own skills and imaginations to the effective use of the "hardware" and "software" in the system. For, like systems anywhere, these in the field of educational technology are only as good as what goes into them.

A Look Ahead

And what about the future? One key question, it seems to me, is whether the educational problems that loom so large today can be made irrelevant through the technical resources we have at our disposal.

The shortage of classroom space, for example, is tied to numbers of qualified teachers and optimum class sizes. But what if we decided to spend the money to train staff people in the use of new media techniques and other learning resources? The teacher-pupil ratio might rise to 50-to-1, the basic instructional unit to more than 100 . . . and "that teacher," with a team of assistants and technicians, would have the time for the individual attention that students and parents are asking for.

In terms of the sheer amount of information and accelerated change in every field . . . in terms of the trend to individualized instruction . . . the teacher today cannot hope to bear the whole burden of instruction. Furthermore, as the emphasis shifts from "teaching" to "learning," there is no reason why he should try to be all things to all students. The teacher who can use technology to advantage—to fulfill his role as a director of learning—surrounds his profession with new prestige.

There is a wide gap today between the promise of educational technology and the day-to-day reality in the classroom. None of us single-handedly can make the sweeping innovations and changes that will close that gap. But we can start, I believe, by seizing every opportunity to help create the "climate of innovation" that observers of the educational scene have found so sadly lacking now.

Summary

In the final analysis, we find that film offers a number of advantages in the educational setting:

1. Motion

2. Sound

3. Color

4. Low Cost

5. Expansion or compression of time and size

6. Flexibility

7. Repeatability

8. Accessibility

9. Universality of film size

10. Creatibility

11. Compatibility with other media—including TV, computers, books, tape recorders, overhead projectors, slides, and filmstrips.

In addition, the super 8 system, as a relative newcomer in the world of film, should be considered for its:

1. Potential for making film readily accessible

2. Bright, clear, and large images in color

3. Compact size and low cost

4. Simpler projection devices.

And finally, if film is to become a viable part of the educational scene, we must take some specific actions:

1. Support the introduction of first-rate audiovisual courses and day-to-day usage in the teacher training institutions. Perhaps incorporate a requirement for "visual literacy" into the state certification procedures for new teachers.
2. Support research into the development and use of specially tailored films and other audiovisuals to meet the needs of the teacher training institutions.
3. Arrive at a "basic standard" of film hardware and software for effective use in each classroom. Perhaps the DAVI recommendation of one super 8 projector (in this case sound) and 50 prints per classroom is a good starting point.
4. Make the support available to school systems to buy the basic equipment, with parallel support for in-service audiovisual workshops for teachers.
5. Provide the support for leaders in subject-matter areas and experts in film production to work together on integrated series of motion pictures for coordinated use throughout a semester or school year.
6. On a larger scale, provide the impetus for the "systems team" from a variety of fields to investigate what we can do now, and what we must do in the future, to make full use of the technology at our disposal, in terms of both accessibility and cost.

The prophetic words of Freeman and Wood in their landmark 1926 study of film seem to sum up our present situation with uncanny accuracy:

"We believe the present experiment has uncovered only a small part of the film contributions, but that the demonstrated contributions amply justify the extensive use of film . . . in our schools . . .

"The classroom film is, or will be, a social agency whose power is felt far beyond the walls of the classroom . . .

"Film has already revolutioned our ideas, customs, tastes, and mores."[37]

REFERENCES

1. Interview at the Green Chimneys School, Brewster, N.Y. "Diana's" name has been disguised at the request of the principal. 1967. From the files of the Editorial Service Bureau, Eastman Kodak Company, Rochester, N.Y.

2. National Education Association. *Teachers Supply and Demand in Public Schools.* (Washington, D.C., NEA, 1967).

3. Goodlad, Dr. John J. *Catholic Education Today and Tomorrow* Washington, D.C., The National Catholic Education Association, p. 67.

4. Allen, William H. "The State of the Art." University of California study prepared for the Committee on Economic Development, sub-committee on Efficiency and Innovation in Education New York, CED, 1968.

5. Newsletter of the Genesee Valley School Development Association, in cooperation with the University of Rochester. *Research and the Classroom Teacher.* Dr. Warren S. Williams, Ed. Rochester, N.Y., April, 1965, p. 3.

6. Ridenaur, Dr. Louis N. "Bibliography in an Age of Science." p. 23, Urbana, Ill., University of Illinois Press, 1952. As quoted in *The Dollars and Sense of Business Films,* Films Steering Committee of the Association of National Advertisers, New York, New York. 1954, p. 39.

7. Gibson, J. J. Ed. "Motion Picture Testing and Research." Report No. 7, Army Air Forces Aviation Psychology Program Research Report. Washington, D.C., Government Printing Office, 1947. As quoted in *The Dollars and Sense of Business Films,* p. 50.

8. From an interview with Robert McClelland, Director of Training, Eastman Kodak Company, Rochester, N.Y., 1968.

9. Quoted from an interview with Clyde Glazer, Director of Instruction for Saginaw Township, 1967. From the files of the Editorial Service Bureau, Eastman Kodak Company.

10. Quoted from an interview with John Larsen, Director of Instructional Media for the Granite School District near Salt Lake City, Utah, 1967. From the files of the Editorial Service Bureau, Eastman Kodak Company.

11. Research supplied from the files of the Editorial Service Bureau, Eastman Kodak Company, 1967.

12. Quoted for an interview with Fred S. Rosengarden, Director of Visual Education for the Chicago Board of Education, 1967. From the Files of the Editorial Service Bureau, Eastman Kodak Company.

13. From an interview with Dr. Jerrold Kemp, Co-ordinator of Production Services, Audio-Visual Services Division, San Jose State College, Calif., 1966. From the files of the Editorial Service Bureau, Eastman Kodak Company.

14. "Shortfilm," like a filmstrip, has no maximum length but does have a specific communication objective. This definition includes such motion pictures as the "single-concept" film and "film loop."

15. From an interview with Jack Miller, Principal of the Sobrante Elementary School, Oakland, Calif., 1967. From the files of the Editorial Service Bureau, Eastman Kodak Company.

16. Quoted from an interview with Carl B. Snow, Director of the Audio-Visual Center, Western Michigan University, 1967. From the files of the Editorial Service Bureau, Eastman Kodak Company.

17. Quoted from an interview with Miss Phyllis Cambre, teacher in Ossining, N.Y., 1966. From the files of the Editorial Service Bureau, Eastman Kodak Company.

18. Steir, Merle. "Films for Youth," a presentation prepared for the American Management Association, 1968. Reprinted in *Youth Concepts,* a newsletter of the organization of the same name, 3 East 40th Street, New York, N.Y., August, 1968, p. 1.

19. Williams, Dr. Warren. *op. cit.*

20. Zornow, G. B. Vice President, Marketing, Eastman Kodak Company. "Educational Technology Shapes the Future . . . Are You Ready?" Speech given before the Superintendents' Meeting, National Catholic Educational Association, October, 1968, Rochester, N.Y.

21. Miller, Neal E. (ed.). *Graphic Communication and the Crisis in Education.* p. 76. Special issue of *Audio-Visual Communication Review,* Department of Audio-Visual Instruction, National Education Association, Washington, D.C., 1957.

22. "Can Kodak Come up with an Encore?" *Forbes Magazine,* Volume 102, No. 9, November 1, 1968, p. 37.

23. Steir, Merle, *op. cit.,* p. 1.

24. Based on telephone interviews with Mr. William M. Gregory; Mr. Johna Pepper, Ford Motor Company; Mr. Win Sears, The Henry Ford Museum; Mrs. Mayfield Bray, Audiovisual Branch, The National Archives, 1968.

25. Based on telephone interview with Dr. Paul R. Wendt, Department of Instructional Materials, Southern Illinois University, 1968.

26. Dates confirmed in telephone conversation with Mrs. Shirley Kupelian, Yale University Press, New Haven, Conn., 1968.

27. Wood, Ben D. and Frank N. Freeman. *Motion Pictures in the Classroom.* Cambridge, Mass., Houghton Mifflin, 1929, p. xviii.

28. *Ibid.,* p. xix.

29. *Ibid.,* p. 191.

30. *Ibid.,* p. 223

31. *Ibid.,* p. 224

32. *Ibid.,* p. 228

33. Ingles, Major General H. C. The Chief Signal Officer, United States Army. "Report on the Army Pictorial Service." *Business Screen Magazine,* Vol. 7, Issue 1, December 30, 1945, p. 31.

34. Ramsey, Rear Admiral D. C. USN, Chief—Bureau of Aeronautics, U.S. Navy Department. "Special Report on the Training Film Program of the United States Navy." *Business Screen Magazine,* Vol. 6, Issue 5, May 15, 1945.

35. Hope, Thomas W. "Market Review: Nontheatrical Film and Audio-Visual—1967." *Journal of the Society of Motion Picture and Television Engineers,* Vol. 77, No. 11, November, 1968, pp. 1210-1220.

36. Department of Audio-Visual Instruction, National Education Association, extracts from *Standards for School Media Programs* Tentative, Washington, D.C.: DAVI, 1968.

37. Wood and Freeman, *op. cit.,* p. 228.

8.

8mm Film in Education
Status and Prospects—1968

by LOUIS FORSDALE
Prof. of English
Teachers College
Columbia Univ.

What is so special about 8mm film—in contrast with 16mm or 35mm or 70mm—that this particular gauge should be singled out for consideration? The special import of "8" in education is that it can help make motion pictures vastly more accessible to teachers and students than they are today.

No case need be made here concerning the value of film in education. The problem is that this value is largely potential, so infrequently and so unwisely have films generally been used. An overwhelming deterrent to the use of motion pictures—effectively or not—is their inaccessibility. Our 16mm prints are expensive and therefore are housed in central libraries, to be distributed to teachers who requisition them, generally well in advance. This is an annoying and time-consuming process, and it puts off most teachers at the outset. But even the teacher who persists and orders a film is confronted with a second problem: when it arrives it must be shown on a clumsy projector which is difficult to locate, move, set up, and operate. Most teachers prefer to live without these irritants.

As compared with the book—the best medium to use as a standard in this respect—film is quite inaccessible to the teacher, and if it is inaccessible to the *teacher*, most educators would never think of asking a *student* to go to the library and study a motion picture on his own.

The difficulties of using film in education can be alleviated through the use of 8mm systems. Reduced costs of 8mm prints and projectors could enable us to establish film libraries in many individual schools, perhaps some day in individual laboratories and classrooms. And even today some 8mm projectors can be used by five-year-olds (or by "unmechanical" adults) after a minute of instruction, literally.

The biggest dream about 8 in education, then, is that this miniature gauge of film will help bring motion pictures geographically closer to the user, and at the same time make the showing of films vastly simpler. One of these goals is keyed to economics; the other is tied to engineering. Both favor 8mm, both work against 16mm, the film gauge which dominates education today. John Flory, an early advocate of the use of 8mm film in school, church and industry, once called 8 "the paperback of films." Flory's analogy is a good one, although it may be conservative. Considering the current inaccessibility of motion pictures in education, 16mm films might better be likened to manuscripts, chained to monastery reading tables, in which case 8 might be the book liberated and made ubiquitous by the invention of print with moveable type.

Whichever analogy eventually serves best, 8mm will almost certainly have a considerable impact on the uses of moving images in education, fundamentally changing our present notions of what kinds of films should be made, how they should be purchased, stored and distributed, and how and by whom they should be used.

Film Gauges In and Out of Education

Some background information will be useful in seeing where we stand now and in making some guesses about what the future might hold. 8mm film and associated camera and projection equipment was introduced by Eastman Kodak in 1932 as a motion picture form for amateurs who wanted to make home movies. It caught on, and 8 has remained overwhelmingly an amateur's gauge since that time. 16mm remains the preeminent gauge for non-theatrical professional purposes; 35mm and 70mm dominate the theatrical field.

A variety of film guages is needed so that the factors of quality, on the one hand, and economy and ease of use, on the other, can be balanced as need requires. In general, the wider the film, the better the picture on the screen: 70mm is elegant for the wide-screen spectaculars. Also in general, the narrower the film, the easier it is to use in a variety of situations: 8mm suits home, school, and library settings. Obviously a 70mm system is more expensive in every way than an 8mm system.

When the move was made in the mid-1920's away from the clumsy 35mm gauge, and toward 16mm as the school standard, there were cries that the smaller gauge could not possibly provide the image quality which was needed. But advocates of 16mm argued, persuasively, that the advantages of portability, space saving, economy, and ease of operation offset the disadvantages of loss in picture quality. Also, those who knew photography understood that improvements in emulsions, lenses, cameras, projectors, and screens meant that the 35mm quality of 1925 would be equalled by the 16mm quality of 1935. It was. (All gauges improve constantly, of course, so one never catches another in absolute quality: the improvement is relative to a point in time.)

The move toward miniaturization which was begun with 16mm film forty years ago continues today with 8mm. Once regarded as adequate only for amateur use, 8 is now considered by photographic engineers to be good enough today for many professional non-theatrical uses. This is particularly true of Super 8, the new form of 8mm which has a 50 percent larger picture area than regular 8.

Although the Japanese have used 8mm film in education for many years, American educational interest in this gauge probably can best be dated from 1960-1961, when two 8mm sound projectors were marketed, one by the Fairchild Camera and Instrument Corporation, the other by the Eastman Kodak Company. Both projectors used standard reel-to-reel theading schemes. Although both were designed primarily for amateurs, they caused a small flurry of interest in education, stimulating, among other things, the convening of a major three-day conference at Teachers College, Columbia University ("8mm Sound Film and Education"), attended by some 150 persons from education, educational film houses, church, government, and the photographic industries. Interest in 8 in education has continued steadily upward since that date, although not only because of the conference, of course.

The Cartridge-8 Projectors

The first gut-level excitement about 8 in education came when The Technicolor Corporation introduced a small, inexpensive 8mm cartridge-loading projector. It was unique in the history of the motion picture. An inexpensive plastic cartridge holding up to four minutes of silent film could be plugged into a projector by anybody, including a five-year-old child. And the projector sold for less than $100. (This cartridge-loading capability is a peculiar technical advantage which 8mm has over wider film gauges. Educators have long complained about the difficulty of using projectors, and have advocated some kind of cartridge-loading system as the solution, but technical difficulties associated with 16mm film have stood in the way of achieving the goal. Because 8mm has one-quarter the mass of 16mm [it is half as wide and half as long], and because it moves within a cartridge at half the linear speed of 16mm, it presents fewer weight and friction problems than does 16, and it can therefore be loaded into inexpensive passive cartridges—casettes which merely contain the film but which are not encumbered by expensive gear arrangements to help drive the film forward. The active [motor driven] cartridges which are needed for 16mm film are quite expensive. Indeed, in the two prototypes 16mm cartridge-loading projectors which I have seen, the empty cartridges cost on the order of $25.00 apiece, a good deal more than the film which they were designed to contain! The cause of accessible film is hardly promoted by doubling or tripling costs!)

The Technicolor silent cartridge-loading projector noted above was instantly attractive to educators who saw it. There was, however, no backlog of films to use with it, primarily because the projector had been designed and first marketed for amateurs. (The decision to limit the cartridge to a four-minute capacity, for example, was made because 8mm home movie cameras generally accommodate four minutes of film in each load.) But the amateur market which was first envisioned for the projector did not materialize, and the Technicolor people turned their attention to the fields of education, training, and sales. Gradually the established educational film houses (and some new ones) began to develop cartridge loop films for the projector, and today the available world-wide total of such films (generally called "single concept films") must number on the order of 7000 titles. The fact that these loops are silent makes traffic across language boundaries possible.

In 1962 the first cartridge-8 *sound* projector was marketed, by the Fairchild Camera and Instrument Corporation. In contrast with the four-minute cartridge of the Technicolor silent machine, the Fairchild sound projector could accommodate up to twenty-two minutes of film in its plastic cartridges. This rear-screen projector (having the appearance of a television receiver) was designed for use by one person or a handful of people, viewing the small image in a lighted room. Like the Technicolor silent projector, the Fairchild sound machine also lacked a library of films ready for use. Subsequently similar rear-screen cartridge-8 sound projectors were marketed by other companies. Recently the Technicolor Corporation has marketed a sound projector which produces a larger image on a wall screen in a darkened room.

The Slow Growth of 8mm Film in Education

Both the silent and the sound cartridge-8 projectors have found their way only slowly into education; 8mm projectors of the traditional threading variety have had almost no impact. The cartridge machines have been used to a much greater extent in business and industry, for sales and training purposes. Among early (and continuing) industrial users of cartridge-8 have been various pharmaceutical houses, automobile and other heavy equipment manufacturers and certain retail chains which conduct continuing employee training programs. It is not surprising that business and industry should turn more quickly to an attractive new communication device. They have greater fiscal mobility than most schools have. Further, to pinpoint a special advantage, many industrial and business firms are quite prepared to make films which are specifically designed for cartridge projectors and to make sufficient copies for widespread use in their sales and training programs. They are therefore generally not disturbed by lack of existing libraries of films for the machines.

General inertia has impeded the growth of 8mm film in American education, of course.

A more specific problem is that 8mm is not a new medium; it is, rather a variation of the established medium of film. From the perspective of an experienced 16mm film maker or film user, 8 can seem terribly tangential: it may be a nice adjunct, but isn't it, after all, at least a little amateurish, rather cute, somewhat gimmicky? 8 always stands in the shadow of its older and bigger brother, 16.

Nor is this true only in the schools. The new "learning industries" have been publicized for half a dozen years now, and, in their planning with respect to educational technology, all of these still emerging enterprises have investigated 8, among other media. Still, their plans for the future, with respect to 8, seem to be unduly cautious. Indeed, the lack of research and development activity (which might lead to greater daring) in educational film houses and in most of publishing is astonishing to behold!). To be sure, the educational photographic market is still an economic peanut compared with the amateur market, and until dollars flow massively in education prudence will doubtless caution against vigorous advocacy of 8mm systems, especially where that advocacy might raise questions about the future role of 16mm prints and equipment.

The Sound Track and Format Debates

Two specific engineering/economic problems have plagued everybody in or around the 8mm field for the past several years, and have therefore slowed the acceptance of 8. One of the problems is still unresolved; the other is largely solved now.

The first problem (and the one which is unresolved) is the question of what kind of sound track, technically speaking, should be used on 8mm prints. Two types of sound tracks are used in motion pictures. Most 16mm and 35mm films have optical tracks, in which the sound is recorded as part of the photographic emulsion, appearing as a strip of varying shades of gray along the edge of the film. The second sound track is magnetic, in which the sound is "stored" on a stripe of iron oxide along the edge of the film. Magnetic tracks are used on 70mm theatrical films, on a very few 35mm and 16mm prints, and on a considerable number of 8mm prints. If all motion picture prints were lumped together, optical tracks would be found on the overwhelming majority of them; optical tracks are cheaper than magnetic tracks to reproduce. Magnetic tracks are inherently superior to optical tracks in quality of sound produced, however, and they have some advantage in prolonging print life, particularly when a print is subject to heavy use. The magnetic track also presents the amateur (and other local producer who has limited resources) with the opportunity of adding a modest sound track to a homemade film with a minimum amount of difficulty. The principal disadvantage of the magnetic track is that it is somewhat more expensive to use in the print-making process than is the optical track, at least when present printing equipment is employed. Advocates of the magnetic track argue, however, that added print life which results from this process more than offsets the added initial cost.

In the early and mid-1960's, when serious talk about professional use of 8mm film started, engineers, controllers and salesmen started a still-continuing debate about which of the sound tracks should be used in making 8mm prints. The magnetic track gained the ascendancy at the outset, and there are probably more 8mm sound prints in use today with magnetic tracks than with optical tracks. Three cartridge-8 projectors use magnetic tracks; one uses the optical tract. Standard reel-to-reel 8mm projectors use both tracks although the magnetic track dominates. Major commitments have been made by photographic laboratories—and labs are a most critical element in the total scheme—for both magnetic and optical printing and processing facilities. In short, the issue is by no means settled. Nor can one necessarily anticipate either a quick or an easy resolution of the problem. While one system may eventually gain commercial superiority over the other, it appears to me that both tracks will exist side by side for some time as we engage in a pragmatic test of the quality and cost questions.

Meanwhile—returning to the reason for talking about sound tracks—financial commitment to 8mm has been slowed by the presence of two tracks and by lack of clear-cut industry support for one over the other. A rather dramatic example of reluctance to invest in 8 because of the unrest over sound tracks involves the Methodist Church of the United States. The Methodists have a centralized purchasing power backed by some 30,000 local churches, and for years their leaders have been interested in using 8mm films for Sunday school and other church work. In the mid-1960's they had in fact nearly committed the church to an experimental program of distributing 8mm prints in a Film-of-the-Month plan, using magnetic sound, and many observers were eagerly awaiting the adventuresome scheme. Then the sound track debate opened. They pulled back, aborting in the early stages of this promising new venture in accessible film. Other groups have doubtless been cowed at the very outset by the ambiguities of the sound track issue.

The second technical problem, now largely resolved, relates to what format should be used on 8mm film. Format means the size and arrangement of the sprocket holes, the picture, and the sound track on the ribbon of film. With the serious attention to 8mm film as a professional gauge came a reevaluation of the capabilities of the regular 8mm format which has been used since 1932. Engineers reasoned that improvements could be made in the quality of the projected picture if the area given over to the picture in the film could be enlarged. As the illustration below shows, the key to making the picture area greater was reducing the size of the sprocket holes.

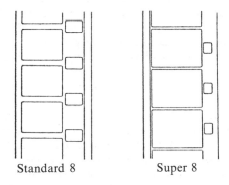

Standard 8   Super 8

Many format proposals were aired and argued in engineering circles, but it soon became clear that Super 8 (see illustration above), the new format which Kodak had designed, would eventually win the day. As a result, traffic in 8 slowed (or failed to rise) while everyone waited to see what impact Super 8 would have. The impact became obvious more quickly then most observers suspected it would. Within a few months after its marketing, it was clear that Super 8 film would in time innundate regular 8 as clearly as LP records had submerged 78 rpm's many years before. The immediate future of 8 lies with Super 8.

There is no doubt that Super 8 is technically superior to regular 8. Its picture is sharper and brighter; its sound is better. It is also doubtless true that the overall economic position of 8mm film has been enhanced by the introduction of Super 8. Amateurs have eagerly accepted the dozens of new, often highly sophisticated Super 8 cameras and projectors. In the professional marketplace (schools, colleges, etc.) many dealers are providing trade-in arrangements for owners of regular 8 films and projectors who now want to switch to Super 8. Almost all new projector designs are for Super 8 films.

While two sound tracks and two formats make for more confusion in the marketplace than anyone likes, if the market for 8mm prints becomes big enough this multiplicity of choices will be possible to live with, as has been the case with phonograph records. In the phonograph recording field, there are two dominant speeds (45 rpm and 33⅓ rpm), and for 33⅓ records, both monaural and stereo versions are often available, although stereo records are gradually taking over completely. For a long time now most record playing machines have been capable of playing both of these speeds, as well as the older 78 rpm speed. The analogy between phonograph records and 8mm films cannot be carried too far, however, partly because multi-speed, two-sound-track, two-format 8mm movie projectors are a good deal more expensive than are multi-speed, two-needle record players. A bigger drawback in the analogy is that the recording industry rests upon a very large, very solid, home market; educational purchases neither make nor break it. The sale of educational films, however, is restricted to a comparatively small institutional market. A big market permits stocking large inventories, which, in turn, permits diversity within the inventory.

Cartridge Incompatibility

The problem of cartridge incompatibility from projector to projector also discourages potential users of 8mm film today. There is only one manufacturer of *silent* cartridge-8 projectors—The Technicolor Corporation. Still, Technicolor makes Super-8 and regular 8-silent projectors and the cartridges are not interchangeable between machines. Although interpretations of the word "major" vary, there are at least three major *sound* cartridge-8 projector manufacturers. (Fairchild, Technicolor and MPO). No cartridge from any of these projectors fits any other projector. If markets were large enough, as noted earlier, the distributor of films could simply stock titles in the various cartridges or load them in designated cartridges on demand, but the market is too small to be fragmented and remain solvent.

Why, then, don't projector manufacturers agree upon a particular cartridge and resolve the indecision? A first answer is that in this country manufacturers are prevented by law from entering into agreements with each other about the characteristics of a product in advance of the production of that product. Such agreements are regarded as collusion in restraint of trade. Standardization and compatibility are achieved when a manufacturer markets a product which is worthy of emulation. If others want to manufacture it they are either licensed (generally at a cost) to do so, or are simply given the necessary plans. What has occurred in the cartridge-8 field, to simplify, is that none of the manufacturers to date has marketed a product which in its design is thought to be so superior that other manufacturers have sought it out. Also, many manufacturers have felt that cartridge compatibility really isn't yet a major issue. This last statement may seem nonsensical unless one recalls that most of the cartridge-8 projectors are used in business and industry, where a company makes its own sales and training films for the projector model which it has purchased.

Some stability is likely to come to the cartridge scene in the Fall of 1969 when Eastman Kodak markets the first of a new series of cartridge-8 projectors. Their system will be quite different from existing cartridge projectors. The endless loop cartridge will be sacrificed in favor of an extremely fast rewind. Because the designs of the Eastman cartridge and projector are unique, they are not likely to be regarded as merely other sheep in the pack. The cost of the Kodak cartridge will be markedly lower than that of other cartridges, and Eastman hopes that it will therefore appeal to both amateur and professional markets, as no existing cartridge does, thus providing that broad base of economic support which is so necessary for lowering the cost of projectors, and, eventually, of prints. As compared with other manufacturers now active in the cartridge 8 field, Eastman is a massive force—in terms of engineering talent as well as manufacturing and marketing ability—and their force has not yet been felt in a major way in the professional 8mm projector field. Further—and this is a point of pivotal importance—Kodak has systematically informed the photographic manufacturers of the world of its cartridge projector plans, and has equipped them with exact plans of key parts of the system (the cartridge, for example) and invited them to design projectors to fit the scheme. As a result of this strategy, projectors designed by several manufacturers should be marketed at the same time—in late 1969, all based on the Kodak cartridge system.

This approach is similar to the demonstrably successful technique which Eastman used in launching Super 8. Kodak began about two years in advance of the date on which they planned to introduce Super 8 to inform the photographic world of their plans, saying in effect, "Here is what we are going to do, charted to the last millimeter; make equipment of your own to fit into this system if you wish." The photographic industry liked the look of the new format, with the result that scores of Super 8 cameras and projectors from the United States, Europe and Japan were introduced to the public in a united front. The photographic manufacturers of the world had volunteered to follow the persuasive lead of the giant of the industry and Kodak gained from its design "give away" plan. With nearly every camera and projector manufacturer in the world turning out Super 8 equipment, Kodak concentrated on its two specialties: producing raw film stock and making new equipment for the low cost mass amateur market.

Many observers feel that Kodak may be able to "pull a Super 8" with their new cartridge-loading projectors. If they can (and I side with those who feel that they can), that fact would be the biggest event in the history of professional 8. It would probably break all kinds of log jams.

An Apology for the Technical Talk

What has gone before in this paper is heavily colored by technological considerations. This is not because human factors are irrelevant, but rather because the motion picture, like still photography or television, exists in and because of technical devices. Erwin Panofsky observed once that the rise of film art ". . . took place under conditions contrary to precedent. It was not an artistic urge that gave rise to the discovery and gradual perfection of a new technique; it was the technical invention that gave rise to the discovery and gradual perfection of a new art."*

Technical advances affect film and its uses vitally. The maturation of 8mm film in education has been rooted in technical advances: better cameras, better films, new projectors. A cartridge projector, for example, was made and we *then* set about finding its uses. (Magnetic tape recorders in an earlier day were marketed and then educators found dozens of uses for them.) This technology-first, use-second pattern is not unique with communication technology, of course, nor do I think it is particularly unfortunate. Educational inventiveness can proceed quite usefully from the stimulation of seeing a gadget and then wondering how the gadget (and modifications of it) can be used. And—though it may be heresy—I am not at all sure that this device-oriented approach is less productive in the long run than the more academically pure need-based approach may be. But, be that as it may, the ups and downs of 8 in education simply cannot be understood without an elementary knowledge of such technical facts as have been presented here.

Where Does 8 Stand Today?

Where, then, do we stand today with respect to the use of 8mm films in American education? (The problems of 8 abroad are somewhat different and are not treated here except by implication.)

First, to touch upon something which has not been alluded to yet, the local production of motion pictures by students and teachers has been stimulated by the growth of 8. More films both dramatic and didactic in nature, are being produced in schools today than were a decade ago. This is a highly visible development, even though the numbers of participants are small; it is exciting to see films produced by children and teachers. The educa-

* *Erwin Panofsky, "Style and Medium in the Motion pictures," in Daniel Talbot (ed.)* Film: an Anthology, *New York: Simon and Schuster, 1959, p. 15.*

tional possibilities of locally produced "grass root" films are many and may be likened to the preparation of local "printed" material via mimeograph, xerox, ditto, or similar means. The day may well come when George Eastman's ubiquitous box will insinuate its way into education as profoundly as it has permeated its way into American family life.

A second observation about the state of 8 today—and a more important one—is that commercially produced 8mm films already firmly occupy a small corner of the educational film world. It is a new corner, furthermore, and thus represents expansion of educational film use, not a significant displacement of traditional uses of 16mm film. The new corner which is occupied by 8 is the rather specialized one of individual or small group use of motion pictures. It is dominated by cartridged films, most particularly by the so-called "single concept" films. "Single concept" films are the short (four minute or under) silent loop films which are used with the Technicolor "Instant Movie Projector," the largest selling 8mm cartridge projector. These films are most frequently sold in packages of, say, four or six or twelve cartridges which treat subjects ranging from fluid mechanics to silk screen processes to life in Afghanistan. Some of these loops have been cannibalized from longer films, but most are now developed from scratch to capitalize specifically on the formal qualities of loops.

I feel that the term "single concept" is somewhat misleading. *No* film can present only a single concept. A far better descriptive phrase for films of this style would be "short, silent loops," for it is the shortness, the silence, and the "loopiness" which are the important formal characteristics. Still, by whatever name, these mini-films are so dramatically different from past film forms that they have invited the extravagant but inaccurate conclusion that the whole future of 8 points in their direction.

No doubt short loop films, silent and sound, will continue to be designed and marketed in 8, but educational planners would be foolish to limit their thinking about 8 to a single film style or genre, including the currently popular "single concept" one. It is more productive to think of 8 as a flexible, inexpensive and highly accessible means of packaging the whole range of moving visual images. (The awkward phrase "moving visual image" is used as a generic term to describe what is packaged by film or video tape, or, for that matter, the new video disc.) 8 can be used today with groups of 25 to 35 with existing inexpensive projectors, and tomorrow 8 can undoubtedly be used with groups up to 500 in size with projectors which can be made if we want them. That is, 8 is actually potentially capable of handling 95 per cent of the needs of film in education; it is, therefore, frontally competitive with 16mm, at least theoretically.

To return to a theme stated early in this paper, the biggest gain which is possible with 8 in education is making film, in all of its forms, readily and randomly accessible to the teacher and student, when it is needed, where it is needed and as frequently as it is needed. We have lived so long with *in*accessible film, however, that it is difficult for most of us to think of the possibility of making a big breakthrough. The most frequently suggested solutions to the problem of inaccessible film—financing existing approaches more heavily, improving such administrative procedures as booking and distribution, training more student projectionists, requiring of all teachers-in-training a course in audio-visual education, etc.—are all useful, but not radical in the sense of getting at the root of the problem. The root of the problem is twofold: dependence on centralized film libraries which are geographically removed from points of utilization and dependence on projectors which are difficult to use. Both problems can be attacked significantly by embracing the emerging 8mm technology.

Other approaches to making the moving image accessible must be considered, of course, particularly the electronic alternatives offered by television and video tape. Television transmission is an efficient means of making a particular moving image available to large numbers of people at a precisely given time. TV programs are delivered in accordance with a centrally determined schedule, of course, not on demand of the learner. In short, they are not randomly accessible, either to groups or to individuals. To stretch the matter, TV is to the moving image what sky writing is to print. Delivery of video tape by mail or local "bicycling" is exactly the process now used with film. Video tape suffers by comparison, however, partly because the tapes are cumbersome, but also because machines are a great deal more expensive and temperamental than motion picture projectors are. Perhaps video discs will mature rapidly as a means of lowering costs, but they will suffer, as do all video systems, from a small image size.

The Future?

No one can foresee the future, not even the future of this tiny corner of our lives. But one can guess.

I think that technical facts point overwhelmingly to the possibility that 8mm film will largely replace our 16mm libraries, in time. This is an opinion which is seldom aired, least of all by photographic manufacturers who have the most intimate knowledge of technical advances. While they would welcome the increased sales which would almost inevitably accompany a transition to 8, they hesitate to speak of such matters for fear of creating panic among the holders of 16mm films. And, interestingly enough, many persons in the photographic industry who can see all of the pieces of an accessible 8mm professional film system right before them fail to put those pieces together in their minds. Eyes are more generally on the big action—the massive amateur market.

There is really little reason to panic at the thought of the obsolescence of 16mm film libraries in education. Our investment there is large only if we think of it that way, and, more importantly, it is not a static investment. If our prints and projectors are used they will wear out, at which time they can be replaced by 8. If they aren't being worn out they aren't being used and we should ask whether *that* is a good investment. Nor would a gradual transition to 8 be disastrous to educational film houses. All of their master negatives can be printed quite easily on Super 8.

To make a difference in the educational film field, 8 must reach mass production proportions. At the present time successful 16mm school films sell, say, 750-1000 copies—during the lifetime of a title. A few extraordinary titles sell as many as 5000 copies. Given the number of schools which we have, these figures are incredibly small; they really do make 16mm prints seem a bit like medieval manuscripts. We should be thinking of 10,000, 25,000 or 50,000 copies of films, a figure which is perfectly possible to achieve in Super 8 with laboratory printers which now exist. The only thing missing is consumer demand in education.

The educational demand for films turns heavily on projector innovation, as I have repeatedly suggested. While low quality pictures and sound will not be acceptable no matter how stunningly simple the projectors are, low quality is not at all necessary with 8 today. Quality is already quite good and the remaining major technical limitation—inadequate image brightness on a classroom or auditorium screen—is about to be solved in a dramatic way. Within a year after this paper is read, the next generation of 8mm projectors will be ready to market, as will a sensational (I choose the word with utmost care) new screen, which is capable of reflecting at about *eight times* the brightness of any screen now in widespread use. It is now being marketed in small typewriter paper size by Kodak, and will shortly be available in a 30" × 40" size which will be suitable for classroom projection. When this screen is used, 8mm films can be shown in *an undarkened classroom!*

At the very minimum, 8mm has already made its mark on education by expanding our uses of the film medium. At the maximum, it can be the vehicle to place film almost literally at our fingertips—in classrooms, laboratory, library, home, office and factory. If we have the chance deliberately to intervene in ways that will enhance the maturation of 8 in education, there is no doubt that we should grasp those opportunities. There is no development in educational media—in television, programming, print with greater promise than this one.

9.
Instructional Radio

by *RICHARD O. FORSYTHE*
Educational Supervisor
WBAA, Purdue Univ.

It is the purpose of this paper to describe the nature, scope, and functions of radio as they relate to instructional applications. This, quite obviously, is a formidable task. The history of radio encompasses a fifty-year technological revolution that defies comprehension. In turn, this technology must be examined as it relates to the practices of a tradition-bound educational system and a science of learning that has not yet discovered the "wheel." The resulting dichotomy has helped to create qualitative discrepancies between hardware and software which make it difficult to explain the promise of one through the accomplishments of the other.

For the purposes of this paper, instructional radio can be defined as the use of radio transmission in any systematic process of education to extend the competence and intellect of the audience. Programming in this category is, for all practical purposes, restricted to stations operated by non-profit educational institutions. It should be noted that this definition excludes the commercial programming which constitutes an overwhelming majority of the radio industry. In a way this is unfortunate because the commercial area of broadcasting represents such a demonstrably potent social force that some even say the mass media themselves have become the "message" and that program content is insignificant in comparison with its mode of transmission.[27] While this represents an extreme positon in some respects, there is little doubt that the broadcast media have profoundly shaped out culture, even though their instructional efforts have for the most part been both unintentional and extracurricular.

Educational Radio: the Beginnings

Educational radio has been part of the American scene for nearly half a century. For the most part, its history is a study in frustration. In the early 1920s, many universities engaged in radio broadcasting, but their efforts were usually an outgrowth of electronic experimentation and bore little relationship to a public service. During the years preceding 1936, there were 202 radio stations licensed to educational institutions; unfortunately, 164 of these licenses were allowed to expire, were transferred, or were revoked. While educators of the day were slow to see the potential of radio, men in the private sector were quick to exploit its commercial possibilities. The expansion of commercial broadcasting during this time rapidly filled the radio channels vacated by educational institutions, and today only twenty educational AM stations remain. If FM broadcasting had been not developed and if the Federal Communications Commission had not reserved part of its spectrum for education, there would be little need to study instructional radio. It probably would not exist.

Other factors which contributed to the frustration of early instructional broadcasters were the apathy of educators toward a device which was transforming the culture around them and the inconstancy of financing provided by legislatures and school boards. The schools of today are often criticized for slowness in adapting to change, but they seem radical in comparison to the prevailing climate of radio's early years. Education's failure to involve itself with radio during this period is reflected in the fact that most broadcasts used in classrooms before World War II were produced by commercial organizations, rather than educational institutions.

Surprisingly, instructional radio has survived and, in several cases, has even flourished. In the course of its development radio has been used successfully to teach subjects ranging from mechanical drawing and mathematics to dental hygiene and music appreciation. It has been successful in providing direct instruction and in supplementing or enriching curricula. It has served to motivate student learning and it has been used successfully for direct instruction, both in school and out, and with people of all ages and backgrounds.

Educational Radio Today

In spite of early difficulties, it would seem that radio is more widely used for instruction today than in the pre-television era. Although the scattered nature of educational radio's development makes it impossible to accurately gauge its audiences, some indication of use can be seen in studies which show radios among the most common audiovisual devices found in schools.[14] A further clue is provided by the general growth of educational broadcasting which is reflected in the following table showing the growth of school-owned FM stations.[18] Significantly, half of these stations have gone on the air since 1960.

1938— 1	1948— 29	1958—151
1939— 2	1949— 48	1959—159
1940— 4	1950— 73	1960—175
1941— 7	1951— 85	1961—194
1942— 8	1952— 98	1962—209
1943— 8	1953—112	1963—237
1944— 8	1954—122	1964—255
1945— 9	1955—123	1965—269
1946—10	1956—125	1966—292
1947—17	1957—141	1967—326 (April)

Most educational FM stations are in the frequencies between 88.1 and 91.9 megacycles, the band reserved for their use, and 134 out of the total of 326 are low-power stations with a broadcast radius of two to five miles. The following table indicates the number and type of educational radio licensees.[18]

	FM	AM
Colleges and Universities	228	16
Public School Systems	50	1
Independent Schools	10	0

Biblical Colleges	10	1
State Councils	10	1
Educational Organizations	13	0
Public Libraries	3	0
Municipally-Owned	2	1
	326	20

As might be expected with such variety, the stations serve many functions. In the broadest sense of the term, all 326 stations broadcast instructional programs; however, if broadcasting directly to classrooms provides the criterion, forty stations could then be described as primarily instructional. In data compiled for *The Hidden Medium,* it was found that,

> "The colleges and higher educational authorities use their stations for cultural enrichment, student training, and in a few cases, for student teaching. In addition, they tend to see their stations as having a public relations purpose. The school districts focus upon direct teaching and supplementary instruction. The non-profit institutions and public libraries are primarily concerned with adult education, particularly cultural enrichment, and the theological groups generally favor informal adult education, with a few accentuating religious education."[18]

Network

The most common network arrangement in educational broadcasting involves the exchange of tape-recorded programs. One such network, the National Educational Radio Network (NERN), has played a vital role in the development of instructional radio in the United States. A project of the National Association of Educational Broadcasters, this tape network regularly selects and distributes outstanding instructional radio series produced by member stations. Since over half of the "instructional" radio stations in the country operate with budgets of less than $20,000 a year they are forced to rely on NERN for much of their programming. Many large university stations also operate localized tape networks which distribute selected programs within their primary service area. While some (e.g., Purdue and Minnesota) include instructional materials, the majority offer general cultural or informational programs.

In addition to the distribution and exchange of recorded programs, there are some live interconnected networks in educational radio. Wisconsin, through its state university and Station WHA, operates a network of eleven stations which covers the entire state. Other such networks include the Eastern Educational Radio Network, a regional grouping of eight stations in four states and the District of Columbia, and the special two-way networks for professional education which exist in several states. Various forms of state-wide networks are currently under study in seventeen states and there is considerable interest in the establishment of a national interconnected educational radio network.

Technological Developments

It is impossible to discuss the instructional applications of radio without considering recent technological advances which have already revolutionized the field. The most important of these is multiplexing, which permits one or more additional signals to be carried in the side bands of a main channel transmission. The best known uses of multiplexing have been for stereo broadcasting and for commercial "Muzak-type" operations, but it is now developing also as a private point-to-point communications system in education. Since multiplex signals can only be received on special radios, they are well suited to the newer professional education networks, such as the one operated by the Albany Medical College.

Other related technological developments now used in conjunction with radio include the electrowriter, various types of speaker-phone arrangements, and slow-scan (still picture) television. Experimental work is also underway which may eventually permit radio stations to utilize computer-telephone systems to gather immediate audience feedback or response.

Instructional Radio in Other Countries

Broadcast systems in other countries can generally be differentiated from those of the United States on the basis of the extent and nature of government involvement. While this does not necessarily mean full government control of broadcasting, it usually does mean a distinct system of financing and the indirect involvement of government in production. These conditions have frequently resulted in greater national commitments to educational uses of the medium. Radio Sweden, for instance, currently broadcasts more than 166 hours of instruction a year to over 12,000 participating schools. School radio publications number approximately two million copies a year in a nation of only eight million people.[24] South Korea has recently instituted a national instructional radio service over KBS and provides programming for elementary schools. Its programs emphasize music, social studies, and anti-communist education. Their Ministry of Education considers the school radio service to be very important in raising educational standards and it has instructed all schools to make maximum use of the broadcasts.[21] Radio is also being used extensively for instruction in Japan and India. In England, 79 percent of the 38,000 schools have and use radios.[41] An example nearer home is Canada, where CBC produces many classroom programs.

Radio is also becoming a vital instructional force in Africa. In Cameroon, radio is used experimentally to combat illiteracy and with good results.[4] Several African countries have conducted anti-malaria campaigns through radio. Radio Omdurman in Sudan carries instructional programs for the general populace and partially compensates for the country's scarcity of schools. Broadcasts include instruction in Arabic, in tribal history, and in social manners.[33] Radio is the primary form of national communication in Nigeria and further plans are developing to have it provide a major instructional service.[1]

Most countries use radio for some instructional purposes and many are more actively involved with the medium at the national level than is the United States. Many "emerging" nations turn to radio both because it offers the most economical means for distributing instructional materials and because it provides an effective means of communicating with a generally illiterate population.

The Instructional Dimensions of Radio

Various analysts have explored radio's potential for instruction and have cited qualities inherent in the medium which make it educationally valuable; they have also listed specific instructional tasks which radio can perform.[11] [23] These qualities and functions are presented here along with programming illustrations selected from current information provided the author by educational radio stations. In essence, this review is an attempt to summarize the theoretical constructs of instructional radio in a manner that will also provide some insight into its present state of development.

A Broadcast Medium

Radio is a broadcast medium which literally provides listeners an ear upon the world. In addition to broadcasting events as they occur, radio also has the advantage of being able to present educational programs that incorporate timely material. Many educational stations provide specially written newscasts for use in current events classes. Station WFBE, Flint, Michigan, produces a dramatized weekly news summary which is used in conjunction with special news maps that are distributed to the classrooms. Station WBAA, Purdue University, produces *News in Review* for the intermediate grades and distributes the series throughout Indiana on its tape network.

Radio's ability to provide timely instructional material is an advantage reflected in the growing quantity of programming for the disadvantaged. KBPS in Portland, Oregon, has received Federal funding for a special instructional radio project aimed at the culturally deprived. The station has been enabled to produce four series for children, including (1) a newscast for slow learners, (2) broadcasts of creative students' work, (3) dramatized biographies of Negroes and whites who have succeeded in spite of difficulties, and (4) a call-in series for the junior high school which discusses student problems. WFBE is producing a creative writing-participation series for the Flint inner city schools. KDPS, Des Moines, has produced *Mr. Achiever* for use in the inner city intermediate grades. Station KSLH in St. Louis and Station WBGO in Newark have both produced series in conjunction with Operation Headstart.

The speed with which radio responds to instructional problems is further mirrored in Station WHA's special week-long broadcast from the ghettos of Milwaukee which led to the passage of an open housing ordinance, and Station WAUP's special instructional programs concerned with the military draft and with venereal disease. Other series, such as WBAA's *Spotlight on Careers* and *The World of Science* feature up-to-date information in fields which are constantly changing.

A Sense of Realism and Participation

Students who listen to an event as it occurs feel a sense of participation which can serve as a stimulus for learning. Broadcasters, in attempting to demonstrate this quality of the medium, frequently ask, "Would you rather listen to a football game or read about it in the newspaper?" Teachers could as easily be asked to make a similar choice about a presidential address or other important events. The voices of actual participants convey shades of meaning that are lost in a written account. In addition, the listener hears background sounds which serve to enhance the effect of realism. A broadcast probably provokes a greater sense of involvement than other types of audiovisual presentation because listeners associate it with something that is happening now—an association that is not made when recordings or films are presented in class. Primary grade pupils can become so involved with radio that they seem to believe the radio teacher "really is in the little box." Series like WBAA's *Discovering Science* capitalize on this by employing direct dialogue with the listeners, allowing pauses for pupil responding.

Emotional Impact

Radio can combine artistic elements in a dramatic form to create an emotional impact which heightens instructional effectiveness. A documentary which uses the sounds of tragedy to teach safety makes a strong impression. Radio dramatization of famous plays and of other great literature abound in educational broadcasting schedules and may be used both as direct instruction and as a means for motivating further study. Radio can also be an emotional force in the creation of attitudes which affect how students utilize knowledge. Some educational stations have approached the problem directly with series designed to improve social attitudes. Some of WNYE's recent efforts in this area include *Out of Many, One, Peter and Pepe, Senorita Jones, People and Places,* and *A World of Brothers.*

It should be noted that dramatized instructional formats are found more frequently in radio than in any other medium because of the ease of production.

Presentation of Authorities

Educators frequently use outside authorities to stimulate student interest and because no teacher is expert in all areas. In such a role, radio provides leading specialists in many subjects. Program series such as *The World of Science,* a series of talks by prominent scientists addressed to junior high school students, and *Speaking of Books,* a series in which authors are interviewed by a panel of students, illustrate ways in which radio can present authorities to supplement the classroom lesson.

Radio also serves instruction by engaging itself directly in the process. School systems may utilize radio to offer specialized subjects which would not otherwise be possible. As an example, the Supervisor of Elementary Vocal Music in Evansville uses Station WPSR to present the core of the primary grade music curriculum. There are a number of foreign language series on educational radio such as *Spoken German* and *Spoken French* produced by Station KUOW at the University of Washington. Also, several stations, such as WHA, KANH in Albuquerque, and KEBS in San Diego broadcast English lessons to local minority groups for whom it is a second language.

Radio has used authorities to present direct instruction in many subjects and at all educational levels. One of the most dramatic success stories in this category has been in the use of radio for continuing professional education. Using FM radio, usually with multiplex equipment, highly specialized programs have been developed for groups of practicing professionals whose duties make it difficult for them otherwise to continue their education. The first and largest of these networks is operated by the Albany Medical College, through Station WAMC. Receivers and transmitters are installed in participating hospitals where doctors then assemble to hear presentations by the Albany medical faculty. Slides, charts, and X-rays are also made available to the listening groups. Doctors in attendance may ask questions by means of transmitters at their reception points and these questions are heard throughout the network. The WAMC operation, described as the largest postgraduate classroom in the world, presently includes 60 hospitals in seven Northeastern states. Other such medical networks are found also in North Carolina, California, Utah, and Ohio, with other states still planning similar activities. The technique is rapidly being expanded to other professional areas. Ohio State University and WOSU are engaged in continuing teacher education using a somewhat similar system. Station WHA is using its multiplex system for continuing education in medicine, law, and veterinary science. To date, only fifteen educational stations have multiplex equipment, but others are proceeding to develop professional educational programs using open broadcasts and telephone "talk-back" arrangements.

Uniqueness of the Medium

Radio is an aural medium and the ear is a channel of communication that is particularly appropriate for certain types of learning. Music appreciation, for instance, is one subject which has been well taught consistently by radio. The advantages of an aural approach to language study are reflected in the recent development of language laboratories and by the number of foreign language series broadcast by educational stations. WMUK in Kalamazoo is only one of several stations which has done extensive work with closed-circuit radio broadcasts of language drill materials.

Instructional programming which involves creative student responses is frequently better treated by radio than by other means, as was vividly demonstrated by the WHA experience with *Let's Draw.* This creative art program had been highly successful on radio and, when television became available, it was transferred there. It was soon discovered that the program was no longer successful because students tended to copy the television artist. The program was returned to radio and is still successful there. In art instruction, radio has also been used successfully at KRVM in Eugene, Oregon, at WBOE in Cleveland, and by CBC, Canada.

In other areas related to creativity, Station WBAA recently produced *Creative Thinking: The American Pioneers,* a series which used social studies as the basis for teaching the principles of creative thinking to third and fourth grade students. Two research projects related to this series indicate that children who used the programs significantly increased their creative abilities. Station WAMU, Washington, D.C., in cooperation with the District of Columbia Public School System, produced programs for disadvantaged children that used common sounds to evoke creative responses. The project was an effort to overcome the language barrier which separates ghetto children from an essentially middle class school system. Initial results of the project seem promising.

Another instructional area that lends itself to an aural medium is listening. Skill in listening is considered so important by educators that it is included in most elementary curricula. While any use of radio tends to focus attention on listening, many instructional radio series have been developed specifically to assist in the teaching of listening skills. WBGO, for instance, indicates that *Learning to Listen* has probably been its most successful instructional series, due largely to the essential identification of the series content with resources of the medium.

It is said by some that radio "plays in the theatre of the mind" because it encourages listeners to use their imaginations to visualize the action. It is this form of listener involvement which makes radio a more personal medium than television and which leads Marshall McLuhan to describe radio as a "hot, active" medium, and television as "cold and passive".[27] Certainly, radio drama demands more of the listener than its television counterpart and in return it gives more. To illustrate the effectiveness of sound alone, students of broadcasting are often asked to name their most terrifying experience. Their responses usually focus on the hearing of ominous, unidentifiable *sounds* at times when their imagination could be particularly active.

Overcomes Space and Time

When audiovisual theorists discuss radio's ability to overcome the barriers of space and time, they are referring to the way in which it transports listeners around the world or back or forward in time. Radio's ability to originate broadcasts from any point on the globe and even from points beyond has been clearly demonstrated. Instructional series have used both on-the-spot accounts and simulated travel in such series as WFBE's *Mike Cable, Special Correspondent,* KBPS's *Exploring Scenic Oregon,* and WBAA's *Our Hoosier Heritage.* Countless instructional series have also broken the time barrier with dramatized history; two of the best known are *You Are There,* produced by CBS, and *The Jeffersonian Heritage,* produced by the National Association of Educational Broadcasters.

Curriculum Innovation

School systems which have made more than a token effort to use radio see it as a valuable way to introduce new materials and new curricula. For example, Newark, Cleveland, St.

Louis, Indianapolis, and Portland stations have all produced radio series designed to acquaint their teachers with the "New Mathematics". Also, Station KUOM has presented a linguistic approach to English in a recent series, *Our Living Language;* WBAA has introduced economic education into the primary grades with *Our Working World* and cultural anthropology into the intermediate grades with *Faces of Man.* Virtually all educational stations oriented to instruction have developed series which fit this category, and there is satisfactory evidence that radio effectively assists with the introduction of new curriculum material or with changes in the emphasis of old materials.

In-Service Training for Teachers

Radio is being used to improve teaching skills in two ways. First, it provides classroom teachers with opportunities to hear selected and experienced teachers who have had more than the usual time and assistance in preparing their lessons. Second, radio provides training programs specifically directed at teachers. KBPS has several series for teachers, all produced in cooperation with the superintendent's staff. Station WDTR in Detroit has had outstanding success with city-wide teachers' meetings, using telephone lines for talkback, while WOSU's professional network uses a similar system to extend in-service training across several school boundary lines.

Extension of the School

Most universities view their radio stations as part of the extension function and many of the stations are thus administered by university extension officers. These stations frequently broadcast college courses either on a credit or non-credit basis. As examples, Stations WAMU and WHA are among those currently broadcasting university courses for credit and both report satisfactory results. Their students are required to enroll in the university and to meet occasionally for discussion and testing. At another level, WNYE operates a "High School of the Air" for more than 600 homebound or hospitalized children.

Community Relations

A school radio station is a logical public relations or community relations arm of the school system and it can function in this capacity in many ways. While parents can and do listen to classroom programming to develop a better understanding of their schools, many stations also prepare special programs just for them. WWHI in Muncie presents interviews with teachers and WEBS in Elgin broadcasts P.T.A. discussions. WMTH in Park Ridge has a program entitled *Main Line* which gives listeners an opportunity to call and to ask questions concerning the school. Several public school stations also broadcast meetings of their local school boards.

Discrimination in Program Selection

The commercial rating services indicate that the average family spends more than six hours a day listening to radio and watching television. A desirable goal of education is the development of good taste and the ability to make intelligent choices, especially in areas which occupy so much of a person's time. One way to teach such selectivity and critical analysis is through selective exposure to mass media within the classroom.

Vocational Training

Educational radio stations are usually involved to some extent in the training of students for careers in broadcasting. Most high school stations depend upon such student assistance and some may even see their primary function as the providing of vocational training. Station WGVE in Gary is an example of an educational station which has undergone a major physical expansion because of its relationship to the vocational educational program.

Non-Broadcast Service

An instructional radio broadcast can obviously be recorded for playback in the classroom. Some stations, such as WHA, WNYE, and WBAA, make program recordings available to schools and individuals. Practically all instructional stations encourage teachers to record programs off-the-air if scheduling problems prevent normal use of the broadcast itself. Actually, educational radio stations constitute aural production centers that can serve many instructional functions that are unrelated to broadcasting.

Radio and the Systems Approach to Instruction

An important trend in instructional technology is toward the design of systems which provide for the use of various communication techniques as each is appropriate to the educational task at hand. This multi-media approach to instruction is reflected increasingly in the broadcasting practices of educational radio stations.

WHA, University of Wisconsin, is currently combining multiplex transmission of lecture materials with telephone question-and-answer periods for continuing education in medicine, law, and veterinary science. The system is also used for high school student science orientations and for meetings of various regional specialists. Another technique, used in conjunction with an art course, is called "radio vision" and involves the use of film strips correlated with instructional radio broadcasts. WHA has also cooperatively produced and simulcast television programs.

WFBE, Flint, Michigan, distributes radio books containing the reading exercises broadcast in their series, *Reading, Writing, and Radio*. Various art prints are also distributed to classrooms for use with their *Symphonic Melodies* series.

WDTR, Detroit, Michigan, has used radio in combination with television to teach English in grades 4, 5, 6, and 11. Radio broadcasts have also been combined with the classroom use of audio tapes in elementary German and Spanish series.

WBOE, Cleveland, Ohio, distributes colored slides that are coordinated with radio programs in fifth and sixth grade art. A similar technique involving the overhead projector is used in senior high classrooms with the CBS series, *Listening to Pictures*. In addition, senior high English programs are related to newspaper and magazine articles, television broadcasts, and motion pictures. Radio programs are also used to prepare students for their exposure to Shakespearean theatre productions.

KLON, Long Beach, California, distributes picture books with their kindergarten language arts program. They also provide listeners with a science kit that is used to perform experiments in conjunction with their two elementary science series.

Several stations have used various combinations of radio and television for instructional purposes. KDPS, Des Moines, has several series on both radio and television. KUOW, Seattle, used the two media for a course entitled *Spoken German*. KRVM, Eugene, has produced a music series for several years using radio programs as a follow-up to television broadcasts. They have also produced a physical education class in folk dancing that used television to present the lesson and radio to provide the music and participation part of the program. KSLH, St. Louis, broadcast a science series in cooperation with KETC–TV, alternating programs between radio and television. KDPS, Portland, has also experimented with radio-television simulcasts.

Several professional education networks, such as the one operated by Albany Medical College and Station WAMC, are using various combinations of FM multiplex channels, telephone or broadcast talkback arrangements, and correlated visual materials distributed directly to listening posts.

An Iowa mathematics project uses telephone techniques in combination with the electrowriter for the transmission of equations and other notes. This particular combination can be directly adapted to FM multiplex transmission and holds great promise as a means of accomplishing those instructional tasks which only require a voice and a "blackboard".

Many techniques initially developed in language laboratories and with audio-tutorial tape recordings can be used in conjunction with instructional radio. Programmed learning techniques are already being used in educational broadcasting with excellent results. Slow-scan television, when fully developed, will make possible the FM transmission of still pictures. Research is also underway to link radio stations, push-button dialing systems, and computers to provide, among other things, a possible answer to broadcasting's perennial problem of feedback.

Instructional Radio Research

There can be no doubt that radio is an effective instructional tool. While it has never been subjected to the intense experimental scrutiny focused on television, the accumulated evidence is no less positive.

Of the studies that have been undertaken many compare the effects of radio with those of other forms of instruction. Phillips[33] compared "face-to-face" presentation with speech via radio and found that more facts were gained by direct listening to a formal speech, but that the reverse was true for an informal speech.

Ewbank,[12] reporting on current events presented by radio, concluded that lessons supplemented with school broadcasts were more effective than those taught by teachers without radio.

Lumley[25] found that pronunciations of students who studied foreign language by radio were superior to pronunciations of students trained by conventional methods.

Harrison,[16] in an experiment with rural-school children, concluded that radio is equal or superior to ordinary classroom instruction in teaching music appreciation and nature study.

Carpenter[5] used radio to teach science to students who ranged from fourth grade through senior high. He found that radio students learned as well or better than those taught by conventional methods.

Brewer[3] also used radio in the science instruction of elementary school children. Post-test scores indicated that the radio students learned significantly more than did the control group and that they had greater interest in and more favorable attitudes toward science.

Heron and Ziebarth[19] conducted an experiment in which a group of 98 college psychology students was divided with one-half attending classroom lectures while the other half listened to the same lectures over radio. Tests conducted throughout the course indicated that radio was as effective as the face-to-face instruction.

Wiles[36] found that junior high school students learned more from listening to a series of news broadcasts than did a comparable group of students studying current events in the classroom.

Miles[28] found advantages for the radio group in the learning of elementary science when their performance was compared with that of a comparable group taught conventionally.

The University of Wisconsin undertook an extensive two-year study of school radio broadcasts at several grade levels and in seven subject areas.[39] Teachers of both the experimental and control groups taught from the same lesson plans. As might be expected, results generally indicated no significant differences although they consistently favored the radio groups in the field of music. In other subjects the comparisons yielded mixed results.

Cook and Nemzek[10] also found no significant differences in the information acquired by radio and non-radio students.

Nelson[30] compared two methods of presenting *Meet the Press* by studying groups who had heard the program on radio or on television. He concluded that for this type of program, radio was as effective as television.

Barrow and Westley[2] presented randomly selected groups of sixth graders with news background programs on both radio and television. Although the television group scored higher on an immediate-recall test, differences between the two groups were not significant on a delayed-recall test administered six weeks later.

Popham[34] reported a comparison of two education classes, one taught by tape-recorded lectures and the other taught conventionally. He found no significant differences in measured learning.

Some of the more recent comparisons of radio teaching with conventional techniques have been undertaken in foreign countries. To cite Chu and Schramm's review of the literature,

> "Radio has been found effective in teaching English to elementary school children in Ghana (Kinross, 1961), and in teaching French to native school children in Tahiti (Medard, 1962). In Thailand, a sample of schools which had access to radio instruction was compared to a control group consisting of schools of similar characteristics, except for the absence of radio instruction (Xoomsai and Rata-mangkala, 1960). Grades two and three were compared in music, grades six and seven in English. For grades two and three, the radio group had a significantly better average performance than the control group. For grades six and seven, the radio group scored significantly higher on reading and writing tests, although no significant differences were found in aural tests between the two groups."[8]

Mather and Neurath[26] equipped 145 villages in India with radios and selected a like number of villages to serve as a control. Twenty special farm programs were broadcast; tests administered before and after the broadcasts showed a significant increase in knowledge in the radio villages and only a negligible increase in non-radio villages.

Two experiments conducted by NHK in Japan both favored radio. In one,[31] two groups of seventh grade pupils were taught English from the same book, but one group listened to regular summary broadcasts on radio. Tests indicated that the radio group learned substantially more than the control group. In the other experiment,[32] elementary school pupils received a fifteen minute music program on radio within their regular music class, while a control group studied in the conventional manner. The experimental group scored higher on all tests but the differences were not statistically significant.

The preceding studies are typical of the experimental investigations that have attempted to assess the instructional effectiveness of radio. Although they suffer from the same ills attributed to most of the recent educational television studies, they collectively represent an important body of evidence attesting to the instructional effectiveness of radio.

Much of the rationale for the use of audio-visual aids in instruction is based on a view which relates instructional effectiveness to the number of sensory channels employed in the teaching process. The use of radio has also been questioned on the grounds that the ear is not the most efficient channel of communication. Carver,[6] in a series of seven experimental studies, used 39 Harvard undergraduates and 52 adults to investigate the relative effectiveness of auditory and visual presentations of identical material. He found among other things that

> . . . "the effectiveness of auditory presentation is limited to meaningful material (as opposed to nonsense syllables), and tends to be superior for subject matter that is concrete and serial in nature. If other conditions are constant, the mental functions of recognition, verbatim recall, and suggestibility seem more effectively aroused in listening; whereas critical attitudes and discriminative comprehension are favored by reading. The human relationship involved in the auditory situation is of value for certain types of communication (e.g., aesthetic and humorous) where the personal factor customarily plays a role."

Cohen[9] investigated the relative effectiveness of silent reading and radio listening in the teaching of facts to several hundred New York City school children. He found no significant difference between the reading and listening groups at any grade level, either on immediate or on delayed-recall tests.

Goldstein[15] attempted to compare reading and listening comprehension at various rates of presentation, using adults as subjects and phonograph records and visual projections to provide materials. He concluded that listening comprehension was greater than reading comprehension and that the difference became increasingly noticeable as the intelligence of his subjects and the difficulty of the material decreased. His findings also indicated that individuals vary in listening ability much as they do in reading ability.

Lanman and Henderson[22] compared the attitudinal change effected by listening to a radio program, by silent reading, and by teacher reading. They found the changes induced by both the radio program and by silent reading to be significant, while those produced by teacher reading were not. No significant differences were found between the radio group and the silent reading group.

Robert M. W. Travers and members of the Bureau of Educational Research at the University of Utah recently reported a review of the research and theory related to audio-visual transmission of information.[35] In summarizing their chapter on the relative efficiency of auditory and visual transmissions of information, they state:

> The information reported on the relative advantages and disadvantages of the visual and the auditory senses in terms of the number of available dimensions for the coding of information point to the conclusion that vision has more codable dimensions than does hearing. On the other hand the transmission of information through the auditory sense has advantages over vision in that the reception of information does not require specific muscular adjustments or head position. Sources of visual information are thus far more easily blocked than are auditory sources which may force themselves on the perceptual system of the person who is exposed to them.
> While the early studies of the value of transmitting redundant material through more than one sensory channel at a given time provided results purportedly to show that simultaneous transmission through more than one sensory modality improves learning, such a conclusion may well be questioned on the grounds that none of these early studies utilized a test of significance.
> Studies conducted at the University of Utah which have attempted to repeat earlier work with the introduction of proper controls have failed to demonstrate any particular advantage for the transmission of redundant information through more than one sensory channel.

Elsewhere in his report, Travers indicates that at any given time during communication, one sensory channel of the receiver seems to predominate and that simultaneous presentations through two channels results in blocking of one. Obviously, a multi-channel communication presents options to the receiver that a single-channel communication does not; however, it seems that the receiver can seriously attend only to one channel at a time.

Chu and Schramm, in their recent review of instructional television research, concluded that the effects of visual images on learning were not uniformly beneficial and seemed to depend on the kind of learning task involved. The evidence indicates that "the use of visual images will improve learning of manual tasks, as well as other learning tasks where visual images can facilitate the association process. Otherwise, visual images may cause distraction and interfere with learning."[8]

Problems in the Use of Radio for Instruction

The major difficulties in the use of radio in the classroom are centered in three areas which can be described as (1) reciprocity, (2) flexibility, and (3) single-sensory communication. Problems in these areas are directly related to the nature of the radio medium in particular and of mass media in general. The other problems commonly cited by educational broadcasters as having an adverse effect on the development of instructional radio can be classified as human, or administrative, failures.

Lack of Reciprocal Relationship

A broadcast is essentially a one-way communication and lacking in the immediate feedback provided in interpersonal discourse. The separation of speaker and receiver imposed by the medium makes it virtually impossible for the broadcaster to adapt to the individual needs of listeners while programs are in progress. Theoretically, it is possible for the classroom teacher to observe the reactions of students as she teaches and to modify her presentation to correct misunderstandings as these develop. (In practice, her ability to do this successfully is open to question.) The broadcast teacher cannot react similarly because audience feedback, if it is forthcoming, is usually available too late.

Educational broadcasters are aware of the problems caused by the lack of feedback and are continually trying to improve the flow of information from the listener to the studio. Some techniques commonly used for this purpose include evaluation forms, questionnaires, interviews, and direct observation techniques. Much effort has also gone into the development of talkback arrangements, using telephone lines or remote transmitters to permit students to question the broadcast teacher.

In summary, reciprocity in the communications process is desirable, but no mass medium provides it. A viewer does not enjoy a reciprocal relationship with a television program, a book, or a film. While it is true that books provide a degree of redundancy through individually controlled exposure as partial compensation for the lack of reciprocity, it is also true that radio can be recorded to accomplish the same purpose.

Lack of Flexibility

As a mass medium, radio must contend with the problems inherent in the presentation of single, fixed instructional messages to large and often heterogeneous groups. Such presentations are difficult to integrate into an ideal curriculum, one which should be related closely to individual student needs and differences. However, ideal situations are rarely encountered in education and instructional materials are commonly developed for large numbers of students, thus, the problems faced by radio broadcasters are hardly different from those encountered by producers in other media.

Since it is possible to develop radio programming correlated with all of the curricular options provided within a school system, the lack of flexibility is most obvious in the delivery system itself. Most educators tend to view a radio program as a "one-shot" presentation and this has made the medium seem more inflexible than it actually is. Tape recordings, central sound systems, and multiplexing equipment now make it possible for a radio station to provide a greatly increased number of scheduling options and the interconnection of school units by coaxial cable would further increase the options for program distribution.

Limitation of the Physical Senses

Most educators believe that teaching effectiveness is positively related to the variety of physical senses employed in the process. Since radio's appeal is to the ear, it is generally considered inferior to the audio and visual medium of television, at least insofar as classroom applications are concerned. As discussed earlier in the review of research, this issue is not as clearly defined as it might seem. For instance, the aural nature of radio makes it particularly appropriate for certain types of instruction. Also, there are several studies which directly challenge the view that multi-channel presentations are inherently superior to single channel.

The usual argument concerning the relative merits of instructional radio and television centers on the importance of pictures and other graphic non-verbal cues. Television producers cite the importance of the visual dimensions in instruction and the totality of television as a broadcast system. Radio producers counter with statements concerning the uniqueness of their medium and the fact that it provides nearly the same services for a fifth of the cost. In this argument, radio broadcasters stress several points. First, television is much more expensive than radio in all areas of its operation. Estimates have placed the cost of television at five times that of radio.[8] Second, they point out that most current instructional television programming could transfer to radio with little or no loss of effectiveness because most instructional television programs use talk-oriented formats. They note that, if necessary, crucial visual materials can be distributed by means other than television. It is common practice in radio, for example, to distribute manuals which contain visual supplements. A similar technique called "Radio-Vision" (radio and correlated slides) has been extensively developed, especially in Scandinavia and Africa. Other alternatives for the distribution of visual materials are provided by facsimile transmission and by electro-writers. Personnel in educational radio point to the fact that extensive post-graduate medical education is successfully being conducted with radio-vision and they contend that the idea can succeed in a variety of other instructional situations. The available evidence supports this contention.

Administrative Problems

Various surveys indicate that scheduling is the largest single problem in the utilization of both instructional radio and television programming. Many factors are involved in getting the proper student group in the proper place at the proper time and radio has been particularly handicapped by educational administrators who rarely consider it when compiling class schedules. As a result of scheduling problems, educational radio stations have tended to concentrate their instructional programming at the elementary school level to avoid the difficulties caused by departmentalized subject matter. They have also emphasized general enrichment programming for the same reason.

The major difficulty facing instructional radio broadcasters must be stated as a lack of administrative support. The failure of many educational administrators to view radio as a viable instructional system has resulted in a group of related problems, the most important of which has been lack of money. Approximately half of the educational radio stations in the United States operate on total yearly budgets of $20,000 or less.[18] With current financing, stations are obviously understaffed and without the means for proper promotion or development of their programming. This, of course, contributes to a general apathy and the establishment of a downward cycle.

Summary

Radio has been part of America's educational scene since its development in the early part of the century. Although its instructional applications were restricted during the twenties and thirties, that situation improved somewhat with the development of FM broadcasting and with the government's reservation of part of the FM spectrum for education. Today there are more than 325 educational radio stations, half of which have gone on the air since 1960. Many of these stations are seriously underfinanced and must rely on outside sources for programming, a condition that is detrimental to their efforts at meeting local needs. Unlike the United States, broadcasting in other countries usually involves more governmental participation and a greater national commitment to educational radio. Many countries, including Sweden, Japan, and Canada, make extensive use of the medium for instruction.

Radio has much to offer education. First, it is a broadcast medium which provides students an ear upon the world. It can broadcast events as they happen, as well as present programs consisting of timely information, because the technical characteristics of radio allow fast response to events. Radio can combine artistic elements to create an emotional impact which may then heighten the effectiveness of instruction. It also evokes in listeners a sense of involvement in the events being broadcast. Radio can be used to present authorities and programs that are beyond the means of individual school systems, and it is particularly appropriate for presenting certain types of subjects, as those requiring creative responses. Radio is currently used for curriculum innovation, for in-service teacher training, and for continuing professional education. Educational radio stations also serve their institutions as extension arms for community service and as aural production or recording centers. In addition, they frequently serve a purpose in vocational education.

The systems approach to education has involved radio in combination with other teaching tools. Instructional radio broadcasts are usually coordinated with printed materials which include many types of visual aids; the use of correlated filmstrips with radio programs is commonly called "Radio-Vision" and has been a highly successful technique. Radio has also been successfully combined with television in many situations. The development of FM multiplex equipment has opened new avenues for cooperative media approaches to instruction which involve facsimile transmission and electrowriters. Until this equipment is more generally available, instructional broadcasters will probably continue to use telephone techniques to provide talkback and conference facilities. Tape recordings and audio-tutorial programmed learning techniques are also being used within instructional radio.

Research clearly indicates that radio is effective in instruction. Experimental studies comparing radio teaching with other means or media have found radio as effective as the so-called "conventional methods". Even though radio has been criticized for being only an audio medium, studies have shown that visual elements in learning are not uniformly important. In many educational situations visuals may be more harmful than helpful. Also, the efficiency of combined audio and visual media has been challenged by studies which show that multi-channel communications may not be inherently more effective than single channel presentations.

The problems directly related to the nature of radio which are encountered in using the medium for instruction are reciprocity, flexibility, and single-senseness. While all mass media lack the reciprocity and flexibility found in interpersonal discourse, the aural nature of radio presents unique problems. Recent technical developments have greatly alleviated some of these difficulties, but instructional radio broadcasters are still faced with the human problems created by apathetic school administrators and inadequate financing.

Conclusions

From the standpoint of instructional technology, radio can be viewed as a delivery system, a piece of hardware that has the capacity to disseminate material from a central location to schools or listeners scattered over a wide geographic area. Recent technological advances make it possible to accomplish this transmission either by open broadcast on a regular AM or FM frequency or by a "closed" broadcast to special receivers via an FM sub-channel. Radio programming can also be distributed over an interconnecting wire system which utilizes telephone lines or coaxial cable, or it can simply be recorded on tape for use by anyone with playback equipment. While it is possible and frequently desirable to utilize all these methods of program distribution, it is radio's broadcast capability that sets it apart from all other educational media except television. In discussing the merits of their own medium, television broadcasters often neglect to mention that radio can also share one good teacher with many classrooms simultaneously, and, in doing so, it can free the faculty for other things; radio can also provide experiences impossible for individual schools to equal. It can carry instruction to places where there are no schools, as in western Australia, for example, and to students who are unable to attend school conventionally. Most importantly, radio makes it possible for schools to extend their resources into the homes and business places of the community. The only other medium which provides this capability is television and it is far less flexible than radio and is at least five times as expensive.

The most reasonable approach to the question of which teaching device to use begins with analysis of the instructional task to be performed. Then, when the needs have been defined, the available alternatives should be considered on the basis of cost effectiveness. Given a sufficient population, radio offers the least expensive means of communication available to schools. When its cost is considered in the light of its demonstrated effectiveness, its unique advantages for certain types of instruction, and its adaptability to various types of technological systems, radio must be accorded a prominent place in the developing educational armamentarium.

Many events in the history of instructional radio are a source of concern for broadcasters, teachers, national leaders, and lay citizens. With some justification, they can contend that radio has not had a fair chance to win consideration and intelligent adoption by educators. In the early days, during the 1930's, friends of instructional radio stood almost alone as advocates of innovation and the use of technology in instruction. Few funds were available to innovators then and little support, financial or otherwise, was invested in exploring or investigating the uses of radio. These early difficulties are compounded now by several recent developments in education. With the advent of educational and instructional television, many broadcasting practitioners and many of the qualified research personnel gravitated to the newer medium; hundreds of ITV facilities were established, hundreds of ITV evaluative studies conducted, and, predictably, interest in the instructional uses of radio declined. If present circumstances were the product of systematic planning and convincing evidence, few would resist them, but that unfortunately is not the case. On the contrary, it is more reasonable today than ever before to regard radio as a versatile, a practical, and an effective instructional medium. In comparison with other media, especially television, radio is impressively economical. Hopefully, now that the climate for consideration of all educational innovations has improved, many educators will achieve the perspective necessary to review carefully the applications of radio in dealing with instructional problems.

REFERENCES

1. Arms, George. "Diary from Nigeria: The Second Year." *NAEB Journal,* January-February 1963.

2. Barrow, Lionel C., And Bruce H. Westley. "Comparative Teaching Effectiveness of Radio and Television." *Audiovisual Communication Review,* Winter, 1959.

3. Brewer, L. "Radio as an Aid to Instruction in Elementary Science." *Science Education,* Vol. 23, 1939.

4. Browne, Don R. "Radio in Africa: Problems and Prospects." *NAEB Journal,* November-December 1963.

5. Carpenter, Harry A. "Teaching Science by Radio." *Junior-Senior High School Clearing House,* March, 1934.

6. Carver, Merton E. "A Study of Conditions Influencing the Relative Effectiveness of Visual and Auditory Presentation." 1924. A doctoral dissertation, Harvard University.

7. Chester, Giraud, Garnet R. Garrison, and Edgar E. Willis. *Television and Radio.* New York: Appleton-Century-Crofts, 1963.

8. Chu, Godwin C., and Wilbur Schramm. *Learning from Television: What the Research Says.* Washington, D.C.: National Association of Educational Broadcasters, 1967.

9. Cohen, Irving L. "The Relative Value of Silent Reading and Radio Broadcasting." 1937. A doctoral dissertation, New York University.

10. Cook, Dean C., and C. L. Nemzek. "The Effectiveness of Teaching by Radio." *Journal of Educational Research,* Vol. 33, 1939.

11. Dale, Edgar. *Audio-Visual Methods in Teaching.* New York: The Dryden Press, 1954.

12. Ewbank, H. L. "The Wisconsin Plan for Radio Development." *Education on the Air.* Columbus: Ohio State University, 1930.

13. Forsythe, Richard O. "Radio Research." *NAEB Journal,* November-December, 1965.

14. Forsythe, Richard O. "A General Survey of the Problems Related to the Utilization of School of the Air Programs." Purdue University, 1966. (Mimeographed.)

15. Goldstein, H. (A doctoral dissertation reported by Woelfel and Tyler in *Radio and the School.)*

16. Harrison, Margaret. "Measures of the Effect of Radio Programs in Rural Schools." *Education on the Air.* Columbus, Ohio State University, 1932.

17. Harrison, Margaret. *Radio in the Classroom.* New York, Prentice-Hall, Inc., 1938.

18. *The Hidden Medium: Educational Radio.* New York, Herman W. Land Associates, Inc., 1966.

19. Heron, W. T., and E. W. Ziebarth. "A Preliminary Experimental Comparison of Radio and Classroom Lectures." *Speech Monographs,* Vol. 13, 1946.

20. Herzberg, Max J., Ed. *Radio and English Teaching.* New York, D. Appleton-Century Co., 1941.

21. Hulsen, A. L. "Radio Education in Korea." *Educational Broadcasting Review,* December, 1967.

22. Lanman, Richard, and John Henderson. "A Comparison of Radio, Reading, and Teacher Presentation in Changing Children's Attitudes." Purdue University 1953 (Mimeographed.)

23. Levenson, William B., and Edward Stasheff. *Teaching Through Radio and Television.* New York, Rinehart and Company, Inc., 1952.

24. Loney, Glenn M. "Swedish School Broadcasts." *NAEB Journal,* November-December, 1964.

25. Lumley, F. H. "Rates of Speech in Radio Speaking." *Quarterly Journal of Speech,* June, 1933.

26. Mather, J. C., and P. Neurath. *An Indian Experiment in Farm Radio Forums.* Paris, Unesco, 1959.

27. McLuhan, Marshall. *Understanding Media: The Extensions of Man.* New York, McGraw-Hill Book Company, 1964.

28. Miles, J. Robert. "Radio and Elementary Science Teaching." *Journal of Applied Psychology,* Vol. 24, 1940.

29. Monahan, Jane E. (ed.) *Radio and the Classroom.* Washington, D.C.: National Education Association, 1940.

30. Nelson, Harold E. "Two Methods of Presentation to Meet the Press Compared." *Journal of Broadcasting,* 1957.

31. NHK Radio-Television Cultural Research Institute. *The Listening Effects of Radio English Classroom, April 1954—March 1955.* Tokyo, Japan, NHK, 1955.

32. NHK Radio-Television Cultural Research Institute. *The Effects of Educational Radio Music Classroom, April-December 1956.* Tokyo, Japan, NHK, 1956.

33. Phillips, C. D. "Radio Broadcasting in Sudan." *NAEB Journal,* July-August, 1964.

34. Popham, W. James. "Tape Recorded Lectures in the College Classrooms." *Audio-Visual Communication Review,* March-April, 1962.

35. Travers, Robert M. W., Mary C. McCormick, Adrian P. Van Mondfrans, and Frank E. Williams. *Research and Theory Related to Audiovisual Information Transmission.* Interim Report, Contract No. 3-20-003. U.S. Department of Health, Education and Welfare, Office of Education, 1964.

36. West, Robert. *The Rape of Radio.* New York, Rodin Publishing Company, 1941.

37. Wiles, M. Kimball. "The Evaluation of School News Broadcasts." 1940. A doctoral dissertation, Ohio State University.

38. Willey, Roy DeVerl, and Helen Ann Young. *Radio in Elementary Education.* Boston, D. C. Heath and Company, 1948.

39. Wisconsin Research Project in School Broadcasting. *Radio in the Classroom.* Madison, The University of Wisconsin Press, 1942.

40. Woelfel, Norman, and I. Keith Tyler. *Radio and the School.* New York, World Book Company, 1945.

41. Wynne, Michael. "Educational Broadcasting in Britain." *Educational Broadcasting Review,* October, 1967.

A RECENT RELEASE OF INTEREST

Madden, Richard. "Educational Radio Bibliography 1954-1967," *Educational Broadcasting Review,* October, 1968.

10.

Instructional Technology and School Buildings— Influences, Conflicts, and Guidance

by ALAN C. GREEN
Secretary
Educational Facilities Laboratories, Inc.

My professional world is architecture, and within that world my special interest is building for education. I read about, talk about, and think about educational facilities every working day and try to spend as much time as possible in and around school buildings, experiencing the physical environment that results when we try to bring the processes of education in out of the rain. And of special concern is that highest order of achievement when the container itself contributes positively to the educational and aesthetic growth of the people who dwell within.

The refinement of buildings for education is particularly challenging today. Educational objectives and processes are in the throes of major change, so the form of the school is itself in a period of rapid change. For a hundred years, from the mid-eighteen-forties to the mid-nineteen-forties, the American graded school was not under much stress. True, the parts of the school were rearranged in different ways—finger plans, compact plans, campus plans—but the basic parts themselves—the classrooms, the library, the gymnasium, and the "office"—remained essentially the same. New materials and finishes—glazed block, vinyl tile, glass block, laminated wood arches, bar joists—did change the way the school was constructed and how it looked. And better lighting, heating, plumbing, and ventilation did improve the climate. Still it was the same basic school, just more attractive and more comfortable.

The last decade has obviously changed much of that, and the schoolhouse, under stress, is emerging as a significant new building type. Curricular and organizational changes—individualization, nongradedness, cooperative teaching, differentiated staffing—have influenced the kinds of facilities that go into schools and the arrangement of schools. And the expanded role of the school in continuing education, job retraining, vocational education, and community extension has created new relationships with its neighborhood.

The classroom as the basic unit for instruction and the basic component in planning is giving way to a variety of facilities—from lecture rooms to pods of open space. The library is taking on new roles, and its services and facilities extend into every corner of the school. Electronic shops and computer centers, art studios and a variety of laboratories indicate the richness of the educational and training opportunities. And the schoolhouse itself no longer stands alone in the midst of fields and fence, but may be part of a high-rise office or apartment building or one unit in a comprehensive educational center. So the shape and content of the school and the school's place in the fabric of the community is changing as education itself changes.

And higher education is not exempt. Christopher Wren designing the original buildings of William and Mary College in the 1600's could have continued to practice his art well into the 20th Century by utilizing the same design vocabulary. No more; even college buildings aren't what they used to be.

High on the list of influences reshaping our educational buildings is instructional technology. The decade since World War II has seen film, tape, and other non-book media, and the hardware that renders them useful—projectors, recorders, television systems—helping reconstitute education. Certainly this is to be expected as the age of electronics affects every area of our society; education has not been left out.

From my observations and investigations,* there are some very real influences that instructional technology is having on the physical form of the schoolhouse. These are readily apparent and fairly well refined. I also observed some conflicts where school buildings have failed to respond appropriately, if at all, to instructional technology, or have not anticipated its use. And these observations would lead me to several overall planning concepts offered as guidance in developing schools that can effectively house instructional technology now and which can respond to change in the future. It is not the purpose here to judge the educational merit of any or all of the technologies; rather, assuming they do have roles to play, here are some thoughts on the physical housing for them.

Influences

The first major applications of instructional media, primarily films and audio materials, came in the military during the Second World War and had as an objective the acceleration of training. So when technology was introduced to civilian education, an early purpose was to make the transfer of information to students more efficient. Eventually, bringing additional resources to instruction and rendering it more effective were added motivations. Several developments in facilities resulted:

    1. *Development of the multi-media large-group room.* Some information, some experiences can be brought effectively to large groups of students at one time; a large group can be appropriate for viewing films, watching demonstrations, and utilizing other electronic means of communication. No single medium can handle all information tasks, so the resulting large-group rooms are provided with multiple ways of introducing information. Architectural research and experience with pilot facilities have led to well-refined design criteria for large-group multi-media rooms—criteria in terms of shape, projection methods, size and location of display surfaces, systems of equipment and controls, lighting, seating, acoustics, and the like. Prototypes are plentiful; schools and colleges are building and equipping exemplary large-group multi-media facilities when instructional efficiency via large group and multiple channels of communication is the objective.

    2. *Demise of the audiovisual room.* For years any "modern" school provided an audiovisual room in its schedule of spaces. This classroom, equipped with devices to cut out natural light (and usually natural ventilation), a screen, and a projection

[1] *Some of these are reported in* Educational Facilities with New Media, New Spaces for Learning, Design for Medical Education, *and* New Building on Campus. *The first was a report of research sponsored by the U.S. Office of Education and the latter three by Educational Facilities Laboratories, Inc. The research was conducted when the author was associated with the Center for Architectural Research, Rensselaer Polytechnic Institute, Troy, New York.*

stand, was to meet the needs of instructional technology. With the arrival of that special film ordered for use in a particular unit of instruction, the class was herded down the hall to the audiovisual room and the film was, hopefully, shown. Utilization of the room was sporadic, conflict inevitable, and certainly the whole process did not reflect integration of non-book media in the curriculum.

As media are used oftener and are better integrated, more and more schools are abandoning the audiovisual room and adapting the conventional classroom for uses of media whenever called for in the curriculum—adaptations such as light-tight blinds, built-in screen, lighting that provides several levels of illumination, and an audiovisual coordinator to service materials and equipment. Even less cumbersome ways of accommodation are being tried—the self-contained rear projection unit is one and the use of a television system as a means of distributing film and tape materials is another. In all of this, the lowly overhead projector, to date, has been accommodated most extensively, and readily, in America's classrooms.

3. *Television as a total communication system.* At first used to bring "the best teacher to the most students," television is performing more and more as a total communication system throughout a school, whether old or new, because of its flexibility, and its ease of accommodation. By simply running coaxial cable to each room, by locating receivers easily seen by all students, and by arranging receiving and distribution equipment at some central control point, live, recorded and off-the-air programs, as well as film and tape materials, can be distributed upon call throughout a building or campus. For many places and purposes such TV systems are a logical, if pedestrian, answer to accommodating media. It is also interesting to note that developments such as inexpensive video recorders and CBS's recently announced EVR system are extending the capabilities of such TV systems.

4. *Introduction of production and support facilities.* Both within the local school and at district and regional levels, production and support facilities are being provided. Clearly, if films and slides are to be shown, if overhead transparencies are to be used, if television is important—then facilities must be provided for maintaining and readying equipment, and for preparing, filming, and originating materials. The "quick and dirty" production facilities serving teachers at the local level as part of an instructional materials center, the district film library, and the regional television center are typical of the new facility types which have emerged in order to support the uses of instructional technology.

The instructional media support sections of the NDEA and Titles III and IV of ESEA have lent emphasis to programs of support, as well as to the variety of facilities to house these programs. It is worth noting that these facilities are generally less complex, less rigidly planned than their predecessors, since many production techniques are simpler and are accomplished under less demanding environmental conditions than in the past. A few years ago all television production took place in carefully prepared studios; today any place with enough light to see and a power supply can be a studio.

5. *New roles for the language lab.* Again through the stimulus of NDEA and its concern with language instruction, the language laboratory was for many schools their first big brush with technology. Although not a great success story, the language laboratory has been a major influence in school buildings. Of importance are the new roles the former language lab is assuming; considered more as an audio laboratory, it is now being used for drama, speech, literature—in any area where audio recording, distribution, and playback can be effective. It is still being used for groups of students

on a scheduled basis, but also more and more by individuals on an informal basis. TV receivers are adding video capabilities to some stations, giving them the functions of the dial access carrel.

6. *Impact on the library.* If instructional efficiency was the prime objective for the early uses of instruction technology, then individualization has certainly been the motive for the later developments. With small, personal, portable recorders, viewers, and projectors, and the various configurations of dial access retrieval systems, a vast wealth of non-book material can be brought to the individual student whenever and wherever required. And so the library—the hub of information for the individual student—has taken on some additional functions and some new names—instructional materials center, resources center, and learning center.

In schools and colleges all over the country the reconstituted library is providing for the storage and access of non-book as well as printed media, through coordinated cataloguing and shelving. Special facilities, such as a variety of carrels and viewing and listening rooms and areas, have joined the reading rooms of the past. The greatest stresses and changes I see in educational facilities today center on that oldest of facilities—the library—stress and change caused in large part by the placing of instructional technology in the hands of the individual student.

Conflicts

But the extent of the influence of instructional technology on school buildings is not what one might be led to believe. There are hundreds and hundreds of schools, very often newly opened schools, completely untouched by instructional technology. There are also many schools where the uses of instructional technology are incompatible with the facilities provided. It should be helpful to review some of these conflicts:

1. *Lack of well-defined roles for technology.* Instructional technology is generally hand-me-down hardware developed for home or commercial use and brought into the schools by manufacturers in order to broaden the market. These are often multi-million dollar corporations with resources for research, development, promotion, and sales. This pressure for hardware sales often causes instructional technology to run way ahead of the educational program. The true role of instructional technology is rarely defined or its integration in the instructional program well planned by a school or a district. No wonder that school buildings are so often unaffected by instructional technology, for no one has spelled out how instructional technology is to be used, much less communicated its significance to the planners and architects. Here then is a major conflict—hardware for its own sake without educational programming and in turn with little or no definition of its impact on the building itself.

2. *Narrow definition of the roles of technology.* Even when instructional technology is mentioned and is reflected in planning, invariably it is reflected at only two points— as used in large-group and individualized instruction. Rarely are the total range of opportunities explored—the accommodation of instructional technology in seminar rooms, laboratories, shops, studios, offices, work centers, clinics, and the myriad of other facilities that make up the contemporary school or college. It may well be that the large group and the individual student are the obvious places to begin to plan, but other avenues will develop, and these influences must also be defined.

3. *Failure to know available and appropriate options.* Visitors to many of the more innovative schools around the country are struck by the realization that often the "hep" educators and planners responsible for these schools are technologically blind. An open plan school catering to a highly individualized program may make no use of cartridge-loaded projectors, cassette recorders, and the like simply because the educators aren't aware of what's available.

And equally frustrating is the job of sorting through the vast proliferation of hardware that has come on the market to find what is appropriate for some learning objectives in terms of performance, maintenance, cost, and availability of software. We have not done well in helping educators and school planners understand their options in technology; likewise we have not done well in reflecting the options in planning buildings.

4. *Inadequate accommodation.* And when instructional technology is to be used in various ways, its accommodation is often cursory and shallow. A too-small screen is hung too high on a wall that catches glare from the lights, a projector is tucked in the middle of the room with wires snaking along the floor to a cheap speaker and a wall receptacle. There are environmental inter-relationships that should be established for students to view and hear instructional media—relationships between where they sit, what they see, the size of what they see, what they sit at, how they get there, and so on.

5. *Failure to anticipate changes in facilities.* And even when planning has provided for technology, the accommodation of change is often not considered. I recently had a call from the principal of a 1966 elementary school, rendered obsolete by the library which was undertaking many new roles—including individualized use of media—but which was hemmed in by the surrounding kitchen, toilets, and other committed spaces. In 1966, no thought was given to planning for change—to the expansion of the library caused by increased use of technology. Constructed space, inadequate sources of power, no place to run conduits, no way to darken rooms, no way to move heavy equipment through a building, are a few of the many conflicts arising from short-sighted planning.

6. *Incompatibility of equipment.* Often when incorporating instructional hardware in school buildings, tremendous problems of maintenance, replacement, and extension are bought by buying equipment haphazardly from various dealers and manufacturers. Poor maintenance, inadequate supply of parts and replacements, inordinate down-time are problems which arise from incompatibility of hardware and create untold setbacks to the effective use of technology.

7. *Failure to follow through on innovations.* In the rush to innovate, or to keep up with the educational Joneses, school districts often fail to follow through with the implications of instructional technology for their new programs. Recently, visiting a very significant open plan middle school, I witnessed the simple act of showing a movie to a group of a hundred and forty students gathered in one corner of the loft. The floor was flat, the projection surface was badly placed, the image was obliterated by stray light, and many of the youngsters were obviously turned off as the switch was turned on. I approached a little girl near the back of the group with her head on the desk and asked if she was interested in what was being shown. She indicated that she really didn't know, that she could never see anyway, and she always used

the showing of a movie as a time to rest. With all of the educational opportunities afforded by the flexibility and freedom of the open plan school, this district had failed to think through the contribution that technology could make in group instruction and had failed to provide for it in planning.

8. *The cult approach to planning.* I recently saw plans for a large city high school organized in four smaller houses. In each house a carrel is provided for every two students where they can work with books, manuals, programmed texts, references, and the like. But when a student is to view a movie or see a set of slides, he will go to the central resource center, check out the materials, and use them in special rooms. If the film or audio material is available on the dial access system, he will go to some other point—to a wet carrel—and dial up the material needed. And in another part of the school is to be the computer center with adjacent carrels for CAI. This school plant is responding to technological cults rather than taking an integrated systems approach.

9. *Failure to provide all needed facilities.* We may plan adequately for technology in large-group instruction, but we forget that such activity will also require production, maintenance, and other support services and facilities. And if instructional media are used in the lecture room, they ought to be made available for individual study—and so the library is affected. This failure has been well documented by the recent evaluation of the performance of multi-media facilities in colleges across the country. The multi-media rooms themselves are generally well planned and equipped, but they often don't function well because supporting services and facilities have been neglected—technical consultive and production services with their shops, maintenance facilities, planning rooms, and studios.

10. *Planning for the technological breakthrough.* And finally we see the schools planned for technology that is not yet proven to be either economically or technically feasible. For instance, some educators are turning from more commonly understood and less expensive technologies, on the assumption that computer aided learning is *the* technological breakthrough. Clearly, leaping from electronic miracle to electronic miracle makes realistic school planning difficult.

Guidance

Based on these observations of the influences of instructional technology on school buildings and in order to avoid many of the conflicts that are equally apparent, I would offer the following points of guidance in physical planning. Hopefully, these points are as appropriate to higher education as to elementary and secondary education.

1. During the development of educational specifications, define the tasks to be performed by instructional technology in all areas of the educational endeavor. This is the responsibility of the educator. Then, before architectural planning begins, define how the buildings must be planned in order to accommodate these uses of media. This is a task to which the architect should bring his experience.

2. If there is little experience with technology on which to base a program, then give all potential roles thorough consideration and anticipate the uses of media in the new school.

3. In anticipating technology be realistic as to what is technically and economically feasible, but don't be shortsighted.

4. Anticipate the directions in which a program of technology will grow, and identify those areas of the school plant where change is most apt to come—probably these will be in the area of the library and in production and support areas. Plan so that expansion and change can take place.

5. Be sure to consider all of the facility components that are necessary to house a program of instructional technology. Planning just for its use in large group or individualized instruction is not enough, because such efforts will also create need for production and support facilities and resource storage and retrieval facilities.

6. Plan around a true learning systems approach to media in education. Avoid the audiovisual cults by planning for the integrated use of media and, in turn, plan for integrated production and support facilities, and integrated resource facilities. Film makers, TV producers, graphic artists should be gathered administratively under a single umbrella as films, videotapes, slides, and audio-cartridges should also be gathered within the resource facility.

7. Plan so that instructional technology is potentially available in every learning situation. Initially at least provide adequate and accessible power, conduits, lighting controls, and the like.

8. Design facilities so that old hardware and equipment can be pulled out and replaced as new equipment and capabilities come on the market. Build in as little as possible—rather suspend, hang, and set-on.

9. School building like education itself must not be considered static; the building must be responsive to change which will take place periodically beginning soon after the buildings are opened and may involve everything from very minor to major rearrangement of processes. Again the less technology that is buried in the fabric of the building, the more that is free standing and relocatable, the better the technology will respond to change.

10. Define the degree of commitment required by the uses of technology in various facilities—define the degree of precision with which the facilities must be designed. Then in every case try to move towards less commitment, for the sake of economy and responsiveness to change as long as the educational processes are adequately served. A multi-media lecture room obviously is a higher degree of commitment than the use of portable rear projection units in an open plan school. In analyzing each situation there is always a conflict between commitment in one dimension and permissiveness in the other. In each, define the appropriate position between these two dimensions.

11. Plan for the various levels of production and support required for effective employment of technology in a school or college—where can a teacher get a transparency made, where is a film produced, where are TV services available.

12. Look to the simple self-contained pieces of the hardware which are personal

and portable and go wherever the student goes with whatever information he needs to accomplish as much of the task as possible.

It should be noted that most of these points in planning guidance deal with people and their responsibilities and decisions at various points in the planning process. The physical accommodation of instructional technology is a relatively simple task once the present and anticipated roles of technology and their purposes in education are defined. When accommodating technology, seek the simple solutions, the solutions that are educationally sound but which require the least commitment in terms of facilities. Above all, don't first plan a school for instructional technology; rather—plan a school for people; plan a pleasant, productive, aesthetically rewarding environment. A school building that is good for people is about as good as a school can be and chances are it will also be good for instructional technology.

11.

The Future of Educational Television

by *ROBERT B. HUDSON*
Sen. Vice President
National Educ. Television

With reference to the future of educational television, if one is permitted to separate it from the interrelated communications complex, I should like to talk first about instructional television, then about public television, including some comments about the applications of communications satellites to television in both industrialized and developing countries.

To plunge forthwith into an obscure future, instructional television, long before the turn of the century, will have little need for today's ETV stations. ITV will not be using the broadcasting band of frequencies. The stations that were sought, reserved and claimed in the name of education will go public, that is, they will be used mainly for public broadcasting. Instructional, or school television, including academic and occupational courses for adults, will be carried mainly by closed circuit transmissions. This prediction is clearly contingent on the assumption that schools exist 30 years hence in much the same physical and functional shape as we know them today, and this by no means is a certainty. Should the education of children and youth be reassigned on some larger dispersal base, computerized and instructional television information flow through CATV—community antenna television systems—could readily augment closed circuit systems.

The physical fact is, of course, that a single TV channel, or even two channels are not adequate to the instructional needs of a metropolitan area, or of a school system, or even of a single school. Subject matter, grade level work, that is often repeated in many sections, and clock hours, all are variables to be reconciled. Already there are more students to be educated than can be handled effectively by current techniques of teaching and administration. The curve is sharply up and the pressure of sheer numbers will force more sophisticated technological innovation in instruction perhaps sooner than schools are ready for it.

We try to have diversified schools quite the opposite of the French pattern where all students in a given grade study the same subjects at the same clock hour—and we need diversified services. Open circuit broadcasting nevertheless is effectively opening up the school arena to electronic inputs and it will continue to service schools in remote areas but, inevitably, it will give ground to the multichannel, closed-circuit system augmented, on a spot basis, by open channels in the 2500 megaHertz band.

Note: This paper was prepared for and presented at "Toward Century 21," a conference at Stanford University. April 4.

Educational administrators and teachers, at least many of them, are finding a variety of ways to improve teaching and enhance the learning experience. That an integrated use of television can help in doing this has been demonstrated over and over again. Why has television proved so effective when other projection and filming techniques have had only lukewarm reception in the past? The Educational Facilities Laboratory answers that question in this way: "Of audiovisual tools available, television appears to offer the broadest potential. The teaching image is easily transmissible by air and cable. It is reproducible from magnetic tape. It is viewable at relatively high ambient light levels without the need for darkening a room. It permits viewing of current events concurrently with the occasion. Taped programs, entire courses or laboratory demonstrations may be banked in libraries for use as required. Such tapes and/or programs for the slow learner or the advanced student may serve to enrich the gifted and help the slow. The viewing and audio instrument itself is relatively inexpensive, easily used, widely available in a variety of sizes and easily maintained. The arts of the industry are rapidly improving and lowering the costs of receiving, transmission, recording and production equipment."[2] But television, like library books, language labs, films, audio tapes, programmed instruction and the like must be available when the teacher needs it and when students are prepared and ready for it. With a single ETV channel, that patently is impossible. With six channels or twelve or more feeding into each school, the distribution problem is solved. It remains only that schools have available television courses and related materials that complement the classroom and make a positive and often a unique contribution to teaching and learning.

Herein lies the rub. One is tempted to say that television courses today are in the McGuffy Reader stage. How to use the medium effectively is the problem. For nearly half a century educational films have compressed large amounts of pictorial information into ten-minute reels with a narrator "telling it." They break the class routine, then it's over and done without much relation to course or lesson plan. Instructional television, on the other hand, was used in its first decade mostly to carry the image of a teacher from one classroom to another with a visual prop only occasionally introduced. It is not enough to simply pick up conventional teaching techniques as practiced within the limiting boundaries of the classroom. New procedures must evolve to capitalize more fully on the unique characteristics of the medium. Things are getting better. Work is being done in many parts of the country on curriculum planning, presentational method and utilization in television courses. The Education Development Center in Massachusetts and the National Center for School and College Television at Indiana University are taking the lead in course experimentation and improvement. In spite of the fact that most ITV producers try to edit into their programs a variety of information streams or tracks, unfortunately the components seldom fall together to best advantage. Usually the problem is too little money, too many programs to produce; too little time, too little staff, too many other things to do; too little planning, too little experience, too little testing.

Up until now efforts in instructional television have been either experimental or "boot straps." A parallel would be asking school systems to write and produce their own text books. Foundations have probed the area and the United States Office of Education has researched the initial decade of experience. Now the big boys have moved in. Education has been discovered for what it is—a multibillion dollar market. A score of years ago, at the end of World War II, education's budget stood at $4 billion; now it tops $50 billion. You need wonder no more at surprising mergers in the corporate world—electronics and publishing are strange bedfellows no longer. Large hardware is married to large software and it foreshadows the shape of the future.

These new enterprises have staked out claims in the educational materials field with heavy emphasis on educational technology. They are concerned with computers, with information storage and retrieval, with feedback, and are seeking ways of giving students ready access not only to great storehouses of knowledge but better ways of assessing and thinking about problems.

The view is widely held among educators that a surgical attitude toward institutionalized education and the logistic problems it faces is in order. Dean John I. Goodlad of the Graduate School of Education at UCLA asserts that "the incidence of nonpromotion, dropouts, alienation, and minimal learning in school is such that one is led to conclude that today's schools are obsolescent. They were designed for a different culture, a different conception of learners and of learning, and a different clientele." He goes on to note, "The era that is in full bloom and is about to fade is human-to-human instruction. . . . The era of instruction that will supersede the era of human-based instruction is to be the one of man-machine interaction. And the machine is the computer."[3] Already the electronic/publishing combines are portraying a picture of great instructional efficiency and hopefully freeing the human teachers to do human instructional tasks. Under today's load of curricular and extracurricular work, perhaps even now many teachers don't have time for human person-to-person instruction. If the computerized system giving students and teachers finger touch command of information, utilizing television monitors (classroom wall size, carrel size and pocket size) along with other devices, matures by the turn of the century and the educational establishment is willing to use it, then teachers will have an opportunity to pursue human instructional goals.

Whereas instructional television is reaching impressive numbers of students in elementary and secondary schools, it is, nevertheless, employed in scores of colleges and universities. It is reported that 28,000 of Ohio State's 41,000 students took some of their work, mostly math and biology, by television during the 1966-67 school year. Michigan State carried 27 courses a term over a TV closed-circuit hookup that interconnected 137 classrooms and 300 monitors, many of which were in dormitories. A 20-page log was required to itemize the offerings.

The wave of the future may further be foreshadowed by a plan put before the current session of the Indiana Legislature by the four state-supported universities—Indiana University, Purdue, Ball State and Indiana State—for a state-wide telecommunications system. The system would interconnect the four major campuses and twelve regional campuses. Eventually 22 private universities and colleges would be tied in. In addition, the system would link 16 clinical-medical teaching centers and community hospitals with the Indiana University Medical School. Agricultural and other non-credit adult education activities would make use of the system.

University students haven't fully endorsed the ITV system. Some just don't like it; some even prefer the T.A.s, but there is ample evidence that information can be transmitted effectively and with good results given the proper motivation at the receiving end.

There are student complaints these days on campuses, in the megaversities, about lack of identity and dehumanization brought about by the application of management systems to academic and student affairs. One answers to a serial number and personality finds expression in a punched card. Don't despair, the road ahead is somewhat brighter. Universities are caught up in a population explosion that they are ill prepared to deal with. The ID card is only a symbol of the problem. Later in this century, by the time your sons and daughters are ready for college, it will not be that way. You won't have to send them to Reed or Swarthmore, or to Stanford Overseas to find their identities. The chief concern of university faculties will be the students—not lecturing to students, but living with students and participating in the life of the college community in much the way that a Master of the College lives with students at Yale today. As Jacqueline Grennan (Wexler) has said, "Learning is not essentially expository but essentially exploratory."

Apart from his research, perhaps 80 percent of a professor's time is wasted in a classroom. The classroom is highly inefficient, there are so many better ways of getting information to students. Already the professor's books convey in one dimension what he knows about his area of specialization. In another generation he will have added other dimensions. And this is where the electronic/publishing mergers will make their contribution. A student in a study carrel through a simple coded system can have delivered instantaneously via a television monitor or a microform or facsimile full information on the subject or the problem that concerns him. He can have information in the form of data, document, case studies, professional opinion by one or more persons, sequential cause and effect processes, a programmed approach, or a filmed vignette, to mention a few formats. These will be single concept learning aids bearing precisely on the student's problem, not fully processed programs containing a load of materials and relationships irrelevant to the student's immediate interests. For example, with a six-minute single concept film or audio tape the student can be in the presence of the best professor or specialist in a given field. Or a micro-reader will place a selection of text or a whole document immediately on his screen in response to the touch of a button.

We have some experience now with the split screen on a television picture tube; we can see four golfers at the Masters playing under stress at four different locations on the course; we can have closeups of the snap of the ball in a football game and of a lonesome end far out on the scrimmage line. Then, of course, there is the instant replay. Television central can isolate picture elements and it can accept multi-channel feeds. Well, these electronic devices, and others even more sophisticated, can be applied to the learning situation too.

If you can divide a picture into four separate parts, why not into a hundred parts? Why not into a moving mosaic in which you can interchange parts or drop them out, thus making for a fascinating and imaginative study in relationships? This can be done now in the laboratory, but for your grandson it will be done in his study carrel.

National Cash Register has succeeded in writing a two-micron line width (a size about half the width of a red blood cell) with a laser beam. In terms of storage, this means that 10,000 pages could be stored on an area the size of one page. It will not be long before microforms will be adapted to computer systems for automatic retrieval of documents.

I should not want to leave the impression that students will be confined to carrels in the pursuit of their studies. Carrels will represent focal points where the student can draw upon the full range of resources. As a matter of fact, he will be far less campus bound than you and I have ever dreamed of being, although we can carry paperbacks, tape recorders, radio and television receivers wherever we go. Cassettes of film and audio tape and microfiche in sizes ranging from wrist watch to cigarette pack that can supply hours of information on almost any subject are emerging even now from the laboratory. Of course, from the carrel he can have full documentary films or artistic performances fed in for the asking. Feedback will be programmed into the system, both self-correcting aids which are central in programmed instruction and discussion with other students and with specialists on duty in one of the information and materials centers.

The system is relatively simple, but it will take a generation before we accord book status and prestige to other information storage devices and organize and encode an ever expanding curriculum suitable for the university man of the 21st Century. As I indicated earlier, instructional television in the elementary and secondary schools is still in the McGuffy Reader stage. At the college level it isn't even that far along. Today's university follows the pattern of the Medieval university; it "tells it" to the student or lets him read it. Perhaps not quite so much learning by rote as in the Middle Ages but not nearly enough premium on independent study. Opportunity for that will come as fast as information the student needs can be selected, processed in a variety of formats, stored, and made available at will.

When that day does come, then the professor can get down to the real business of education. He will spend his time with students, individually and in groups. He will be a generalist, not a specialist, and life, ideas and experience will be examined unfettered of 50-minute bells and numerical grades.

In short, by the beginning of Century 21 instructional television, in concert with memory banks containing mankind's useful knowledge accessible in a variety of attractive and meaningful forms, will free the university to pursue its central mission of human to human interactive education.

Let's turn now to the future of what the Carnegie Commission on Educational Television has labeled "public television." Incidentally, the label will stick. Already it is taking on a distinctive connotation. In creating the term, the Commission provided a context. It said, "All television, commercial television included, provides news, entertainment, and instruction; all television teaches about places, people, animals, politics, crime, science. Yet the differences are clear. *Commercial television* seeks to capture the large audience; it relies mainly upon the desire to relax and to be entertained. *Instructional television* lies at the opposite end of the scale; it calls upon the instinct to work, build, learn, and improve, and asks the viewer to take on responsibilities in return for a later reward. *Public Television.* . . . includes all that is of human interest and importance which is not at the moment appropriate or available for support by advertising, and which is not arranged for formal instruction."[4]

The National Educational Television Network and most of the ETV stations have been working that street for a number of years although the concept wasn't quite as sharp; nevertheless they welcome the creation of the Corporation for Public Broadcasting and the prospect of substantial funding.

The Public Broadcasting Act of 1967 contains a Congressional declaration of policy, a sharp reversal of the policy of 1934, and one that foreshadows the shape of television services for home reception as we approach the 21st Century. Section 396(a) of the Act states:

"(1) that it is in the public interest to encourage the growth and development of noncommercial educational radio and television broadcasting, including the use of such media for instructional purposes;

"(2) that expansion and development of noncommercial educational radio and television broadcasting and of diversity of its programming depend on freedom, imagination, and initiative on both the local and national levels;

"(3) that the encouragement and support of noncommercial educational radio and television broadcasting, while matters of importance for private and local development, are also of appropriate and important concern to the Federal Government;

"(4) that it furthers the general welfare to encourage noncommercial educational radio and television broadcast programming which will be responsive to the interests of people both in particular localities and throughout the United States, and which will constitute an expression of diversity and excellence;

"(5) that it is necessary and appropriate for the Federal Government to complement, assist, and support a national policy that will most effectively make noncommercial educational radio and television service available to all the citizens of the United States;

"(6) that a private corporation should be created to facilitate the development of educational radio and television broadcasting and to afford maximum protection to such broadcasting from extraneous interference and control."

That private corporation—The Corporation for Public Broadcasting—has been created but at this date (April 1968) has not been funded.

When one considers the kind of program service that a people have a right to expect from television broadcasting in the limited and publicly owned spectrum space available, it is interesting to compare the policies followed in Great Britain with those of the United States. In 1927 the British Government created the BBC and thus consolidated all broadcasting functions under this chartered corporation. The BBC did not accept advertising and its revenues derived from a tax on receiving sets. Its first director-general, Lord Reith, and his successors set the standards and the public exerted little influence on programming. The U.S.A. took the low road. At first the big four in the electronics group—Westinghouse, General Electric, AT&T and RCA—used their radio transmitters to broadcast programs that could be heard on the receiving sets that they, in turn, sold to listeners. Soon, however, the idea caught on that radio programs were splendid carriers for commercial messages. Government policy followed a tortuous course but in the end the commercial system became dominant and operated free of all but technical controls except, of course, for some elastic rules covering matters of common decency.

These policies held in both countries, respectively, for two decades of radio and were carried over into the television era. Then, in the early '50s, seemingly both countries recognized that they were not getting the optimum service from the television medium. Britain thereupon created the Independent Television Authority as a commercial television service, and in the U.S.A. the Federal regulatory body reserved 250 television channels for noncommercial, educationally oriented programming. Now, after nearly a score of years and with the advent of the Corporation for Public Broadcasting, one may say that the U.S. is ready to beef up its noncommercial service and, like Great Britain, bring the two into some appropriate equilibrium. One may say so, but it may not necessarily be true. The British Government has a long tradition of hands off its chartered instruments. Prime Minister Anthony Eden was effectively rebuffed when he tried at the time of the Suez crisis to bring the BBC under direct Government control. Not so in the United States. The Government here likes to retain fiscal control of the instruments it creates—a dedicated tax is an anathema to it—and sometimes these controls are subject to buffeting by political winds.

I predict that public television will grow and mature during the last quarter of this century. The Corporation for Public Broadcasting will obtain substantial Federal funding after some lean early years; its direct financial assistance will strengthen the stations in a basic network, and it will provide a line of distinctive programs to the stations and to the nation, but programs largely non-controversial in nature.

The range and depth of the Federally supported program service will depend in large measure on the degree to which the Corporation is insulated from political pressures. If the Congress should take the advice of the Carnegie Commission and dedicate a tax source to the Corporation's support (e.g., an excise tax on radio and television receivers), then one could expect the exercise of considerable boldness in the underwriting of programs that scrutinize and probe the cause and effect aspects of political, economic and social problems. Lacking a dedicated tax—it would take a minor miracle to bring it off—Corporation-supported programs will tend to avoid controversial subjects except on issues where there is substantial consensus.

But high controversy is the engine of democracy, the essence of the democratic process. These are the issues that matter in our society and institutions that ignore them soon atrophy. Perhaps some of our universities and churches and political institutions are suffering dry rot because of their unwillingness or inability to face new issues and resolve them in the white light of public discussion from which none are barred.

If public television is to be worth its salt it must deal with vital matters. If support for those programs doesn't come from the public treasury, it must come from private sources. But through what mechanism? One might say, parenthetically, that it is far easier to predict technological change than it is to design social mechanisms. Private funds also have masters, and a private source in and of itself does not guarantee an optimal use of freedom or a full and balanced exploration of all that is relevant in a subject. To neutralize the threat of privately imposed biases, public television has two precedents from the past that can guide it in the future. One is the principle of diversity and the other is the doctrine of fairness.

Throughout its 15-year history educational television, now called public television, has relied upon a wide variety of program sources and an even wider mustering of producers in conceiving and creating programs. Sources of support also run the gamut from foundation grants to business corporations to labor unions to state legislative appropriations. In the next decades as private funds are fed into public television to round out a program service primarily supported by Federal funds, their influence and credibility will vary directly with the diversity of their sources.

Another safeguard for public television, regardless of the source of funds, lies in the fairness doctrine. This doctrine was enunciated by the Federal Communications Commission as an interpretation of The Communications Act of 1934. In short, it requires that when a broadcasting station presents a point of view on a controversial issue of public importance "reasonable opportunity must be afforded for the presentation of contrasting views." The doctrine is being reexamined on public policy and constitutional grounds just now, but for our purpose it expresses the spirit of fair play to be observed by the managers of the public airways. This doctrine will apply also to CATV systems if they finally are ruled subject to FCC regulation.

I noted early on in my comments that it is in the cards for instructional television to gravitate toward closed circuit, or wired transmission facilities. This trend inevitably will affect the numbers and kind of public television stations. There are now about 150 ETV stations on the air and some people forecast upwards of 200 in 1970. But instructional services provide the financial floor for three-quarters of these stations and the removal of that floor when schools abandon open-circuit broadcasting will result in substantial shrinkage in the number of stations. The Corporation for Public Broadcasting will assist many of the local stations, the number depending in large measure on the magnitude of funds available to it, but it seems unlikely that it will become the prime underwriter of hundreds of public TV stations. When Federal funds are dispensed there is apt to be mandatory support in some measure for at least one station in each state. Population density will be another controlling factor, and the nature and quality of the local or regional service should weigh heavily in the allocation of funds. One hopes that other criteria will apply in the Corporation's grant making for program production.

In looking 30 years into the future, three possible developments cast faint shadows. The first is that of a public television network—perhaps one should say a group—of roughly a hundred powerful noncommercial stations, plus many translators, largely supported by Federal funds. In addition, there may be a scattering of locally supported stations. The second is the allocation of one or more channels on a domestic communications satellite feeding directly into home television receivers programs produced mainly under the aegis of the Corporation for Public Broadcasting, plus other programs required to round out the service. The third shadow shows the Corporation's and other programs being fed into homes through a nation-wide linkage of CATV systems. These, of course, like the satellite, would be multi-channel carriers and viewers would enjoy a wide range of choices in selecting what they want to see and hear.

A further development that is more than a shadow is the television recorder and playback. Already Dr. Peter Goldmark of CBS Laboratories is demonstrating EVR—Electronic Video Recording—a system that for the first time makes it possible to show on conventional TV sets prerecorded programming from motion picture film and videotape at low cost. The time isn't far away when you will be able to set your recorder to automatically pick up and store the program that is on any given channel at any given time. It is then yours to have and to hold and to play at your option. You will be able, also, to purchase video programs in much the same way as you now buy audio tapes and records.

One need hardly comment on the pressures the Corporation will feel in deciding which local noncommercial stations to support with Federal funds. Many a head will be bloodied before a rational and a tenable policy can be devised that will reconcile at least some of the urgent and pressure-laden demands.

Assuming the availability of an adequate number of frequencies, the communications satellite plan has the most going for it—a single television antenna in synchronous orbit 22,300 miles above the earth, in line of sight of and receivable by every television receiver in North America. Synchronous communications satellites are operating now over the oceans but at such low power that highly sophisticated and expensive ground stations are required for sending and receiving their signals. Professor Wilbur Schramm of Stanford forecasts the advent of "direct" satellites, that is, satellites emitting a sufficiently powerful signal to be picked up by a home TV receiver, by 1975. That gives us 25 years, then, to the end of the century in which to adjust our conventional broadcasting policies and patterns to opportunities opened up by the new technology.

As has been noted, this will affect noncommercial stations in some important ways; indeed, the satellite could supersede these stations or it might be used to interconnect them. Even in the latter case the marginal ones may die off for want of operational support. But what of commercial stations? Will there be some kind of tariff policy that protects them in their market areas? The American system of local television stations presently is based on the physics of television signal propagation. Without going into the precise location in the spectrum of the public broadcast bands—VHF and UHF—which, incidentally, are now under review by the President's Task Force on Communication Policy, suffice it to say most TV stations effectively cover a circular area that has a radius of about 75 miles. A station may have competition in that area from other stations on other channels, but they, too, are local stations. Other coverage areas are assigned to other Federally licensed stations. Thus, when an advertiser wants to reach the whole country with his commercial message he must contract for as many stations as are necessary to give him effective national coverage. Networks, as we know, make this easy for him.

But when the state of the satellite art develops to the point where it alone can give total national coverage, what will happen to the local TV station, be it commercial or noncommercial? Will public policy permit a sizable private enterprise industry to be emasculated? Will it countenance the elimination of a prime vehicle through which local voices can be heard, sacrificing them on the altar of one all-powerful national communications system? I do not believe that public policy will take that road (also, old technologies, like ingrained behavior patterns, die hard!) There is a powerful American tradition for local participation, for giving local voices access to the public forum. As our country becomes more densely populated there will be increasing need for keeping the democratic base both informed and articulate and interactive.

There are other reasons, too, for not abandoning our system of local broadcasting stations: they are not as vulnerable as a satellite. You can lose a few stations and still maintain a full coverage communications system; if all of your bets are placed on a bird in orbit, you must remember that birds can be shot out of the sky.

By the turn of the century the odds are that we will enjoy a highly efficient integrated communications system. Satellites to be sure, not only for broadcasting but for computer linkage and other common carrier functions, but also broadcasting stations for radio, television and facsimile; coaxial cables, microwaves, lasers and other magic devices that only Bell Labs knows about.

If I appear to be downgrading the importance of communications satellites on the American scene, one must remember that this country has developed over the years a communications grid second to none. Information can move instantaneously to every hamlet in America. Information flow is the blood stream of business, industry and government. It is one of the stronger cohesive forces in our social structure. A satellite, at best, complements the land based system and, like other ingenious technological breakthroughs, it will substitute for inefficient and uneconomic parts of it as performance dictates.

The potential role of the communications satellite in developing countries, however, is of a quite different order of magnitude. It can provide the basic service, not merely complement an existing one. In countries like India, Indonesia and Brazil, for example, there are no comprehensive communications grids. Trunk lines exist only between major cities and they are overloaded. The message simply doesn't get through to the town, the village, or the countryside. Education doesn't get through, agricultural information doesn't get through, family planning information doesn't get through. Neither is there rapid and effective communication between central governments and local, state and regional authorities. Without current market and weather information the farmer is at the mercy both of the broker and of the elements.

In these developing countries a communications satellite can make the difference, and by 1975 they can be in business. By the year 2000 their national systems will rival those of industrial nations—as a matter of fact, by that time, they may be industrial nations. What the communications satellite can mean to them is the quantum leap toward national development. All India Radio's fifteen year plan for television station construction calls for 56 stations by 1982 and, significantly, those stations would cover only 19 percent of the country and only 25 percent of the population. The cost would be more than double that of a satellite. It will take India until the beginning of the 21st Century to have enough television stations to reach 80 percent of her population. India's development problems, human and physical, are such that she can't wait 15 years or 30 years for conventional technology to service her information needs. Such is her quandary.

This paper has dealt mainly with prospective technological developments in communications as they may shape the future of educational television. The hardware is important because it not only serves society, it changes society. In education, both at school and at home, it promises to free us from our traditional routines and inhibitions. We are earth-bound no longer. As the remarkable prognosticator of the space age, Arthur C. Clarke, has said, "The communications network, of which the satellites will be nodal points, will enable the consciousness of our grandchildren to flicker like lightning back and forth across the face of this planet. They will be able to go anywhere and meet anyone, at any time, without stirring from their homes. All knowledge will be open to them, all museums and libraries of the world will be extensions of their living rooms. Marvelous machines, with unlimited information-handling capacity, will be able to speak directly into their minds."[5]

Technology can open up this bright future, but in what measure will social institutions accept it and adapt to it? What will be the ground rules governing access to public television's cameras? To an international, people to people, television system? Who are the gatekeepers? On what basis is the work and product of creative people made available for public television and global television? The Register of Copyrights in Washington has not yet found an equitable formula for satisfying both the creator and user of unique works—the number of users being raised to the nth power through modern communications technology. The talent unions and the technicians also will have a voice in how their contributions are exploited.

A further consideration: What will people be doing in the 21st Century? How many will there be? How much leisure will they have? What about their economic status and living conditions? What languages will they speak and how mobile will they be in moving around the world? Obviously we have few answers for these questions, but the answers, when they are found, will have important bearing on the shape of television and on the tasks that society assigns to it.

Perhaps television potentially is the greatest unifying force ever to act upon man, but to attain that potentiality we must try to find a way to unfetter it, a way to let it operate in the free market place of ideas.

REFERENCES

1. Erik Barnouw. *A Tower in Babel.* New York: Oxford University Press, 1966, p. 78

2. *Design for ETV: Planning for Schools with Television.* Educational Facilities Laboratory, 1968, p. 22

3. John I. Goodlad. *The Future of Learning and Teaching. AV Communication Review,* Vol. 16, No. 1, Spring 1968, pp. 5, 6, 7

4. The Carnegie Commission on Educational Television, *Public Television: A Program for Action.* Bantam Books, 1967, p. 1

5. Arthur C. Clarke. *Voices from the Sky.* Pyramid Books, 1967, p. 121

12.

Dial Access Information Retrieval Systems

by RICHARD B. HULL
Director
Telecommunications
Center
Ohio State Univ.

An increasing number of schools, colleges and universities are demonstrating interest in electronic dial access information retrieval systems (DAIRS) to support programs of instruction in various subject matter areas. Most present installations provide audio services but some have video capability as well. While equipment suppliers frequently use the term "random access" in describing these systems, only a few such installations now have this desirable capacity. The basic DAIRS objective is to serve individual students in semi-private listening or viewing situations with a kind of "non-book" library resource almost instantaneously available at the student's option.

As a concept, electronic information storage and retrieval is considerably less awesome than it may appear to be although the variety of storage media and technologies now employed or projected for this purpose does comprise a formidable listing.

The mass production of printed books was the first large scale expression of a mechanical storage and retrieval process. Paper was the storage medium, the printing press the recording device, and the human eye was the retrieval mechanism.

Phonographic recording devised early in the 20th Century established the basic principles for all subsequent non-book information storage and retrieval. Sound, transmitted through a microphone was translated into a series of "vibrations" which was physically etched or encoded into "cue" patterns within the circular grooves on a wax or plastic disc. Information, either voice or music, which had been stored on the disc could then be retrieved or decoded by the phonograph needle which retrieved the information by translating the groove markings into intelligible "vibrations" which in turn were amplified through a phonograph horn or loud speaker for easier comprehension by the human ear.

While this whole "phonographic" process was soon to become electronic rather than mechanical and would embrace the recording and retrieval of print-out data and television pictures with magnetic plastic tape as the basic storage medium, the essential process has remained unchanged. This concept of transferring or encoding information into a storage medium and retrieving and decoding or translating into a form which the human eye or ear can perceive is applied through a variety of devices to any number of present day applications—business data processing, stereo and video recording and playback, analogue and digital computer systems and, of course, to DAIRS installations.

DAIRS simply represents the combination of two now long established communications techniques—magnetic tape information storage and retrieval and telephone exchange switching. Automated magnetic tape record and replay devices are linked to telephone dialing switching devices which in turn are connected to individual reception points. In some instances a small computer is employed to expedite switching, to control program flow, and to provide a record of DAIRS usage.

Typically a DAIRS installation functions as an electronic non-book library or facility. An assortment of instructional materials pre-recorded on magnetic audio or video tape are collected in a central repository connected to various individual reception points at varying distances from the central facility interconnected by wire or coaxial cable. The interconnections terminate at each reception point in an automatic switching or selection device like those used for dial or "touch-tone" telephones.

A typical user will employ a reference directory or an instructor's assignment sheet to determine the code or dial number of the particular instructional item. When he dials the number, a tape transport (playback) machine at the library is automatically cued by the dial impulse through a switching system. This selects and sends the requested information to the acoustically treated study booth or carrel from which the "call" originated.

Although these installations have been widely referred to as "random access" systems, until very recently none of them actually had this capability and only a relative handful of DAIRS audio installations (at considerable additional cost) now offer this feature. "Random access" implies that the user can select any information item at will from the repository and hear it or see it relayed to his reception point immediately. In most cases, however, a user actually has only "serial access," i.e., if a given lesson or segment of information already dialed by one user is being transmitted, a second or third dialer seeking that information will "join a program already in progress." Thus the user will have to wait for the tape cycle to end and start again before he can hear the beginning of the lesson.

Theoretically, any desired amount of information on audio and video tape may be stored in a DAIRS library, and any number of reception points established nearby or remote from the library. However, there are both cost and technological limitations (particularly in video systems where the problems can be overwhelming) which enthusiasts may tend to underestimate or overlook.

Indeed, early planners envisioned individual learners throughout a metropolitan area calling into a school or university DAIRS center, using normal residential telephones. Unfortunately, most telephone exchange switching systems are not designed for extended tie-ups of subscriber lines at a single access point as in a DAIRS information bank. Telephone exchanges assume no more than 15 per cent of the subscribers will be using the circuits at one time, but DAIRS users may employ the system 100 per cent of the time. Mass dial-in for the general public through normal telephone exchange facilities is limited to recorded 10-15 second weather and temperature messages, etc. Each DAIRS lesson or informational playback may run 15 minutes or more, while many different informational packages are playing back at the same time to different users at many reception points. Thus the DAIRS installation must have its own "telephone exchange" or switching system. It must have its own circuits on a campus or within a school system or, if they are leased from a telephone company, must be leased as "dedicated" or sole-use circuits. As sole-use circuits they are not subject to the limitations of the standard telephone exchange.

Equipping a reception point for group rather than for individual carrel listening or viewing is quite feasible where desired. However, the primary concern of educators interested in these systems is not in group instruction but rather in the real or imagined potential which DAIRS has for improving individual and self-study. In some cases the requirements for tapping this potential have not been fully understood especially where video display service has been attempted.

With no known exceptions, DAIRS facilities are used to supplement, not to replace, the teacher in the classroom. Neither is it used as an alternative to required programs of reading and research. Almost any academic discipline may be involved. In school systems lesson materials would typically include English, foreign languages, history, mathematics, science and vocational education. In university applications, DAIRS libraries would include English and the full range of classical and modern foreign languages, various history sequences, education, music, biological and physical science materials. Repository library content varies from school to school and from campus to campus. Usage involves collections of audio materials most of which is locally prepared by faculties who use the DAIRS facilities and correlate them with regular courses of instruction. Use of DAIRS facilities for central video distribution is by comparison sharply limited. Some of the instructional material is prepared locally where television and film production facilities are available, but much of it is procured on film or tape from outside sources. Surprisingly, little concern has been expressed about copyright and royalty considerations, possibly because so much DAIRS activity is localized and still considered experimental, and perhaps because instructors relate the supplementary materials they prepare so closely with the basic course that they see them as integrated support items rather than separate activities. With any increased use of syndicated materials, however, one may expect this situation to change rapidly.

There are perhaps more than 150 DAIRS installations in school systems and institutions of higher education throughout the country. They vary greatly in size, capability, capacity, complexity and cost. A simple audio-only system with limited information storage capacity and 10 or 15 listening posts may be established for $10,000 or less. More elaborate systems, many with video facilities and computerized switching and program equipment and large information storage capacities equipped to serve several hundred listening and viewing posts, call for capital investments of $500,000 or more. However, a true random access audio only DAIRS with 25 individual carrels can call for an investment on the order of $350,000.

In most instances the reception stations, whatever their number, tend to be located in the same building or in buildings near the central library or tape repository. While this self-contained adjacency may be a normal expectation in the first phase of DAIRS installations, because of shorter wire and cable runs and perhaps no more than 150 reception points, other considerations also apply.

A DAIRS installation may also be self-contained because it is considered to be a specialized facility by some administrators. Thus it might be under the aegis of the audio-visual center at a single location in a school system, or regarded as an instructional media laboratory at a College of Education in a university.

When a DAIRS facility is planned as an instructional aid on a university-wide basis, metropolitan area institutions with highly congested campuses may prefer to have all audio-visual instructional aids located in a single building. This central building may be planned as a "learning resource center" equipped with television and radio studios, a graphics department and film department where all instructional materials for DAIRS and other applications are produced. A large centralized facility of this kind conceivably could service 1,000 or more reception terminals. If a video dial access service is involved, centralization of repository and reception stations is logical because much shorter television coaxial cable runs (considerably more expensive than the wired circuits used for audio only facilities) are required.

However, some of the larger university DAIRS installations have adopted a deliberate policy of extending their resources throughout and sometimes out of the campus area. One university facility serves 415 stations, 18 of which have video capability. While the video stations are now immediately adjacent to the tape repository and comprise part of the original central carrel complex of 140 terminals, there are an additional 240 reception stations at various campus locations including the student union building, the library, and various residence halls as well as single reception points at each of 25 fraternity and sorority houses. Plans call for extension of the system to buildings now under construction on a new undergraduate campus. Further extension of the dial access facility services to branch campuses in other cities has been discussed but a decision has been postponed because of costs and technical problems.

Some observers argue that whatever the desired DAIRS service and reception capacity, it should be regarded as a master facility for an institution and housed at a single central point. Expansion of services then would occur, not by the continual addition of diffused reception points, each of which was connected to the master facility, but rather through the establishment of sub-central DAIRS facilities with adjacent reception stations at various strategic locations throughout a campus. A sub-center might have wire and cable interconnections to the master facility for the purpose of dubbing off master tapes to store in its own tape repository, or it might decide to forego interconnection and physically transport master tape copies instead. The sub-center concept also suggests the possibility of developing specialized tape storage depots keyed to the subject matter of primary concern at a given location.

Technology for audio only DAIRS systems appears to be well advanced, and the basic components for the most part, reliable, provided the purchaser employs competent engineering counsel and understands that equipment dependability is not obtained at bargain prices—either in acquisition of the original equipment or for its continuing maintenance. System designers have now had many years of experience with the basic system elements, automated audio tape recording and playback mechanisms and automated dial select switching systems, in other applications.

A DAIRS installation with many listening stations and the need to provide repository access to as many individuals as possible, may employ a small digital computer control unit to speed up switching; to program segments of repository tapes in different combinations at different times for different reception locations; and to provide a cumulative statistical record of use. Backup computer capacity may also be desirable since these control units are complicated and extremely difficult to repair quickly when problems develop. A faulty computer can bring the entire system to a halt and a system will remain out of operation until the computer is restored and reprogrammed. Use of computer switching, however, should not be regarded as experimental.

DAIRS attempts to provide a viable video dial access retrieval service have been somewhat disappointing since fully adequate technology for this purpose is still being developed. DAIRS video installations now in operation employ compromise designs which are partly electronic, partly mechanical, and partly manual. The systems, semi-automated at best, are not reliable where continuous high volume use is attempted. Both video tape players and motion picture film projectors feed pictures into the video system. Machines are hand loaded for the most part and cued or switched by hand. Picture quality is below television broadcast standards, the low cost video tape machines employed in these systems were not designed for the kind of heavy work load which continuous usage of the video circuits requires. Even so, the capacity of these installations to distribute pictures exceeds the supply of instructional materials presently available from any combination of sources. A true random access dial capability would further extend that capacity. Some observers believe if user efforts to achieve random or serial video access were abandoned temporarily and the facilities employed to display instructional units on a scheduled basis, some very useful outcomes could be achieved while work on reliable automated video dial access technology continues.

The older more familiar language laboratory, the forerunner of present DAIRS systems, runs the gamut from the simple to the sophisticated. Originally the laboratory merely consisted of collections of disc recordings with examples of the language under study to which an individual student might listen with earphones or a loudspeaker. Later the disc recordings were replaced by magnetic tape recordings. The tape recorder could also be used to record and play back the student's own voice as he practiced phrasing and pronunciation in a study cubicle or carrel, attended from time to time by the supervising language instructor. Subsequently all of these elements were combined through an electronic interconnection and switching system so that the supervising instructor could speak or listen to any individual student; direct the sound from pre-recorded language tapes to individuals or to the class as a whole; criticize or compare the student's pronunciation with that on the pre-recorded tape. In addition, the student could record his own pronunciation, compare it with the pre-recorded tapes, or discuss it with the instructor in a live dialogue. Some laboratories have individual tape recorders with delay circuits which permit the student to hear his own words repeated back almost immediately. All of these factors make it possible for the student to work individually at his own pace and to use supplementary resources as desired. Some language laboratories also employ visual aids utilizing slides, motion pictures and video tape materials either in a modified classroom setting or in the study carrels.

At this point, it becomes increasingly difficult to clearly distinguish between a sophisticated language laboratory (which may also have dial access switching capability) and a sophisticated DAIRS system. The study carrel in the DAIRS may incorporate motion picture and television tapes and be employed in language as well as other kinds of instruction. Indeed, many writers in instructional technology use the term "learning laboratory" and "learning resource center" to describe what were formerly regarded as language laboratories but are now employed in the teaching of subjects other than languages.

Those language laboratories which provided individualized instruction and utilized individual study carrels clearly set the pattern for what are now regarded as totally innovative instructional departures characterized by terms such as "auto-tutorial instruction," "audio-tutorial instruction," "auto-didactic instruction," etc. Recent examples of the latter incorporate the familiar carrel now equipped for audio tape recording and playback, motion picture and video tape playback.

A number of the companies who now manufacture and install DAIRS equipment were and are involved in the construction and sale of electronic "language laboratories," "listening centers," and "learning centers," as they are variously termed. Several manufacturers of cross-bar switching and automatic dialing equipment are involved as are some of the major multi-product electronic manufacturers whose equipment offerings run the gamut from television transmitters and studio equipment to microwave systems, tape recording equipment and generating plants.

Singly or in combination with the manufacturers of telephone switching equipment, they are prepared to provide a DAIRS (or "Datagram" as one supplier terms it) installation complete with tape recording and playback gear and radio and television studio facilities for the preparation of software. Many smaller suppliers also provide and install equipment complexes. All of this reflects in part the burgeoning ambitions of industry in the as yet unconsummated marriage of industrial hardware and educational software and still find hopeful expression in the names of some companies such as "Continuous Progress Education," "Omnilab," etc. The implicit promises which the supplier infers and the educational purchasers seem only too willing to believe are even more marked in the nomenclature which the "language laboratory" and "learning laboratory" manufacturers apply to some of their various systems—"The Preceptor," "Transolab," "Electronic Educator," "Select-a-Lesson," "Electronic Learning Center," "Learning Laboratory System," etc.

Assessment of the "real and the imagined" instructional potential in DAIRS and the scores of other electronic "instructional systems" which are literally flooding the market is a formidable task which too few educational purchasers are really qualified to undertake. It is important to find out what these systems are and what they can do what they are not and what they cannot do.

It would seem to be obvious that an assessment of the educational problem should precede an assessment of electronic systems. A thorough analysis of the educational objectives and step-by-step spelling out of the procedures necessary to attain those objectives are factors which logically should determine the specifications of the "instructional system" which is ultimately selected.

Surprisingly, these analytical procedures are sometimes neglected altogether. An instructional system or an array of electronic devices which purportedly will solve some generally recognized but not carefully specified educational needs of an institution will be acquired. The specific procedures to tap this "educational potential" will actually be devised after the fact. This posture would almost suggest the machine or the system itself is expected to provide elements of the creative function which only its users can supply.

The ongoing search in American education to find more efficient ways of deploying instructional personnel and resources, to individualize instruction and to improve its quality, to keep abreast of the geometric increase in new knowledge, at times takes on almost panic aspects. Compared with business, industry and the military, the educational establishment has been a laggard in developing and employing new ways and means of analyzing, processing, storing, retrieving and distributing information, which is really one of its most basic concerns.

Now, as education without much previous experience in electronic information systems, begins to grope for a kind of "instructional technology" of its own, it sometimes appears to act as if it were "re-inventing the wheel." While the endeavors of education to employ technology for instruction may be unique, the technical requirements and operational principles which information systems employ are not.

Institutions on every instructional level tend to greatly overestimate the actual scope and degree of the educational establishment's present involvement with "instructional technology." Because computers are widely used in processing educational data and in making research computations, some observers infer that a parallel application in computer assisted instruction is underway. Because a carrel designed to foster self-study has usefully employed an audio or video dial access system, enthusiasts rush forward to construct more and separate carrels, each of which is dedicated to a different media application, i.e., motion pictures, teaching machines, a computer terminal, etc., ignoring the fact that the same reception point might embrace *all* of these facilities.

Often these institutions, feeling they are falling behind in the "instructional technology" process react too readily to the appeals of equipment suppliers and grasp for "instant solutions." They fail to differentiate between the many widely reported experimental projects where outcomes are still to be determined and some of the solid demonstrations of technology applied to educational purpose which have become integral parts of the instructional process.

Obviously, the future will bring a combination of the various attributes of each of these systems related to multi-branching systems of logic in computer assisted programs of instruction. Undoubtedly, the sophisticated libraries of the future will incorporate dial access storage and retrieval information banks with both print out and pictorial reproduction capacity which, on the one hand, will be used by the computer in instructional patterns, and on the other will be available for simple and collated reference purposes as conventional libraries are used today. The future libraries will be disseminators as well as collectors of information.

Over-riding all of the technical factors noted thus far, the major and most important problem is planning and producing the necessary instructional materials at high levels of quality and in sufficient quantity to make DAIRS or any of the related or comparable systems truly effective teaching instruments. Electronics firms and photographic equipment manufacturers are purchasing textbook publishing companies in the hope that effective programmed sequences for machine instruction will emerge. General Sarnoff explained RCA's merger with Random House by saying, "They have the software and we have the hardware." FORTUNE magazine, along with many other observers, responded by saying "as far as education is concerned, *neither* side has it yet."

13.

Information Science: Media Implications of the New Means of Information Organization

by ALLEN KENT
Director, Knowledge Availability Systems Center
Prof., Library Science, Computer Science and Education,
University of Pittsburgh

A. The Library and Information Science Field: A Review

The field of information science is derived from the struggle of man to control his environment, or at least to avoid being destroyed by external forces. The struggle articulates into requirements to make decisions continually. The quality of the decisions is dependent fundamentally on the problem-solving capability of the decision-maker, but initially on the quality and relevance of information brought to bear on the problems. Here, then, is the fundamental rationale for man to accumulate and organize information relating to past accomplishments of civilization.

Emphasis on the information science field has grown in the past several decades because of five interrelated factors:

(1) *Time Scale Changes*
The time scale of information gathering for decision-making and control has been reduced drastically. This change corresponds to increases in the rates with which competitive activity, international aggressive action, and changes in public opinion can deteriorate economic, military, and political situations.

(2) *Changes In Quantity Of Available Information*
There has been a dramatic increase in the amount of information that is freely available (i.e., published in one form or other), resulting in the characterization of the situation as an information explosion. This situation has three dimensions of frustration:

  (a) The impossibility of an individual reading and remembering all of the literature that has a reasonable probability of being of later use.

  (b) The economic impossibility of individuals or their organizations processing for later retrieval the majority of literature of probable pertinent interest.

  (c) The breakdown of traditional library tools in coping effectively with the detailed requirements of individuals in identifying information pertinent to a given problem.

(3) *Changes In Nature Of Information Requirements*
The increasing complexity of the problems of society has led to a consequent requirement for information from an ever-widening diversity of fields. This has resulted in the need to achieve insight into otherwise obscure or uncertain situations through the use of large amounts of fragmentary information from widely scattered sources.

(4) *Changes In Importance Of Information Sources*
The increasing internationalism of industrial, educational and political organizations has been leading ta increasing emphasis on information for decision-making and control derived from many sources and geographic areas not formerly considered important. This trend has increased the need for obtaining and providing information quickly which heretofore could be transmitted on a more leisurely basis.

(5) *Increase In Number Of Information Processing Agencies*
The four changes described above have resulted in various agencies undertaking information processing and disseminating functions. These include governmental agencies, professional and trade associations, universities, and profit-making industries. This trend has led to an unquantifiable overlap in processing and services.

In consequence of these changes, new tools, new communication systems, new means of information organization, and new means of dissemination have been proposed and developed. Each in turn has both helped alleviate the problems, and uncovered new and fundamental problems.

(1) *Influence of the Computer*

(a) Logical Capabilities
The use of computers to search indexes to large files based on logical combinations of subjects has led to the trend to increasing depth of analysis of source materials, which in turn has increased the cost of such analysis to the point where few organizations have the wherewithal to process for their own use the information that would be of possible use in the future. This has led to centralization of information processing activities, e.g., by government agencies and professional societies, and an attempt to amortize the cost over many users. But centralized services have been imperfect, and decentralized as well as specialized information centers have been developed in an attempt to overcome some of their limitations.

(b) Processing Speed Capabilities
The speed with which computers can search large files carries with it a consequent high cost. In an attempt to amortize this cost over many users, there has been a trend to utilize the batch processing capabilities of computers to handle as many questions as possible at one time. But the consequences of this trend is a decrease in effective speed of search, since time elapses while a sufficient quantity of search requests are accumulated. This has led to consideration of how time-sharing computers may be utilized to provide search results in real time. The processing speed of computers has also led to consideration of how whole texts may be searched to advantage. But this consideration brings up the problem of whether algorithms can be developed which apply the test of significance of information as opposed to mere identification of words that may appear in a given text.

(2) *Influence of Communication Systems*

Modern communication technology offers the opportunity to transmit information in the form of data, voice, and images. Theoretically, this technology would permit the information resources of all organizations to be shared by permitting remote inquiry through an appropriate network mechanism. The availability of time-sharing computer systems with their ability to tie into network systems makes it possible to contemplate an inquirer sitting at a remote console interacting with a multiplicity of information resources in real time. However, in considering how to translate theory into practice, it becomes obvious that fundamental knowledge is lacking with regard to the following questions:

(a) How can the differing philosophies of analysis of source materials and differing means of vocabulary control be rationalized when several resources are to be exploited to serve a single inquiry?

(b) What criteria would inquirers use in judging relevance of information provided in an interactive mode when networking systems employing modern communication technology are used?

(c) What will the behavior of an inquirer be if he has the opportunity to conduct information searches personally through a console? What training problems will be involved? What programs need be written to provide an adequate conversational mode in this regard?

(3) *Influence of New Means of Information Organization*

The pressures for greater and greater penetration into the subject matter of source materials have been evident as the quantity of published information has reached the point where traditional classifying and indexing methods are not able to provide literature search results with the precision, relevance, and quantity limitations being demanded. In other words, the requirement for precise specification of problems and questions of inquirers has led to consideration of corresponding means for precise specification of the subject matter of the source materials. This consideration has led to increased pressure for subject analysis expertise which approaches the expertise of the inquirer. On the other hand, the personnel requirements for processing the increasing quantity of source materials have not been matched by available skilled manpower. Consequently alternative methods of processing have been considered, proceeding successively through the use of:

(a) generalists rather than specialists; and

(b) automatic means for analysis of information, involving either portions or the entire text of the source materials.

Study of the results of application of both of these methods indicate that imprecision and inconsistency in analysis is not avoided, leading to uncertainty in the exploitation of large files. Accordingly, other means have been sought to overcome the consequences of this uncertainty. Explorations have resulted in the development of various vocabulary control and search strategy techniques. Testing and evaluation of these techniques has become a matter of increasing attention, leading to the identification of increasingly fundamental problems relating to:

(a) the nature of information transfer from source materials to the inquirer;

(b) the criteria for relevance judgments of inquirers, and their dependence on incremental learning;

(c)   the nature of concept formation; and most basic of all;

(d)   the learning and thinking processes.

(4)   *Influence of New Means of Dissemination of Information*
It has been interesting to observe the development of means for dissemination of information in such a manner as to correspond selectively to the "profile" of interests of inquirers, thus keeping them informed periodically of published materials in the precise areas of their professional work. However, the changing interests of many inquirers requires that careful attention be paid to means for obtaining feedback which permits dynamic response to indications of changes, or even saturation of interests. The need for development of means for observing inquirer behavior without undue interference with normal work habits has led to consideration of the methodology of the behavioral sciences. But this methodology must take into account the fact that the average information user can spend only minor fractions of his time relating to information services. Accordingly, the mass effects of new dissemination methods can be discerned only with large populations of users, leading to the need for the careful application of statistical methods to discern real effects and their significance.

The foregoing have stimulated consideration of matters relating to the traditional libraries, and the very significant investment that has been made by society in their development and maintenance. Increasing demands for library service, even of a traditional nature, have led to investigations of how the new tools and communication systems might streamline these functions, which despite the growing importance of information storage and dissemination centers, still is the main instrument of society for democratic access to recorded knowledge. Resulting has been the application of computers and other data processing equipment to the control of circulation records, serial records, and even to the conversion of catalog information to machine-processable form. Initially this latter application was considered for purposes of convenient up-dating and publication of book catalogs. However, the availability of this information in machine-processable form has led to some effort toward providing real-time access by library users. And attempts have been made to exploit the logical capabilities of the computer for identifying books and monographs in a manner that is analogous to the way in which they are used for information retrieval in depth for documents and published papers. But the paucity of subject headings normally provided during subject cataloging has made this approach unrewarding. So methods are being investigated for more detailed analysis of books and monographs, a problem that is far from trivial.

The advanced communications technology has been exploited in connection with inter-library loan procedures (the traditional library response to resource-sharing requirements). The location of desired materials has been facilitated by the mechanism of almost real-time communication systems such as teletype. In addition, image-transmission systems are being considered for the provision of copies of materials without physical removal from existing collections.

But the services that are emerging and will develop are much more costly in visible expenditures than traditional activities, and the question must be explored regarding how to market these services, either through filling overt requirements or through stimulating interest that did not exist before. This has not been a trivial problem, since the library function has been considered to be free to society ever since the principle was established by Andrew Carnegie toward the end of the 19th century.

There are also legal implications involved in the application of the new technology in the library and information sciences. The convenience of providing copies of published materials and the accelerating trend toward conservation of storage space through the use of microform brings up consideration of violation of copyright through promiscuous processing, copying, and transmission of such materials. This legal problem, and the related economic problems is causing concern and investigation of the consequences to various elements of society: the publisher, the authors, and the user public.

B. The Library and Information Center of the Future

1. Introduction

Information science programs are being designed to respond to the problems incurred by the information explosion by hypothesizing that the library which is to serve future generations is more than bricks and mortar. It will not be useful if it is to be a book *warehouse*—manned by book *keepers*. Rather, the library of the future must be created as an organism for performing work, for providing service, and for conducting research. This organism will be responsive to the changing requirements of a dynamic field, with responsibilities in education, in research, and in practice. The most modern and flexible mechanisms will be available for exploiting recorded knowledge in the interests of professional advances.

The director of the library of the future will be a library and information scientist, an educator, and a research director. He will draw about himself a constellation of specialists from a number of professional disciplines.

Some new libraries have been designed modularly (to permit physical expansion); functionally (to facilitate the performance of technical services); reader-oriented (to better serve the client); and librarian-oriented (to convenience the internal staff). The new programs must consider a new need—for a library designed for intellectual growth through research.

The articulation of information science programs is based on the thesis that there is need for access to recorded knowledge that must be satisfied by providing rapidly, conveniently, economically, and with precision, that portion of the current or previous literature that will be useful
- —to a particular individual
- —at a particular time
- —for a particular problem or interest
- —and in a form that is useful to him

regardless of
- —where it was generated
- —in what form or language
- —or how it must be located and processed

The utopian dream is to have information available on the day of publication, neatly translated into one's mother tongue, and packaged in quanta which are of infinitely variable size and content.

The translation of this dream into a program involves changing concepts of information handling. Some of these concepts are discussed in the following:

    a. *Information as a Physical Commodity*

        Library materials, including books, periodicals, and reports, have traditionally been stored physically on shelves and selected on a "custom" basis, either by library staff or by the reader. In more modern terms, the significant amounts of library materials to be moved into and out of storage can be considered from an industrial engineering point of view as:

(1) a warehousing and materials handling problem, with selection, delivery, and return to storage conducted mechanically

(2) a manufacturing problem, with materials stored in microform, and access provided locally and to distant locations through:

    (a) provision of returnable copies by mail or other physical means of transfer

    (b) provision of disposable copies by mail, or by telecommunications techniques

    (c) transmission of materials by means of television techniques with option of preparation of copies locally from the face of cathode ray tubes

    (d) stocking of subwarehouses with microform copies and providing access to information via mail or telecommunication media.

b. *Information Retrieval as a Data Processing Problem*

The available stockpile of information can be considered in modern terms as a data processing problem, with various types of equipment available for manipulating indexes to the physical storehouse of information from a multidimensional point of view. By this is meant that source documents may be characterized from more than one point of view and also identified for delivery by combining more than one aspect of subject matter—by applying clerical, mechanical, or electronic means to perform selecting and correlating operations.

c. *Information Retrieval as an Intellectual Problem*

In traditional terms, the library activity has been an art, with analysis of documents and reference services considered to be techniques which are learned through apprenticeship after suitable training. However, the greater demands being placed on the library have resulted in the realization that specialists in other fields can make a significant contribution to the intellectual problems facing the field. Accordingly, there has been an infusion of linguists, logicians, mathematicians, electronic engineers, psychologists, and other specialists who have been considering means for the solution of theoretical and practical questions that are encountered in communicating via the written record. These specialists have been deeply involved in the forward research work leading to the development of more sophisticated automatic information retrieval systems.

d. *The Library in Terms of Technical Processes*

A library represents different things to different people. To many library staff members, the library consists of a number of technical processes involving: selection of books, periodicals, or other materials; ordering of materials; binding; cataloging; copying; etc. These technical processes can be considered from an engineering point of view as unit operations, which are conducted in a "production" environment, with modern business methods being applied to carry them out and to keep track of them. Various methods of automation are now being considered for each technical process of the traditional techniques and for many of the unit operations newly identified in more modern approaches.

2. Development of Campus-Based Information Systems

The scholarly community is becoming increasingly aware of its information environment. This awareness has been stimulated by a number of factors, not the least of which is the increasing realization that keeping up to date through reading the book and periodical literature in its classical form is becoming less and less convenient as the scope of interest of scholars becomes increasingly interdisciplinary and the quantity of literature of potential relevance becomes greater.

Communication among scholars through personal contacts, although increasing dramatically, is not likely to provide assurance that even the most fruitful contacts can be assured in a timely way through serendipitous discovery of communities of interests.

An impressive array of centralized and specialized information services, both discipline- and mission-oriented, are available, under development, or being planned. It has been hypothesized that these services will be augmenting or, in some cases, replacing the traditional library services that have been used by scholars in many or even most fields of endeavor. But exploitation of each of these new services, many computer-based, involves overt expenditures of funds which, in a university, may often equal and, sometimes, exceed the budgets for purchases of books and other materials of the library system. These overt expenditures, when multiplied by the number of services that are now, and may soon be, available present a budget dilemma that has not often been contemplated seriously by university administrations.

It is not enough to say that funds are not available to support these new services that will be demanded by the scholarly community. Rather, like the conclusion reached in contemplating increasing budgets for conventional libraries, that some academic programs cannot be maintained without ready access to adequate library collections, so it may be said for these new services that some programs should be excluded from the curriculum if ready access to these new services cannot likewise be assured.

Nor is it enough to rely on grant support to establish campus-based information centers, since interest in services from these centers stimulated during the grant period will have to be satisfied following the period of sponsored development.

Rather it is necessary to predict the dimensions of the information problem; to design an information system which not only brings replicas of files to the campus but also provides remote access to other files when it is more convenient or economical to do so, and to develop plans for financing the operation of the system.

In developing such plans, the starting premise must be that faculty and students are to be provided with the most effective secondary information services that may be technologically feasible. It is known that any given educational institution will never be able to create such services *de nova* and that each would always wish to interrelate, on some basis or other, with many discipline- or mission-oriented services. This relationship would involve acquisition of, or remote access to, search-ready files, mostly involving the use of computers for exploitation purposes.

It is assumed that the costs of providing such service at the level and frequency desired will eventually exceed the ability of the institution to cover such costs when the expected lease, royalty, capital, and operating expenses are all taken into account, once the period of sponsored research has passed. Accordingly, a basis for amortizing basic operating costs over a group of users larger than any single educational institution must be sought.

Accordingly, successive expansion of the base of users must be considered so that resource-sharing economies may be achieved.

But, it has become obvious that many, or most, organizations are not willing to pay the full costs of obtaining services unless a "one-stop" service is offered. That is, assurance is demanded that the services to users are based on exploitation of all of the resources relevant to a given interest.

It is entirely reasonable for fee-paying users of information services to demand such assurance, since otherwise other sources would have to be exploited by the users independently, with attendant substantial fees, but without obviating uncertainty as to the extent of overlap in coverage among the services exploited.

This situation provides an additional incentive to the educational institution to inter-relate with as many services as are willing and able to provide access to their data bases for purposes of local or regional exploitation.

C. Information Science and Learning

Discussions of the information explosion and its consequences have emphasized primarily the increasing difficulty of any professional being able to read all of the published literature that is of interest and of consequence. This situation has led to a trend toward increasing specialization in an attempt to reduce the amount of information that must be assimulated by any individual to manageable proportions.

It comes as no surprise that this trend toward specialization has led to increasing difficulties in communication among specialists. Furthermore, the specialist, when he must exploit literature peripheral to his specialty, finds it more and more difficult to use traditional library facilities to penetrate the subject matter and to obtain information relevant to his requirements.

This problem has provided impetus to the development of information storage and retrieval systems, involving the use of non-traditional techniques and devices, particularly computers.

However, there is another matter that may not be as evident that is related to the knowledge explosion problem. One of the consequences of information overload has been, and continues to be, increasing emphasis on teaching of principles rather than facts, at all levels of the education continuum. This shift in emphasis does not relieve the student from the burden of being able to locate facts which may be needed during his educational experience and later, which relate to the principles he has learned, and which can be related to the intellectual framework of the subject matter that a student has acquired. This implies an increasing burden on libraries and information retrieval activities to permit ready identification of information on demand.

The problem is complicated by another factor relating to this shift in emphasis. When certain information has not been provided to a student during his educational experience, questions directed to the library or information center are no longer based on a "recall" function, since the student may never have been exposed to the information which he wished to locate. Rather, questions are now derived from the student's knowledge of principles, leading to the identification of characteristics of the desired information rather than the information itself. This change in the nature of question-asking leads to the requirement that information stored for later retrieval must be analyzed in sufficient depth so that this new type of question can be asked with some confidence in effective searches being performed.

More and more, then, learning and information retrieval become interrelated as the information explosion develops further, with an increasing requirement that students be taught how to exploit effectively the libraries of the past and the information centers of the future. How to infuse into the educational experience a thorough knowledge of the library and information sciences of the future, is a challenge that must now be faced.

The increasing availability of time-sharing computer facilities has made it possible to consider the development of conversational programs which provide instruction regarding formulation of strategies for exploiting computer-processable files. Although several such efforts are now underway, the programs are still untested and not generally available. However, it may be anticipated that as these programs become increasingly available, there will be stimulated a demand for on-line files, so that searches may be performed by an individual through a console following successful negotiation of a search strategy. This, in turn, would lead to demand for provision of images of printed materials via a console, presenting a requirement for image transmission capabilities from remote locations.

D. Media Implications

From the foregoing, it may be obvious that there has been a shift in media involved in the library and information science field, with regard to: (1) generation and storage of records; (2) inquiry; and (3) response to inquiries.

(1) *Generation and Storage of Information*

Traditionally, the printed page has been the primary medium for storage of information. Although this medium will probably continue to handle the bulk of storage requirements, other media are being used increasingly including: film (including microform); magnetic tapes; and discs.

(2) *Inquiry*

Reference to information-locating tools has traditionally been dependent on printed records, e.g., catalog cards, and printed indexes. However, it may be expected that increasing use will be made of consoles, which permit direct inquiry via other media, such as keyboard inputs to computer-based files or cathode ray tube displays which permit formulation of requests based on light pen selections from available alternatives.

(3) *Response to Inquiries*

Traditionally, delivery of materials in response to inquiries has used the medium of hard copy. Now, the opportunity presents itself to display images via consoles with an option to produce hard copy locally. Also, for materials stored in an audio medium, audible signals may be transmitted in response to an inquiry.

The technology that permits communication systems to handle these media has been developed to the point where it is possible to demonstrate the efficacy of such approaches. However, the economic impact of such technology seems, on the surface, to be destructive. Nevertheless, network development to permit the provision of data, voice, and image transmission capabilities is contemplated as the way to share costs (as well as information resources), so that, given full loading of the proposed and developing systems, the cost of each use should be well within plausible limits.

The development of a telephone network, which has illustrated this principle, provides hope that media of various sorts can be handled efficiently and economically.

14.
Programming and Programmed Instruction

by SUSAN MEYER MARKLE
Head of Programmed Instruction
Office of Instructional Resources
Univ. of Ill. at Chicago Circle

The programming of instruction is a process of designing instructional materials and systems which results, if followed to its full extent, in a rationally constructed and empirically validated product or set of procedures. The process consists of five basic steps:

1. Determining the objectives of instruction in order to, a) describe an observable performance of a student who has completed the instruction, b) make clear the conditions under which students will demonstrate mastery of the material and c) establish a standard of acceptable performance.

2. Designing and evaluating the "criterion measures" which would rate students individually on a scale of attainment of the desired knowledge or behavior.

3. Testing potential student groups to learn their characteristics which will determine, in turn, the design of the lesson.

4. Selecting instructional media and preparing instructional material in draft form.

5. Refining the product through try-outs with individual students until effectiveness reaches satisfactory levels. This process is then continued with increasingly large groups of students until effectiveness proves satisfactory in approximately "real" situations. The materials are finally "validated" by publication of a complete description of their performance in terms of their effect on specified groups of students under carefully described conditions.

Programmed materials, therefore, cannot be identified by any single format. The only observable distinguishing characteristic is a product description, providing the consumer with the complete set of objectives, matching criterion measures, and data, drawn from research with students, which support the claims for the teaching effectiveness of the materials.

The impact of programmed instruction on the educational system has been minimal

Note: This paper was prepared as an addendum to a chapter submitted to the Macmillan Company for publication in The Encyclopedia of Education *in 1971.*

quantitatively and qualitatively. "Software" is one very important problem: when considered in relation to their proposed intent to truly individualize instruction, the quantity of programmed materials available to the schools is still miniscule. On the other hand, schools generally do not require effective products and methods because administrative innovation has not proceeded at the same rate as instructional innovation.

In sum, programmed instruction is not fully ready for the schools and the schools are even less ready for programmed instruction. In the interface between education and programming there are serious weaknesses in the designing of the materials, severe problems in the economics of design and use, and an almost insurmountable gulf between the philosophy or point of view on which programming is based and the present thinking of most school systems.

Weaknesses in the Technology

A significant problem in the design stage is the selection of appropriate objectives. In industry and in military organizations, where programming has had considerable success, there exists an ultimate reference against which the appropriateness of the objectives can be tested, namely the job for which the man is being trained. This is not to say that such job descriptions are necessarily simple, especially when interpersonal relations are involved, such as with salesmen or management trainees. However, where such a job exists as a reference against which instructional decisions may be validated, lean programming makes obvious sense. One can determine standards, which may include efficiency as well as effectiveness (see D. Markle, 1967b), and build instruction from this endpoint backwards. In the educational setting, with no such outside reference, the instructional designer is usually thrown back upon the more or less illogical content coverage found in existing texts and syllabi. With a few possible exceptions in some of the curriculum projects now underway, this content coverage is an irrational patchwork of topics bearing little relation to what students have already learned or to what they will need to know in future courses. The fractionation and lack of articulation between and within subject matters has been noted many times; the problems created are serious for teachers and instructional materials developers who have to "cover" material. For programmers, oriented to student performance, the problems are critical. Buried in the patchwork are two areas where the technology is not yet mature.

The first area we might call the "structure of knowledge," in the sense intended by Bruner (1960) and others. It hardly needs saying that we have no firm grasp of what happens to students when various elements in the mathematics or science or social science curricula are moved up or moved down in the academic progression. For instance, on a speculative note, if set theory is taught in the first grade, would this not in some way affect the ability to form logical categories—which is included in the "process approach" to science several grades later? Or might it not interfere with the child's ability to grasp the essentially illogical categories of traditional grammar when he meets them in seventh grade? No research designs exist at present for expanding the measuring procedures used in validating programmed materials to take account of these possible transfer effects. No pressure exists to do so, of course, since the teaching profession does not itself do so. What I see needed here is some long-term development studies paralleling some of the pioneer work done in individual language development, where individual children are intensively followed over long periods. Such an approach is implicit in the orientation of operant conditioners who tend to study single organisms intensively for long periods of time. It does not generally exist in educational research, where a developmental study is more likely to include a sampling at one point in time of different individuals at different ages. (The work of Piaget and Gesell illustrate this latter approach; Terman's studies of the gifted is a rare example of the former.)

Programmers have begun work on the types of analytical procedures needed to improve objectives. There are, however, no published papers or results as yet from the work of persons like Philip Tiemann and myself, Richard Anderson at the University of Illinois, Urbana, or James Popham and Eva Baker at the University of California, Los Angeles. Similar in intent, but not fully adequate to this purpose, is Gagné's analysis (1965). The absolute necessity of new techniques of analysing knowledge has become apparent from the weaknesses in the kinds of objectives which predominate in available educational programs. In other words, there must be a way to attack rationally the question of what ought to be taught. But the technology for deriving better objectives does not yet exist in educational subjects to the same extent as in task analysis for industrial objectives.

A second and related area in which the technology needs further development is in the analysis of what might be called "cross-curricular skills", among which would be "critical thinking," "inference techniques," "creativity", and others. Skinner (1968) points out that the attempt to teach thinking, in the sense intended by proponents of discovery learning, often leads to inefficient teaching of the subject matter being "discovered". The conflict is real, in that students undoubtedly should be led to think for themselves and yet the method of discovery often leaves them with precious little knowledge to think about. A few direct attacks on the problems of teaching thinking or creativity (James Holland's program on inference, Richard Crutchfield's program on critical thinking, and Sidney Parnes's work on creative analysis) have had little effect on the design of programs aimed at subject-matter knowledge. The technology of empirical testing—the revision cycle based on student errors—almost guarantees dropping any frames and sequences which require much thinking skill, since the error rate generally goes up. As a consequence, remarkably little is known about how to produce such skills reliably.

The computer as a magnificent branching tool comes to mind in discussions of teaching thinking. The prognosis for computer assistance with this problem would be more hopeful, however, if we had a better software technology for producing thinkers. Most of the "dialogue" mode software now used as illustrations of what computers will be able to do in teaching thinking are really nothing more than tests of skills already learned.

The technology of analysis is incomplete in these two areas. Until these puzzles can be solved, the products of the programming process will not come up to the fond hopes of the educators. It is, of course, readily apparent that present educational techniques are not achieving such results either, although educational goals promulgated by school systems would lead us to think they are. The average educator, unconcerned by the gap between the goals claimed and any evidence that students are achieving such goals, tends to reject as beneath consideration products which, if appropriately administered, can reliably achieve the lesser objectives claimed for them.

Economic Problems

There have been many references in the literature to the remarkable amount of development time invested by programmers in producing reliable products. Estimates of 50 to 75 hours per hour of student time are frequent, even for the so-called "simple" skills of military and industrial training. The economic advantages of such an extensive investment of programmer time have been calculated in an industrial setting where students are paid while learning and production losses due to ineffective instruction can be at least estimated. (K. Brethower, 1966. See also, Rummler et al., 1967.) No such economic basis for improving instruction has been agreed upon for education.

A short perusal of a bibliography such as Hendershot's (1967) reveals that most programs, including those with a sound research basis, are being sold to schools at prices competitive with traditional textbooks. Some programs aimed at the industrial market appear to have more meaningful price-tags. Given the small distribution of any programmed material whatever in the schools at present, as mentioned in the article, and the small per unit price, it is indeed small wonder that so few fully researched effective products have appeared on the market.

The financing of the capital development required is still problematical. Fractionated school districts certainly cannot afford it, nor do they generally have either the talent or technical knowledge to produce such materials. Publishers, accustomed to reimbursing authors by royalties based on sales, are wary of the immense investment required by the research. Authors do not recover their investment of time (I have calculated a returned wage of 50 cents per hour on one of mine) and the financial woes of the programming companies which concentrated solely on the school market is well-known.

Considerable discussion of government priming of the pump has taken place (see Subcommittee on Economic Progress); at least one of the regional laboratories backed by the Office of Education is officially in the business (see Popham, 1967). There is, of course, also the risk capital available in the "education industry", the effects of which at the moment are unknown. Much has been said about the concentration of that industry on glamorous hardware; it is well known that software, if available at all for these new machines, is rarely a product of behavioral technology at a level of sophistication consonant with the hardware.

As one wit said "If education had produced the Edsel, they still wouldn't know it was a failure." It is difficult to see how appropriate pricing of effective products backed by expensive and extensive research can be fostered when the consumer is apparently incapable of making the appropriate discriminations.

Economist Donald Paden (1967) has theorized that, at least at the college level, a severe problem exists in providing the resources to enable instructors to take advantage of the new technology. A professor who is caught up in the cycle of frequent lectures, last-minute construction of tests, and management of increasing numbers of students has, in the publish-and-perish world, little time and less incentive to invest the required effort in instructional improvement. He talks of the notion of "critical mass"—of developing enough replicable (though not programmed) instruction via film, TV, tapes or whatever, so that a course may be, in a sense, self-operating or run by assistants. When, for instance, a sufficient number of lectures are on videotape, the instructor is then freed to devote time to improving them, making do with less than perfect performances in most lectures while he upgrades one at a time. To do so, the instructor needs not only the time released by his previous investment of time but also considerable technical help in the production process. Paden has also emphasized the impossibility of the educational system repeating this experiment on every campus in every university, because of the cost.

Such an investment of capital resources and talent suggests that the resulting improved products should command wide distribution. In reality, university instructors tend to give little consideration to using other instructors' validated lectures, though they feel no qualms about adopting texts. The widely used phrase "not invented here" (the NIH syndrome) puts the finger on the probable cause—the ego satisfaction of the instructor in his role as purveyor of information and his unfamiliarity with the role of manager of learning. This phenomenon is parallel to the still-prevalent fear of teachers at lower levels of the educational system that programmed instruction will somehow replace them. The economic loss represented by the cottage-industry approach to instruction—every professor across the country writing the same formula on the blackboard for thirty students in front of him—has the parallel in what I call the "prima donna" approach to course development, in which neither administrator nor department head nor even colleagues teaching later courses would presume to tell a professor what his course should achieve.

The "critical mass" phenomenon was obliquely mentioned on p. 17 of the article. The significant capital investments in education lie in buildings and wages for the staff, not in teaching materials. When the number of students increases in such a system, the system adds new classrooms and new staff. Little thought is given to increasing the efficiency of the system's use of its resources. Efficiency cannot be calculated with any meaningful accuracy, however, until effectiveness is established, and this basis is still lacking. Until a sufficient number of products exist to enable a shift to a criterion-referenced system, there is little incentive for educational systems to endure the pains and problems of operating partially on time-accounting and partially on effectiveness-accounting. Until there is a discriminating market for fully researched materials, it is unlikely that many will be developed. The result is a stand-off between these two realities. It seems, in concurrence with the findings of the Harvard University Program on Technology and Society (1967) that, barring some revolutionary development, especially in the administrative area, substantial and sophisticated use of educational technology is not likely to occur in the near future.

Philosophical Issues

It is not clear at the moment how many of the arguments bandied about are a function of a true difference of opinion and how many are purely a function of the preferred language of each side. The use of the term "technology", the emphasis of operant conditioners on "behavior" and especially upon "control" have undoubtedly created violent reactions where the intent and even the methods would be fully acceptable to the opposition. Any attempt to "improve" instruction is, of course, implicitly an attack upon its present state and is so interpreted by its practitioners.

There does, however, seem to be a basic divergence in point-of-view between the tough-minded empiricism of the product-oriented programming fraternity and the tender-minded idealism irrespective-of-evidence of the process-oriented educational philosophers. Skinner (1968, p90) points out again, as he has before: "We fear effective teaching, as we fear all effective means of changing human behavior." The technology of instruction, based on a scientific and experimentalist approach to human behavior, will probably remain in conflict with other positions for quite some time. It remains to be seen whether its existence will, as Mesthene suggests technology can (1968), determine a change in the value system and administrative organization of the school system or whether the "educational establishment in the United States /is so/ ideally designed to resist change" (Harvard Program, 1967) that the technology itself will be kept outside the doors.

BIBLIOGRAPHY

Markle, David G. *The Development of the Bell System First Aid and Personal Safety Course.* Final Report. AIR-E81-4/67-FR. Palo Alto, American Institutes for Research, 1967.

Bruner, Jerome S. *The Process of Education.* Cambridge, Harvard University Press, 1960.

Gagne, Robert M. *The Conditions of Learning.* New York, Holt, Rinehart & Winston, 1965.

Brethower, Karen. "Individual testing as a guide." *NSPI Journal, V,* April, 1966.

Harvard University Program on Technology and Society. *Third Annual Report.* Cambridge, Harvard University Program, 1967.

Hendershot, Carl. *Programmed Learning: A Bibliography of Programs and Presentation Devices.* Fourth Edition, 1967. (Distributed by NSPI.)

Mesthene, Emmanuel G. *How Technology Will Shape the Future.* Reprint #5. Cambridge, Harvard University Program on Technology and Society, 1968.

Rummler, Geary A., Yaney, Joseph P., and Schrader, Albert W. *Managing The Instructional Programming Effort.* Ann Arbor, U. of Michigan, Bureau of Industrial Relations, 1967.

15.
Television-in-Instruction: The State of the Art

by The Research and Development Office
National Association of Educational Broadcasters

The term "state of the art" is susceptible to varying interpretations. For us in the context of this paper it means surveying the general conditions of contemporary practices as a way of determining the highest level of achievement which is reasonably practical within the constraints of the technical and skill capabilities available.

If we were concerned with the state of the art of the knife-in-kitchen-work, rather than of television-in-instruction, we should probably proceed briskly to an incisive examination of all the many cutting, chopping, slicing, paring, carving, coring, peeling, mincing, scoring, scalloping and other such culinary operations possible with the various sharp-bladed instruments comprising the *genre* in question. It is likely we would give but glancing attention to the multifarious stirring, squeezing, mixing, patting, measuring, tasting and spearing tasks which are also potentially in the repertory of those same handy implements. This would be for the perfectly sensible reason that the highest virtue of the knife is universally recognized to be that of *cutting:* the single category of kitchen tasks by which the state of the "knifely" art could be discerned and examined with greatest cogency and precision. The other functions would be seen as strictly secondary to the knife; some even a touch exotic, useful only in rare scullery emergencies, and all likely to be performed rather better by some other kitchen tool. It is not that these secondary functions are totally unimportant, but rather that they are not of prime worth in understanding the essence, significance and potentials of the knife-in-kitchen-work.

All of which brings us around to emphasize the vital importance of determining the highest virtue (or what the Greeks called the *arete:* the chief excellence) of television-in-instruction as the best means of trying to assess the "state of its art." It is a point on which there is something less than universal accord throughout the new field of instructional technology. Yet the disagreements probably arise more from confusion than conviction.

Television can be employed "effectively" for so many "useful" teaching jobs that assigning primacy among them may seem somehow arbitrary and procrustean. What does it matter if television's chief virtues are numbered in the dozens—or more? Why must we distill them down to some solitary essence? No reason, indeed, if it were really true that television could accomplish a long list of vitally significant teaching tasks "better" than any other means available. We believe it can be shown, however, that such diversity of virtue is not in fact the case.

It would appear valuable at this starting point to take a look at a typical catalogue of the many (sometimes overlapping) applications of television-in-instruction, so that we might winnow out the genuinely significant.

Current Television Applications

Television devices, of one kind or another, can be arranged to provide:

Magnification and Visual Display   Simple video systems can be used as convenient magnifying and display implements for group viewing. Laboratory materials, graphic pieces, book pages, etc. are placed under a magnifying lens and the resultant image is fed to TV receivers placed in classrooms or laboratory areas.

Specimens for Behavioral Analysis   In such academic areas as speech training, acting, practice teaching, music performance and athletic development, portable helical-scan video-tape devices are employed to record student performances for analysis by the student himself, his classmates or his instructor. These relatively inexpensive machines permit instantaneous and repetitive showings of the recorded "behavioral specimens."

Alternate Means for (Mass) Film Distribution   In a few schools, television closed-circuit systems exist primarily for the purpose of allowing easy distribution of film materials from a central point to many classrooms. The technique offers not only a logistical advantage but also enables films to be used in a class setting without dousing the lights or requiring the teacher to undertake irksome machine operations. Nevertheless there are serious legal problems attendant to the practice which have not been resolved on a national basis. Film distributors are reluctant to allow wholesale distribution of single prints on large closed-circuit systems because they feel the procedure could drastically reduce the sale of duplicate prints.

Communications Channels for Administrative Prescription   Some institutions are finding television effective for passing on instructions. For example, at the Pennsylvania State University, students coming into a science laboratory are shown brief video-tape programs which tell them exactly how to proceed with the scheduled experiments. (In the Southeast, the Agricultural Extension Service has experimented with administrative "briefings" for its agent specialists through statewide ETV networks. In some instances, long-distance telephone lines were used to provide "two-way" communication between the parties involved.)

Materials for Drill Exercise   Television can be employed as a mechanical "drill master" in such areas as language training and calisthenics. The audio-video system cues class groups to make responses on an appropriate, iterative schedule. The technique frees teachers from the burden of having to conduct such rote-learning activities in person.

Data Storage and Retrieval   Videotape can be a useful archive medium for the storage of certain aural-and-visual resource "data" in a convenient retrieval form for direct, instructional use: lectures by visiting authorities, music performances by famous guest artists, interviews with primary sources in history, etc.

Testing Materials   Television can be employed to devise special test materials. The technique is particularly valuable where the student needs to be tested for his discrimination of phenomena which are not reducible to writing, as for example, the specification of a particular microorganism in a "mixed" culture or the identification of certain stage-craft techniques manifest during the actual presentation of a play. (The CBS Network has used a sort of testing format successfully on several occasions in connection with informal "lessons" about highway safety and current events.)

Descriptive and Solution Elements for Simulation and Gaming Experiences Videotape materials can be utilized as elements in Simulation-and-Gaming exercises. One of the most effective uses is found in teacher education. A typical classroom behavior problem is screened for a teacher-trainee. He is then asked to decide which corrective steps should be taken. Standing by are three or four "solution" tapes. The one representing the course of action suggested by the trainee is then projected on the screen so that he can see for himself the probable consequence of his judgment.

Materials for Auto-Tutorial Study Television can be linked up as a display system in the new study-carrel configurations springing up in "media centers" all across the country. These arrangements allow students to "dial-up" videotape or film materials for individualized study. Customarily the materials available through these private channels are "repeats" of televised elements previously used in group class situations, although special learning elements can be devised as well. The expense of videotape equipment keeps this from being a large-scale application; however, less expensive audiotape equipment is being used very extensively for this same kind of individualized study.

An Electronic Blackboard There are on the market now several so-called "slow-scan television" devices which enable the transmission of static pictorial and diagrammatic materials over regular telephone lines. These devices are especially helpful in such academic areas as mathematics, because they enable a television receiver to become an "electronic blackboard" on which written figures can appear (at interval rates of about five seconds, far too slowly to give the effect of natural motion). Occasionally regular television equipment is also employed to devise "electronic blackboard" effects in teaching mathematics.

Computer-Related Visual Displays Videotape systems can be linked with computers so that visual cueing can be provided at various points in a sophisticated branch program; however, the videotape machinery presently available is not really flexible enough for the frequent and rapid "seek-frame" operations requisite to proper computerized branching. Technological advances will likely remedy this defect in the next few years.

The Communication Means for Direct Interchange A few institutions make use of television as a two-way communications device. They have installed a "true" circuit between two or more meeting locales, each having audio/video pick-up capability. Persons gathered at each of the locales are able to communicate aurally and visually with persons at the other locales. The technique is notably valuable in conducting graduate seminars and the like; it is, however, a rather expensive procedure.

Topics for Class Assignment One of the oldest academic uses of television is that of assigning a particular program to serve as a topical basis for student themes or classroom discussion. Documentary and fine arts programs from ETV and commercial stations are especially suitable for this purpose.

Materials for Diversion Some schools make regular use of television as a diversion during out-of-class periods. Students are allowed to watch mass appeal programs from local commercial channels, or the school uses its own CCTV system to feed a special "educative" film with high attractant value for the age group involved.

Mechanism for Visual Surveillance   Simple video systems can be used for "security and discipline" surveillance of corridors, library areas, laboratories and the like. While this application is only indirectly related to instruction, it could prove very valuable in large schools with severe staff shortages.

Materials for Curricular Enrichment   The most frequent application of television in instruction nowadays comes under this general rubric, by which is meant the classroom showing of unitary (or series) programs structured to heighten the student's interest in some topical compartment of the regular curriculum. Customarily programs of this kind are not considered *sine qua non* components of the courses with which they are used. Instead, they are regarded as supplementary and extraordinary, with their main emphasis being on special motivation and affect. The usual practice is to allow teachers to opt the inclusion of such enrichment materials on a purely individual basis. Measurability of the effects of these offerings is extremely difficult, if not impossible.

Articulable Teaching Elements   Television can be used to supply teachers lesson elements which are substantially articulable with other components of course operations, including textbook materials. Such television programs are assigned some more-or-less specific part of the total presentational load. In too many situations, unfortunately, the design of the televised elements is determined only along the lines of an arbitrary "content allocation;" coordinated "performance objectives" for the courses affected are seldom relied on to provide the mechanism for a genuinely rational articulation of all the elements into an efficient whole. Use of the materials by teachers is often permissive.

Electronic Adjunct Materials for Correspondence Course Teaching   Television can be used as an adjunct to the familiar correspondence course format. In some instances, enrolled students are advised that they should tune in to televised lectures and demonstrations which will be very helpful in their understanding of certain concepts to be treated through the regular (correspondence) format. In other instances, students are actually required to accept a part of their instruction electronically, or, at least, they are responsible for examination on content handled largely in that form. (The Chicago Junior College has made an outstanding showing in this overall category, although students enrolled in the "televised courses" offered by that institution do have direct—as well as correspondence—access to teachers or tutors.)

All the Elements for Total Teaching   In certain rather special circumstances, students can be taught exclusively by televised materials. The technique is employed in "extension education" situations where there are serious logistical blocks in the way of providing students with printed materials or in having them come together to meet with live instructors. (North Carolina State University has made use of this kind of televised training as in-service education for professional agriculturalists.)

Linear Programming Materials for Groups   It has been established (by C. R. Carpenter, George Gropper, Kenneth Komoski and others) that television can be used in the "lock-step" regulation of linear (Skinnerian) programming for groups of students. The television system submits cue frames, students make responses on printed answer sheets, after which the system provides knowledge of results. The technique requires that the instructional program be validated to a highly efficient "pass rate" for each and every response point. The length of each response interval is determined by averaging the actual answer times required by sample students during the "testing out" phase. There is some evidence that this "optimum" response interval is a more efficient one for learning than is the purely self-determined rate, characteristic of regular Skinnerian programming.

Branch Programming for Groups   Some limited work could be done with television equipment designed to feed out simple "branch programming" to classroom groups. In such an arrangement, each student would be supplied with a pair of audio headsets and a special scoring box with push-buttons. The television system would submit cue frames separated by active response intervals. The frames would be written so that the student would be led to choose one of several alternatives as the only "correct" answer. If the key button he depressed represented the correct response in a given case, he would receive through the main audio channel confirmation of his result phrased in "reward" terms. If, on the other hand, he pressed a button representing an "incorrect" response, he would be shifted over to a second audio track which could provide him an appropriate, corrective step. While this kind of simple branch programming is certainly less sophisticated than most of the Crowderian books and punch-button machines, it would allow for "incorrect" responses in a way not possible with the purely linear design. It is possible to imagine that more sophisticated equipment in the future will allow production of fairly elaborate branch programs.

The Facilitating Mechanism for New Instructional Systems   In several respects, each of the uses of television described thus far permits the integration of new and more effective teaching materials into the basic and familiar educational setting. Taking many of these separate uses together, however, it becomes possible to understand how television as a communications instrument can be tailored to effect quite different and promising instructional operations.

In this situation, television and classroom activities are seen as *one* task, with several components that interact with each other. This concept is increasingly called *co-operative instruction*, since it involves an assignment of "team" duties among the members of a total teaching force who *co-operate* in order to develop and carry out instructional plans.

This instructional strategy is based on the need to bring the most suitable instructional resources to a given learning situation and derives from a familiar model of human behavior:

a) a person senses a need and sets an objective to satisfy it,

b) he engages in some kind of activity designed to produce the desired results,

c) he monitors outcomes to determine how closely he has come to achieving the wished-for result, and

d) he makes appropriate changes in his "strategy" to try to improve the efficiency of outcome.

The term "closed-loop" describes the cyclic structure of the events involved:

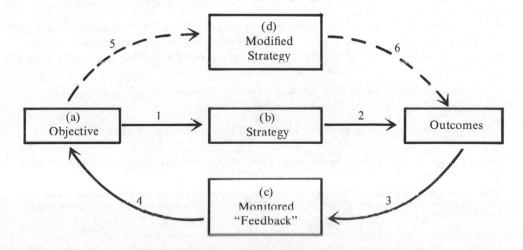

More often than not the efficiency of the "closed-loop" in systematic instruction is sharply reduced through a failure to manage it on a "short interval" basis. Monitoring is irregular and feedback is protracted. In truly efficient operations results are monitored on a daily basis and feed back data are used systematically to modify instructional strategies on an equally "short interval." In effect, lesson B is directly contingent on the student performance resulting from lesson A, etc.

How does co-operative education differ from traditional education? First, because co-operation is involved, curriculum cannot take the form of an "ordering of content," arranged according to some arbitrary interpretation of ambiguous (non-operational) "teaching" objectives. Second, individual classroom teachers are neither required nor permitted to interpret and implement curriculum as they deem best, within the often-impoverished confines of a so-called "self-contained classroom." Third, curriculum development is accomplished by design teams, composed of content and methods specialists brought together to work co-operatively. Fourth, the teams establish precise "learning objectives" based on identified needs. These objectives then become the operational basis for a systematic analysis of the kinds of *interactive* experiences (or instructional strategies) which appear most likely to lead to efficient and desirable learning outcomes.

In such a system concerned with a truly *comprehensive* approach to curriculum and instruction, television and support technologies are used to transmit carefully-structured materials of uniform value. Modulated learning elements replace the differentiated, variable and frequently inefficient "talking-teacher-cum-textbook presentations" of traditional education.* In the co-operative process, based on the integrated use of electronic technology, activities of classroom teachers are carefully defined and co-ordinated. Hour-to-hour activities which must provide the vitally important "frame" and reinforcement for the mediated learning elements are spelled out for the teachers, and adaptive guidance techniques are provided for individual students.

The whole system is developmental in that day-to-day-characteristics of the instructional output are contingent upon actual student response and behavioral change. Daily testing and feedback must be designed into the "short interval closed-loop." These characteristics do impose certain reasonable, practical limits on the size of the system in terms of the numbers of students and teachers—but not in terms of geography.** In fact, a school "district" organized co-operatively could include a number of different school units located in several, non-contiguous areas—united by objectives, methodology and technology rather than by land proximity.

Putting "Televised Instruction" in Perspective

It could probably be well argued that television could be "gainfully" employed in any of the application categories previously listed. What criteria then can be applied to separate the truly significant from the contrived or routine? It seems to us that the discriminating tests are two:

1) the teaching/learning task involved must be intensely valuable, even critical, to contemporary educational operations;

2) the task could not be performed as well—if at all—without television mediation.

*It should be noted that the television elements referred to here would closely parallel many of the applications shown previously, albeit in a radically different kind of educational framework.

**It would be difficult to generalize as to the practical limits imposed on the size of such a system. Much depends upon local circumstances. Systems have been planned for areas with fewer than 3,000 students and for other areas with as many as 250,000 students.

Before moving on into considerations of issues affecting significant uses of television-in-instruction, it is important to point out that *the current sum-total of all applications of television to instruction has not made any lasting, important or basic impact on any part of American education.* The significances we find arise from "exceptions not rules." Three years ago, Judith Murphy and Ronald Gross of the Academy for Educational Development turned out a milestone study of ITV entitled "Learning by Television." Its opening paragraphs, widely read and hotly quoted, are still as apposite today as they were at the time of publication.

"After more than a decade of intensive effort and the expenditure of hundreds of millions of dollars, has television made a real impact on America's schools and colleges? Has it made a worthwhile contribution to education?

"The short answer to such a sweeping question would probably have to be 'No.' Whether measured by the numbers of students affected, or by the quality of the product, or by the advancement of learning, televised teaching is still in a rudimentary stage of development. The medium can take credit for helping understaffed schools to cope with ever increasing enrollments. But television has not transformed education, nor has it significantly improved the learning of most students. In short, TV is still far from fulfilling its obvious promise. Television is in education all right, but it is still not of education."

There are undoubtedly many ways of explaining this condition, but the observation that seems increasingly valid is this: we have not yet matched the state of technology's art with the state of education's art. Virtually all innovative and promising educational techniques have been molded, bent, squeezed, or otherwise contorted so as to "take their proper place" in the traditional educational systems.

What seems to be different about television, in concert with other electronic means of communication *(e.g.,* radio, audio, facsimile computer-managed-instruction), is that it affords the possibility of operating instructional systems that are organized, authoritative, scientific, and effective. And it can do so, if properly designed in a manner that places in a central position at last, the needs and requirements of the learner.

In order to place "televised instruction" in perspective, then it is important to examine the formal teaching/learning process in a fundamental model:

a. A teacher arranges for a student to experience a complex "stimulus" of some kind, to which the student can respond in some sort of appropriate format.

b. If the response is unsuitable to the teacher, he goes through various adaptive motions of "shaping" the student's behavior to bring it up to an acceptable level. (This critical phase often includes "directed self-study" of one kind or another. It is by no means limited to group drill formats.)

c. The student then "learns" the new behavior through having it "positively reinforced" by the teacher.

Man does much of his learning by means of *symbols.* An instructional technologist regards a symbol as a special sort of stimulus (like a word, gesture or picture) which "refers" to some separate-but-associated stimulus for its response contingency (or meaning). Symbols are the convenient means by which one person elicits responses—meanings as well as certain resultant behaviors from another person in the social process termed communication. Responses elicited in a communication can be learned if conditions appropriately reinforce the behavior, as through reward or punishment. *The control of symbols and reinforcement conditions is a fundamental operation of all instruction. The efficiency of that operation is a primary concern of instructional technology.*

The varieties of symbols are many. A primary category can be said to be made up of those produced directly by the person of the communicator: speech, gesture, facial expression, song, hand-clapping and the like. A second category comprehends symbols which are produced (or reproduced) and extended by means of some intervening device or material called a *medium:* television, radio, books, films, photographs, diagrams, phonograph recordings, billboards, stone monuments, sky writing, etc.

Mediation is an important, even central, principle of the new *instructional technology,* which can best be defined as *a rational methodology for designing media-facilitated learning systems.*

In theory, television, being a mediating device, can be used at any strategic point in the teaching/learning process which requires its kinds of symbol capabilities. In fact, operational conditions have made it practicable to use television almost exclusively in connection with presentations of "initiating content." * Adaptive and reinforcement activities are usually reserved for direct handling by a teacher in person.

The "atomic" model of instruction given on page 303 might seem to support the use of television and the other media so long as they effectively assist a teacher in putting symbols before a student. The efficiency of such a "one-to-one" use would be a different matter, of course. As it is, however, "free instructional atoms" do not often exist in nature—and almost never in modern mass education. *The classroom is not a place in which an individual teacher interacts persistently with an individual student. A single teacher must guide the learning behavior of a number of students, usually a fairly large number.* The fact that education is a "social" event makes mediation all the more valuable when it facilitates group learning while allowing a teacher to spend time at shaping the performance of individual students.

The latter of these conditional constraints often goes unacknowledged. For example, currently fashionable audiovisual doctrine has it that an overriding value of mediation in the classroom lies in the variant "sensory approaches" made possible. A richly varied "multi-media mix" presumably can expose students to so many alternatively redundant stimuli that, surely, one of them will "work" for each and every learner in the group.

This may or may not be a valid educational technique. Evidence is not significantly clear on the claims. But this form of multi-media practice carries within itself a serious management danger. Classroom teachers, generally speaking, are certainly unable alone to contrive, choose and serve out the admittedly complicated and widely varied multi-media elements necessary in a single instructional unit. Many teachers are unable even to keep up with the content and methodological burdens required of them by the traditional, relatively "unitary" textbook system. To expect them to become masters of multi-media legerdemain is to be operationally unrealistic.

Moreover, teachers desperately need more time to conduct suitable, adaptive and reinforcement activities for their many students including activities of the "directed self-study" category. Media processes, even if they could be managed on classroom basis, would significantly cut back on time for these vital elements. Therefore, what is needed increasingly is a mass mediation technique which can provide suitable "sensory approaches" without enmeshing a classroom teacher in irksome, highly sophisticated and often operationally impossible methods.

The value of mediation in permitting teacher redeployment has been largely disregarded by the educational community; yet it seems to many that it constitutes a critically important task for television. In modern mass-education, anything which provides a teacher with the means and opportunity to apply more time and skill at "shaping and reinforcing" the learning of his students should have a very high value. Especially is this true as the force of ris-

---

* *The term "presentation" sometimes causes concern because it seems to suggest a one-way, passive classroom condition: being talked at/being made to listen to, etc. This notion arises from our familiarity with the "time-honored" lecture technique. Actually, the fundamental model of the teaching/learning process we are using merely establishes that the initial "presentation" phase involves offering students stimuli to which they can respond. It does not specify the interval. In properly managed situations, the presentational intervals are fairly brief, each quickly succeeded by some kind of active student response. The total effect is one of back-and-forth interaction. Well-designed televised materials nowadays are apt to be structured in this same operational format. They do not consist of long presentations which are essentially passive in learner terms.*

ing student numbers tends significantly to increase the need for such activities while at the same time perniciously decreasing the opportunities for them.

It can be shown that television materials can be effective in eliciting objectified learnings while at the same time providing teachers time and guidance to "shape and reinforce" the learning performance of students.* Detailed arguments supporting the learning effectiveness of televised materials are not needed in this paper. Suffice it to say that there is a veritable mountain of research findings to indicate that people can learn any number of skills from television-facilitated instructional systems.**

What we wish to stress here is that the evidence does not point to an extensive use of television in instruction merely because it is an effective "audiovisual" learning implement. Instead we believe the evidence suggests that television should be used in those situations in which it greatly reduces the requirement that a teacher have substantial responsibility for planning, making, or selecting basic presentations—and does so to such an extent that a system can re-invest the time and energy of its classroom teachers in the other vital parts of the instructional process.

Employing television conventionally as a classroom "visual aid" or as a convenient source of casual "enrichment" materials does *not* contribute appreciably toward the establishment of more time and opportunity for teachers to spend in vitally important adaptive and reinforcement pursuits. Therefore, all the television application of these kinds must be taken to be of lesser significance. *Only those applications which allow for television to provide systematic learning experiences to (masses of individual) students in a way which beneficially reduces the "content" responsibility of (many) classroom teachers should be said to capture the fundamental virtue of television-in-instruction.*

Putting Television and Other Media in Perspective

The first of the two criteria shown on page 304 is met when television is used as a primary source of symbol presentation for active learning, assuming, of course, that the classroom teachers involved are actually released to carry out important adaptive and reinforcement tasks with individual students. In such an application, the teaching/learning activity involved is indeed "intensely valuable, even critical, to contemporary educational operations." The second criterion—that of the essentiality of television mediation—may appear as yet unanswered. Why cannot many of the other media perform as well as television in the role of presentational surrogate?

Television systems are capable of carrying a very wide range of different kinds of symbols, including many originating through other media: speech, music, alpha-numerics, sound effects, pictures, diagrams, cinematics, gestures and more. It is a "multi-medium" in itself. But so is the sound film. This is clearly not the critical dimension.

Television systems are able to produce their symbols quickly and then to replicate them instantaneously (or after convenient time-storage) over long distances and at relatively low unit costs. Related media do not possess these same important characteristics in the same degrees.

Television, when linked with other media like radio, telephone and high-speed print, is readily adaptable to the establishment of short-interval "closed-loop" instructional systems. These allow learning designs to be diagnostically monitored and improving changes to be made directly contingent on actual outcomes measured frequently at critical points in the process. These characteristics are not peculiarly related to television, of course. But when

---

*In American Samoa and elsewhere.

**Note in particular the recent HEW-commissioned study "Learning from Television: What the Researcher Says," Godwin C. Chu and Wilbur Schramm: NAEB, Washington, D.C. 1968.

the logistical conveniences of television are added to this "cybernetic" adaptability, the resultant instructional system takes on a set of synergistic attributes which are unique: "It does many things and it does each of them better because it does all the rest."

Television is not only useful for producing and distributing a wide range of effective symbols, but, used properly, television also enables us to accommodate and react to regular, coordinating feedback procedures without immobilizing delays. Most importantly, television can be operated on a mass scale; which means that it can be used to provide systematic instruction to large numbers of students and classrooms simultaneously. Further, such use can free comparable numbers of individual classroom teachers for adaptive and reinforcement tasks which are functionally prescribed by uniform presentations. Its use can lead to wholly new organizational· and administrative patterns for improving the effectiveness of the total educational enterprise.

One highly consequential result of these attributes is particularly relevant nowadays to educational systems which are faced with demands for "decentralization." Television can enable such administrative "complexes" to group their individual schools—or even classrooms—into numbers of different, operating "districts," each with its own special curricular patterns. Furthermore, because of the very nature of the electronically-facilitated co-operation which can be established between the elements of these new school units, they need not be geographically contiguous to function effectively.

Television and Today's Educational Realities

Really fine "teaching scholars" are as rare as great poets. The number in a given place at a given time will always be extremely small. Without access to instructional mediation of any major kind, the educational institution of a society would have to be very narrowly elitist, as was the case in Europe before Gutenberg. The printed book, by virtue of the heavy content load it could help bear, has been able in recent centuries to extend the educational process to many more students. Books enable numbers of skilled and dedicated persons of less-than-highest-scholarship to conduct academic activities with at least adequate teaching effectiveness. The new expectations for contemporary mass-education are of such magnitudes, however, that the limited size of our effective book-facilitated teaching force has become woefully inadequate to the enlarging task. For all its mediating helpfulness, the book imposes on many teachers content and related methodological responsibilities which go beyond their abilities. Many pupils in the inner-city and remote-rural areas now study under the academic management of persons for whom books are inadequate and incomplete content facilitators and who, therefore, must proctor more than teach.

Television mediation, coupled with that of print, can make it possible for these persons to function suitably in an effective educational effort. It can do so by consistently taking over an ever larger share of presentational responsibility, thus very sharply reducing the content load borne by local classroom personnel. Proper instructional television design can also enable classroom teachers to put a great deal more time and effort into carefully co-ordinated "shaping and reinforcement" activities which are essential to learning. Furthermore, television is critically useful in helping establish specific methodological practices and in training teachers at the skills requisite to effective learning management.

But can we really expect persons who are less-than-adequate in content skills to develop adequate methodological skills? The answer is: *when technology truly facilitates educational effort, classroom teachers are directed in system-defined "adaptive and reinforcement" activities on a day-to-day, even hour-by-hour, basis.* Therefore, common sense, dedication to their students and the ability to carry forward carefully structured tasks are the really essential traits for these teachers. The new division of labor in such a program obviates the necessity for each classroom teacher to manifest sophisticated psychometric, counseling and pedagogical skills. If nothing else, the educational system designed by Vernon Bronson for American Samoa has abundantly demonstrated the "personnel" advantages of an educational effort organized along these lines.

It is sometimes urged that improved and re-oriented training programs in our colleges of education would virtually eliminate the acknowledged short-comings noted about teacher performance in "content" areas and classroom uses of media. Presumably, a welter of new courses in specific content disciplines and "audio visual" * would provide all members of the American teaching force with the full range of impressive pedagogical skills needed for highly efficient classroom operations. To be candid, this argument is nothing more than educationist "guildism." It is unsound for the reason that it plainly ignores the blunt fact that such high-level teaching skills as would be universally required cannot be "cultivated" in the large numbers of persons actually needed to staff our schools. Without casting aspersions at anybody, we must face up to the reality of the human situation: high-level teaching skills will ever be scarce in our population. We must devise an educational system which accommodates itself to that condition. Television, systematically designed into co-operative teaching/learning programs, holds the real promise of letting us do just that.

Television provides the potential of allowing mass-scale educational programs to be carried forward with uniform, basic opportunities and standards for all participants. It can be the facilitating means of mass-education in a genuinely democratic age.

The fact that the medium has been seldom used to carry out this important function in no way denies the truth of these assertions. If one looks about in the world to find instances of "exemplary" television usage, one is invariably attracted to such places as American Samoa, Hagerstown, Chicago Junior College and South Carolina. Even a cursory examination of those "successful ETV operations" reveals that in each, television has been used fundamentally to provide effective and systematic learning experiences to numbers of students in a way which has beneficially reduced (or readjusted) the content load of local teachers while (potentially) facilitating a needed role change for them.

On the basis of all these things, we believe that by the end of the 1970's American universal education can become, at last, an operating reality. Schools in the inner-city and remote rural areas need no longer be "skeletons in our educational closet." They, too, could be operating at an efficiency and productivity suitable to the demands of a great democratic people. The social dynamism represented by a combination of the "population explosion, the knowledge explosion," and the technical development of American society can lead to a new national condition: More people will be able to learn more quickly and more effectively—and with a conscious, new efficiency on the part of our multi-faceted educational system.

Because the multiplication of traditional resources (teachers, classrooms, laboratories, and such) to meet the demands implicit in this projected educational growth pattern is neither feasible—nor possible, it is absolutely necessary for education to turn to innovating techniques that facilitate equal and adequate learning opportunities for all citizens. This obviously means technology—and especially communication technology.

Technical Considerations

If technology is going to play so important a role in educational operations in the future, is the "technical state of the art" high enough for the heavy traffic loads to be imposed? It is not the purpose of this paper to explore these questions in any great depth. That is being

Nowadays often termed "educational communications."

done elsewhere.* But because these issues loom so large, they should be dealt with, at least, in a general perspective.

Technically, television operations have three inter-relating aspects: production, storage and transmission. While most systems involve all three, it is more orderly to examine them separately.

1. Production Planning and producing material to be used for systematic instruction is a fairly complicated kind of undertaking. The cannons of art, the strictures of the learning psychologist, the regulations of the electronics engineer, and the cost-accounting principles of the industrialist all must bear on the process. Materials must be effectively structured for learning; suitably attractive to the eye and ear; devised within carefuliy drawn technical parameters; and managed with high efficiency toward carefully defined goals. That fact that we have experienced many failures in these regards should surprise no one. Yet we are gradually improving. Instructional production practitioners are beginning to acquire a much higher level of professional competence which enables them to cope with the great number of demands faced in day-to-day instructional output.

Origination equipment is becoming more versatile and reliable—but no less expensive. Quite the contrary. Although substandard television equipment is available cheaply, the cost of professionally equipping an instructional television studio (and related graphic/film facilities) is much higher now than it was ten years ago. Moreover the increasing demands for color apparatus—instructionally justifiable or not—have intensified some of these cost strains.

Color in an instructional system poses some uncomfortable questions. Current research as to the significance of color cueing in lesson materials is inconclusive if not downright negative. The attractant value of color is fairly well demonstrated no doubt, but at the same time any heightening of attention seems to be offset by some sort of stimulus distraction that interferes with desired response. In any case, there will probably be a drift toward color in instructional production in the years ahead simply because the electronics manufacturing industry will make color equipment "the standard of their lines."

There are those who believe local production of a proper quality is not feasible because of rising costs. Consequently, the argument is frequently advanced that emphasis should be only given the development of regional, or even national, production centers. The several videotape libraries currently in operation (at Bloomington, Lincoln, etc.) are sometimes seen as the grains of sand around which to spin such production "services." At the moment there may even be a trend in that general direction. But whether it will carry forward in the long run is another matter. The real obstacle is probably not so much local pride as the essential requisites of the "short interval closed-loop" design scheme which is fundamental to high-level technology. It is true that "pieces of curriculum" can be—and will be—attractively devised and properly validated (through samples) on large-regional or even national levels. But the sheer complexity of curricular inter-relationships necessary for comprehensive, pluralistic school/college programs would certainly appear likely to frustrate the operation of a whole curriculum—or any significant part—on any such large-scale, unitary basis.

Some authorities now believe that the central purpose of the "ITV libraries" should be one of collecting, indexing and distributing "single-concept" materials for appropriate integration within locally produced lessons and courses. Such elements, available as short films, videotapes, audiotapes, discs, etc., would be supplied local centers at low rates.

Production by local instructional centers is a long way from disappearing—or needing to. Instead, it will probably begin to flourish as the new design methodologies we have discussed make a full impact on our educational communities. (This assumes, of course, that

---

Particular attention is called to W. J. Kessler's treatise entitled "Fundamentals of Television Systems," NAEB, Washington, 1968.

the educational power structure comes to recognize the relevance of comprehensive technological applications to our widening instructional tasks. The Commission on Instructional Technology will have an important influence in this regard.)

We now can forecast that psychological strictures about the necessary simplification of symbol content will lead to a deliberate reduction of cues in the synergized aural-and-visual output of program systems. This does not mean, however, that electronic materials will be unadorned, dull, and unattractive. Rather, that they will be composed only of those production and academic content elements which are essential to the motivated learning prescribed. Spurious attractants which do not contribute positively to that unity of behavioral purpose will not be allowed to creep into the production as so many distracting flourishes.

This approach is fundamentally unlike that used to concoct affective ("show biz") materials in which attending responses are of the first magnitude. In instructional applications, the attending response—while essential—is not quite so urgent because of the "captive audience" context. *The proof of the academic pudding is the learning not the viewing. Behavior, not "circulation."* Therefore, programs which are merely "fun to watch" can become colossal failures in terms of any real learning achievement; consequently, lesson production—live or videotaped—will be much more rationalized and much less intuited than at present.

2. Storage   The television medium became much more useful to education with the invention of the storage techniques possible with videotape (VTR) devices. The earlier film-process kinescope machinery was expensive, relatively unreliable, complicated and of a lesser "technical" effectiveness. Nowadays instructional television operations virtually depend on videotape, be it the "professional" quadrature sort or one of the newer, less expensive helical-scan systems. Currently lessons are more-often-than-not produced on, and transmitted from, videotape; although the storage of most such materials is for temporary, day-to-day convenience not for purposes of extended re-use. High cost of the tape itself as well as loss of content currency and validity precludes long-period storage.

The time is probably not far distant when academic buildings of every kind (including those now called dormitories) will be equipped with internal distribution networks and with numbers of small videotape recorders, probably of the helical sort. (The as-yet-unmarketed EVR—Electronic Video Recorder—designed by CBS may also link into these building-level networks. Our current understanding of these new devices would make it appear that they will be less expensive than helical machines, although program materials for them may have to be factory-processed rather than locally "dubbed" from in-coming air or cable signals.) These various storage devices will probably be used to release instructional materials to individual classes and students on system-managed schedules—not on teacher or pupil whim.

This new kind of system-managed storage of instructional content will facilitate the introduction of cooperative education methods by eliminating the "tyranny of the clock." Materials transmitted during night time hours will be automatically recorded for later scheduling, thus tremendously extending the traffic potentials of "real-time" transmission devices. The technique will also broaden the offerings of materials to include more "multi-track" elements for students of greatly variant achievement levels.

3. Transmission   The key to the most efficient application of television-in-instruction is found in mass, instantaneous replicability. Fortunately, the ways of accomplishing such distribution of "cinematized" signals are conveniently plural. There are three *wireless* techniques: broadcasting (VHF and UHF), Instructional Television Fixed Service (ITFS-2500 mHz radiation), and microwave (a point-to-point beam). There are two *wired* techniques as well: RF-CCTV (closed circuit systems capable of multiplexing up-to-82 channels on a single coaxial cable) and Video-CCTV (closed-circuit systems which can "coax" single-channel video signals of very high quality over relatively short distances). The much-discussed community antenna TV (CATV) systems are RF-CCTV networks used primarily to relay signals from broadcasting stations to receivers in homes, schools, factories, etc. The same cables may carry especially originated programming as well.

All of these techniques—except Video-CCTV—are employable for mass replication of instructional signals. No one of them is inevitably superior to the rest; no one is necessarily less expensive; no one is cause for inferior production standards. The selection of the machinery depends on the specific job to be done. The expected linkage of VTR/EVR storage devices into transmission "paths" will intensify the value of each by raising potential traffic capacities. Of course, comprehensive application of technology in impacted urban school areas may necessitate traffic capacities considerably beyond those possible with any of those transmission systems which are limited to a few channels. In such circumstances, we would expect RF-CCTV multiplex networks to carry the main burden of instructional distribution.

Transmission by satellite is frequently cited as a most promising means of overcoming the logistical difficulties faced in routing television signals by normal line-of-sight and land-cable techniques. Satellites might enable programs to be "broadcast" on a nation-wide basis without incurring the technical and institutional complexities of traditional relay networking. There are practical obstacles, however, which will not disappear upon the resolution of the purely technical problems involved. The inherent demands of the "closed-loop" design format have been previously discussed. The regional time-zones will generally require staggered transmission schedules, even from national satellite systems, thus necessitating traffic capacities of four-fold complexity. The traditional fear of a "single national curriculum" will undoubtedly inhibit the acceptability of any direct, large-scale distribution scheme. Indeed, satellites may come to serve only as convenient variants in the relay processes now dependent on land-delivery methods.

It is quite likely that special community—or state—agencies will eventually emerge to manage electronic distribution complexes which will offer access to a variety of transmission facilities. Under such a scheme, school systems, colleges, training centers and other educational agencies will have privileged use of appropriate audio, video and data channels. A concerted arrangement of this sort could mean an efficient, maximized exploitation of available spectrum and cable circuits. There are those who predict that existing organizations like ETV stations, Educational Media Centers and Regional Laboratories may serve as administrative nuclei around which these valuable transmission complexes might be formed. Embryonic developments of the sort are already "in the works" in Cleveland, Appalachia, and Northern Virginia. All this points up the oft-omitted fact that *one properly designed technical system can facilitate a number of different instructional and data systems,* thus greatly enriching investment returns.

* * *

In the years to come we shall experience a greatly intensified use of instructional technology at every level of education. We are probably going to see the electronic media become basic components of a new "Nerve system" for schools, universities and training facilities: a development which will help make possible the higher levels of instructional productivity and efficiency needed for effective implementation of truly universal educational opportunities.

16.

"Dial-Access" as an Instructional Medium

by R. STAFFORD NORTH
Dean of Instruction
Oklahoma Christian College

In 1964 when Oklahoma Christian College first began serious consideration of a dial-access system which would allow a thousand dialing stations to select from any of more than a hundred programs, many said it could not be done within the normal limits of educational enterprises. Costs would be too high, maintenance impossible, materials unavailable, and faculty unwilling. In just four years, however, it is clear that the project not only is possible, but that it has worked successfully.

In fact, the use of dial-access* educational facilities, which began in 1961,[1] has now grown to more than a hundred twenty operational systems with above fifty more being developed.[2] About half of these systems are in elementary or secondary schools, and the other half in higher education.[3] Thirty-six percent are used for language study only with the remaining sixty four percent employed for multi-subject purposes.[4]

The rather rapid spread of dial-access systems in educational facilities is a clear indication that this mode is both electronically possible and financially feasible. This increase is also an indication that there are many who believe that this form of remote-access to information is instructionally sound.

Like almost every new plan, however, dial-access is not without its opponents. Some suggest that it is an unnecessary cost, others that it does not provide sufficient flexibility, and still others that it is too difficult to maintain in working order.[5]

A review of the systems in use and of the literature, then, would warrant the conclusion that dial-access can provide some useful instructional experiences, but that it is not useful in all conditions and for all purposes. The aim of this paper, therefore, is to explore those circumstances in which dial-access retrieval is effective as part of an instructional program and, in such cases, just what contribution it can make. In considering this topic, four questions must be asked:

(1) What learning media can be made available by dial-access?
(2) What special qualities does dial-access give these learning media?

---

* "Dial-access" is used in this paper to designate any remote-access system whether it is activated by dial, pushbuttons, or other device.

(3) What learning modes can be provided by these media?
(4) What types of access are required for using these media?

What Learning Media Can Be Made Available by Dial-Access?

The most common media used on dial-access systems are audio and video tape recordings. All present dial systems are designed to receive audio tapes and twelve, in addition, can receive video.[6] But any system which can receive audio tapes can also easily be adapted to receive live radio, a live speaker, a telephone conversation, and disc recordings. Any system with video capability, likewise, can be adapted to receive live broadcast-television, live closed-circuit television, slides, filmstrips, and moving pictures.

But making these media available to a carrel, a classroom, a home, or a dormitory room just by dialing does not, by any means, exhaust the possibilities of remote-access systems. And, indeed, it may well be that some of these additional uses eventually may become the most valuable. Although it has not yet been done in any current installations, a response system can be built into a remote-access system—particularly one which uses push buttons. This response system can allow a student to give his answer to questions or problems presented by the material on the system. This response may be received by the same computer which controls the switching system, and a graded printout can be prepared for the teacher listing each student's responses. Item analyses can even be provided giving the teacher feedback on the overall progress of the class.

Branching systems are also a possibility through remote-access. In this case, a student's response on a question can determine which material he receives next. Response "A" might be programmed to send him to one track of a tape while response "B" might be programmed to lead him through another. In this way, the remote-access system takes on some of the qualities of computer assisted instruction.

Not only, then, can a dial-access system make available all types of audio and visual materials, but it can also incorporate such other media as response systems and branching techniques. Future developments, undoubtedly, will produce still other uses. Particularly will progress in the remote-accessing of documents bear watching for instructional dial-access systems.

What Special Qualities Does Dial-Access Give These Learning Media?

The media which can now be made available by dial-access are well known as instructional methods. For years, for example, we have used films, television, and recordings for teaching purposes. While each of these media has its own character when used in its usual form of presentation, the use of each of these on a dial-access system gives it certain additional qualities.

A. The first quality imparted by the dial-access system is *immediacy*. A textbook is often two or three years in the making, and journal articles may be many months in preparation and printing. It even takes several days for a teacher to write material and have it reproduced for class distribution. A recorded interview or information just available, however, may be disseminated immediately through a dial-access system. And when students are dialed-in to live radio or television coverage of an event, they are in contact with it at the very moment it occurs.

The quality of immediacy is also seen in the fact that while one copy of a book, or recording, or film may take weeks to circulate among a large group of students, one copy of a recording or film on dial-access may be made available to hundreds or thousands at the same moment. In this way, for example, a movie can easily be seen by the students of a large class within a day or two without occupying class time or teacher time. Or, to take another example, an important speech occurring out of class hours can be heard live or by recording before the next class meeting.

B. A second important quality of materials on dial-access is *ease and efficiency of presentation.* One of the major deterrents to the use of many instructional media is the difficulty and waste involved in their use. Many teachers, for instance, do not like to "waste" time setting up equipment; others have never learned to use it; some are even afraid of it. A dial system, however, makes either audio or video material easily available. With a dial position located in a classroom, for example, a teacher may have a film or a recording with no more difficulty, training, or fear than dialing a telephone.

With the same ease, students may dial materials for use in their carrels. One music teacher, for instance, has estimated that students in his music appreciation class listen to ten times as much music with the dial system as when they had to go to a listening room and operate the record player themselves.

Still another factor relating to ease and efficiency of presentation is that students can use material on a dial system without the presence of the teacher. A great waste of teacher-time occurs, for example, during a forty-minute film in class as the instructor sits idle. His time can be used far more efficiently if he prepares the students for the film and then lets them see it without taking his time.

Another obvious saving of teacher-time occurs when the teacher can record certain experiences to be made available to students through a dial system, thus being relieved of repeating that particular material for several sections of students. At OCC, for example, much of the beginning speech course utilizes audio-taped materials on the principles of speaking. This relieves the teacher of repeating the same lecture to successive sections and allows him to use class time more effectively and efficiently.

Of course, it takes a teacher's time to prepare material for use on a dial system, but this initial investment of time can be more than regained through the use of the recordings or films.

C. The third quality which dial-access imparts to the media used on it is *flexibility.* A teacher can be in only one place doing only one thing at any given point in time. The materials on a dial-access system, on the other hand, can be in many different places at once—carrel, dormitory, home, classroom, or even a car. And those dialed-in can all be doing different things. Each student can, therefore, be studying material best suited to his own needs. In addition, different students may access the same materials at different times, thus making scheduling simpler.

An obvious example of this flexibility is in the use of recorded shorthand drills. If the teacher dictates in class, all must go at the same speed. If the teacher wishes to save his time by using a recording in class, still all must go at the same speed. But if dictations at 40, 50, 60, 70, and 80 words per minute are placed on different dial numbers, then each student may dial the particular speed which best suits his particular need. This same principle applies, of course, to a wide range of subjects and materials.

But not only is the flexibility seen in that it allows different students to be dialed to different programs at the same time, but it also allows one student to use a given set of materials more times than another, should this be beneficial to him.

D. This flexibility leads directly into the next special quality, *individualization.* Most dial-access positions now in use in school systems are located in individual carrels, and this is no coincidence. A dial system certainly affords a student the opportunity to utilize material in the way best suited to his own needs.

Sitting in a location that provides him partial sight and sound isolation and with earphones masking the "outside" world, the student has an experience that is really quite personal. Not only can he dial a program adapted to his particular needs, and at the time most suitable to him, but he has the sense of doing it alone. Often this experience becomes a rather personal encounter between a student and his teacher. One student at OCC, moreover, commented to a visitor that she liked working in a carrel located near others because she could have a sense of partial isolation and yet not feel completely alone.

What Learning Modes Can Be Provided by These Media?

Having seen what media can be made available by dial-access and having seen some of the special qualities which dial-access gives these media, let us next explore the various learning modes which can be provided by this approach. Or, to phrase it another way, what learning conditions and procedures are especially suited to use through a dial-access system? Those learning modes discussed here are not exclusive to dial-access and are, of course, used in other settings. It is important to note, however, that these are particularly appropriate for dial-access.

A. Dial-access can be used to *present information.* In almost any learning system there must be some provision for disseminating information. Sometimes this is done by a "class lecture," sometimes by a textbook, sometimes by "outside reading." Another possibility, however, is to use a dial-access system to tapes and films.

Probably the most obvious example of the use of an audio or video format for presenting information is the radio or television newscast. Particularly in nations where literacy is low and distribution of printed media slow, the audio mode via transistor radio is used for large-scale dissemination of information.

Some schools with dial systems record classroom lectures and make them available to students for replay, thus giving them more than one opportunity to obtain the information presented. An even more effective use of this mode, however, is to make available, through dial-access, speeches or interviews by experts or the recording of some actual event related to the topic being studied. Music, drama, or literature are other types of informational presentations which can be dialed.

This learning mode, then, is primarily concerned with simply presenting information to students which they are either to remember or to write down for later study. Dial-access is one of the ways students may have the necessary contact with this information they are to receive and learn.

B. A *programmed format* can also be utilized on dial-access. In addition to making information available, as suggested above, the teacher may wish to present information in a form designed to assist the student in mastering the information as he receives it. Such an approach may take the structure of formal programmed instruction with the presentation of a "frame" of information, the opportunity for a response to this information, followed by feedback for reinforcement.

Material presented in this form by recordings frequently uses not only an audio or video tape, but also a workbook in which the student can record his responses. In such a case, the procedure might be as follows: the recording presents two or three sentences of information followed by a multiple-choice question over the material; there is a brief pause on the recording during which the student looks in his workbook at the possible answers and marks his choice; then the recording provides the correct answer for reinforcement.

But why would there be an advantage in presenting this in sound or sight rather than in print? In subject matter areas dealing with sound or sight such as music, speech, literature, drama, shorthand, physical education, foreign language, education, or art, the answer is obvious. Since sound and sight are involved in the desired learning outcome, they should be involved in the learning process.

Even in subjects not involving sound directly, however, audio or video may be useful. Greater variety in the presentation can be obtained by combining the printed workbook with the sound or sight on tape than could be achieved with the print alone. Often, too, the recording can add different voices, recordings, of actual events, simulations, musical backgrounds, and other special effects to the words. In addition, many teachers feel that the warmth and personality of voice can add a personal touch.

This is not to suggest, of course, that all programmed instruction should be presented by the audio or video mode, but rather that it is one possible mode for such a presentation. And in this form, it can be utilized on dial-access systems.

An additional word should be added about programmed instruction on recordings. Many teachers have found a "semi-programmed" format to be quite useful for recordings prepared for dial-access. In this case the presentation of information departs somewhat from the strict programmed style and yet retains some of its principles. Thus a teacher might provide an outline map in a workbook, discuss it on the recording as the student fills in points of interest, and then provide a blank map on the next page of the workbook which the student is to fill out from memory. After a brief period of silence during which the student works, the teacher resumes by giving the correct answers as reinforcement.

There are many variations on this "semi-programmed" style. In some cases a presentation of perhaps five minutes in length may be followed by a true-false or matching quiz. In other cases a problem may be worked in step-by-step fashion as the student follows in his workbook. Then, while the recording is silent, he works the next problem by himself and is given the correct answer either by the recording or by the next page of the workbook. While this "programming" is not as concentrated as the more formal style, it is simpler and faster for the teacher to prepare.

C. *Drill* is another learning mode which is easily adapted to dial-access. While education certainly must involve much more than rote memorization, absolute mastery of certain material provides the foundation for many learning experiences. Studying shorthand, foreign language, multiplication tables, chemistry symbols, dates and places, parts of animals, phonetic symbols, and any number of other materials requires the drill and repetition which a recording can provide. In this mode a recording has special benefits for it can repeat as many times as necessary without tiring or losing patience and it can offer the individualization of different speeds or levels should this be necessary.

D. Another learning mode possible on dial-access is *"audio-tutorial."* This form of recordings has not usually been employed on dial-access systems because it normally requires the student to start and stop the recording himself. It has now become possible, however, for a dial-access system to provide "exclusive" access to students by allowing the first student dialing a tape to lock out other users until he is through. Another approach provides each student with his own "dubbing" of the master tape so that he can stop and start as he wishes. Because of these new capabilities, audio-tutorial is possible on dial-access and so is here listed among its possible learning modes.

In audio-tutorial instruction, the tape becomes the tutor to guide a student through a learning program. The teacher converses with the student on the tape and directs him to various other resources as necessary. Science laboratories, in particular, have been developed in this way. The student comes to a carrel in a science laboratory, turns on his tape recording, and listens to the teacher. After some background, the teacher may tell him to take out slide No. 27 and place it on the microscope. The student stops the machine and follows this instruction, then turns on the recorder again and is guided as he looks at the slide. The recorder then directs him to Table No. 3 where he is to make a particular observation which the teacher describes to him on the tape. He stops the machine, goes to Table

No. 3, makes the observation, and returns to write down his observations. Having started the machine again, the student learns the nature of the observations he should have made.

This plan, developed by Dr. S. N. Postlethwait of Purdue University for botany instruction, has been adapted to many other fields. Particularly have Oakland Community College of Bloomfield Hills, Michigan, and Meramec Community College of St. Louis, Missouri, made extensive use of this approach.

E. It is also very important to notice, however, that the more presentational types of instruction do not exhaust what can be done on dial-access. *Problem-solving* and *discovery* experiences are also possibilities. In many cases a student can analyze, critique, reason, and search while using materials available on dial-access.

Students in oral interpretation, for example, may analyze various styles of reading as they listen to different samples. Counselling students may critique a variety of guidance techniques. Students of group dynamics and communications may observe a group crisis develop and be brought to a solution. Students of music, drama, art, teaching, laboratory techniques, physical education, or any other type of observable performance may watch or hear the performances of others and seek to determine their strong and weak points.

While it may be simpler to use recorded materials in a presentational or drill mode, some of the most effective use of recorded materials has been in the problem solving and discovery mode. Not nearly as much use has been made of this aspect as of others, but it seems to offer important promise for future developments.

F. A final learning mode possible on dial-access is *accessibility to resource material.* At the present state of the art this use of remote-access must be confined to those resource materials which need to be available to several students at about the same time. There is, of course, little value in using a dial-access system when only one person may need a recording and that at an unknown time. Eventually, however, it will be possible to dial a page from a newspaper, periodical, or book, as well as to dial a recording of a historical event, music, speeches, drama, discussions, interviews, and other such information. At the present time, then, the use of dial-access in the resource mode is limited, but likely, this will be one of the eventual major uses of dial-access retrieval of information.

These six modes of learning—presentation, programmed, drill, audio-tutorial, problem-solving, and resources—summarize the various types of uses on dial-access systems today. While one recording might combine as many as three or four of these modes into one 30-minute experience, they still serve as useful separate categories for thought in either examining or preparing audio-video materials. By far the greater use now being made of dial-access systems is for two of these categories: presentation and drill. Other uses, however, particularly that of the programmed or "semi-programmed" and problem-solving, appear to be developing rapidly as more instructors and institutions gain experience. Audio-tutorial is also developing rapidly, but more on direct-access machines than on dial-access. The extensive use of dial-access for research into resource materials appears to be awaiting more technological developments.

What Types of Access Are Required in the Use of These Media?

In considering types of access to audio and video materials, the following three pairs of terms should be considered:

Random	Exclusive	Remote
Scheduled	Common	Direct

A. *Random access* refers to a system which allows a student to obtain any program he wishes at any time. In the fullest sense of the term, random access implies that a student is assured of getting his choice of material from its starting point and without the possibility that it may be in use by someone else at the time he wishes it. In a more limited sense, random access may be applied to a system which allows students to access materials when they desire with only an occasional possibility of that material's already being in use. One might suggest, for comparison, that although a student has random access to books in a library, he runs some risk that another student will have checked out the book he desires.

Currently the system offering the most in random access is the recently opened facility at Oak Park and River Forest High School.[7] In this push-button system, a student punches in his program, waits only a few seconds while an ultra high-speed duplicator copies for his personal use the tape he has chosen, and then allows him not only to listen to the tape but to start, stop, and rewind as he wishes.

This degree of random access offers many advantages although it is, as yet, quite expensive. Particularly it facilitates the instructional modes of audio-tutorial, problem-solving, and the use of resource materials. For straight presentations, programmed materials, and drills, however, *scheduled access* may be quite adequate and much less expensive. In this case, tapes are scheduled to be played several times a day or as often as necessary to accommodate the users. While a student must be present at a scheduled time to start a tape, he does have a choice among the several times the tape will be played. In this way there may be fifty, a hundred, or more listening to one copy of a tape at the same time. Scheduled access, while being less flexible, is a more economical way of making materials available, and for some modes of instruction and some student situations, it is sufficient.

B. In addition to the "random-scheduled" duality, investigation of the types of access must also include consideration of whether access needs to be *exclusive* or *common*. When used in this context, exclusive refers to the provision for one student to obtain complete control of a playback machine so he may start, stop, and rewind at his own discretion. Common access, of course, refers to the opposite of exclusive control and indicates that two or more students can use material at the same time.

Scheduled access and common access, obviously go together for if a tape is scheduled for a given time, it cannot be started and stopped by a single student. It is desirable, likewise, that random access and exclusive access go together, but this is not absolutely necessary. A tape needed by only a few students, for example, may be available on dial start at any time with little likelihood that two would dial it at the same time. Should this occur, there still is no great problem for the second user can either choose to continue listening if the material allows one to begin in the middle, or to dial it at some later time.

Exclusive access has, up to this point in time, been provided primarily through direct access to machines rather than through any remote system. As mentioned earlier, however, the remote system at Oak Park, Illinois, allows exclusive access, and other systems are now being manufactured which will achieve the same result through computer programming rather than through the "rapid duplication" approach.

C. A final duality in types of access is *direct* or *remote*. While there are times when it is advisable for a student to have the playback machine and the tape in his own hands, there are also times when it is impractical or impossible to provide each student with this opportunity and thus a remote system becomes feasible. What factors, then, determine at what point one should cease providing tapes and machines to individual students and move to a remote-access system?

    1. The first and most important factor in deciding between direct and remote access is *cost,* and the key ingredient in determining cost is the quantity of traffic expected for listening or viewing.[8] If class sizes, for example, are expected to be small, then five copies of a tape might be sufficient and the direct provision of machines would be less

expensive. On the other hand, if there are five hundred in the class and a tape needs to be seen or heard by all of them within the period of three or four days, making individual copies of the tape and making sufficient machines available would be impractical. With the low cost cassette machines now available, the breaking point at which remote-access becomes feasible is a higher number of students than it was before, but one still reaches the "break-even" point at some quantity. And if the remote system has to be available for some large classes, then it will likely be feasible to place tapes for smaller groups on the system too.

2. But cost is not the only consideration in determining whether to choose remote or direct. *Expansion* is another important element. If one ever anticipates a system which will be of such a size to make a remote system feasible, then he should start with such a plan. Converting to a dial-access system after having invested in five hundred tape playback machines, for example, would involve a large loss.

3. A third factor to consider in deciding whether to move toward a direct or a remote system is the *amount of student control* required when using the tapes.

Theoretically, the control factor is not a distinction between direct and remote access for any type of control which can be made available in the direct use can be done remotely. At the same time, it is less expensive and usually simpler to provide such controls as start, stop, rewind, record in a direct fashion than in a remote.

If one expects students frequently to need the capability of start, stop, and rewind, then this factor would tend to favor the direct use. On the other hand, if most of the material is to be used without stopping and is presentation, programmed, or drill rather than audio-tutorial, problem-solving, or resource material, then the remote access would work quite well. One can, of course, have both by utilizing a remote-acess system for the bulk of the material, then making special provision for those uses that require the student to have greater control over the tape.

4. Another factor to be weighed in deciding between a direct and a remote system is *maintenance.*

A dial system is a rather sophisticated piece of electronic equipment and requires persons with special training to keep it running well. When it fails, the whole program suffers and major adjustments must be made. At OCC, we have found that a large audio system will require one or two full-time men plus student help for adequate operation. Video systems, of course, require much more in terms of operational staff for they are more delicate and require additional equipment.

A small, direct system would, of course, require less maintenance than a dial-access system. Yet there is a point at which upkeep on a large number of individual tape-players becomes a major task. In the OCC system, for example, there are 1,024 positions, 46 tape decks, and the switching system to maintain. The student position has little to fail except headset cords, loose connections, or a sticking dial. The 46 tape decks are operated only by qualified people and do not require much time in maintenance except cleaning heads, occasional adjustment, and replacement of a relay; and since these are close together, all this is relatively easy. A direct system our size, on the other hand, would require 1,024 tape decks which would, of course, be a major maintenance task.

5. A final factor for consideration here is that of *convenience.* Convenience to the user must be a matter of prime importance. Students will not use materials that are difficult to access. Their time is important just as is the time of their teachers, and they do not wish to waste it walking great distances or waiting long periods for something to become available.

In some cases the dial-access system has made listening more convenient by allowing students to have carrels available at many points on the campus. Thus they are saved a ten or fifteen minute walk to the listening laboratory and the same walk back. The remote system serves their needs all over the campus without requiring the staff to carry tapes to all these points and to keep them there in good order. The Ohio State University experience has indicated that the usage of tape-recorded materials will increase dramatically when it is made more convenient to the students.[9]

On the other hand, if the number of tapes to be used is not large and the campus is not sizable, a direct access system in a central place would be convenient and simpler to operate than a dial-access system.

6. These, then, are five basic factors to be weighed in deciding whether one should make audio and video available to students through a direct or a remote access system. *It is not enough to make the decision on any one factor alone;* rather, all of these must be weighed together.

Conclusion

The rapid increase of dial-access systems for instruction since their advent in 1961, along with the millions invested in them, is clear evidence of the value many see in this learning approach. Yet, there have been opponents and disappointments.

At the least, dial-access, along with other recent technological developments, has placed new emphasis on the values of audio and video recordings as instructional tools regardless of the manner in which access is provided. On this point there seems to be general agreement.

On the other hand, dial-access retrieval itself appears to provide an effective way to meet certain instructional conditions. Particularly is dial-access useful when the quantity of the traffic is heavy, the distance separating users is great, or the approach to instruction is flexible.

In sum, there appears to this observer to be a place for dial-access in future instructional systems. It cannot do everything or even all that some have thought it might. But in certain circumstances, it provides the answer to important instructional needs.

REFERENCES

1. Ofiesh, Gabriel D. *Dial Access Information Retrieval Systems: Guidelines Handbook for Educators.* Final Report of Project No. BR-7-1042, U.S. Dept. of Health, Education, and Welfare, Office of Education, Bureau of Research, July, 1968, p. 23. Don Stewart, in his *Dial-Access Information Retrieval and Systems for Education Newsletter* of Sept., 1968, places the date of the first dial-access system in 1960.

2. *Ibid.,* p. 25.

3. *Ibid.,* p. 92.

4. *Ibid.,* p. 25.

5. Theumay, Jean R. "Is Dial Access a Fad?" *Audiovisual Instruction,* XII December, 1967, p. 1079.

   Lalime, Arthur W. "Tape Teaching: Dial Select or Auto Library?" *Audiovisual Instruction,* XII May, 1967, p. 441.

6. Ofiesh, *Dial Access Information Systems,* p. 94.

7. "Random access learning equipment can serve these students and others in school or at home." *School Product News,* September, 1968, p. 69.

8. Stewart, Donald K. "The Cost Analysis of Dial Access Information Retrieval Systems." *Audiovisual Instruction,* XII, May, 1967, pp. 43-44 and pp. 492-494.

9. Blemesderfer, William E. "Ohio State University's DATAGRAM." *Audiovisual Instruction,* XII, May, 1967, p. 459.

17.

Computer Assisted Instruction in Elementary/Secondary Education: The State of the Art

by *LAWRENCE PARKUS*
Manager, Visual Education
Westinghouse Learning Corp.

Introduction

Computer assisted instruction has been subject to a good deal of definitional confusion. For some, CAI capaciously describes *any* application of the computer in an educational institution. Others rigidly apply the term to include only that tiny fraction of computer applications marked by intensive and highly sophisticated student-computer communication. A realistic definition—in terms of the state of the art now and in the near future—lies somewhere between the generalized and particularized versions mentioned above. For the purposes of this report, CAI is defined as a process which exploits the memory capacity and computational capabilities of a digital computer to allow a *unique* interaction between a student and curricular subject matter. Typically, this involves a terminal, which allows a student to receive and transmit information, linked to a computer which stores and regulates the flow of information to and from the student. There are several distinguishable forms, or *modes,* of CAI: these are briefly described below. The development and growth of CAI—in all its configurations—is, above all, a function of its rich potential to support the individualization of instruction.

The depth, intensity, and flexibility of *student-computer interaction* define both the CAI mode and the nature of the equipment (hardware) and curricular programs (software) required. The simplest mode of CAI, i.e., the lowest interactive level, is *Drill and Practice.* In this application, the presentation of *concepts,* indeed, of all *new* information, remains the sole responsibility of the teacher. Here, the role of CAI is to evaluate a given student's understanding of the material which has been presented and then to present a program of drill and practice which is most applicable to his particular needs. The overall function of the drill and practice mode is to provide maintenance of skills and retention of concepts. Because this is the dominant application of CAI in elementary/secondary education, it will be further explored below.

In the *tutorial* mode of CAI, the computer system *introduces* concepts and new information in varying degrees as well as provides maintenance of skills and retention of concepts. Although, as will be seen below, both drill and practice and tutorial systems provide branching to varying levels of difficulty, the student, in both systems, is quite restricted in his ability to really manipulate the subject matter being studied. The student is limited to constructed responses: he is rigidly limited in the case of drill and practice (e.g., "yes",

"2 + 2 = 4"), less limited in some tutorial applications (e.g., "The Chief Executive Officer of the U.S. is the <u>President</u>" or "<u>The President of the United States</u>").

Problem-Solving is a CAI mode which permits a greater degree of flexibility in the interaction of student and subject matter. By the use of a computer language, the student may exploit the enormous calculating capability of a modern computer in manipulating large and complex data bases necessary to the solution of problems in science and engineering. System Development Corporation, for example, has developed a college-level statistics course—implemented at UCLA—which allows a measure of realism in student handling of complex data unavailable in traditional teaching situations. The necessity for student knowledge of a computer language and the general paucity of software has severely restricted the application of problem-solving CAI in the public schools.

Simulation and *Gaming* applications of CAI too allow for a more rigorous and flexible student-curriculum materials interaction. Typical of experimentation in this area is the development of economic games by the Board of Cooperative Educational Services (BOCES) of Westchester County, New York. At the BOCES Center in Yorktown Heights, a CAI system simulates diverse economic environments—as diverse as the ancient kingdom of Sumer and the contemporary nation of Sierra Leone—and sixth grade students on terminals are provided the opportunity to make critical decisions effecting these simulated economic systems. While the Yorktown Heights experiment has demonstrated real promise, very few similar applications are to be found in the public schools—again, the funding and the expertise necessary for the development of simulation programs have not been available.

A *Dialogue* mode would be an ultimate in CAI development. Such a system would permit a student to input free-form questions and statements and, in so doing, would create a totally flexible interaction, a curricular dialogue, between pupil and computer. Elements of existing CAI programs approach this ideal. A logic program developed by Patrick Suppes at Stanford, for example, will accept *any* line in a proof or derivation if such a student response does not violate the rules of logic. Generally, however, free interaction in CAI is very much in the research stage and no existing CAI system can be accurately categorized a dialogue system.

This report will concentrate upon the application of drill and practice CAI in elementary/secondary education. In focusing upon the public schools, this report falls within an emerging consensus—recently stated in forceful terms by the new national administration—which recognizes the critical relationship between the improvement of public elementary/secondary education and the attempt to confront the socioeconomic crises which plague us. Drill and practice CAI receives special attention in this report because, within the public school environment, it *is* the state of the art. State of the art is defined here quite simply as that which is possible—and has been proven so by extensive, relatively efficient applications. Another way of saying this is that selective emphasis is placed upon *operational* CAI—installations where a meaningful number of students receive a significant portion of their instruction in at least one subject area under computer control—rather than CAI locations which are of a research or demonstration nature.

CAI in the Schools: An Overview

The introduction of CAI in elementary/secondary education has been a slow process. As early as 1961, Professor D. L. Bitzer of the Coordinated Science Laboratory of the University of Illinois was employing a one terminal CAI system, PLATO I, to provide instruction in a variety of curriculum areas. Some eight years later, however, there are fewer than one thousand CAI terminals in the public schools serving fewer than twenty thousand students. When we subtract from these totals terminals and students involved in limited experimental and demonstration projects, we find that the parameters of operational CAI shrink to less than five hundred terminals and sixteen thousand students. This situation is summarized in Figure 1.

Figure 1: Operational CAI Installations, January 1969

Installation	Number of Terminals	Number of Students	CAI Subjects	Grade Level(s)	CAI Mode(s)
New York City (Board of Education)	192	6,000	Mathematics	2–6	Drill & Practice
Philadelphia— Project GROW	32	464	Biology, Reading	Junior High School Senior High School	Drill & Practice/ Tutorial
Eastern Kentucky Consortium	32	1,920	Mathematics	2–6	Drill & Practice
McComb, Mississippi	60	2,500	Mathematics	2–6	Drill & Practice
Waterford, Michigan INDICOM Project	32	400	Mathematics	2–6	Drill & Practice
San Francisco Bay Area Schools (Stanford Computer)	122	4,880	Mathematics, Reading, Computer Programming, Logic	2–12	Drill & Practice/ Tutorial (52 terminals used for mathematics drill and practice)
Commonwealth Consortium: Pittsburgh, Philadelphia, Pennsylvania State University—to be operative in September 1970.	64	512	General Mathematics Algebra	9	Tutorial
TOTAL	534	16,676			

Figure 1 clearly shows that mathematics drill and practice at the elementary school level accounts for a large percentage of what has been defined as operational CAI. All of these mathematics drill and practice programs have a common derivation: the materials were originally developed at The Institute for Mathematical Studies in the Social Sciences at Stanford University under the leadership of Dr. Patrick Suppes and Mr. Max Jerman. The original Suppes-Jerman program is used by the CAI installations in Eastern Kentucky; McComb, Mississippi and the San Francisco Bay Area. The L. W. Singer Company has published the Suppes-Jerman program in computerized form and this version is utilized by the New York City CAI project. Given the relative pervasiveness of the math drill and practice program, a description of its operation is necessary to an understanding of CAI in the schools.

The math drill and practice program is structured as follows: The content of the mathematics curriculum for the entire year is divided into twenty-four concept blocks—at each grade level. Each block is comprised of seven drill lessons. Each lesson exists in five versions representing five levels of difficulty. The first drill lesson in each concept block is a pretest: the student's score on the pretest determines the difficulty level (1-5) of the lesson drill which will be presented to him on the following day. The levels of difficulty for subsequent drills are similarly determined by the performance of the individual student. If the student's score falls in the range of 60-84% correct, he remains at the same level of difficulty on the following day. If, however, the student scores 85% or better on a drill lesson, he is automatically raised one level of difficulty on the following day; if he scores below 60%, he is lowered one level. This branching structure is depicted in Figure 2.

Figure 2: Branching Structure for Regular Drill on a Concept Block

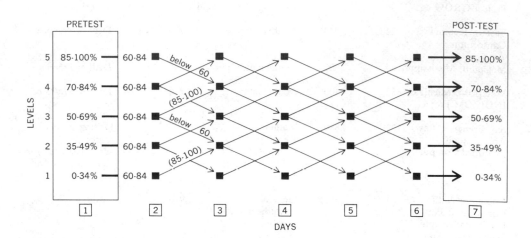

CAI drill and practice also provides for a system of individualized review lessons. A computerized record is kept of a student's performance on block post-tests (see Figure 2), and, on the basis of those performances, review lessons at the appropriate level of difficulty are prescribed. There is an extensive attempt to individualize the reviews: four separate sets of reviews of each concept block have been written and each review has been constructed at five levels of difficulty. Further, a series of review *tests* are designed to measure the effectiveness of the review lessons and provide the basis for continuing diagnosis. Generally, these procedures appear to ensure that a student, throughout the year, is reviewing his weakest areas.

A daily drill varies in duration from four to ten minutes. Problems are presented in a variety of formats thus encouraging the student to broadly apply his understanding of concepts and to recognize those concepts in various guises. A teletypewriter serves as the instructional terminal: problems are displayed in hard copy print-out form and student responses are effected via the keyboard. Typically, student responses are instantaneously reinforced. If the student's response is incorrect, "No, try again" is typed out and the problem is displayed again. If a second error is made, the correct answer is displayed and the student is instructed to "Try again". The problem is once again displayed and the student is permitted to insert the correct answer. The daily lesson which is reproduced in Figure 3 consists of drill on a new concept block followed by a review of an earlier concept block on which the student had performed poorly. The drill is Grade 4, Concept Block 19, third level of difficulty and is a mixed drill treating arithmetical functions as well as the commutative, associative and distributive laws.

Figure 3: Sample Mathematics Drill 2
Practice Lesson

```
PLEASE TYPE YOUR NUMBER.   164

NOW YOUR FIRST NAME.   JOHN SMITH

THIS IS A MIXED LESSON.

27 × (13 + 15) = (27 × 13) + (27 × 15)

8 × 70 = 570

NO, TRY AGAIN.

8 × 70 = 560

IF JEFF ATE 1 5 OF THE 450 COOKIES AT THE PARTY,

HOW MANY COOKIES WERE LEFT FOR THE OTHERS?

90 COOKIES

9 × 30 = 270

IF MARY PUT 30 DONUTS IN EACH OF 9 BOXES, HOW MANY

DONUTS WERE THERE ALL TOGETHER?

___DONUTS

TIME IS UP. TRY AGAIN.

___DONUTS

TIME IS UP.   THE ANSWER IS 270.   TRY AGAIN.

270 DONUTS

6/3 6 3      60
  3 6 0
      3

80 × 9 = 720

17 29 − 9/29 = 6 29

NO, TRY AGAIN.

17/29 − 9/29 = 9/29

NO, THE ANSWER IS 8   TRY AGAIN
```

17/29 − 9/29 = $\underline{8}$/29

57 − 47 = 47 − $\underline{37}$

$9\overline{)2\ 7\ 9}$ $\underline{30}$
    2 7 0 $\underline{1}$
       9

   3 0
+   1
  $\overline{3\ 1}$

24 × (16 + 19) = ($\underline{4}$ × 16) + (24 × 19)

TIME IS UP. TRY AGAIN.

24 × (16 + 19) = ($\underline{14}$ × 16) + (24 × 19)

NO, THE ANSWER IS 24. TRY AGAIN.

24 × (16 + 19) = ($\underline{24}$ × 16) + (24 × 19)

IF THERE ARE 48 CHILDREN IN THE CLASS AND 1/4 OF
THEM ARE GIRLS, HOW MANY BOYS ARE IN THE CLASS?

$\underline{36}$ BOYS

4 × 60 = $\underline{240}$

(27 + 70) + 83 = 27 + ($\underline{27}$ + 83)

NO, TRY AGAIN.

(27 + 70) + 83 = 27 + ($\underline{70}$ + 83)

END OF LESSON NUMBER   11431902

15 PROBLEMS CORRECT, 75 PERCENT, IN 242 SECONDS

72 PERCENT CORRECT FOR ALL LESSONS THIS YEAR

THIS IS A REVIEW ON UNITS OF MEASURE.

1 2 YEAR = $\underline{6}$ MONTHS

3 NICKELS = $\underline{15}$ CENTS

2 PINTS = $\underline{5}$ CUPS

NO, TRY AGAIN.

2 PINTS = $\underline{3}$ CUPS

NO, THE ANSWER IS 4. TRY AGAIN.

2 PINTS = $\underline{4}$ CUPS

1 2 DAY = $\underline{12}$ HOURS

1 YEAR = $\underline{365}$ DAYS

1 2 FOOT = $\underline{8}$ INCHES

NO, TRY AGAIN.

1 2 FOOT = $\underline{6}$ INCHES

END OF REVIEW NUMBER   12411701 OCT. 6, 1967

4 PROBLEMS CORRECT, 67 PERCENT, IN 69 SECONDS

GOOD—BY, JOHN. PLEASE TEAR OFF AT THE DOTTED LINE.

••• ••• ••• ••• ••• ••• ••• ••• ••• ••• •••

The results that have been achieved with CAI math drill and practice will be summarized in the section that follows. Before turning to this subject, however, a few comments on several of the installations summarized in Figure 1 are offered because of their relevance.

There are plans within the New York City project to employ their computer in administrative data processing applications during time periods when the CAI system is not in operation. Computerized test scoring, for example, is one area receiving serious consideration: well over five million tests per year would be compatible with computer-scoring. A pattern of utilization which combined CAI with ADP applications could significantly reduce the high per-student CAI costs which are detailed in the costs section of this report.

Twenty-eight elementary schools in seven counties participate in the Eastern Kentucky CAI project. Created by an ESEA Title III grant, this project offers a unique opportunity to gauge the effectiveness of CAI with children living in an economically depressed rural area—the seven counties fall squarely within Appalachia. In addition to elementary school children, many of whom fall far below their formal grade levels in mathematics achievement, the system will be used by Neighborhood Youth Corps trainees, by Upward Bound enrollees, by adults taking basic education courses and by special education students. There is a good reason to believe that the Eastern Kentucky project will, over time, provide a basis for evaluating the effectiveness of CAI in remedial education.

The Commonwealth Consortium project (Philadelphia, Pittsburgh, Pennsylvania State University) promises to offer the most extensive test to date of tutorial CAI in the public school environment. Commencing in September, 1970, five hundred twelve ninth-grade pupils will spend a total of 2,560 hours per week on computer terminals in the study of general mathematics and algebra. These will truly be "stand-alone" CAI courses—teachers will not be assigned to the experimental groups. The development of the CAI programs in the CAI Laboratory at Pennsylvania State University and the results achieved in the classrooms of Philadelphia and Pittsburgh should provide the kinds of data necessary for a cost-effectiveness analysis of tutorial CAI.

CAI in the Schools: Acceptance and Results

There has been relatively little CAI in the schools; there has been practically *no* systematic assessment and evaluation of the effects of the medium where it has been employed. In some cases, CAI installations have not had access, either internally or externally, to personnel qualified to conduct valid evaluations; in other instances, the individuals responsible for CAI have been preoccupied with the myriad problems accompanying the introduction of a highly innovative program and, therefore, have postponed evaluation. It would be unrealistic to assume that this situation will change, that, in some way, systematic evaluation will automatically be built-in to future CAI projects. Accordingly, there is an urgent need to deeply involve specialists in learning research from the university community in the systematic assessment and evaluation of present and future CAI applications in the public schools. Federal and state educational funding authorities must assign a higher priority to this need than they have in the past.

The relatively few studies which have been conducted on CAI effectiveness do create a basis for optimism about the eventual contributions of the medium. These studies, as well as the reactions of those who have experienced the application of CAI in the schools are summarized below.

Eastern Kentucky According to Dr. Leonard Burkett, Program Coordinator and Professor of Education, Morehead State University, the introduction of CAI has resulted in widespread educational benefits. Students, on the whole, are strongly motivated by the medium: this new enthusiasm and motivation to learn was reflected in marked improvement in student attendance at schools where terminals were installed. A number of observers reported that experience on the terminals appeared to have increased the confidence of particularly disadvantaged students with long histories of failure. The judgments of the computer, impersonal and private, appear to cause such students much less embarrassment and frustration than did their previous experiences with classroom teachers. This observation, when coupled with a number of other factors, strongly suggest that CAI may have the ability to reach those students who are unresponsive to traditional instruction. Of similar interest is the observation that a significant number of students with CAI experience made marked gains in reading and language arts skills, although the CAI curriculum was exclusively in the area of mathematics. This "spin-off", which has been observed in several other CAI projects, appears to result from the 'general motivation to learn engendered by the medium as well as the systematic, relatively fast manner in which the instructional material is presented and the ability of this procedure to increase student concentration.

On balance, CAI has had a positive effect upon the performance of classroom teachers. The logical and sequential nature of the CAI programs has made a significant contribution to the planning and execution skills of a number of teachers involved in the project: as a result of their experiences, they are better prepared, on a daily basis, to specify their instructional objectives and to systematically plan the sequence of activities which will achieve those objectives. Also, the program has resulted in significant economies of time for the classroom teacher by eliminating the routine of classroom drill and the burden of preparing, correcting and recording large numbers of drill and practice exercises. More than ever before, this has freed teachers to work with students in individual and small group situations. In these individualized or small group situations, the CAI system has proven a powerful diagnostic tool: by typing in a simple code on the teletype terminal, the teacher can receive a summary of the work of a class, the class's work on a given concept, or the work of an individual pupil. The teacher has been in a position, therefore, to go beyond even the individualized CAI review routines in attacking specific areas of individual weakness.

The Kentucky project has been positively received by parents. The printouts of students' daily drill lessons are taken home and this, according to Dr. Burkett and others, has resulted in much greater parental interest and involvement than had been the case in the project schools before CAI. Special observation and demonstration programs for parents have been extremely well attended.

Nothing approaching a comprehensive evaluation has been conducted in Eastern Kentucky; however, the limited measures taken of the effectivness of CAI are suggestive of promising potential. One study involved the seventh grade class at the Morehead State University Laboratory School. The Stanford Achievement Test was administered to the twenty-six class members. The class mean for arithmetic concept formation was 7.8 (seven years, eight months) while the class mean for computational skills was 6.3. Each student then received 3.3 hours of the Suppes-Jerman math drill and practice CAI program. This was *not* supplemented by any other form of instruction. When the Stanford Achievement Test was administered after completion of the CAI programs, the computational mean was 7.4, a mean *growth* of *one year, one month,* and the concept mean was 9.8, a mean *growth* of two *full years.* A similar experiment conducted with a small group of Upward Bound enrollees yielded almost identical results. That these studies are both limited and crude is obvious; taken together with other evidence, however, they are suggestive of a potential measure of effectiveness of drill and practice CAI in remedial instruction, that is, in reaching students who have been derailed from the instructional track.

California Schools   The research team at the Institute for Mathematical Studies in the Social Sciences (Stanford) is in the process of completing an extensive evaluation of their CAI program in drill and practice mathematics. Fragmentary results of these surveys have been made available and may be briefly summarized as follows. During the 1967-68 school year, experimental and control groups were established at seven different schools in grades one through six. The regular mathematics instruction of the experimental group students was supplemented throughout the entire school year with the Suppes-Jerman CAI drill and practice program while the control groups' instruction was not so supplemented. A battery of the Stanford Achievement tests in elementary level mathematics was administered to both groups, first in October, and then at the end of May. The results were: the students receiving CAI drill and practice had a statistically significant greater increase in performance level than the control students on the *computation* section of the SAT in grades 2, 3 and 5. Also, the CAI students achieved a significantly greater increase in performance level than the control students on the *Concepts* section for Grade 3 and on the *Applications* section for Grade 6. A very similar comparative survey has been conducted in McComb, Mississippi: the results of that survey provide an interesting comparison with the Stanford results.

McComb, Mississippi The McComb evaluation is almost identical in design with the Stanford study. The Stanford Achievement tests were the standard of measurement: they were administered at the start of the experiment in the form of pre-tests and at the termination of the experiment as post-tests. Control groups and experimental groups were established in twelve different schools and included grades one through six. As in California, the regular mathematics instruction of the experimental students, over the entire school year, was supplemented by regular CAI drill and practice sessions while the control group students were not exposed to CAI. The results of the experiment are represented in Figure 4.

Figure 4: Statistical Results

Experimental vs Control Groups—Suppes (Stanford) Mathematics Drill and Practice

Location and Grades: McComb Public Schools, McComb, Mississippi, Grades 1–6
Dates: Pre-test September 1967   Post-test May, 1968
Test: Stanford Achievement

	Mean Pre-test			Mean Post-test		Mean Post-Pre		t score post-pre	p	df
	Control N^6	Exp.	N^6	Control	Exp.	Control	Exp.			
Computation										
Grade										
1	1.32*	63	1.41*	52	1.46*	2.55	.206*	1.135*	10.56	<.01	113
2	1.96	54	1.99	25	2.80	3.37	.84	1.42	5.23	<.01	77
3	2.76	56	2.82	22	4.04	4.85	1.26	2.03	4.64	<.01	76
4	2.45	77	2.26	58	3.17	3.36	.69	1.10	2.63	<.01	133
5	3.71	134	3.09	83	4.60	4.46	.90	1.37	3.43	<.01	215
6	4.36	160	4.82	275	5.48	6.54	1.13	1.72	5.18	<.01	433
Concepts										
Grade										
3	2.97	56	2.83	22	4.26	4.78	1.29	1.95	3.01	<.01	76
4	2.31	77	2.65	58	3.06	3.01	.74	.36	2.25		
5	4.00	134	3.42	83	5.24	4.78	1.29	1.37	.50		
6	4.88	160	5.34	275	5.39	6.31	.52	.98	3.74	<.01	433
Applications										
Grade										
4	2.88	77	2.89	58	3.28	3.33	.41	.44	.22		
5	4.12	134	3.36	83	4.73	4.33	.63	.77	.88		
6	4.52	160	5.06	275	5.06	6.13	.61	1.08	4.09	<.01	433

*grade equivalence in years and months
0 number of students

The impact of CAI, as Figure 4 shows, was considerably more pronounced in Mississippi than in California. The performance growth of the experimental students on the *Computation* section of the SAT was significantly better (at the .01 level of statistical significance) than the performance growth of the control students *in all six grades.* The most dramatic difference was at the first grade level where the average increase in grade placement for the experimental students was more than *one year and one month* while the average increase for the control students was less than *two months.*

The performance of the experimental students was significantly better (at the .01 level) than the control group students on the *Concepts* section for Grade 3 and Grade 6, and on the *Applications* section for Grade 6.

The Mississippi results, once again, are strongly suggestive of the potential of the drill and practice mode of CAI in upgrading the mathematical skills—especially critical computational skills—of low-achievers: in Figure 4 note the extent to which experimental group students were brought to or near their formal grade level *after* a year's exposure to CAI.

The responsible officials in McComb discern a number of educational benefits as a result of the introduction of CAI. These improvements were, in most cases, very similar to those observed in Eastern Kentucky. There was, throughout the year, a high degree of student enthusiasm and motivation for the CAI program and, in many cases, toward the entire instructional process. There was no evidence of teacher fear or of skepticism toward CAI; rather, the teachers who were interviewed universally expressed, in very positive terms, gratitude for the benefits which they felt accrued both to the students and themselves as a result of CAI. As a result of the time made available and the diagnostic aid rendered by CAI, the teachers felt that they had more closely approximated the individualization of instruction than ever in the past. The attitude of the teachers toward the contributions of CAI were summarized by Mrs. Gayden Stovall, a sixth grade teacher, who said that she would perfer a CAI terminal in the classroom to the services of a teacher's aid and that she would accept a larger class, e.g., thirty-three rather than thirty student, if a terminal were available.

Some of the potential benefits of CAI have been indicated above. A final comment on this subject will be offered in the concluding remarks. Now, however, let us turn to the costs of CAI.

The Costs of CAI

The halting growth of CAI in elementary and secondary education has been, above all, a function of the high, indeed exorbitant costs of the medium. These costs include hardware, software, and general operating expenses. Until these costs are significantly reduced, it is impossible to predict when, if ever, CAI will be absorbed into the mainstream of the instructional process at the elementary and secondary levels. Contrary to my judgment, there are those who take the view that the impressive pedagogical benefits suggested by CAI research and demonstration projects will somehow result in the expenditure of the large sums necessary to widely disseminate state of the art CAI systems throughout the public school establishment. This is fallacious reasoning and its acceptance will retard the advent of operational, effective computer assisted instruction in the schools. First, one must consider the meager body of research on the learning effectiveness of CAI that exists—and that is summarized within this report. On balance, this research indicates that, indeed, *when* CAI is more effective than traditional methods of instruction the learning gains are to be measured in arithmetical and not exponential terms; and, further, that CAI has proven more effective than traditional methods of instruction in the acquisition of a *limited* number of skills. Past experience as well as ongoing research strongly suggests that the perfection of CAI as an instrument of learning will be a lengthy, difficult and tedious process: It is illusory to await a "Sputnik effect" to sustain the growth of this process.

Unfortunately, misconceptions about the financing of CAI do not end here. There is a rather widely held belief within the educational community—by those who are involved in CAI research and development as well as those who are users or potential users of the medium—that the advancing state of the art of computer technology will significantly reduce the costs of computers and peripheral equipment. This belief reflects a serious misunderstanding of the computer industry and its major marketing thrust. It is crucial to grasp this misunderstanding for it leads to an awareness of one of the major factors—though not the only factor—in the high cost of CAI.

Data processing equipment has, is, and will continue to be designed to serve the needs of extensive and well endowed commerical and scientific markets. The users in these markets require data processing equipment that possesses extremely sophisticated and complex capabilities. Existing CAI systems are created from this equipment which, in many cases, offers capabilities not needed, in other cases lacks required capabilities, and is extremely expensive. The computers currently employed in state of the art CAI systems, for example, possess extremely large core memory capacity, extremely high computational speed, the ability to accommodate a wide variety of input-output devices, and frequently multiprogramming capability. The RCA Spectra 70/45 computer, the heart of the RCA IS 70 CAI system, for example, is a general purpose digital computer designed to handle data infinitely more voluminous and computations infinitely more complex than the drill and practice algorithms which it processes in the New York City CAI project. Similarly, the computer which serves as the central processor for the IBM 1500 CAI system is a special purpose digital computer designed for process control. In truth, this computer fulfills its anticipated role in systematically ordering and monitoring the complex sequence of operations in an oil refinery and not in supplementing the teaching of economics to elementary school children as at Yorktown Heights, New York. In short, CAI systems are created with hardware designed for much different purposes and, to some extent, are priced on the basis of data processing capabilities and features which are irrelevant to computer assisted instruction.

Unfortunately for CAI, the general trend in the computer industry is toward even larger, more powerful, more sophisticated systems with enormous core memory capacities and increased computational speed. This trend, for example, is at the heart of the recent lawsuit brought by Control Data Corporation against International Business Machines Corporation. CAI, in short, is caught in a vicious cycle. As long as the market for CAI systems remains small, industry cannot be expected to invest the necessary funds to develop a specially designed system which will be functionally relevant and significantly less costly. The CAI system market, however, will remain small as long as expensive hardware designed for commercial and scientific applications form the basis of CAI systems. The problem of the cost of CAI will not be eliminated either by "the invisible hand of the marketplace" or by the advancing state of the art of computer technology. Affirmative action is required to solve the problem. I shall return to this subject at the conclusion of this discussion of CAI.

Let us turn now to an examination of the precise hardware costs of CAI systems presently available in the marketplace.

IBM 1500 System

In terms of major components, this system consists of two computers which are provided with additional memory capacity by two disc storage units. The system provides sixty-four student instructional terminals of a "rich" nature. That is, the terminals are equipped to provide the student with both audio and visual displays and allow the student to input information by means of both typewriter keyboard and lightpen. In this configuration, the sale price of the system is approximately $1.2 million (maintenance charges included). The annual rental charge for this system is approximately $380,000, including maintenance.

These costs are itemized in Figure 5 below:

Figure 5: IBM 1500: Itemized Costs

Description & Model No.	Quantity	Monthly Rental	Price	Monthly Maintenance Charge
1131—CPU 2B (Central Processing Unit)	2	$2,172	$ 29,170	$ 150
1132—Printer	2	536	22,700	50
1442—Card Reader/Punch	2	530	29,150	104
2310—Disc Storage	2	700	27,000	53
1501—Station Control	2	4,100	194,000	45
—Display Adapter	2	1,000	42,800	22
—Display Control	2	1,140	48,500	72
—Light-Pen Adapter	2	220	9,600	4
1505—Audio Adapter	8	560	20,400	20
—Audio Tape Drive- Play/Record	64	6,400	255,360	1,344
1510—Instructional Display	64	3,520	118,400	768
—Light-Pen	64	1,408	61,440	96
1512—Image Projector	64	5,760	227,840	912
TOTAL		$ 28,046	$1,149,360	$ 3,640
ANNUAL TOTAL		$336,552		$43,680

Philco-Ford 102 System

There is a serious question as to whether this system is available in the open market. There is but one installation—in the Philadelphia schools—and there the system has been radically transformed in configuration. I include the cost figures on this system only in the interest of providing a broad view of state of the art CAI systems' costs. In terms of major components, this system is configured much like the IBM 1500: that is, two medium size computers, upgraded in memory capacity by two disc storage units, control 64 student terminals. These terminals, as in the IBM system, permit the student to receive visual materials which are displayed on a modified television receiver and to receive audio messages which are transmitted via headsets. The student may input information by means of a typewriter keyboard arrangement. In the configuration described above, the system was priced at $1.1 million. This total price is itemized below in Figure 6.

Figure 6: Philco-Ford 102 System

Device	Quantity	Price
CPU	2	$ 230,000
Magnetic Tapes	6	36,000
Printer	2	50,000
Card Reader/Punch	2	72,000
ASR (Teletype)	2	8,000
Input/Output Interface	2	72,000
Terminal Control Unit	2	290,000
Terminals	64	200,000
Disc Storage	2	140,000
TOTAL		$1,098,000
ANNUAL MAINTENANCE CHARGE		$ 24,000

RCA Instructional 70 System

This is the largest system which, at the present time, may be commercially procured. At the heart of the system is a large processor, the memory capacity of which is upgraded by a number of auxiliary storage units. The computer is linked to 192 instructional terminals. These terminals are modified teletypewriters: students receive information in the form of hard copy teletypewriter print-out and communicate with the computer by means of the teletypewriter keyboard. The annual rental fee for this system is $720,000. The rental costs are itemized below in Figure 7.

Figure 7: RCA Instructional 70 System

Description	Quantity	Total Monthly Rental
CPU (Spectra 70/45)	1	$11,125
Memory Protect	1	129
Elapsed-Time Clocks	1	52
Selector Channel	1	385
Console	1	340
Card Reader	1	670
Magnetic-Tape Unit	3	1,860
Tape Controller	1	720
Random-Access Controller	2	1,080
Input-Output Attachment Feature	2	N/C
Disc Storage Unit	2	1,180
Disc Pack	10	150
Communication Controller M. C.	1	720
Synchronous Buffers	8	344
Record Overflow Feature	1	10
Card Punch	1	465
Printer	1	720
Line Concentrator	4	20,360
Instructional Terminals	192	18,642
TOTAL		$59,652

Returning to the broader perspective of *total* CAI operating costs, let us focus upon the largest such system in existence and the pattern of expenditures which supports it. The New York City Board of Education Computer Assisted Instructional System consists of a total of one hundred ninety-two student terminals installed in sixteen elementary schools in The Bronx, Brooklyn and Manhattan. Six thousand students, Grades 2 through 6, receive individualized drill and practice on a daily basis.

The annual equipment rental totals $720,000 (see Figure 7 above). The annual communications costs, that is, the costs of the many telephone lines which link the remotely located instructional terminals to the central computer in Manhattan, are $144,000. The major software component, the mathematics drill and practice curriculum materials, are leased from the L. W. Singer Company at an annual cost of $19,200. The overall administrative costs associated with the project, including the costs of space rental, operating personnel, supplies, etc., are approximately $125,000 annually. The inclusive costs of CAI in the New York City schools, therefore, is just over $1 million a year.

In effect, New York City is incurring an annual per student cost of just over $183 for a CAI system which supplements instruction in one curriculum area at five of the thirteen formal learning levels. It is sobering to compare this figure with other educational expenses. For example, the national median annual per student expenditure for textbooks in 1968 was $5.58. On a national average, in 1968, we spent $328.63 per student for classroom teachers, and only $20.98 for administration. These comparisons merely serve to provide added emphasis to the thesis expressed at the outset of this section: the costs of CAI must be radically reduced before there can be any reasonable expectation that the medium will be introduced into the mainstream of the instructional process at the elementary and secondary levels.

Several potential paths toward cost reduction deserve serious consideration. In the equipment of hardware area, one point of clarification is perhaps in order. Nothing that I have said should be interpreted as casting the manufacturers of data processing equipment into the role of the culprits responsible for high cost of CAI. This, for two reasons. These costs are the result of *multiple* causation, as I trust the analysis above makes abundantly clear. Second, it is unreasonable and unjust to expect industry to invest millions of dollars of risk capital in the design and development of an optimum CAI system for a market that has shown such limited potential. It is my judgment that a functionally relevant, moderately priced CAI system—a cost-effective system—would be created by an intensive collaborative effort of representatives of the computer industry, engineers, learning theorists, and educators. Such an effort could become a reality were the federal government to supervise the design of specifications, organize a competitive bidding process, and subsidize the project. While this course of action raises serious questions of public policy, I am unable to envision alternative means of efficiently and expeditiously reducing CAI hardware costs.

Communications costs are a major factor in CAI expenses: in the New York City project, the leasing of telephone lines results in expenditures equivalent to twenty per cent of total equipment costs. The New York situation is symptomatic, for virtually all CAI projects will involve linking remote terminals to central computers. A subsidized tariff schedule similar to the GSA TELPAK program—where the GSA leases and subleases interstate telephone lines at less than half the commercial rates—would be a powerful stimulant to CAI cost reduction and growth. Several existing *interstate* CAI projects, e.g., the McComb-Stanford project, have benefited from participation in the GSA TELPAK program. These benefits, however, are not currently available to purely *intrastate* projects.

The problem of software costs is dealt with elsewhere; however, several factors bear brief consideration. The fact that, at the present time, only one major publisher offers but one CAI program for sale is not surprising in light of the extremely high program development costs and the severely restricted existing market. Should, however, it become clear that the appearance of efficient and reasonably-priced hardware was imminent—as a result of a federally subsidized program or any other means—a number of major publishers would be prepared to invest significant capital in software development. This conclusion results from "off the record" interviews with responsible representatives of major publishers. Such a development, in turn, would result in the availability of a broad range of lower cost CAI programs. The crucial point is that (commercial) software availability and cost reduction *follows hardware*. In the past, there has been a belief that CAI software could and should be developed locally by the educational user, e.g., a school district. Abortive attempts in this direction at several installations are a matter of record. The inability of schools to attract and pay the curriculum design, systems analysis, and programming personnel needed to do the job make it clear that software must be developed either in the publishing industry or in regional centers which pool broadly invested material and intellectual resources.

A Note on Software

In effect, the outlines of the CAI software situation, by implication, have been sketched in other sections of this report. Precious few CAI programs, suitable for use in operational elementary/secondary installations, are available from any source. As mentioned above, only one CAI program, math drill and practice is available from a commercial publisher. While some two hundred thirty CAI programs have been developed over the past decade, the overwhelming majority of these were created in academic research centers and bear little relevance to the elementary and secondary curricula. Presently, there are several research centers concentrating on the development of CAI programs for the public schools. The most prominent of these centers are located at Stanford University under the leadership of Professor Patrick Suppes, at Florida State University under the leadership of Professor Duncan Hansen, and at the Pennsylvania State University under the leadership of Professor Harold Mitzel. In light of the limited financial resources available to these centers, however, it is unrealistic to assume that their efforts will result in the availability of a significant number of CAI programs in the near future.

The development of CAI materials in the publishing industry can be briefly summarized. The L. W. Singer Company, which offers the *Computer-Based Drill and Practice in Arithmetic* program, has no additional programs under development. Harcourt, Brace Jovanovich has developed an elementary level English drill and practice program (Grades 4, 5 and 6) and a drill and practice program in Remedial Reading at the junior/senior high school levels. These programs, however, will be validated in the field and not available for sale for at least one year. Harcourt, at the present time, plans no new course development. No other publishers involved in CAI development were identified. As emphasized previously, however, this situation would quickly change with the appearance of moderately-priced CAI hardware systems. One caveat, however, should be made. Publishers are extremely concerned about the lack of adequate copyright protection for CAI program materials. Under existing copyright regulations, there is a widespread fear that these materials would be reproduced without compensation to the publisher of origin. In summary, the key to software availability lies in the development of lower cost hardware *and* copyright protection of CAI materials.

A Concluding Note

Intensive, systematic, interdisciplinary studies of the effectiveness of operational CAI projects are urgently required. If such studies validate the findings of the fragmented and limited studies which have been conducted, state of the art CAI systems might well make a dramatic impact upon remedial education at various levels: in the schools of our economically depressed urban and rural areas as well as in the skill and job training of the disadvantaged.

While this report has consistently qualified the limited evidence supporting the pedagogical potential of CAI, there is little doubt in the mind of the author—based on extensive experience with the application of educational technology—that the medium possesses tremendous potential for supporting the individualization of instruction. If this potential is to be realized within a reasonable time, a CAI system must be developed which possesses the data processing capabilities peculiarly required by the CAI process and the system must fall in a much lower price range than state of the art systems. Federal and state educational funding authorities must supply the initiative for this program of research and development.

18.

At Will and At Once: The Audio-Video Dial Access Information Retrieval System

by IRA J. SINGER
Asst. Superintendent
Instruction and Special Services
West Hartford Public Schools

The Purposes of Dial Access

The need to retrieve information "at will and at once" grows more pressing with each passing day. Although computers have been effective in solving vexing storage problems, relatively little companion technology has been developed for high-speed selection and retrieval of information in familiar audio and video modes. Students learning job skills at school, expectant mothers in the ghetto administering self-care during prenatal periods in pregnancy, teachers observing student (and teacher) behavior in a variety of teaching-learning situations, citizens requiring transportation directions to a nearby hospital—all are seekers of selected information at specific times for specific purposes. Relatively few packages of such information exist to satisfy these needs, but even where they do, they are not readily available to potential users on a demand basis. The major purpose of a dial access information retrieval system, then, is to enable learners at remote locations to dial and receive instantaneous access to a wide range of selected audio and video materials.

By the twirl of a mounted dial, the school-based student sitting in the privacy of a dial access carrel (or booth), can signal into action audio tapes containing poetry and dramatic readings, instrumental and vocal music, foreign language and art lectures, and countless other instructional programs. A change in the dial code can bring any film, video tape, slide or other visual material into view on the user's personal television screen. For example, the student studying urban development might dial a filmed interview of Robert Moses on urban planning, an audio tape by Louis Mumford on the impact of the automobile upon urban life, video-taped interviews of families awaiting eviction or relocation as a result of a redevelopment project, a chamber of commerce sound-slide program extolling the virtues of the project and a video tape of other local areas slated for future redevelopment.

In other carrels, or in classrooms where dial access programs may be viewed by groups of students on larger viewing screens, students pursuing an in-depth study of air and water pollution might dial a preselected segment of the film, "Poisons, Pests, and People," a video taped interview of Rachel Carson, recorded readings from "Silent Spring," a series of slides depicting lung and other respiratory ailments related to polluted air, a video tape of local sources of polluted water and smoke poisoned air, audio interviews of local businessmen justifying their dumping of wastes into inland waterways, and a video taped discussion of political leaders recommending corrective legislation and other possible remedies.

In addition to such special purpose materials, learners could dial video tapes containing instructional procedures basic to the school curriculum. For example, a student might obtain skill instruction in painting and sculpture techniques, the typing keyboard, wiring of circuit boards, repairing small appliances or fingering stringed or brass instruments via a dial access system. Originating in regional information centers, selected messages may be transmitted in audio and video modes via coaxial cable to individuals or groups dialing from a far-ranging cross-section of strategically placed remote locations.

The system can be useful for a variety of individuals dialing in from non-school locations. Medical, legal, and instructional tapes could be dialed by ghetto tenants from store fronts, laundromats, bus terminals, tenement lobbies and, eventually, living rooms. Users might include an unemployed family head requiring guidance for receipt of welfare benefits, a police suspect seeking legal aid, a high school youth needing information concerning the availability of after-school employment. Information basic to life itself but generally unavailable in convenient form to the ghetto resident can be made available on demand.

The Operation of Dial Access

The school based dial access system serves independent learners and groups of students. The major components of a dial access system are: a) a program origination center housing such equipment as video tape recorders, switching gear, audio tape decks, intercom console, and instructional software; b) coaxial cable required to carry programs from the originating center to the remote receiving points; c) the receiving locations (carrels and classrooms) containing the remote switching and demodulation equipment, television monitors, audio headsets.

The student using an independent study carrel would first obtain the title and description of any desired information through the school library file or special catalogue containing program descriptions. The desire to dial an audio or video tape may originate with the student doing an in-depth study of a specific topic or with his teacher assigning the program as part of a class project. Upon entering the carrel (a three-sided acoustically treated booth approximately 48" high, 42" wide, 36" deep with a 24" by 42" writing surface), the student is confronted by a 9" transistorized television receiver, double earphones with an attached microphone, and a telephone-type dial plate. The dial control plate has a conventional telephone dial, an on-off power switch, audio volume control knob, two headphone jacks, a three position intercom microphone switch, and an intercom signal lamp. The student may then dial a number as listed on his library or catalogue card and receive the picture or sound he requires. He may, if he wishes, call the origination center by intercom and ask for special programs. Another alternative open to the user is to dial a reference number and receive a TV scanning of all programming available at that particular time. The *variety* of programming that can be transmitted simultaneously is determined by the availability of pertinent software, the number of different pieces of originating equipment on hand (video tape recorders, audio tape decks, film chains), and the number of channels available via a single video cable.

The act of dialing the correct program number of a specific video tape in a remote carrel activates a video tape recorder in the origination center. The video signal is transmitted from the origination center via coaxial cable to the receiving location where it is converted to the images and sounds seen and heard by the learner.

A classroom is equipped with a 25" video monitor, a high fidelity sound column and a dial plate. The dial control plates in the classroom and carrels have the same telephone type dial, intercom facilities, and audio volume control.

One major difference between the carrel and classroom dial panels is the addition of audio and video input jacks. On each classroom panel, provisions have been made to connect a camera and microphone. This allows the system to make video and audio tapes by taking only a camera and sound system to the classroom. The bulky video tape recorder remains in the media center where it receives and records audio and video signals transmitted by cable from any one of the classroom panels.

School-Based Dial Access Network

In West Hartford, Connecticut, students in nine interconnected schools may select from a range of eight video channels and 32 audio channels simultaneously. In 1970, the program capacity of the system will be increased to 20 video programs and 100 audio programs. To serve such a system, the origination center must contain 20 different pieces of video equipment (video tape recorders, film chains, etc.) 100 audio tape decks, a video cable capable of carrying 20 video messages at one time, and related switch gear. The number of users is determined by the number of carrels and group areas receiving the signal. In West Hartford, approximately 1,500 students can dial into a single program generated by one video tape recorder. Or, since there are 40 different audio and video programs currently available, all 40 can be used simultaneously by students throughout the network with different purposes in mind. Through the use of regional networks incorporating schools, museums, seats of government, universities, community centers and other neighborhood gathering points, new and useful dialogues could begin. The advantages and drawbacks of such developments will be treated in detail later in this paper, but the potential of national and international (via satellite) systems interconnecting school and nonschool agencies is an intriguing prospect at this time.

The Dial Access Independent Study Carrel—A Rationale

Since modern teaching strategies stress the education of the individual, the development of an instant access electronic system was, perhaps, inevitable. Through the years, students have either surmounted or been submerged by the obstacles of the lockstep school and curriculum. In order to avoid controversy, assign "equal" teacher loads, conform to Carnegie units and grading demands, and cling to beloved but obsolete grouping practices, many educators have worshipped form rather than function. Uniform structures, self-contained classrooms, seven-period days, 50-minute periods, etc. have dictated the functions of learning. A unique feature of the American system is that the kindergartener enjoys greater freedom of choice than does the high school senior.

However, in recent years, several schools served as proving grounds for innovation in such areas as curriculum design, staff utilization, flexible schedule, and functional architecture. Teachers and administrators investigating traditional approaches to grouping, class size, facilities design, teacher role, and the utilization of technology have found many existing practices to be illogical, irrational, and without validity. Dissatisfied with their conclusions, these educators designed new patterns for instruction assigning introductory, provocative messages to large groups of students, conflicting points of view to small group discussion, and in-depth investigations to independent learners. The large group lecturer used additional planning time to present once that which he previously repeated five times each day. The teacher most capable and at ease in informal settings with small groups was encouraged to capitalize on these special talents. Time, materials, and facilities were provided teacher and student engaged in tutorial exchanges requiring privacy and concentration. New schools were designed with the high degree of flexibility essential to the instruction of groups of varying sizes and purposes.

Still, something was missing. Large group instruction threatened as a new orthodoxy; it contained a fatal fascination for schoolmen and tended to become terminal. The dynamic lecture personality, stimulating visual material, and additional planning time overshadowed the insulation and isolation of the individual in the large group. The large group method had a proper place in the strategy for change but, at best, performed only a fractional role.

Since small group work defied the lecture style of most teachers, administrators were hardput to staff seminars with capable personnel. Most small group meetings degenerated into facsimiles of teacher dominated large group lectures. Finally, many principals were unwilling to depart from the accepted daily pattern of 45-minute packages for all instructional tasks.

Independent study was confounded by unimaginative architecture, rigid staff deployment patterns, and the outdated nature of many instructional resources. Locker benches, library tables and study hall desks were not conducive to independent study. Little professional help, a lack of materials, and an excruciating need for privacy characterized these situations. The "dry" carrel (not equipped for electronic information retrieval) provided privacy and a partial answer to the use of nonprint media. Outlets were incorporated in some carrels to provide access to conventional audiovisual devices. However, this arrangement became impractical as many students, switching from medium to medium, moved in and out of carrels carrying various types of bulky devices. The student was limited to printed material and conventional "audiovisual" equipment. Hence, the advent of the "wet" carrel with electronic access to a variety of audio/video material.

The potential benefits of immediate access to selected segments of audio and video material, instruction in specific skill areas, and transmission of video programs containing legal, medical, insurance, transportation, voting and employment information to inner city areas have already been enumerated. There are, however, other arguments that could be mounted for expansion of the dial access system.

Reduction of Time Lag

For one thing, dial access reduces the time lag between the occurrence of an event and its perception by the learner. Despite the promise of television as an efficient means for mass dissemination, it has become increasingly apparent that students do not need the same thing at the same time. Put more precisely, they need what they need when they need it. Single-channel, fixed-schedule, educational TV cannot satisfy this diverse array of individual demands. For example, via dial access, a youngster performing on the football field can dial his performance immediately after the contest and review it with his coach; a group of young actors can dial themselves in action scene by scene following the day's rehearsal; a job applicant can view her manner and conversational technique following a role-played employment interview episode; a youngster with speech defects can view his lip movements after a speech exercise; a teacher can dial his own teaching performance following a session with small or large groups of students; an absentee can dial a lesson he missed; cultural events occurring in the vicinity of the school, taped by a mobile production crew, can be made immediately available for student viewing; educational "specials" taped off the air can be offered to individuals or groups the very next day for study and review.

Dial access enables a student to relive important experiences, albeit vicariously. In most conventional programs for the disadvantaged, the child visits an art gallery or a zoo when the teacher decides it is time for the group to take such a trip. The logistics of most school agencies require participation in large numbers in order to bring costs down and spread the benefits to all. Laudable purposes, no doubt, but contrary to the requirements of students expressing needs as individuals rather than as a group. The youngster returning from the art gallery must wait for the next trip (perhaps a year) before seeing a certain painting again. A child trying to re-create his trip to the zoo through an original sketch, song, or poem, might want to take another look at the funny giraffe's ungainly legs, loping stride, and quizzical look. Through dial access, he can dial his painting or giraffe on film or video tape without having to wait for next year's field trip.

Teacher Role

Use of the dial access system enables the teacher to spend more instructional time pursuing ideas and concepts with individuals and less time on rote and drill with groups. A science teacher can devote more time to the scientific concepts of a lesson when he does not feel compelled to spend such time demonstrating the proper use of lab equipment; an art teacher can spend more time studying the style and meaning of a student's work and less time in teaching that student how to hold the brush, mold the clay, etc.; the electronics instructor can do more tutorial and small group work on the theories of solid state circuitry while students learn the manual skills of circuit construction in the carrel through slide and video tape presentations.

The development of a remote control mechanism enabling the learner to control the start, stop, forward, reverse and pace of a tape, would also enhance the use of programmed learning techniques and materials through the presentation of sequential frames in audio and video modes. Programmed learning techniques remove some of the abrasive human contact suffered by ghetto-bound learners and offer, instead, infinite patience, success, and a "tutor" incapable of discriminating against a student because of his color, appearance, or wealth.

Catalyst for Dialogue

Perhaps the greatest promise of dial access lay in its potential as a catalyst for an electronic dialogue between poverty areas and health, education, and welfare agencies; between school systems and public libraries, museums, planataria, and hospitals; between community services centers and people at home; between classroom teachers, and university scholars—in short, a spectacular exchange between strangers. In the near future, professionals at home and abroad, via satellite, could dial into pre-packaged programs racked in international program banks and receive video and audio transmission in strategically placed remote carrels. Display facilities installed in hospital centers could provide interns, students, and general patients with medical, academic and occupational instruction. Teachers in training at schools of education equipped with dial access systems could dial into nearby public school classrooms to keep informed about current practices in urban, suburban and rural schools. The possibilities are truly limitless.

Liabilities of Dial Access

The comments thus far could be characterized as idealistic space age prose if not balanced by a rundown of the current limitations and liabilities of dial access systems. Therefore, such factors as high cost, teacher attitude, scheduling difficulties, lack of software, passive environment and hardware limitations should be carefully considered.

Costs and Related Factors

Dial access systems are expensive. Capital, installation, and transmission costs run high. Capable staff is difficult to find and must be paid accordingly. Since dial access installations are mechanical conveyances for instructional matter, they must be manned by technical as well as educational experts. An administrative director, technical staff, curriculum specialist and systems analyst are basic to any successful dial access operation. If local program production is part of the system, then a production supervisor, graphics specialist and camera crew must be employed. In addition, funds must be allocated for the purchase and development of software*.

An educators handbook, recently compiled at the Catholic University of America contains a survey showing the existence of 121 operational dial access systems in the country. Only 12 of these have a video capability with six of the 12 currently installed in elementary and secondary schools. The majority of systems are audio only and range in initial costs from $10,000 to more than $100,000, the median initial cost being $56,000. All video systems are in the $50-$100,000 initial cost range**.

Although initial costs are high, they begin to stabilize when the user population expands. The highest long-term continuing cost is for program transmission. In fact, the single greatest financial and technical obstacle to coast-to-coast or other long range interconnections for dial access, computer assisted instruction, or facsimile transmission is the cost of transmission. Line costs vary from area to area throughout the country and are often computed without rhyme or reason. Some AT&T subsidiaries can accommodate dial access systems, others cannot. Rates in our poorest states often exceed those in the wealthiest sections of the nation. Relief can come only through the establishment of special, low cost public service networks for schools and other public agencies***.

Teacher Attitudes

Conservative attitudes toward change and technology have been instrumental in retarding the use of dial access in education. Teachers are not dazzled by technology. Some are frightened, some are indifferent, some are enthusiastic. But all are somewhat skeptical and suspicious of the steel and antisepsis represented by a dial access system. They are primarily interested in:

1) the quality of the software displayed in the system
2) student reaction to this software
3) convenience in displaying the software
4) time allotted for program planning
5) additional compensation for dial access planning and activity extending beyond the school day
6) inservice knowledge of production techniques
7) current and complete data concerning content and location of available software
8) scheduling of system facilities
9) the right to decide, with the student, the nature of the content to be transmitted
10) the "feeling" that they are controlling the system and are part of its development.

*See Appendix A for sample costs of dial access components

**Ofeish, Gabriel, D. "Dial Access Information Retrieval Systems: Guidelines Handbook for Educators," Office of Education, Bureau of Research, U.S. Department of Health, Education and Welfare, July 1968.

*** In West Hartford where distance is moderate and 12-channel video cable is available, sample costs for transmitting eight video and 40 audio channels from originating point to 50 installations in eight satellite school buildings over a cumulative distance of 12 miles, amount to $360/month for video and $250/month for audio rental with a one time network and headend installation charge of $35,000. This will increase in 1970 when the new Hall High School opens and offers 100 audio and 20 video channels to program users.

These ends can be accomplished through some of the traditional communications techniques—committees, demonstrations, newsletters, etc. However, the most important attitude to engender is the desire to use the system or to advise a student to use it. A teacher who takes part in the planning of the system's development, attends content-oriented seminars taught by content (not audiovisual) experts using components of the new technology, and is offered incentive for such participation is a likely supporter and user of the dial access system. The teacher pressed into participation, after the fact, through promotion and demonstration of hardware only, will merely confim initial suspicions of the entire enterprise. An inservice program committed to the proposition that teachers who learn via the new technology tend to teach that way, will enhance the probability of developing positive teacher attitudes.

The Software Problem

The very accessibility of dial access to individual users in remote areas offers exciting new possibilities for testing the effect of media (as an isolated variable) upon the lives of individuals and institutions. However, Marshall McLuhan notwithstanding, teachers, students and other potential users continue to seek the message; and much of the message incorporated in the current software catalogue is weak, limited, obsolete, and dull. Terrible gaps in important instructional areas have given credence to the charge that education is software poor.

A headlong dash to design sophisticated hardware has preoccupied the education industry. The subordinate and defensive position assumed by software producers has confirmed the jittery attitudes of many already reactionary educators. Unwilling to depart from the profit proven software staples, producers prefer to cater to this conservatism. Until recently, few significant attempts have been made to produce provocative, short burst (30 seconds—5 minute) items for the educational market. The traditional 28-50 minute format of the educational film is generally unacceptable for dial access viewing.

Software deficiencies and the uniqueness of the dial access system make school based production centers more important than initially envisioned. The paucity of good material, the uneasy status of copyright legislation, and the natural bent of staff members to produce original visuals have resulted in the establishment of local studios. However, it would be foolhardy for school systems, or even regional centers, to compete with commercial or ETV stations and education industries, in the production of software. Therefore, a new and unorthodox liaison between the schools and industry is important. Software producers must conduct a scientific, grass roots search for new types of educational materials tailored for a rich mix of learning styles and behaviors as defined by educators working in innovative school systems. Such a strategy encourages experimentation and production based upon curricular needs. The incentive for the corporation is access to a fertile laboratory where identification and field testing of instructional materials for quality and marketability may occur. For the school system, the rewards may be found in the industry's production resources and specialized personnel.

If the "partnership" between industry and education continues to be a front or showcase, rather than a fact, many school districts already pressed to the limit in taxing for school purposes, will continue to shun change. Categorical subsidies from federal or state sources to private companies, small and large, for funding the design and manufacture of experimental materials as loss items might provide some relief. After a reasonable testing period, financial aid could be withdrawn and the materials left to stand on their own. Such subsidies could be requested by local agencies through categorical grants available under ESEA 89-10, NDEA or the National Science Foundation.

Another possible solution to the problem of software poverty is a string of federally funded production centers staffed with competent TV and production specialists, artists, and script writers, producing programs and low cost materials upon request from regional education laboratories and supplementary services centers. The success of federally funded National Science Foundation project materials has dispelled many fears of federal intrusion in curricular matters. Although the federal production center is political dynamite (and a last resort) it may be the only way to insure a steady output of custom tailored high quality, low cost materials to schools and other public institutions.

Copyright Problem

If the school is to prescribe individualized programs for all students, then pertinent bits and pieces of existing materials must be utilized. The copyright laws will have to be molded to fit this radically new apparatus for independent learning. Although the creator of an educational product should be guaranteed a fair return for his work, the public school should not be expected to pay royalties similar to those paid by commercial networks or publishers. It is imperative that legislators look carefully at systems which allow thousands of students to dial a series of maps, diagrams, or recordings before deciding on what the school must pay for this privilege.

The Carrel—Active or Passive Environment

The dial access carrel has been justly criticized as a passive environment. Although a convenient multisensory dimension has been provided through the combination of viewing screen and headphones, little active physical involvement is required of the student. Carrels at some installations contain record-active microphones which permit students to record responses to audio stimuli and to redial the tape after it recycles for comparison of master and student tracks. A similar feat may be accomplished for video purposes by placing a camera in some carrels in order to video tape student performances of various physical skills. These tapes could then be redialed, played back and compared to the master tape for self correction by the student.

   Computer terminals can also be located in carrel areas making for a more active environment. The ratio of terminals to carrels would depend upon the nature of the training agency and the emphasis of its curriculum. The display properties of the dial access screen could be combined with the manipulative, problem solving functions of a data set connected to a high speed computer. Problems, exercises, and games could be presented in the carrel. The learner could then proceed to a convenient computer terminal to complete his assignments.

   Another companion system available to the dial access carrel is the student activated multiple response system. Tests and other stimuli can be presented via the dial access screen soliciting multiple choice responses through the provision of a four or five position button selector at each carrel. This can be connected, in turn, to a master console visible to an instructor, or to a computer for the generation of student achievement or attitude data necessary for student growing, profiles, and similar purposes.

The High Cost of Limited Access

Current dial access systems suffer restrictions on the number of channels available to individuals with different interests simultaneously vying for available channel time (limited access). The ultimate in individualized instruction would enable each student to gain access to his own video and audio program source at anytime during the school day (random access). Due to technical limitations and high costs, however, it is unlikely that 500 students in a given school would be able to dial into different video programs simultaneously. Five hundred pieces of originating equipment is simply not affordable by single school districts. Government funding and regionalization are potential alternatives for relief from the high cost dilemma. For example, ten school systems within a given state could apply for state and/or Federal assistance for a regional network of dial access programs. Each system could reserve a given number of video and audio channels for its exclusive use. School system A could reserve 10 video and 50 audio channels; system B might desire 20 video and 100 audio channels, etc. One large program center could provide the switching, intercom, originating equipment, graphics, TV studio and software storage space. If no such building was available in the region, several centers could be established in order to decentralize some of the functions.

Mechanical Conflicts

Dial access hardware contains other built-in limitations. Although instant access is possible, any channel may be tied up by one student dialing a program from any carrel. Another student dialing into the middle of an ongoing program must "join" it at his point of entry or wait for the recycling of the sequence. Particularly vexing is the four track tape deck. Once an audio signal contained on one track is dialed, all four begin simultaneously. This has the effect of forcing new dialers into ongoing sequences on the three remaining tracks. Although an economy in operation, the four track tapedeck is a hindrance to individualized instruction.

Computerized Random Access

Several new developments promise to add some flexibility to the system. A random search device developed by several companies permits the student to dial any pre-selected tape segment over an open channel. Another evolutionary step in giving each student full control over the selection and operation of any program is a random access high speed slave tape system. Now being developed for audio dial access systems in Oak Park, Illinois, the computer controlled random access storage bank contains several multiple-track master tapes on which individual 15-minute lessons have been recorded. The carrel is equipped with a high speed recording device able to copy any one 15-minute program in the storage bank, make the copy available to the student, and free the master tape for another student immediately. Once the slave tape is made, the student has complete control at his carrel. While it remains to be seen whether video tapes can be reproduced in similar speed and fashion, the high speed copy technique should add a highly desirable aspect of flexibility to dial access systems.

Other attempts at providing flexibility are stop-gap. They involve imaginative scheduling and programming arrangements, reserved information channels, assigned time segments of individual channels, extended group use of basic programs, and staggered carrel assignments for daily use. Computer controlled search, retrieve, and load devices are sorely needed. Most program orders are now being placed in writing or via an intercom. Upon receipt of the written or verbal request, an assistant must locate the desired item, retrieve it and load it before the automatic dial start goes into action. The time involved in such activity is wateful and restrictive.

The need for random access is particularly apparent in West Hartford, Connecticut where Hall High School, slated to open in 1970, will contain a production and media center transmitting 120 programs (20 video, 100 audio) to 100 dial select carrels and 50 group stations. This expanded program capacity will also be made available to nine other dial select schools (including one in the city of Hartford) through a cable network system currently offering eight video and 32 audio channels. One is staggered by the enormous potential of such an installation. If the optimum length for a single program is 20 minutes, then a single channel is capable of carrying three programs per hour. With 120 channels the system capacity becomes 120 (channels) × 3 (programs) or 360 programs per hour. A five-hour day would theoretically provide the setting for 1,800 programs daily; and a five-day week would mean a weekly capacity of 9,000 programs. The mathematics is stunning and, at best, suggests that electronics has provided a feasible way for individualizing instruction within a mass educational system. However, before any such conclusions may be reached, random access and retrieval is required.

Dial Access and EVR

Many of the current technical limitations cited above may be solved by the advent of electronic video recording (EVR). Invented by Dr. Peter Goldmark, President of CBS Laboratories, EVR promises to cut hardware costs by 75 percent while increasing program capacity a minimum of tenfold. The EVR device contains a small cartridge incorporating one hour of black and white or one half hour of color programming on EVR film. Individual frames on each of two tracks can be scrolled by the viewer frame-by-frame as a reader turns the pages of a book. The viewer may switch at any time from track to track, controlling the action through a single lever mounted on the EVR device. The device itself is similar in appearance to an audio tape recorder weighing approximately 35 pounds. By connecting the EVR device to the terminals of any home TV receiver, a viewer can see the program of his choice played back on the receiver screen. The racking of EVR devices (instead of video tape recorders) in dial access program centers can lead to greater program flexibility as well as system economy. It is anticipated that users dialing into EVR devices from a variety of locations, could control the pace and sequence of EVR programs through the simple manipulation of a control lever mounted on the remote carrel's dial plate. The combination of remote control EVR with a computer controlled search, retrieve and load device (similar to the ordinary jukebox) could remove many of the limitations of current dial access systems.

Evaluation of Dial Access

Actually, little evaluation of dial access systems of an empirical nature has been done. That is best explained, perhaps, by the nature of the system itself. Since dial select is a synthesis of a variety of multi-media techniques, it does not seem immediately appropriate to repeat traditional studies of TV vs. conventional methods of instruction, since such studies are already available. For example, Wilbur Schramm in 1964 reported a comprehensive analysis of the evidence on learning via ETV in his "What We Know About Learning From Instructional Television"*. In 1964, the Schramm Institute also compiled some 300 abstracts of research on instructional television and film representing a substantial sampling of research done between 1950 and 1964. Mere replication of such studies for dial select would add little to the literature. However, developmental studies concerning the application of this research in terms of the system and its components can be significant. Dial access is a system, more like a library than a single book, and is as difficult to evaluate with precision

---

*Schramm, Wilbur, "What We Know About Learning From Instructional Television," Education Television: The Next Ten Years. *Stanford: Institute for Communication Research, 1962.*

as is the library. To assess, for example, the precise educational output of a library is an impossible task. A perfectly controlled experiment to "prove" that the library produced certain valuable outputs would be near impossible. For the same reasons, the nature of dial access as a system precludes its evaluation through "definitive" small scale tests here and there.

Finally, the focus on developmental evaluation must be on *how* to affect certain things through dial access not on *what* are effects. For example, one might ask "What are the effects of dial access on student interest?" If initially, dial access affects student interest positively, so much the better. But the developmental evaluation question will probably be 'more like this: "How is dial access used to affect student interest positively—if 'student interest' is a serious and long range issue relative to dial access?" Since considerable research has been done on the effects of television and other components of dial access on learning, a more useful technique would be to determine how student learning might be enhanced through a variety of creative uses of the dial access system and a description of such uses. Future developmental investigations should attempt to depict the current position of dial access relative to two poles, namely the teaching and learning conditions pre-dial access, and teaching and learning conditions as they "should be" when dial access is fully developed.

Summary

It seems clear that the following developments must occur if dial access audio-video systems are to succeed and proliferate:

> a) A concerted attempt must be made by education and the new education industry to produce high quality, provocative software based on student and curricular needs.

> b) A program must be constructed stressing a positive, content oriented approach to teacher training. Teachers impressed by the message should be treated to a synthesis of content, method, and media in their in-service training.

> c) Hardware must be designed and produced stressing flexibility, economy, durability, and reliability. Subservient to the needs of the program, the hardware must be dependable enough to contribute to the development of positive user attitudes. Particularly important now is the development of computerized random access system controls, lower costs components and a merged EVR and dial access system.

The federal government can contribute to dial access research and development through projects and agencies funded under the Elementary and Secondary Education Act of 1965 and the Educational Professional Development Act of 1968. Specifically, the government should urge that selected Title III supplementary services centers, regional laboratories, and other centralized agencies serve as urban communications centers incorporating audio and video program banks available through dial access to people living throughout the city.

It is also urgent that dial access communication centers extend beyond the borders of "education". New instructional techniques and technology should be employed to convey information and service in the areas of health, welfare, law, transportation, housing and employment. Community centers incorporating manpower recruiting offices, housing exchanges, medical clinics, legal aid societies, facilities for training in the performing arts, and vocational training facilities should be located in the vicinity of school-oriented audio-video program banks, handicapped children's programs, in-service teacher training centers, film libraries, data retrieval centers, graphics and publications services, and modest television production facilities for the preparation of special video tapes to be transmitted to the community as new needs arise.

The appetite of Americans for information is enormous. Negative attitudes toward mechanical delivery of such information are not quite as prevalent as they once were. Better software is beginning to appear. New sources of funding are being tapped. Approached in a systematic manner, assigning first priority to user needs, the future development of dial access systems can bring significant benefits to all.

Appendix A
Sample Cost Estimates for Dial Access Systems
(Approximate)

Component	Unit Cost	Costs for 10 positions receiving 6 video and 20 audio programs	Costs for 40 positions receiving 6 video and 20 audio programs
Video tape recorder*	$4,000	$24,000	$24,000
Audio tape decks	350	7,000	7,000
Film chain	3,000	3,000	3,000
Intercom	2,500	2,500	2,500
Demodulator video	350	2,100	2,100
Video input amplifier	150	900	900
Video output amplifier	100	600	600
Telephone line equalizers	100	600	600
Carrels (including dial plate, microphone and headset)	250	2,500	10,000
Carrel 9" TV monitor	225	2,250	9,000
Classroom 23" TV monitor with amplifier**	325	–	–
Miscellaneous (frames, cabinets, etc.)		1,500	2,500
Video switching		4,800	14,000
Audio switching		3,500	9,500
TOTAL		$55,250	$85,700
Plus installation costs —approximately 10%		5,500	8,500
GRAND TOTAL		$60,750	$94,200

The reader will note that the system becomes more economical to install as the number of positions increases. The allocation of certain equipment (video tape recorders, amplifiers, etc.) is based upon the number of *inputs* and can serve any number of positions. This equipment increases in quantity (and gross cost) as new program channels are added. Other

---

*New dial access video playback decks have been developed for approximately $1,500. The $4,000 video tape recorder above receives in color—a $500 modification enables it to distribute color. (For remote color reception, the installation of color receivers is necessary.)

**All positions are considered as individual carrels—no classroom monitors are included. However, one can estimate that one classroom installation serves from 25 to 125 users.

equipment (carrels, monitors, etc.) is based upon the number of *positions* and will increase in quantity (and gross cost) as the user population grows.

The above estimate does *not* include cost estimates for staff, consultants, local production facilities, or software—all necessary considerations when planning for a dial access installation.

See Appendix B for transmission and installation costs.

Appendix B

Sample Transmission Rates for Dial Access Systems in the New England Area*

Audio Rate (Monthly)

voice grade—	$1.50 for the first quarter mile
	.40 each additional quarter mile
signal line—	1.10 for the first quarter mile
	.30 each additional quarter mile

Installation (one time)

voice grade—	$10 per circuit
signal line—	7 per circuit

Cable Video Rate (Monthly)

		Installation (one time)
first channel—	$9.50/ ¼ mi.	$760/ ¼ mi.
second channel—	1.00/ ¼ mi.	$475/ ¼ mi.
third channel—	1.00/ ¼ mi.	$375/ ¼ mi.
channels four through twelve—	1.00/ ¼ mi. per channel	No installation charge

Input Video Rate (at Head End)

first input—	$10.00/ month	$850
second input—	9.00/ month	$475
third input—	9.00/ month	$475
inputs four through twelve—	8.00/ input per mo.	No installation charge

Output Video Rate (at Receiving End)

output one through twelve—	$ 2.00/ month per output	No installation charge

RELATED REFERENCES ON DIAL ACCESS SYSTEMS

Arnoff, Mary S. "Nova's Dial Access Retrieval System." *Audiovisual Instruction,* XII, No. 5 (May 1967), 470–71.

"Beverly Hills Schools' Experimental Information Retrieval System" *Audiovisual Instruction,* XII, No. 5 (May 1967), 478–79.

Brish, William M. "Five Years with Television Instruction," *Report on Washington County Schools* Closed-Circuit Television, Hagerstown, Maryland. 1964.

Brown, James W. and Kenneth Norberg. *"Administering Educational Media."* New York, McGraw-Hill Book Company, 1965.

*These rates are approximate and subject to change.

Green, Alan C., Ed. *Educational Facilities with New Media.* Washington, Department of Audiovisual Instruction, National Education Association.

Howe II, Harold. *"Realities of the Learning Market."* School Library Journal, January 16, 1967, 29–33.

"The Impact of Technology on the Library Building." *Educational Facilities Laboratories,* New York, New York, 1968.

Lieberman, Myron. "Big Business, Technology, and Education." *Phi Delta Kappan* January 1967, 185–86.

McClendon, Paul I. "Oral Roberts University's Dial Access Audio-Video System." *Audiovisual Instruction,* XII, No. 5, May 1967, 464–66.

North, R. Stafford. "Oklahoma Christian College's Dial Access Retrieval System." *Audiovisual Instruction,* XII, No. 5, May 1967, 468–69.

Ofiesh, Gabriel, D. "Dial Access Information Retrieval Systems: Guidelines Handbook for Educators." *Office of Education,* Bureau of Research, U.S. Department of Health, Education and Welfare, July 1968.

Schramm, Wilbur. "What We Know About Learning From Instructional Television." *Educational Television: The Next Ten Years.* Stanford: Institute for Communication Research, 1962.

Singer, Ira J. "The Dial Select Story—West Hartford, Connecticut." *Audiovisual Instruction,* XII, No. 5, May 1967, 446–49.

Singer, Ira J. "Media and the Ghetto School." *Audiovisual Instruction,* XII, No. 5, October 1968, 860–864.

Skornia, Harry J. "What We Know From New Media Research." *NAEB Journal,* XXV, No. 2, May/April 1966, 26–37.

Trump, J. Lloyd. "Images of the Future." *National Association of Secondary School Principals,* Washington, D.C. 1959.

Trump, J. Lloyd, Baynham, Dorsey. "Focus on Change: Guide to Better Schools." *Rand McNally,* Chicago, 1961.

Wisniewski, Ray. "Grand Valley State College's Dial Access Retrieval System." *Audiovisual Instruction,* May 1967.

19.
Adaptive Machine Aids to Learning

by *JOHN A. STARKWEATHER*
Dir., Off. of Information Systems
San Francisco Medical Center
Univ. of California

Instructional technology is a topic which includes consideration of a wide array of devices developed as aids to learning. Some of these, most notably those which make use of computers, have the capacity to interact with their users. They may make use of feedback information to adapt to the user's needs and to improve their future performance. It is with this emphasis on man-machine relationships and on machine evolution that I address the question: "What is the outlook for the development and application of cybernetics in instructional technology?"

In comparison with man's evolution, the presently observable rate of change of the machine capability is many times faster. We must assume that there will continue to be a rapid reduction in size and cost of computers, for example, while at the same time they increase in speed, reliability, and functional capability. It seems possible that machines will become self-sustaining, with self-regulated growth, automatic repair, and reproduction of further related machines. A machine system will make use of information about the needs of its users to regulate its functioning in a self-adaptive manner. Computers and their related end-organs and communication devices will in turn become simulated counselors, mathematicians, clerks, designers, reference librarians, tutors, etc. as the specific need for assistance changes.

The Background of Machine Assistance to Learning

The present level of interest in programmed instruction and automated teaching received its major impetus from a paper by B. F. Skinner in 1954 (Skinner, 1954), although Pressey had been attempting to arouse interest in the field since the 1920's (Pressey, S.L., 1926, 1950). At a symposium in 1958, Rath, Andersen, and Brainerd reported work done by them at the IBM Corporation Watson Research Center in which a digital computer was used not as a teaching device itself, but as a means of simulating teaching machines (Rath et al, 1959). They felt at the time that the ideal of putting a student in direct contact with a computer was economically unsound. Only a year later Lumsdaine, in referring to their work said, "This may seem like a fantastic degree of instrumentation, but it actually has practical possibilities for future development." (Lumsdaine, 1960).

Work did continue towards relating the computer to teaching not only at IBM, but at such places as Bolt Beranek and Newman and Systems Development Corp. At the University of Illinois, Bitzer and Alpert began designing learning stations which linked the student or curriculum author with the computer. In 1961 a conference on computers and education was sponsored by System Development Corp. and the Office of Naval Research. Zinn (1968) counted 11 curriculum packages finished or underway at the time of the conference.

Today, with developments in computer design and construction and in systems programming, there has been a great amount of work both in this country and abroad in this field which has come to be called "Computer-Assisted Instruction" (CAI). A recent survey (Hickey, Newton, 1967) listed 240 publications concerning CAI that had appeared between 1959 and 1967, and identified 20 major centers in the United States where large digital computers were dedicated for instructional systems.

Ten years back, when the ideas for computer teaching were first materializing, placing a student in real-time communication with a large scale computer for purposes of learning was thought wildly unfeasible on economic grounds. Now the hardware exists to accomplish this relationship at a cost no greater than that of an individual tutor. Ten years from now, it seems safe to predict, the cost of providing computer-assisted instruction will be no greater than the cost of instruction in classes of ten or less.

This optimism is reflected in the August 1, 1968 issue of Forbes magazine, its reporter claims CAI will become big business, bigger in fact than textiles, rubber, or paper. He notes: ". . . But the sharpest rate of gain (in educational expenditures) is almost certainly going to be in spending for machines and programs to enable teachers to teach more effectively and efficiently. At present, total spending in this area is only about $2 billion a year, most of it in textbooks. That $2 billion could easily swell to $10 billion within the next six years, with old-fashioned textbooks getting a smaller and smaller proportion."

A number of writers have noted that tomorrow's education will become less and less a matter of imparting facts to be learned and it will more and more involve teaching the skills of inquiry and problem solving. To do this we must have ways to give the student practice in inquiry and in problem solving and we must have ways to give him greater initiative in the teaching and learning process. Three potential characteristics of computer-based systems will be particularly relevant in providing greater control to the student. These are: a.) the capacity to analyze and respond to relatively unconstrained input from the student; b.) rapid access to extensive capabilities for information storage and retrieval, graphic displays, mathematical analyses and transformations; c.) potentially unlimited competence in the field of instruction by access to the collected insight, experience, and creativity of large numbers of teachers.

As we delve deeper for the potentials of CAI, it will be increasingly useful to look at the teaching-learning process. This process involves the presentation to a student of the material to be learned, the evoking of an active participation by the student in response to this presented material, the evaluation of the student's response, a decision on the part of the teacher as to what material should be presented next, and finally, in good teaching, an evaluation of the teaching process and modification of the whole scheme in light of the outcomes attained. This process may be represented briefly as a seven-stage process:

1) Initial presentation.   5) Collection of outcome data.
2) Student response.   6) Analysis of outcome data.
3) Evaluation of response.   7) Modification of the teaching program.
4) Modified presentation.

We can evaluate each of the common teaching techniques in each phase of the teaching-learning situation. The devices we shall consider are: books, lectures, non-computerized

Teaching Method

	Books	Lecture	Tutorial or small group	Noncomputerized programmed instruction	Computer-Assisted learning
1. Initial Presentation	Efficient maybe elegant (1)	Efficient maybe elegant (2)	Costly, maybe elegant (3)	Inefficient, few elegant examples (4)	Potentially as efficient and elegant as books & lectures since they may be used (1.5)
2. Student response	Un-programmed (4)	Un-programmed (4)	Optimal, but subject to un-programmed variations (1)	Limited (3)	Minimum limitations (2)
3. Evaluation of student response	None (5)	Limited to gross evaluation (restlessness, sleeping) (4)	Limited only by teacher's ability to divide attention (1)	Linear programs, student compares his response with answer(s) given; branching programs, some flexibility (3)	Substantial flexibility (2)
4. Modified presentation possible to accommodate individual student needs	No (4)	No (4)	Can be modified (1)	Linear programs, "tracking"; Branching programs, some modification (3)	Can be modified (2)
5. Collection of outcome data	Tests only (4)	Tests only (4)	Tests, teacher's memory of participation (3)	Recording of responses on paper (2)	Recording of responses in computer compatible form (1)
6. Analysis of outcome data	Typically, test statistics may be compared with those from other years, other courses, other schools (3)	(3)	(3)	Typically item statistics examined frequently during development. (2)	On line analysis possible (1)
7. Re-design of teaching	Select different book or revise (5)	Revise lectures for next year, or next week (4)	Intuitive changes in course design. (3)	Revise program frames where difficulties have been pinpointed (2)	On line modifications could be built into system. Students can be prompted to "challenge" the program in order to improve it. (1)
Sum of ranks	26	25	15	19	10.5

teaching machines, individual tutorial relations with a live instructor, and computer-assisted instruction. Chart 1 presents a summary comparison of the various phases of the teaching-learning process. If ranks (the numbers in parentheses) are assigned in terms of relative merit at handling each phase and summed over seven phases, computer-assisted instruction appears to have an advantage over the next best method, tutorial or seminar presentation. Of course, this result is achieved only by introducing functions that the tutorial method has not traditionally attended to in an explicit way. Variations in weighting the different phases could alter this conclusion, but the potential advantages of computer-assisted instruction are sufficient to warrant considerable efforts at exploration.

Current Status

Computer-assisted instruction is suffering some ill effects in reputation as a result of the overpromotion which occurred with programmed instruction (booklets, multiple-choice filmstrips, branching books, etc.) in the last few years. For example, a former principal of a school where many new methods were tried, recently wrote that ". . . programmed learning has been oversold, overrated, overpriced and underproductive." (Meyer, 1968). As a result of early predictions that programmed learning would offer individualized instruction for those with different abilities and match or exceed the efficiency of teachers, almost a third of all secondary schools now use some form of programmed instruction. These materials were promoted, however, long before carefully developed programs were designed. Individualized instruction was usually sacrificed to a standard instructional sequence and to the use of standard, centrally produced materials. The mismatch of materials and students has led to complaints of boredom and frustration by students, and the materials have not been built with internal mechanisms capable of response to such problems.

Computer assistance to learning, or computer-assisted instruction, is presently suffering from some similar problems. The methods of program development are cumbersome and still costly in relation to other learning aids. The programs do not handle free conversational interaction as easily as responses which are rigidly formatted as true-false or multiple-choice. Once the programs are specified, they are not easily changed to fit local needs. Most examples of computer instruction in present use are therefore characterized by multiple-choice responses which engage a student in drill of basic skills. Such operation is not a great advance beyond a programmed instruction booklet, though the computer can be used to collect automatically a great deal of information about individual student progress and to analyze it for secondary data on program efficiency.

A book of readings on computer-assisted instruction is currently in press, to be published by Academic Press in the first half of 1969. The editors, R. Atkinson and H. Wilson, have included a paper of their own which is probably the most extensive study to date of student progress as seen in automatically collected data.

Directions of Development

The development of methods of interaction with computers which are more global, more problem-centered and more human-like is coupled with the development of remotely connected terminal hardware or separate small computers. The combined effect is to make more likely the personal use of the computer, perhaps in some ways like we make personal use of the automobile. Orr (1968, preface) describes an imaginary development of the internal-combustion engine as if it had been developed in a way analogous to what is happening with computers. He imagines that transportation methods remained very primitive until about 1944. Then, as part of wartime needs, someone invented the internal-combustion engine and hitched it to a huge trailer to carry big guns for the Army. Engineers then began to use it for heavy laboratory equipment. Next business developed uses for it, perhaps about 1953, and highways, service stations, and related facilities were built. The technology then rapidly improved to the point that it became practical to provide individual transportation. Quite aside from the mixed blessing represented by the personal automobile, its assimilation on this kind of timetable would have produced a good deal of cultural shock, perhaps similar to what we will experience with the computer. Like the automobile, computer systems used for aids to learning will not require that the user know very much of what goes on "under the hood."

To carry the analogy a step farther, we seem to put up with many disadvantages of the automobile, mostly physical problems, because it offers a measure of personal autonomy, freedom, and mobility. We can feel that we drive the machine rather than the reverse. As we develop a personal relationship with an adaptive computer assistant, we may be able to have similar feelings about it. While past frontiers for man have been physical ones, and our heritage has emphasized values of independence and individual initiative in overcoming them, the new frontier for man has to be seen in the area of intellectual rather than physical effort. Man's initiative must be applied to adaptation to increasingly complex technology, an excellent description of the challenge facing education in general.

Can educational technology assist in meeting the educational challenge which is largely the result of technology? Those who work in technological areas and who face the need for constant learning of new skills, techniques, and knowledge are those most likely to answer positively. During the same time that employment figures for scientists, engineers, technicians, and science teachers has been growing at a rate more than three times that of the United States population, an engineer's knowledge has been estimated to be sufficient for only 50 percent effectiveness after between five to ten year post graduation. Unless an engineer continues to re-educate himself, he may find himself unemployable. Technology's rapid growth thus creates a direct need for continuing education. As we increase the amount of computer-aided thinking, we will increase the rate of technological growth, and also increase the demand for technically trained people, who, of course, use computer-aided thinking. They are most likely to seek their education by similar means. A report by The Commission on College Physics (1965) serves as an example.

It appears that computer-based access to self-assessment as well as instructional material has particular usefullness at the continuing education level. Areas of weakness or gaps in knowledge are likely to be individually different, and a professional who is already at work may be much more comfortable in exploring his own competence in private than in public. At other levels of education as well, an especially effective use of computer assistance will likely be through the development of short programs which will be used as the student needs them and chooses them to fill discovered gaps in knowledge. It is one way that education may become more flexible and responsive to the needs of students. It is also a way that education will find many more "students" in the general public than are now apparent.

The mass market of the general public provides a potentially huge spectrum of possibilities and problems. The public has a tremendous appetite for learning and has a clear need for easy access to increasing amounts of information. The availability of television receivers is so widespread that it seems most likely that public access to information technology in the future will develop with some relationship to television. Information of special interest to the viewer is of course currently a matter of station scheduling and a viewer's ability to match that schedule. Even modest attempts to involve television viewers, such as the self-administered testing used in the nation-wide driver tests during 1967 and 1968, seemed to increase the television viewer's motivation and his ability to learn the material. While there is undoubtedly a motivational aspect to live television there will be considerable advantages to the viewer-learner with the advent of easily handled videotape cartridges which he can schedule to meet his own needs. If this technology further develops without undue expense to allow fairly rapid random access to different portions of such videotape material, the more individual aspects of computer-assisted instruction then become possible.

The Development of Criteria

Anyone who sets out to improve instructional methods soon realizes that objectives and criteria for successful instruction are seldom specified in sufficiently specific terms that they can be useful for measurement and evaluation of the instructional process. When the process is an experimental one, such as various means by which the computer is involved in learning and instruction, a specific listing of objectives and criteria of performance is especially valuable. Such information can be fed back to a program author who may be in a position to compare more than one method of presentation of the curriculum materials. If the criteria are sufficiently objective and measurable then statistical techniques such as discriminant function analysis or factor analysis may be used to discover which items of input are especially relevant to the outcome. Such measures are also of course necessary to make comparisons of methods which have different costs and to develop a relationship between costs and outcomes.

A good case can be made for the belief that instructional objectives should be stated in terms of observable behavior that can be expected from a student at the completion of the sequence. During the course of learning, a student should be in a position to practice the behavior which he is trying to master. This may seem to be a platitude, but medical students for example, are too often asked to give a list of signs and symptoms associated with a disease, and get less practice in attempting to solve a diagnostic problem on the basis of presented symptoms. Interactive instruction can allow a student to practice behavior which is closer to his eventual goal.

Meeting the Needs of Users

Corrective feedback can be a powerful mechanism in the control of any dynamic process and an especially valuable one in the development of new procedures which cannot be completely predicted in advance to their operation. In developing a programmed interaction between man and machine we must be particularly cautious in settling on a method which seems to work well in one instance. A change in context and setting seems to have a powerful effect on such interaction, and sometimes with disruptive results. This concern can be addressed by arranging for such systems of man-machine interaction to have a mechanism by which the user can record comments about its handling of his responses or comment on its occasional malfunction. Such comments should be put to use as rapidly as possible with a resulting improvement in succeeding interactions. A developer of such systems should leave matters of curriculum content in the hands of professionals in the specific subject matter area, but he should provide them with methods by which they can receive corrective feedback information from students who face the material and with methods which make it easy for them to review such feedback and take corrective action. It is possible and usual for human instructors to make use of centrally produced standard text books and other curriculum aids and it is possible for them to interpret such materials in a specific local context and assist the student to understand them. It is exceedingly difficult, and it seems to me impossible, for computer programs in their present stage of development to accomplish this same task. We should therefore not expect to produce centralized standard curriculum materials for computer presentation except in very basic areas of routine drill. We may produce examples and a point of departure for the local instructor by providing centrally-produced materials. He should be in a position, however, to test these materials and modify them easily to meet the needs of local context and local customs.

An interesting variety of this problem occurs in arranging for a computer program to recognize and "understand" the language produced by a student or other user in a conversational situation. We may assume that the author of such a program will have such versatile mechanisms at hand. Even so, he cannot predict the entire range of possible responses to a question which does not severely limit the format of the reply. If the situation is such that the author can expect feedback from test subjects who face his program, then it is sufficient for him to write only an initial skeleton which he expects will fail on first attempts. Information from the user will then let him quickly add other elements of recognition so that the program rapidly improves.

One can imagine improving this process in a way which might make program development much less painful from the author's standpoint. Future versions of an author language might have provision for an active monitor or proctor terminal where an author-instructor would sit and converse with a student who sits at a separate terminal. It is conceivable that a program could be written to not only record appropriate portions of this interaction but also abstract, from the spontaneous return from the author, elements necessary for the construction of automatic replies. On successive runs with new students the program would first attempt to recognize the student's reply by virtue of these previously recorded elements and in the event of failure indicate at the monitor terminal that the author should insert a new human response. An iterative process of this sort might result in the building of a functioning program which would progressively handle more and more responses. Before long the author could step aside from the process.

If a program were to be transplanted and used in a context where the language characteristics of students were different from its original location, then a similar process would have to be undertaken in order to bring the program into line with the new setting. For example, it is clear that the language background of students in central city schools is likely to be quite different from those found in suburban districts. A computer program which recognizes the language in one setting will quite likely fail in the other. The required process of translation for such a program may result in new knowledge about language habits in the two environments. In any case, the program should be readable and easily modified by someone who is on the scene in the new setting.

Requirements for a Computer System to Handle Conversational Interaction

The preceeding discussion suggests that a language for writing conversational interaction, built to recognize appropriate elements of naturally occuring language, should have a high level of readability and editing methods which make it as easy as possible for a person who has curriculum concerns at the local level to make changes in the program to meet local needs. He should have a means to record comments about its operation from students and users and make use of these to change and improve the program. It would be especially valuable for the system to have a subset of mechanisms for simple operation and easy entry to its use. With such mechanisms, a local teacher or a curriculum coordinator could make use of the language with little effort. We expect that the system should itself instruct new users in learning the basic aspects and initial operation that would be necessary. The system should be capable of handling and storing text in a very flexible fashion and at the same time should make use of rapid recognition methods in tracking the meaning of responses from subjects. Basic recognition methods should be sufficiently rapid so that the pace of conversational interaction is not badly distorted. While it should be possible to designate a specific sequence of program responses to subjects, there also exists a need for a random choice mechanisms so that an author can call on a varied output. Future systems should probably have the development of adaptive mechanisms to improve their responses as a result of increased experience with many subjects.

The appendix contains a paper descriptive of PILOT, a language being developed for the recognition of conversational interaction and for the control of computer programs by means of such interaction (Starkweather, 1968). It is initially being used for the development of demonstration instructional programs, simulated diagnostic interviews and specialized inquiry systems. It is also being explored for its usefulness in assisting a remote user of the computer to avoid the complexities of job control language or the control statements required for operation of prepackaged statistical programs. We also expect to explore a variety of terminal devices and the possible interaction of PILOT as a communication link to many other programs useful to a variety of people who need computer services.

As executive monitors for time sharing systems become more elaborate they tend to develop rudimentary languages facilities to allow easier interaction with their users. Our approach is from the opposite side, to build upon our history of developments since 1962 in constructing a programming system which is flexible in the handling of language recognition problems. PILOT is now adding control functions so that the system can aid users in gaining access to other programs and computer facilities which now require cumbersome coding and knowledge of computer complexity. Our future goal is an ability to handle the problem of a naive user who makes a request for computer assistance, perhaps one of an arithmetic nature or perhaps an information retrieval request from a remote point. If he does not know the appropriate coding for obtaining the use of a program necessary for his purpose the computer will be capable, via PILOT, of understanding his request and teaching him what he needs to know to accomplish his purpose.

Feedback and Adaptation of Machine Systems

Mechanisms described in the previous section suggest that means can be provided to program an instructional sequence so that feedback and appropriate reinforcement to a student may be immediate and progressively more accurate. A somewhat less immediate feedback has been arranged for improvement of the program itself but it was not imagined that this feedback circuit could be made automatic and self-correcting. I have no doubt, however, that self-regulatory machines will eventually be capable of this kind of self-improvement. Wiener (1948) and Ashby (1960) described a variety of systems operating under different forms of feedback control, and more recently Miller (1965, a,b,c) has worked out an organized terminology for systems which he has applied across a wide range of system levels. These are attempts to abstract general principles about feedback and cybernetic devices. The use of feedback implies a measurable criterion, always a difficult matter to specify for instructional efforts. Criteria for instructional materials are often found to differ markedly between three involved people: the author of the materials, the teacher who hopes it will assist in his instructional endeavors, and the pupil who hopes it will aid him to learn something relevant to his needs. For each such person in the situation, we must consider some form of judgment and measurement of results to be necessary. Teachers have often been reluctant to have such criteria developed, because such specification implies the requirement that something measurable be produced by their activity. The schools have not often liked to be judged on measured results, and they have a valid point that such measurement is often misinterpreted.

J. R. Pierce (1968) has recently pointed out that increasing need to find means with which to assess educational technology has increased the urgency for developing methods of measurement for older methods of instruction.

> "Computerized instruction has raised a clear challenge in all of instruction. We cannot afford either poor teaching or expensive teaching. How good are various means of teaching and for whom? What do various options cost? For example, what are the objectives of a given textbook? Can a student with some specified preparation, intelligence or other measurable prerequisite reach the objectives by

reading the textbook? Or must a teacher make up for deficiencies of the book or of its use? Such questions must be raised and answered concerning all courses and all modalities of instruction if we are to evaluate computerized instruction."

As has been pointed out in a recent review of papers on computer simulation and artificial intelligence (Hunt, 1968), there are very few programs which have been written to simulate directly the presumed mechanisms of human cognition. On the other hand, there have been a number of attempts to construct artificial intelligence systems to augment human intelligence, and while the programs are not psychological models, they may provide analyses of cognition which have implications for psychology and the understanding of human cognition. Fogel and his colleagues (1966) have developed a rather extensive system of programs which may be described as evolutionary machines. Such a machine is in the form of a computer program, thought of as a simulated and somewhat arbitrary logical organism. A supervisory program then initiates a random mutation of the existing organism, producing a number of offspring, that is, new simulated organisms with somewhat different properties from their parent. These offspring, acting as new machines, are observed (by the supervisory program) while reacting to the existing variables and their available history. They are each evaluated in terms of their individual ability to accomplish a given goal. The best of the offspring is selected to serve as the new parent, and such mutation and selection is continued to the point of some predetermined level of cost or the point at which a real-time decision is required. The authors hope that their method will open the door to self-programming of computers with methods which improve themselves. They would probably look upon adaptive instructional programs as a special case of this principle.

The Choice of Man or Machine for Educational Tasks

Whatever generalizations we make about the advantages of human authorship, human tutoring, and human review of student performance, or about the advantages of a machine doing any of these, there are likely to be special types of students who might benefit from one or the other. We usually expect that elementary school pupils will perform best in response to a human teacher, but our schools contain some youngsters who for a variety of reasons have given up trying to communicate with adults, particularly those who are in positions of authority. Their general suspicion of adults is coupled with a belief that teachers single them out for harsh treatment. I have watched seventh and eighth grade pupils with this kind of problem respond with remarkable motivation and interest to instructional material presented by machine. The machine seems to be seen as utterly impartial, communicative and yet unemotional. Colby (1968) has described some interesting and encouraging effects of a computer-based method for aiding language development in nonspeaking mentally disturbed young children. These children reject the use of linguistic communication with people, but he hoped that they would find the computer keyboard and display to be more acceptable as a way to practice and play with language. Colby makes the point that disturbed children are not resistant to learning, but to being taught by people, particularly people who are inconsistent, or who become angry or bored in the course of communication. The computer, on the other hand, is patient, consistent, and unreactive to emotional display.

If the computer can be made truly adaptive to the special needs of individual users, and adaptive to the particular language habits which may make a pupil especially difficult for a human teacher, then it may have a decided advantage over the teacher for serving such a pupil. Landers (1966) suggests that the telephone appeals to many people because talking on the telephone is almost like talking to an intelligent machine. Two women who barely speak to each other when they meet on the street will spend hours doing so on the tele phone. In this situation they need pay no attention to the other person's facial expression or gestures, and they are free to carry out minor tasks while listening. Landers believes that when conversation machines are developed, many people will prefer them as conversational partners to humans, particularly when the machines become "tunable" to one's personality.

It appears to me that when the machines have reached this stage of development, then they will no longer necessarily serve us very well as a first step in talking to those who we hope will move on to communicate better with other people. Such pupils may not have any desire to talk with difficult and variable humans after developing a satisfying relationship with such a paragon machine. It will clearly become trustworthy, loyal, helpful, friendly, courteous, kind, obedient etc.

We have not yet reached this state of affairs, however, and man's greater variability is still linked with greater adaptiveness. The choice between using men or machines can perhaps be seen today in its most advanced stage in the space program. Man's adaptiveness to the unexpected has so far kept him an active participant. In the instructional arena, the computer will more and more become an intellectual partner for learning, but processes of feedback will work best for the human learner's advantage if he, in the role of teacher or pupil, is a part of the feedback loop.

It may be a particular advantage to use the computer to allow students to play the role of teacher or the author of instructional materials early in his career of learning. If the mechanisms of program authorship are sufficiently easy to handle, then even pupils in the early primary grades can benefit from writing the machine side of a conversation with their classmates. Such a program author should receive feedback information from the system and from the students, and be motivated to improve the program's operation. In an elementary school setting where I have seen pupils involved both as authors of computer-presented instruction and as responding students, the total interaction has appeared to prompt a refreshing spirit of self-directed inquiry and exploration of the subject matter. As automation continues to lead us to describe more of our future time as "leisure" rather than "work", then it will be helpful to foster attitudes about learning that will lead us to classify it as a leisure activity. Involvement of students with adaptable machine assistants to self-directed learning is likely to help in developing this attitude. Future students will learn to use the computer as an intellectual partner early, and it will be a great advantage throughout their lives.

Likely Results of Increased Machine Intelligence on Instruction

Major improvements of methods by which a computer system can better recognize the messages of a user, understand his requests and adapt itself to them, are required and can be expected. These improvements will be found in the area of human engineering, and do not require marked additions to computer technology. Individualized instruction will be possible, and students who are poorly prepared in specific areas will be able to learn material which is required for advanced work. This will be possible where basic curriculum materials are matched to the local need and the local context. Instructors will find that their role has changed when the use of instructional technology is widespread. They will place more emphasis on a definition of goals and an accompanying development of criteria with which to measure student performance. It may be possible for schools to interchange their materials more directly and meaningfully, and it may be possible for teachers at different schools to collaborate in the development of course sequences better than they could produce independently. When the programming systems become truly adaptive in their ability to profit from new experience with new students in a new setting, then the movement of materials from one school to another will result in steadily increasing value of the materials.

Adaptive machines of the future will have a problem similar to that which men face today: how can they be secure while in the process of constant change, rather than secure while relying on fixed belief, knowledge, and procedures?

BIBLIOGRAPHY

Ashby, W. R. *Design for a brain.* New York: Wiley, 1960.

Colby, K. M. "Computer-aided language development in nonspeaking children." *Arch. Gen. Psychiat.,* 1968, *19,* 641-651.

The Commission on College Physics. *The computer in physics education.* Report of a conference on the uses of the computer in undergraduate physics instruction. University of California, Irvine. November, 1965.

Forbes Magazine, August 1, 1968. "Tools for Teaching." pp. 38-44.

Fogel, L. J., Owens, A. J., & M. J. Walsh. *Artificial Intelligence through Simulated Evolution.* New York: John Wiley & Sons, 1966.

Hickey, Albert E. and John M. Newton, *Computer-Assisted Instruction. A survey of the Literature.* ENTELEK, Inc., Newburyport, Mass., 1967, 2nd edition.

Hunt, E. "Computer simulation: Artificial intelligence studies and their relevance to psychology." *Ann. Rev. Psychol.,* 1968, *14,* 135-168.

Landers, R. R. *Man's Place in the Dybosphere.* Englewood Cliffs, N.J.: Prentice-Hall, 1966.

Lumsdaine, A. A. 1960. "Teaching machines: an Introductory Overview." *In* Lumsdaine, A. and Glaser, R. (Eds.), *Teaching Machines and Programmed Learning.* National Education Association, Washington, D.C.

Meyer, J. A. "Programmed learning: Education's turkey?" *The Amer. Sch. Board J.,* 1968, *V. 156, No. 4 (Oct.),* 26-27.

Miller, J. G. "Living Systems: Basic Concepts." *Behavioral Science,* 1965, *10,* 193-237.

Miller, J. G. "Living Systems: Structure and Process." *Behavioral Science,* 1965, *10,* 337-379.

Miller, J. G. "Living Systems: Cross-level Hypotheses." *Behavioral Science,* 1965, *10,* 380–411.

Orr, W. D. *Conversational Computers.* New York: John Wiley and Sons, 1968.

Pierce, J. R. *What really works to help learning—The Challenge of Computers to Education.* Address to the American Educational Research Association. Feb. 9, 1968.

Pressey, S. L. "A simple apparatus which gives tests and scores—and teaches." *School and Society,* 1926, *23,* No. 586 (March 20).

Pressey, S. L. 1950. "Development and apparatus of devices providing immediate automatic scoring of objective tests and concomitant self-instruction." *J. Psychol.* 29: 417-47.

Rath, G. J., Andersen, N. S., and R. C. Brainerd. 1959. "The IBM Research Center Teaching Machine Project." In Galanter, E. H. (Ed.), *Automatic Teaching: The State of the Art.* John Wiley & Sons, New York.

Skinner, B. F. 1954. "The science of learning and the art of teaching." *Harvard Educ. Rev.* 24: 86-97.

Starkweather, J. A. *A common language for a variety of conversational programming needs.* Paper presented at IEEE International Conference on Communications, Philadelphia, June, 1968.

Wiener, N. *Cybernetics.* New York: John Wiley & Sons, 1948.

Zinn, K. L. "Instructional Uses of Interactive Computer Systems." *Datamation.* 1968, *14,* 22-27 (September).

20.

Education and
The Communication of
Scientific Information

by DON R. SWANSON
Dean, Grad. Library School
Univ. of Chicago

If it is worthwhile for scientists to communicate with one another concerning the results of current research, then surely the results of research are worth teaching to students. To place knowledge newly gained from research into the context of previously existing knowledge is of course part of the task of research, but clearly it can also be considered part of the education process. It follows that the problems of communicating scientific and scholarly information, and in particular the results of current research, are also educational problems. The subject of this paper is essentially scientific communication, information services, and libraries, but an attempt is made here to identify those aspects which are of probable relevance to "educational systems,"* even though much additional work is needed to translate such probable relevance into a definite plan of action.

As the backlog of recorded information accumulates, each succeeding generation has effective access to an ever decreasing fraction of the total. Unless the right countermeasures are taken, we run the risk that each generation will take progressively longer to learn what has gone before. This is the central problem of scientific communication and it is the central problem that will face education within the next several decades.

Solutions to this basic problem will not spring from new technology, though sound approaches to these problems may well result in the formulation of requirements to which technology can be expected to respond. There is little doubt, for example, that technology in principle will soon be able to put the world's recorded information in the palm of our hand, and that certain limited advantages might even result from so doing. But to achieve in practice what can be done in principle requires that a favorable environment (of libraries and information centers) be created which allows adequate scope for initiative and innovation. Unfortunately the present economic, institutional, and organizational environment does not encourage technological innovation and development in the providing of information services to the degree that might reasonably be expected. This is so at least in part because most information services are financed in such a way that there is no direct connection between the price the user pays and the benefit he receives. Even in those areas where-

---

*"*Educational system*" is defined here, for better or worse, as an aggregate of teachers, students, institutions, machines, instructional materials, and communication links which function as a whole—i.e. in a more or less coordinated manner and for commonly recognized goals.*

in modern technology could result in improved services for a higher price, the option to purchase such "extra" services does not exist (in general, and on any large scale) for the users of libraries and information services. Yet this problem is being recognized to an increasing degree, and it seems likely that the future will see important innovations in the methods of financing information services. As the economic environment improves, the technology of large capacity rapid access storage, microform reproduction, print reading, communications, and displays will gradually be adapted to and incorporated in information systems and services. "Educational systems" can benefit to a like degree, provided that planning takes place on a broad, probably national, basis.

Problems of communication and education will not be solved by the development of any single system or single approach. The system presently in existence is pluralistic, not monolithic. It consists of many organizations and institutions producing a variety of products and services. This fact is of central importance in any overall plan for the improvement of information and educational services, for effective coordination depends strongly on voluntary co-operation rather than upon establishing lines of organizational authority. Some idea of the complexity of the pluralistic system in the provision of information services can be gained from noting that over 1800 separate indexing and abstracting services in the field of science and technology exist throughout the world. Each of these "secondary" services covers some segment of the primary literature, usually with a particular viewpoint or a particular audience in mind. For the most part these services operate independently, though increasing efforts are in progress to secure a greater degree of coordination.

The very large number and complexity of the library and information services in the world, and the many efforts under way to improve these services, preclude any adequate description in a brief paper. Yet there are at least two major categories in which these efforts can be grouped which seem of particular significance for educational systems, and so deserve some discussion. The first of these concerns the need for universal bibliographic tools and for better coordination among the various libraries and other institutions which provide information services, so that the aggregate functions more as a cohesive 'system' or 'network'. The second category concerns the need for more responsive and individualized services for relatively small user groups which share common interests, and in particular the need for more and better reviews, summaries, and compendia which serve the end of condensing or 'packing down' knowledge.

Library and Information Networks

Academic libraries of course attempt to develop collections and services that are responsive to the needs of the institution to which they belong. Yet to define such needs is a difficult matter, and it is even more difficult to evaluate the effectiveness of a library in meeting those needs. There are some 100 or so research libraries in the United States (most, but not all, at universities) each of whose individual holdings and resources are so much larger than other libraries that these may be considered in a class by themselves as a major national resource. Even the largest of these major libraries however cannot realistically hope to be self sufficient, in the sense of collecting everything its users might conceivably need. They must somehow seek to optimize the usefulness of what they do collect and arrange with other institutions to share resources and to develop complementary acquisition policies. Such sharing is usually effected through interlibrary loan, a practice which, although quite old, is still in a primitive state. Yet it is conceptually of extraordinary importance for it must be the forerunner of larger and more systematic developments toward systems and networks.

Technology can be expected to play an important role in network development (especially computer, microform, and communication technology), but to assess the rate and nature of development we must look not so closely at technology per se, but at organizations and institutions and at their specific plans and efforts, particularly those addressed to identifying needs and requirements. Just as in the case of instructional technology, it is more profitable to ask not "what has technology to offer?", but rather "how can we identify and define the needs of education, and create the kind of economic environment, so that suitable technology can be adapted or developed to respond to these needs?"

The number of separate network-planning efforts presently under way is too great for individual discussion here, nor is there any necessity for presenting a survey. Instead, a brief outline of a few of these efforts will serve to point up the significance of what is happening more generally.

The Library of Congress in effect functions as a national library in that it provides a variety of bibliographic services for other research libraries; indeed that is perhaps its most important activity apart from directly serving the Congress itself. Foremost among the services to libraries is the production and sale of catalog cards. Through such centralized cataloging, not only is labor saved at the subscribing libraries, but of more fundamental import is the resulting standardization of cataloging practices and wide acceptance of the Library of Congress classification system and subject heading list. Certainly standardization of cataloging and classification is prerequisite to network development, and much has already been accomplished in this direction, at least for monographs. (Subject access to individual articles in scientific and scholarly journals is another matter however). Equally important, in principle, to the production of catalog cards is the maintenance of the National Union Catalog. This catalog covers the joint holdings of the major research libraries in the country (with certain limitations), and so permits one to ascertain in which library a book not locally held can be found. An extension of this concept leads to the notion of "universal bibliographic tools", that is, catalogs and indexes to the world's knowledge, (i.e. not limited by the holdings of any particular collection), and accessible from any point where information requirements originate.

The Library of Congress is taking positive steps to expand its services, and its role as a national library. One of the recommendations of the President's National Advisory Commission on Libraries, incidentally, is that the Library of Congress be declared the National Library of the United States. (Congressional Record, Oct. 21, 1968, p. E9363.)

The Library of Congress has carried out (under a contract with United Aircraft Corp.) an automation system study and it has implemented its MARC (Machine Readable Catalog Record) programs in which digitally coded catalog records on magnetic tape are made available to other libraries. It is clear that the Library of Congress will play a central role in the future coordination of various automation programs in other major research libraries.

The National Library of Medicine has also assumed leadership in developing a national program of biomedical information services, primarily through its MEDLARS (Medical Literature Analysis and Retrieval System) programs. The present version of MEDLARS provides two main services; a) the publication and distribution of the Index Medicus, and b) the creation of a machine language data base, corresponding largely to the contents of Index Medicus, but including more detailed indexing, for retrospective searching and for the production of various specialized bibliographies. Of particular interest in this connection are the similarities as well as the differences between the printed product and the machine data base. Each is, of course, a store of information to be searched. Machine searching has the advantage of producing a printed list as output and is faster for a search of multiple categories, or a complex logical combination of categories. The printed Index Medicus however is available to many thousands of widely dispersed users for whom it would be impractical to provide access to machine input and printing terminals. Even in those cases for which the latter may indeed be possible, it is nevertheless clear that the printed Index Medicus is faster, more convenient, and cheaper for certain large categories of requests that are not overly complex. The same issues of comparison between printed storage and machine storage are relevant in most information retrieval systems, and in connection with programmed instruction. *While printed and machine storage each may have its own special merits, the presumption that a dialog with a machine system is necessarily better than reading a textbook presenting the same or similar material is questionable at best.* The issues are complex, but the rich variety of useful printed materials (reference books, index journals, etc.) associated with the services of libraries and information centers has many important lessons and implications for the planners of mechanized information retrieval and educational systems.

A network of regional libraries with the National Library of Medicine as the center is being developed. Existing libraries are receiving increased support in order to develop their collections and facilities to serve other medical libraries in their region. Services will not only include MEDLARS searches, extensive sharing of resources through interlibrary loans, but in addition a full range of library services and functions similar to those provided by the National Library of Medicine. Numerous other cooperative library ventures have been implemented in part through support available under the Higher Education Act of 1965, the Library Services and Construction Act, and the State Technical Services Act.

Cooperative library networks which in some form have long existed are gaining increasing attention and accelerated development.

Various indexing and abstracting services are also taking steps toward increased cooperation and plans for network activities on both a national and an international basis. Cooperative arrangements are active among the abstracting and indexing services in biology, engineering, chemistry and physics. These efforts include studies of indexing procedures as well as the exchange of abstracts in order eventually to achieve common formats and reduce unnecessary redundancy.

The International Council of Scientific Unions Abstracting Board (ICSU AB), founded in 1952, attempts to strengthen and coordinate worldwide secondary publication in physics, chemistry, biology, and astronomy. Under the joint sponsorship of ICSU and UNESCO a study is now in progress of the feasibility of a worldwide science information system (UNISIST), that will be based essentially on voluntary cooperation among existing national and private information systems.

Recommendation 1. Broad studies of educational systems should be carried out, and prior studies reassessed, in the context of the assumption that libraries and information systems are evolving toward large scale networks, and national systems. The development of universal bibliographic tools, increased library and information system coordination, sharing of resources, and improved communications present the opportunity for planning educational systems on an increasingly purposeful, systematic, and coordinated basis.

Review, Summary, and Condensation of Knowledge

As recorded knowledge accumulates, it becomes increasingly important to condense, review, simplify and summarize. If this is not done, it would seem that progress must virtually cease when it becomes impossible to define a specialty narrow enough so that one can learn in a lifetime all, or most, of what has gone before. It is important that scientists, engineers, and scholars become increasingly involved in sifting, reviewing, interpreting, and summarizing the literature, and that society somehow reward these kinds of endeavors adequately in recognition of the fact that they are often as important as original or new contributions to knowledge. This need was emphasized in the 1963 'Weinberg report'.[1] Since that time the subject has received increased recognition, and the federal government has stepped up its support of reviews, summaries, and compendia.

One example of a much needed publication is the NSF supported "Annual Reviews of Information Science." Several studies have shown that the percentage of material devoted to state of the art studies and reviews at recent annual meetings (in a number of science and engineering disciplines) ranges from about twenty-five to fifty percent,[2][3] which seems (impressionistically) to be much higher than any comparable statistic ten years ago. Evidence for the increasing recognition of the importance of reviews is provided by a recent action of the Society of Civil Engineers which now offers an annual state of the art civil engineering award for outstanding review papers.

As important a function as the review literature serves, it is not easy to identify. It is thus of especial importance to educate scientists, scholars, and teachers, both when they are students and later on in their careers, in the means of access to review literature.

The compilation of critically evaluated and updated scientific data is another aspect of the needed continual summary review function. In 1963 the Federal Council for Science and Technology recommended to the President's Science Advisory Committee the establishment of a government wide compilation effort to promote and coordinate systematic data compilation and evaluation activities in the physical sciences. The responsibility for administering this program was assigned to the National Bureau of Standards which then set up the National Standard Reference Data System.[4] The system operates in a pluralistic manner and depends on the cooperation of numerous institutions throughout the country. The principle activity of the system is to locate data within the literature, to evaluate and compile it systematically and then to prepare critical reviews concerning the data. Most importantly perhaps, the NSRDS determines the need of the scientific and technical community for data, and coordinates and surveys existing compilations and evaluation efforts.

In 1966 the International Council of Scientific Unions established the Committee on Data for Science and Technology (CODATA).[5] It is the purpose of this group to foster international coordination of data compilation and evaluation efforts and to encourage the scientific and engineering community to greater efforts in these directions. During the past five years data evaluation efforts have been gradually evolving toward programs coordinated at the national and international levels.

It is particularly in the area of reviews and summaries that it would be difficult to make a distinction between the requirements for effective communication of new knowledge and the requirements of educational programs. Yet a still broader and more systematic effort is needed to identify areas in need of review and summarization and to take the steps necessary to bring them into being. A parallel effort is needed then to associate these with college and university curricula, and thus to identify the types of instructional materials, including particularly textbooks, that indeed serve to relate newly gained knowledge to that which was previously known.

Special Information Centers and Services

It is characteristic of our diverse, decentralized, and pluralistic "system" of scientific and technical communication that the most effective and sophisticated information services are those developed by highly specialized, relatively small groups of users to meet their own immediate needs. A variety of primary and secondary sources is searched, filtered, and reprocessed to produce detailed indexes, abstracts, bibliographies, and selective dissemination services. Federal programs have financed and encouraged the development of specialized information analysis centers and services, and it seems clear that these efforts can and should be expanded.

The purpose of these centers is essentially to create new information, not by original research but by sifting through existing data and studying and examining it, evaluating, analyzing, synthesizing, and repackaging hopefully so that new generalizations and new insights can be gained. In general the work is carried out by small groups of subject specialists working within the framework of existing research institutions.

The very diversity of services however creates a broader problem of effective coordination and systemization, in order that the services become known and thus more broadly effective beyond the confines of the immediate group for which they were developed.

The Federal Committee on Scientific and Technical Information (COSATI) published in 1968 a census of information analysis centers listing over a hundred that were currently active and over half of which were established during the past five years. Most of these are in the areas of physical sciences, education, engineering, medicine and health, and environmental sciences. All of these may be regarded as potential resources for educational materials but of particular importance perhaps is the extent to which they represent a pattern or model of organizational effort that has significance for education. Incidentally these include educational information analysis centers themselves, namely the National Center for Educational Statistics and a system of clearinghouses under the Educational Resources Information Center (ERIC).

It is of some interest to relate certain of these specialized centers to the broader national systems which they depend upon. For example, the MEDLARS system, as extensive as it is, cannot adequately meet highly specialized needs and accordingly the system in effect becomes an input for further analysis and processing to smaller more specialized centers. One example is the Neurological Information Network of the National Institute of Neurological Diseases and Blindness, which itself includes the Brain Information Service, the Information Center for Hearing, Speech and Disorders of Human Communication, the Parkinson's Disease Information and Research Center, and the Vision Information Center. These centers maintain systematic efforts to encourage the production of summaries and reviews of major topics in the neurological sciences.

Certain information analysis centers sponsored by the Department of Defense are developing plans for a schedule of user charges in the near future. Such centers will attempt to recover costs through sales of publications and special charges for services. This effort to associate costs directly with the services provided and thus giving users the option of allocating their resources toward the most valuable services is of very great importance in the evolving picture of national information systems. The idea of financing information services directly through users may well establish a prototype or pattern of significance to educational technology. What is clearly needed, for information centers, libraries, and educational systems is an environment allowing wide scope for initiative and innovation, which might best be brought about through new and imaginative methods of financing.

Recommendation 2. The processes, and procedures for condensing, summarizing, and reviewing the scientific literature should be studied in the light of their implications for educational programs. In particular, similar processes and procedures might be useful in identifying areas of need for textbooks, and in promoting or encouraging high quality authorship.

The Need for Education in the Use of Information Services

The overall picture of scientific communication, libraries, and information services, only a small part of which has been touched upon here, is clearly one of enormous complexity and diversity. There is no evidence that the situation is growing any less complex in the course of time, notwithstanding the various efforts toward networks and cooperative arrangements. On the contrary, it is steadily becoming of increasing importance that users become more knowledgeable about library and information resources as the total backlog of recorded knowledge accumulates relentlessly, and as specialized access services proliferate. In general, scientists and engineers do not now make effective use of existing information services, even while deploring the slow progress toward sophisticated pushbutton systems of the future. Students at all levels must be increasingly exposed to the nature and extent of the information and library services available to them, and this exposure should be woven into the fabric of essentially all educational programs and curricula.

Recommendation 3. Throughout all educational programs, especially at the college level, more thorough and systematic efforts should be made to acquaint students and faculty with the use of library and information services. These services clearly will become increasingly numerous and increasingly complex in the future, and the need increasingly great for detailed knowledge on the part of the user.

Appendix

Relevant Areas of Technology

The main theme of this paper has been to develop an analogy, in terms of institutions, activities, and concepts between education and the communication of scientific information. As a related but subordinate matter, it might now be of use to identify the major areas in which new technological developments are likely to have an impact.

The cost and speed of reproducing page images, particularly in microform, have been improving in recent times to the point where this technology is beginning to have significant influence on the availability and flow of scientific and technical information. One implication is that, to an increasing extent, libraries will be able to distribute expendable copy instead of lending materials. Already in many large libraries and information services, this practice is prevalent. For example, the National Library of Medicine fills most of its requests for published journal articles by sending Xerox copies of the original. Other agencies, including the Clearinghouse for Federal Scientific and Technical Information, send either full size expendable copy or microfilm copy. The economic advantage of microfilm over hard copy is illustrated in the prices charged by the Clearinghouse, namely hard copy at $3 per report and microfiche at 65¢. It is estimated that the various government document centers (The Department of Defense, the Federal Clearinghouse, the ERIC Clearinghouse, the NASA Technical Information Center, and that of the Atomic Energy Commission) distribute over fifteen million copies of reports per year, about a third of which are hard copy and two thirds microform.

The economic implications of document reproduction, as projected into the future, are remarkable, for it is not implausible to assume that before too many years microform copies of books can be made (once the original master has been prepared) for perhaps as low a cost as 10¢ or 20¢ per book. Thus every small college might reasonably aspire to developing a major research library collection.

One of the areas in which computer technology is likely to have significant impact on information systems and on educational systems is in the selective dissemination of information. At present although a hundred or so experimental selective dissemination services exist most of these are too costly to be practical. However an important trend in this field is that of identifying groups of users with common dissemination interests, which then offers hope for improved tailoring of subscription packages to the requirements of users without the extreme degree of refinement (and cost) of individual dissemination systems.

One of the major bottlenecks of course in the large scale use of computers for information handling concerns the initial transcribing of textual information into machine language. However, new information services are increasingly becoming available which depend upon machine readable document texts and bibliographic records. In many cases these records are created as a by-product of the publication process. Some of the government information activities which maintain bibliographic records in machine readable form include the MEDLARS system for the National Library of Medicine, the Library of Congress catalog records (Project MARC), Scientific and Technical Aerospace Reports for NASA, Nuclear Science Abstracts for the Atomic Energy Commission, and U.S. government Research and Development Reports Index for the Federal Clearinghouse. Private professional organizations also are beginning to expand their activities in the maintenance of mechanized bibliographic records. Those presently existing include, for example, Psychological Abstracts, Applied Mechanics Review, Biological Abstracts, International Aerospace Abstracts, Documentation Abstracts, Engineering Index, and several types of machine readable records from Chem Abstracts Services. Mechanized citation indexes are maintained and sold by the Institute for Scientific Information, as well as a number of bibliographic records maintained by the R. R. Bowker Co., including Publishers Weekly and the Subject Guide to Books in Print.

The monumental task of converting textual records to machine readable form of course suggests the importance of automatic character recognition for print reading. Developments in this area of technology are extensive and would require a separate treatment in themselves, but the complexity and variety of type fonts in common use clearly indicate that at this time large scale application (i.e., on the scale on which libraries and information services operate) is still some distance in the future.

Communication technology is also of crucial importance to information systems of the future, but still tends to be overshadowed by the economic problems of input-output and the organization of large scale services. For example, time delays in the delivery of most library materials are often much longer than the time it takes to fly a book by jet plane from coast to coast. Thus it is clear that high speed transmission of data alone is not likely to have significant impact on our information systems until the broader problems of organization and information flow within institutions are at least partially solved.

The technology of cathode ray type (CRT) and other types of display terminals for information systems is also an important area for consideration, but the obvious (though often overlooked) fact should be noted that these techniques are in competition with the printed page. At present they suffer by comparison with the printed page from high costs and relatively poor quality of image. Furthermore, and equally obvious, but even less often remarked, is that a printed page is *both* storage and display.

However obstacles to the further development and widespread use of CRT displays are economic rather than technical, and the central problems are those of identifying the requirements and the extent of need for such terminals in the context of future information systems.

A trend with numerous implications for computer display, and communication technology is evident in the growing development of large scale bibliographic information systems which employ on-line interaction from remote terminals. Some of the corporations and institutions active in this area include the Systems Development Corporation with a highly developed time sharing system, the Massachusetts Institute of Technology (Projects MAC and TIP), Stanford University, Lockheed, Bunker Ramo, and Bolt, Beranek and Newman.

BIBLIOGRAPHY

Brady, E. L. and M. B. Wallenstein. "The National Standard Reference Data System." *Science,* 1967, 156, pp. 751-756.

Brown, H. "International Cooperation: The New ICSU Program on Critical Data." *Science,* 1967, 156, pp. 751-754.

Compton, B. E., and W. D. Garvey. "Preliminary Findings on Dissemination Practices of Scientists and Engineers and Their Implications for Documentalists." In *Proceedings of the 33rd FID Conference and International Congress on Documentation.* Tokyo, FID 1967.

Johns Hopkins University Center for Research in Scientific Communication. *The Nature of Program Material and the Results of Interaction at the February Semiannual Meeting of the Amer. Society for Heating, Refrigerating, and Air-Conditioning Engineers.* JHU CRSC Report #8. Baltimore, Md., Johns Hopkins Center for Research in Scientific Communication, 1968.

Weinberg, A. L., et. al. *Science, Government and Information. The Responsibilities of the Technical Community and the Government in the Transfer of Information.* Washington, D.C., President's Science Advisory Committee, 1963.

21.

The Generation of Images

By ROBERT W. WAGNER
Prof. and Chrmn.
Dept. of Photography and Cinema
Ohio State Univ.

A State of the Art Report on Sixteen-Millimeter Film

Ours is an *image generation*—a time when people, young and old, are being subjected to more forms of imagery than ever before; a time when young people, in particular, seem to have found in the film experience a unique, and perhaps the only way of expressing themselves in an ambiguous world, short of mass demonstration or individual withdrawal. Film and television imagery seems to offer some kind of organizational refuge from a flood of empty verbalisms on the one hand and a torrent of senseless reality on the other.

This *generation of images* must be considered in another sense. It is a time when images beget other images—one visual form becoming another—making it important for the critical educator to identify not only how the original image is generated (by whom, for what purpose, in what medium, for what audience, with what effects), but also to identify the generation of image which reaches the student, the nature of its transformation, and what might have been lost—or added—in the translation. A motion picture may become a still picture through freeze-frame; a series of still photographs becomes an iconographic film or a television image; an electronic image is transformed to silver halide, perhaps passing through stages of wire or satellite transmission on the way, finally appearing in several half-tone reproductions of varied compositions; film becomes videotape; 16mm becomes Super-8mm; and in this process messages are changed, modified, displayed to different audiences in different viewing environments, by different users for different purposes. The possible consequences of these "dissolving forms" are partially but effectively explored by Boorstin in his book, *The Image*[1] and in more recent expositions including those of McLuhan.

In the Generation of Images described, it is obviously impossible to isolate the "sixteen-millimeter" film except as a point of relative focus. It must rather, be regarded in relationship to other image systems, both photographic and electronic, and will be discussed here under the following headings: 1) Technological Factors (the hardware); 2) Environmental Factors (display settings); 3) Audience Factors (the student, the teacher); 4) Design Factors (the "software"); 5) Philosophical Factors (research, theory, and practice).

Technological Factors

The term "sixteen-millimeter" came into being in 1923 as the expression of the lateral di-

mension of a reversal motion picture film developed for the amateur market by the Eastman Kodak Company. At the time, the international motion picture standard was 35mm—a
format originally selected by Thomas A. Edison for use in his peep-hole Kinetoscope which
he displayed at the Chicago World's Fair of 1893. For forty years, the history of film in
education was the history of the 16mm film, and although 8mm film came on the market in
1932, it was not until the emergence of Super-8 (and many other conditions) in the early
1960s that the non-theatrical role of the 16mm medium was challenged and changed.

History is not necessarily "bunk" as Henry Ford once put it, and there is much to be
learned from the history of film in education. The fact is, however, that the im-
age-consuming and image-generating culture of the United States today—educators
included—appears to have little reason, time, or patience for excursions into the past of
either 16mm or 35mm. The current surge of interest and funds for Super-8mm developments, and for television, and programmed instruction has nearly totally obscured what has
been learned about the production, use, and research of films in education from 1918-1950.
The automation and systematization of photographic and electronic image production and
utilization has, in fact, obsoleted many conceptions, techniques, and research growing out
of the older 16mm experience. Yet, in process, there is a curious similarity between the
early development of the 16mm film and the renaissance of 8mm in its Super-form some
thirty years later, which could lead educators and technologists alike to a broader concept
of how technological change comes about, and possibly save time for those who feel they
are ploughing new ground when, in reality, they may be toiling in an old field they have
just never seen before.

Both 16mm and Super-8 quickly became not only a size of film, but also a state of mind.
Both were departures from a well-established standard. Sixteen-millimeter became synonymous with "safety" film, being on an acetate base, compared to the highly inflammable ni-
trate-based 35mm film of the period. Sixteen-millimeter also became associated with terms
such as "non-theatrical," "documentary," and "educational," as, like the latter-day saints of
8mm, the evangelists for 16mm sought a separate identity for this format compared to the
35mm film. Early professionally-produced 16mm prints were actually generated from
35mm originals just as professionally-produced Super-8 prints are struck from 16mm, and in
some cases 35mm, originals today. Advocates of 16mm were saying that it was not "merely
to be scaled-down 35mm apparatus and methods"[2] just as Super-8 enthusiasts insist today
that this format is "not just little 16." Professional 35mm film makers expressed the same
repugnance about handling 16mm that professional 16mm film makers today feel about the
"spaghetti-like" characteristics of Super-8mm.

Both formats provided an entre into the media field for a whole generation of aspiring
young film makers with little or no experience in the production and use of film in education, and with very little concern for, or interest in historical, theoretical, or technological
precedents of the medium, (only to rediscover many of them later on). Both 16mm and
8mm opened new potentials for a generation of teachers and students caught in a set of circumstances in which technological developments were brought to bear on education only in
the context of major national pressures and needs for rapid, efficient instruction of large
numbers of learners. (World War II in the case of 16mm film and Sputnik in the case of
Super-8).

In both cases there were bench-mark publications growing out of an invitational conference or symposium which formalized the secession from the proceeding format,[3] each em-
phatically asserting its immediate and, looking backward, somewhat obvious point—"16mm
is not 35mm;" and "8mm is not 16mm." Both publications appeared about thirty years after the development of the format they featured; a fact indicative of educational lag in the
field of instructional technology.[4] While focussing on 16mm and 8mm respectively, the true
significance of these reports was really the public visibility they generated; the stimulus they
provided for the further exploration of the potential of film in education on the part of
educators; a quickening of the pace on the part of hardware manufacturers, and a reassess-

ment of film design on the part of perceptive producers of educational software.

Eight-millimeter equipment, especially the development of Super-8 formats, underwent rapid sophistication, surpassing 16mm especially in some aspects of projector design. In 1967, 16mm sound projector sales to schools fell 20%, and laboratories reported a slight decline in the amount of 16mm processed compared to 1966, while the amount of 8mm film increased.[5] However, it appears that the two formats will exist compatibly and necessarily, for the foreseeable future since all professionally-produced 8mm release prints presently originate on 16mm or 35mm film. Improvements in 16mm camera and projector design may also make significant differences in their application in educational settings. Bell and Howell and Bauer, among others, have produced, improved, and simplified auditorium projectors; the Viewlex Sound-16 is designed for both large and small-group use and loads like an audio tape recorder; the Graflex model 930 may be used to play a 16mm film directly into a TV camera for CCTV use or for classroom conversion to videotape.

There is considerable speculation that the photographic image may be replaced by an electronic image recorded on magnetic tape, obsoleting both 16mm and 8mm films in educational systems.[6] Higher silver prices have stimulated research in alternative systems of image formation including electrostatic, thermographic, electronic, and other non-halide methods.

Informed opinion, however, indicates that it is unlikely that silver images will be replaced for many years, especially in applications requiring high light or wide spectral sensitivities, or continuous tone reproduction.[7] Photographic film also has rather good stability as a storage medium, which, together with improvements in color stocks and the increasing reliability of color motion picture film systems strongly suggests its continued existence for some time to come, along with videotape and other types of non-silver materials now being developed.

In the 1968-69 television season, approximately 90% of network and regional television commercials were produced on film with distribution in 16mm. Although film shows on television in prime time of the major networks declined from 69% in the 1967-68 season to 56% in the 1968-69 season, film-to-tape transfers rose from 12½ to 20% in the same period.[8] Sixteen-millimeter color may be expected to increase as the original recording material for television features *(Death Valley Days* was one of the first); while nearly all television news footage on both the local and network levels is also 16mm color.

Duplication and distribution of original images in a variety of formats—photographic and electronic—is an inevitable consequence of the competitive proliferation of new and generally incompatible image systems which already exist in the 8mm and VTR fields. There is a system for transforming black and white originals to color, through electronics, with the light values being recorded in coded form on standard 16mm monochrome—also requiring special play-back equipment. There is a new 17½mm film format with properties similar to Super-8, including self-rewinding features, multiple optical tracks with audio quality above that of standard 16mm, and a condensation of 40 minutes of images on a single 400-foot reel at a predicted cost of only about 25% the price of a 16mm equivalent.[9] The CBS Electronic Video Recorder (EVR) uses an 8.75mm film designed for use in existing black and white (and later, color) television receivers in schools, hospitals, industries, and the home.

At the time of this writing, the 16mm format seems to lend itself to the requirements of the immediate future in a unique way. It translates well to other generations of images and to a variety of image systems. It stores well, and preserves the original investment reliably. It is compatible with national television transmission standards as well as with larger and several smaller film formats found throughout the world. In this connection, one European authority points out:

> It is obvious that the 16mm film has a great future with regard to both the 8mm
> film and television providing that it adapts and takes advantage of the opportunity
> it has to play a new, vital role in education.[10]

Sixteen millimeter has great usefulness as an original recording medium for the moving image in the many forms in which it might finally appear in instructional settings. It is, of course, a temporal form, as are all other known media of communication. We are already beyond the day of the transistor and can expect entirely new forms to replace not only silver halide image formation systems—which, after all, go back to 1839—but also electronic image systems. The communication problem remains the same—a fact recognized in *Sixty Years of 16mm Film* where a writer, fifteen years ago, stated:

> Some will probably object that electronic recordings have no place in a discussion of the future of 16mm films. On the contrary. Sixteen-millimeter is not just the width of a film, it is a state of mind. The same people, the same aims, the same drives would be present thirty years from now even if the physical form of the medium were altered.[11]

And in *8mm Sound Film and Education* it is suggested that the future of the film medium relates not only to technical standards, but more significantly to quality, purpose, and developments in the field of general education during the next ten to fifty years:

> It really doesn't matter whether moving images are ultimately written or printed or recorded on film, videotape, thermoplastic materials, or captured on Jello, as far as that's concerned. The important thing is to close up the technological lag in education by anticipating technological developments beyond the present . . . Perhaps improved television receivers of the future will also incorporate playback devices and thereby become a primary "projector" for all kinds of images including "home-movies" produced on film, videotape or other material.[12]

Sixteen-millimeter or not, purposeful, creative design of original materials of instruction in a format which makes possible the generation of images in many formats; useful in a variety of display systems; with multiple audiences; for many different purposes, would seem to be the problem of central importance to the future of media in education.

Environmental Factors

Decisions about the future of any image system, and particularly projected photographic images, will increasingly depend not simply upon film dimensions, projector capabilities, and screen-surface characteristics, but rather upon the total display situation of which they are parts. Hardware and software will need to be considered in a larger architectural and engineering context; in terms of a total *environment* (as distinguished by the somewhat more limited concept of *system*) deliberately intended to optimize the conditions for human learning (both programmed and non-programmed), and to match specific instructional objectives. It is appalling to consider the consequences of the variety of isolated software and hardware formats which appear to be proliferating without much regard to this larger problem of environment design.

The role of 16mm film, then—or any other medium—is related to a number of specific requirements which appear to be influencing the design of learning environments today. While it is doubtful if any single setting could ever be expected to meet all the possible requirements, many will probably include most of the conditions suggested below:

a) *More images.* These will need to be delivered individually and sequentially as well as simultaneously as multiple images. Both modes will need to be programmed but will also require random access as well. There will be more comparative and critical viewing of images; more repetition of these images for study in depth. This will require both small screens for individual viewing and large screen surfaces where group studies are concerned. It will raise to the level of the practical, what have up to now been largely theoretical, questions about definition or "sharpness" image size, brightness, ambient light (with regards to both intensity and color), shape, and the generation of images so compared.

b) *More light*. Whereas the history of audiovisual education has been a struggle to establish room-darkening conditions in the schools, there will be the necessity for *adding* light to learning environments, especially in comparative imagery involving a variety of media. The development of the quartz-halogen projection lamp; high-gain projection screens with greatly improved ambient light rejection; projection lenses with improved transmission characteristics; the success of the overhead projector; the use of rear-screen image systems both photographic and electronic, coupled with controlled, directional room lighting have combined to change the traditional requirements for the viewing environment. Since some of the images involved in multi-media presentations may be seen by transmitted light and others by reflected light, it may be necessary to add spotlight sources to increase the brightness of the latter to equalize the illumination of the various elements of display, including demonstration areas. With new front-screen designs already producing approximately six times the brightness of the best existing lenticular screens the need for more, not less, light in many learning environments seems a promising possibility.[13]

c) *More detail*. The need for image systems which will carry more detailed, magnified images has been expressed in the sciences where high-definition CCTV equipment is used. Large-screen television and film images will yield this definition only if the original image system (16mm in the case of film and 800-plus television-lines) is adequate to support the information required. Since "definition" or the condition of sharpness involves several variables, including the relationship of the viewer to the image, this factor becomes part of the total environmental design.

d) *More color*. While black and white images will continue to play an important role in education, the trend towards color in both film and television will undoubtedly continue to increase. Where color is used effectively and purposefully, it will need to be recorded and reported out accurately. Conditions of comparative viewing will make the viewer aware of differences in color from tape to film, for example, and from original to print stages in some cases. Sixteen-millimeter color films and processes yield excellent results when properly handled and can be reliably transferred to videotape, reduced to 8mm format, or even blown up to 35mm. In addition to the critical importance of the original recording and duplicating methods involved in color will also be the affective conditions of the viewing environment which may, under conditions of relatively high ambient light, induce perceptual color shifts in the eye of the viewer. The color temperature of the room illumination (tungsten, fluorescent, daylight), the reflected colors from walls, floors, and ceilings, and the comparative color of adjacent images will become environmental factors of increasing importance.

e) *More sound*. Once experienced in the classroom only through audio-tape and earlier disc recordings, sound is becoming a more vital part of the educational environment through 16mm film and videotape. There is a definite trend to 8mm sound even for single-concept films, once considered to be ideal subjects for silents. The ambiguity resulting from the desire of manufacturers' to serve both the amateur and professional markets has put both optical and magnetic tracks on 8mm films. Reel-to-reel Super-8 sound projectors are currently magnetic; those using cartridges are both magnetic and optical. While the relation of the picture to the track is a separation of 18 frames for Super-8 magnetic sound and 22 frames for optical Super-8, it remains standard at 26 frames in the 16mm format whether the track is optical or magnetic. Informed technical opinion is that "the method of sound reproduction that will achieve the greatest customer acceptance is not yet predictable."[14] Again, any image environment for the immediate future will have to provide for multiple sound as well as visual images, including the possibility of multiple (and stereo) tracks (and multiple images) on the same film. The magnetic film used in 70mm film systems accommodates six tracks. Sixteen-millimeter film can accommodate six tracks using the Maurer optical system. If half the track is coated with magnetic oxide, foreign language translations also become possible and teachers or students using magnetic 16mm projectors, could record their own narration. Optical-magnetic projectors have existed in 16mm for some time thus combining features desired by both the professional film maker who tends to prefer the optical track as a permanent, and less expensive way to record sound on prints, and the educator who would like to adapt the interpretation to meet his own needs. The Elmo ST-8 is one of the first projectors of this type in the small-format field. The capacity for local recording directly on a commercially-produced 8 or 16mm film using a magnetic stripe could make it useful as a feedback system in the mode of the language lab tape. Videotape, because it is magnetic, has better sound fidelity than film systems, but as original image and sound recording material, 16mm again has the virtue of standardization which makes it possible to transform it to other formats which are likely to appear in learning environments in the near future. Such environments will need to be considered in terms of acoustics; individual listening devices; a choice of optical or magnetic sound determined by the fidelity required, local recording and feedback requirements; stereophonic sound (especially if there is a revival of three-dimensional projected motion picture images); and—more sound, accompanying more visual modes.

f) *More flexibility.* Given the conditions mentioned previously, the total environment, including its image system components, will need to be very flexible. Wall structures will need to be adjustable both to accommodate images which could appear anywhere, and to control acoustics. Materials will need to be accessible to both student and teacher in large group, small group, and individual environments. A condition of such environments would be their design not only for information retrieval but also for the generation of images copied by teachers or students from video or audio playback systems as a form of what might be called "visual note-taking." This suggests camera and recording equipment for use by students in all audiovisual environments, either as part of the system, or as standard equipment owned by each student as he now owns pencil, notebook, and typewriter. Students in the Department of Photography and Cinema at the Ohio State University, for example, have used automated 8mm cameras fastened to their desk-chairs to take "notes" directly from films on the screen. Sixteen-millimeter cameras could be used to record still images, such as slides, frame by frame. Such copies represent a generation of images which will come into being out of the necessity for remembering visual images accurately through serious and repeated study by students and should not be regarded as violation of copyright any more than the notes they copy from print forms by Xerox or other methods. Repeatability of images for detailed study is the essence of the loop projector. It will be more necessary for students to own or have copies of key materials which he can study at his leisure. The 8mm format offers more promise here than either 16mm or, at the moment, videotape. The principle condition of flexibility in the environment, however, is that it be considered not only as a playback-center, but also in terms of its capacity to generate images to be copied for further use and study, and as a testing center as well—a condition which the capacity to record as well as play back audio and visual images would make possible.

These environmental factors suggest 16mm as an excellent primary medium especially regarding image size, brightness, capacity for detail, fidelity of color, and multiple sound tracks. Its greatest importance, however, is a standardization which makes it possible to translate it to the many other generations and formats of images required in an increasing number and variety of learning situations.

Audience Factors

The "target" audience for any film (or other medium) is difficult to define in this image generation because of rapidly shifting visual and perceptual values; the increasing types and numbers of individual viewers; and the increasing proliferation of varieties of situations in which the intended audience might be found.

Audience research, complicated by these factors, is badly needed. Reliable information on the effects of film experience from 8mm to wide-screen and multiple image presentations, for example, is almost totally lacking. Most educators, however, would agree with film critic Arthur Knight who points out that ". . . television has made this a particularly eye-minded generation" with "a new speed of perception." "Not only are we seeing faster than ever these days," he claims, "but apparently we can see more—if the film-makers will give us more to look at. The experience of Expo 67 has provided ample confirmation of this . . ."[15]

While recent research on multiple-channel information transmission would appear to make Expo 67 questionable as an absolute "confirmation" that audiences *are* seeing more and faster,[16] the influence of the theatrical film on youth is no news to educators who recall the Payne Fund Studies of more than 30 years ago, and the preachments of early prophets whose voices, lost in the wilderness of indifference and time, are now being echoed by latter-day-saints in the film "revival" of today:[17]

> The better we understand how young people view film, the more we have to revise our notion of what film is . . . The new multisensory involvement with film as total environment has been primary in destroying literary values in film.
>
> Perhaps one sense of the symptomatic word 'grooving', which applies to both sight and sound environments, is that a new mode of attention—multisensory, total, and simultaneous—has arrived. When you 'groove' you do not analyze, follow an argument, or separate sensations; rather, you are massaged into a feeling of heightened life and consciousness.[18]

The Reverend Schillaci's interpretation via Culkin, out of McLuhan must be taken seriously because what he is saying has been said in other ways by perceptive educators and students of film for thirty years.

It has never been difficult for an audience—especially a young audience—to "groove" with a good entertainment film, or to become involved in it as a "multisensory," "total," or "simultaneous" experience. A good story film has always involved its audience. But if the experience is nothing more than a "massage" then film may, indeed, be the opiate of the people and we can all repair to a Magic Fingers bed, watch *Petulia* on the late show, while listening to the background music from *The Yellow Submarine* without having to remember, or be responsible for, or critical of, any of it in the morning.

The classic problem of education, of course, is involvement on *different* levels of sensation. It means empathetic engagement as well as critical disengagement, a Brechtian sense of aesthetic distance; the discipline of stepping *out of* as well as *into* a situation. The motion picture can achieve both, when artfully designed (as discussed in the next section of this report), and when the audience is at once appreciative and critical of both medium and message.

Research on the nature of the audience, including studies of subgroups in terms of perceptual abilities and other variables, is needed to help the designer of media reach his target audience more efficiently.[19] Research on how to develop the ability of the audience to learn from these media is also in order.

Much has been made recently, for example, of what has been called "screen education" and "visual literacy." Consideration has been given to "the language" of film; of "grammar" and "syntax" in cinema.[20] Whether, in fact, film can be considered in literary terms at all, is questionable, but the study of how to get students to learn from film and other visual media should be continued in a serious vein and not just as an exercise in semantics on the part of enthusiasts of the feature film.

Most theorists who have contributed to the best thinking and writing in this field, describe motion pictures in education as "audio-visual film"—non-cinematic, pedantic, ineffective; produced by amateurs or unimaginative professionals for unimaginative educators who simply use dull films as substitutes for dull lectures. Whatever exaggeration there is in the position of the believer in "cinematic values," is matched by the exaggerated idea held by educators that instructional films should be free of "frills," "embellishments," or other non-informational content which would clutter the perceptions of the viewer and weaken the precise instructional point to be made.

The real change in the nature of the audience for educational films, however, may arise from the influence of visual experiences outside the educational system, as suggested earlier. Students will be affected before teachers, most of whom seldom see a theatrical film, or even much television, thus cutting themselves off from experiences which could help bridge the generation gap.

The change could also be implemented by the increasing number of local productions being undertaken by both students and teachers, and by multi-media experimentation going on at the public school level. The principal of an elementary school in New York, for example, describes how third-graders were immersed in a multi-media experience on an individualized study basis, resulting in the distillation of one unit from four weeks to seven days. He also reported that most of the software is "open end" material and that teachers are constantly adding to this by making their own materials.[21] Single-concept film making on 8mm by teachers is not uncommon, and film making by teen-agers in both 8mm and 16mm has reached the stature of a national movement. Creative film making by young people is recognized and stimulated by The Kodak-University Film Foundation Teen-Age Awards, the CINE Golden Eagle Youth Film Awards, and an increasing number of student film festivals for high-school and college age youth.

At the college and university level, the use and production of films lagged historically until the present decade. The audience for serious films was limited to film societies and a few departments making occasional use of the medium when time could be spared from the traditional and academically respectable business of reading, writing, and listening to lectures.

Today, films are being used and produced in greater variety and quantity than ever before in higher education, where the audience for film is being developed and sophisticated at the same time. University teachers who once looked down on this medium are now seeking it out as an answer to their instructional problems—and their professional aspirations. They are interested in "publishing" on film, and are actually willing to learn to operate a camera if necessary to express their ideas. Often starting out in the production of single-concept 8mm films, like students in film courses, their technical and visual requirements quickly escalate. From 8mm silent experiments they go to 16mm work. Color, sound, optical effects, animation, and ultimately release printing are soon involved. Colleagues and students react to their work which is now public, and a whole new set of appreciations and understandings of the medium arises as the university instructor becomes a "film author"—a producer as well as consumer of motion picture images. The camera has beome a typewriter.

Another generation of film makers has come into being—and another generation of film audiences.

As we focus on the audience for the 16mm film, it is important to remember that nearly all feature films and nearly all television documentaries and dramatic series are still released and made available to schools, film societies, and other educational institutions in 16mm form. Nearly all industrial, military, business, and religious films are designed for 16mm audiences. Most serious film students and teachers producing their own films, move from the 8mm format to 16mm in order to accomplish their purposes more professionally and in order to reach a larger audience. The "16mm industry" in the United States is big, being composed of laboratories, studios, distribution organizations, and producers who see the audience for films in this gauge expanding as the whole field—8mm and 35mm— expands.

The influence of today's visual imagery is affective. Television and theatrical images, multi-media, and multiple-image experiences outside the schools, will affect the perceptual capacities and tastes of the in-school audience, student and teacher alike.

The nature of the film experience needs to be explored in both its affective and informational aspects and educators should know much more about how film theorists have come to regard the medium and why they deplore the kinds and uses made of films in education. Teachers need to become part of the motion picture and television audience with their students in order to appreciate the kinds of images that are currently making an impact on youth. They must also recognize the different kinds of (often multiple) imagery, with different points of view, with different levels of involvement, and different kinds of viewing situations which make up the complex film experience of today.

Audience research must be revived at a level which takes into account the increasing number of variables in the contemporary situation. Audience, or screen education must include the cultivation of a sense of aesthetics as well as critical judgements about instructional values. Learning how to learn from film is involved. Learning how to make films may be an important development in the improvement of the audience for films of all types.

Finally, the changing nature of the audience for films of all types may change the design of films of all types, including films in education. The nature of the young audience, the nature of media, and the nature of contemporary film experiences certainly must be studied if Arthur Knight's description is accurate:

> An older generation is inclined to think of the media hardware as 'machines' to be screwed to the floor or locked in a booth while they produce images and sounds. The young, in contrast, recognize this hardware as part of the information environment of electronic technology, and they use it accordingly. Spontaneity, the chance synchronization, overload that leads to breakthrough—these are all part of the excitement that draws people to media rather than film alone.
>
> The young look at film is a revolutionary one, motivated more by love of the medium than hatred of the Establishment. In a sense, the new taste is liberating film for a free exploration of its potential, especially in the area of humanizing change. The hunger for a relativity of time and space will extend to morality, producing films that explore problems rather than package solutions. Nevertheless, the very intensity of young involvement gives promise of profound changes in the youth audience as people open themselves to the reality of the medium. Whether as young film-maker or multi-media entrepreneur, the young will have their say. If we take the time to cultivate their perspective, we may learn an interesting view of the future of media, and a fascinating way to stay alive.

The professional educator is not noted for the alacrity with which he has moved in education's oft-quoted "race with disaster", nor have the makers and users of educational film exhibited much ingenuity in helping win that race. For example, the evolution of the theory of quantum mechanics and the introduction of 16mm film both took place in the early 1920's, but it was nearly forty years before either development made any impact on the teaching of physics, even at the introductory level.

The changing nature of the "audience" may speed changes both in media and in education itself and help bring about a consideration of form-content relationships from which a new concept of design in education may emerge.

Design Factors

The first problem in creating excellence in 16mm films, or any other instructional medium, is in their original "design"—a term which, as Dewey once pointed out, connotes both purpose *and* form, arrangement, or mode of composition.[23]

The factors involved in the design of superior instructional materials obviously include much more than the classic ones of how to get the right message to the right audience in the right medium. As suggested earlier, hardware, architecture, curriculum, and an increasing number of human and societal conditions both in and outside the school, together with problems of generations of images in multiple forms, are involved. The fact that media are being built into total technological systems whose potential effectiveness is considerable, makes imperative a deep consideration of the art of teaching and a definition of the design in terms of the thoughtful, artful, organic application and creative control of necessary systems. The focus here is on film design, but behind these observations is their applicability to *all* media and their relationship to the larger concept of design in education.[24]

"The systematic study of design in exposition is one of the most strangely neglected fields of educational inquiry," stated the Harvard Report on General Education nearly 25 years ago. It also posed a challenge for the investigation of the unique qualities of the motion picture:

> The challenge to the text is given when the screen ceases to be a mere illustration or adornment to the language and becomes the equal or superior medium of communication . . . In the making of a good instructional or documentary film the duties of language are searchingly looked into and the needless obscurities of traditional texts are exposed. A healthy criticism is started and language, gaining a rival in its new partner has now new standards of lucidity to live up to.[25]

The Report describes film as an "awakener of interest", characterized by "massiveness of impact", and concludes with the judgement: "The movie has proved itself to possess the power, if there is the wisdom to use it."

Contemporary comment continues to reinforce the widely-held belief in the power of the film, but how to make and use films wisely is still a "strangely neglected field of educational inquiry."

The reason may well be that because of the intricate interaction of content and form, film making, like teaching, remains an art not explainable solely in terms of the myopia of the subject-matter specialist, or the mania of the form-centered cineaste, or the laboratory-oriented behavioral scientist. The problem of generating images in an image-oriented generation is further complicated by the multiple, transitional, and transactional forms in which sounds and images now appear.

On the simplest level, the design of a successful informational film is a kind of program, or logic—with frame, sequence, beginning, middle, and end. It is hopefully intended for a known audience to match specified outcomes related to instructional objectives. There is often an introduction ("tell them what you're going to tell them"), and a summary ("tell them what you've told them"), and some additional redundancy in the body of the film itself. Pictures and words are closely related, the vocabulary is geared to the intended audience level, the film is often allied to a text, and there is usually a teacher's or study guide.

Yet, film producers and most teachers know that it is not all that scientific; that there is an art to the making of an instructional film in the same way that Norberg regards "programming" as "a art in the sense that it allows for stylistic variations, but also because of the present state of learning theory and the science of human behavior."[26] A. A. Lumsdaine, who has done a great deal of research on what makes an educational film effective also once pointed out that:

> ". . . the principles that research can come up with will always be nothing more than statements about film methods; and it's important to remember that a film

method is not a film. It's only an approach to a film which still has to be implemented by the creativity of the film writer and director . . . I think that what research provides in the way of dependable facts and principles about the relation of film methods to educational outcomes will increasingly permit more opportunity, not less, for the application of creative talent in the construction of more effective films."[27]

The distinctions between the creative educational film and the film as an "entertainment" experience tend to blur—a fact which the writer along with a few others pointed out nearly twenty years ago.[28] Today, films designed for education may appear in 70mm, 35mm, 16mm, or 8mm formats. They may vary in length, style, and purpose, and be designed for a variety of types of viewing situations with a variety of audiences in competition with a variety of other audiovisual images. The short 8mm single-concept film on *The Cavendish Experiment* made by a teacher of physics, will be compared to the economy, lucidity, and compelling power of a television commercial; the time-tested documentary, *The River,* will be seen, drawn from the shelf of the audiovisual center, alongside an hour-long television study of the waste of our natural resources today, done in the hard style of the new visual journalism. Theatrical films reflecting the social scene in brutal, often imbalanced, but unquestionably powerful ways, will be seen by young adults who will also see more balanced, but often less affective, and generally less relevant, "educational" films on some of the same subjects in social science classes.

This current interaction of artful film form and audience perception is seen in the theatrical and instructional film alike. The pace in both has quickened. The "single-concept film" and the television commercial alike are swift-moving, fragmented, limited in length, and devoted to a close-up intensive treatment of one main idea, displayed on a small screen. The reference to "visual-squeeze" in TV spots by the ad agency man, finds its counterpart in the educator who refers more pedantically, but no less accurately, to ". . . the new rhetoric of the 8mm loop film . . . which invites dense packing of pictorial information."[29]

The "open-ended" film, popular in university programs in educational administration and teacher training, contains basically the same ambiguity and absence of closure (or "happy ending") found in films like *The Graduate, 2001: A Space Odyssey;* or even in a three-minute silent 8mm cartridged film of a demonstration which ends not with the question of what happened, but *why* it happened. In each case, the requirement is that the viewer finds his own resolution; that he become an extension of the film maker; that he, in fact, complete the film. This point of view is compatible with that philosophy of education which holds to the "discovery approach" to learning; with the "low-pressure sell" referred to by the commercial communicator; and with the theory of those students of cinema who believe there should be much less "telling" and much more "showing" in films—especially with young audiences.

"As far as the 'point' of films is concerned," reflects the Reverend Schillachi, "young people will resist a packaged view, but will welcome a problematic one. The cry, 'Please, I'd rather do it myself,' should be taken to heart by the film-maker. It is better to use understatement in order to score a personal discovery by the viewer. Such a discovery of an idea is a major part of our delight in the experience of film art."[30]

Miller and Bollman, predicting that 16mm in educational usage will become a medium-length film, suggest a design which will ". . . provide motivation by providing very few facts, concentrating instead on creating a state of mind in which the child wants to use his own efforts to fill in the deliberate gaps in information created by the film."[31]

While length is not always an essential quality of the provocative, open-ended film, it does take time to establish a mood and a sense of involvement which goes below the surface of the screen. The effect is also enhanced by amplification of image size—a view expressed by Cahaney, referring to the industrial film:

I think the 16mm color film offers industry the single most powerful and compelling device to communicate with the public, and I see no reason to think it won't continue to do so in the years ahead. The 16mm film is really a remarkable instrument. It's bigger than life. Its power to absorb the viewer is second only to the 35mm theatrical picture. Given a combination of the right story line for the right audience, it's nearly equal to it.[32]

The "mind-boggling" films intended by form and content to generate "total involvement" through high visual density, swift-paced delivery of audiovisual information (or in some cases, non-information), and intentional (or in some cases, accidental?) gaps in continuity at best fulfill a need for creative educational experiences which stimulate intellectual discovery and promote critical thinking. At worst, the psychedelic film experience and multi-media happening may "leave no more trace of their existence than a burnt-out firecracker."[33]

The critical need for experiences which *fill the gaps* in a world of ambiguities requires films which help put Humpty-Dumpty together. The degree to which new cinematic forms may be put to this purpose is questioned even by film critic and enthusiast, Arthur Knight:

These new techniques . . . cannot be forced upon traditional subject matter. Content and form are not separable; and nowhere is this more evident than in pictures that attempt to engraft Expo's multiple screen effects or Resnais' swift flashbacks and flash-forwards, onto stories that follow a conventional formula.[34]

There is "traditional subject matter" enough to be transmitted today. Film and television, in a world of increasing entropy, hold forth one of our few, last hopes of organizing and structuring an increasing mass of information; for bringing some clarity out of ambiguity; for narrowing the ever-widening gaps between theory and practice, between fields of human knowledge, between generations of human beings, and between nations and cultures.

In religion, for example, it is hoped that these media ". . . can be used by the Church as a kind of catalytic agent that has the potential of transforming the Church's whole relationship to society."[35] The Physical Science Study Commission expressed the belief that ". . . films will serve to solve a teaching problem that is not peculiar to physics but that runs through the entire educational process: the problem of the gap that so frequently arises between a science or a humanity as it is actually carried on by its practitioners."[36] If the technological gap between the advanced and less developed nations increases by the predicted 50 percent during the next half-century, foresight in designing simple informational films with regard to their potential use in other nations and other cultures is immensely significant.[37] Even more difficult may be the making of films which communicate with sub-groups in our own culture—films which bridge the generation gap, which reach shifting, heterogeneous audiences at home and abroad—perhaps with what Norbert Weiner once referred to as "to whom it may concern" messages.

We have much to learn about the design of films which fill, as well as create gaps in information. Nearly all of what has been written, researched, and produced in the field of the educational film up to now has been devoted to the problem of how to organize, present, and test information in film form, and we still know too little about how to make effective didactic films, let alone more complex, multi-imaged forms.

The major consideration in film design in education in the future may not be in terms of the kinds of specific factors studied in the past, but rather in more generalized, creative, philosophical studies involving films whose function is the systematic transmission of information; the clarification of abstracts, and the closing of perceptual gaps, and those designed for the transformation of information and experience; deliberately intended to create ambiguity, to open gaps in the viewer's existing perceptions of things and ideas. The first design suggests 8mm cartridged prints used as part of a "program function" in the logical manner of a Socratic dialogue. The second implies the use of non-programmed 16mm films which serve a "pointing function" in the style of Cratylus, one of Plato's teachers who so doubted the exactness of words that he decided he was only going to point the way to learning.[38]

Remembering that this is a grey-scale rather than a formula, the technical, aesthetic, and pedagogic elements of design for films to be displayed in the 8mm and 16mm modes may be suggested as follows:

SMALL FORMAT	LARGE FORMAT
Informational function	Transformational function
Small screen	Large screen
Individual or small-group viewing	Large-group viewing
Short attention span required	Long attention span required
Specific content	Generalized content
Precise, parsimonous	Ambiguous, provocative
Short, repeatable fragments	Long, total experiences
Close-up images for limited screen	Long-shot images for expanded screen
Logical, linear, continuity cutting	Non-logical, dynamic cutting
"Straight" photography	Non-representational photography
Supportive use of sound	Psychological use of sound
Daylight or room light projection	Darkened environment projection
Programmed use	Non-programmed use
Immediate feedback	Delayed feedback
Continuous usage and accessibility	Limited usage and accessibility

The construction of films which serve both ends of this educational log was a major concern in the production of a series of films on communication and the new media of education developed at the Ohio State University for the U.S. Office of Education.[39] This consisted of a collection or repertoire of films which could be considered a "package" or program which, because each film and each sequence in each film was designed as a self-contained module, could also be "unpackaged" since the films were designed to be recut and rearranged for individualized use by different instructors in different fields with different target audiences.

This type of modular film, produced originally on 16mm, has been used as parts of other films, transferred to videotape, transmitted by open-and closed-circuit television, and, as intended, completely rearranged by individual users. Segments which are inappropriate or which may contaminate other parts of the film because of obsolescence, may be removed without violating the continuity of the remainder. Instructional time may be saved by selecting one or two short sequences in a given film which fulfill the immediate instructional objectives with a specific audience without having to run the entire film.

The ends of necessary organization and desirable ambiguity may thus be theoretically served by this design, and the generation of these 16mm images to other forms is technically simplified as well. A study of usage patterns to check the validity of these propositions is being made in locations in which this set of films is in use throughout the nation and in certain international situations as well.

The ultimate and most fruitful uses of films designed in the modular, open-ended, single-concept, or any other form, depends upon the perceptivity and creativity of the individual user. Producers, teachers, students, administrators, librarians, media specialists, and all those involved in the Nation's most important business of teaching and learning must come to regard film (and other media) as a generative, interactive, and challenging *process* rather than a mechanical system of unalterable fixed images and ideas.

The study of design in exposition, with regard to film and other media as well, is central to the problems faced by professional educators, statesmen, industrial, religious, and political leadership, and to our international as well as our domestic well-being. Creative films are needed to serve both the "programmed" as well as the "pointing" function of which they are capable. The dynamic contributions of the moving-image-media are yet to be explored.

The new forms emerging on theatrical, art-house, underground, and Expo screens are affecting what is seen on classroom walls, in carrels, and instructional auditoria. Yet, we are still primitives in the art of the moving image, not far removed from the imagery of other, more primitive communicators whose work created on the walls of the caves of Altamira and Lascaux and first seen 30,000 years ago by the uncertain light of a torch, may appear as a flickering image seen by the light of a tungsten-halogen bulb on a local motion picture screen.

Man's innate need to express himself pictorially—in wide-screen, color, multiple images—is vividly portrayed in the glowing portrayals of bison, reindeer, and woolly mammoth, designed by Upper Paleolithic man. These images, infused with what anthropologists refer to as "sympathetic magic"—may have been similar in effect to projected images of today, for very possibly the same reasons. Makers of 16mm films for education face the same basic design problem as the Magdelenian cave artists whose task, through their draftsmanship, was to create images of animal realities and, through their artistry, to transform as well as instruct their viewers in what was, doubtless through associated ceremony, a totally-involving audiovisual experience.

Thus, while the ancient problem of design in exposition is complexed by technological changes in image-making, it seems, as critic Judith Crist observed, after reviewing the spectrum of contemporary film, that ". . . the more it changes, the more it is of the same old thing."[40] And the more we realize that we, too, are still the ancients in the art of audiovisual imagery.

Philosophical Factors

The subject of film is not accurately describable in terms of 16mm or any other gauge, or even as "film." The topic is a philosophical and creative consideration of the moving image in an image-oriented generation with images which generate other images, combining and dissolving from one form to another for different purposes in different systems both within formal learning environments and without.

We need thoughtful *Media Philosophers* with a sense of "art as experience," and responsible *Designers in Exposition* with superb skill in the organic use and creative control of necessary system. Only through the philosophical approach can we effect what Dr. Don Bigelow, of the U.S. Office of Education once referred to as "the detribalization" of media-specialists, content-experts, instructional-technologists, curriculum-makers, programmers, systems-analysts, and hierarchies of educational theorists, and schools of research, thus opening the windows for fresh thinking. (How else explain the societal effect of McLuhan?) Only through the expertise of designers in exposition, familiar with the entire palette of what is humanly required and technologically possible in communication, can the conceptions of the media philosopher be given meaningful form. (How else explain the influence of Charles Eames, Buckminster Fuller, and Frank Lloyd Wright?) In each—philosopher and designer—there must be some of the capabilities of the other.

Woven into the texture of this report are inter-acting technical and philosophical considerations which make 16mm, in many respects, what may be described as "a happy medium."

As a primary recording material, it fulfills a number of technical requirements of today, and of the foreseeable future. It is a kind of universal image system, compatible with existing film and television projection systems throughout the world. It is reducible to smaller as well as to larger screen formats; transferrable; storageable; and capable of satisfying demands for images with more light, more color, more exquisite detail, multiple sound tracks, and multiple-imagery.

Sixteen-millimeter meets design requirements for flexibility in a multiplicity of learning situations, and can produce a harvest of many modes from a universally-conceived original design. It may, for example, be structured and restructured to serve either a "programming" or "pointing" function; to close information gaps, or to open information gaps; to inform, or to stimulate. While such films may become longer in format, they may also be designed as modules which may be taken apart and reformed as a new generation of images, extending the physical act of "film-making" to the teacher, and even to the student himself. The *use* of film thus becomes the kind of creative function described by Filip in terms of computer-assisted instruction:

> An individual may gain a sense of "molding" his instruction in much the same way a potter molds clay. The presentation is responsible to his replies, and he can see a set emerging which is modified by his input. The "hands-on" quality of typing and/or using a light-pen also give him feedback through the tactile senses. These experiences may fulfill a need for contemporary man to be a "craftsman" or at least actively participate in the highly personal process of learning . . . Perhaps in this interaction "work of art" from start to finish as did the craftsmen of old with their products. The person sitting at the terminal is involved in the process of creating *his* instructional "urn."[41]

Sixteen-millimeter production is increasing among advanced amateurs, teachers, and students, though they typically begin with 8mm filming. While 16mm projection equipment lags behind 8mm in sophistication and simplicity, 16mm production and laboratory facilities are well established, highly professional, and increasingly accessible to the independent producer at almost any level. For example, a professor of mathematics is making his own films on a professional animation stand; a college student is producing art films with his own 16mm camera and sound equipment; teen-age movie makers are submitting 16mm films in national competitions. Seven- and eight-year olds such as those in the Early Childhood Center of the Bank Street College of Education in New York are making 8mm films from which may evolve 16mm prints for study by students of education throughout the country. Some serious professionals are turning from 35mm to 16mm for economic reasons, because film festivals are receptive to 16mm work, and because of creatively-related technical interests, some of which are explained in a publication catering to the growing cadre of underground, independent, and non-establishment film makers:

> The 16mm filmmaker has an advantage over his 35mm big brother when his film reaches the laboratory. The 35mm filmmaker using color is basically limited to one camera stock (5251, Eastman color negative) and one print stock (5385, Eastman color positive). But there are several roads open to the producer of 16mm color motion pictures, some that were not available six years or even six months ago.[42]

The shifting nature of "target" audiences can be met only by an image system and a medium which may be put into many modes, as mentioned earlier. One of the modes for which 16mm seems to be ideally suited is the large group, extended viewing experience, requiring a large picture in a semi-darkened condition. This film image may be seen, in some instructional settings, in combination with other juxtaposed images such as front- or rear-screen slides, or with other 16mm films.

The 16mm film in education may become longer, perhaps approaching feature length. It will be affected by the nature of the contemporary cinema screen in style and possibly in function, and will actually be increasingly competitive with 16mm theatrical and television films released for use in education. The 16mm educational "feature" film will contrast in length, purpose, design, and setting with the 8mm cartridged film which in its professional form will continue to originate as first generation 16mm image. The longer 16mm will typically employ a "shotgun" approach to a general, or "to whom it may concern" audience, while the short-3 cartridge will take a rifle-like aim at a more specific target.

The versatility of the 16mm medium has never been fully exploited in educational research; multiple-versions and changes have been expensive and time-consuming. However, linked with other forms of image making, and with the computer, stimulus material originally produced on 16mm has extensive research usage. At the Ohio State University, for example, Basic Chemistry is taught using material which originates on 16mm color film to which a magnetic sound track is added. This film is played directly into a CCTV system, or may be converted directly to a 1-inch videotape for testing in student laboratories. The tested material (with necessary revisions on the 16mm original) is then reduced to Super-8 prints for use in carrels, may be converted to the CBS-EVR system for wider electronic distribution, and also be used in 16mm with large groups.[43] Computer-made films promise even greater potential for testing, re-testing, and modifying the image and producing generations of image for transmission in a variety of modes, where they may be tested in diverse settings. For example, artist Charles Csuri draws a picture of a hummingbird which is programmed into a computer, changed to a 35mm image recorded from an oscilloscope screen, modified by an animation camera, converted to a standard 16mm print seen on a screen in the Museum of Modern Art, as a videotaped image on a major television network, as a 16mm classroom film, or perhaps later in 8mm form. The basic 16mm image could be tested in these settings, and changed by computer-based methods which may, for the first time, make possible the necessary multiple-factor analysis needed to find out what films can really do in education in both the cognitive and the affective domains.

For fifty years empirical evidence has supported the popular truism that children and adults learn from film, that they are involved in the medium, and that they are influenced by what they see in informal as well as formal learning situations. We are on a new wave of film interest with a myriad of new and challenging possibilities for research related to the influence of the moving image; the effects of multiple-imagery; the proliferation of generations of images and their interpretations; and the nature of the Image Generation itself.

A number of such research possibilities may be posed in conclusion, many of them perhaps in the domain of the philosopher rather than the psychologist; the designer rather than the behavioral scientist. Yet, all must necessarily be involved in exploring the many complex, fascinating, and critical facets of two basic questions which are at once ancient and contemporary: 1. the nature of the generation of images, and 2. the nature of our own generation—an image generation.

What are the real sources of power of the film (or "the moving image" including television which is largely film) with children and how they learn? A lot is said and written about the subject by adult experts. We have yet to hear much from the children themselves.

What are the effects of "the *same* image" when transferred from 16mm to 8mm, to videotape, to television, when transmitted by satellite? Should we be concerned with losses or gains in the meaning and *integrity* of the image as well as losses or gains in *technical quality* in the transfer?

What are the influences of the viewing environments in which these images appear? How do variations in the physical and psychological settings in which images are now being seen affect the nature of the image itself? Do we need a new conception of "gallery", of the ways in which images can be displayed, ways which do not simply put an image where a teacher used to stand and deliver?

How good are existing studies of the learner's ability to absorb a barrage of images? Is man really a limited-input animal, or are we testing only one response to his many modes of information processing because we have not yet developed the test instruments to measure his full capabilities?

What use of multiple-images and cross-media can we really make in designing instructional materials? Is Richard Fleisher, director of *The Boston Strangler,* correct when he says: "The multi-image screen should not be used for informational purposes. It should be used to get over a mood and atmosphere."[44]

What is the significance of the number of people, from 8 to 80, who are now making their own films? Is there a new visual language in the making that transcends generation gaps, national boundaries, and subject matter fields? Is what used to be a public art becoming private expression—even personal therapy? How important is the apparent escalation from 8mm to 16mm technology among amateurs and what does it mean?

What are the implications of films (and other materials of instruction) designed in a modular mode? What psychological factors become operative when films, books, and other once protected, "on-shelf" materials begin to be regarded by teachers, students, and administrators as truly generative, interactive, and expendable items rather than a collection of authoritative, unalterably fixed images and ideas?

Does the concept of flexibility inevitably lead to destructability—to the total expenditure of media and material once hoarded beyond the point of obsolescence? Should the design of instructional materials include a built-in "destruct element" thus insuring the larger purpose of planned change? Is the element of destruction a basic characteristic of our image generation, the end of the mechanical age, symbolized in Tinguely's mechanical assemblage titled "Homage to New York", which destroyed itself in the Sculpture Garden of the Museum of Modern Art in the Spring of 1960?

Is the fact that a few photographs of its self-destruction are all that's left of Tinguely's artistic happening, symbolic of the ultimate role of the camera in "capturing and holding in a state of permanency" (as the early announcements of photography 130 years ago described the process) the fleeting, transitory, multiple images of our times? Is it possible that only through photography, film, and television may we really be able to know what is going on at all? Will more teachers come to use these media like the football coach who understands that his only chance of knowing, let alone analyzing and reflecting on what happened in the field, is through slow-motion films or extended videotape replays of the game?

Is our image generation exhibiting the first visible signs of how technology really affects human biology? Are we on the threshold of a new phase of an evolutionary process in which, as one writer claims, the whole image-making drive may be a means for preparing man for physical and mental changes which he will, in time, make upon himself?[45]

These are fundamentally philosophical questions—like Dewey's reference to "design" as both purpose and mode of expression; McLuhan's oft-maligned "medium is message", questions of "realism" vs. "symbolism" in film; "form" vs. "function", and the relationship of man and machine in a world where we already seem to be passing from the mechanical and electronic period into biological and chemical modes which will change the technology of imagery and theories of learning as well.

In the meantime, film (or its future equivalent) seems to create excitement by exploding perceptual traditions, by its "photographic realism", by its facility for the reconstruction as well as the dissection of experience, and because film, like a particular value philosophy in which a felt-response is the core, can bridge both a cybernetic model of reality and a purely sensory experience.[46]

Film may close gaps and open gaps, and serve a universal communication function, with 16mm being a kind of universal medium given the present conditions and requirements for image-generation in a Generation of Images.

REFERENCES

1. Boorstin, Daniel. *The Image: or What Happened to the American Dream.* Atheneum, New York, 1962.

2. Offenhauser, William H., Jr. *16mm Sound Motion Pictures.* Interscience Publishers, Inc., New York, 1949, p. 8.

3. *Sixty Years of 16mm Film 1923-1983. A Symposium.* Edited by Paul Wagner, Film Council of America. Practical Offset Inc., Des Plaines, Illinois, 1954.

   8mm Sound Film and Education. Edited by Louis Forsdale. Horace Mann-Lincoln Institute of School Experimentation. Bureau of Publications, Teachers College, Columbia University, 1962.

4. Sound-8 projectors had been introduced by both Eastman and Fairchild in 1960, but as early as 1952 Lloyd Thompson, of the Calvin Company in Kansas City, developed and marketed an 8mm sound projector which operated at both 16 and 24 frames per second, using a magnetic track.

5. Hope, Thomas W. "Market Review: Nontheatrical Film and Audio-Visual—1967." *Journal, SMPTE,* Vol. 77, No. 11, Nov., 1968, pp. 1210-1220.

6. Abrahamson, Albert. "Picture Quality: Film vs. Television." *Journal, SMPTE,* Vol. 77, June, 1968, pp. 613-621.

7. *1966-1969 Perspective World Report of the Photographic Industries, Technologies, and Science.* Edited by L. A. Manneheim, The Focal Press, London and New York, 1968, p. 128.

8. *Rewind.* General Film Laboratories. Hollywood, Vol. 10, No. 10, Oct., 1968, p. 2.

9. Brudner, Harvey J. and William E. Bowen. "A Suggestion for a New Film Format for Educational Use." *Journal, SMPTE,* Vol. 77, Oct., 1968, pp. 1050-1051.

10. LeFranc, Robert. "L'Avenir du film d'Enseignement de 16mm." *Moyens Audio-Visuals, Revue Internationale,* Vol. 2, 1968, pp. 23-30.

11. *Sixty Years of 16mm Film 1928-1938.* p. 18.

12. Forsdale, Op. cit., pp. 152-154.

13. Chandler, J. S. and J. J. DePalma. "High Brightness Projection Screens with High Ambient Light Rejection." *Journal, SMPTE,* Vol. 77, Oct., 1968, pp. 1012-1024.

14. "Progress Committee Report for 1967." Edited by Richard E. Putnam. *Journal, SMPTE,* Vol. 77, May, 1968, p. 494.

15. Knight, Arthur. "Engaging the Eye-Minded." *Saturday Review,* Dec. 28, 1968, pp. 18-19.

16. See "Expo-67—A Retrospect," and other related information in the *Journal of the University Film Association,* Vol. 21, No. 1, 1969.

17. Charters, W. W. *Motion Pictures and Youth.* The Macmillan Company, New York, 1935.

18. Schillachi, Anthony. "The Now Movie." *Saturday Review,* Dec. 28, 1968, pp. 8-10.

19. Snow, Richard E. and Gavriel Salomon. "Aptitudes and Instructional Media." *AV Communication Review,* Vol. 16, No. 4, Winter, 1968, pp. 341-355.

20. Pryluck, Calvin. "Structural Analysis of Motion Pictures as a Symbol System." *AV Communication Review,* Vol. 16, No. 4, Winter, 1968, pp. 372-401.

21. "They Like Working There." *Educational Screen & AV Guide,* Sept., 1968, pp. 20-21.

22. Knight, op. cit.

23. Dewey, John. *Art As Experience.* Minton, Balch & Co., New York, 1934, p. 116.

24. Wagner, Robert W. "Design in Education." *The Newsletter.* The College of Education, The Ohio State University, January, 1968.

25. *General Education in a Free Society, Report of the Harvard Committee.* Harvard University Press, Cambridge, Mass., 1945, pp. 262-264.

26. Brown, James W. and James W. Thorton, Jr. *New Media in Higher Education.* National Education Assn., Washington, D.C., 1963, p. 20.

27. Lumsdaine, A. A. "Experimental Research as a Aid to Creative Film Making." *The Aperture,* Vol. 2, No. 6, 1951.

28. Wagner, Robert W. *Design in the Educational Film: An Analysis of Production Elements in Twenty-One Widely Used Non-Theatrical Motion Pictures.* Ph.D. Dissertation. Unpub. The Ohio State University, 1953.

29. *Newsletter of 8mm Film in Education.* Teachers College, Columbia University, No. 3, April, 1966, p. 1.

30. Schillachi, op. cit., p. 11.

31. Miller, Elwood, and Charles Bollman. *Journal, SMPTE.* Vol. 77, 1968, pp. 1046-1048.

32. Cahaney, G. Roger. "The Industrial Film: Its Status and Prognosis." *Audiovisual Communications,* October, 1968, p. 22.

33. "Sound and Fury in the Arts." *Look,* January 9, 1968, p. 13.

34. Knight, op. cit., p. 19.

35. Lowe, Clayton K. *The Protestant Use of Television as a Means of Social and Spiritual Reconciliation.* M.Sc. Thesis. Unpub. Butler University, Indianapolis, 1966, p. 22.

36. *First Annual Report of the Physical Science Study Committee.* Vol. 1, 1958, p. 36.

37. Wagner, Robert W. "The International Educational Film." *Audiovisual Communication Review,* Vol. 6, 1958, No. 1, pp. 49-55; No. 2, pp. 140-146.

38. Wagner, Robert W. "In Search of Design." *Education Technology.* Donald P. Ely, Ed. Syracuse University Press, 1966, pp. 81-96.

39. Wagner, Robert W. *A Galaxy of Motion Picture Documents on Communication Theory and the New Educational Media.* USOE Project B-131-A. Contract No. OE-3-16-020. Final Report, December, 1966, p. 82.

   Wagner, Robert W. "Flexible Films." *Educational Screen and Audiovisual Guide,* May 1967, p. 22f.

40. Crist, Judith. "Movies Where Anything Goes." *Look.* January 9, 1968, p. 23.

41. Filip, Robert. "Individualized Instruction and the Computer: Potential for Mass Education." *AV Communication Review,* Vol. 15, No. 1, Spring, 1967, p. 104.

42. Zeobi, Nick. "Equipment News." *Filmmaker's Newsletter,* Vol. 2, No. 2, 1968, p. 5.

43. Barnard, Robert, and Rod O'Connor. "Teaching Aids: Television for Modern Chemistry Classroom, Part III." *Journal of Chemical Education,* Vol. 45, No. 11, November, 1968, pp. 745-748.

44. "Symposium: Adding to the Director's Tools." *Action,* The Director's Guild of America, November-December, 1968, p. 26.

45. Burnham, Jack. *Beyond Modern Sculpture: The Effects of Science and Technology on the Sculpture of This Century.* Braziller, 1968.

46. McGuire, Jerimiah C. *Cinema and Value Philosophy.* Philosophical Library, 1968, p. 1.

   Huss, Roy, and Herman Silverstein. *The Film Experiences.* Harper and Row, New York, 1968.

   Bazin, Andre. *What is Cinema?* The University of California Press, 1967.

   Kracauer, Siegfried. *Theory of Film: The Redemption of Physical Reality.* Oxford University Press, 1960.

22.

The Adoption and Distribution of Videotape Materials for Educational Use

*by KEN WINSLOW**
Dir. of Educational Services
Reeves Actron Corp.

Introduction

The present commitment of American Education to the use of instructional materials of a motion visual-aural nature is undeniable. Dollar expenditures by public, private, and parochial elementary and secondary schools plus public and private institutions of higher learning as well as business and trade schools for the use of 8mm and 16mm film materials involving production, purchase, and distribution of such materials amounted to $94.6 million in calendar 1967.[1]

Before 1956: Period Prior to Development of Videotape Technology

In contrast to the history of film techniques for education, the development of television techniques for education has been relatively short in years but rapid in technological progress. The adoption by education of television communication techniques took hold by the middle 1950's in an operating context which was "live" and which lacked at the outset a satisfactory storage and retrieval capability. The only means available for recording was that of kinescoping, i.e. the recording on motion picture film the television image from the face of a television picture display tube—technically known as a kinescope.

Early investigations and uses made of television by education involved facilities ranging from single building and campus-wide closed-circuit wire distributions systems to city and state-wide broadcast transmissions. Of the most notable among the very many demonstrations were those at Hagerstown, Maryland (commencing Fall, 1956) for the public school level and at Pennsylvania State University (commencing Spring, 1955) for the college level. Apart from a relatively few exceptions, all these demonstrations used live television camera presentations simultaneously distributed by wire means to closed-circuit viewers or by wireless means to broadcast transmission viewers. During these very extensive and pioneering efforts almost every conceivable aspect of the use of television by education was investi-

*At the time the paper was written, he was manager of Ampex Tape Exchange, Consumer and Educational Products Division, Ampex Corporation.

gated.[2] Conclusions were drawn about costs, educational effectiveness, and curricular design at a time when the condition of the technology of television communication was—in retrospect—relatively quite primitive.

In many of the early investigations and uses of television by education where the objective was to reach viewers over a large geographic area extending anywhere from a city to the entire nation in size, commercial television time was purchased or public service time was used. The first purely educational television station (KUHT-ETV8) was jointly licensed to the University of Houston and the Houston Board of Education and placed into regular operation on May 12, 1953. The Fund For Adult Education of the Ford Foundation through matching grants was instrumental in establishing many of the first ETV stations.[2]

1956-1961: Period of Broadcast Standard Videotape Development

It was not until 1956—after experience had been accumulated by education with a large variety of live closed-circuit and broadcast transmission uses—that videotape recording and playback capability was first introduced and demonstrated at a meeting of the National Association of Radio and Television Broadcasters in the form of a commercially available and satisfactory means for television electronic storage and retrieval.[3] The videotape technique was developed for the entertainment broadcasting industry initially as a delay device. The first videotape machines gobbled up by the commercial television broadcasters were —from the point of view of educational agencies per se—expensive to acquire and complicated to operate. As first a short term time delay device and then a long term storage/retrieval delay device, the videotape machine became the unchallenged essential tool for the television broadcaster. In the late 1950's the Ford Foundation provided a grant through the National Educational Television and Radio Center to provide one broadcast standard videotape machine to all NETRC affiliated ETV stations. Accordingly, in the late 1950's where an educational agency either operated an ETV broadcast station or used the broadcast time provided by an ETV broadcast station for transmission of instructional course material . . . the relative sudden availability of widespread videotape record/playback capability made an initial and significant impression on the production, transmission, and utilization by educational agencies of television course materials.

During this period in response to the Meierhenry-McBride survey conducted in 59/60 and published in 1961 the then 53 operating ETV stations throughout the country reported that a total of 199 elementary (K-6) courses were recorded; 103 secondary (7-12) courses were recorded; and 135 college level courses were recorded. Only 88 of the known 222 closed-circuit activities replied to the survey. Of these 88 reporting closed-circuit installations, there were only reported 83 recorded *programs*.[4] The study does not indicate whether these recordings were made on videotape or film. The study reports that of the 53 replying stations, 35 reported having kinescope recording facilities and that 50 reported having videotape record/playback capability. It is the experience of the author that the ETV stations turned en mass to the use of videotape. The only limiting factor in committing instructional courses and programs to videotape was the availability of enough videotape and situations where a recorded presentation was to be subsequently used at a time or place where a videotape machine was not available for playback. Clearly both the focus and initiative for the recording for education of instructional courses and programs at this time lay in the hands of the ETV broadcast station. Videotape technology was not yet feasible to the point of being generally available as an "in-house" device for education.

1961 And On: Period of Helical Standard Videotape Development

In March, 1961 a major manufacturer of broadcast standard videotape equipment demonstrated in the form of a commercially available device a heretofore new and different videotape record and playback process exhibiting a helical scan characteristic which was by neither design or intent to be compatible with the by then well established broadcast quadruplex standard. The helical scan videotape machine was announced as specifically designed for the closed-circuit education and training community. This event showed the way to many other manufacturers.[3] The result today is a large array of low cost, physically compact, highly portable, and easy to operate helical scan videotape machines in model types for almost every conceivable nonbroadcast closed-circuit educational application.[6][7] Each manufacturer has developed his own unique helical videotape record/playback standard . . . in some cases two or more different standards . . . with the result that videotapes recorded on one helical machine standard are not directly retrievable on another helical machine standard of the same or another manufacturer. There is a regular cry for a universal helical videotape machine standardization agreement among manufacturers. The major argument is to provide for complete mechanical interchange of recorded videotape materials among all helical machines irrespective of manufacturer's make and model. The major counter argument is that to fix a universal helical recording standard—if such could in fact be done—would stop competition and thereby freeze technological developments, cost reduction programs, etc. Any individual or agency contemplating the acquisition of a videotape machine for educational applications must undertake his own investigations in a methodical, objective, and dispassionate manner.[8] In point of fact all established distributors of pre-recorded instructional videotape materials make their materials available for use on one or more helical standard machines. Major distributors (see below) make their materials available for several different helical standard machines.

The Adoption of Videotape Technology By Education

In the years since 1961 the appreciation and utilization of the helical scan videotape machine has continued to mature as a result of continued technological development by many manufacturers[7] plus the growing number of uses to which the helical scan machine has been put by education. The purchase by education of television videotape and associated origination and display equipment increased 13% in 1967 over 1966 while in the same period the purchase of film projection and associated equipment decreased.[1] At the November 1968 technical meeting of the Society of Motion Picture and Television Engineers, Washington, D.C., Dr. Sam M. Lambert, Executive Secretary, NEA, reported that the number of television receivers in the nation's schools has exceeded for the first time the number of film projectors. It is estimated that by 1970 every school in the United States will have at least one television receiver.[9]

An important reason for the capture by videotape and related equipment of an increasingly larger share of educational media equipment expenditures is the multi-application potential of helical videotape equipment systems as compared to the single "retrieval" ability of the film projector.

A review of the experience of education has shown that the helical scan videotape machine and associated television camera, microphone, and monitor/receiver equipment is devoted by educational users to three general categories of applications singularly or (most often) in combination.[7] In *recording applications* the helical machine is used to store visual/aural presentations: 1) created locally with recording input obtained by the machine from a television camera and microphone; 2) created remotely and received locally as a recording input obtained by the machine from a closed-circuit, telephone company, or CATV wire source; or 3) created remotely and received locally as a recording input obtained by the machine from a VHF/UHF broadcast; point-to-point microwave; multiple address ITFS: or (future) satellite-to-ground wireless source. In *interactive feedback applications* the helical machine with associated equipment is used as an instant record/replay means in almost every conceivable situation involving self-development of cognitive and mechanical skills by students, teachers, and administrators. In *distribution applications* the helical machine is used to retrieve previously recorded visual/aural presentations: 1) created locally with available resources of technical facilities, trained and knowledgeable personnel, and budgetary support; and 2) acquired outside as a pre-recorded videotape course-series, lesson-title, or subject module.

The commitment of education to the use of videotape—communication techniques is firm. The initiative being taken throughout the country at the various levels of education is typified by a distributed mimeograph publication of the Los Angeles City Schools which states that, "The uses of the Video Tape Recorder are applicable to every area of (instruction) education. It can be used as a motivational tool to create enthusiasm and greater understanding of instructional material." The publication goes on to identify and recommend to school personnel 13 combinations of videotape recording and playback activities under the heading of "evaluation", 15 combinations under the heading of "presentations", and 7 combinations under the heading of "skill development".[10]

The Forms, Uses, and Needs for Pre-Recorded Instructional Materials by Education

Recorded materials—whether on film or videotape—can take the form of a complete course-series, individual lesson—titles, or specific subject oriented materials ranging in programmatic form from being self-sufficient and independent in their ability to stand alone in an instructional context to materials of a highly dependent, impersonalized, and subject-oriented nature in segment or module form requiring extensive teacher and/or cross media support. The uses to which these various types of materials have been put by education have been categorized[4][11] as being: 1) total teaching or major resource in which all major content and basic concepts are presented; 2) supplementary in which the recorded material does not present major content but rather correlates with the locally conducted course of study and provides unusual resource treatments of course content not ordinarily possible; 3) enrichment in which the recorded material is not related to the principle course of study but rather to other subject areas deemed desirable; and 4) remedial in which the recorded material provides for make-up or concentrated attention in narrow subject areas.

From the statistical sample of the school population constructed for the 1961 Meierhenry-McBride study, 49% of the schools reported the use of pre-recorded instructional television materials. Of these reporting schools: 57% identified their use as supplementary; 38% identified their use as enrichment; 5% identified their use as remedial; and none identified their use as total.[4] Subsequent studies of the National Instructional Television Center (previously the National Center For School and College Television) verify the continued majority of uses as being supplemental.[11] Additional information gained by the 1961 study indicates that the reasons stated by the schools for using televised instruction were: to improve instruction—54%; to extend curriculum—30%; for increased enrollment —6%; alleviate teacher shortage—6%; and for cost reduction—4%.[4]

The summary conclusion is that the use of television in courses of instruction—first as a live presentation and then with the advent of videotape as a recorded presentation—has typically taken the programmatic form of complete course-series used as a supplement to school-room conducted courses for the declared purpose of improving instruction. There are inferences contained in this summary conclusion which are both intriguing and speculative. For one it is to be noted that investigations of education vis-a-vis the use of television techniques and the great body of related research were completed by 1961. It is also to be noted that the result of technological development of television videotape recording had progressed no further by 1961 than to equip agencies essentially external to schools i.e. ETV stations, with videotape machine capability. The salient point to be identified for the purposes of this paper is that for whatever reason, the vast majority of videotape pre-recorded materials offered for inter-institutional use by either the ETV stations or the developing ITV Libraries (see below) were then and are now of the course-series form (see Appendix). A critical question is whether this present preponderance of materials in the television course-series form of the past and present times has been a positive or reluctant choice on the part of the school. The implications are important to the future viability of the course-series form . . . its continued use by the schools . . . and its continued provision by inter-institutional sources of pre-recorded materials.

The increasing use by education of on-site media production equipment in which the videotape machine is taking a center role has in part maneuvered the concerns of many school media administrators from piecemeal equipment questions to questions overall application strategy.[12] This manifestation centers in electronic random access retrieval systems (often termed "dial") which are being constructed in a great variety of forms at all levels of education about the country to support small group (about 25 maximum—the number generally regarded as a desirable optimum for viewing a single 21—23 inch television screen) and individual student self-paced access to visual/aural programmatic materials which are modularized and segmented in conformance to highly specific and localized curriculum design. Systems illustrating the great variety in design and application are to be found at Oklahoma Christian College, Beverly Hills (Calif.) Unified School District, Orange Coast College (Costa Mesa, California), University of California at Berkeley, Evanston High School (Illinois), New York State University at Brockport, and West Hartford Public Schools (Conn.). The simple programmatic objectives in this trend are to employ the very latest in sophisticated electro-communications technology to provide to individual students at any time or locale individually designed media experiences in modular and segment form.[13]

The question of the form and structure of pre-recorded aural/visual motion materials—whether on videotape or film—is critical for this random access trend. The pre-recorded materials made available by recognized distributors fall in the course-series or lesson-title programmatic form (see appendix). Rather than for, "Regular ETV or ITV programs in consecutive order . . .," the need is for, ". . . materials (on videotape) which are meaningful, direct, concise, and simple. This may sound like a big order, but what we are looking for is something between the 8mm single concept loop and the conventional 16mm classroom film."[14] "Programming for dial access is in its infancy. Software producers are still cranking out lengthy, comprehensive films and TV programs. The supply of short-burst video (tape) treatments of skills, concepts, and ideas is meagre."[15]

Although the above suggests a perspective gap in the form and structure of existing pre-recorded videotape instructional materials in the eyes of a number of forward moving media developments about the country, it is interesting insofar as pre-recorded film materials are concerned to note that the number of short films (defined as having no maximum length but containing a specific communication objective, i.e. as in the "single-concept" film and "film loop")[1] released in 1967 was double the number turned out in 1966 and the sales of 8mm silent short film prints jumped 77% in 1967, going from $1.8 million to $3.1 million in 1967.[1] The traditional tendency for the production by the film industry of individual titles as distinguished by the developed conventions to apply television production efforts toward complete series would seem at the moment to direct the attention of newer media activities toward film materials rather than videotape materials. But the widespread misunderstanding and fear of the film distributors to inquiries for the use of their film format materials in electronic distribution systems for the moment nullifies this potential advantage of film over videotape materials.[16]

NDEA Study of In-School Use and Exchange of Television Materials—1961

Title VII of the National Defense Education Act of 1958 focused on improving instruction through the uses of educational media such as motion pictures, programmed instruction and television. Under Title VII research projects and dissemination activities were devised. The question of how effective television materials could be made readily available to schools was identified and divided itself into three parts: 1) how to locate and gather useful ITV materials; 2) how to ensure continuing availability and production of quality materials; and 3) how to devise a system for the nationwide interchange of selected materials.[17]

In response to these and similar questions a study contract between the U.S. Office of Education and the University of Nebraska was developed for which Meierhenry and McBride were the principle investigators. The scope of the study was outlined in part by the proposal which observed that there had been to date a large development of television programs for direct and/or supplementary instruction at all school levels; activities throughout the country were unrelated; there was a minimum of information exchanged; there was practically no exchange of actual programs; and there was prospect for an increasing number and variety of program subjects to be covered by the use of television. It was further stated that in order to conserve time, energy, and money it was urgent to study the present status of the field; determine likely future developments; and recommend a distribution plan.[4] The work of Meierhenry and McBride conducted prior to and released in 1961 amassed a large amount of evidence relating to the development and use of the materials for televised instruction; how television was used in school curricula; the amount and availability of recorded television materials; the reasons for and against the availability of already recorded materials; dispositional factors regarding the use of television for instructional purposes; and factors pertaining to the feasibility and organization for inter-institutional exchange and distribution of recorded instructional television materials.

Although approximately ten years old and conducted at a time prior to the availability directly to the schools of present day videotape technology and techniques, this study nevertheless established a bench mark in the crystalization of the concept of the inter-institutional exchange of materials directly pertinent to courses of instruction. One recommendation of the study was to establish a nonprofit national center for recorded televised instruction to: 1) encourage studies to determine curriculum objectives best served at a national level by recorded televised instruction; 2) encourage production of needed high quality recorded television programs and related materials; 3) support experimentation with the utilization of recorded televised instruction; 4) serve as a cataloguer, disseminator, and distributor of recorded televised instructional programs and supplementary materials; and 5) facilitate selection and training of personnel needed for all types of instruction by television. A second recommendation was to establish nonprofit regional production and distribution centers for recorded televised instruction to serve the same purposes as those recommended above but keyed to the region.

The study suggested problems needing further study: 1) legal problems—most notably residual fees for teachers participating in the recording of materials and the use of commercially prepared materials; 2) State and local laws affecting the use and distribution of recorded materials; 3) cost factors bearing on decision between live and/or recorded televised instruction; and 4) effect of new industrial developments bearing on such factors as cost, scheduling flexibility, and the ease of undertaking the recording of instruction. If anything, the problems suggested for further study by Meierhenry-McBride are more pertinent today than they were ten years ago. The factor pointed to of new industrial developments is perhaps the most sensitive of them all. The opinion of the writer is that lack of proper attention here has in certain important cases found developing educational media programs left waiting at the wrong gate.

NDEA/National Library Project First Demonstration Period—1962-65[11] [17]

Acting on the recommendations of the Meierhenry-McBride study to establish a non-profit national center for recorded televised instruction the U.S. Office of Education under provision of NDEA Title VII in January 1962 funded a three-year demonstration project to examine the status and needs of instructional television programming in the United States. The contract was made with the National Educational Television and Radio Center to establish the National Instructional Television Library in New York City. Two regional libraries were established at the same time—one at the University of Nebraska called the Great Plains Regional Instructional Television Library and the other in Cambridge, Massachusetts at the headquarters of the Eastern Educational Television Network and called the Northeastern Regional Instructional Television Library. The purpose of this demonstration project was to study the educational desirability and economic feasibility of exchanging recorded instructional materials through the mechanisms of a national library system.

Under its mandate for the three year demonstration project (62-65) the National Instructional Television Library (NITL) set about to: 1) appraise the exchange potential of existing instructional television programming; 2) develop and demonstrate policies and procedures regarding the evaluation, acquisition, and exchange of recorded programming; 3) make available selected series for widespread use; 4) study economic feasibility for exchange; 5) research the character and needs of instructional television;/and 6) identify and assess factors regarding a permanent national instructional television system. By late 1963 NITL researchers had surveyed the kind of instructional fare offered on educational television stations. They concluded that relatively few of the courses examined were suitable for nationwide distribution. The survey also showed that existing sources of programs, i.e. ITV production centers could not supply quality ITV materials in the amount required. In September, 1963 at regional meetings called by NITL with authorization of the Educational Media Branch of the USOE there was complete agreement that the areas of greatest concern were: 1) the urgent need for high quality television materials; and 2) the need to supplement local resources with the most useful materials available from other sources. It was further urged that consideration be given to an enlarged and permanent national and regional instructional television library service of the highest quality.

It was found that the NITL demonstration project could not be completed in the three-year (62-65) period. More time was needed to: 1) identify and assess the considerable accumulation of recorded instructional course material; 2) intensively involve numerous educational leaders; 3) acquire courses for pilot distribution through actual negotiation; 4) repeatedly disseminate information to potential users; 5) await the decision of local preview committees; 6) provide broadcast materials consistant with school schedules; 7) gauge the acceptance of course materials through analysis of user reactions and patterns of subsequent use; and 8) judge the operational and economic practicability of a national system by studying cost and income over a meaningful number of years.

Toward the end of the initial demonstration period the NITL Advisory Board and staff plus carefully solicited opinion from instructional television leaders throughout the country concluded that: 1) high quality recorded materials were essential to effective use and future development of instructional television; 2) the necessary high quality can only be obtained at the local level only if limited local resources are supplemented by readily available television materials produced in other places; 3) sole reliance on existing sources of recorded instructional programming will not assure the availability of the necessary high quality materials; 4) installation of new facilities (closed circuit) is increasing and will continue to do so; 5) significant effort will be required to assure the satisfactory growth of instructional television; 6) improvement is needed in wise classroom utilization of television; and 7) the demonstration project had a beneficial impact upon the development and projected character of instructional television. Because of the identified need for more time and the findings of the reporting and reviewing authorities, it was recommended that the demonstration be continued beyond the scheduled termination in 1965.

Matters were somewhat complicated by the fact that as the end of the 62-65 demonstration was approached the National Educational Television and Radio Center was obliged to request release from its contractual obligation because it was under direction to give up its activities in instructional television as well as in several other areas. The USOE consented. In formulating the proposal for both continuing and relocating the demonstration project it was agreed that both the objectives and findings of the first demonstration period must continue to be observed. Added to the second demonstration phase was the plan to take more specific initiative in the matter of the acquisition and distribution of recorded course materials on videotape plus extensive information services to users in particular and to education in general. Accordingly it was recommended that the demonstration would have the best prospects if it were relocated for the following major reasons to an established educational agency: 1) experienced in the production and national distribution of quality instructional materials for all educational levels; 2) possessing a national reputation for leadership in the educational media field; 3) whose administration expressed a genuine and long term interest in the concept of an instructional television library; and 4) centrally located with respect to transportation. The requested extension period was to be two years. There was deep concern that the agency accepting the NITL project could and would in some way work to continue the activity of the NITL in whatever way might prove necessary beyond the second two year demonstration period until such time that the project might become self-sustaining. Indiana University became the site of the relocated NITL project for a second two-year period (actually 28 months) beginning May 1, 1965 and the contracting agent with USOE became the Indiana University Foundation. The NITL was renamed the National Center For School and College Television.

NDEA/National Library Project Second Demonstration Period—1965-67[11] [17]

The demonstration project was in good company. The Indiana University Foundation also contributed to the establishment of the Educational Television Stations Program Service of the National Association of Educational Broadcasters which also was organized in 1965. A third program service has also been made available for national distribution through the Indiana University Audio-Visual Department. The NET-Film Service transfer to 16mm film selected NET programs which are made available to schools, civic, and private organizations. Recent conversations between this writer and the administration of both the NET-Film service as well as the general motion picture film distribution activities at Indiana University indicate that there has been long consideration about the release by the University of many of its produced and distributed film titles in the form of one or more helical videotape standards. Reasons cited were the growing needs of schools for such materials in various of the videotape formats.

The relationship between the National Center For School and College Television (NCSCT) continued with regional libraries through a newly established reciprocal representation agreement which included financial support from the USOE via the NCSCT with the Great Plains Instructional Television Library, the Northeastern Regional Instructional Television Library, and the Western Radio and Television Association. At the conclusion of the first demonstration period the Great Plains Library had moved into activities heavily leaning toward actual exchange of recorded videotape course materials. Using the facilities and logistic support of the University of Nebraska and its Radio-Television activities which included ETV station KUON, the Great Plains Library had aggressively pursued the avenue of finding potentially good materials used in one section of the country and making them available on a cost plus overhead basis to other sections of the country. At the conclusion of the second demonstration period, Great Plains continued as an independent and self-supporting library (see below).

The Northeastern Library during the first demonstration period had grown as a corporate extension of the various services of the Eastern Educational Network (EEN). An extremely strong interstation curriculum development and assessment activity evolved. The Northeastern Library during this period served as an ITV program management link among the EEN stations, regional ITV authorities, and regional, state, school, and educational agencies. Many of the courses first distributed by the NCSCT came from ETV station constituents of the Northeastern Library. At the end of the second demonstration period and upon the conclusion of the representational agreement with NCSCT and its modest financial support, the Northeastern Library cut back severely its strong central initiative and reverted to an inter-station ITV Association of the member stations of the EEN. Newly designated as the third regional representative in the second demonstration period was the Western Radio and Television Association (WRTA) which used the contributed financial support to establish an office in San Francisco to carry out its representational responsibilities for the NCSCT. Without prior activities of any sort to build upon, the WRTA embarked upon activities which were mainly information oriented about the specific recorded instructional television programs and related services of the NCSCT as well as general information felt to be of value to the instructional television community. Aside from travel correspondence, and direct support of NCSCT needs, the WRTA Office distributed a wide range of information in the form of a newsletter, equipment specification guidelines, a collated listing by subject and grade level of all available recorded instructional materials cleared for television usage, a summary report covering an NEA sponsored ITFS assessment conference, and a handbook guide of information for educational agencies interested in the ITFS service. At the conclusion of the second USOE demonstration period and the funds provided through the NCSCT, the Office maintained by the WRTA in support of the NCSCT ceased to operate in early 1967.

In the second demonstration period the NCSCT developed an image of its own and moved actively into the phase of service and operations with the aims of: 1) acquiring existing courses completing successive and stringent evaluations by MCSCT staff, instructional television specialists, and subject matter authorities; 2) improving where determined feasible to do so those aspects of existing courses evaluated as "near misses" for national distribution; 3) developing new courses and materials in curriculum areas where through the conduct of assessment conferences it was determined that either nothing existed for which there was a clear need or what did exist was not satisfactory for either acquisition or improvement; and 4) serving as a central information agency for the field of ITV. NCSCT evaluated the submission of existing materials by owner-producers for purposes of potential NCSCT acquisition and national distribution at mainly the elementary level. From 1962 through 1967 (through both NDEA demonstration periods) of one hundred seventy-two elementary courses in the subject areas of music, art, health and physical education, foreign languages, mathematics, science, and social studies 14 (8.1%) were considered directly suitable; 39 (22.7%) were considered near misses but tentatively suitable; and 119 (69.2%) were considered unsuitable for national distribution. Because of the large need indicated for what were considered by the NCSCT to be suitable materials, during the second demonstration period (65-67) NCSCT was able to additionally augment and enhance seven of the initially judged tentatively suitable courses through reorganization of lesson material, improved production and technical recording, improved presentations, and acquisition of clearances for nation-wide use of music and other copyrighted materials. Agreements for the remodelling of an additional five courses were entered into. During the 62-67 period evaluative judgements of actual or tentative unsuitability for national distribution obtained from NCSCT staff, instructional television authorities, and subject matter authorities were based on: 1) technical quality; 2) restricted investments in research, planning, and consultation because of the pre-production assumption of only local use; and 3) tendency of teacher communication to be more concerned with the material presented rather than effect upon learners. Suitability criteria identified as required of courses for national distribution consisted of: 1) course subjects of a content and a manner as commonly taught in most places; 2) ability to impress educators responsible for determining what is to be offered in their locales; 3) required high technical quality because of the necessity for duplication for distribution; 4) necessity of exceptional teaching and production quality to meet the human double standard which exaggerates local confidence and diminishes outside achievement.

In order to determine the needs for new courses and material NCSCT held an extensive series of assessment conferences widely involving ITV and content authorities and covering basically same subject categories (with some additions) as above. From 1965 through 1967 a total of 441 already recorded elementary courses produced and in use by schools were submitted to the National Center Assessment Conferences: Music—98; Art—82; Foreign Language—73; Science—66; Social Studies—55; Mathematics—34; and Physical Education—33. Similarly, a total of 93 secondary courses were submitted: Social Studies—41; Foreign Language—13; Science—13; Mathematics—11; Physical Education—7; Art—6; and Music—2. Of the courses submitted for assessment: 88% of the elementary grade lessons were 15 or 20 minutes in length; course-series ranged in number from 2 to 120 lessons; and more than 60% of the time the courses were transmitted at the rate of one new lesson every week for a full academic year.

NCSCT reported that the number of hours devoted to instruction each week by ETV broadcast stations increased from 754 in 1961 to more than 2500 in 1967; the average hours each week per station increased from 14 in 1961 to more than 22 in 1967; the use of local production to create in-school programming decreased from 82% in 1962 to 40% in 1967; and of the 134 operating ETV stations in 1967, 115 offered instructional television lessons for elementary and secondary grades. The above figures as well as others pertaining to students using television were reported by the NCSCT through its research and dissemination functions and participation with other educational agencies in a variety of studies.[18]

During the second demonstration period extensive field services were undertaken to establish and strengthen liaison with teachers, administrators, and instructional television personnel throughout the country. Centered at Bloomington Indiana, the field services were undertaken in conjunction with the representational arrangements with the three regional organizations described above. Direct mail campaigns, personal visits, regional workshops, and previewing of specially constructed course kits containing three representative lessons plus a sample teachers guide were carried out as a part of the field service activity.

National Library—1967 and On

The USOE contract with the Indiana University Foundation For Support of the National Center concluded in May 1967. Until self support is attained, receipts from NCSCT course users and the Indiana University foundation will support the NCSCT. The NCSCT currently projects that it will become self-supporting by the year 1973. NCSCT materials have grown in distribution to a point where they are now used by almost every educational television station serving schools in the country and by a growing number of closed circuit installations and instructional television fixed service systems. NCSCT predicts a continually expanding use of materials related directly to the growth in techanical facilities. Seen as most important is the re-use pattern that has emerged after the second demonstration period. Re-use patterns for several elementary courses for 1967 show that in 70% of the cases in which Center course material is used, it is being reused in a successive academic period.

In July 1967 three regional centers directly under National Center supervision and operation were established in San Francisco, Milwaukee and Boston. A National Center representative will visit periodically every major instructional television installation in the United States. The Center will continue and expand close contact with sources of programming and information. Center regional representatives will gather data concerning each installations physical plant, production capacities, personnel, review and selection practices, existing program schedules, materials available for acquisition. The field services activity is additionally concerned with course promotion techniques, proper use of Center materials, and the development of efficient techniques of duplication and distribution of materials. By September 1, 1967 the Center was providing programming in Music, Art, the Humanities, Health, Language Arts, Mathematics, Science and the Social Sciences. In 1968 NCSCT placed the Harvard produced college series in circulation (see Appendix.) For each of its television offerings the Center provided related materials for classroom teachers. When required, materials are offered for the use of students. In late 1968 the NCSCT was renamed the National Instructional Television (NIT). The overall conclusions contained in the March 1968 evaluative report of activity find that much of existing instructional television material continues to be of modest quality. Reported opinions solicited by NIT from panels of disinterested educators widely concur in the judgement that much of existing television courses produced and used locally have only limited instructional effectiveness.

National Instructional Television—Currently Announced Distribution Practices

Courses are available on broadcast quadruplex and several helical videotape standards for rental only as a part of the regular instructional television activities of schools and colleges. The rental fee applies to all forms of electronic transmission including open-circuit (broadcast by ETV or commercial VHF or UHF television station), closed-circuit, and 2500 Mhz/ITFS facilities. Fees are based upon the total student enrollment of all schools participating in the general school television service of the contracting agency. The fee provides for unlimited use of each course-lesson during one calendar week. In and outgoing transportation is extra with a standard out charge of 50 cents per lesson. Teacher's manuals and student exercise books are available for a large majority of the course offerings at extra charge. Preview materials for each course consisting of representative lessons (on 16mm film or videotape) plus a copy of teacher's manual and student exercise book as appropriate are available upon request without fee to qualified contracting agencies. Requirements other than above and agreements for acquisition covering conditions for specific use are individually negotiated. For a list of availabilities see the appendix.

For the currently available series, *Patterns In Arithmetic* the per lesson unit rental cost at the maximum rate (for a participating school population of 800,000 and more) ranges from approximately $62 to $68. The per lesson unit rental cost at the minimum rate (for a participating school population of 50,000 and less) ranges from approximately $26 to $29.

NDEA/Regional Library Demonstration Project—1962-65[19][20]

The Meierhenry-McBride study[4] called for the establishment of one or more pilot regional production and distribution centers at the same time a national center was established. In January 1962 coincidental to the establishment of the National Instructional Television Library pilot Demonstration Project, the U.S. Office of Education contracted with the University of Nebraska to establish and operate as a pilot demonstration project the Great Plains Regional Instructional Television Library to serve the twelve-state midwestern region. At the same time the Northeastern Regional Instructional Television Library was established at the headquarters of the Eastern Educational Television Network to serve the Northeastern region (see above). The Meierhenry-McBride study recommended the same set of objectives for the regional demonstration libraries as were recommended for the national demonstration library. It is therefore not surprising that there is great similarity between the initially declared aims and objectives of the national and regional demonstration library projects. By the end of the first three-year demonstration period (62-65) each library project had developed its own characteristics. The description that follows of the Great Plains Regional Instructional Television Library (GPRITL) will build on the initially declared aims and objectives already discussed in detail above under the national library project and additionally highlight certain distinguishing characteristics.

At the outset it should be noted that the principle investigators of the basic Meierhenry-McBride study were from the University of Nebraska. Dr. Meierhenry at the time of the study was Associate Dean of the University Teachers College and Mr. McBride was Director of Broadcasting at the University of Nebraska with major administrative responsibilities for the closed-circuit use of television at the University as well as the developing role of the University in the state-wide ETV broadcasting and closed-circuit television network. While neither undertook or exercised operational authority in the organization and conduct of the affairs of GPRITL, each served on the Policy Board and each (particularly McBride) was regularly available for advice and consultation. In retrospect this has proven an invaluable link between the very extensive Meierhenry-McBride study and its translation into a viable library demonstration project.

The general findings of the Meierhenry-McBride study acted as points of departure for the design, establishment, and practical operation of GPRITL. In brief the findings were that 1) many schools by 1962 had produced viable television courses for their own use through the means of television broadcast transmission (and were thereby accustomed to the use of television techniques for course instruction); 2) a good number of courses were being "saved" by means of recording on videotape at the broadcast standard; and 3) many of these videotape recorded courses featured teachers of excellence who used highly effective methods for the television medium. One of the implicit findings of the Meierhenry-McBride study was the relatively widespread willingness at the public school levels of education to make locally recorded material available for outside use where appropriate clearances could be obtained and provided logistics, promotion, and similar details did not fall upon the producing school agency.[21] The prospect that the producing school agency might obtain some modest return as an unplanned windfall to its production budget from rental fees obtained through the efforts of an intermediate distribution agency further encouraged the availability of recorded course materials. The development during the first demonstration period (62-65) of GPRITL flowed from this premise, i.e. the prior existence of viable educational materials for exchange. On the other hand during this same first demonstration period the National Instructional Television Library (NITL) almost immediately came to the conclusion that relatively little of the existing materials in use by the schools was suitable for distribution as is.[11] [17] Consequently it appears that the attention of the NITL during the first demonstration period was directed to appraisal of materials and needs and establishing lines of communication with the administrative and curriculum elements of the educational community. The GPRITL immediately moved into an operating phase involving actual exchange of recorded materials.

It is to be noted that NITL and GPRITL were physically situated in different types of operating contexts which undoubtedly conditioned their growth and activities. NITL during the first demonstration phase was headquartered at the National Educational Television and Radio Center in New York City. This was the administrative location of the central agency for the evening programming concerns of ETV broadcasting stations. The elaborate videotape duplicating and support facilities servicing the nationwide group of ETV stations were located at Ann Arbor, Michigan. GPRITL on the other hand was located in an actual operating context which: 1) was not overshadowed by a larger entity engaged in a somewhat different endeavor; 2) which had a more easily definable and cohesive regional geographic area to serve; and 3) had relatively easy physical access to modest but effective videotape duplication and distribution facilities. That this conclusion is justified is seen in the requisites developed for the relocation and extension of the NITL at the time when the National Educational Television and Radio Center requested release from its contractual obligation to the USOE for the NITL demonstration project and the declaration by the Staff, Board, and consultants of the NITL that more time was needed to effect the demonstration (see above reference). The choice of the Indiana University location for the second demonstration period gave to NITL the resources obtained by GPRITL during the first period and has overall proved most judicious. (It would be most productive to further compare the location situation of the Northeastern Instructional Television Library in the context of an active regional ETV station network but in the interests of brevity this is omitted.)

During the first library demonstration period the GPRITL demonstrated the actual feasibility, need, and practicality of sharing quality instructional television recordings on a multi-state and regional basis by successfully developing a working structure for duplication, storage, distribution, promotion, utilization, and costs. GPRITL was advised by an eighteen man policy board comprised of school superintendents, college presidents, state department of education representatives, and educational media specialists from the region. An Operations Committee composed of the small GPRITL staff, field agents, and experienced ITV administrators formed a GPRITL Operations Committee. During the first demonstration period GPRITL obtained endorsement from the North Central Association of Colleges and Secondary Schools, the largest regional educational accrediting association in the United States.

At the time an extension was requested by the NITL for an additional time period to conduct the demonstration project, a representational agreement was negotiated to provide for continued support of the GPRITL beyond the first demonstration period. The support for the NITL was extended for a second twenty-eight month demonstration period beginning May, 1965. The second period of support for the GPRITL began this time as well as did similar periods of support for the Northeastern Regional Instructional Television Library and the newly involved Western Radio and Television Association. The GPRITL discontinued its fiscal relationship with the USOE on November 1, 1966 thus becoming the first self-supporting activity of this nature in the United States. At about this same time, the GPRITL began to change both its name and avowed scope of activities.

The Library dropped the term "regional" and then adopted the term "national" and is now known as the Great Plains National Instructional Television Library (GPNITL). Additional field representatives have been added to its staff. A recent report[20] indicates there are course users in 40 of the states including Alaska and Hawaii plus Canada. The school agency and system users of GPNITL materials are reported to number considerably in excess of 400. More than 38,000 recorded lesson units have been distributed since the start of the Library in 1962. Course re-use rate continues at about 95% over the years. A large offering covering all grade levels and a wide selection of subject matter is available (see appendix). As at the NITL, the staff of the GPNITL predict continued growth in course use as more educational CCTV facilities are installed yearly. New material is being added in the form of course sequences.

The GPNITL makes a special effort to assemble and distribute materials for teacher training, ITV utilization, and archival purposes. GPNITL produces teacher guides for many of its courses. An annual catalogue containing complete outlines of all of its available library materials is published. A Newsletter offered free upon request continuously updates the annual catalogue as to new acquisitions and availabilities and offers noteworthy information, advice, and guidance for the use of television techniques in education.

The University of Nebraska continues to provide facility support. A large videotape duplication and distribution facility is maintained. Upon reaching an agreement for distribution by the GPNITL, broadcast standard videotape masters are received and held at the headquarters Lincoln, Nebraska and are used to issue individual and fresh recordings for each user in whatever broadcast or helical scan videotape standard is required. The Library encourages the user to provide his own videotape. However, the Library will under certain conditions lease the videotape as well as the use of the course. The user fee is designed to cover the overhead costs of the Library, the costs of duplication and distribution, and a fee to the producing agency for the right to use the series.

Great Plains National Television Library—Currently Announced Distribution Practice[22]

Courses are available on the broadcast quadruplex and a large variety of helical videotape standards for rental by qualifying educational agencies and activities. The rental fee applies to all forms of initial and subsequent electronic transmission in any combination of VHF and UHF broadcast, 2500 Mhz, inter- or intra-building closed-circuit, and CATV system. The fee provides for unlimited use of each course-lesson during one 7 day period. Fees are based upon the actual cost of producing the recording plus additional variables covering: 1) the number and length of lessons; 2) the number of transmission points from which a lesson is telecast; 3) the total span of time during which all telecasts of a single lesson occur; and 4) whether the user or the Library supplies the physical videotape used to contain the recorded material. Where appropriate, return shipping charges are extra. Teacher's manuals and student workbooks are available for a large majority of the course offerings at extra charge. Preview materials consisting of a representative lesson (on 16mm film or videotape) for each course (excepting utilization and in-service materials) plus copies of teacher's manual and student workbook as appropriate are available upon request without fee to interested educational institutions. Requirements other than above and agreements for acquisition covering specific conditions of use are individually negotiated. For a current list of availabilities see the appendix.

Where the user supplies the videotape the per lesson unit rental cost for initial use of a 15-minute lesson is $45.00. If the user has retained the recordings on his own videotape the per lesson unit rental cost for use in a subsequent semester or year is $32.50. Where the user does not supply his own videotape and the Library is required to supply the videotape, the per lesson unit rental cost for use of a 15-minute lesson is $50.00.

The Midwest Program on Airborne Television Instruction[9] [23]

Parallel and seemingly independent of the Meierhenry-McBride study and the two demonstrations of national/regional instructional television libraries was the organization and growth of the Midwest Program on Airborne Television Instruction (MPATI). MPATI was centered in the Midwest and directly served schools in parts of six states (Illinois, Indiana, Kentucky, Michigan, Ohio, and Wisconsin—plus a small portion of Canada) by means of two-channel broadcast transmissions on UHF frequencies 72 and 76 operated from an airplane and essentially completely independent of the ground based ETV broadcast stations in the six-state area.

Instead of a library, MPATI (until 1968) could best be characterized as a regional programming cooperative operated by an interlocking organization controlled by the school agencies which it serviced through the means of a non-profit corporate entity. From its inception in 1959 MPATI was conceived as a centrally operated agency for the design, production, transmission, and evaluation of recorded instructional television programs. Participating school and educational entities which formed MPATI produced anew their own series of instructional courses to meet the subject and grade level needs of the six-state region. The result was then and still is today the best example of an agreed upon body of inter-institutional curriculum materials for use at the public school level. The hypothesis of MPATI from the very beginning has been that a single transmission channel such as offered by an ETV broadcast station for the distribution of instructional programs to schools is not enough. Looking ahead in technological developments, should the prospect of direct-to-the-school satellite transmissions become possible over a national or regional area, the MPATI experience could be considered a very apt demonstration.

MPATI: 1959—May 1962

This period covers the organization and operation of MPATI as a demonstration. MPATI was first announced as a service for transmission direct to the television sets in the classrooms of participating schools throughout the region. Enunciated purposes were to: 1) broaden the range of educational offerings heretofore available; 2) increase the quality of offerings were existing resources unavailable or inadequate; 3) undertake the above at a cost less than that for a comparable improvement of quality by any other means; and 4) conduct the demonstration program in a manner to assist the development of a permanent facility for the long range management and financing of an airborne instructional program by local and state educational agencies. The essence of the MPATI plan was the need for a multi-channel transmission facility. The MPATI rational described a typical twelve grade school system as offering anywhere from 100 to 175 separate courses, some divided into differentiated sections of student ability. A single broadcast television channel can provide only 12 half-hour units of instruction on the 6 hour school day, enough for only one-half hour per day for each grade level. The disparity between broadcasting potential and the size of curriculum is even greater at the college level. MPATI transmitted on two UHF channels during the demonstration year. The fully operating MPATI program called for transmission on six channels from a single orbiting airplane. The region to be served in the six-state area consisted of more than 127,000 square miles and contained (at the time) 17,000 schools and colleges enrolling about 7,000,000 students. It was expected that by the end of the first year of demonstration (1962) that as many as 2,000,000 of these students would have received some part of their education from the MPATI program.

An MPATI Curriculum Policy and Planning Commission served to recommend new courses and to update recorded courses as needed. For purposes of two-way communication and coordination the total region was divided into twenty resource areas administered respectively by area committees and staff coordinators. Wide consultation was encouraged at every step of the design, production, transmission, and evaluation process. An intensive teacher talent search was conducted throughout the United States in order to select those teachers who would prepare and record the needed course materials. Kinescoped auditions of about 300 candidates were received. A two-step selection process chose the eleven actual teachers who began by attending workshops at Purdue University in the summer of 1960 to prepare the actual courses for production starting in late 1960 at nine different ETV Station and Closed Circuit production centers in the Midwest and East. The teachers spent an average of 20 hours preparing and recording each lesson. Once the production schedule started, two and three lessons a week were completed at each of the production centers. Every MPATI course is accompanied by a teacher's guide providing a daily outline, suggested pre- and post-program activities, helpful aids, and collateral activities to reinforce the learning process. Guides were made easily available to participating classrooms. Sample lesson telecasts from the orbiting airplane (see below) were first offered in May, 1961. In June and July 1961 special telecasts were broadcast to 6,000 teachers and administrators attending professional assistance workshops in 43 locations in the six state area. A series of broadcasts were made to pre-school opening conferences in July and August. The first full academic year of demonstration transmissions in which MPATI materials were to be used as a regular part of the school curriculum began on September 11, 1961. Sixteen courses were scheduled in the first semester and twenty-one courses were scheduled in the second semester. Transmissions were on two channels for six hours a day—four days a week. Courses varied from 15-20 minutes for elementary and secondary to 30 minutes for college level.

A videotape processing and duplicating center consisting of five broadcast standard machines was established at Purdue University to handle the materials. Based upon the successful stratovision experiment by Westinghouse Corporation in 1948, one DC6 AB aircraft—with a second identically equipped plane as a standby—based at the Purdue University Airport orbited in a 10 mile radius circle at 23,000 feet over Montpelier in North Central Indiana. The plane was equipped with two broadcast standard videotape machines and a 50 kilowatt transmitter for each of the two UHF channels for which the original construction permits were granted in December, 1959. The broadcasts covered a radius of approximately 200 miles reaching students in over 13,000 separate building locations. About one-third of these were estimated to be in school systems of less than 2,000 pupils. The UHF transmissions from the airplane were designed for direct reception by properly equipped television receivers in school rooms. Additionally, local ETV stations in major cities of the area were encouraged to receive the MPATI broadcasts for simultaneous or videotape delay re-transmission to solve fringe reception or time delay schedule problems.

The total project cost through the end of the first demonstration transmission school year (May, 1962) of $8,500,000 was largely met by the Ford Foundation ($7,200,000), with the balance coming from other foundations and private industry. Approximately half of these monies went for acquisition and operation of technical facilities (excepting that the two aircraft at $900,000 each were deferred for financial support after conclusion of the demonstration period by the ensuing organization). During this experimental period the schools paid only for location receiving equipment and for classroom lesson guides at $2.00 each. It was estimated that starting June, 1962 that MPATI could be operated on an annual budget of approximately $3,750,000 or at about $1.00 per student if the estimated potential users of between 3,500,000 and 4,000,000 students would participate. The initial proposals in 1959 called for a self-sustained financial activity to take over after June, 1962.

MPATI: June 1962—May 1968

In 1962 the participating schools joined to form a non-profit-making organization to permanently continue the MPATI program as already described. Participating schools paid an annual per pupil charge of approximately $1.00. Additional funds were received from the Ford Foundation for a period of time. Activities in the main continued as in the first demonstration year. A significantly new activity was the encouragement in a purposeful way of the use of the recorded MPATI courses by schools outside of the six-state region. In the 61/62 school year seven stations are reported to have scheduled the equivalent of 15 courses for an annual rental income of $21,000. By 1967/68 this had grown to 70 stations scheduling the equivalent of 172 courses. Orders were reported on hand for 1968/69 from 83 users in 31 states.

In July 1965 the Federal Communications Commission ruled that MPATI could not continue to use the UHF band for airborne transmissions beyond the conclusion of the 1969/70 school year citing the need for ground based use of these frequencies in the six state area. MPATI had been preparing to move from two UHF channel to the planned-for six UHF channel operation. The steady growth in numbers of schools participating in MPATI of about 35% per year stopped. As an alternate means of wireless transmission for the orbiting airplane, six 2,500 Mhz/ITFS channels were applied for and received. ITFS transmission of a nature to serve the already established coverage area of MPATI services was untried. MPATI felt strongly that an extensive propagation study for the proposed ITFS was needed. An adequate amount of money for this was not forthcoming. Even if ITFS transmissions of satisfactory strength and coverage area could be obtained, the considerable added expense of reception facilities for the ITFS band which would have to be borne by each individual school was disheartening. Accordingly, the Corporation membership voted in December, 1967 to conclude the MPATI service as an airborne transmission activity in May, 1968 upon the conclusion of the 1967/68 school year. It was further voted to attempt to reorganize the Corporation as a producer/distributor of pre-recorded instructional materials.

MPATI: June 1968 and On

This period represents a transition from a broadcast transmission agency to that of a corporately organized production and distribution organization designed to serve the needs of its members. A successor corporate organization has been formed which now sees the entire United States as its market. In general the plan is to enter into a series of agreements with states and or schools systems which would 1) give the participating entity complete access to the entire MPATI library of pre-recorded materials for a per pupil annual cost ranging from $0.03 and up plus cost of duplication, and which would 2) commit the participating states (school systems are exempt in lieu of a higher cost-per-student rate) to additional financial support for at least one new series per participating state per year.

A rational for the need for a central programming organization to create new materials which would not otherwise probably be produced has been developed by MPATI and is quite similar to the underlying rationales stated and pursued by the National and Regional Instructional Television Libraries already discussed. But rather than operating apart from the "customer" as a take-it-or-leave-it exchange in the fashion of NIT and GPNITL, MPATI is clearly pursuing the avenue of participating cooperative State and large school system membership with centralized corporate control. MPATI will continue to make available its library of materials to individual users such as ITV Authorities using ETV station channels or school agencies using their own ITFS and CCTV distribution systems. But the structure of the rather ingenious MPATI plan is to encourage amalgamation either before dealing with MPATI or as a result of dealing with MPATI.

MPATI is distinguished from the NIT and the GPNITL by what seems to be an emphasized concern for the availability of its materials for use in the school room. This is not to say that NIT and GPNITL are not so concerned. Perhaps this is a result of the background of MPATI because of its operation of its own distribution facility (the transmitting airplane) plus the fact that all of MPATI materials are produced and owned outright by MPATI. The latter is not the case with NIT and GPNITL. Another reason may be that MPATI does not have technical commitment to anyone particular means of course distribution, as does NIT and GPNITL to basic physical distribution in the broadcast videotape format. Any means of distribution which will not serve to defeat the prior commitments or continued economic viability of MPATI has been termed appropriate for consideration. Recognizing the developing need for the extended availability to locally maintained helical scan videotape libraries, MPATI and a manufacturer of one of the helical videotape machine standards are now exploring a procedure wherein an individual school might annually subscribe to a specified list of individual subject titles by: 1) purchasing outright the videotape; 2) paying a very modest fee for duplication of the requested title onto the purchased videotape; and 3) paying to MPATI an annual use license fee of a dollar a minute. Such fee would continue to apply until revoked in writing by the subscribing school by means of returning to MPATI a notarized certificate of erasure of the specific subject title. The subscribing school is then free to re-use the reel of videotape for any other application.

As of the 1968/69 year two states—Illinois and Ohio—have joined MPATI as participating States obtaining complete access to the entire MPATI library for all bona fide school agencies within the State. Having obtained access to the MPATI collection, on the state level each State has developed a wide variety of distribution means for participating schools for these materials using in part ETV broadcast stations, ITFS systems, CATV systems, CCTV systems, and actual physical distribution throughout the state of pre-recorded MPATI videotapes. Schools within such states have been encouraged to obtain the materials and participate by whatever means most suits their classroom needs. Course usage by individual users in states not covered by agreements continues to grow (see above). A new 32 lesson course in basic economics for junior high is in final stages of preparation. Three existing elementary level sciences courses and one elementary level language arts course are under revision. The newly developed state participation plan (discussed above) assures a continued supply of newly recorded instructional course materials.

MPATI—Currently Announced Distribution Practices

In geographic areas and situations not covered by a specially designed state plan, courses are available on broadcast quadruplex and several helical videotape standards for rental by qualifying educational agencies and activities. The rental fee applies to all forms of electronic distribution and relay except commercial television stations. The fees apply to one time use—repeat charges quoted on request. Fees are based upon the number of educational institutions served by the coverage area of the primary and secondary transmitters.

CCTV, ITFS, and similar means of transmission fall within the minimum schedule for institutional coverage. A videotape usage charge is waived if the customer provides his own videotape stock. Return shipping charges are extra. Teacher's manuals and student materials are available where appropriate for an extra charge. Preview lessons on quadruplex videotape or 16mm kinescope plus sample teacher's guide are available to qualifying educational agencies for no charge except the cost of shipping. Requirements other than above and agreements for acquisition covering specific conditions of use are individually negotiated. For a current list of availabilities see the appendix.

For a currently available series, *Space Age Science,* containing thirty-two, 20 minute lessons where the user supplies the videotape, the per lesson unit rental cost at the maximum rate (for 2001 educational institutions and more) is $57.50. The per lesson unit rental cost at the minimum rate (for 300 educational institutions and less) is $30.00.

Western Video Industries

Organized in 1967 as a commercial venture of the Hollywood Video Center of Los Angeles, Western Video Industries is indicative of the movement of private enterprise into the field of providing pre-recorded courses and materials on videotape for instructional and training uses.

Western Video employs experienced and competent teachers to plan course sequences, write teacher guides and student workbook materials, and appear before the camera in the process of recording the course presentations. Consultants are engaged. The recordings are made initially on broadcast standard videotape in color using first-rate technical and production support facilities and staff. No other producer and distributor of contemporary videotape instructional materials has recourse to such technical and production resources.

Courses are available on broadcast quadruplex color and black and white quadruplex standard as well as on most helical standards for rental only. The rental fee applies to broadcast, closed-circuit, and 2,500 Mhz/ITFS transmission. Fees are based upon the total school population from grades 1 through 12 in the district or districts viewing the provided materials. The fee applies to a three day use period. Teacher's manuals are available at extra cost. Preview lessons are available on videotape. Requirements other than above and agreements for acquisition covering conditions for specific use are individually negotiated. For list of availabilities see the appendix.

For the currently available series, *Exploring the World of Science* containing 85 fifteen-minute lessons, the per lesson unit rental cost at the maximum rate (for a school population of 100,000 or more) is $80.00 for black and white and $100.00 for color. The per lesson unit rental cost at the minimum rate (for a school population of 50,000 and less, is $35.00 for black and white and $50.00 for color.

Telstar Productions, Inc.

Organized in 1968 as a non-profit venture by persons experienced in educational and instructional television broadcast matters in the Minneapolis and Minnesota area of the country, Telstar Productions has begun its activities with a pre-existing series of recorded materials initially designed for ETV station transmission. Their existing materials lie in two essentially different areas, i.e. personal skill development and nursing education.

Courses are available on broadcast color and black and white quadruplex standard as well as on several helical standards for rental only. Fee information is obtained by specific inquiry. Period length of use is determined by specific inquiry. Student materials consisting variously of textbook, study guides, etc. are available as appropriate at a specified unit cost. A preview lesson on videotape is available upon request. Requirements other than above and agreements for acquisition covering conditions for specific use are individually negotiated. For a list of availabilities see the appendix. For the currently available series, *Success Through Effective Writing* containing ten thirty-minute lessons the per lesson unit rental for any ETV station is $7.50 for black and white and $15.00 for color.

Network For Continuing Medical Education

The Network For Continuing Medical Education (NCME) is a free educational service in the form of an inter-institutional exchange of produced videotape materials under NCME direction linking medical schools and hospitals for the post-graduate medical education and instruction of doctors, nurses, technicians, and paramedical personnel. The Network is headquartered in New York City and services locations throughout the United States and Canada. The Network has been in operation for several years and is entirely supported by the Roche Laboratories. Proprietary messages regarding pharmaceutical product development and research which are unrelated to the program content of the reel and clearly distinguishable are included at several positions in each distributed reel of videotape material. Each participating institution receives a one-hour videotape reel containing an average of three separate presentations which are predominantly clinical but include research, paramedical subjects, and recent news of medical developments. A monthly reel exclusively for nursing and paramedical subjects is additionally distributed. NCME provides a great variety of assistance of a utilization nature for participating institutions: 1) TV Guides distributed in advance of each bi-weekly and monthly videotape; 2) poster and display materials; 3) visiting representatives who provide advice regarding maximum use of the television and related display facilities and greater viewer participation; 4) technical advice regarding installation and use of videotape and related equipment; 5) utilization clinics at locations throughout the country to help actual and potential participants learn about the NCME services; and 6) a periodic newsletter reporting latest developments of interest to participating members. Where proper procedures are followed course credit can be obtained from the American Academy of General Practice by viewing the videotapes. After the videotape materials have circulated, many are placed into a library method of circulation wherein each presentation is on a separate reel and is available for rental to qualifying agencies.

Pre-recorded videotape materials are available on broadcast quadruplex as well as on many helical standards variously in color and in black and white. Current videotapes are distributed without charge to participating institutions. Library videotapes (those which have previously circulated) are available for rental. Current and library videotapes may be used over the television distribution facilities normally available to and used by the participating institution at scheduled times convenient for viewing by staff, attending physicians, nurses, and paramedical personnel. Both current and library videotapes are not meant for public viewing. The fee for library videotapes provides for a use period of two weeks. Return postage and requested insurance is extra. Utilization and information materials for each current and library videotape are provided as needed without charge. Requirements other than above and agreements for acquisition covering conditions for specific use are individually negotiated. For a list of availabilities see the appendix.

Currently distributed videotape reels containing up to three distinct presentations plus several institutional messages are available without charge to participating institutions. Library presentations, each on an individual reel, are available to qualifying institutions at $12.00 for each title received in available helical scan formats. Quadruplex scan formats are higher.

Medical Television Network

The Medical Television Network (MTN) of Southern California began in 1964 when a microwave broadcast from the Univeristy of California at Los Angeles to the San Bernardino County Hospital was successfully accomplished. In April and March, 1965, an experimental encoded program consisting of ten two-hour sessions was broadcast over KCET-ETV28, Los Angeles, to 425 doctors in fifteen selected hospitals. The encoded broadcast of medical programs continues on a weekly basis. From September 1968 through June 1969 an estimated 120 participating hospitals throughout California will receive the now twice weekly broadcasts which have been expanded to include nursing.

Videotapes are being physically distributed to participating institutions in 16 states throughout the country. In late 1968, 8,000 hospitals in the United States were contacted for purposes of expanding the program of the physical distribution of pre-recorded videotapes. An annual package of thirty-six 30 minute pre-recorded videotapes is offered—twenty-seven for the physicians and nine for the nurses. They are on current subjects and provide information for use in daily practice. Physician oriented programs are planned in consultation with the American Academy of General Practice and are approved for credit provided proper procedures are followed. After the current videotape materials are circulated they are placed in a library method of circulation.

Pre-recorded current videotape materials are available on several helical standard in black and white for rental by hospitals. The library videotapes are available on quadruplex and helical quadruplex variously as color and black and white. The rental fee for current videotapes applies to any mode of distribution excepting VHF and UHF broadcast which is normally available and used by the hospital. Library videotapes are available for rental. The videotapes are not meant for public viewing. Each received videotape is retained for a one-week period for viewing convenience. A twelve program description schedule is distributed shortly before each cycle with enough time allowed for intramural program promotion. Requirements other than above and agreements for acquisition covering conditions for specific use are individually negotiated. For a list of availabilities see the Appendix.

Currently distributed videotape materials are available through an annual agreement for receipt of the total series of thirty-six programs at a per unit program cost of $20.83. Library videotapes are available upon inquiry.

Video Nursing

Video Nursing began distribution in 1968 several course series produced on videotape at WTTW ETV11, Chicago and intended for nursing students and graduate nurses in continuing education and refresher programs. The course series plus supplementary materials was supported by a grant for the Improvement In Nurse Training, from the Division of Nursing, USPHS, Department of Health, Education, and Welfare.

Only certain of a larger number of course series being distributed on 16mm film are simultaneously being distributed on two helical scan videotape standards in black and white. The videotapes are available for rental only. The rental fee applies to all forms of electronic distribution excepting VHF and UHF broadcasting and 2500 Mhz/ITFS which are normally available and used by the subscriber. The fee provides for a single class viewing covering one day's use. Return postage plus requested insurance is extra. Student syllabus, instructor guides, and audiotapes of videotape presentations are available at extra charge. There is no provision for preview of either videotape or supplementary materials. Requirements other than above and agreements for acquisition covering conditions for specific use are individually negotiated. For a list of availabilities see the appendix.

For the currently available series, *Nursing In Psychiatry* containing twenty-four forty-four minute lessons, the per lesson unit rental cost is $15.00.

ANA-NLN Center for Videotape

The American Nursing Association and the National League for Nursing have for some time operated a film distribution service. In 1968 a program for the distribution of materials in the form of pre-recorded videotape materials was initiated. Initial arrangements are now underway to distribute a television refresher course for registered professional nurses. This series was first produced for the State University of New York by the Russel Sage College Department of Nursing and ETV station WMHT of Schenectady, New York.

Information regarding distribution practices is not available.

Advanced Management Research

In early 1968 the Advanced Management Research Corporation announced an executive series of pre-recorded videotape courses for business and industry encompassing a full range of subject areas. This activity is an outgrowth of the work of AMR in seminars and group educational meetings.

Courses are available on a color and black and white helical videotape standard for rental or purchase. The fee applies to electronic closed-circuit distribution only which is normally available and used by the subscriber or purchaser. Fees are set for rental or purchase for each particular course-series. Requirements other than above and agreements for acquisition covering conditions for specific use are individually negotiated. For a list of availabilities see the appendix.

For the currently available series, *Marketing and the Computer* containing eight lessons ranging in time-length from twenty-five to forty-five minutes the per lesson unit cost for purchase of the complete series is $346.88 in black and white and $396.88 in color. For the same series the per lesson unit cost for rental of the complete series is $106.25 in black and white and $106.25 in color.

Office of Public Affairs and Education, Republic Steel Corporation

In 1968 the Republic Steel Corporation through an educational subsidiary arranged to make available on videotape certain of its course-series previously available for management training in business and industry on 16mm film. This program is still under development.

Distributed courses are available on broadcast quadruplex and several helical scan videotape standards for sale and rental. The fee applies to various types of electronic transmission as a result of specific negotiation. Fees are based upon either a set cost per course-series or alternately the number of individual users as a result of specific negotiation. Conference leader/teacher guides, textbooks, audits, and related materials are available for each course-series. Requirements other than above and agreements for acquisition covering conditions for specific use are individually negotiated. For a list of availabilities see the appendix.

For the currently available series, *Exploring Basic Economics* containing ten thirty-minute lessons, the approximate per lesson unit cost for purchase of the complete series is reported as $120.00.

Educational Systems & Designs, Inc.

In 1968 Educational Systems and Designs began to make available on videotape certain of its course-series previously available for management training in business and industry on 16mm film.

Courses are available on various videotape playback standards for long term lease covering a minimum three-year period at a price which varies according to the particular type of videotape desired and a per capita charge based upon the number of student guides in each order. The fee applies to various types of electronic transmission as a result of specific negotiation. Shipping charges are extra. Conference leader guides are available.

For a minimum three year lease period of the currently available series, *Management By Objectives* containing six thirty-minute lessons, the per lesson unit cost of $200.00 plus a per capita charge based upon the number of guides (workbooks) in each order ranging from a per unit guide cost maximum (for twenty-four and fewer guides) of $30.00 each to a minimum (for 500 and more guides) of $16.00 each.

Professional Development Corporation

The Professional Development Corporation was organized in late 1968 to develop by means of videotape production and provide course-series of a professional and continuing education nature to engineering and scientific management. Higher level mathematics and computer technology are subject areas of first attention. Lecturers are experienced teachers. A bound set of detailed lecture notes for each participant is to be made available. Consulting services by the Professional Development Corporation will be provided to organizations interested in establishing their own continuing education programs. Each course-series is described as being a self-contained educational package structured to appeal to the heterogeneous nature of the industrial community and allowing for differences in backgrounds, experience, academic training, capabilities, and specialities.

Courses are available on various standards of helical scan videotape as well as 16mm film for rental. The rental fee applies to all forms of electronic distribution excepting VHF and UHF broadcasting which are normally available and used by the subscriber. Fees are set at a flat per lecture hour rate. The fee provides for unlimited use of each course-lecture by a subscriber for a two-week period. Twenty sets of bound notes covering the lecture material are supplied free with each lecture. Additional sets are supplied for a fee. Preview lectures from currently available courses are available by arrangement. Requirements other than above and agreements for acquisition covering conditions for specific use are individually negotiated. For a list of availabilities see the appendix.

For the currently available series, *Basic Unified Calculus* containing twenty-four sixty minute lectures, the per lecture unit rental cost is $300.00.

Modern Videotape Library

Long a source of free loan 16mm film titles sponsored by business and industry for use by educational organizations and others, The Modern Talking Picture Service has specifically organized a free loan videotape library which began operation in late 1968. A number of business documentary and public relations presentations heretofore available on 16mm film are now being distributed on several helical scan videotape standards. The individual titles listed as being available are identical to the 16mm versions which continue to be distributed. All presentations carry some sort of institutional message provided by the sponsor. Thirty-four titles are available. They range widely in subject matter and interest level. These materials are available as unrelated subject titles—not in course sequence form. A brochure describing the service is readily available from Modern.

Individual subject titles are available in the form of pre-recorded videotape variously in color and black and white in several helical scan standards without charge for use excepting return postage. The videotapes are provided for use on closed-circuit electronic transmission systems only. The videotapes are to be returned promptly after use. The number of viewers using the videotapes is to be reported. Requests well in advance are encouraged. Alternate use dates are encouraged. Time lengths individually range from thirteen to thirty minutes.

Ampex Tape Exchange

As a major manufacturer of helical scan videotape equipment, the Industrial and Educational Products Division of the Ampex Corporation has organized a program exchange service in response to the requests of educational, instructional, and training agencies. The purpose of the Ampex Tape Exchange is to: 1) assist producers and distributors of materials who are contemplating the distribution of series or program titles on the one-inch Ampex helical scan videotape standard; 2) collect and distribute information to present and future users of the Ampex one-inch helical scan equipment about sources of pre-recorded videotape materials available for use on their equipment; and 3) undertake the distribution of pre-recorded videotape materials in the Ampex one-inch helical scan format. A Videotape Duplicating Facility specializing in the duplication of black and white and color videotape and film materials into the Ampex one-inch helical scan standard complements the efforts of the Ampex Videotape Exchange.

Pre-recorded Ampex one-inch helical standard videotapes in a variety of course and individual titles sequences are available variously in color and black and white for rental and sale. The fee applies to specifically indicated forms of electronic transmission set for each series or title. In and outgoing transportation and insurance is extra. Requirements other than above and agreements for acquisition covering conditions for specific use are individually negotiated. For a list of availabilities see the appendix.

For the currently available series, *AACTE Workshop In Teacher Education* consisting of four lecture-demonstrations ranging in length from forty-five to sixty minutes, the per reel unit sale cost is $60.00 plus shipping.

Summary Statement and Proposals

There can be little doubt of the rapid adoption by education of the use of television communication techniques in teaching and learning activities. Education has accepted the premises leading to the use of television techniques; dollar expenditures by education for television equipment capability are significant and rising; and equipment capability for the storage and retrieval of instructional materials which is in a manner peculiar to and most favored by education's use of the television medium and which is relatively inexpensive to acquire and use, portable in transport and application, and simple to operate and maintain has been developed and is being widely adopted. The growth of collections of pre-recorded instructional materials in the medium peculiar to television—videotape—has been steady and in recent years has accelerated. The cause for the inter-institutional development, exchange, and distribution of pre-recorded videotape materials first investigated and demonstrated by a series of government supported pilot projects has in substance proved viable and has been joined by a growing list of private entrepenures. There is every prospect for the continued and rapid growth in education of the use of television techniques incident to the teaching learning process and the adoption of the videotape machine and accompanying techniques of application as the prime mode of intra- and inter-system communication.

From the point of education's need—growth has not been fast enough. But judged from the increasingly fragmented experiences of education with developing electro-communications capabilities—growth has been too rapid. Techniques of application have overrun understandings. The capabilities of technology have overrun techniques.

It is the thesis of this paper that with the advent of helical scan videotape technology in the early '60s we have now clearly arrived at a time in electro-communications when the technological capability to "publish" has moved full swing out of exclusive domain of the producer or creator of materials into the hands of the consumer or user of materials. *(Xerox* and *Polaroid* similarly mark an almost identical advent for print and photography.) What is proposed below is not new in the context of thought . . . but it is new in the matter of the adoption of electro-communication concepts and the context of the technological times in which we live.

> *PROPOSAL NUMBER 1:* Study disposition toward, adoption by, means employed, and results obtained by schools embracing electro-communications capabilities centering on the use of videotape recorded materials.

A notable contribution was made by the Meierhenry-McBride study in the technological context of its time. A contemporary study along the subject lines suggested and organized and conducted in the fashion of the Meierhenry-McBride study is urged. Particular attention should be given to new educational philosophies, new technological capabilities, and new needs for programmatic forms of recorded materials.

> *PROPOSAL NUMBER 2:* Stimulate the creation of a greater quantity of pre-recorded videotape materials which are more widely diverse in form, content, and structure.

The day of the "best" telecourse for national use at a particular subject and grade level is gone—if in fact it was ever here. It is urged that a matching fund support scheme be developed for the acquisition and use by school systems of pre-recorded videotape materials widely diverse in form, content, and structure. The operation of the Farr-Quimby Act in California which provides 50% of the cost of program materials used by schools in ITV programs provides an excellent guide. The program has placed fund support at the decision point i.e. the classroom, of need in terms of the form, content, and structure of the needed materials; has made possible the upgrading of resident school instructional programs; and has stimulated a greater number of competitive sources of more diverse types of pre-recorded instructional television materials.

> *PROPOSAL NUMBER 3:* Establish on a regional basis joint and cooperative supplier/user agencies to serve the growing needs of education for impartial and systematic information for the design, establishment, operation, and assessment of electro-communications systems.

Properly conducted dialogue between suppliers of goods and services and the educational users of these goods and services is sadly lacking. There have been some attempts in the USOE (Equipment Development Branch) and through the efforts of non-profit and private enterprise. These have failed because either one side from the beginning had the better of the other or the undertaking was not adequately organized and funded. A properly established organization is urged with distinct regional lines of organization and opportunities of broad participation by users and suppliers. This should be basically an educational and communications effort. Activities could develop to cover such diverse activities as jointly agreed upon supplier/user standards; a centralized information activity pertaining to technological developments as well as user applications of the technology; a rights clearance bank for print, film and electronic materials subject to actual and potential use by education in electro-communication systems—particularly in the matter of local videotape recording and reproduction; operation of media transfer facilities, i.e. among the mediums of print, film, and tape servicing all the different standards; and a clearing house for the organization and dissemination of research pertaining to the electro-communications facilities, media, and—methods.

REFERENCES

1. Hope, Thomas W. "Market Review: Nontheatrical Film and Audio-Visual—1967." *Journal of the SMPTE,* Vol. 77, November 1968, pp. 1210-1220.

2. *Teaching By Television.* New York: Fund For The Advancement of Education and the Ford Foundation, May 1959, 87 p.

3. Mooney, Jr., Mark. "The History of Magnetic Recording." *Hi Fi Tape Recording,* Reprint M-DL 110(271)BPH, 17 pages.

4. Meierhenry, W. and J. McBride. "Exchange of Instructional Television Materials: Report of the Nebraska Survey (1961)." *Educational Television: The Next Ten Years.* Stanford, California, Institute For Communication Research, 1962, 375 p.

5. Bretz, Rudy and K. Winslow. "Compatibility in CCTV—How Important Is It?" *Journal of the National Association of Educational Broadcasters,* Vol. 20, No. 3, May/June 1961, pp. 58-65.

6. Winslow, K. "Technology and Technique of Videotape—Part 1." *Educational/Instructional Broadcasting,* Vol. 1, No. 2, April/May 1968, pp. 18-26.

7. Winslow, K. "Technology and Technique of Videotape—Part 2. *Educational/Instructional Broadcasting,* Vol. 1, No. 4, September/October 1968, pp. 33-39.

8. Winslow, K. (Editor). *The Specification and Selection of a Videotape Machine for Educational Applications.* San Francisco, California, Western Radio and Television Association, June 1966. 16 pages.

9. Fall, William R. *State Plan For Production and Distribution of Television Materials.* Lafayette, Indiana, Midwest Program On Airborne Television Instruction, Inc., 8 pages, Mimeograph, July 18, 1968.

10. *Guidelines For The Use of a Videotape Recorder.* Audio-Visual Department, Los Angeles City Schools, 12 pages, mimeo.

11. Jordan, J. *The National Center For School and College Television: A Demonstration of a National Program Agency For Instructional Television.* Final Report, Project No. 50273, Contract No. OE-5-16-015, U.S. Department of Health, Education, and Welfare, Office of Education, Bureau of Research. Bloomington, Indiana, Indiana University Foundation, March 1968, 203 pages.

12. North, R. S. "Three Exceptions To The Rule—The Key: Strategy, Not Equipment." *College Management Magazine,* October, 1968. See also: "Learning Center Gives Each Student a Study Carrel," *College and University Business,* May, 1966.

13. "Instructional Resources A Major Tool At State University of New York." *Visual Views* (Visual Electronics Corporation, New York City), November 1968.

14. Correspondence with Mitchell Garret Jr., Project Director, Dial Select System, West Hartford Schools, West Hartford, CN, October 31, 1968.

15. Singer, Ira J. "Media and the Ghetto School." *Audiovisual Instruction,* October, 1968.

16. Winslow, K. "Survey of Policies Governing the Use of Film Materials for Television Projection." Unpublished paper presented to the University Interest Session of the annual meeting of the National Association of Educational Broadcasters at Denver, Colorado, November, 1967.

17. Cohen, E. "A Center For ITV." *American Education,* June 1966.

18. a) National Instructional Television Library. *The Status of Instructional Television.* New York, National Instructional Television Library, 1964.

    b) Morse Communication Research Center and the National Center for School and College Television. *One Week of Educational Television. Number Four. April 17–23, 1966.* Bloomington, Indiana, The National Center for School and College Television, 1966.

    c) Department of Audiovisual Instruction, National Education Association. *A Survey of Instructional Closed-Circuit Television 1967.* Washington, D.C. Department of Audiovisual Instruction, National Education Association, 1967.

    d) McKune, Lawrence E. (ed.). *National Compendium of Televised Education.* Vol. XIV, 1967. East Lansing, Michigan, Michigan State University, 1967.

19. McBride, Jack G. "Sharing Instructional Television On A State-Wide Basis And On A Regional Basis." *Improvement of Teaching By Television,* Proceedings of the National Conference of Educational Broadcasters at the University of Missouri, March 2–7, 1964, Edited by Griffith and Maclennan. Columbia, Missouri, Univ. of Missouri Press 1964.

20. *A Growing Service To Education.* Lincoln, Nebraska, Great Plains Instructional Television Library, University of Nebraska, 1968, 4 pages.

21. Series of conversations in 1960 with E. G. Sherburne, Jr. who was one of the regional field consultants for the Meierhenry-McBride Study.

22. *The 1969 Catalog of Recorded Television Courses.* Lincoln, Nebraska: Great Plains National Instructional Television Library, Univ. of Nebraska, November, 1968, 112 pages.

23. a) *Midwest Program On Airborne Television Instruction.* Includes transmittal letter by John E. Ivey, Jr. dated April, 1960. Lafayette, Indiana, Midwest Program On Airborne Television Instruction, Purdue University, 28 pages, 1960.

    b) *This is Airborne.* Lafayette, Indiana, Midwest Program On Airborne Instruction, Purdue University, 16 pages, 1962?

    c) *Inside The Flying Classroom.* Lafayette, Indiana, Midwest Program On Airborne Instruction, Purdue University, Multifold brochure, 1962?

    d) *Viewpoints On Airborne.* Lafayette, Indiana, Midwest Program On Airborne Television Instruction, Inc., Purdue University, 12 pages, 1963?

    e) *What is MPATI.* Lafayette, Indiana, Midwest Program On Airborne Television Instruction, Inc., Purdue University, Multifold brochure, 1967.

    f) *Classroom Television Courses.* Lafayette, Indiana, MPATI, Inc. Multifold brochure, 1968.

    g) Letter from William Fall, MPATI, Inc., to K. Charles Jameson, San Diego State College dated April 8, 1968.

    h) Fall, William R., *After Airborne Television, What?* Lafayette, Indiana, Midwest Program On Airborne Television Instruction, Inc., 5 pages, Mimeograph, August 5, 1968.

    i) Fall, William R. "Letter To The Editor." *Educational Television,* November, 1968.

Appendix

VIDEOTAPE MATERIALS IN DISTRIBUTION BY THE GREAT PLAINS NATIONAL
INSTRUCTIONAL TELEVISION LIBRARY, UNIVERSITY OF NEBRASKA, LINCOLN,
NEBRASKA 68508

RECOMMENDED STARTING LEVEL: Primary (K–3)

	Series Name / Program Title	Number In Series	Time Length
1.	Time For Music	30	15:00
2.	Language Corner	30	15:00
3.	Sounds Like Magic	30	15:00
4.	Mathematics—1	35	15–20:00
5.	Just Wondering	31	15:00
6.	Sounds To Say	25	15:00
7.	Around The Corner	35	15:00
8.	The Magic of Words	25	15:00
9.	Children's Literature	30	15:00
10.	Art About Us	30	20:00
11.	Word Magic	16	15:00
12.	Mathematics—2	35	20:00
13.	Neighborhood Explorers	15	15:00
14.	Just Curious	30	15:00
15.	Language Lane	31	20:00
16.	Mathematics—3	34	20:00
17.	Land and Sea	15	15:00
18.	Our Changing Community	28	15:00

RECOMMENDED STARTING LEVEL: Intermediate (Grades 4–6)

	Series Name / Program Title	Number In Series	Time Length
1.	Time For Art	30	20:00
2.	Geography—4	34	20:00
3.	Mathematics—4	31	20:00
4.	Search For Science	32	15:00
5.	Americans All	31	20:00
6.	Rails West	5	30:00
7.	Quest For The Best	32	20:00
8.	Bill Martin	15	15:00
9.	Let's Explore Science	15	15:00
10.	Hablo Espanol	100	15:00
11.	Mathematics—5	31	20:00
12.	Adventures In Science	52	30:00
13.	Geography For The Gifted	12	30:00
14.	Places In The News	weekly	20:00
15.	Mathematics For The Gifted	12	30:00

RECOMMENDED STARTING LEVEL: Intermediate (Grades 4–6)

	Series Name / Program Title	Number In Series	Time Length
16.	The Science Room	32	20:00
17.	Astronomy For The Gifted	12	30:00
18.	Cultural Understandings	14	30:00
19.	Hablo Mas Espanol	64	15:00
20.	Mathematics—6	35	20:00
21.	The World of Science	52	30:00

RECOMMENDED STARTING LEVEL: Secondary (7–12)

Series Name / Program Title	Number In Series	Time Length
1. New Dimensions In Science	26	30:00
2. English Composition	15	30:00
3. Earth And Space Science	48	20:00
4. Office Career Training	13	30:00
5. TV Shorthand ABC Stenoscript	39	30:00
6. Sportsmanlike Driving	30	30:00
7. Americans From Africa: A History	30	30:00
8. Approaching Poetry	15	20:00
9. The Peaceful Uses of Nuclear Energy	14	30:00

RECOMMENDED STARTING LEVEL: College (Undergraduate)

Series Name / Program Title	Number In Series	Time Length
1. Gregg Shorthand	30	45:00
2. Business Law	30	45:00
3. Marketing	30	45:00
4. Communications & Education	30	30:00
5. Data Processing—Introduction	30	45:00
6. A Programmed Introduction to Economic Analysis	26	50:00
7. American Public School	30	45:00
8. Educational Psychology	30	45:00
9. Overview of Human Relations Problems	30	45:00
10. Measurement And Evaluation	30	45:00

RECOMMENDED STARTING LEVEL: College (Undergraduate)

Series Name / Program Title	Number In Series	Time Length
11. Philosophy of Education	30	45:00
12. Introduction to the Visual Arts	30	30:00
13. Fundamentals of Music	30	45:00
14. Spanish—First Course	30	45:00
15. History of American Civilization by Its Interpreters	94	30:00
16. History of the American People From 1865	30	45:00
17. Humanities—First General Course	30	45:00
18. Humanities—Second General Course	30	45:00
19. English Composition	30	45:00
20. Fundamentals of Speech	30	30:00
21. Shakespeare	30	45:00
22. American Literature From Colonial Period to Civil War	29	45:00
23. American Literature From Civil War to 20th Century	30	45:00
24. Fundamentals of Mathematics	30	45:00
25. College Algebra	30	45:00
26. Logic	30	45:00
27. Physical Science—First General Course	30	45:00
28. Mechanics and Heat	30	45:00
29. Physical Geology	30	45:00
30. Descriptive Astronomy	30	45:00
31. Weather and Man	20	60:00
32. Social Science—First General Course	30	45:00
33. Social Science—Second General Course	30	45:00
34. National Government	30	45:00

RECOMMENDED STARTING LEVEL: Professional & Continuing Education

	Series Name / Program Title	Number In Series	Time Length
1.	Channels To Learning	10	30:00
2.	TV In The Classroom	1	28:00
3.	Approaching Poetry	1	30:00
4.	Showcase	14	30:00
5.	The Role of the Classroom Teacher (Kinescope)	1	30:00

RECOMMENDED STARTING LEVEL: Professional & Continuing Education

	Series Name / Program Title	Number In Series	Time Length
6.	The Second Classroom (Kinescope)	1	25:00
7.	Discovering Discovery (Kinescope)	1	30:00
8.	The Studio Teacher (Kinescope)	1	47:00
9.	Television Techniques For Teachers (Film)	1	24:00
10.	Television In Your Classroom (Sound Film Strip)	1	12:00
11.	Enrichment Programs For Intellectually Gifted Students (Film)	14	30:00
12.	Ford Foundation Kinescopes (Kinescope)	100	10–45:00
13.	ITV Humanities Project (Kinescopes)	5	30–120:00

RECOMMENDED STARTING LEVEL: Adult

	Series Name / Program Title	Number In Series	Time Length
1.	Modern General (Secondary) Math for Parents	10	30:00
2.	TV High School: Natural Sciences	12	30:00
3.	TV High School: English Grammar	12	30:00
4.	TV High School: Social Studies	12	30:00
5.	TV High School: Literature	12	30:00
6.	TV High School: General Mathematics	12	30:00

VIDEOTAPE MATERIALS IN DISTRIBUTION BY MPATI, MEMORIAL CENTER, PURDUE UNIVERSITY, LAFAYETTE, INDIANA 47902

RECOMMENDED STARTING LEVEL: Primary (K–3)

	Series Name / Program Title	Number In Series	Time Length
1.	Scienceland	32	20:00
2.	Science Corner I	64	20:00
3.	Let's Go Sciencing	32	15:00
4.	Science Is Fun	32	15:00
5.	Science Is Everywhere	32	15:00
6.	Science Is Discovery	32	15:00
7.	Rhyme Time	16 / 32	10:00
8.	Initial Teaching Alphabet	48	20:00
9.	Your Community	16	20:00
10.	Singing, Listening, Doing	64	20:00
11.	Music For You	64	20:00
12.	All That I Am	16	20:00
13.	Listen and Say	32	15:00
14.	Learning Our Language	64	20:00

RECOMMENDED STARTING LEVEL: Intermediate (4–6)

Series Name / Program Title	Number In Series	Time Length
1. Science Corner II	64	20:00
2. Exploring With Science	64	20:00
3. Adventures of Science	64	20:00
4. Space Age Science	32	20:00
5. Exploring Mathematics	64	20:00
6. Que Tal, Amigos	128	20:00
7. Hablemos Espanol	64	20:00
8. Paso A Paso	64	20:00
9. Bonjour Les Enfants	128	20:00
10. En Avant	64	20:00
11. Freedom To Read	16	15:00
12. Reading Through Television	24	15:00

VIDEOTAPE MATERIALS IN DISTRIBUTION BY MPATI, MEMORIAL CENTER, PURDUE UNIVERSITY, LAFAYETTE, INDIANA 47902

RECOMMENDED STARTING LEVEL: Secondary (7–12)

Series Name / Program Title	Number In Series	Time Length
1. Nature of Matter	32	30:00
2. Investigating The World of Science	64	30:00
3. Adelante Amigos	128	20:00
4. Our Adventure In Freedom	64	30:00
5. Our Changing World	128	30:00
6. Franklin to Frost	64	30:00
7. Your State Today (Suitable Midwest Social Studies)	32	20:00

RECOMMENDED STARTING LEVEL: College (Undergraduate)

Series Name / Program Title	Number In Series	Time Length
1. Living Russian	64	30:00

RECOMMENDED STARTING LEVEL: Professional & Continuing Education

Series Name / Program Title	Number In Series	Time Length
1. Initial Teaching Alphabet	6	30:00

VIDEOTAPE MATERIALS IN DISTRIBUTION BY THE NATIONAL INSTRUCTIONAL TELEVISION CENTER, BOX A–BLOOMINGTON, INDIANA 47401

RECOMMENDED STARTING LEVEL: Pre-School

Series Name / Program Title	Number In Series	Time Length
1. Roundabout	52	15:00
2. Tell Me A Story	30	15:00
3. Imagine That	15	15:00

RECOMMENDED STARTING LEVEL: Primary (K–3)

Series Name / Program Title	Number In Series	Time Length
1. Physical Education For "Doers" and "Viewers"	30	20:00
2. Patterns In Arithmetic—Level 1	32	15:00
3. Patterns In Arithmetic—Level 2	48	15:00
4. Patterns In Arithmetic—Level 3	64	15:00
5. Sing, Children, Sing	15	15:00
6. Stepping Into Melody	30	15.00
7. Stepping Into Rhythm	30	15:00
8. All About You	20	15:00

RECOMMENDED STARTING LEVEL: Intermediate (4–6)

Series Name / Program Title	Number In Series	Time Length
1. You And Eye	30	20:00
2. Meet The Arts	15	30:00
3. Cover to Cover	30	20:00
4. The WordSmith	15 / 28	20:00
5. Patterns	33	20:00
6. Patterns In Arithmetic—Level 4	64	15:00
7. Patterns In Arithmetic—Level 5	64	15:00
8. Patterns In Arithmetic—Level 6	64	15:00
9. Let's Investigate	15	15:00
10. The World of Change	20	20:00

RECOMMENDED STARTING LEVEL: Secondary (7–12)

Series Name / Program Title	Number In Series	Time Length
1. Look To The Future	10	30:00
2. The Communists	8	20:00
3. Project: History	10	20:00

RECOMMENDED STARTING LEVEL: College (Undergraduate)

Series Name / Program Title	Number In Series	Time Length
1. Chemistry I: Basic Principles of Chemistry	15	30:00
2. Chemistry II: Chemical Equilibrium	15	30:00
3. Chemistry III: The Covalent Bond	15	30:00
4. Chemistry IV: Some Elements and Their Compounds	15	30:00
5. Physics I: Introductory Mechanics	15	30:00
6. Physics II: Introductory Electricity	15	30:00
7. Physics III: Introduction to Wave Motion, Light, and Sound	15	30:00
8. Physics IV: Introduction to Modern Physics	15	30:00
9. Physics V: Mechanics and Heat	15	30:00
10. Physics VII: Electricity and Magnetism	15	30:00
11. Physics VIII: Electronics	15	30:00
12. Mathematics I: College Algebra	15	30:00
13. Mathematics II: Coordinate Geometrics	15	30:00
14. Mathematics III: Introduction to Calculus I	15	30:00
15. Mathematics IV: Introduction to Calculus II	15	30:00
16. Mathematics V: Introduction to Calculus III	15	30:00
17. Mathematics VI: Introduction to Statistics	15	30:00

RECOMMENDED STARTING LEVEL: College (Undergraduate) (Continued)

18. Mathematics VII: Boolean Algebra and Computers	15	30:00
19. Mathematics VIII: Probability	15	30:00
20. Engineering I: Introduction to Computer Science I	15	30:00
21. Engineering II: Introduction to Computer Science II	15	30:00
22. Engineering III: Introduction to Metallurgy	15	30:00
23. Engineering IV: Elect Eng: Circuit Analysis	15	30:00

RECOMMENDED STARTING LEVEL: College (Undergraduate)

Series Name / Program Title	Number In Series	Time Length
24. Government I: American National Government	15	30:00
25. Government II: Ideologies in World Affairs	15	30:00
26. History I: World History I	15	30:00
27. History II: World History II	15	30:00
28. History III: History of the United States I	15	30:00
29. History IV: History of the United States II	15	30:00
30. Psychology I: Principles of Behavior	15	30:00
31. Psychology II: Man and His Motives	15	30:00
32. Sociology I: Introduction to Sociology	15	30:00
33. Economics I: Economics and the Public Interest	15	30:00
34. Geography I: Introduction to Geography; The Geographer's World	15	30:00
35. English I: Expository English I	15	30:00
36. English II: Expository English II	15	30:00
37. English III: Major American Books: American Literature	15	30:00
38. English IV: The Critical Reader: English Literature	15	30:00
39. Slide Rule Seminar	5	15:00

RECOMMENDED STARTING LEVEL: Professional & Continuing Education

Series Name / Program Title	Number In Series	Time Length
1. English—Fact and Fancy	15	30:00
2. English For Elementary Teachers—First Course	15	30:00
3. English For Elementary Teachers—Second Course	15	30:00
4. Pathways to Discovering Music	4	30:00
5. Sets and Systems	15	30:00
6. Tell Me a Story	1	
7. Physical Education For "Doers" and "Viewers"	2	
8. Patterns	8	

VIDEOTAPE MATERIALS IN DISTRIBUTION BY WESTERN VIDEO INDUSTRIES, INC., 1541 NORTH VINE STREET, LOS ANGELES, CALIFORNIA 90028

RECOMMENDED STARTING LEVEL: Primary (K–3)

Series Name / Program Title	Number In Series	Time Length
1. Exploring The World of Science	85	15:00
2. English As A Second Language	30	15:00
3. Holiday Specials	6	15:00

RECOMMENDED STARTING LEVEL: Intermediate (4-6)

Series Name / Program Title	Number In Series	Time Length
1. Sing Along With Me	32	15:00
2. This—Our Country	32	15:00

RECOMMENDED STARTING LEVEL: Secondary (7-12)

Series Name / Program Title	Number In Series	Time Length
1. Demonstrations In Physics—First Series	15	15:00
2. Demonstrations In Physics—Second Series	15	15:00

VIDEOTAPE MATERIALS IN DISTRIBUTION BY TELSTAR PRODUCTIONS, INC., 366 NORTH PRIOR AVENUE, SAINT PAUL, MINNESOTA 55104

RECOMMENDED STARTING LEVEL: Professional & Continuing Education

Series Name / Program Title	Number In Series	Time Length
1. Nursing Education: Nursing In Society	12	30:00
2. Nursing Education: Pharmacology	24	30:00
3. Nursing Education: Anatomy and Physiology	48	30:00
4. Nursing Education: Chemistry	60	30:00
5. Nursing Education: Communication	24	30:00
6. Nursing Education: Microbiology	48	30:00
7. Nursing Education: Social Science	36	30:00
8. Nursing Education: Psychology	48	30:00

RECOMMENDED STARTING LEVEL: Adult

Series Name / Program Title	Number In Series	Time Length
1. Success Through Efficient Reading	12	30:00
2. Success Through Effective Writing	10	30:00
3. Success Through Word Power	10	30:00

VIDEOTAPE MATERIALS IN DISTRIBUTION BY THE NETWORK FOR CONTINUING MEDICAL EDUCATION, 342 MADISON AVENUE, NEW YORK, N.Y. 10017

RECOMMENDED STARTING LEVEL: Professional & Continuing Education

Series Name / Program Title	Number In Series	Time Length
1. Medical subject series provided to participating hospitals and schools.	Biweekly	60:00
2. Nursing and paramedical subject series provided to participating hospitals and schools.	Monthly	60:00
3. Master Videotape Library available to qualifying institutions and agencies.	250	various

VIDEOTAPE MATERIALS IN DISTRIBUTION BY THE MEDICAL TELEVISION NETWORK, CONTINUING EDUCATION IN MEDICINE, UNIVERSITY OF CALIFORNIA EXTENSION, 10962 LE CONTE, LOS ANGELES, CALIFORNIA 90024

RECOMMENDED STARTING LEVEL: Professional & Continuing Education

Series Name / Program Title	Number In Series	Time Length
1. Res Medica (Medical Series) provided to participating hospitals	27 annually	30:00
2. Speaking of Nursing (nursing series) provided to participating hospitals	9 annually	30:00
3. Videotape Catalogue listing library of medical and nursing recordings available to qualifying hospitals	77	30–60:00

VIDEOTAPE MATERIALS IN DISTRIBUTION BY VIDEO NURSING, INC., 2645 GIRARD AVENUE, EVANSTON, ILLINOIS 60201

RECOMMENDED STARTING LEVEL: Professional & Continuing Education

Series Name / Program Title	Number In Series	Time Length
1. Nursing and the Law	10	44:00
2. Nursing In Psychiatry	24	44:00

VIDEOTAPE MATERIALS IN DISTRIBUTION BY ANA-NLN CENTER FOR VIDEO-TAPE, 342 MADISON AVENUE, NEW YORK, N.Y. 10017

RECOMMENDED STARTING LEVEL: Professional & Continuing Education

Series Name / Program Title	Number In Series	Time Length
1. Return To Nursing	25	30:00

VIDEOTAPE MATERIALS IN DISTRIBUTION BY ADVANCED MANAGEMENT RE-SEARCH, INC., 1604 WALNUT STREET, PHILADELPHIA, PENNSYLVANIA 19103

RECOMMENDED STARTING LEVEL: Professional & Continuing Education

Series Name / Program Title	Number In Series	Time Length
1. Fundamentals of Finance and Accounting for Non-Financial Executives	10	30–38:00
2. Marketing and the Computer	8	25–44:30

VIDEOTAPE MATERIALS IN DISTRIBUTION BY OFFICE OF PUBLIC AFFAIRS AND EDUCATION, REPUBLIC STEEL CORPORATION, POST OFFICE BOX 6778, CLEVE-LAND, OHIO 44101

RECOMMENDED STARTING LEVEL: Professional & Continuing Education

Series Name / Program Title	Number In Series	Time Length
1. Exploring Basic Economics	10	30:00
2. Understanding Government	7	30:00
3. Understanding Politics	7	30:00
4. Modern Management Methods	14	30:00

VIDEOTAPE MATERIALS IN DISTRIBUTION BY EDUCATIONAL SYSTEMS AND DESIGNS, INC., 136 MAIN STREET, WESTPORT, CONNECTICUT 06880

RECOMMENDED STARTING LEVEL: Professional & Continuing Education

Series Name / Program Title	Number In Series	Time Length
1. Developing Communication Skills	6	30:00
2. Management By Objectives	6	30:00
3. Interviewing For Results	6	
4. Controlling Labor Turnover and Absenteeism	8	
5. Job Instructor Training	8	
6. Supervisory Leadership	8	
7. Quantitative Approaches to Decision Making	6	
8. Looking Into Leadership	8	

VIDEOTAPE MATERIALS IN DISTRIBUTION BY PROFESSIONAL DEVELOPMENT CORPORATION, 233 BROADWAY, SUITE 1375, NEW YORK, N.Y. 10007

RECOMMENDED STARTING LEVEL: Professional & Continuing Education

Series Name / Program Title	Number In Series	Time Length
1. Basic Unified Calculus	24	60:00
2. Applied Differential Equations	24	60:00
3. Fundamentals For Modern Analysis	12	60:00
4. Modern Analysis and Transform Methods	24	60:00
5. Numerical Methods and Computer Techniques	24	60:00
6. Thermodynamics of Phase Equilibrium	10	60:00

VIDEOTAPE MATERIALS IN DISTRIBUTION BY MODERN VIDEOTAPE LIBRARY, MODERN TALKING PICTURE SERVICE, 1212 AVENUE OF THE AMERICAS, NEW YORK, N.Y. 10036

RECOMMENDED STARTING LEVEL: Intermediate (4–6)

Series Name / Program Title	Number In Series	Time Length
1. Your Share In Tomorrow	1	27:00
2. The Mayflower Story	1	25:00
3. The Time Of Our Lives	1	27:00
4. Main Street U.S.A.—Today	1	22:00
5. The Wondrous World of Sight	1	28:00
6. Ski Country, USA	1	28:00
7. Ski With Buick	1	29:00
8. Chocolate Crossroads of the World	1	27:00
9. The Invisible Power of Coal	1	28:00
10. The World is One	1	28:00
11. Light!	1	18:00
12. Happy Holidays . . . Camping In The Smokies	1	28:30
13. Occupation—Auto Mechanic	1	13:00
14. Discover Hawaii	1	28:00
15. Poised For Action	1	30:00
16. The Six Deadly Skids	1	27:00
17. Yoo Hoo! I'm A Bird	1	27:30

RECOMMENDED STARTING LEVEL: Intermediate (4-6) (Continued)

18.	You're The Judge	1	18:00
19.	From Cow To Carton	1	20:00
20.	The Name of the Game is—Fun!	1	27:30
21.	The Dangerous Years	1	30:00
22.	Horizons Unlimited	1	28:00
23.	The Answer is Clear	1	14:00
24.	Cream of the Crop	1	13:30
25.	The Name of the Game is . . . Baseball	1	28:30
26.	Olympic Skates and Skis	1	13:30
27.	1968 Buick Open	1	28:00
28.	21st Century: The Laser—A Light Fantastic	1	30:00
29.	21st Century: Atomic Medicine	1	30:00
30.	21st Century: The Computer Revolution, Part I	1	30:00
31.	21st Century: The Computer Revolution, Part II	1	30:00
32.	21st Century: The Four-Day Week	1	30:00
33.	21st Century: Bats, Birds and Bionics	1	30:00
34.	21st Century: Miracle of the Mind	1	30:00

VIDEOTAPE MATERIALS IN DISTRIBUTION BY AMPEX TAPE EXCHANGE, AMPEX CORPORATION, 2201 LUNT AVENUE, ELK GROVE VILLAGE, ILLINOIS 60007

RECOMMENDED STARTING LEVEL: College (Undergraduate)

	Series Name / Program Title	Number In Series	Time Length
1.	AACTE Workshop In Teacher Education	4	44-52:00
2.	Professional Public Relations	12	30:00

RECOMMENDED STARTING LEVEL: Professional & Continuing Education

	Series Name / Program Title	Number In Series	Time Length
1.	44th NAEB Highlights	3	30:00
2.	44th NAEB Videorecord	6	45-60:00

RECOMMENDED STARTING LEVEL: Adult

	Series Name / Program Title	Number In Series	Time Length
1.	Interski	1	56:00

Instructional Course-Series and Lesson Titles Available on Videotape—Jan 1969

	Recommended Starting Level													
	Pre-School		Primary (k–3)		Intermediate (4–6)		Secondary (7–12)		College (ug)		Prof & Cont Education		Adult		
Source	crs	lsn	crs	lsn	crs	lsn	crs	lsn	crs	lsn	crs	lsn	crs	lsn	Total
Great Plains			18	505	21	677	9	230	34	1069	2	26	6	70	90/2577
MPATI			15	576	12	776	7	512	1	64	1	6			36/1934
NIT	3	97	8	269	11	378	3	28	39	575	7	75			71/1422
Western Video			3	121	2	64	2	30							7/215
Telstar											8	300	3	32	11/332
NCME											2	286			2/286
MTN											2	113			2/113
Video Nursing											4	73			4/73
ANA-NLN											1	25			1/25
AMR											2	18			2/18
Republic											4	38			4/38
Educational Sys											8	56			8/56
Prof Dev Corp											6	118			6/118
Modern											0	34			0/34
AMTEX									2	16	2	9	0	1	4/26
TOTALS	3	97	44	1471	46	1929	21	800	76	1724	49	1143	9	103	248/7267

#1 Designation of use is at recommended starting level. Majority of materials are multi-level.

#2 Must have two or more sequentially related titles for listing as a course-series. All individual program titles (whether qualifying as a course-series or not) counted in lesson-title totals.

#3 In two cases shorter course-series made up and distributed separately from longer course-series of lesson-titles are counted as additional course-series and lesson-titles.

Index